JOSEPH'S BIBLE NOTES

Society of Biblical Literature

# TEXTS AND TRANSLATIONS
## EARLY CHRISTIAN SERIES

edited by
Harold W. Attridge

Texts and Translations 41
Early Christian Series 9

*JOSEPH'S BIBLE NOTES*
(Hypomnestikon)

# Joseph's Bible Notes
## (Hypomnestikon)

Introduction, Translation, and Notes by

ROBERT M. GRANT AND GLEN W. MENZIES

Greek Text Edited by
GLEN W. MENZIES

Scholars Press
Atlanta, Georgia

# Joseph's Bible Notes
## (Hypomnestikon)

Introduction, Translation, and Notes by
ROBERT M. GRANT AND GLEN W. MENZIES

Greek Text Edited by
GLEN W. MENZIES

**Library of Congress Cataloging-in-Publication Data**
Hypomnestikon biblion Joseppou. English & Greek.
   Joseph's Bible notes =Hypomnestikon / introduction, translation, and
notes by Robert M. Grant and Glen W. Menzies ; Greek text edited by
Glen W. Menzies.
      p.   cm. — (Texts and translations / Society of Biblical Literature ;
41. Early Christian series ; 9)
      The author is unknown; the work was previously thought to be by a certain
Joseppus or Josephus Christianus, but this was a misunderstanding of the title,
which probably means that the work is a summary of points culled from the
writings of the Jewish historian Josephus ; cf. Introd.
      Includes bibliographical references and indexes.
      ISBN 0-7885-0195-X (cloth : alk. paper)
      1. Bible—Introductions—Early works to 1800. I. Josephus,
Christianus, 4th/5th cent. II. Grant, Robert McQueen, 1917–   .
III. Menzies, Glen . IV. Title. V. Series: Texts and translations ;
no. 41. VI. Series: Texts and translations. Early Christian
literature series ; 9.
BS474.H9713   1996
220.6—dc20                                                                95–42144
                                                                                      CIP

Printed in the United States of America
on acid-free paper

This Volume is Dedicated to the Members of the North American Patristics Society in recognition of their quarter century of service to scholarship.

# TABLE OF CONTENTS

## ABBREVIATIONS

| | |
|---|---|
| ALGHJ | Arbeiten zur Literatur und Geschichte des hellenistischen Judentums |
| *Ant.* | Josephus *Antiquities of the Jews* |
| Arm | Armenian version |
| *CAG* | *Commentaria in Aristotelem Graeca* |
| CChr | Corpus Christianorum |
| *Chr* | Hippolytus, *Chronicon* |
| Cod. A | Codex Alexandrinus |
| Cod. B | Codex Vaticanus |
| Cod. D | Codex Cottonianus |
| Cod. G | Codex Colberto-Sarravianus |
| GCS | Griechischen christlichen Schriftsteller |
| *HE* | *Historia Ecclesiastica* |
| *Her.* | *Adversus Haereses* |
| ICC | International Critical Commentary |
| *JBL* | *Journal of Biblical Literature* |
| *JTS* | *Journal of Theological Studies* |
| *KP* | *Der Kleine Pauly* |
| LCL | Loeb Classical Library |
| NHS | Nag Hammadi Studies |
| OCT | Oxford Classical Texts |
| *Pan.* | *Panarion (The Medicine Chest Against Heresies)* |
| PG | Migne, Patrologia Graeca |
| *PGL* | Lampe, *Patristic Greek Lexicon* |
| PL | Migne, Patrologia Latina |
| *RAC* | *Reallexikon für Antike und Christentum* |
| *PWRE* | Pauly-Wissowa *Realencyclopädie der classischen Altertumswissenschaft* |
| SPCK | Society for Promoting Christian Knowledge |
| *Str.* | *Stromateis* |
| TU | Texte und Untersuchungen |
| *VC* | *Vigiliae Christianae* |

# BIBLICAL ABBREVIATIONS

Gn, Ex, Lv, Nm, Dt, Js, Jd, Ru, 1-4 Rg, 1-2 Par, 1-2 Esdr, Ps, Prv, Ec, Job, Is, Jer, Ez, Dn, Mic, Hab, Zch, Hos, 1 Macc; Mt, Mk, Lk, Jn, Ac, Ro, 1 Cor, 1 Jn, Rv, 1 Cl, Barn

## SHORT TITLES

Bauer, *Die Chronik*
  Adolf Bauer, *Die Chronik des Hippolytos*. TU 29.1; Berlin: Akademie, 1905.

Cavallera, *Saint Jérome*
  Ferdinand Cavallera, *Saint Jérome: Sa vie et son œuvre*. 2 vols.; Spicilegium sacrum lovaniense: Études et documents 1 and 2; Louvain: Spicilegium sacram lovaniense, 1922.

Dean, *Weights and Measure*
  James E. Dean, *Epiphanius' Treatise on Weights and Measures: The Syriac Version*. Chicago: University of Chicago Press, 1935.

Diekamp, *Hippolytos von Theben*
  Franz Diekamp, *Hippolytos von Theben:Texte und Untersuchungen*. Münster i.W.: Aschendorff, 1898.

Feldman, *Josephus* 9
  Louis Feldman, *Josephus* 9. LCL; Cambridge: Harvard University Press, 1965.

Gelzer, *Sextus Julius Africanus*
  Heinrich Gelzer, *Sextus Julius Africanus und die byzantinische Chronogrphie*, vol. 2: *Die Nachfolger des Julius Africanus*. Leipzig: Teubner, 1885.

Goranson, "The Joseph of Tiberias Episode"
  Stephen Craft Goranson, "The Joseph of Tiberias Episode in Epiphanius: Studies in Jewish and Christian Relations." Ph.D. dissertation, Duke, 1990.

Hahn, *Bibliothek*
August Hahn, *Bibliothek der Symbole und Glaubensregeln der alten Kirche*. 3rd ed., rev. L. Hahn, Breslau: Morgenstern, 1897.

Helm, *Die Chronik*
Adolf Bauer, *Hippolytus' Werke*, vol. 4: *Die Chronik*. 1st ed.; GCS 36; ed. Rudolf Helm; Leipzig: Hinrichs, 1929; 2d ed.; GCS 46; ed. Rudolf Helm; Leipzig: Hinrichs, 1955.

Hopfner, *Offenbarungszauber*
Theodor Hopfner, *Griechisch-ägyptischer Offenbarungszauber* 2.1 Amsterdam: Hakkert, 1983.

Kelly, *Jerome*
J.N.D. Kelly, *Jerome: His Life, Writings, and Controversies*. London: Duckworth, 1975.

Menzies, "Interpretive Traditions"
Glen W. Menzies, "Interpretive Traditions in the *Hypomnestikon Biblion Ioseppou*." Ph.D. diss., University of Minnesota, 1994.

Moreau, "Observations"
Jacques Moreau, "Observations sur l'Hypomnestikon Biblion Ioseppou," *Byzantion* 25–27 (1955–57) 241–76

Opitz, *Athanasius' Werke*
Hans-Georg Opitz, ed., *Athanasius' Werke*, Vol. 3: *Urkunden zur Geschichte des arianischen Streites*. Berlin: DeGruyter, 1934.

Schermann, *Prophetarum vitae*
Theodorus Schermann, *Prophetarum vitae fabulosae*. Leipzig: Teubner, 1907.

Sodano, *Lettera ad Anebo*
Angelo R. Sodano, *Porfirio Lettera ad Anebo*. Naples: Arte Tipografica, 1958.

Sodano, *Giamblico*
Angelo R. Sodano, *Giamblico I misteri egiziani*. Milan: Rusconi, 1984.

Usener, "Vergessenes,"
Hermann Usener, "Vergessenes, IX," *Rheinisches Museum* 28 (1873)
430–33.

Williams, *The Panarion of Epiphanius*
Frank Williams, *The Panarion of Epiphanius of Salamis* (2 vols.; NHS
35-36; Leiden: Brill, 1987–1994)

# INTRODUCTION

## MANUSCRIPT, TITLE, CONTENTS

What we have called "Joseph's Bible Notes" really bears the title *Hypomnestikon Biblion Ioseppou*[1] or "Notebook of Josephus." The name Josephus is a biform of the biblical name Joseph, and for convenience we will call the author Joseph, although this may not have been his name.[2] Traditionally, the author has been designated "Josephus Christianus" to distinguish him from the Jewish historian. Except for a few brief snippets of text employed in commentaries and catenae, the *Hypomnestikon* is known from only one manuscript, Codex Ff. I.24 of the Cambridge University Library.[3] This rather prominent tenth-century codex has achieved some notoriety since it also contains the best extant witness to the text of the *Testaments of the the Twelve Patriarchs*. It probably came to England from Athens about 1241 C.E. through the efforts of Robert Grosseteste.[4] H. J. de Jonge has argued that it had

---

[1]*Lemmata* to selections from our document embedded in a few manuscripts call it the *Hypomnemata Ioseppou*. This *lectio facilior* is to be rejected.

[2]The issue turns in part on how the short poem which appears at the end of the book is understood. If this is the work of the *Hypomnestikon*'s author, then his name was Josephus. If this is a scribal colophon, then it merely indicates that the scribe (mis)understood the title to attribute authorship to a Josephus.

[3]The Utrecht manuscript (Rijksuniversiteit Ms. 17 [1 C. 7]) is not really an exception since it was copied from the Cambridge manuscript in 1706. In his 1678 *editio princeps* of Iamblichus' *De Mysteriis* Thomas Gale mentions the short section of Porphyry's *Letter to Anebo* which is quoted in the *Hypomnestikon*. In addition to the Cambridge manuscript of the *Hypomnestikon*, he says that he knows of two others: a copy of the *Cantabrigiensis* which he has in his possession, and another manuscript held in the possession of F. Crojus. Nothing more is known of Crojus' manuscript and apparently it has disappeared. For more on the manuscripts, see Glen W. Menzies, "Interpretive Traditions in the *Hypomnestikon Biblion Ioseppou*," (Ph.D. diss., University of Minnesota, 1994) 4–35.

[4]Grosseteste knew about the manuscript through John of Basingstoke. According to a colophon found in a number of manuscripts of the Latin translation of the *Testaments*, Grosseteste sent "diligentissimos exploratores" to Greece with instructions to obtain the manuscript at any cost. See Marinus de Jonge, "Robert Grosseteste and the Testaments of the Twelve Patriarchs," *JTS* 42 (1991) 118–119.

previously been brought to Athens from Constantinople by Michael Coniates, the Orthodox Metropolitan of Athens, who had studied at Constantinople.[5]

The *Hypomnestikon* occupies the second place (folios 104a-196a) in the codex, following a text of First and Second Chronicles (1a-103b; 1 Par.12.32–21.16 is not there[6]). The codex continues with "verses of the Emperor Leo for an Enigma of Christ the Lord" (196a-197a),[7] a poem on the Rich Man and Lazarus (197a-198a), and then the famous text of the Jewish-Christian *Testaments of the Twelve Patriarchs* (203a-262b).[8] The contents of the manuscript are obviously miscellaneous, but their center lies in the moral lessons of the patriarchal and post-patriarchal ages of Israelite history. This is also the center of the "Bible Notes."

The *Hypomnestikon* was edited for the first time in 1723 by the great eighteenth-century polymath Johann Albert Fabricius, with a second edition appearing in 1741.[9] He seems to have worked from apographs of the Cambridge manuscript, although he clearly felt at liberty to emend quite freely. In 1781 the fourteenth and last volume of the *Bibliotheca Gallandii* printed a text of the *Hypomnestikon* edited by Giovanni Batista Gallicciolli.[10] While his text is clearly based on Fabricius' edition (and not on consultation with manuscripts),

---

[5]See Herman J. de Jonge, "La bibliothèque de Michel Choniatès et la tradition occidentale des Testaments de XII Patriarches," in M. de Jonge, ed., *Studies on the Testaments of the Twelve Patriarch* (Leiden: Brill, 1975) 99.

[6]Brooke-McLean-Thackeray, *The Old Testament in Greek* II 3 (Cambridge: Cambridge University Press, 1932) v.

[7] The emperor Leo VI Sapiens (886–911), whose epigrams 1–11 are in PG 107, 661–66 (not including the Enigma).

[8]R. H. Charles, *The Greek Versions of the Testaments of the Twelve Patriarchs* (Oxford: Clarendon, 1908) x; Marinus de Jonge (ed.), *Testamenta XII Patriarchum. Edited according to Cambridge University Library MS Ff 1.12 fol. 203a–262b* (Leiden: Brill, 1964); idem, "Robert Grosseteste and the Testaments of the Twelve Patriarchs," *JTS* 42 (1991) 115–25; idem, "The Transmission of the Testaments of the Twelve Patriarchs by Christians," *VC* 47 (1993) 2–6.

[9]Johann A. Fabricius, *Codex Pseudepigraphicus Veteris Testamenti* (Hamburg: Felginer, 1723), part 2 (separate pagination at the end of the volume). See also the notes of Gallicciolli reprinted in PG 106, 9–14; George T. Stokes, "Josephus (31)," *Dictionary of Christian Biography* 3 (1882) 460–61; Jacques Moreau, "Observations sur l'Hypomnestikon Biblion Ioseppou," *Byzantion* 25–27 (1955–57) 241–76; Hans Georg Beck, *Kirche und theologische Literatur im byzantinischen Reich* (Munich: Beck, 1959) 799.

[10]Andreas Gallandi, ed., *Bibliotheca Veterum Patrum Antiquorumque Scriptorum Eccesiasticorum Græco-Latina* (1st ed.; 14 vols.; Venice: Albriti, 1765–81; 2d ed.; 14 vols.; Venice: Zatta & Sons, 1788). Each item in the *Bibliotheca Veterum Patrum* is numbered separately.

Gallicciolli felt free to emend and improve the text as he saw fit. He also includes different notes to the text, although many of the observations are borrowed from Fabricius. Gallicciolli's text, notes, and introduction were later reprinted with only the most infrequent changes in Migne's Patrologia Graeca, Vol. 106, pp. 15ff. The Greek text presented here is a diplomatic transcription of the Cambridge manuscript text with notes detailing divergences and emendations in the editions of Fabricius, Gallicciolli, and Migne. The punctuation and accentuation of the text generally follow Migne's edition. Of necessity, the translation reflects an eclectic text, i.e., the various emendations proposed by previous editors have been taken into consideration, although a microfilm copy of the text of the Cambridge manuscript has been continuously consulted.

The *Hypomnestikon* has not survived the ravages of time intact. This is made evident by the few short selections of its text which appear in medieval catenae and which reflect a textual tradition independent of the Cambridge manuscript. In these texts, material from C. 73 of the Cambridge manuscript is identified as being from "Chapter 100 of the *Hypomnestikon*"–a difference of twenty-seven chapters. Nine or ten additional chapters, summaries of the prophets Ezekiel through Habakkuk, seem to have fallen out between Cc. 76 and 77 of the Cambridge manuscript. This would nearly account for the *lemmata* which identify material from C. 120 in the numeration of the Cambridge text as being from "Josephus, from the *Hypomnestikon*, Chapter 158." These *lemmata* suggest that at least thirty-eight chapters have fallen out of the Cambridge text. Additionally, in the Cambridge manuscript there are only four chapters between the beginning of Book II and the beginning of Book IV, and there is no indication as to where Book III should begin. This evidence also suggests that a substantial amount of text has been lost.

Our book shares the rare title *Hypomnestikon* with the fifth-century *Hypomnesticon against the Pelagians and Celestians* .[11] Although traditionally attributed to Augustine, this work is actually a pastiche of material dealing with the Pelagians and Celestians taken from Augustine's genuine writings by a later editior. The *Hypomnestikon Biblion Ioseppou* is, perhaps, similar in that it also is a pastiche of material taken taken from other authors and arrainged conveniently by a later editor/author. The word *hypomnestikon* may also indicate something of its summary nature.[12] It is not a theological treatise like the *Hypomnesticon against the Pelagians and Celestians*; rather it deals almost

---

[11]PL 45, 1611–64; modern edition by John Edward Chisholm, *The Pseudo-Augustinian Hypomnesticon against the Pelagians and Celestians* (2 vols.; Paradosis 20–21; Fribourg: Fribourg Univeristy Press, 1967–80).

[12]See, for instance, *Adversus Rhetores* 106 (*Adversus Mathematicos* 2.106), where Sextus Empiricus uses the adverb ὑπομνηστικώτερον to mean "in more summary fashion."

exclusively with biblical-historical questions. And while most of the biblical *Quaestiones* studied by Bardy[13] deal with contradictions, Joseph discusses such matters infrequently. Moreover, in *Joseph's Bible Notes* the form of the answers, generally given as lists, seems more fundamental to the character of the work than the fact that most chapters have a question for the title.[14]

Most of Joseph's lists are related to the Old Testament, often viewed through the eyes of the Hellenistic Jewish historian Flavius Josephus, sometimes coordinated with the New Testament. He also takes an explanation of the Hebrew alphabet from Eusebius' *Gospel Preparation*, other materials from the *Chronicon* by Hippolytus of Rome, a list of early Christian martyrs mostly from Eusebius' *Church History*, brief notes on sixty-two heresies drawn largely from the lost *Syntagma* of Hippolytus of Rome and the *Epitome* (*Anakephalaeosis*) of Epiphanius' *Panarion*, equally sketchy notes on five Jewish and four Samaritan sects, a list of Greek philosophical sects from "Heraclides the Pythagorean," and fifty-eight varieties of divination taken mostly, perhaps exclusively, from Porphyry's lost *Letter to Anebo*. The points he is making with these lists are not always clear (we shall discuss them later). His intermittent diligence outweighs his critical ability, though Jacques Moreau went too far when he referred to his "fratras d'érudition inutile." (Compare Usener's comment cited below.)

## RELATION TO THE GREEK OLD TESTAMENT

Joseph uses biography and adventure to give moral lessons, and therefore briefly summarizes significant and interesting biblical stories, sometimes supplying longer lives of such heroes as Samuel, David, and Solomon, and teachings of various prophets (not including Ezekiel), especially as related to Christian doctrines, and a rather full description of the Temple (mostly from Josephus). The biographical sketches do not resemble the Christianized lives

---

[13]Gustave Bardy, "La littérature patristique des '*Quaestiones et Responsiones*' sur l'Écriture Sainte," *RB* 41 (1932) 210–36, 341–69, 515–37; 42 (1933) 14–30 (Isidore of Seville asks how many, p. 22) 211–29, 328–52; see also Robert Devreesse, "Anciens commentateurs grecs sur l'Octateuque," *RB* 44 (1935) 166–91; 45 (1936) 201–20; 364–84.

[14]While the list as a genre has not received much scholarly attention, there is some literature on the subject. See Jonathan Z. Smith, *Imagining Religion: From Babylon to Jonestown* (Chicago Studies in the History of Judaism; Chicago: University of Chicago Press, 1982) 44–52; and Jack Goody, *The Domestication of the Savage Mind* (Cambridge: Cambridge University Press, 1977) 74–111.

collected by Schermann,[15] though somehow Joseph's interests are related to those of Eusebius, who discussed the structure of the Temple and may have written a questioned fragment "on the names in the book of the prophets."[16] In dealing with such historical-factual matters both Eusebius and Joseph make little use of allegorization.

In his lists and summaries Joseph copies many obscure proper names from the Greek Old Testament as well as from the *Jewish Antiquities* of Josephus. The historian Josephus and other Greek authors were reluctant to use transliterated Hebrew names and claimed to be making them Greek to please readers fond of euphony,[17] but our Joseph rarely does so. His readers, though obviously Greek, are concerned with religion and morality, not euphony. His names are not just his own inventions, however, for they often occur in the early fifth-century Codex Alexandrinus (Cod.A), the Armenian translation (Arm), as our notes will show, or a few minuscule manuscripts. Montgomery claims that Alexandrinus is not "physically Constantinopolitan; it is Egyptian, an Alexandrian copy of the Textus Receptus of the Melchite Church in Egypt, the faithful daughter of Byzantium."[18] On the other hand, Skeat pointed out that the evidence for Constantinople was fairly strong.[19] The fact that it contains works by the fourth-century bishops Eusebius and Athanasius proves nothing either way. But it must be noted that Joseph, unlike the Codex, counts 150 Psalms, not 151.[20] He is not a slavish follower of Alexandrinus or one of its ancestors.

Sometimes Joseph's transliterated names agree with the Armenian version of the Septuagint against other witnesses, though his eclectic use of this version shows that it, or the Greek underlying it, was not a primary source, since "with few exceptions the Armenian version maintains throughout the same form for

---

[15]Theodorus Schermann, *Prophetarum vitae fabulosae* (Bibliotheca Scriptorum Graecorum et Romanorum Teubneriana; Leipzig: Teubner, 1907); another edition by C.C. Torrey, *The Lives of the Prophets: Greek text and translation* (SBLMS 1; Philadelphia: SBL, 1946), emphasizing Jewish features. Contrast Marinus de Jonge, "Christelijke elementen in de Vitae prophetarum," *Nederlands Theologisch Tijdschrift* 16 (1961–62) 161–78.

[16]Eusebius *De vitis prophetarum*, PG 22, 1261D–72A. He discussed the Temple in the lost part of his *Onomasticon* (p. 2, 9–11 Klostermann).

[17]Henry Cadbury, *The Making of Luke-Acts* (New York: Macmillan, 1927) 123–25; Jos 1.120, 11.68.

[18]James A. Montgomery, "The Hexaplaric Strata in the Greek Text of Daniel," *JBL* 44 (1925) 300.

[19]Theodore C. Skeat, "The Provenance of the Codex Alexandrinus," *JTS* 6 (1955) 233–35; cf. F.C. Burkitt, "Codex Alexandrinus," *JTS* 11 (1910) 603–6.

[20]C. 73(16); see Milne-Skeat, *The Codex Sinaiticus and the Codex Alexandrinus* (2d ed., London: British Museum, 1955 [1963]) 30–41 (Psalms, 35).

each proper name,"[21] while Joseph does not do so. H.S. Gehman's study of "the Armenian version of I and II Kings" concludes that "the Armenian translator used a text which was very similar to A."[22] Joseph could be writing in the early fifth century and adding his own errors, but more probably he is using ancestors of Alexandrinus or the Armenian version. It should also be noted that Adolf Bauer and Rudolf Helm have shown textual affinities between the Armenian form of the *Liber generationis* and the *Hypomnestikon*.[23] This really suggests a relationship between the Greek *Vorlage* of the Armenian and the *Hypomnestikon*.

Gehman's study of "the officers of King Solomôn" (C. 103) shows that Joseph can go his own way against all our manuscript evidence. The first part of the list is rather accurately copied. It begins with "Banaias general in place of Iôab" (3 Rg 2:34-35) and thus suggests that it is part of a larger narrative. Next come "the priests Sadôk and his son Azarias, Zambouch another priest of Solomôn,[24] Eliareph, and Achiab, sons of Sisa" (3 Rg 4:2-3),[25] then "Iôsaphat, son of Achillid, and Adôneiran, son of Abdôthô (Abaô, Cod.A), over the tax-collection" (4:3-6 with omissions). Confusion reigns, however, in the list of "those who supplied the provisions every month" (4:7). The first name is Beour in Mount Ephraim (4:8); he is called "son of Kakôn." But this is a garbled version of the second name in the LXX, "son of Dakar" (4:9 Cod.A, Arm). The next name, Emmakmes, is really the location, *en Makmas*, for the son of Dakar, and "he" is called "son of Esde" ("Esd" in 4:10 Cod.A, Arm). Another place name that becomes personal is "Errabôth" (for *en Arabôth*, 4:10, Cod.A, Arm), identified as "second (?) son of Aminas (Aminadab) in the land of Taassé" (Nephaddôr, 4:11, Cod.A, Arm). After him comes the real name Benaan (Baana, Cod.A), son of Aliouth (Eloud, Cod.A), in Thaanas (4:12). Unfortunately the

---

[21] A.E. Brooke-N. McLean, *The Old Testament in Greek* 1.1 (Cambridge: University Press, 1906) iii n.4.

[22] Henry S. Gehman, "The Armenian Version of I and II Kings," *Journal of the American Oriental Society* 54 (1934) 54.

[23] Adolf Bauer, *Hippolytus' Werke*, vol. 4: *Die Chronik* (1st ed.; GCS 36; ed. Rudolf Helm; Leipzig: Hinrichs, 1929) 5–10 (2d ed.; GCS 46; ed. Rudolf Helm; Leipzig: Hinrichs, 1955) XI–XIV. (Hereafter cited as Helm.) According to Helm the *Hypomnestikon* tends to follow the *Liber generationis I*, and, in fact, never agrees with the *Liber generationis II* (the text from the Vienna manuscript of the *Chronicle of 354*) against the *Liber generationis I*. There are times, however, when it agrees with the Armenian against the *Liber generationis I*, and in at least one instance, the *Hypomnestikon* agrees with the Armenian against all other witnesses (the bare Ἑβραῖοι rather than Ἑβραῖοι οἱ καὶ Ἰουδαῖοι in *Chr* 200 = *Hypomnestikon* C. 24).

[24] Cod.A calls him Zabouth a priest of the king (4:5).

[25] Cod.A gives the names as Enareph and Achia.

list then returns, to place names with "Megedô" (Megiddo) for "Mekedô" (4:12), identified (by means of a long omission) as "son of Gaber" (so 4:13); "Erramoth" for Eremath (*en Ramôth*, 4:13, Cod.A,), identified as son of Addé (4:14, Ainadab son of Addô, Arm; Ainadab son of Sadôk, Cod.A); and "Emmaenô" for Maanaim (Cod.A) = "in Mahanaim." Accuracy now almost emerges, with the mention of Acheimaas in Nephthaleim (4:15), but the LXX statement that he had married Basemmath (Masemath, Cod.A) the daughter of Solomon (4:15) underlies the next personal name, that of "Chousé, son of the queen, in Asér and in Baalaôth." In 4:16 Cod.A this is "Baanas son of Chousei, in Asér and in Maalôt." Joseph's list takes "Iôsaphat son of Pharrou in Isachar, Semeé son of Éla in Beniamin, and Gaber son of Adaé in Galaad" from 4:17-18 Cod.A. On the other hand, Joseph's "and in the land of Géôn king of the Amorites and of Og king of Basan" is closer to Arm and the MT than to Cod.A. Finally, "and Naseph[26] stood by in the land of Iouda, receiving what was ordered of each one" (4:18 and 21). Clearly the list reflects a minimal understanding of the Greek text, while the Hebrew remains incomprehensible. (Josephus' transcription of this text is better, but not much.[27])

It was Joseph's misfortune to copy a text, and badly, from which were absent the names of those defined as "son of" (*ben*) in 3 Rg 4:8-11 and 13. He did not know that this was the case, and he was also unaware of the mechanical cause for the situation, explained by Montgomery. "A vertical break at the right hand of the papyrus (?) left blank the initial names in vv. 8-11, with a further blank in v. 13. In v. 12 there has been some shuffling of the geographical data; in vv. 13. 19a some glosses have been added."[28] Joseph thus compounded chaos.

Since he relies on the Greek Old Testament and the Greek text of Josephus, we can follow him only through exact transliterations of the significant proper names. This is not so important when the names are very common or raise no questions about sources, as in the New Testament. We usually cite those names in conventional English translations, unless distinctions are important, as between the patriarch Iakôb and the apostle Iakôbos. Since there are no problems with such names as Moses (Môysés), Ruth (Routh), Saul (Saoul), and David (Dabid), we give these in English.

---

[26]The LXX identifies the *naseph* or "governor" as "Iôsaphat son of Phouasoud in Issachar."

[27]Josephus *Ant.* 8.35–36, much closer to 3 Rg 2:35; 4:1–19; cf. Alfred Rahlfs, *Septuaginta-Studien* 3 (Göttingen: Vandenhoeck & Ruprecht, 1911) 224–39, but Joseph is certainly not following the "Lucianic" text.

[28]James A. Montgomery (ed. Henry S. Gehman), *The Books of Kings* (Edinburgh: Clark, 1951) 120–26.

## JOSEPHUS

Joseph explicitly refers to a chapter from the *Jewish War* of Josephus in his own C. 125 (cf. 141) and elsewhere often uses the *Jewish Antiquities* without naming it. Such is the case especially in regard to the complete list of high priests (2), the detailed descriptions of the Temple, the sanctuary, and the ark of the covenant (106-11), the captures of Jerusalem (123-25), and the accounts of Jewish sects (141). He also takes the prophet's name "Iadôn" (15[22], 89) and minor details about Samouél and David from Josephus (72, 74). Indeed, Josephus appears very frequently, in Chapters 2, 15, 22, 31, 43, 63, 72-74, 89, 102, 104, 106-9, 120, 123-126, 130, 141, and 165. He did not say, however, that "Melchi" was a name given Moses at circumcision, though Joseph says he did (63).

## HIPPOLYTUS

Joseph's oldest patristic source is the *Chronicon* by Hippolytus of Rome. According to the Greek text (Ms. *Matritensis* 4701, ed. Adolf Bauer), the *Chronicon* concluded with a series of eight appendices that took the form of lists. Only the titles of these appendices survive in Greek, but the lists themselves have been preserved fairly well in the Latin *Liber generationis I* and *Liber generationis II*.[29] Chapters 7–10 and 12–18 of the *Hypomnestikon* appear to contain edited versions of the bulk of this material. In addition, the material in Chapters 1, 11, and 24 may have been extracted from the body of the *Chronicon*,[30] and Chapters 3–6 contain such basic information that they could have been assembled from the Septuagint, Josephus, Hippolytus, or some other source; there is no way to tell. Such a heavy concentration of material taken from the *Chronicon* of Hippolytus in the first twenty-four chapters of the *Hypomnestikon* suggests that the *Chronicon's* appendices not only provided the nucleus around which the *Hypomnestikon* was formed, but also that the form which these appendices took–that of the "list"–provided the inspiration for the remainder of the work. Based on this evidence, it was Pierre Nautin who first suggested that the *Chronicon* "gave birth" to the *Hypomnestikon.*[31]

---

[29]See the standard edition of Theodor Mommsen, "Chronographus Anni CCCLIIII" in Idem, ed., *Chronica Minora Saec. IV–VII*, Vol. 1 (Monumenta Germaniae Historica, Auctorum Antiquissimorum 9; Berlin: Weidmann, 1892) 39–148.

[30]Chapter 124 (Israelite Captivities) also appears to have come from the *Chronicon.*

[31]The words "gave birth" are from Pierre Nautin, *Lettres et écrivains chrétiens des II^e et III^e siècles* (Paris: Cerf, 1961) 189, but already in 1952 he had said

The lost *Syntagma* of Hippolytus was also used to construct Chapter 140 (Christian Heresies). The outline of this work has survived in a Latin summary known as the *Adversus omnes haereses* of Pseudo-Tertullian.[32] The *Syntagma* can also be reconstructed from the agreements between the heresiologies of Epiphanius and Filaster, who each independently used it as a source.[33]

## EUSEBIUS

Joseph uses the *Church History* of Eusebius extensively, turning there for information about the Hebrew names of Old Testament books (25),[34] the sieges of Jerusalem (123-125), Jacob bishop of Jerusalem (47, 134, 153), the married apostles (116), and the evangelist Mark (135). He also mines the *Church History* for material from Clement of Alexandria (116, 137, 153[4]), information about the persecutions (139) and some of the heresies (140[5-6, 33, 38, 39, 41], 141) He also uses Eusebius' *Gospel Preparation* for information about the Hebrew alphabet (26). In addition, two chapters seem to echo Eusebius' lost treatise *On the Polygamy with Many Offspring (polypaidia) of the Ancients Beloved by God* (30, 38).

## EPIPHANIUS AND THE *EPITOME (ANAKEPHALAIÔSIS)*

In Chapter 141 Joseph provides a list of Jewish sects: Pharisees, Sadducees, two classes of Essenes, Judas the Galilean. It does not come directly from Epiphanius, who has Sadducees, Scribes, Pharisees, Hemerobaptistai, Nasaraioi, and Ossaioi (14-19). Joseph is a litle closer to the list in the *Anakephalaiosis* or *Epitome* (15-19, I 167,8-168,10): Pharisees, Sadducees, Hemerobaptistai, Ossenoi, and Nasaraioi (followed by #20, Herodianoi), but apparently does not use it. There may also be some influence from the reports about Jewish sects found in Flavius Josephus.

---

essentially the same thing. See idem, "La controverse sur l'auteur de l'«Elenchos,»" *Revue d'histoire ecclésiastique* 47 (1952) 39–42.

[32]Because it has generally been transmitted in the manuscript tradition appended to Tertullian's *De præscriptione* as the final part of Chapter 45 through Chapter 53, it has sometimes been printed along with that work. The best text of the *Adversus omnes haereses* is Aemelius Kroymann, ed., "Adversus omnes haereses" in *Tertulliani Opera*, part 2: *Opera Montanistica* (CChr, Series Latina 2,2; Turnholt: Brepols, 1954) 1399–1410.

[33]See Richard Adelbert Lipsius, *Zur Quellenkritik des Epiphanios* (Vienna: Braumüller, 1865) 4–32.

[34]This would be odd if Joseph were a Jew.

Chapter 142 of the *Hypomnestikon* describes the Samaritans and lists four sects of the Samaritans. The initial paragraph of this chapter, which describes Samaritanism taken as a whole, is an amalgam of information gathered from *Antiquities* 9.288–290 and *Antiquities* 10.184. Josephus, following the account in 2 Kings (LXX = 4 Kings) 17:24, claims that the Samaritans were Persians imported into the North of Israel by Salmanezer the Assyrian king, in contrast to the purity which was maintained in the South. This basic presentation is retained in the *Hypomnestikon*.

The names of the four sects of Samaritans listed by the *Hypomnestikon* accord with those listed by Epiphanius, although much of the content differs from what Epiphanius says about the Samaritan sects. The order of presentation is the same as that found in Proem 1 of the *Panarion* (*GCS* 25, 157) and in *Epitome* 10–13, but differs from that found in the body of the *Panarion*.[35] Since according to Holl, Epiphanius' list is unique, it must be Joseph's source, even if at some remove.[36]

Chapter 140 contains a list of sixty-two heresies. This list is similar to Epiphanius' *Panarion* of 376 which was aimed at eighty heresies,[37] each compared to a species of snake or wild beast.[38] Except for the final heresy in the *Hypomnestikon*'s list (the Athropomorphites), each heresy can be found either in the *Panarion* (or the *Epitome*) or in Eusebius' *Church History*. Nevertheless, the order of the inital heresies (through the Melchisedekians, Heresy 34) suggests that Joseph also relied on the lost *Syntagma* of Hippolytus of Rome.

Joseph avoids some of the idiosyncracies of the *Panarion*. Epiphanius connects the Quintillians and the Taskodougitai who put their forefinger on their nose when they pray or sprinkle themselves with an infant's blood (48.14.3–6) with the Kataphrygians or Montanists. Joseph does not. Epiphanius' treatment of the Gnostic Epiphanes, worshiped as a god, is literary and comes from

---

[35]In *Panarion* 10–13 (GCS 25, 203–207) the order given is Essenes, Sebuaeans, Gorthenians, and Dositheans.

[36]Regarding Epiphanius on Samaritan festivals, see T.C.G. Thornton, "The Samaritan Calendar: a source of friction in New Testament times," *JTS* 42 (1991) 580 n. 12.

[37]Cf. Aline Pourkier, *L'hérésiologie chez Épiphane de Salamine* (Paris: Beauchesne, 1992) esp. 84–114; Gerhard Vallée, *A Study in Anti-Gnostic Polemics*: *Irenaeus, Hippolytus, and Epiphanius* (Waterloo, Ont.: Wilfrid Laurier University Press, 1981) 63–91. On later influence cf. Jean Gouillard, "L'hérésie dans l'empire byzantin des origines au xiie siècle," *Travaux et mémoires* 1 (1965) 300–1.

[38]Cf. Jürgen Dummer, "Ein naturwissenschaftliches Handbuch als Quelle für Epiphanius von Constantia," *Klio* 55 (1973) 289–99. He had already listed eighty heresies in his *Anchored* (cc. 12–13) of 374.

Clement of Alexandria.[39] Joseph mentions him only from the *Epitome* (140[19]).

Joseph did not use the *Panarion* directly. He omits almost all the significant details that Epiphanius provides, whether taken from the tradition of anti-heretical writing or from personal observation. Indeed, Joseph (in C. 139[7]) comes close to the *Panarion* only when he refers to Origen's penance, which according to Epiphanius (*Pan.* 64.2) was made necessary by his apostasy.

Joseph bypasses all Epiphanius' first-hand information. Epiphanius had come from Eleutheropolis in Palestine to live as a young monk in Egypt, and his listing of Gnostic groups is oriental in origin. Some details come from his personal knowledge of Egypt. Thus he tells exactly where Basilides[40] and Valentinus originated.[41] Among the living Gnostics he had encountered in Egypt were Borborianoi, probably his own name for antinomians, since *borboros* means "mud" or even "sewer." Information from their writings and trustworthy witnesses enabled to inform on the group of eighty he proudly mentions.[42] In addition, in Palestine he met a woman who supplied information on the "Origenians."[43] In the Egyptian countryside he also met some Sethians, but he could not remember just where. Because of memory lapses he had to get some of his information from books.[44]

Joseph neglects Epiphanius' detailed and probably reliable information about these sects and also about the Palestinian Archontics. Epiphanius knew that their leader Eutaktos brought them from Palestine to Armenia Major and Minor in the reign of Constantius (337-361), and that they were first known in Palestine in the village of Kapharbaricha, near Eleutheropolis and Jerusalem and three miles beyond Hebron. An ex-presbyter who had been deposed for Gnostic heresy propagated their views. Later Archontics lived in the same Kokaba in Arabia as the matrix of the Ebionites and Nazoraioi.[45] Joseph C. 140 (51) repeats none of what Epiphanius says about the Apostolici, also called Antitacti, but with the *Epitome* simply locates them in Pisidia.[46]

---

[39]*Pan.* 32.3.4–7 (from Clement *Stromata* [abbreviated *Str*] 3.5.2). Kephallénia was a league of four cities but Samé, one of the four, no longer existed, according to Strabo *Geography* 10.2.13,455.

[40]*Pan.* 24.1.1; cf. Strabo 17.1.20, 23–24, p. 802.

[41]*Pan.* 31.2.3; A.H.M. Jones, *Cities of the Eastern Roman Provinces* (Oxford: Clarendon, 1937) 346–48.

[42]*Pan.* 26.3.6–7; 26.17.4–18.4.

[43]Pan. 63.1.3–3.3.

[44]*Pan.* 39.1.2.

[45]Epiphanius *Pan.* 40.1.1–5. They used Allogeneis books (*Allogenes*, Nag Hammadi XI 3) and the *Ascension of Isaiah*.

[46]*Pan.* 61.1.1, 2.1; Pisidia in *Epit.* 61 (II 213,18 Holl).

The reason he rarely comes anywhere near Epiphanius' text is that he follows the *Epitome*, a later – early fifth century – collection of descriptive notes also used by Augustine, the *Doctrina Patrum*, and John of Damascus in the epitome *On Heresies*. The *Epitome* makes use of Epiphanius' own summaries included in the *Panarion*, though not correctly, and like Joseph it provides no refutations of the heresies.[47]    (The incorrect name Nauatos for the Roman schismatic [C. 140(35)] comes from Epiphanius, but it is found in the *Epitome* as well.) As already noted, Joseph sometimes supplements this information with materials taken from the *Church History* of Eusebius (C. 140 [5-6, 33, 39, 41]), just as Augustine once does.[48]

Epiphanius himself verges on the absurd when he reports on the mysterious Angelics. "We have heard just the name, and we do not know definitely what such a heresy is." Since he cannot explain the name, he suggests that Angelics might say that angels made the world, or perhaps consider themselves angels, or come from Angeliné beyond Mesopotamia.[49]    For the same group Joseph (C. 140[53]) certainly does not follow Epiphanius but gives a different explanation, based on the *Epitome*. They "think highly of themselves as having their own angelic rank, shared with those ranked with them."[50] Later on, John of Damascus was also at a loss and noted with the *Epitome* that these heretics had completely vanished. They claimed angelic rank or else invoked angels.[51]

## OTHER GREEK LITERATURE

Joseph specifically names only two Greek sources: a list of philosophical schools ascribed to the the Pythagorean Herakleides (143) and a quotation-paraphrase from Porphyry's *Letter to Anebo* against divination (144[57]).

---

[47]On the lateness of the *Anacephalaiosis* cf. Karl Holl, *Die handschriftliche Überlieferung des Epiphanius (Ancoratus und Panarion)* (TU 36.3; Leipzig: Hinrichs, 1910) 95–98. Holl notes that it was used much more often than the original work (p. 98); cf. Franz Diekamp, *Hippolytos von Theben:Texte und Untersuchungen.* (Münster i.W.: Aschendorff, 1898) lxx–lxxi, 266–69. For its influence, Gustave Bardy, "Le 'de haeresibus' et ses sources," *Miscellanea agostiniana* 2 (Rome, 1931) 395–416; Berthold Altaner, "Augustinus und Epiphanius von Salamis," *Mélanges J. De Ghellinck* 1 (Gembloux: Duculot, 1951) 265–75; also Wilhelm Schneemelcher, "Epiphanius," *RAC* 5 (1965) 919–20; I. Opelt, "Epitome," *RAC* 5 (1965) 944–73 (specifically 963 [no. 129] and 968).

[48]Augustine *Her* 83 from Eusebius *HE* 6.37 (Bardy, 411).

[49]Epiphanius *Pan.* 60.1.1–2.

[50]*Epit.* 60 (II 213,16–17).

[51]*Her* 60 (PG 94, 713A).

Apart from these items, however, the format of the *Hypomnestikon* is paralleled in Hellenistic/Roman materials, for it reflects "Alexandrian" scholarship. In the papyrus called "Laterculi Alexandrini" by Diels[52] we find short lists of legislators, painters, sculptors, architects, and technicians, followed by the seven wonders of the world, the largest islands, the tallest mountains, and rivers, springs, and lakes. (Such questions are also discussed in the third-century Christian *Chronicon* by Hippolytus, a source of our Joseph.) Diels compared it with the anonymous *Tractatus de mulieribus*, which lists women courageous in war, houses ruined because of women, those who showed brotherly affection, those who showed comradely affection, and transformations.[53]

Diels noted similar lists found in the second-century Greek mythography (*Fabulae*) by Hyginus, including the seven wise men, the seven lyric poets, and the seven wonders of the world (221-23). The first forty-seven chapters deal with individuals and are followed by a list of Athenian kings (48), then individuals again (50-69),[54] then seven kings against Thebes (70), the fifty-five sons and daughters of Priam (90), a list based on the Homeric catalogue of ships (97), who fought with and/or killed whom (in Homer, 112-15), the Titanomachy (150), the offspring of the Giant Typho and the Gorgon Echidna (151), sons of Zeus and other gods (155-62), what daughter of Danaus killed whom (170), and mostly individuals up to the daughters of Oceanus (182) and the names of the horses of the Sun and the Hours (183). Not for forty chapters do we leave mythological names for lists: the seven wise men (221), the seven lyric poets (222, missing), the seven wonders of the world (223), who became immortal from mortals (224), and who first built temples to the gods (225; 226-37 missing). The subject changes to death in c. 238, with fathers who killed daughters, then mothers who killed sons (239), wives who killed husbands (240), husbands who killed wives (241), male (242) or female suicides (243), those who killed relatives (244) or fathers-in-law and sons-in-law (245), those who consumed their sons in banquets (246) or were consumed by dogs (247) or died when pierced by a boar (248). Similar topics appear thereafter, including "those who came back from Hades by permission of the Fates" (251). Moral questions arise with "those who had unlawful intercourse" (253) and "those women (or men) who were most pious" or "impious" or "chaste" (254-56) or were the closest of friends (257). At the end we find "who discovered what"

---

[52]Hermann Diels, "Laterculi Alexandrini aus einem Papyrus ptolemäischer Zeit," Abhandlungen der königlich preussischen Akademie der Wissenschaften, Philosophisch-historische Classe, II (Berlin: 1904) 1-16.

[53]A. Westermann, *Paradoxographi Graeci* (Brunswick: Westermann, 1839) 213-23. See further Otto Regenbogen, "Pinax," *PWRE* 20 (1951) 1409-82 (1470-72 on Hyginus).

[54]Individuals again in cc.71-89, 91-96, 98-111, 116-49, 152-54, 163-69A.

(274), "who founded which towns" (275), "the largest islands" (276), and "the first inventors of things" (277).[55] C.J. Fordyce claims that Hyginus' "absurdities are partly due to the compiler's ignorance of Greek."[56] Joseph has some difficulties with Greek, more with Hebrew.

Joseph provides a Christian equivalent for such a pagan *pinax* or "catalogue" as these *Fables*. Indeed, both Hyginus and Joseph were mythographers than scholars, sharing a love of information arranged more or less statistically. In addition, the popular fables of Aesop and such a work as the *Pinax* of Cebes resemble Joseph's moral lessons, often ambiguous and illustrated by biblical texts.[57]

## FUNCTION OF THE NOTEBOOK

The use of biblical examples for moral teaching has a long history in Christian writings. One of the earliest witnesses is the Epistle to the Hebrews, with its "roll-call of faith" in Chapter 11.[58] A little later (and influenced by Hebrews) comes 1 Clement, where we find jealousy exemplified by Kain and Ésau, affecting Iôséph, Moses, Aarôn, and Mariam, making Dathan and Abeirôn rebel against Moses, and Saul persecute David (4; the examples of Peter and Paul follow). Repentance was preached by Nôe and Iônas (7.6-7), while fidelity is illustrated by Enôch and Nôe, faith and hospitality by Abraam, Lôt, and Raab (9-12), humility by Élias, Elisaie, Iezekiél, Abraam, Iôb, Moses, and David (17-18), and heroism by the women Ioudith and Esthér (55.3-6). This use of examples is related to the "Hellenistic synagogue sermon," which Thyen studied. His best examples are Christian and use biblical figures as moral examples.[59] The same approach to the biblical materials appears in Joseph's work. It may be noted that 1 Clement, Thyen's primary source, was included in Codex Alexandrinus, to which Joseph is often close.

---

[55]H.J. Rose, *Hygini Fabulae* (Leiden: Sijthoff, 1933; 2d ed., 1963); later literature, P.L. Schmidt, "2. H. Mythographus," *KP* 2 (1967) 1263.

[56]C.J. Fordyce, "Hyginus," *Oxford Classical Dictionary* (2d ed., Oxford: Clarendon, 1970) 533–34.

[57]See Ben E. Perry, ed., *Babrius and Phaedrus* (LCL; Cambridge, MA: Harvard University Press, 1965).

[58]The heroes and heroines of faith are Abel, Enoch, Nôé, Abraam, Sarra, Isaak, Iakôb, Iôséph, Moses, [Iésous], Raab, Gedeôn, Barak, Sampsôn, Iephthaë, David, Samouél, "and the prophets" (Heb 11:4–32).

[59]Cf. Hartwig Thyen, *Der Stil der jüdisch-hellenistischen Homilie* (Forschungen zur Religion und Literatur des Alten und Neuen Testaments, N.F. 47; Göttingen: Vandenhoeck & Ruprecht, 1955) 11–26 (*1 Clement*, James, Hebrews, *Didache* 1–6 and 16, *Barnabas*, *Testaments of the Twelve Patriarchs*).

In 1882 G.T. Stokes described the work as "in part a commentary on, in part a paraphrase of the Scripture history, with some chapters added on the persecutions and heresies which afflicted the church." A clue to the function of such a book may lie in Usener's scornful and only partly justifiable description of it as "ein recht triviales Compendium für theologischen Unterricht."[60] Early documents on the requirements for ordination point toward the need for such compendia. Coptic ostraca show that prospective deacons had to memorize portions of the scriptures, single gospels, for example, such as Matthew, Mark, or John. The more demanding Aphou, anchorite and bishop of Oxyrhynchus in Egypt, required a deacon to memorize twenty-five psalms, two apostolic epistles, and part of a gospel, while a presbyter had to memorize portions of Deuteronomy, Proverbs, and Isaiah.[61] And in the *Chronicon* of Hippolytus, closely parallel to parts of Joseph, we read that the servant (*diakonos*) of the truth must be instructed from the sacred scriptures and know the historical meaning of wars, judges, kings, prophets, captivities, priests, etc.[62] Though here *diakonos* does not mean "deacon," Joseph's treatise could easily introduce deacons to the scriptures and help them memorize details.[63]

The *Apostolic Constitutions* tell us that like the baptized, the deacons were to learn "how those initiated into Christ ought to live," and therefore consider how "God punished the wicked with water and fire but glorified the saints in each generation — I mean Séth, Enôs, Enôch, Nôe, Abraam, and his descendants, Melchisedek and Iôb and Moses, Iésous and Chaleb and Phinees the priest, and the holy ones in each generation."[64] Origen describes the pleasure simpler Christians found in hearing the moral teaching of Esther or Judith or Tobias or "the mandates of Wisdom," and Athanasius states that books like the Wisdom of Solomon, the Wisdom of Sirach, Esther, Judith, and Tobias, not to mention the

---

[60]Hermann Usener, "Vergessenes, IX," *Rheinisches Museum* 28 (1873) 430–33; similarly Adolf Bauer, *Die Chronik des Hippolytos* (TU 29.1; Berlin: Akademie, 1905) 152.

[61]W. C. Crum, *Coptic Ostraca* (London: Egypt Exploration Society, 1902) nos. 29, 30, 31, Ad.7, 44 (pp. 9–11). He is citing Francesco Rossi, *Trascrizione di tre manoscritti copti del Museo Egizio di Torino* (Memorie della Reale Accademia delle Scienze di Torino, 2.37; Torino: Loescher, 1885) 21 (fragment 30); 88 (Italian translation).

[62]Hippolytus *Chr.* 17; *LG* 1.21–22 (see Bibliography).

[63]Special cases are the deacon Valens of Aelia (Eusebius *Martyrs of Palestine* 11.4) and Didymus the Blind, who were said to have memorized all the scriptures; Richard Reitzenstein, *Historia Monachorum und Historia Lausiaca* (Göttingen: Vandenhoeck & Ruprecht, 1916) 160–61, 164. Origen too had an amazing memory, stimulated by a drug according to some critics (Epiphanius *Pan.* 64.3.12).

[64]*Apostolic Constitutions* 7.39.3 (Funk p. 440).

*Didache* and the *Shepherd of Hermas*, none of them canonical, were to be read to converts.[65]

Since Joseph's manual was based on a Hellenistic Jewish or Christian (or Hellenistic-Jewish-Christian) biblical foundation, it might be possible to disentagle Christian additions[66] from a Hellenistic Jewish original.[67] The analogy of 1 Clement, where both Jewish and Christian elements are already combined, does not suggest that such a project would be useful.

## DATE OF THE NOTEBOOK

In the late seventeenth century William Cave observed that Joseph mentioned no heresy later than the fourth century and reasonably claimed that C. 136, from Hippolytus of Thebes, was an interpolation.[68] Fabricius himself argued that the author had no information later than Epiphanius. (His use of the *Epitome* could not make him much later.) Previously, in 1680, Isaac Voss had argued that the author was Count Joseph of Tiberias, mentioned by Epiphanius (*Her* 30.4-12).[69] In 1781 G. B. Gallicciolli in the introduction to his edition of the *Hypomnestikon* defended Voss' proposal, and then again in this century both Jacques Moreau and Stephen C. Goranson[70] have forcefully reiterated and expanded Voss's argument, dating the work in the late fourth century and relating it to this Joseph. Adolf Bauer in his edition of Hippolytus (ed. Rudolf Helm) stated without argument, that Joseph wrote "at the earliest at the turning of the 5th and 6th centuries."[71] Franz Diekamp places the date even later–sometime

---

[65]Origen *Homilies on Numbers* 27.1 (Baehrens p.256); Athanasius, *Festal Epistle* 39 of 367 (PG 26, 1177D).

[66]C. 1, 25–28, 63(12–15), 64(9–11), 65(4)–67, 97–101, 115, 118, 120–35, 137–43, 145–46, 148–53, 156(3–4), 157, 161(3), 163(13), 164(5–7), 165(5).

[67]C. 3–24, 29–62, 63(1–11), 64(1–8), 65(1–3,5–8), 68–96, 102–4, 112–15, 117, 119, 154–67.

[68]William Cave (Guilielm Cavius), *Scriptorum Ecclesiasticorum Historia Literaria* (1st ed.; 2 vols.; London: Richard Chiswell, 1698) 2.138–42. This same material appears unaltered on pp. 397–99 of Vol. 1 of the 1741 Basel edition.

[69]Isaac Voss (Vossius), *De Sibyllinis...Oraculis* (Oxford: Sheldonian Theatre, 1680) 29.

[70]Stephen Craft Goranson, *The Joseph of Tiberias Episode in Epiphanius: Studies in Jewish and Christian Relations* (Ph.D. diss.: Duke, 1990). Prof. Grant wishes to thank Prof. Goranson for sending him a copy of his dissertation.

[71]Helm, *Die Chronik*, 221 (2d ed., p. 135).

between the sixth and ninth centuries.[72] Diekamp has more recently been followed by Beck.[73]

The work has also been set in the fifth century because its list of heretics ends with the Anthropomorphite heresy, extremely controversial around 399 and later strenuously attacked by Cyril of Alexandria.[74] Despite this, Galicciolli, Moreau, and Goranson have attempted to preserve a fourth-century date and the attribution of authorship to Joseph of Tiberias. They have attempted to show that the term "Anthropomorphites" can be taken as a reference to the Audians, thus evading the problem. (Audius died about 370 C.E.) This identification of the *Hypomnestikon's* Anthropomorphites and Audians cannot be correct, however. Not only does the *Hypomnestikon* itself distinguish the two groups (Heresies 54 and 62), but when the Audians are discussed, they are not even accused of having an anthropomorphic conception of God.[75] Moreover, the *Hypomnestikon* locates the origin of Anthropomorphism "in the land (τὴν χώραν) of Eleutheropolis, in which (ἐν ᾧ) is . . . ."[76] Unfortunately, at this point the text is interrupted. A not unreasonable conjecture is that the text here

---

[72]Diekamp, *Hippolytos von Theben,* 151.

[73]Hans-Georg Beck, *Kirche und theologische Literatur im byzantinischen Reich* (Handbuch der Altertumswissenschaft 12.2.1; Munich: Beck, 1959) 799.

[74]Cyril of Alexandria's *Letter to Calosirius* (Epistle 83) can be found in PG 76, 1065–1152 and in a better edition with an English translation in Lionel R. Wickham, ed. and trans., *Cyril of Alexandria: Select Letters* (Oxford: Clarendon, 1983) 214–21. The anthropomorphic conception of God is also discussed in Cyril's *Doctrinal Questions and Answers* and *Answers to Tiberius*: Editions of these works are available in P. E. Pusey, *Sancti Patris Nostri Cyrilli Archiepiscopi Alexandrini in D. Joannis Evangelium. Accedunt Fragmenta Varia necnon Tractatus ad Tiberium Diaconum duo* (3 vols; Oxford: Clarendon, 1872; reprinted Brussels: Culture et Civilisation, 1965) 3.549–66 and 3.577–602.

[75]The Audians may have believed that God has a body since Epiphanius reports this in the *Panarion.* This peculiarity is described as being secondary to the rigorism which was the chief mark of the Audians, and in the *Epitome* no reference is made to the belief that God had a body. Moreover, the Audians are not called Anthropomorphites, even in the *Panarion.* The confusion of the Audians with the Anthropomorphites can be traced to Augustine. In Chapter 50 of his *De haeresibus,* Augustine draws on a source which describes Egyptian Anthropomorphites and also the *Epitome's* description of the Audians. He mistakenly identifies these two groups on the basis of a vague statement from the *Epitome* that the Audians interpret "in the image [of God]" most harshly. Augustine's error has continued to be perpetuated.

[76]This could also be translated "in the land of Eleutheropolis, in whom is . . . ." Moreover, it is important to note that as the text stands neither "land" nor "Eleutheropolis" can be the antecedent of "which/whom." However, since no satisfactory antecedant presents itself, perhaps the text should be emended.

originally mentioned "the monastery of Besanduc (Βησανδούκη)" or perhaps "the monastery which Epiphanius founded," since this is the only site related to both Eleutheropolis and Anthropomorphites known from other sources. The monastery of Besanduc was located in the "land" (χώρα), as the *Hypomnestikon* puts it, or "district" (νομός), as Sozomen and Nicephorus Callistus put it,[77] of Eleutheropolis. Since Sozomen explains that Besanduc was the birthplace of Epiphanius,[78] and Jerome can speak of "the monastery of the holy pope Epiphanius—which is called Becos Abacuc,"[79] it appears that Epiphanius founded this monastery.[80] The anonymous preface to the *Ancoratus* which appears in some ancient manuscripts states that Epiphanius "became the abbot (Πατήρ) of monks" who lived at Eleutheropolis when he was twenty years of age.[81] The *Letter of Acacius and Paul*, prefixed to the text of the *Panarion*, is addressed to "Epiphanius of Palestine and Eleutheropolis, <sometime> abbot in the district of Eleutheropolis, now bishop of the city of Constantia in the province of Cyprus."[82] Even after being called to serve as bishop in the city of Salamis (Constantia), the principal see of Cyprus, Epiphanius continued to use Besanduc as a base of operations in his native Palestine.

---

[77] Sozomen *HE* 6.32; Nicephorus Callistus *HE* 11.39.

Peter the Deacon's *Book on the Holy Places*, which was composed in the twelfth century, mentions "Bycoyca in Eleutheropolis," where the tomb of Habakkuk was located. See John Wilkinson, *Egeria's Travels* (London: SPCK, 1971) 202.

[78] Sozomen *HE* 6.32.

[79] Jerome *Epistula* 82,8. He also agreed that it was located *in Eleutheropolitano territorio*. His point was that Besanduc was not located in the diocese of Jerusalem and therefore was not under the authority of Bishop John of Jerusalem.

While the significance of *Becos* in the name which Jerome uses is unclear, *Abacuc* is certainly a reference to the prophet Habakkuk. According to Sozomen (*HE* 7.29), the relics of Habakkuk were discovered at the village of Κηλά by Zebennus bishop of Eleutheropolis during the reign of Theodosius I (379–395 C.E.).

Prior to the discovery of the relics, this Κηλά (previously called Κεειλά) had already been recognized as the site of Habakkuk's burial, for Eusebius in his *Onomasticon* (s.v. "Κεειλά"; p. 114 in Klostermann's edition) makes reference to this identification. See also the separate entry in the *Onomasticon*, apparently to this same village, under the biform "Εχελά" (p. 88 in Klostermann). In both of these references the village is described in terms which locate it near to Eleutheropolis.

[80] This is also suggested by the anonymous preface to the ancient editions of the Ancoratus. See Frank Williams, *The Panarion of Epiphanius of Salamis* (2 vols.; NHS 35-36; Leiden: Brill, 1987–1994) 1.xi–xii.

[81] A text of this ancient preface may be found in PG 43, 12. Williams' discussion of this text may be found in *The Panarion of Epiphanius*, 1.xi–xii..

[82] This translation is from Williams, *The Panarion of Epiphanius*, 1.1.

The first stage of the Anthropomorphite Controversy began in 393 C.E. when a monk by the name of Atarbius went to Bethlehem to find Jerome and to the Mount of Olives to find Rufinus, intending to make them renounce Origenism.[83] His efforts directed toward Jerome were immediately successful, but Rufinus would not even see him. In the face of this rebuff, Atarbius began "barking against [Rufinus],"[84] to use the words of Jerome, but soon afterwards he "promptly retreated."[85]

While nothing is known of Atarbius' background or pedigree, J. N. D. Kelly has argued convincingly that it was Epiphanius who put Atarbius up to this examination of Jerome and Rufinus. He says: "Most biographers assume that Atarbius was acting on his own initiative, but Jerome clearly alludes to someone

---

[83]This episode is described in only one ancient source, Jerome's *Apologia adversus libros Rufini* 3.33. Cavallera, Kelly, and Murphy all date this incident to 393. See Ferdinand Cavallera, *Saint Jérome: Sa vie et son œuvre* (2 vols.; Spicilegium sacrum lovaniense: Études et documents 1 and 2; Louvain: Spicilegium sacrum lovaniense, 1922) 2.33, J.N.D. Kelly, *Jerome: His Life, Writings, and Controversies* (London: Duckworth, 1975) 198–200, and Francis X. Murphy, *Rufinus of Aquileia (345–411): His Life and Works* (Studies in Mediaeval History [New Series] 6; Washington, DC: Catholic University of America, 1945) 68.

Since Jerome renounced the teachings of Origen when pressed by Atarbius, but in his *De viris illustribus* he still praises the Alexandrian theologian, the Atarbius incident must postdate the writing of the *De viris illustribus*. On the basis of the phrase "usque ad XIV Theodosii imperatoris annum" found in the preface of Jerome's biography of illustrius men, Cavallera believed that it was written in 392 or the beginning of 393 with the latter being more probable. See Cavallera, *Saint Jérome,* 2.31. Nautin dates it in the year 393, sometime after sea navigation has resumed. See Pierre Nautin, "Études de chronologie hiéronymienne (393–397): Part 4," *Revue des études augustiniennes* 20 (1974) 277.

The *terminus ante quem* for the Atarbius episode is the arrival of Epiphanius in Jerusalem to confront Rufinus, John of Jerusalem, and the other Origenists, which is mentioned specifically in Jerome's *Apologia adversus libros Rufini* 3.33. Cavallera dated to Passover 393 the confrontation between Epiphanius and John of Jerusalem at the Church of the Resurrection, which is described in Jerome's *To Pammachius Against John of Jerusalem* 9 and which formed a part of Epiphanius' trip to Jerusalem. See Cavallera, *Saint Jérome,* 2.31–36. Nautin, however, has argued persuasively that this confrontation took place at the Dedication festival in September of the same year. See Pierre Nautin, "Études de chronologie hiéronymienne (393–397): Part 4," *Revue des études augustiniennes* 19 (1973) 69–73. Thus if both the *terminus post quem* and the *terminus ante quem* are located in the year 393, this is the year in which the Atarbius episode occurred.

[84]Jerome *Apologia adversus libros Rufini,* 3.33.

[85]Jerome *Apologia adversus libros Rufini,* 3.33.

whose agent he was, and it can hardly be doubted that this was Epiphanius."[86] The Bishop of Salamis, who saw links between Origenism and Arianism and every other pernicious doctrine, had to work carefully in a diocese which was not his own, but he seems to have been unable to resist meddling in the affairs of the Jerusalem church with its Origenist bishop, John. At first, Atarbius, who may very well have lived as a monk at Besanduc, was his surrogate, but soon Epiphanius himself would step out from behind the veil.

Thus, the *Hypomnestikon's* statement that Anthropomorphitism began at Eleutheropolis meshes nicely with what we know about the Anthropomorphite controversy of the 390's, and it provides a bedrock *terminus post quem* of 393 C.E. for the *Hypomnestikon*. While we cannot be certain that the *Hypomnestikon's* author knew about the Egyptian phase of the controversy, which erupted in 399, nothing precludes this and it seems likely that he did. Since Nestorianism is not mentioned in the *Hypomnestikon's* catalogue of heresies (which does claim to be complete), the emergence of the Nestorian controversy as a significant issue in the Church and its repudiation at the Council of Ephesus in 431 C.E. provide a reasonable *terminus ante quem* for the document, although like every argument from silence, it is not iron-clad. Aside from possible interpolations, the book certainly predates 500 C.E. as Chapters 1 and 150 assume the chronological schema of Julius Africanus which held that the first advent of Christ occurred on or about 5500 *Anno Mundi* and that the second coming of Christ would occur five hundred years later, at the close of the sixth millenium.

Other evidence points to the late fourth or early fifth centuries. First, Joseph pays inordinate attention to the high priests and to the Temple at Jerusalem with its vast consumption of gold (C. 2 and 107-11). This is odd in a Christian document, since the high priests have been replaced by Christ the heavenly high priest (C. 53[3]) and the ruined temple (C. 2[81], 123-25) by the church. The emperor Julian (mentioned in C. 139 [12]) planned to rebuild the temple at Jerusalem and, presumably, to restore the high priests.[87] Is Joseph indicating how expensive his plan would have been?

Julian noted that Christians killed heretics but considered their debates inconsequential; indeed, he called together the dissident bishops in the palace

---

[86]Kelly, *Jerome*, 198 n. 12. Typical of those scholars against whom Kelly argues is Cavallera, who says: ". . . the incident of Atarbius is prior to the arrival of St. Epiphanius in Jerusalem and has no connection with it." See Cavallera, *Saint Jérome*, 2.33.

[87]For Julian's scheme see Johannes Lydus *Months* 4.53 (Wünsch, p. 110, 5); Ammianus Marcellinus 23.1.2–3; church writers, e.g. Theodoret *HE* 3.20. For Julian's awareness that the Temple had been destroyed three times, *Epistle* 89 (Bidez-Cumont p. 135, 18).

with the people, urging them to lay aside differences and stop opposing individual forms of worship.[88] Joseph, on the other hand, insists that such heresies were highly divisive for Christians, Jews, Samaritans, and even Greeks (C. 140-143).

The concern with divination (C. 144) also points to Julian's reign and after.[89] Ammianus justifies his use of prophetic signs and dreams but admits that many thought he was "too much devoted to considering predictions" and "superstitious rather than a legitimate observer of rites."[90] Indeed, he tried without success to reanimate the Delphic oracle,[91] though he viewed divination as a substitute for oracles and wrote (*Against Galilaeans*) that

> the prophetic spirit has ceased among the Hebrews, and it is not preserved among the Egyptians to the present. It is obvious that the native oracles [of Greece], too, have grown silent with the passage of time. But our gracious Master and Father Zeus had this in mind, and so that we might not wholly lack fellowship with the gods has given us through the sacred arts [divination] a means of inspection by which we may obtain the necessary help.[92]

He praised the Jews as Chaldaeans of a theurgic race, who sleep among tombs for the sake of dream visions, and their forefather Abraham, whose divinations were based on meteors.[93] Cyril replied, just as Joseph does, by naming and criticizing "many and various" kinds of divination,[94] and like Joseph, Cyril knew and used Porphyry's *Letter to Anebo* against it.[95] Presumably, then, Joseph's lengthy discussion of divination, including an attack

---

[88]Julian *Against Galilaeans* 206A; Ammianus Marcellinus 22.5.3.

[89] Cyril of Jerusalem had been far less concerned with the topic (*Cat.* 4.37 [PG 33, 501A–B]), while the later Cyril of Alexandria would go into detail, writing against Julian and providing most of the fragments of *Against Galilaeans*.

[90]Ammianus Marcellinus 21.1.6–14; 22.12.7; 25.4.17.

[91]Oracle in Georgius Cedrenus (Corpus Scriptorum Historiae Byzantinae 34; Bonn: Weber, 1838) 532, 8–10; also the Castalian spring at Daphne near Antioch (Ammianus Marcellinus 22.12.8), mentioned by Gregory Nazianzen (PG 35, 704C; less probably at Delphi).

[92]Julian *Against Galilaeans* 198C–D.

[93]Julian *Against Galilaeans* 354B, 339E–340A, 356C, 358D.

[94]Julian *Against Julian* (PG 76, 815D).

[95]PG 76, 691–92C = Angelo R. Sodano, *Porfirio Lettera ad Anebo* (Naples: Arte Tipografico, 1958) xlv–xlvi, 16,7–17,6. Cyril was led to Porphyry by Eusebius but read the *Letter* himself; cf. Robert Grant, "Greek Literature in the Treatise *De Trinitate* and Cyril *Contra Julianum*," *JTS* 15 (1964) 265–79 (273).

on inspiration at Delphi, counters Julian's enthusiasm, with appropriate use of the philosopher Porphyry's criticism of "mechanical" or "technical" divination. We know that Julian strongly admired and praised Iamblichus but merely mentioned Porphyry as a Neoplatonist whose works he made no effort to read.[96]

In short, Chapters 2, 105-11, and 139-44 appear to address issues raised by the policies of Julian. They speak of the magnificence (and cost) of the Jerusalem Temple and its priesthood, methods of pagan divination, the sectarian division of Christianity, and how this division was fomented by Julian. These chapters should therefore be dated to an age when the memory of Julian and the threat of paganism had not yet passed–probably the early fifth century.[97]

One might imagine that Joseph's reference to "pseudo-Saracens" related to Ishmael (C. 147) could even reflect the Christian-Muslim debates of the eighth century. "What nations and how many arose from Abraham? First from Agar and Ismaél were born the Agarénoi and the Ismaélites, called the pseudo-Sarakenói, who devoted the name of Sarra to themselves, though they were not from her." But the name "Saracen" appears in the first century, when Dioscorides uses it to identify Arabs living on the Sinai peninsula, and as early as the fourth century Eusebius and others referred it to the descendants of Ishmael.[98] It is true that Joseph speaks of controversy over descent from Abraham's wife Sarra. This occurs later in the attack on Muslims by John of Damascus. "The Ishmaelites are descendants of Ishmael, born of Agar to Abraham....They call them Sarakénoi as 'empty *(kenoi)* from Sarra.'"[99] This is a reference to Mohammedans; John speaks of "Mamed."[100] But the claim that the Saracens were descended from Agar, not Sarra, was already known to Jerome (about 412) and Sozomen (mid-fifth century), long before the time of Mohammmed.[101]

---

[96]Iamblichus: Julian *Orations* 4.146A–B, 157D; 7.217B, 235A–B; Porphyry: Julian *Orations* 5.161C (though in the Neoplatonic succession, 7.222B).

[97]Compare William J. Malley's remarks about the very general occasion for Cyril's fifth-century treatise against Julian (*Hellenism and Christianity* [Rome: Università Gregoriana, 1978] 239–41).

What Joseph says about Moses is not related to Julian's comments; see John Gager, *Moses in Greco-Roman Paganism* (SBLMS 16; Nashville: Abingdon, 1972) 101–11.

[98]Full details by J.H. Mordtmann, "Saracens," *Brill's First Encyclopaedia of Islam 1913–1936* (7 vols.; Leiden: Brill, 1987) 7.155–56.

[99]*Her* 101 (PG 94, 764A).

[100]Cf. B. Kotter, "John Damascene, St.," *New Catholic Encyclopedia* (7 vols.; 1967) 7.1048 (cc. 100, 102, 103 interpolated).

[101]Jerome *Commentary on Ezekiel* 8 (cf. Kelly, *Jerome*, 305–8) on Ezek 25 (PL 25, 233C); Sozomen *HE* 6.18 (PG 67, 1412B).

Joseph's use of an amalgam of the *Chronicle* (*Syntagma*) by Hippolytus of Thebes, dated by Diekamp to between 650 and 750 C.E.,[102] and a fragment from Cosmas Vestitior probably dating from the ninth century, might suggest a date in the ninth century or later,[103] but the chapter (136) looks like an interpolation.[104] Other chapters may also be later interpolations. Diekamp mentions several chapters quoted anonymously in Byzantine manuscripts.[105] They deal with the lost books mentioned in the Old Testament (C. 120), with Greek versions of it (C. 122), with the captivities of the Israelites (C. 124),[106] with the number of Johns and Zechariahs (C. 135), with Jewish fasts (C. 145), and with the ten epiphanies of the risen Lord (C. 152). Chapter 125 is quite atypical and probably is an interpolation. It consists of an extract from the *Jewish War* of Flavius Josephus and bears a heading which reads either "A Chapter of the Other Josephus" or "Another Chapter of Josephus."

## AUTHORSHIP

The date for which we have argued eliminates Joseph of Tiberias as a possible author of the *Hypomnestikon*, but other factors point away from him as well. The sources used to produce the *Hypomnestikon* seem inappropriate for a former protege of Jerusalem's Patriarch, whom Epiphanius styles "a leading

---

[102]Diekamp, *Hippolytos von Theben*, 157. For early 9th-century use of Hippolytus see Diekamp, *Hippolytos von Theben*, xi–xiii, 134–45; Achelis (Helm, *Die Chronik*, 33 n.1) noted that Codex Parisinus bibl. nat. 48 (f.18v), an uncial of the late 9th century, cites (this) Hippolytus; Diekamp, *op. cit.*, xxv–xxvi.

[103]For this date Diekamp (*Hippolytos von Theben*, LVI n. 1) follows A. Ehrhard ("Forschung zur Hagiographie der griechischen Kirche," *Romische Quartalschrift* 11 [1897] 173).

[104] Diekamp's analysis of the text does not support the notion that Hippolytus himself refers to the tenth-century Symeon Metaphrastes (*Hippolytos von Theben*, 38, 25; 39, 7, 10 [itself doubtfully genuine]; cf. 112–13). Pierre Nautin views the *Hypomnestikon* as a witness to the *Chronicle* of a certain "Josipos," author of the *Philosophoumena* ascribed to Origen or Hippolytus (*Lettres et écrivains chrétiens des iie et iiie siècles* [Paris: Du Cerf, 1961] 188–90; Aline Pourkier, *L'Hérésiologie chez Épiphane de Salamine* [Paris: Beauchesne, 1992] 64). "Joseph" did not write Malley's "Four Unedited Fragments of the *De Universo* of the Pseudo-Josephus found in the *Chronicon* of Georgius Hamartolus (Coislin 305)," *JTS* 16 (1965) 13–25.

[105]Diekamp, *Hippolytos von Theben*, 149 n. 1.

[106]A number of Byzantine Octateuch manuscripts have three three short works appended: a discussion of the various translations of the Hebrew Scriptures into Greek, a list of the deportations of Israel and Judah, and a discussion of the various divine names. For more on this, see Robert Devreesse, *Introduction à l'Étude des Manuscrits Grecs* (Paris: Imprimerie Nationale, 1954) 101.

man" of the Jews and fluent in Hebrew. Why would such a man need to rely on Eusebius (*Hist. Eccl.* 6.25) in order to produce an Old Testament canon (Chapter 25) complete with muddled Hebrew names of the various books? And again, why would he need to rely on the Greek-speaking Eusebius in order to teach the names of the letters of the Hebrew alphabet (Chapter 26)? The lack of familiarity with Hebrew on the part of the *Hypomnestikon*'s author is perhaps demonstrated most clearly in Chapter 151 which speaks of the "mystical and ineffable name," two letters of which have been inscribed on the "crown" of the ark of the covenant. These letters are reported to be the letters ἰώδ and ἤδ. The numerical value of these letters is given as ten and eight so there is little doubt that *yodh* (ʾ) and *chet* (ח) are intended. The point of supplying this information is to show that the ark points to Ἰησοῦ" since the first two letters of his name also have values of ten and eight. The problem, of course, is that *yodh* (ʾ) and *he* (ה) are the initial letters of the Tetragrammaton, not *yodh* (ʾ) and *chet* (ח).

The knowledge of the geography of Palestine reflected in the *Hypomnestikon* has impressed some, particularly Moreau and Goranson. It is contended that this specialized knowledge points to Joseph of Tiberias or someone with a background much like his. In fact, virtually all of the *Hypomnestikon*'s geographical references come from the Septuagint, Josephus, or the *Chronicon* of Hippolytus.

The language employed in the *Hypomnestikon* suggests that its author held an Alexandrian christology and as Diekamp first observed[107] there are clues that he may have been Apollinarian. Alexandrian theology tended to emphasize the unity of Christ and his divine nature, whereas Antiochene theology emphasized that Christ had two complete natures, divine and human. Another way of saying this is that the theologians of the Antiochene school would not would not tolerate any infringement on Christ's full humanity. rist's full humanity, for "that which he has not assumed, he has not healed."[108] As a result of these competing emphases, somewhat divergent vocabularies developed. Alexandrian theology characteristically spoke of "the incarnation of the Word," or the divine Word being united with human "flesh" (the Logos-Sarx christology). Antiochene theology in contrast tended to speak of the Word's ἐνανθρώπησις, or of Christ being united with "man" (the Logos-Man christology).

That the author of the *Hypomnestikon* was probably schooled in Alexandrian theology is suggested by the beginning of Chapter 140 where the phrase ἐπὶ τῇ ἐνσάρκῳ τοῦ Κυρίου παρουσίᾳ is used in a rather spontaneous, unreflective manner. Similarly, in Chapter 37 Rahab is said to have "contributed

---

[107]Diekamp, *Hippolytos von Theben*, 148.

[108]Τὸ γὰρ ἀπρόσληπτον, ἀθεράπευτον. Gregory of Nazianzus *Epistula* 101, 32 (PG 37, 181).

to the Savior's being born of flesh," and Chapter 40 states that "Mary aided in the salvation of the world by bearing for us in the flesh the only begotten Son of God, our Lord Jesus Christ." Finally, as was mentioned in Chapter 3, the expression Θεοτόκος occurs twice outside of the interpolated Chapter 136. This expression was more congenial to Alexandrian theologians than to Antiochene theologians even before the Nestorian Controversy.

Diekamp observed that there may be an Apollinarian *Tendenz* in the listing of heresies found in Chapter 140. The Dimoirites (Apollinarians) are listed as a heresy in the heresiologies of Epiphanius, but not in the *Hypomnestikon*. The same is true of the Antidikomarianites,[109] who, according to Epiphanius, claim that their "doctrine was sounded forth from the presbyter Apollinarius himself."[110]

There is also the matter of the epithet "Anthropolater" found at the close of Chapter 139 in the description of the attacks made upon Christians during the reign of Julian. In its context the word is linked with the term "Arians" and may simply be another way of referring to them. Gallicciolli suggested that the Anthropolaters were Nestorians,[111] and the term was used later as an anti-Nestorian slogan, but there were no Nestorians in Julian's day.

Diekamp concluded that Anthropolater was an insult hurled by Apollinarians at those who disagreed with them. The evidence for this is substantial. In Gregory of Nazianzus' *Epistula 101*, which is a short polemic against Apollinarianism, an echo of the Apollinarian slogan is found: "You are a Sarcolater (i.e., flesh-worshipper), if I am an Anthropolater (i.e., man-worshipper)."[112] Similarly, in the *De incarnatione contra Apollinarium*, which was written about 380 C.E. and has been wrongly attributed to Athanasius,[113] the same disparaging label is recalled: "You call us Anthropolaters."[114] For an

---

[109]The distinctive doctrine of this group was that they denied the perpetual virginity of Mary. There are no references to the perpetual virginity of Mary in the *Hypomnestikon* outside of Chapter 136, the interpolated material from Hippolytus of Thebes and Cosmas Vestitior.

[110]Epiphanius *Pan.* 78.1 (GCS 37, 452, line 14).

[111]Gallicciolli, "Joseppus: Notitia," 14.III. (See n. 10 above).

[112]Gregory of Nazianzus *Epistula* 101 (SC 208, 48).

[113]On the date and authorship of this work, see Johannes Quasten, *Patrology*, vol. 3: *The Golden Age of Greek Patristic Literature* (Utrecht: Spectrum, 1960; reprinted Westminster, MD: Christian Classics, 1983) 29.

[114]Pseudo-Athanasius *De incarnatione contra Apollinarium libri ii* (PG 26, 1129).

Apollinarian document which uses the term directly, consult the long Apollinarian recension of Ignatius' *Epistle to the Trallians* 11.1.[115]

It is doubtful that the *Hypomnestikon's* author was a monk. Chapter 116 is entitled "Who among the apostles had wives?" This does not seem to be the type of material which an author committed to celibacy and monasticism would want to include in his work.

It is unlikely that the author of the *Hypomnestikon* will ever be identified precisely. Based on the title and the epilogue/colophon found at the end of the work most scholars have assumed that he was called Joseph or Josephus, but this hardly affords a complete identification. What is more, it is probable that the title should be understood as an objective genitive ("Someone summarized Josephus") rather than a subjective genitive ("Josephus summarized"). Thus we would have a *hypomnestikon* or summary of Josephus, not a *hypomnestikon* by Josephus. This usage is paralleled in the title of the *Hypomnesticon sancti Augustini episcopi contra Pelagianos et Caelestianos*, which is drawn from the works of Augustine, but is not by him. This suggestion becomes all the more likely when it is recognized that without further qualification the bare name Josephus would almost universally have been understood to refer to Flavius Josephus the Jewish historian. The colophon at the close of the book could then be explained as a misunderstanding of the significance of the title, a misunderstanding not unlike that of modern scholars.

## PROVENIENCE

The *Hypomnestikon* was written by someone with access to a fairly substantial library, so Alexandria, Constantinople, Antioch, Caesarea, and Jerusalem (Aelia) quickly come to mind. The fact that the Cambridge manuscript, as well as several other manuscripts which quote from the *Hypomnestikon*, probably came from Constantinople speaks in favor of that city, as does the existence there of a tradition of chronography. Certain other factors speak against it, however. There is no particular interest in the succession of emperors as might be expected from a work written in the imperial capital; they are only mentioned in a significant way in relationship to the persecutions of the church. If the author of the *Hypomnestikon* is an Apollinarian, then he is unlikely also to be from Constantinople, for Apollinarianism did not flourish there.

---

[115]In F. X. Funk and Franz Diekamp, *Patres apostolici*, vol. 2: *Epistulae spuriae* (3d ed.; Tübingen: Laupp, 1913).

A better candidate is Alexandria. There was a good library there. A strong chronographic tradition is known to have existed in Alexandria,[116] and fragments from a papyrus *Weltchronik*, which has some similarities to the *Hypomnestikon*, have been discovered in Egypt. The works of Hippolytus were known in Alexandria. Moreover, since the Anthropomorphite Controversy affected the church at Alexandria along with Nitria and Scetis, it can be said to have had a special relevance there.

If there is a problem with claiming an Alexandrian origin for the *Hypomnestikon*, it is the manner in which Alexandria is mentioned in a couple of passages. There is a direct reference to the city found in the discussion of the translation of the Septuagint in C. 122. In a work intended for Alexandrian readers, a more oblique reference might be expected. Similarly, C. 140(42) refers to "Origen of Alexandria." Nevertheless, these modest impediments are insufficient to rule out the possibility of an Alexandrian origin.

## MANNER OF COMPOSITION

Because a compendium, by definition, draws from a variety of sources, the material that it contains will not all be of the same age. The greater question relative to "authorship" is on the one hand whether there was a single "authorial moment" in which these diverse materials were brought together, or whether, on the other hand, the editorial process was more complex. Perhaps the question could be stated in this way: Does the noticeable variety in the *Hypomnestikon* simply reflect the diversity of its sources, or does it signal multiple redactional stages in the production of the *Hypomnestikon* itself? For instance, the evidence might be construed to suggest that an earlier Jewish edition was expanded into the Christian document known today. Many of the *Hypomnestikon's* chapters make no obvious Christian references. In addition, it constantly refers to Hebrews or Jews as "the people,"[117] and it teaches that after the Jews are

---

[116] As Adler (following Gelzer) has noted, the monks Panodorus and Annianus were doing important chronographic work in Alexandria of the late fourth and early fifth centuries. Unfortunately, most of their work has perished. See p. 499 of William Adler, "The Origins of the Proto-Heresies: Fragments from a Chronicle in the First Book of Epiphanius' *Panarion*," *JTS* 41 (1990) 472–501 and Heinrich Gelzer, *Sextus Julius Africanus und die byzantinische Chronogrphie*, vol. 2: *Die Nachfolger des Julius Africanus* (Leipzig: Teubner, 1885) 193–96.

[117] However, even in chapters which are obviously Christian, Israel is referred to as "the people" (e.g., C. 75). The Jewishness of certain chapters may be due simply to the fact that the Hebrew Bible was accepted by the Church as its own scripture. Scholarly discussion of such material by Christians will not necessarily appear to be overtly Christian.

punished for their rejection of Christ they will be recalled from the dispersion and the promises given them will be fulfilled (C. 75).[118] Unfortunately, even were it to prove possible to disentangle Christian additions from a Jewish original, it is not likely that such a project would be useful.

It has already been suggested that the lists appended to the *Chronicon* of Hippolytus provided both the nucleus and inspiration for the *Hypomnestikon*. In Alexandria, the tradition of biblical scholarship which, no doubt, began with the Hellenistic Jewish community flourished later in Christian circles as well. The result is apparent in material such as the *Chronicon*.[119] Once the headings to the lists from the *Chronicon's* appendices were converted to appropriate questions, there was little difficulty in mining other works of erudition in order to produce similar lists of questions and answers. Chief among these other works were the writings of Josephus, especially the *Antiquities*. As a result, our document came to be seen as a compendium extracted from Josephus and accordingly received the name *Hypomnestikon Biblion Ioseppou* .

## TRANSLATIONS

The *Hypomnestikon* has not previously been translated into English. The editions of Fabricius, Gallicciolli, and Migne each contained a Latin translation. A German translation, based on Fabricius' edition, was published under the direction of J. H. Haug in 1742. The "Josephi Gedächtnis-Büchlein" is found in the eighth and final volume of the Berlenburg Bible, published between the years 1726 and 1742.

## II CONTENTS OF THE NOTES

### BOOK I

1.    Generations from Adam to the Savior's advent
2.    High priests
3.    Descendants of Cain to the seventh generation
4.    Those saved in the ark
5.    Sons of Jacob, patriarchs
6.    Seventy-five who migrated to Egypt with Jacob

---

[118]Although perhaps idiosyncratic in the fifth century, such an understanding is not incompatible with Christian theology.

[119]While Hippolytus (or whoever authored the *Chronicon*) may not have spent his entire life in Alexandria, the Alexandrian features of this work, and especially the *Stadiasmos* which is embedded in its Greek text, are readily apparent.

7.    Priestly ancestors of Samouél
8.    Priestly ancestors of Éli
9.    Priestly ancestors of Ezekiel the prophet
10.   Priestly ancestors of Jeremiah the prophet

11.   Judges of the people after Joshua
12.   Kings of the people
13.   Kings of Israel after the division

14.   Writing prophets mentioned in the divine word
15.   Other prophets who did not write
16.   Women who were prophetesses

17.   Pious kings (vs Solomon and Uzziah, foreign wives)
      Impious kings
18.   False prophets

19.   Leaders of the people in Exodus
20.   Sons of Moses, from whom
21.   Sons of Aaron
22.   Nations from whom the people inherited
23.   Kings of what nations killed by the people
24.   Nations descended from sons of Nôe

25.    Twenty-two books of the Old Testament
26.    Names of the Hebrew letters
27.    Months of the Hebrews, Egyptians, Macedonians, Romans
28.    Making sacred chrism
       Making sacred incense

29.    Who were giants
30.    Who were prolific (*polypaides*)

31.    Division of promised land
32.    Cities of refuge
33.    Cities for Levites
34.    Cities and kings taken by Joshua and Caleb
35.    What kings came out in salt plain, killed by Abraham
36.    Kings saved by Abraham with Lot

37.    Hebrews with gentile wives
38.    Polygamists
39.    Women who corrupted their husbands
40.    Women who helped their husbands, hence pleasing to God
41.    Men admirable for wisdom
42.    Women admirable for wisdom

43.    Perished because too clever
44.    Wise who concealed truth
45.    Justice through guile
46.    Death through claim of goodness or piety
47.    Just people killed
48.    Killed brothers
49.    Perished because merciful
50.    Death for justice, life for impiety
51.    To die though not ill
52.    Died blind
53.    Preserved without dying
54.    Dead live again
55.    Sterile women bore offspring
56.    Dishonored father
57.    Overthrown for arrogance
58.    Glorified for humility
59.    Murderers accepted by God
60.    Stoned for sins
61.    Stoned though virtuous

94.  Predictions of Oziél (Jahaziel)
95.  Predictions of Eliad son of Obdia
96.  Predictions of Olda wife of Selim

### \<CHRISTIAN, 97-101\>
97.  Predictions of Zacharias the [high] priest
98.  Predictions of Symeôn
99.  Predictions of Elisabet
100. Predictions of the Virgin Maria
     Predictions of Iôannés the Baptist
101. Involuntary prediction in the Gospel ("and in the Old")

## BOOK V
### \<DAVID AND SOLOMON, 102-4\>
102. David's mighty men
103. Solomôn's princes
104. Solomôn's daily consumption

### \<THE TEMPLE, 105-11\>
105. Solomôn's temple
106. Dimensions of the temple
107. Sacred vessels in the sanctuary
108. Precious vessels dedicated by Solomôn
109. Vestments prepared by Solomôn
110. Tabernacle constructed by Moses
111. Sanctuary constructed by Moses

### \<DAVID\>
112. Census of David
113. Deaths due to David's sin

### \<MEN AND WOMEN\>
114. Prostitutes who married well
115. Celibate prophets
116. Married apostles (Christian)

### \<KINGS\>
117. Impious kings not buried in David's tomb
118. Davidic kings omitted from Savior's genealogy (Christian)
119. King died trusting physicians not God

148.    Predictions of the apostle Paul
149.    Predictions of John the Evangelist
150.    Years from creation to the birth of Christ [cf. C. 1]

151.    Names of the Lord in the scriptures
152.    Ten epiphanies of the risen Lord
153.    Appearances of the Lord after the ascension

<Mostly Hebrew 154-67>
154.    Idols worshiped by the people
155.    Closest friendships
156.    Soul changed to beast (3-4 Christian)
157.    Good from evil (Christian)

158.    Long-lived after Moses
159.    Killed lions with hands
160.    Killed by lions
161.    Killed for sacrilege (3 Christian)
162.    Put in pits to be killed
163.    Paid penalties for sins (13 Christian)
164.    Obtained mercy for sins (5-7 Christian)
165.    Supposed they acted rightly but sinned

166.    Nôe's descendants identified (5 Christian)

167.    Powers of the stones on the high priest's girdle (cf. 2, 109)

        Epilogue/Colophon

# Text and Translation

## Sigla used in the Text

< > Additions by editors
[ ] Deletions by editors; or references
( ) Corrections; folio numbers (approximate
for Greek text) of MS. Cambridge University Library Ff.1.24E

## Abbreviations Used in the Apparatus

C – Cambridge University Library Ms. Ff. I.24
F – Edition of J.A. Fabricius in Part 2 of *Codex Pseudepigraphicus Veteris Testamenti* (2d ed.; Hamburg: Felginer, 1741).
G – Edition of G. B. Gallicciolli in Vol. 14, pp. 2–84 of Andreas Gallandi, ed., *Bibliotheca Veterum Patrum Antiquorumque Scriptorum Ecclesiasticorum Græco-Latina* (2d ed.; 14 vols.; Venice: Zatta & Sons, 1788).
*Lc* – *Lege cum* (Read with)
M – Edition printed by J. P. Migne, *Patrologia Graeca*, Vol. 106, pp. 15–176.

In the following text, the folio and column numbers of the Cambridge manuscript are given in parentheses. For the sake of readability, wherever a word spans columns, the reference has been placed following the word.

(104a1) Ὑπομνηστικὸν βιβλίον α' Ἰωσήππου.[1]

**Α'.** +[2] "Οσαι γεγόνασιν ἀπὸ τοῦ Ἀδαμ ἕως τῆς τοῦ Σωτῆρος παρουσίας γενεαί;
α' Ἀδὰμ, β' Σὴθ, γ' Ἐνὼς, δ' Καϊνᾶν, ε' Μαλελεὴλ,[3] ϛ' Ἰάρεδ.
ζ' Ἐνώχ. Οὗτος μετετέθη καίπερ ἔτι ζῶν καὶ φυλαττόμενος.
η' Μαθουσάλα, θ' Λάμεχ.
ι' Νῶε. Οὗτος ἐκ τοῦ κατακλυσμοῦ διασώζεται ἐν λάρνακι μετ' οἴκου παντός. Τρεῖς δ' αὐτῷ γεγόνασι παῖδες, Σὴμ, Χὰμ, Ἰάφεθ. Ἡ δὲ γενεαλογία εἰς τὸ Ἑβραίων ἐρχομένη γένος, ἀπὸ (104a2) τοῦ Σὴμ συνίσταται.
ια' Σὴμ, ιβ' Ἀρφαξὰδ, ιγ' Σάλα, ιδ' Ἔβερ.
ιε' Φαλέκ. Ἐπὶ τούτου ἐμερίσθη ἡ γῆ. Πληροῦται[4] γὰρ ἐπ' αὐτὸν ἀπὸ Ἀδὰμ ἔτη ‹ ͵γ›.[5] ὡς[6] εἶναι τὸ ἥμισυ τοῦ χρόνου τῆς παρούσης ἐν ἑξάδι χιλιάδων καταστάσεως.[7]

---

[1]F (in his text) Ὑπομνηστικον βιβλιον Ἰωσηππου; F (in his title) GM Ἰωσηππου Ὑπομνηστικον βιβλιον. Elsewhere C places the book divisions in the margin. Here it is in the body of the text.
[2]In C, the heading to each chapter is set off with a cross.
[3]GM Μαλαλεηλ.
[4]*lc* FGM Πληρουνται.
[5]C is lacunose here, has space for 5 letters; *lc* FGM ͵γ.
[6]FGM ὥστε.
[7]Emend to ἀποκαταστασεως?

## NOTEBOOK OF JOSEPHUS, BOOK I

Joseph begins abruptly, in the manner of a chronicler but without a preface such as we find in Hippolytus' *Chronicon* or the examples noted by Helm: Hippolytus' treatise *On Christ and Antichrist*, Polybius, the evangelist Luke, Theophilus of Antioch, and Irenaeus — not to mention the more relevant *Jewish War* and *Jewish Antiquities* by Josephus and *Church History* by Eusebius. Because of this lack we do not know just what he thought his subject matter was. The *Hypomnestikon* begins with folio 104a in the Cambridge manuscript.

### <LEADERS OF THE PEOPLE 1-24>

**1.** – How many generations were there from Adam to the coming of the Savior?[1]

1. **Adam**. 2. **Seth**. 3. **Enôs**. 4. **Kainan**. 5. **Maleleél**. 6. **Iared**.

7. **Enoch**, who, alive and kept safe, was translated.

8. **Mathousala**. 9. **Lamech**.

10. **Nôe**. In the ark he was preserved from the deluge with his whole house. He had three sons, Sém, Cham, Iapheth. The genealogy that comes down to the Hebrew people proceeds from Sém.

11. **Sém**. 12. **Arphaxad**.[2] 13. **Sala**. 14. **Eber**.

15. **Phalek**. Under him the land was divided [Gn 10:25]. For from Adam to him are completed three thousand years[3] so as to be half the time of the restoration which comes in six chiliads

---

[1] Words and sentences from Joseph's source (here Hippolytus *Chr* 718 = *LG* 1.332) are in **bold** type.

[2] With *LG* 1.332 and Julius Africanus, Joseph omits Cainan after Arphaxad.

[3] Fabricius reasonably places ,γ ΄ (= 3,000) in the blank space and cites Procopius of Gaza on Gn 11:18 (PG 87, 316C): "From the creation to Phalek is 600 (X'; emend to ,γ΄ ) years, half the whole time of the existence of the world; for not only the land but the time was divided with him." The figure 3,000 is only approximate (correct to 2,791) but would place Joseph's date before 500. Note William Adler's discussion of the witnesses to the chronological position of Phalek in Africanus' thought on pp. 491–92 of his "The Origins of the Proto-Heresies: Fragments from a Chronicle in the First Book of Epiphanius' *Panarion*," *JTS* 41 (1990) 472–501.

ιϛ' Ῥαγαῦ, ιζ' Θροὺχ,[1] ιη' Ναχώρ, ιθ' Θάρα.[2]
κ' Ἀβραάμ, ὃς ἀπὸ τῆς Χαλδαίας εἰς τὴν Χαναναίαν θείῳ μετοικίζετο[3] προστάγματι.
κα' Ἰσαάκ.
κβ' Ἰακώβ. Οὗτος ἐγέννησε τοὺς δώδεκα φυλάρχους, ἐξ ὧν τὸ δωδεκάφυλον τοῦ Ἰσραὴλ συνίσταται. Ἀπὸ δὲ τοῦ Ἰούδα, ὃς ἦν τέταρτον[4] (104b1) αὐτῷ γόνος, τὸ βασιλικὸν παράγεται γένος.
κγ' Ἰούδας, κδ' Φαρὲς, κε' Ἐσρώμ, κϛ' Ἀράμ.
κζ' Ἀμηναδάς.[5] Ἐπὶ τούτου ἡ Αἰγύπτου ἔξοδος[6] τοῦ λαοῦ, Μωϋσέως ἡγουμένου, γεγένηται.
κη' Ῥαασσών.[7]
κθ' Σαλμών. Ἠγάγετο[8] τὴν Ῥαάβ, τὴν τοὺς κατασκόπους κατακρύψασαν.
λ' Βοός.[9] Οὗτος τὴν Μωαβίτιν Ῥοὺθ ἠγάγετο, ὅστις δέκατος ἀπὸ Ἀβραάμ. Καὶ πληροῦται ἐπὶ τῆς Ῥοὺθ[10] τὸ προρρηθὲν ὑπὸ Μωϋσέως· Μωαβῖτις οὐκ εἰσελεύσεται εἰς ἐκκλησίαν[11] Κυρίου μέχρι γενεᾶς δεκάτης.
λα' Ὠβὴδ, λβ' Ἰεσσαί.
λγ' Δαβὶδ, (104b2) ὃς χρίεται τοῦ λαοῦ βασιλεὺς, δι' ἐπιείκειαν εὑρεθεὶς[12] ἀπὸ[13] Θεοῦ ἄρχειν τοῦ λαοῦ.
λδ' Σολομὼν, ὃς τὸν ναὸν, τὸν ἐν Ἱεροσολύμοις ἐδείματο.
λε' Ῥοβοάμ, ἐφ' οὗ[14] ἡ βασιλεία τοῦ Δαβὶδ διηρέθη. καὶ τὸν Ἱεροβοὰμ ὁ Ἰσραὴλ ἔστησεν ἑαυτῷ βασιλέα, μερισθεὶς ἀπὸ τοῦ Ἰούδα.

---

[1] *Lc* FGM Σερουχ.
[2] *Lc* FGM Θαρρα.
[3] FGM μετοικιζεται.
[4] *Lc* FGM τεταρτος.
[5] *Lc* FGM Ἀμιναδαβ.
[6] FGM ἡ ἐξ Αἰγυπτου ἐξοδος.
[7] *Lc* FGM Ναασσων.
[8] FGM Οὗτος ἠγαγετο.
[9] *Lc* FGM Βοοζ.
[10] FGM ἐπι Ῥουθ.
[11] FGM εἰς την ἐκκλησιαν.
[12] *Lc* FGM, who in their notes suggest emending to αἱρεθεις.
[13] Emend to ὑπο.
[14] FGM ἐφ' ὁν.

16. **Ragau**. 17. **Serouch**. 18. **Nachôr**. 19. **Tharra**.

20. **Abraam**, who by a divine command migrated from Chaldaea into Chanaanea.

21. **Isaak**.

22. **Iakôb**. He generated the twelve founders of the twelve tribes of which Israel consisted, and from Ioudas, his fourth (104b) son, proceeds the royal family.

23. **Ioudas**. 24. **Phares**. 25. **Esrôm**. 26. **Aram**.

27. **Aminadab** [Ex 6:23]. Under him the exodus of the people from Egypt took place, with Moses as leader.

28. **Naassôn**.

29. **Salmôn**. He married Rahab who concealed the spies.

30. **Booz**. He married the Moabitess Ruth and was tenth from Abraham. And in Ruth was fulfilled what was spoken by Moses: "A Moabitess shall not enter the congregation of the Lord to the tenth generation" [Dt 23:3].

31. **Ôbéd**. 32. **Iessai**.

33. **David**, who was anointed as king over the people, who because of his modesty was chosen by God to rule the people.[1]

34. **Solomôn**, who founded the Temple in Jerusalem.

35. **Roboam**, under whom the kingdom of David was divided and Israél, divided from Iouda, set up Jereboam as king for itself.

---

[1] Thus far the list is the reverse of Lk 3:31–38 (omitting the Kainam of Lk 3:36, as in *Liber generationis* I).

λς' Ἀβιὰ, λζ' Ἀσὰ, λη' Ἰωσαφὰτ,[1] λθ' Ἰωράμ, μ' Ὀχοζίας, μα' Ἰωὰς, μβ' Ἀμασίας, μγ' Ὀζίας, μδ' Ἰωάθαν,[2] με' Ἀχάζ.

μς' Ἐζεκίας, ἐφ' οὗ ὁ Ἰσραὴλ αἰχμάλωτος ἤχθη.

μζ' Μανασσῆς, μή Ἀμών, μθ' Ἰωσίας.

ν' Ἰεχονίας, ὁ καὶ Ἰωακεὶμ,[3] (105a1) αἰχμάλωτος ἤχθη εἰς Βαβυλῶνα. να' Σαλαθιήλ.

νβ' Ζοροβάβελ, ἐφ' οἷς ἡ τοῦ Ἰούδα αἰχμαλωσία ἀνήχθη ὑπὸ Κύρου[4] Βασιλέως Περσῶν.

νγ' Ῥησὰ, νδ' Ἰωαννὰ, νε' Ἰωλὰ, νς' Ἰωρὴχ, νζ' Σεμεὴ, νη' Ματθὰν, νθ' Ναγγαὶ, ξ' Σελὴμ, ξα' Ναοὺμ, ξβ' Ἀμὼς, ξγ' Ματταθὶ,[5] ξδ' Ἰωσὴφ, ξε' Ἰαννὰ, ξς' Μελχὶ, ξζ' Λευΐ, ξη' Ματθὰν, ξθ' Ἠλή.[6]

ο' Ἰωσὴφ,[7] ὁ τῆς παρθένου Μαρίας τῆς Θεοτόκου μνηστήρ, τῆς τὸν Κύριον ἡμῶν Ἰησοῦν Χριστὸν, τὸν προϋπάρχοντα Θεὸν Λόγον, Θεὸν συναΐδιον τοῦ[8] τῷ Πατρὶ τετοκυίας. (105a2)

**Β'.** + Ὅσοι γεγόνασιν ἀρχιερεῖς ἀπὸ τοῦ Ἀαρῶνος ἀρξάμεν;[9]

Τοῦ Ἰακὼβ τρίτος γέγονε παῖς Λευΐς,[10] τοῦ δὲ Λευΐ Καὰθ, τοῦ δὲ Καὰθ Ἀμβρὰμ, ἐξ οὗπερ γίνονται Ἀαρὼν καὶ Μωϋσῆς. Καὶ ὁ μὲν Μωϋσῆς ἡγεμόνευσε τῆς τοῦ λαοῦ ἐξ Αἰγύπτου πορείας, Ἀαρὼν δὲ πρῶτος ἀρχιερεὺς ὑπὸ τοῦ Μωϋσέως χρίεται.

α' Ἀαρὼν, β' Ἐλεαζὰρ,
γ' Φινεὲς, δ' Ἐβιέζερ, ε' Βοκχὶ,

---

[1] FGM Ἰωσαφαθ.
[2] Lc FGM Ἰωαθαμ.
[3] FGM Ἰωακειμ, ος.
[4] GM omit Κυρου.
[5] Lc GM Ματταθιας.
[6] Lc FGM Ἠλι.
[7] M mistakes the numeral ο' for the definite article, thus Ὁ Ἰωσηφ.
[8] FGM omit του.
[9] Lc FGM ἀρξαμενοι.
[10] GM Λευι.

36. **Abia**. 37. **Asa** (Asaph, Mt). 38. **Iôsaphat** (so Mt). 39. **Iôram**. 40.
**Ochozias** (so Lk, Codex Bezae; Ozias, Mt). 41. **Ioas**. 42. **Amasias**. 43. **Ozias**.
44. **Iôatham**. 45. **Achaz**.
46. **Ezekias**, under whom Israél was led into captivity.
47. **Manassés**. 48. **Amôn**. 49. **Iôsias**.[1]
50. **Iechonias** also known as (105a) Iôakeim, who was taken to Babylon as
a captive.[2]
51. **Salathiél**.
52. **Zorobabel**, under whom [plural] the captivity of Iouda was removed by
Cyrus king of the Persians.[3]
53. **Resa**. 54. **Iôanna**. 55. **Iôla**. 56. **Iôrech**. 57. **Semeé**. 58. **Matthan**.
59. **Naggai**. 60. **Selém**. 61. **Naoum**. 62. **Amôs**. 63. **Mattathias**. 64. **Iôseph**.
65. **Ianna**. 66. **Melchi**. 67. **Leui**. 68. **Matthan**. 69. **Héli**.
70. **Iôséph, to whom the Virgin Maria** the God-bearer **was betrothed,
who bore** our Lord **Jesus Christ**, the preexistent God-Logos, God coeternal
with the Father.[4]

**2.** – How many high priests were there, beginning from Aarôn?
The third son of Iakôb was Leui, who begot Kaath; Kaath's son was
Ambram, from whom Aarôn and Moses were born [1 Par 6:1-3]. Moses was the
leader of the people on the way from Egypt, and Aarôn was the first high priest,
anointed by Moses.[5]
1. Aarôn [Josephus *Ant.* 3.188; 20.225], 2. Eleazar [1 Par 6:3-4; Josephus
*Ant.* 5.361],
3. Phinees [1 Par 6:4; Josephus *Ant.* 5.361], 4. Ebiezer [Abeisou, 1 Par 6:4-
5; Abiezerés, Josephus *Ant.* 5.362], 5. Bokchi [Bôe, 1 Par 6:5; Bokki, Josephus
*Ant.* 5.362],

---

[1] From this point to the end Joseph diverges from the *LG*.

[2] Hippolytus *Chr.* 718 = *LG* 1.332 says that "Iosias genuit Ionaam et Ioachim et
fratres eius Heliachim, qui et Ioachim, et Sedeciam, qui et Ieconias dictus est, <et>
Salum."

[3] So far (up through Zorobabel) the list is close to both Mt 1:2–11 and the *Liber
generationis*. The material that follows, however, appears to be based on the genealogy
of Lk 3:23–27 in reverse order. Cf. C. 118, which purports to explain why certain kings
of David's line were omitted from the gospel genealogies.

[4] On *theotokos*, PGL 639–41 (Eusebius and Epiphanius); on *proüparchôn*, ibid.
1191 (as early as Justin); on *synaïdios*, ibid. 1297 (Epiphanius). The idea of seventy
generations from Adam to Christ is a commonplace of early Christian eschatology.

[5] Cf. C. 10 on the ancestors of Ieremias; also Hippolytus *Chr.* 741 = *LG* 1.341:
nomina sacerdotum.

ϛ' Ὀζὴ, ζ' Ἠλή.[1]

η' Ἀχιτώβ. Ἐφ' οὗ Σαμουὴλ[2] προφήτης ἦν, καὶ ἱερεὺς ἅμα καὶ[3] κριτὴς τοῦ λαοῦ.

θ' Ἀχιμέλεχ, ὃς ἀναιρεῖται ὑπὸ τοῦ Σαοὺλ[4] μετὰ (105b1) τριακοσίων πεντήκοντα ἱερέων, διὰ τὴν τοῦ Δαβὶδ δεξίωσιν.

ι' Ἀβιαθὰρ, ὃς μόνος διασωθεὶς ἀπὸ τῶν ἀναιρεθέντων ἱερέων, κατέφυγεν ἐπὶ τὸν Δαβίδ.

ια' Σαδὼκ, ἐφ' οὗ ὁ ναὸς ὑπὸ Σολομῶνος ᾠκοδομήθη.

ιβ' Ἀχιμάας, ιγ' Ἀζαρίας, ιδ' Ἰωράμ.

ιε' Ἰωδαέ. Οὗτος ἔζησεν ἔτη ἑκατὸν τριάκοντα, ὃς καὶ τὴν Γοδολίαν ἐξαλεῖψαι τὸ τοῦ Δαβὶδ γένος βουλομένην ἀνεῖλεν.[5]

ιϛ' Ἀζιωρὰμ, ιζ' Φειδαῖος, ιη' Σωβαῖος, ιθ' Ἰῆλος, κ' Ἰώθαμος.

κα' Οὐρίας. Οὗτος ἐπὶ Ἄχαζ καὶ Ἐζεκίου ἱεράτευσεν.

κβ' Ἰκρὴ, (105b2) κγ' Ἰωασσῆ, κδ' Σελούμ.

---

[1] Lc FGM Ἠλι.

[2] FGM ὁ Σαμουηλ.

[3] FGM omit και.

[4] FGM place ὑπο του Σαουλ after ἱερεων.

[5] FGM ἀνειλε.

6. Ozé [Ozei, 1 Par 6:5-6; Ozis, Josephus *Ant.* 5.362], 7. Éli [not 1 Par; Éleis, Josephus *Ant.* 5.362, 6.122; *b. Pes.* 57a].[1]

8. Achitôb, under whom Samuel was prophet and at the same time priest and judge of the people [1 Par 6:7–8; Josephus *Ant.* 6.122].

9. Achimelech, who was killed by Saul with (105b) three hundred fifty priests because they supported David [Josephus *Ant.* 6.242, 6.260; cf. C. 73].

10. Abiathar, who alone was saved from the slain priests and fled to David [Josephus *Ant.* 6.269; 7.110].[2]

11. Sadôk, under whom the Temple was built by Solomôn [1 Par 6:12, omits names 9-10; Josephus *Ant.* 10.152-53 lists names 11-27].[3]

12. Achimaas [1 Par 6:9; Achimas, Josephus], 13. Azarias [1 Par 6:9, Josephus], 14. Iôram [Iôanas, 1 Par 6:9; Iôramos, Josephus].[4]

15. Iôdaë [4 Rg 11; = Azarias, 1 Par 6:10?; Iôs, Josephus], who lived 130 years [Josephus *Ant.* 9.166] and killed Godolia [Othlia, 9.150-52], who wanted to obliterate the family of David [9.140].[5]

16. Aziôram [Axiôramos, Josephus], 17. Pheidaios [Phideas, Josephus], 18. Sôbaios [Soudaias, Josephus], 19. Iélos [Iouélos, Josephus], 20. Iôthamos [Josephus].

21. Ourias [Josephus], who was priest under Achaz and Ezekias.

22. Ikré [Nérias, Josephus], 23. Iôassé [Ôdaias, Josephus], 24. Seloum [Selloum, 1 Par 6:12 Cod.A; Salloumos, Josephus].

---

[1] Josephus mentions two high priests who served between Éleis and Achitôb: Iésous and Achias. He shows some confusion about Iésous since in *Ant.* 8.12 it is implied that he served prior to Éleis, not after, as indicated here. There Bokki (Bokchi) is described as his son, so Iésous may have been confused with Abiezerés (Ebiezer). On the other hand, Josephus' subtotals require an additional name in this section.

[2] In *Ant.* 7.110 Josephus actually lists Zadok ahead of Abiathar, but he records that they served at the same time. In the list of high priests found in *Ant.* 10.152–53, however, it is assumed that Zadok immediately preceded Achimas. Moreover, 2 Rg 8:17 states that Abiathar was the son of Achimelech, the previous high priest.

[3] According to Josephus' reckoning (*Ant.* 20.228) thirteen high priests served beginning with Aaron and extending down to the construction of Solomon's temple. Since the *Hypomnestikon* omits Iésous and Achias, only eleven are listed.

[4] "From here on Josephus' list diverges considerably from Scripture" (Thackeray-Marcus, *Josephus* 6 [LCL; Cambridge: Harvard University Press, 1937] 242 note d), and Joseph diverges from Josephus.

[5] Josephus calls her Othlia (Athaliah, Hebrew), while her name is Gotholia in 4 Rg 11:1–16 (Godolia, Arm). See Index A s.v. Godolia, Gotholia. Josephus has Iôramos' son Iôs after him.

κε' Χελκίας, ὃς ἐπὶ τοῦ Ἰωσίου τοῦ εὐσεβοῦς βασιλέως ἱεράτευσεν.
κϛ' Σαραίας.
κζ' Ἰωσέδεκ, ἐφ' οὗ ὁ λαὸς αἰχμάλωτος ὑπὸ τοῦ Ναβουχοδονόσορ ἤχθη.
κη' Ἰησοῦς ὁ τοῦ Ἰωσέδεκ, ἐφ' οὗ Ἰούδας ἀπὸ τῆς αἰχμαλωσίας ὑπὸ[1] Κύρου ἀνήχθη, καὶ μετὰ τοῦ Ζοροβάβελ τοῦ λαοῦ προέστη.
κθ' Ἰωακείμ. Ἐπὶ τούτου νόμους Ἔσδρας ἀνέγνω.
λ' Ἐλιασήφ.
λα' Ἰώσχας,[2] ἐφ' οὗ τὰ κατὰ Ἐσθὴρ καὶ Μαρδοχαῖον.
λβ' Ἰωάννας.[3]
λγ' Ἰαδδαῖος, ἐφ' οὗ ὁ ἐν Γαρίζῃ ναὸς ᾠκοδομήθη.
λδ' Ὠνίας, λε' Σίμων. (106a1)
λϛ' Ἐλεάζαρος, ἐφ' οὗ αἱ βίβλοι τῶν Ἑβδομήκοντα δύο,[4] Πτολεμαίου τοῦ δευτέρου βουληθέντος, ἡρμηνεύθησαν.

---

[1] FGM ὑπερ.
[2] Lc FGM Ἰωαχας.
[3] Lc FGM Ἰωαννης.
[4] FGM omit δυο.

25. Chelkias [1 Par 6:13; Elkias, Josephus], who was high priest under Iôsias the pious king.[1]

26. Saraias [1 Par 6:14; Azaros, Josephus].[2]

27. Iôsedek, under whom the people was led captive by Nebuchadnezzar [1 Par 5:15; Iôsadakos, Josephus *Ant.* 10.150, 153; 20.231].[3]

28. Iésous son of Iôsedek, under whom Ioudas was led back from captivity by Kyros and with Zerobabel ruled the people [2 Esdr 22:10; Josephus *Ant.* 11.73; 20.234].

29. Iôakeim, under whom Esdras read the laws [2 Esdr 22:10; Iôakkeimos, Josephus *Ant.* 11.121, 158].[4]

30. Eliaséph [Eliaseib, 2 Esdr 22:10; Eliasibos, Josephus *Ant.* 11.158, 297].

31. Iôachas, under whom were the events related to Esther and Mordecai [Iôda, 2 Esdr 22:11; Iôdas, Josephus *Ant.* 11.297; events under Eliasibos].

32. Iôannés [Josephus *Ant.* 11.297; Iônathan, 2 Esdr 22:11].

33. Iaddaios, under whom the Temple was built in Gerizim[5] [Iaddou, 2 Esdr 22:11; Iaddous, Josephus *Ant.* 11.302,347].

34. Ônias (I) [Josephus *Ant.* 11.347], 35. Simôn [Josephus *Ant.* 12.43, 157] (106a).

36. Eleazaros (Ônias II), under whom the books of the Seventy-two were translated by the will of Ptolemy II [Josephus *Ant.* 12.44].[6]

---

[1] Joseph here omits the Azarias of 1 Par 6:13–14.

[2] It is possible that at this point the *Hypomnestikon* reflects influence from the list of Aaron's descendants found in 1 Par 6 and the name Saraios has been substituted for Azaros. However, in 1 Par two separate figures are mentioned, one after the other, and it seems odd that one would be substituted in favor of the other. Moreover, Josephus' subtotals also seem to require an additional high priest at this point. Concerning this problem, a note in the edition of Ralph Marcus states: "In *Ant.* 20.231 Josephus mentions eighteen high priests of the first temple. In the present list there are only seventeen. Possibly the name Saraias (bibl. Seraiah) has been accidentally omitted after Azaros (bibl. Azariah) because of the similarity."

[3] Josephus (*Ant.* 20.231) states that eighteen high priests served in Solomon's temple. The figure fits his list if one begins with Zadôk, ends with Iôsedek, and counts Saraias and Azaros serarately. Since the *Hypomnestikon* lists only Saraias, its total for this period is seventeen.

[4] Joseph does not accept the claim of 1 Esdr 9:40 and Josephus *Ant.* 11.121 that Esdras was high priest around this time.

[5] Joseph does not mention Manassés, Iaddaios' brother and rival (Josephus *Ant.* 11.310, 324, 346).

[6] Also see C. 122.

λζ' Μανασσῆς.

λη' Ἀνανίας. Ἐπὶ τούτου τὰ δεινὰ ὑπὸ τοῦ Ἀντιόχου τοῦ Ἐπιφανοῦς ἐπὶ τῶν Μακκαβαίων συμβέβηκε.

λθ' Σίμων, μ' Ὀνίας, μα' Ἰησοῦς, μβ' Ὀνίας.

μγ' Ἄλκιμος, ὃν Ἀντίοχος κατέστησεν, οὐκ ὄντα τοῦ ἀρχιερατικοῦ[1] γένους, ἀνελὼν τόν Ὀνίαν, ἐπὶ τούτου Ὀνίας ὁ τοῦ Ὀνίου υἱὸς φυγὼν εἰς Αἴγυπτον, ναὸν ὅμοιον τὸν[2] ἐν Ἱεροσολύμοις ᾠκοδόμησεν ἐν τῷ Ἡλιοπολίτῃ νόμῳ.

μδ' Ἰούδας **(106a2)** ὁ Μακκαβαῖος ἐκ τῶν Ἀσαμωναίου, με' Ἰωνάθης ἀδελφὸς, μϛ' Σίμων ἀδελφὸς, μζ' Ἰωάννης, ὁ καὶ Ὑρκανός.

μη' Ἀριστόβουλος, ὃς καὶ διάδημα πρῶτος περιτέθηται.[3]

μθ' Ἰανναῖος, ὁ καὶ Ἀλέξανδρος.

ν' Ὑρκανὸς, ἐφ' οὗ Πομπήϊος ὁ Ῥωμαίων βασιλεὺς εἰς[4] τὸ ἱερὸν ἐπιβὰς τὰ κειμήλια ἀφείλετο.

να' Ἀντίγονος, ὃς Πάρθους ἐπηγάγετο κατὰ Ὑρκανοῦ, ὑπὸ Ἡρώδου ἐκβάλλεται τῆς ἱερωσύνης.

νβ' Ἀνανῆλος, ὁ ὑπὸ Ἡρώδου κατασταθεὶς οὐκ ὢν τοῦ ἀρχιερατικοῦ γένους.

νγ' Ἀριστόβουλος, ὃν Ἡρώδης **(106b1)** καθίστησι τὸν Ἀνανῆλον ἐξομοσάμενος· καὶ πάλιν δολοφονήσας τὸν Ἀριστόβουλον, καθίστησι τὸν Ἀνανῆλον.

---

[1] FGM ἱερατικου.
[2] Lc FGM τω.
[3] Lc FGM περιτιθεται.
[4] FGM omit εἰς.

37. Manassés [Josephus *Ant.* 12.157].

38. Ananias, under whom the disasters were brought about by Antiochos Epiphanés for the Maccabees [Ônias (III), Josephus *Ant.* 12.157].

39. Simôn [Josephus *Ant.* 12.224], 40. Ônias [Josephus *Ant.* 12.225], 41. Iésous [= Iasôn, Josephus *Ant.* 12.239; also see 12.237], 42. Ônias [= Menelaos, Josephus *Ant.* 12.239,383].[1]

43. Alkimos, whom Antiochos appointed after killing Ônias, though he was not of the high priestly family [Josephus *Ant.* 12.385-87; 1 Macc 7:9]. At that time Ônias son of Ônias fled to Egypt, and there built a temple like that at Jerusalem in the Heliopolitan nome [12.388; 13.62-72; 20.236].

44. Ioudas Makkabaios from the Hasmonean family [Josephus *Ant.* 12.434; not 1 Macc], 45. Iônathés his brother [Josephus *Ant.* 13.46,238; Iônathan, 1 Macc 10:21], 46. Simôn his brother [Josephus *Ant.* 13.213; 20.239; 1 Macc 13:36], 47. Iôannés, who is also called Hyrkanos [Josephus *Ant.* 13.228; Hyrkanos, 20.240; 1 Macc 16:24].

48. Aristoboulos, who first put the (royal) diadem on himself [Josephus *Ant.* 13.301; 20.241].

49. Iannaios, who is also called Alexander [Josephus *Ant.* 20.241; Iannaios, *Ant.* 13.320].

50. Hyrkanos [Josephus *Ant.* 20.242], under whom [Aristoboulus, *Ant.* 20.243-44] Pompéios king [general, Eusebius] of the Romans occupied the Temple and took away the precious vessels.[2]

51. Antigonos, who brought the Parthians against Hyrkanos, was deposed from the priesthood by Herôdés [Josephus *Ant.* 20.245-46].

52. Ananélos, who was appointed by Herôdés though not of the high priestly family [Josephus *Ant.* 15.22].

53. Aristoboulos, whom Herôdés (106b) substituted for Ananélos [Josephus *Ant.* 20.248]. But after murdering Aristoboulos in a plot, [15.55] he restored Ananélos.

---

[1] According to Josephus (*Ant.* 20.234), fifteen high priests served from the return from exile until the time of Antiochus Eupator, Antiochus Epiphanes' son. The *Hypomnestikon* agrees.

[2] Dio Cassius 36.16.4 agrees, against both Cicero *For Flaccus* 67 and Josephus *Ant.* 14.72; see below, C. 123(3). According to *Ant.* 20.243, Hyrkanus' brother Aristoboulos through armed attack succeeded him as both king and high priest. The Roman general Pompey then returned the high priesthood to Hyrkanus. The *Hypomnestikon* does not count Aristoboulos among the high priests, while Josephus does.

νδ' Πάλιν Ἀνανῆλος, νε' Ἰησοῦς ὁ τοῦ Φαυβῆ, νϛ' Σίμων ὁ Ἡρώδου κηδεστὴς, νζ' Ματθίας.

νη' Ἰώσηππος, τὴν τῆς νηστείας ἡμέραν,[1] ἀντὶ Ματθίου.

νθ' Ἰώζαρος.

ξ' Ἐλεάζαρος, ἐφ' οὗ Ἡρώδης ἀπέθανε.

ξα' Ἰησοῦς ὁ τοῦ Σεέ.

ξβ' Ἄνανος. Οὗτός ἐστιν ὁ Καϊάφα πενθερός.

ξγ' Ἰσμαῆλος ὁ τοῦ Βιαβῆ, ξδ' Ἐλεάζαρος Ἀνάνου, ξε' Σίμων Καθήμου.

ξϛ' Καϊάφας, ὁ καὶ Ἰώσηππος, ἐφ' οὗ τὸ σωτήριον ἡμῶν[2] πάθον[3] (106b2) ὁ Κύριος[4] ὑπέμεινε.

---

[1] *Lc* FGM κατα την της νηστειας ἡμεραν.

[2] FGM omit ἡμων.

[3] FGM παθος.

[4] FGM ὁ Κυριος ἡμων.

54. Ananélos again [Josephus *Ant.* 15.56],[1]   55. Iésous son of Phaubé [Josephus *Ant.* 15.322],[2]   56. Simôn brother-in-law of Herôdés [Josephus *Ant.* 15.322, 17.78],[3]   57. Matthias [Josephus *Ant.* 17.164, 167].

58. Iôsép[p]os on the fast-day in place of Matthias [Josephus *Ant.* 17.165].[4]

59. Iôzaros [Josephus *Ant.* 17.164; Iôazaros, 339; 18.3,26].

60. Eleazaros, under whom Herôdés died [Josephus *Ant.* 17.339].

61. Iésous son of Seë [Josephus *Ant.* 17.341].

62. Annas [Ananos, Josephus *Ant.* 18.26]. He was father-in-law of Kaiaphas [John 18:13]

63. Ismaélos son of Biabé [Phabi, Josephus *Ant.* 18.34],[5]   64. Eleazaros son of Ananas [Josephus *Ant.* 18.34],   65. Simon son of Kathémos [Kamithos, Josephus *Ant.* 18.34].[6]

66. Kaiaphas, who was also called Iôséppos, [Josephus *Ant.* 18.35, 95] under whom the Lord underwent the passion which achieves our salvation.

---

[1] Josephus, who was no supporter of the Herods, depicts Herod as setting the insignificant Ananélos up as high priest because of his own insecurity. Herod then deposed Ananélos and installed Aristoboulus as high priest for political reasons. When Aristoboulus became too popular with the people, Herod's insecurity reasserted itself and he had the young man drowned while swimming. At that time Ananélos again became high priest.

Josephus does not count Ananélos twice in his subtotal of high priests who served from the time of Herod the Great until the destruction of the second temple (*Ant.* 20.250). The *Hypomnestikon* counts him twice.

[2] Ralph Marcus (with Wikgren), *Josephus* 8 (LCL; Cambridge: Harvard University Press, 1963), notes the reading Phaubé from Joseph, following Niese; cf. Heinz Schreckenberg, *Die Flavius-Josephus-Tradition in Antike und Mittelalter* (ALGHJ 5, Leiden: Brill, 1972) 89: Niese "occasionally uses J. as a witness for the readings of names" (i.e. at *Ant.* 15.322, 18.34 [twice], 20.179 and 196).

[3] Josephus calls him Simon son of Boethus, and *b. Pesach.* mentions that the house of Boethus was a high priestly family.

[4] Josephus (*Ant.* 17.164–67) describes how Iôséppos the son of Ellémos was chosen to replace Matthias for the observance of a fast when Matthias experienced a nocturnal emission and was thereby rendered unclean. Although the replacement of Matthias was only supposed to last for a single day, Herod did not allow him to reassume his responsibilities and appointed Iôazaros in his stead.

[5] Louis Feldman, *Josephus* 9 (LCL; Cambridge: Harvard University Press, 1965) 28 n.6, mistakenly cites Joseph after Niese as writing "Biobe." CFGM rightly read "Biabé."

[6] Feldman, *Josephus* 9, 28 n.7.

ξζ' Ἰωνάθης Ἀνάνου, ξη' Θεόφιλος ἀδελφὸς, ξθ' Σίμων Βοήθου, ο' πάλιν Ἰωνάθας[1] ὁ Ἀνάνου, οα' Ματθία[2] ἀδελφὸς, οβ' Ἡλεὶ[3] ὁ νέος, ογ' Ἡσίωπος[4] Κάμη, οδ' Ἀνανίας ὁ τοῦ Νεβεδαίου, οε' Ἰωνάθης, ος' Ἰσμαῆλος Φαβίου, οζ' Ἰώσηππος ὁ Κάμης.

οη' Ἄνανος Ἀνάνου, ὁ Ἰάκωβον ἀποκτείνας τὸν δίκαιον, τὸν ἀδελφὸν τοῦ Κυρίου. Τούτῳ καὶ ὁ Παῦλος εἶπε· Τύπτειν σε μέλλει ὁ Θεὸς, τοῖχε κεκονιαμένε.

‹Ἰησοῦς ὁ τοῦ Δαμναίου.›[5]

οθ' Ἰησοῦς ὁ Γαμαλιήλ.

π' Ματθίας Θεοφίλου, ἐφ' οὗ ὁ πρὸς Ῥωμαίους πόλεμος ἀρχὴν εἰλήφει, (107a1) ἔτους ὀγδόου Κλαυδίου.

---

[1] Lc FGM Ἰωναθης.
[2] Lc FGM Ματθιας.
[3] Lc FGM Ἡλι.
[4] Lc FGM Ἰώσηππος.
[5] Not found in CFGM. Omitted due to haplography. Note the name which follows.

67. Iônathés son of Ananas [Josephus *Ant.* 18.95], 68. Theophilos his brother [Josephus *Ant.* 18.123; 19.297],[1] 69. Simôn son of Boéthos [Josephus *Ant.* 19.297],[2] 70. Again Iônathés son of Ananas [Josephus *Ant.* 19.313-16, refused second appointment],[3] 71. Matthias his brother [Josephus *Ant.* 19.316, 342], 72. Éli the younger [Éliônaios son of Kanthéras, Josephus *Ant.* 19.342, cf.20.16],[4] 73. Iôséppos son of Kamé [Josephus *Ant.* 20.16, 103], 74. Ananias son of Nebedaios [Josephus *Ant.* 20.103, 131, 213],[5] 75. Iônathés [killed, Josephus *Ant.* 20.162-66], 76. Ismaélos son of Phabios [Josephus *Ant.* 20.179],[6] 77. Iôséppos son of Kamés [Kabi, son of the high priest Simon, Josephus *Ant.* 20.196].[7]

78. Ananos son of Ananas, who killed Iakôbos the Just, brother of the Lord [Josephus *Ant.* 20.197-203]. To this Ananos Paul said, "God is going to smite you, whitened wall" [Acts 23:3, really Ananias, # 74].

<78a. Iésous son of Damnaios> [Josephus *Ant.* 20.203],

79. Iésous son of Gamaliel [Josephus *Ant.* 20.213].

80. Matthias son of Theophilus, under whom the war with the Romans began [Josephus *Ant.* 20.223] (107a) in the eighth year of Claudius.[8]

---

[1] Although not mentioned by either Josephus or the *Hypomnestikon*, Issachar of Kefar Barkai, mentioned in *b. Pesach.* 57a may have served following Theophilos. His name may have been omitted because of his irreverence to the royal family. On account of this both of his hands were amputated.

[2] Josephus suggests that this Simon is related to both the house of Boéthos and the house of Kathros (Kanthéras). Both are recognized as high priestly families in *b. Pesach.* 57a.

[3] The *Hypomnestikon* counts Iônathés son of Ananas twice, although Josephus does not.

[4] A problem arises here. Josephus (*Ant.* 20.16) states that "Herod accordingly removed the high priest surnamed Kanthéras from his position and conferred the succession to this office upon Joseph the son of Kamés." This description sounds as if it would apply to Simôn the son of Boéthos who was surnamed Kanthéras, but it probably refers to Eliônaios (Éli ho neos) the son of Kanthéras.

[5] Yochanan the son of Narbai is mentioned in *b. Pesach.* 57a. It is possible that he is to be identified with Ananias son of Nebedaios.

[6] See Feldman, *Josephus* 9, 484 n.3. Ismaélos son of Phabios is mentioned as a high priest in *b. Pesach.* 57a, although this could refer to the Isamaélos who is sixty-third in this list.

[7] Feldman, *Josephus* 9, 494 n.1.

[8] Josephus carefully dates the beginning in the 12th year of Nero (*Ant.* 20.235, 259); but Christians connected it with the death of Iakôbos in 62, Nero's 8th year. Josephus too dates under Claudius an event that belongs under Nero (*Ant.* 3.320).

πα' Φιναῖος, ἐφ' οὗ ἡ πόλις καὶ ὁ ναὸς καὶ τὸ ἔθνος ὑπὸ Τίτου εἵλω,[1] καὶ πάντα τὰ[2] κατὰ τὸν ναὸν κατελύθη.

**Γ.** + Τίνες οἱ ἐκ τοῦ Κάϊν γεννώμενοι,[3] καὶ εἰς ἑβδόμην γενεὰν ἀνέθηκεν;[4] α' Κάϊν, β' Ἐνὼχ, γ' Γαϊαδὰδ, δ' Μαϊὴλ, ε' Μαθουσάλα, ϛ' Λάμεχ, ζ' Ἰωβὴλ καὶ Ἰουβὰλ καὶ Θοβέλ. Ἐπὶ δὲ τούτων ἡ πανόλεθρος τοῦ Κάϊν γέγονε διαφθορά.

---

[1] FGM print ἑάλω. Emend to εἵλοντο?
[2] GM omit τα.
[3] FG γεινομενοι; lc M γενομενοι.
[4] Lc FGM ἀνεκαθεν.

81. Phinaios [Phanasos, Josephus *Ant.* 20.227],[1] under whom the city, Temple, and nation were destroyed by Titus and everything associated with the Temple was demolished.

> The preceeding list has been extracted from the works of Flavius Josephus. A priest himself and a descendant of the Hasmonian king-priests (See *Ant.* 16.185–87), Josephus has a particular slant on priestly matters. It is also likely that he had access to archives removed from the Temple prior to the Roman destruction of 70 C.E. In *Against Apion* 1.32–36, he speaks of records of "the names of our high priests, with the succession from father to son for the last two thousand years."

**3.** – Who were born of Kain from the beginning to the seventh generation [Gn 4:17-22]?

1. Kain. 2. Enoch. 3. Gai[a]dad. 4. Maiél [Arm]. 5. Mathousala. 6. Lamech. 7. Iôbél, Ioubal, and Thôbel, in whose time the all-consuming destruction of Kain occurred.

---

[1] Phanni (*War* 4.155).

Josephus (*Ant.* 20.250) gives the subtotal of high priests who served from the rise of Herod the Great until the destruction of the second temple as twenty-eight. This works if Anannélos and Iônathés son of Ananos are each counted only once. Josephus omits the Iônathés who follows Ananias the son of Nebedaios in the *Hypomnestikon*'s list. The *Hypomnestikon* omits Iésous the son of Damnaios, who follows Ananos son of Ananas in Josephus.

The grand total of high priests should be eighty-three, according to Josephus (*Ant.* 20.227). Two names are missing from the *Hypomnestikon*'s list in the period from Aaron to the construction of Solomon's temple, and another name is missing from the period when the Solomon's temple was still standing. In addition, Aristoboulos the brother of Hykanos is not counted by the *Hypomnestikon* during the Maccabean period. At the rise of Herod, then, the *Hypomnestikon*'s list is four names shorter than Josephus' list. From Herod to the destruction of the second temple, the *Hypomnestikon* lists two more names than Josephus because Anannélos and Iônathés son of Ananos are each counted twice. The discrepancies regarding Iônathés (who follows Ananias the son of Nebedaios) and Iésous the son of Damnaios cancel each other out with respect to the tally. Thus, the *Hypomnestikon*'s list ends up being two names shorter than that of Josephus.

**Δ'.** + Τίνες εἰσὶν[1] οἱ ἐκ τοῦ κατακλυσμοῦ ἐν τῇ κιβωτῷ διασωθέντες; Νῶε, καὶ υἱοὶ τρεῖς, Σὴμ, (107a2) Χὰμ, Ἰάφεθ, καὶ αἱ τούτων τέσσαρες γυναῖκες.

**Ε'.** + Τίνες εἰσὶν οἱ τὸν ιβ' Ἰακὼβ παῖδες,[2] οἱ τοῦ λαοῦ πατριάρχαι; Ἐκ μὲν Λείας· Ῥουβὶμ, Συμεών, Λευΐ, Ἰούδας, Ἰσάχαρ, Ζαβουλών. Ἐκ δὲ Ῥαχιήλ·[3] Ἰωσὴφ,[4] Βενιαμίν. Ἐκ δὲ Βαλλίς·[5] Δὰν, Νεφθαλήμ[6]. Ἐκ δὲ Ζελφίς·[7] Γὰδ, Ἀσσήρ. Οὗτοι ἐν οε' ψυχαῖς κατέβησαν εἰς Αἴγυπτον.

**F.** + Τίνες εἰσὶν οἱ οε' οἱ μετὰ τοῦ Ἰακὼβ εἰς Αἴγυπτον καταλύσαντες; α' Ῥουβὶμ ὁ πρωτότοκος, καὶ οἱ υἱοὶ αὐτοῦ· Ἐνὼς, Φαλλοὺς, Ἀσρὼμ, Χάρμης.

β' Συμεὼν, καὶ οἱ υἱοὶ αὐτοῦ· Ἰεμουὴλ, Ἰαμηναὼθ,[8] Ἰακεὶμ, Σαὰρ, (107b1) Σαούλ.

γ' Λευῒς,[9] καὶ οἱ υἱοὶ αὐτοῦ· Γεδεὼν, Καὰφ,[10] Μεραρί.

δ' Ἰούδας, καὶ οἱ υἱοὶ αὐτοῦ· Σηλὼμ καὶ Φαρὲς ‹καὶ Ζαρά›.[11] Υἱοὶ δὲ Φαρές· Ἐσρὼμ, Ἰεμουήλ.

ε' Ἰσάχαρ, καὶ οἱ υἱοὶ αὐτοῦ· Θωλὰ, Φουὰ, Ἰασοὺμ, Ἀμράμ.

ς' Ζαβουλὼν, καὶ οἱ υἱοὶ αὐτοῦ· Σέδερ, Ἀλλὼμ, Αἰήλ. Οὗτοι ἐκ Λείας, λ'.

ζ' Γὰδ, καὶ οἱ υἱοὶ αὐτοῦ· Σαφὼν, Ἀγγὴς, Σαυνὴς, Βοασαμὰν,[12] Δίδης, Ἀρὼ, Ἀδδὴς, Ἀροήλ.

---

[1]FGM omit εἰσιν.
[2]FGM οἱ του Ἰακωβ παιδες.
[3]Lc FGM Ῥαχηλ.
[4]F Ἰωσεφ και; GM omit Ἰωσηφ, but note the omission in their notes.
[5]Lc FGM Βαλλης.
[6]Lc FGM Νεφθαλείμ.
[7]Lc FGM Ζελφης.
[8]FGM Ἰαμηνωθ.
[9]Lc FGM Λευι.
[10]Lc FGM Καὰθ.
[11]CFGM do not have και Ζαρα. Emend to include.
[12]Lc FGM Βοασαμων.

**4.** – Who were saved in the ark from the deluge?[1]
Nôe and his three sons Sém, Cham, Iapheth, and their four wives [Gn 7:13] (continued in C. 24).

**5.** – Who are the sons of Jakôb, the patriarchs of the people [Gn 35:23-26]?
From Leia: Roubim, Symeôn, Leui [Arm.], Ioudas, Isachar [Arm.], Zaboulôn.
From Rachél: Iôséph, Beniamin.
From Ballés: Dan, Nephthaleim.
From Zelphés: Gad, Assér. These were among the seventy-five people who went down into Egypt.

**6.** – Who are the seventy-five who lived with Iakôb in Egypt?
1. Roubim the firstborn and his sons: Enôs, Phallous, Asrôm, Charmés [Gn 46:8-9].
2. Symeôn and his sons: Iemouél, Iaménaôth,[2] Iakeim, Saar (107b), Saul [46:10].
3. Leui and his sons: Gedeôn, Kaath, Merari [46:11].
4. Ioudas and his sons: Sélôm and Phares <and Zara>.[3] The sons of Phares: Esrôm, Iemouél [46:12].
5. Isachar and his sons: Thôla, Phoua, Iasoum, Amram [46:13].
6. Zaboulôn and his sons: Seder, Allôm, Aiél [46:14].
These are from Leia: <a total of> 30 (LXX 33) [46:15].[4]
7. Gad and his sons: Saphôn, Aggés, Saunés, Boasamôn (Thausobam, Arm.), Didés (Aédis), Arô/Addés,[5] Aroél<eis> [46:16].

---

[1] Cf. Hyginus 153 on Deucalion and Pyrrha after the deluge.

[2] Two separate names in the LXX: Iamin and Aôd.

[3] The LXX lists Ér, Aunan, Sélôm, Phares, and Zara. Ér and Aunan have been eliminated because Gn 46:12 states that they died while still in Canaan. Zara has apparently fallen out in transmission.

[4] Spellings vary, but Enos (1), Esrom (4), and Seder (6) appear in *Anon*.2 (= Paul de Lagarde, *Septuagintastudien*, Part 2 [Göttingen: Dieterich, 1892]).

[5] The two names Arô and Addés are one name in the LXX.

η' Ἀσὴρ, καὶ οἱ υἱοὶ αὐτοῦ· Ἰεμναεσσοῦ,[1] Ἰεοὺλ, Μαρία, Σάρρα ἀδελφή. Υἱοὶ δὲ Μαρίας· Χορὲβ,[2] Μελχιήλ.[3] Οὗτοι ἐκ Ζέλφις,[4] ιζ'.

θ'. Ἰωσὴφ, καὶ οἱ υἱοὶ αὐτοῦ οἱ[5] τεχθέντες ἐν Αἰγύπτῳ· Μανασσῆς καὶ Ἐφραΐμ. ‹ὁ υἱὸς τοῦ Μανασσῆς· Μαχίρ. Καὶ ὁ υἱὸς τοῦ Μαχὶρ· Γαλαάδ. Οἱ υἱοὶ τοῦ Ἐφραΐμ·›[6] Σουτὰλ, (107b2) Ταλιμμέδεμ.[7]

ι' Βενιαμὶν, καὶ οἱ υἱοὶ αὐτοῦ· Βαλλὰ, Φοὺς, Ἐβήλ. Υἱοὶ Βαλλά· Γηρὰ, Νεομὰν, Ἰαχὴς, Ῥὼς, Μαμφήν. Υἱοὶ Γηρά· Ἀράδ ‹καὶ . . . . .›[8] Οὗτοι ἐκ τῆς Ῥαχὴλ, ιη'.

ια' Δὰν καὶ ὁ υἱὸς[9] αὐτοῦ· Ἀσώμ.

ιβ' Νεφθαλὴμ,[10] καὶ οἱ υἱοὶ αὐτοῦ· Ἀσιὴλ, Γωϋνὴ, Ἀσσὰρ,[11] Συλλήμ. Οὗτοι ἐκ Βαλλὶς,[12] ζ'.

Ὁμοῦ οβ'. Καὶ ὁ πατὴρ Ἰακὼβ, καὶ Δείνα ἡ θυγάτηρ, καὶ Λία· [13] ὁμοῦ ψυχαὶ οε'.

---

[1] Emend to Ἰεμνα, Ἰεσσου.
[2] FGM Χορεβ, και.
[3] Lc GM Μαλχιηλ.
[4] Lc FGM Ζελφης.
[5] FGM omit οἱ.
[6] The text appears to be lacunar at this point and requires emendation.
[7] FGM Σουταλ, Ταλιμμεδεκ; LXX Σουταλααμ, Εδεμ, Τααμ.
[8] A name has fallen out here.
[9] GM οἱ υἱοι.
[10] Lc FGM Νεφθαλειμ.
[11] Lc FGM Ἀσσας.
[12] Lc FGM Βαλλης.
[13] Lc FGM Λεια.

8. Asér and his sons: Iemna, <I>essu, Ieoul, Maria (Baria), sister Sarra. The sons of Maria (Baria): Choreb (Chobor), Malchiél [46:17]. These are from Zelphés, seventeen (LXX sixteen) [46:18].

9. Iôseph and his sons born in Egypt: Manassés and Ephraim. <The son of Manassés: Machir. The son of Machir: Galaad. The sons of Ephraim brother of Manassés:> Soutal, Talim/medek (LXX inserts here: Taam and son Edem, 46:20)

10. Beniamin and his sons: Balla, Phous (Chobôr), Ebél (Asbél). Sons of Balla: Géra, Neoman, Iachés (Ancheis), Rhôs, Mamphén, (Some LXX mss. insert here: Ophimin). Sons of Géra: Arad [+ Anonymous]. These are from Rachél, eighteen [46:22].

11. Dan and his son: Asôm [46:23].

12. Nephthaleim and his sons: Asiél, Gôuné, Assas, Sullém [46:24]. These are from Ballés, seven [46:25].

Altogether 72; with the father Iakôb and the daughter Deina, and Leia, 75 souls [see C. 128].

> Josephus *Ant.* 2.176 (but usually with Greek word-endings) comments thus on the biblical list (Gn 46:8-27): "I was inclined not to recount all their names, mainly on account of their difficulty; however, I have thought it necessary to mention them to confute those persons who imagine us to be not of Mesopotamian origin, but Egyptians," With the Hebrew text he lists seventy.
>
> Our Joseph makes use of the LXX rather than the MT or Josephus and lists seventy-five names, but he interprets that material independently and in a way designed to solve problems raised by the biblical text. The LXX specifically states that "all the people of the house of Jacob, those who entered into Egypt with Jacob, were seventy-five in number." Nevertheless, according to the LXX sixty-six people, not counting wives, accompanied Jacob to Egypt. The text then states that nine additional children were born to him while in Egypt (66 + 9 = 75), but it does not mean this exactly, because Joseph and Jacob himself are counted as part of that nine. An additional problem is that the subtotal of Leah's children in the LXX is given as thirty-three, while only thirty-two names are listed.
>
> The *Hypomnestikon* resolves part of the problem by making the catalogue describe not "those who entered into Egypt with Jacob,"

Ζ. + Τίνες εἰσὶν[1] οἱ τοῦ Σαμουὴλ πρόγονοι ἱερατικοί;
   α' Κορὲ, ὁ ἐπισυστὰς ἐπὶ Μωϋσῆ.
   β' τούτου υἱὸς, Ἐλκανά.
   γ' Ἐναέδ.
   δ' Ἐλιάδ.
   ε' Ἱεραάμ.
   ϛ' Ἐλκανά. **(108a1)**
   ζ' Σαμουὴλ, ἐξ οὗ γεγόνασιν υἱοὶ δύο Ἰωὴλ καὶ Ἰσαμινά. Καὶ δωροληπτοῦντες, οὐκ ἀξίους[2] τῆς πατρικῆς διαδοχῆς εἶναι ἐκρίθησαν.

Η. + Τίνες οἱ τοῦ Ἡλεὶ[3] πρόγονοι ἱερατικοί;
   α' Καάθ.
   β' Ἀβιτώμ.
   γ' Ἀβιμέλεχ.
   δ' Ἀβιάθαρ.
   ε' Οὐριοῦ.
   ϛ' καὶ Ναθάν.

---

[1] FGM omit εἰσιν.
[2] FGM ἄξιοι.
[3] Lc FGM Ἡλι.

but rather "those who lived with Jacob in Egypt." Leah's "sons" are reduced in number to thirty (with the sons of Judah Ér and Aunan, who according to Gn 46:12 died while in Canaan, and Dinah Jacob's daughter being omitted), and Zilpah's children are increased from sixteen to seventeen. The children of Rachel and Bilhah remain at eighteen and seven respectively. This gives a total of seventy-two, which is then filled out to seventy-five by the addition of Jacob, Dinah, and Leah. This scheme remains problematic, however, for it requires Jacob to be counted as "living with" himself, and it seems odd that Leah alone among the wives is counted.

**7.** – Who are the priestly ancestors of Samouél?[1]
    1. **Kore, who revolted under Moses** [1 Par 6:22; Nm 16:1-2].
    2. **His son Elkana** [1 Par 6:23].
    3. Enead [**Souphei**, 6:26].
    4. Eliad [**Eliab**, 6:27].
    5. **Ieraam** [6:27].
    6. **Elkana** [6:27] (108a).
    7. **Samouél, from whom were born two sons, Iôél** [Arm, cf. 6:33] **and** Isamina [**Habia**, 6:28], **who as takers of bribes** were judged unworthy of the succession [8:1-5].

**8.** – And who were the priestly ancestors of Éli?[2]
    1. Kaath [1 Par 6:1].
    2. Abitôm (Ambram) [6:2].
    3. **Abimelech.**
    4. **Abiathar.**
    5. **Ouriou.**
    6. And **Nathan.**

---

[1] *LG* 1.358. A. Dillmann noted the comparison for Mommsen, while Helm claimed that this text, like the parallels to C. 8–9, was an interpolation into Hippolytus' *Chr.* Cf. the two lists in Procopius of Gaza on 1 Rg 1:1 (PG 87, 1081A): Kaath-Isaar-Kore-Elkana-Samouél; and Kaath-Aminadab-Kore-Aseir-Elkana-Souph-Eliou-Ieraam-Elkana-Samouél.

[2] *LG* 1.357; not Hippolytus according to Helm, *Die Chronik* (p. 222n.; 2d ed., p. 135n.), but he may be mistaken. Joseph disagrees with Josephus *Ant.* 5.361–62 (Éli descended from Ithamar), although he is followed in C. 2.

ζ' Ἡλεὶ,[1] ἐξ οὗ γεγόνασιν υἱοὶ δύο, Ὀφνὴ καὶ Φινεὲς, οἳ τὰς θυσίας ἐντρυφῶντες ἀναιροῦνται ἐν πολέμῳ τῶν ἀλλοφύλων.

**Θ.** + Τίνες δὲ[2] οἱ τοῦ Ἐζεκιὴλ[3] τοῦ προφήτου πρόγονοι ἱερατικοί;
α' Ἰωδαέ.
β' Φαδναίας.
γ' Ἀμορρίας.
δ' Ζαχώρ.
ε' Σαμουέ. **(108a2)**
ϛ' Ἐφεδλά.
ζ' Μελχιοῦ.
η' Ἀλώμ.
θ' Γομορρίας.
ι' Βαρούχ.
ια' Σοφονίας.
ιβ' Μασσαίας.
ιγ' Χελκίας.
ιδ' Βουζή.
ιε' Ἐζεκιὴλ,[4] ὁ ἐν τῇ αἰχμαλωσίᾳ τοῦ Ἰούδα προφητεύσας ἐν Βαβυλῶνι.

**Ι.** + Τίνες οἱ Ἰερεμίου τοῦ προφήτου πρόγονοι ἱερατικοί;
α' Ἀαρών.
β' Φινεές.
γ' Ὀζίας.
δ' Ῥαζαζᾶς.
ε' Μωριάδ.
ϛ' Ἀμωρίας.
ζ' Ἀμητώβ.
η' Σεδούκ.
θ' Ἀχιμάς.
ι' τούτου υἱὸς Ἡλίας ὁ προφήτης καὶ Σαλώμ.
ια' Σαλώμου Ἰωρὰμ υἱός.[5]

---

[1] *Lc* FGM Ἡλι.
[2] FGM omit δε.
[3] *Lc* FGM Ἰεζεκιηλ.
[4] *Lc* FGM Ἰεζεκιηλ.
[5] FGM Σαλωμου υἱος, Ἰωραμ.

7. **Éli**, from whom were born two **sons, Ophné and Phineës** [1 Rg 1:3, 2:34], **who** when they **treated the sacrifices contemptuously**, were killed in battle with the Philistines [2:12, 4:11].

**9.** – Who were the priestly ancestors of Iezekiél the prophet? [1]
1. **Iôdaé**.
2. **Phadnaias**.
3. **Amorrias**.
4. **Zachôr**.
5. **Samouë**.
6. **Ephedla**.
7. **Melchiou**.
8. **Alôm**.
9. **Gomorrias**.
10. **Barouch**.
11. **Sophonias**.
12. **Massaias**.
13. **Chelkias**.
14. **Bouzé** [Ez 1:2].
15. **Iezekiél**, who prophesied during the captivity of Judah in Babylon [1:3].

**10.** – Who were the priestly ancestors of Ieremia the prophet? [1 Par 6:3-15, 50-53] [2]
1. **Aarôn** [1 Par 6:3]. [3]
2. **Phinees** [6:4].
3. Ozias [Ozia, 6:5-6 Arm].
4. **Razazas** [Zaraia, 6:6; Razaza, Hippolytus].
5. **Môriad** [Maraiôth, 6:6-7 Cod.A].
6. **Amôrias** [Amarias, 6:7 Cod.A,Arm].
7. **Amétôb** [Acheitôb, 6:7-8].
8. Sedouk [Sadôk, 6:8].
9. **Achimas** [Acheimaas, 6:8-9].
10. **His son Elijah the prophet, and Salôm** [6:12-13].
11. **Iôram** son of Salôm.

---

[1] *LG* 1.356; not Hippolytus according to Helm, *Die Chronik* (p. 222n.; 2d ed., p. 135n.), but again he may be mistaken.

[2] Hippolytus *Chr* 741 = *LG* 1.355.

[3] Joseph omits Eleazar, found here in Hippolytus *Chr* 741.

ιβ' Ἀμὼς καὶ Ἰωδαέ.
ιγ' Σεδεκίας υἱὸς Ἰωδαέ.
ιδ' Ἰωήλ. **(108b1)**
ιε' Οὐρίας.
ιϛ' Νηρή.
ιζ' Σαλώμ.
ιη' Χελκίας.
ιθ' Ἰερεμίας, ὁ τὴν αἰχμαλωσίαν ἐν τῇ Ἰουδαίᾳ προφητεύσας.

**ΙΑ'.** + Τίνες οἱ τοῦ λαοῦ κριταὶ μετὰ τὴν διανέμησιν τὴν ὑπὸ Ἰησοῦ τοῦ Ναυῆ τῆς γῆς γεγενημένην, γενόμενοι;[1]
α' Χουσαραθὼν ποταμῶν Συρίας Βασιλεύς.
β' Γοθονιὴλ κριτής.
γ' [Ἰησοῦς τοῦ Ναυῆ.][2] Αἰγλὼν Βασιλεὺς Μωαβιτῶν.
δ' Ἀὼδ κριτής.
ε' Ἰαβὴς Βασιλεὺς Χαναάν.
ϛ' Δεβόρρα προφῆτις σὺν Βαράκ.
ζ' Μαδιναῖοι ἔθνος.
η' Γεδεὼν κριτής.
θ' Ἀβιμέλεχ **(108b2)** κριτής.
ι' Θωλὰ κριτής.
ια' Εἲρ κριτής.
ιβ' Ἀμμονῖται ἔθνος.
ιγ' Ἰεφθαὲ κριτής.
ιδ' Ἐσσεβὼν κριτής.
ιε' Ἀλλὼν κριτής.
ιϛ' Ἀβδὼν κριτής.
ιζ' Ἀλλόφυλοι.
ιη' Σαμψὼν κριτής.
ιθ' Σεμογὰρ[3] κριτής.
κ' Ἀναρχία καὶ Σαμεὶρ[4] κριτής.[5]

---

[1]FGM μετα την υπο Ἰησου του Ναυη γεγενημενην της γης διανεμησιν, γενομενοι.
[2]Emend to omit.
[3]Lc GM Σεμεναρ.
[4]GM Σαμιρ.
[5]Through typographical error (as the Latin translation indicates) F omits ιθ' Σεμογαρ κριτης. κ' Ἀναρχια. κα' Και Σαμειρ κριτης. GM number Σαμιρ as κα' and Εἰρηνη as κβ'.

12. **Amôs** and **Iôdaë**.
13. **Sedekias son of Iôdaë**.
14. **Iôél** (108b).
15. **Ourias**.
16. **Néré**.
17. **Salôm**.
18. **Chelkias** [Jer 1:1].
19. Ieremias who in Iudaea predicted the captivity.

**11.** – Who were the judges of the people after the division of the land by Iésous son of Naué?[1]

1. **Chousarathôn**, king of the rivers of Syria (Mesopotamia) [Jd 3:8].
2. **Gothoniél**, judge [3:9].[2]
&lt;3&gt; **Aiglôn king of the Moabites** [3:14].
4. **Aôd**, judge [3:15].[3]
5. **Iabés** king of Chanaan [4:1].
6. **Deborra** the prophetess, with Barak [4:4-10].
7. The **Madinaian** people [6:1].
8. **Gedeôn**, judge [6:11].
9. **Abimelech**, judge [9:22].
10. **Thôla**, judge [10:1].
11. **&lt;Ia&gt;eir**, judge [10:3].
12. The **Ammonite** people [10:7].
13. **Iephthaë**, judge [12:7].
14. **Essebôn**, judge [12:8, Cod.A].
15. **Allôn**, judge [Ailôn, 12:11, Cod.A,Arm].
16. **Abdôn**, judge [12:13].
17. The **Philistines** [13:1].
18. **Sampsôn** the judge [16:31].
19. Semenar, judge [16:31, some mss: Semegar].
20. Anarchy and Sameir judge.

---

[1] Hippolytus , *Chr.* 632–52 = *LG* 1.249–67.

[2] Here C mistakenly adds "3. Iésous son of Naué."

[3] Here Joseph omits Samegar [3:31], as do Theophilus *To Autolycus* 3.24 (perhaps adding later as Samera) and Clement *Str.* 1.110.1.

κα' Εἰρήνη, καὶ Σαμανίας κριτής.
Μετὰ δὲ τούτους, ἱερεῖς ἔκριναν τὸν λαόν, Ἡλεὶ[1] καὶ Σαμουὴλ, μεθ' οὓς βασιλεῖς.

**ΙΒ'.** + Τίνες ἐβασίλευσαν τοῦ λαοῦ;
α' Σαούλ.
β' Δαβίδ.
γ' Σαλομών.[2]
δ' Ῥοβοὰμ, ἐφ' οὗ ἐμερίσθη ἡ Βασιλεία.
ε' Ἀβιά.
ϛ' Ἀσά.
ζ' Ἰωσαφάτ.
η' Ἰωράμ.
θ' Ὀχοζίας. **(109a1)**
ι' Γοδολία γυνὴ, μήτηρ τοῦ Ὀχοζίου.
ια' Ἰωᾶς.
ιβ' Ἀμασίας.
ιγ' Ὀζίας.
ιδ' Ἰωθάμ.
ιε' Ἀχάζ.
ιϛ' Ἐζεκίας.
ιζ' Μανασσῆς.
ιη' Ἀμώς.
ιθ' Ἰωσίας.
κ' Ἰωακείμ.
καὶ Ἰεχονίας κα'.
κβ' Σεδεκίας,[3] ἐφ' οὗ καὶ ἡ δευτέρα αἰχμαλωσία τοῦ Ἰούδα γεγόνει,[4] καὶ ὁ ναὸς ἐνεπρήσθη.

---

[1] Lc FGM Ἡλι.
[2] Lc FGM Σολομων.
[3] Lc FGM κ' Ἰωακειμ, κα' Ἰεχονιας, κβ' Σεδεκιας.
[4] FGM ἐγεγονει.

21. Peace, and Samanias, judge.[1]

After these, **priests** judged the people: **Éli** and **Samouél**, after whom there were kings.

**12.** – Who were kings over the people?[2]

1. **Saul** [1 Rg 11:15].
2. **David** [2 Rg 2:4].
3. **Solomôn** [3 Rg 1:39].
4. **Roboam, under whom the kingdom was divided** [12:19].[3]
5. **Abia** [14:31].
6. **Asa** [15:8].
7. **Iôsaphat** [15:24].
8. **Iôram** [22:51].
9. **Ochozias** (109a) [4 Rg 8:24].
10. The woman **Godolia** [11:1 Arm.], **mother of Ochozias**.
11. **Iôas** [12:1].
12. **Amasias** [12:21].
13. **Ozias** (Azarias) [14:21].
14. **Iôtham** [15:7].
15. **Achaz** [16:1].
16. **Ezekias** [18:1].
17. **Manassés** [21:1].
18. **Amôs** [21:19].
19. **Iôsias** [22:1].
20. **Iôakeim** [23:34].
21. **Iechonias** [24:8].
22. **Sedekias** [24:17-18], under whom the second captivity of Judah occurred and the Temple was burned [25:9-11].[4]

---

[1] According to Josephus *Ant.* 5.318 Sampsôn was succeeded by the high priest Éli. Theophilus (*To Autolycus* 3.24) speaks of peace and then Samera; Clement (*Str.* 1.111.3) of anarchy, then Eli.

[2] List, Hippolytus *Chr* 721 (another list, with dates, ibid. 653–79) = *LG* 1.335; cf. Hyginus 48: "Athenian kings."

[3] Hippolytus *Chr.* 656 = *LG* 1.271.

[4] On problems with Ioachim, Sedecias, Ieconias, cf. Pierre Nautin, *Lettres et écrivains chrétiens des iie et iiie siècles* (Paris: Cerf, 1061) 193–202. Joseph sensibly ends his list without discussing them.

**ΙΓ'.** + Τίνες Βασιλεῖς γεγόνασι τοῦ Ἰσραὴλ μετὰ τὴν ἀπὸ Ἰούδα διάρεσιν;
α' Ἱεροβοάμ.
β' Ναδάβ.
γ' Βαασά.
δ' Ἐλά.
ε' Ζαμβρή.
ϛ' ‹Ἀμβρή›.[1]
ζ' Ἀχαάβ.
η' Ὀχοζίας.
θ' Ἰωράμ.
ι' Ἰκοῦ.[2]
ια' Ἰωάχας.
ιβ' Ἰωάς.
ιγ' Ἱεροβοὰμ.
ιδ' Ζαχαρίας. **(109a2)**
ιε' Σελλίμ.
ιϛ' Μανασσῆς.
ιζ' Φακεσίας.
ιη' Φακεέ.
ιθ' Ὡσηὲ, οὗ ἐννάτῳ ἔτει ἡ καθαίρεσις τῆς βασιλείας γέγονε.

**ΙΔ'.** + Τίνες προφῆται γεγόνασιν ἐν τῷ θείῳ λόγῳ, οἳ καὶ τὰς προφητείας ἐγγράφους πεποίηνται;
α' Μωϋσῆς.
β' Ἰησοῦς ὁ τοῦ Ναυῆ.
γ' Δαβίδ.
δ' Σαλομών.
ε' Ἡσαΐας.
ϛ' Ἱερεμίας.
ζ' Ἰεζεκιήλ.
η' Δανιήλ.
‹θ› Ὡσηέ.
‹ι› Ἰωήλ.
‹ια› Ἀμώς.
‹ιβ› Ἀβδιοῦ.

---

[1] C here numbers a vacant space.
[2] *Lc* FGM Ἰηου.

**13.** – Who were kings of Israél after the separation from Iouda?[1]

1. **Ieroboam** [3 Rg 12:20].
2. **Nadab** [14:20].
3. **Baasa** [15:33].
4. **Ela** [16:8].
5. **Zambré** [16:10].
6. **Ambré** [16:23].[2]
7. **Achaab** [16:29].
8. **Ochozias** [22:51].
9. **Iôram** [4 Rg 3:1].
10. **Iéou** [9:6].
11. **Iôachas** [10:35].
12. **Iôas** [13:10].
13. **Ieroboam** [14:23].
14. **Zacharias** [15:8].
15. **Sellim** [Sellem, 15:13, Anon.1].
16. **Manassés** (Manaém) [15:14].
17. **Phakesias** [Phakesias, 15:24; Phakeia, Arm; Phakias, Hippolytus].
18. **Phakee** [15:25].
19. **Ôsée**, in whose ninth year the kingdom was overthrown [17:6].

**14.** – Who were the prophets who made prophecies in writing and were mentioned in the divine word?[3] (continued from C. 10)

1. **Moses** [C. 69].
2. **Iésous son of Naué** [C. 70].
3. **David** [C. 73].
4. **Solomôn** [C. 74].
5. **Ésaias** [C. 75].
6. **Ieremias** [C. 76].
7. **Iezekiél** [no separate discussion].
8. **Daniél** [no separate discussion; see index].
<9> **Ôsée** [C. 114(4), 151(11)].
<10> **Iôél** [C. 10(14), 130(2)].
<11> **Amôs.**
<12> **Abdiou.**

---

[1] Hippolytus *Chr* 722–39 = *LG* 1.336–55.

[2] Hippolytus omits this name.

[3] Hippolytus *Chr* 719 = *LG* 1.333 (42 writing and non-writing prophets combined); relation to Joseph's two lists: Helm, *Die Chronik*, 212n (2d ed., 127n).

‹ιγ› Ἰωνᾶς.
‹ιδ› Μιχαίας.
‹ιε› Ναούμ.
‹ιϛ› Ἀββακούμ.
‹ιζ› Σοφονίας.
‹ιη› Ἀγγαῖος.
‹ιθ› Ζαχαρίας.
‹κ› Μαλαχίας.¹ Οὗτοι μὲν οἱ εἴκοσι ἐγγράφους κατέλιπον αὐτῶν τὰς
(109b1) προφητείας.

ΙΕ'. + Τίνες δὲ γεγόνασιν ἄλλοι προφῆται, οἱ μὴ ἐν γράμμασιν αὐτῶν καταλείψαντες τὰς προφητείας;
α' Ἀδάμ.
β' Νῶε.
γ' Ἀβραάμ.
δ' Ἰσαάκ.
ε' Ἰακώβ.
‹ϛ› Ἐλδὰδ, ‹ζ› καὶ Μηδὰδ, ‹η› Σαμουὴλ, ‹θ› Γὰδ, ‹ι› Νάθαν, ‹ια› Ἀχίας ὁ Σιλωνίτης,² ‹ιβ› Σαμαίας υἱὸς Ἀνανὶ, ‹ιγ› Σαλαμὶν, ‹ιδ› Ἀνανίας, ‹ιε› Ἠλίας, ‹ιϛ› Ἐλισσαῖος, ‹ιζ› Μιχαίας υἱὸς Ἰεμβλὰ, ιη' Ἀβδαδὼν, ιθ' Βουζῆ, κ' Οὐρίας, κα' Σαμαίας.
‹κβ› Ἰαδὼν, ὁ ἐπὶ τοῦ Ἱεροβοὰμ τὴν πτῶσιν τοῦ ἐν Βεθὴλ τοῦ³ θυσιαστηρίου, καὶ τὴν καθαίρεσιν τῆς τοῦ Ἰσραὴλ πολιτείας προφητεύσας.
Καὶ ἐπὶ τῆς παρουσίας (109b2) τοῦ Κυρίου· ‹κγ› Ζαχαρίας, ὁ τοῦ Βαπτιστοῦ Ἰωάννου πατὴρ, ‹κδ› Συμεὼν, ‹κε› Ἰωάννης ὁ Βαπτιστής, ‹κϛ› Ἄγαβος.
Καὶ ἄλλοι ἐπὶ τοῦ Ἰσραὴλ γεγόνασι προφῆται· ‹κζ› Ἀΐας, ‹κη› Ἰκοῦ⁴ υἱὸς Ἀνανί.⁵

---

¹C does not number the entries from Ὡσηε to Μαλαχιας.
²Lc GM Σιλονιτης.
³Lc FGM omit του.
⁴FGM omit Ἰκου; GM insert in brackets [ Ἰηου]; lege Ἰηου.
⁵C stops numbering the entries in this chapter after ε' Ἰακωβ.

<13> **Iônas**.
<14> **Michaias**.
<15> **Naoum**.
<16> **Abbakoum**.
<17> **Sophonias** [C. 77].
<18> **Aggaios** [C. 78].
<19> **Zacharias** [C. 79].
<20> **Malachias**.
These twenty left their (109b) prophecies in writing.

**15.** – Who were the other prophets, who did not leave their prophecies in writing? (cf. C. 14)
1. **Adam**.
2. **Nôe**.
3. **Abraam**.
4. **Isaak**.
5. **Iakôb**.

<6> **Eldad and** <7> **Médad** [Nm 11:27], <8> Samouél [C. 72], <9> Gad [C. 85], <10> **Nathan** [C. 86], <11> **Achias the Silonite** [C. 87], <12> **Samaias son of Anani** [C. 88], <13> Salamin, <14> **Ananias**, <15> **Élias** [C. 81, 83], <16> **Elissaios** [C. 82, 84], <17> **Michaias son of Iembla** [C. 91], <18> **Abdadôn (Addo, Cod.A)** [2 Par 12:15], <19> **Bouzé** [father of Ezekiél, Ez 1:2], <20> **Ourias** [Jer 26:20-23], <21> **Samaias** [Jer 29:29-32].

<22> Iadôn,[1] who in the time of Ieroboam predicted the fall of the altar of Bethél and the overthrow of the state of Israél [3 Rg 13:1-10].

And upon the coming of the Lord: <23> Zacharias the father of Iôannés the Baptist [Lk 1:5], <24> **Symeôn** [2:25], <25> **Iôannés the Baptist** [3:16], <26> Agabos [Ac 11:28].

There were other prophets in Israél: <27> Aias (Achias, Cod.A) [3 Rg 14:18], <28> Iéou son of Anani [16:1].

---

[1] Named not in 3 Rg 13:1 but in Josephus *Ant.* 8.231.

**ΙϚ΄.** + Τίνες προφήτιδες γυναῖκες γεγόνασιν;
α' Σάρρα.
β' Ρεβέκκα.
γ' Μαρία ἡ τοῦ Μωϋσέως ἀδελφή.
δ' Σεπφόρα ἡ τοῦ Μωϋσέως γυνή.
‹ε'› Δεβόρρα, ἡ τὸν Βὰκ¹ ἐπὶ τὸν πόλεμον στείλασα.
‹Ϛ'› Ὀλδᾶ.
‹ζ'› Ἄννα ἡ τοῦ Σαμουὴλ μήτηρ.
Καὶ ἐπὶ τῆς παρουσίας τοῦ Κυρίου· ‹η'› Ἐλισάβετ, ‹θ'› καὶ Μαρία ἡ
Θεοτόκος, καὶ ‹ι'› Ἄννα θυγάτηρ Φανουὴλ ἐκ φυλῆς **(110a1)** Ἀσήρ.²

**ΙΖ΄.** + ‹Α'.›³ Τίνες εὐσεβεῖς γεγόνασι βασιλεῖς;
α' Δαβίδ.
β' Ἀσά.
γ' Ἰωσαφάτ.
δ' Ἐζεκίας.
ε' Ἰωσίας.
Σολομὼν δὲ καὶ Ὀζίας πρὸς τὸ γῆρας ὠλιγόρησαν,⁴ ὁ μὲν γυναιξὶν
ἐθνικαῖς ὑπαχθείς, ὁ δὲ ἱερατεύσασθαι ὑπερηφανήσας.

+ ‹Β'.› Τίνες βασιλεῖς ἐδυσσέβησαν;
α' Ἰωράμ.
β' Ὀχοζίας.
γ' Ἰωάς.
δ' Ἀμασίας.
ε' Ἰωάθαμ.
Ϛ' Ἄχαζ.
ζ' Μανασσῆς.
η' Ἀμών.
θ' Ἰάχας.
ι' Σεδεκίας.

---

¹ *Lc* FGM Βαρακ.
² C stops numbering the entries in this chapter after δ' Σεπφορα. FGM stop
numbering the entries after η' Ἐλισαβετ.
³ CF do not number the two sections of this chapter; G numbers only Β'; M numbers
both.
⁴ *Lc* M ὠλιγωρησαν.

**16.** – What women were prophetesses?[1]
1. **Sarra.**
2. **Rebekka.**
3. **Maria sister of Moses.**
4. Sepphora wife of Moses [om. Lib. gen.].
<5> **Deborra**, who sent Barak into the war.
<6> **Olda.**
<7> **Anna mother of Samouél.**

**And upon** the coming of the Lord: <8> **Elisabet**, <9> and **Maria the** God-bearer, <10> and **Anna**, daughter of Phanouél, from the tribe of (110a) Asér.[2]

**17.** – <A.> What kings were pious? (from C. 13)
1. David [C. 73].
<2> Asa [2 Par 14:2].
<3> Iôsaphat.
<4> Ezekias.
<5> Iôsias.

But Solomôn and Ozias in their old age were regarded lightly, the one subject to gentile wives and the other seizing the high priesthood.

<B.> What kings behaved impiously?
1. Iôram.
2. Ochozias.
3. Iôas.
4. Amasias.
5. Iôatham.
6. Achaz.
7. Manassés.
8. Amôn.
9. Iachas.
10. Sedekias.

---

[1] Hippolytus *Chr.* 720–21 = *LG* 1.334 (2.170).

[2] Cf. the list in Clement *Str.* 1.136.1–2, as well as Theodorus Schermann, *Prophetarum vitae fabulosae* (Leipzig: Teubner, 1907) 3, 3–7.

Σαοὺλ δὲ ὁ τῆς βασιλείας ἐναρξάμενος, φθονῶν τῷ Δαβὶδ ἐξέπεσε τῆς εὐσεβείας, καὶ Θεοῦ ἀνηκούστησε, καὶ τέλος ἐγγαστριμύθῳ προσπέφευγε. **(110a2)**

ΙΗ'. + Τίνες ψευδοπροφῆται ἐν τῷ λαῷ γεγόνασι;
‹α'› Σεδεκίας υἱὸς Χανὰ, ὁ μετὰ τῶν τετρακοσίων ψευδοπροφητῶν τῆς Ἰεζάβελ ἀπατῶν τὸν Ἀχαὰβ εἰς τὴν Ῥεμὼθ, πόλιν τοῦ Γαλαὰδ, παράληψιν.
‹β'› Οἱ υ' τῆς Ἰεζάβελ προφῆται, οὓς Ἠλίας ἀπελέγξας, διὰ τοῦ λαοῦ διεχρίσατο.[1]
‹γ'› Πασχώρ, ὁ τὸν Ἰερεμίαν ἐγκλείσας ἐν φυλακῇ, ὡς πρὸς τὸν Ναβουχοδονόσορ καταφεύγοντα.
‹δ'› Ἀνανίας υἱὸς Ἀλώμ, ὁ τὰ τοῦ Ἰερεμίου ξύλινα χλοιὰ συντρίψας, ἐν ὑποδείγματι τοῦ τὸν Βαβυλώνιον συντρίβεσθαι.
‹ε'› Σαμαίας, ὁ **(110b1)** ἐν Βαβυλῶνι αἰχμάλωτος, ὁ καὶ Σοφονίᾳ τῷ ἱερεῖ γράφων ἐν τῇ Ἰερουσαλήμ, τιμωρείσθαι τὸν Ἰερεμίαν, ὡς τοῖς ἐν Βαβυλῶνι γράφοντα, τὴν αἰχμαλωσίαν ἀποτείνειν.
‹ς'› Ἀχαὰβ[2] υἱὸς Κουλίου
‹ζ'› Καὶ Σεδεκίας Μαλσίου[3] κατὰ τοῦ Ἰερεμίου προφητεύοντος.[4]
‹η'› Ἰεζονίας ὁ τοῦ Ἀσσούρ.
‹θ'› Καὶ Φαλτίας ὁ τοῦ Βεναίου, παρὰ τοῦ Ἰεζεκιὴλ σημαινόμενοι.[5]

ΙΘ'. + Τίνες ἐξῆρχον τῶν φυλῶν κατὰ τὴν ἔξοδον τῆς Αἰγύπτου;
α'› Τῆς μὲν Λευϊτικῆς φυλῆς, Μωϋσῆς καὶ Ἀαρών.
‹β'› τῆς δὲ Ἰούδα, Ἀμηναδάβ.[6]
‹γ'› τῆς δὲ Ῥουβὶν, Ἐλιούρ.[7]
‹δ'› τῆς δὲ Συμεών, Σαρισαλαί.

---

[1] *Lc* FGM διεχειρισατο.
[2] GM Ἀχαβ.
[3] *Lc* FGM Μαασιου.
[4] *Lc* FGM προφητευοντες.
[5] CF do not number this chapter. GM do number it.
[6] *Lc* FGM Ἀμιναδαβ.
[7] *Lc* FGM Ἐλιουζ.

But Saul who first reigned envied David and fell from piety, and finally resisted God [1 Rg 15:22] and fled to a ventriloquist [28:7]. (to C. 117)

**18.** – Who were false prophets among the people? (from C. 16)

<1> Sedekias son of Chana, who with four hundred false prophets of Iezabel deceived Achaab to lead an expedition to Remôth, a city of Galaad [3 Rg 22:6].

<2> The four hundred prophets of Iezabel whom Élias denounced and killed through the people [18:22, 40].[1]

<3> Paschôr, who shut Ieremias up in prison as wanting to flee to Nabouchodonosor [Jer 20:1-2].

<4> Ananias son of Alôm, who broke the wooden yokes of Ieremias as a symbol of of the breaking of Babylon [28:10-14].

<5> Samaias the (110b) captive in Babylon who wrote to Sophonias the priest in Jerusalem to punish Ieremias, because he had written to those in Babylon in order to endure their captivity [29:24-28].

<6> Achaab son of Koulias

<7> and Sedekias son of Maasios, who prophesied against Ieremias [29:21].

<8> Iezonias son of Assour

<9> and Paltias son of Benaios, noted by Iezekiél [11:1].

**19.** – Who were the leaders of the tribes in the Exodus from Egypt? (continued from C. 6)

<1> Of the Levitical tribe the leaders were Moses and Aarôn.

<2> Of Iouda, <Nassôn son of> Aminadab.[2]

<3> Of Roubin, Eliouz.

<4> Of Symeôn, Sarisalai.

---

[1] 3 Rg 18:22 mentions 400 prophets of the asherah; cf. Josephus *Ant*. 8.338.

[2] Joseph's list continues with the names of the fathers of the leaders (none from Cod.A).

‹ε›› τῆς (110b2) δὲ Ἰσάχαρ, Δωγάρ.
‹ς›› τῆς δὲ Ζαβουλών, Χελλών.
‹ζ›› τῆς Ἐφραΐμ, Σεμιούλ.
‹η›› τῆς Μανασσῆ, Φαλασσούρ.
‹θ›› τῆς Βενιαμὶν, Γαδεών.
‹ι›› τῆς Δὰν, Ἀμισαλᾶν.
‹ια›› τῆς Ἀσὴρ, Ἐχρᾶν.
‹ιβ›› τῆς Θὰδ,[1] Ῥαγουήλ.
‹ιγ›› τῆς Νεφθαλήμ,[2] Ἐλάμ.
Οὗτοι οἱ ἐν τῇ ἐξόδῳ ἡγούμενοι, φύλαρχοι τοῦ λαοῦ, οἳ καὶ ἐν τῇ ἐρήμῳ ἀπέθανον.[3]

**Κ΄.** + Τίνας ἔσχε Μωϋσῆς υἱοὺς, καὶ ἐκ τίνος;
Ἐκ Σεπφόρας τῆς θυγατρὸς Ἰωθὼρ ἱερέως Μαδιάμ·[4] α΄ Γηρσὼν, β΄ Ἐλιέζερ.

**ΚΑ΄.** + Τίνας δὲ[5] Ἀαρὼν ἔσχεν υἱούς; (111a1)
Ἐκ τῆς Ἐλισάβετ, θυγατρὸς Ἀμιναδὰβ, ἀδελφῆς δὲ Νααασσὼν· οἳ καὶ ἐκ τῆς φυλῆς Ἰούδα κατάγονται· α΄ τὸν Ναδὰβ, β΄ τὸν Ἀβιοὺδ, γ΄ τὸν Ἐλεάζαρ, δ΄ τὸν Ἰθάμαρ.

**ΚΒ΄.** + Τίνα ἐστὶ τὰ ἔθνη, ἃ ὁ λαὸς ἐκληρονόμησεν;
‹α›› Χαναναῖον.
‹β›› Εὐαῖον.
‹γ›› Γεργεσαῖον
‹δ›› Ἰεβουσαῖον.
‹ε›› Χεταῖον.
‹ς›› Ἀμορραῖον.
‹ζ›› Φερεζαῖον.[6]

---

[1]*Lc* FGM Γαδ.
[2]*Lc* FGM Νεφθαλιμ.
[3]CF do not number this chapter. GM do number it.
[4]*Lc* GM Μαδιαν.
[5]FGM omit δε.
[6]The items in this chapter are not numbered in CFGM.

<5> Of Isachar, Dôgar.
<6> Of Zaboulôn, Chellôn.
<7> Of Ephraim, Semioul.
<8> Of Manassé, Phalassour.
<9> Of Beniamin, Gadeôn.
<10> Of Dan, Amisalan.
<11> Of Asér, Echran.
<12> Of Gad, Ragouél.
<13> Of Nephthalim, Elam [Nm 1:5-15].
These are the ones who led in the Exodus, the tribal rulers of the people, who also died in the desert.

**20.** – What sons did Moses have and by whom?
By Sepphora daughter of Iôthôr priest of Madian: 1. Gersôn [Ex 2:22, 18:3], 2. Eliezer [18:4].

**21.** – And what sons did Aarôn have? (111a)
By Elisabet [Cod.A] daughter of Aminadab, sister of Naassôn, the following who descended from the tribe of Iouda: 1. Nadab, 2. Abioud [Abisour, Cod.A], 3. Eleazar, 4. Ithamar [Ex 6:23].

**22.** – What are the nations from whom the people inherited?
<1> Chanaanaion.
<2> Euaion.
<3> Gergesaion.
<4> Iebousaion.
<5> Chettaion.
<6> Amorraion.
<7> Pherezaion. [1]

---

[1] All from Dt 20:17 (Gergesites from Cod.B); cf. Josephus' list of seven Canaanite cities destroyed by the Hebrews (*Ant.* 1.139).

**ΚΓ'.** + Τίνας βασιλεῖς καὶ τίνων ἐθνῶν [1] ὁ λαὸς ἀπέκτεινεν; ‹α'› Ἐπὶ τοῦ Μωϋσέως ἐκτάσει τῶν χειρῶν αὐτοῦ,[2] τὸν[3] Ἀμαλήκ. β' Διὰ Ἰησοῦ τοῦ Ναυῆ, τὸν Ἀδωνιβέζεκ βασιλέα Ἱερουσαλήμ. ‹γ'› Καὶ (111a2) τὸν Ἰλὰμ βασιλέα Χεβρῶν. ‹δ'› Καὶ τὸν Φειδὼ βασιλέα Ἱεριμούς. ‹ε'› Καὶ τὸν Σιφὰ βασιλέα Λάχης. ‹ϛ'› Καὶ τὸν Δαμὶς βασιλέα Ὀδαλλάμ. ‹ζ'› Καὶ τὸν Ἰαβὶν βασιλέα Ἀσσόρ. ‹η'› Καὶ βασιλέα Σομόρων. ‹θ'› Καὶ βασιλέα Ζίφ.[4]

Καὶ ἄλλους βασιλεῖς ἕως τῆς Σιδωνίας, τοὺς πάντας ὁ Ἰησοῦς ἀνεῖλε,[5] βασιλεῖς κθ'.

Τὸν δὲ Σηὼν βασιλέα τῶν Ἀμορραίων Μωϋσῆς ἀνεῖλε, καὶ τὸν Ὢγ βασιλέα τῆς Βασάν.

Καὶ ὁ Ἰούδας δὲ ἀπέκτεινε τὸν Ἀδωνιβεζέκ, οὗ τὰ ἄκρα τῶν ποδῶν πρότερον ἐξέτεμεν.

Ὁ τε Γοθονιὴλ ὁ κριτής, τῶν Χουσὰρ (111b1) ἐλθὼν[6] βασιλέα Συρίας.

Καὶ ὁ Ἀὼδ ὁ ἀμφοτεροδέξιος τῶν[7] Αἰγλὼν βασιλέα Μωαβιτῶν, δόλῳ διαχρησάμενος αὐτὸν τῇ λαιᾷ χειρί.

Δεββόρρα δὲ διὰ[8] τοῦ Βαρὰκ, τὸν Σισάρα βασιλέα Ἰακὶς, ὃν Ἰαὴλ γυνὴ πασσάλῳ διὰ τῶν ὤτων διήλασε.

Γεδεὼν τε[9] τὸν Ὠρὴμ Μαδιὰμ βασιλέα.

Καὶ Ἰεφθαὲ τὴν τοῦ Ἀμαλὴκ βασιλείαν.

---

[1]FGM Τινας, και τινων ἐθνων βασιλεις.
[2]GM omit αὐτου.
[3]GM omit τον.
[4]CF number only entry β'. GM number entries α' through θ'.
[5]GM ἀνειλεν.
[6]*Lc* FGM τον Χουσαρ ἑλων.
[7]*Lc* FGM τον.
[8]FGM omit δια.
[9]*Lc* FGM δε.

**23**. – What kings, and of what nations, did the people kill?

<1> Under Moses, by the extension of his hands, Amalek [Ex 17:11-13].

2. Through Iésous son of Naué, Adônibezek, king of Jerusalem.

<3> And Ilam king of Chebrôn.

<4> And Pheidô king of Ierimos.

<5> And Sipha king of Lachés.

<6> And Damis king of Odallam [Js 10:3-5].

<7> And Iabin king of Assor [Jd 4:2].

<8> And the king of the Somori [Js 12:20].

<9> And King Ziph.

And other kings as far as Sidônia [13:6], all of whom Iésous slew, twenty-nine kings.

But Moses killed Seôn king of the Amorites [Nm 21:34] and Og king of Basan [21:35].

Ioudas killed Adônibezek, the end of whose great toes he first cut off [Jd 1:6-7].

Gothoniél the judge destroyed Chousar (111b) king of Syria [3:10].

And the ambidextrous Aôd (Ehud) killed Aiglôm king of the Moabites, by a trick slaying him with his left hand [3:15, 21; C. 71].

Deborra through Barak killed Sisara king [general, 4:7] of Iakis, whom the woman Iaél killed with a peg through his ears [4:21].

And Gedeôn killed Ôrém king of Madiam [7:25], and Iephthaë took the kingdom of Amalék (Ammonites) [11:33].

**ΚΔ'.** + Πόσα ἔθνη καὶ τίνα συνέστη ἀπὸ τῶν τριῶν τοῦ Νῶε παίδων, Σὴμ, Χὰμ, Ἰάφεθ;
&lt;α'&gt; Ἑβραῖοι.
&lt;β'&gt; Ἀσσύριοι.
&lt;γ' Χαλδαῖοι.&gt;[1]
&lt;δ'&gt; Πέρσαι.
&lt;ε'&gt; Μῆδοι.
&lt;ϛ'&gt; Ἄραβες.
&lt;ζ'&gt; Μαδιανοί.
&lt;η'&gt; Ἀδιαβηνοί.
&lt;θ'&gt; Ταϊηνοί.[2]
&lt;ι'&gt; Ἀλαμοστινοί.[3] **(111b2)**

---

[1] Insert Χαλδαιοι by emendation. It is not found in CFGM.
[2] FGM Ταϊνοι.
[3] FGM Παλαιστινοι.

**24.** – How many, and what, nations arose from the three sons of Nôé: Sém, Cham, Iapheth?[1] (Continued from C. 4)

    <1> **Hebraioi** (All other texts add: who are also Jews).[2]

    <2> **Assyrioi.**

    <3. Chaldeans>[3]

    <4> **Persai.**

    <5> **Médoi.**[4]

    <6> **Arabes** (the H₁ recension of the *Chronicon* [i.e., Cod. Matritensis 4701 and Scaliger's Barbarus] adds: first and second).[5]

    <7> Madian<ai>oi (the H₁ recension of the *Chronicon* adds: first and second).[6]

    <8> **Adiabénoi.**

    <9> **Taiénoi.**

    <10> Alamostinoi (Palaistinoi/**Salamosénoi**).[7]

---

[1] Hippolytus *Chr.* 200, from the *Diamerismos* preserved in Codex Matritensis Graec. 4701 (ed. Bauer; TU N.F.14.1); Ludwig Dindorf, *Chronicon Paschale* 1 (Corpus Scriptorum Historiae Byzantinae 16; Bonn: Weber, 1832) 57, 5–9. See also Bauer, *Die Chronik*, 136–37, 203 n.11.

[2] The *Hypomnestikon* here agrees with the Armenian against the other witnesses to the *Chronicon* in omitting οἱ καὶ Ἰουδαῖοι. For a German translation of the Armenian, see J. Markwart, "Übersetzung aus Moses Kaghankatuatsi und der armenischen Chronik vom J. 686 bis zum Ende der Kaiserliste," in Helm, *Die Chronik* (1st ed.) 482–86. Markwart's entire translation was not included in the second edition.

[3] The other texts which were based on the *Chronicon* here include the Chaldeans. This name has apparently fallen out of the text of the *Hypomnestikon*.

[4] In listing the Persians before the Medes, the *Hypomnestikon* here agrees with the H₂ recension of the *Chronicon* (witnessed by the *Liber generationis I,* the *Liber generationis II,* and the *Armenian Chronicle*) against the stemmatically prior H₁ (witnessed by Cod. Matritensis 4701 and Scaliger's Barbarus [Parisinus Lat. 4884]) as it typically does. For more about the filiation of witnesses to the *Chronicon*, see Helm, *Die Chronik*, XI–XIV.

[5] While Cod. Matritensis 4701, which is the only extensive Greek manuscript of the *Chronicon*, probably retains the original reading of Hippolytus' composition, it is unlikely that "first and second" was ever in the text of the *Hypomnestikon*, since this addition does not appear in either the *Liber generationis I* or the Armenian, i.e., the H₂ recension. The same situation holds for the additions to the Madianaioi, Indians, Ethiopians, Egyptians, and Libyes.

[6] See the above note to Arabes.

[7] It is reasonable to suppose that *Palaistinoi* was the original reading of the *Chronicon*, but the name had already been corrupted to Alamostinoi prior to its incorporation into the *Hypomnestikon* as the evidence of the *Liber generationis I* and the

‹ια› Σαρακηνοί.
‹ιβ› Μάγοι.
‹ιγ› Κάσπιοι.
‹ιδ› Ἀλβανοί.
‹ιε› Ἰνδοί.
‹ις› Αἰθίοπες.
‹ιζ› Αἰγύπτιοι.
‹ιη› Λύβιες.[1]
‹ιθ› Χαγγαῖοι.[2]
‹κ› Χαναναῖοι.[3]
‹κα› Φερεζαῖοι.
‹κβ› Εὐαῖοι.
‹κγ› Ἀμορραῖοι.
‹κδ› Γεργεσαῖοι.
‹κε› Ἰεβουσαῖοι.
‹κς› Ἰδουμαῖοι.
‹κζ› Σαμαρεῖς.
‹κη› Φοίνικες.
‹κθ› Σύροι.
‹λ› Κίλικες.
‹λα› Καππαδόκαι.
‹λβ› Ἀρμένιοι.
‹λγ› Ἴβηρες.
‹λδ› Βεβρανοί.
‹λε› Σκύθαι.
‹λς› Κολχοί.
‹λζ› Σαμνοί.
‹λη› Βόσποροι.
‹λθ› Ἀσσιανοί.[4]
‹μ› Ἴσαυροι.
‹μα› Λυκάονες.

---

Armenian Chronicle suggests. Cod. Matritensis 4701, Scaliger's Barbarus, and the *Liber generationis II* read Salamosénoi.

[1] *Lc* FGM Λιβυες.
[2] Emend to Χετταιοι.
[3] Emend to Χανααναιοι.
[4] FGM Ἀββιανοι.

\<11\> **Sarakénoi**.[1]

\<12\> **Magoi**.

\<13\> **Kaspioi**.

\<14\> **Albanians**.

\<15\> **Indians** (the H$_1$ recension of the *Chronicon* adds: first and second).[2]

\<16\> **Ethiopians** (the H$_1$ recension adds: first and second).[3]

\<17\> **Egyptians** (the H$_1$ recension of the *Chronicon* adds: and Thebans).[4]

\<18\> **Libyes** (the H$_1$ recension of the *Chronicon* adds: first and second).[5]

\<19\> **Chettaioi**.

\<20\> **Chana\<a\>naioi**.

\<21\> **Pherezaioi**.

\<22\> **Euaioi**.

\<23\> **Amorraioi**.

\<24\> **Gergesaioi**.

\<25\> **Iebousaioi**.

\<26\> **Idoumaioi**.

\<27\> **Samareis**.

\<28\> **Phoinikes**.

\<29\> **Syroi**.

\<30\> **Kilikes** (All other texts add: who are also Tharseis).[6]

\<31\> **Kappadokai**.

\<32\> **Armenioi**.

\<33\> **Ibéres**.

\<34\> **Bebranoi**.

\<35\> **Skythai**.

\<36\> **Kolchoi**.

\<37\> Samnoi (**Saunoi**).

\<38\> **Bosporoi**.

\<39\> **Assianoi**.

\<40\> **Isauroi**.

\<41\> **Lycaones**.

---

[1] The term appears as early as Dionysius of Alexandria (in Eusebius *HE* 6.42.4) as well as in Hippolytus; see Albert Dietrich, "Saraka," *KP* 4 (1972) 1548. Cf. Pseudo-Sarakénoi in C. 147(1). See also Introduction, pp. 23–24.

[2] See the above note to Arabes, item 6.

[3] See the above note to Arabes, item 6.

[4] See the above note to Arabes, item 6.

[5] See the above note to Arabes, item 6.

[6] The *Liber generationis I* reads Cilices Tharsenses.

‹μβ'› Πισσίδαι.[1]
‹μγ'› Γαλάται.
‹μδ'› Παφλαγόνες.
‹με'› Φρύγες.
‹μς'› Ἕλληνες οἱ καὶ Ἀχαιοί.
‹μζ'› Θεσσαλοί.
‹μη'› Μακεδόνες.
‹μθ'› Θρᾶκες.
‹ν'› Μαυσοί.
‹να'› Βεσσοί.
‹νβ'› Δαρδανοί.
‹νγ'› Σαρμάται.
‹νδ'› Γερμανοί.
‹νε'› Παννόνιοι. Παίονες.[2]
‹νς'› Νωρικοί.
‹νζ'› Δαλμάται. (112a1)
‹νη'› Ῥωμαῖοι.
‹νθ'› Λίγυρες.
‹ξ'› Γάλλιοι[3] οἱ καὶ Κεντοί.[4]
‹ξα'› Ἀκυατινοί.›[5]
‹ξβ'› Βριτανοί.›[6]
‹ξγ'› Σπανοὶ καὶ Τυρηνοί.[7]
‹ξδ'› Μαργοί.
‹ξε'› Μακουακοί.
‹ξς'› Σελουκοί.[8]
‹ξζ'› Ἄφροι.
‹ξη'› Μάζικες.

---

[1] Lc FGM Πισιδαι.

[2] FGM list Παννονιοι and Παιονες.as separate items. However, as Cod. Matritensis 4701 and the Armenian make clear, these were originally combined in one entry in Hippolytus' *Chronicon*. This entry read: Παννονιοι ὁ και Παιονες. Emendation is not indicated, since the evidence of the *Liber generationis I* suggests that ὁ και had fallen out prior to the inclusion of this material in the *Hypomnestikon*.

[3] Lc FGM Γαλλοι.

[4] Lc FGM Κελτοι.

[5] Insert Ἀκυατινοι by emendantion. It is not found in CFGM.

[6] Insert Βριτανοι by emendation. It is not found in CFGM.

[7] Lc FGM οἱ και Τυρηνοι.

[8] Lc FGM Σελευκοι.

<42> **Pisidai** .
<43> **Galatai.**
<44> **Paphlagones.**
<45> **Phryges.**
<46> **Hellénes also called Achaeans.**
<47> **Thessaloi.**
<48> **Makedones.**
<49> **Thrakes.**
<50> Mausoi (All other texts: **Mysoi**).
<51> **Bessoi.**
<52> **Dardanoi.**
<53> **Sarmatai** .
<54> **Germanoi.**
<55> **Pannonioi** (Cod Matritensis 4701 and the *Armenian Chronicle* add: also called) **Paiones.** [1]
<56> **Nôrikoi.**
<57> **Dalmatai** (112a).
<58> **Rômaioi** (the H[1] recension of the *Chronicon* adds: also called Latins and Kit<t>aioi). [2]
<59> **Ligures** .
<60> **Galloi also called Keltoi** .
<61. Aquitanians.>
<62. Britons>.
<63> **Spanoi also called Tyrénoi.**
<64> Margoi (All other texts: **Mauroi**).
<65> **Makouakoi.**
<66> Seleukoi (Cod. Matritensis 4701, Scaliger's Barbarus, and the *Liber generationis I* read: Gaituloi). [3]
<67> **Aphroi.**
<68> **Mazikes.**

---

[1] The *Liber generationis I* agrees with Joseph almost exactly: Pannoni Peones. Cod. Matritensis 4701 (a witness to H[1]) and the *Armenian Chronicle* (a witness to H[2]) suggest the *Urtext* of the *Chronicon*, but the text has been corrupted by the time Joseph encounters it.

[2] The *Liber generationis I* and the *Armenian Chronicle* read: Rômaioi also called Latins.

[3] The *Armenian Chronicle* conflates the readings to: Gaituloi, Seleukoi.

‹ξθ'› Γαράμαντες οἱ καὶ ‹ο'› Βοράδες, ἕως τῆς Αἰθιοπίας ἐκτείνουσιν.[1]

The list or *Diamerismos* is not arranged according to patriarchs (as are the lists in Gn 10:1-32 and Josephus *Ant.* 1.122-47) but is found in the third-century *Chronicle* of Hippolytus, pp. 79-90 Helm (2d. ed., pp. 31-33), and the *Paschal Chronicle* (written around 630), as Helm noted. The names from Pisidians to Dalmatians (excepting 49. Thrakes) appear in Oxyrhynchus Papyrus VI 870 (6th-7th century); cf. Daniel Serruys, "Un fragment sur papyrus de la Chronique d'Hippolyte de Rome," *Revue de Philologie* 38 (1914) 27-31; Wilhelm Bannier, "Ein Papyrusfragment aus der Chronik des Hippolytus," *Philologus* 81, N.F. 35 (1926) 123-27; Joseph van Haelst, *Catalogue des Papyrus littéraires juifs et chrétiens* (Paris: Sorbonne, 1976) 239, no. 669. Since Bannier identified the fragmentary lines from the verso with a passage found only a few pages farther on in Hippolytus and the *Paschal Chronicle*[2] but not in Joseph, the papyrus is not based on our work but, as Helm correctly claimed, a chronicle based on Hippolytus.[3] Contrast the different and largely incorrect list in C. 166.

The figure of seventy or seventy-two nations was quite important to the original form of the list, but even the shorter form of the list has been imperfectly transmitted in the Cambridge manuscript. The shorter form of the list probably resulted from haplography. For more on this, see the notes to the final two nations listed in the chapter.

---

[1] CFG do not number this chapter. M does number it.

[2] Hippolytus *Chr.* p. 83,7–84,7 Helm; *Chronicon Paschale* p. 58 (Dindorf 3–13).

[3] Helm, *Die Chronik*, 80–81.

<69> (Cod. Matritensis 4701 adds: the interior) **Garamantes** (Taramantes),[1] **who extend to Ethiopia;** also called <70> Borades (**Sporades**).[2]

---

[1] At this point the *Hypomnestikon* and its textual relatives, the *Liber generationis I* and the *Armenian Chronicle* omit "the exterior Taramantes, Borades also called Makores, Keltiones also called Sporades, Nausthi also called Nabotai," although later the Sporades do reappear. Perhaps this omission can be explained by haplography, the scribe's eye having passed from one Taramantes to another. Since the "interior Taramantes" no longer needed to be distinguished from another kind of Taramantes, the qualifier was then dropped. At about the same time another error was introduced, Taramantes being corrupted to Garamantes. In this matter once again, the *Hypomnestikon*, the *Liber generationis I*, and the *Armenian Chronicle* agree against the other witnesses.

[2] It is likely that the author of the *Chronicon* originally wrote Sporades, although the corruption to Borades must have occurred early, since only Cod. Matritensis 4701 retains Sporades. Only the *Armenian Chronicle* agrees with Joseph in identifying the Sporades/Borades with the Taramantes/Garamantes. The reason for this identification is obscure, but perhaps is related to the fact that Sporades/Borades immediately follows the first reference to Taramantes/Gaaramantes in those texts which do not suffer from the haplography suggested in the previous note. It is possible that early manuscripts of the *Chronicon* linked these two groups, but it is more likely that they were linked through the mistake of a later editor or copyist.

**ΚΕ΄.** + Τὰ ἐν τῇ Παλαιᾷ ἐνδιάθετο βιβλία κβ΄.
α΄ Βρισὴθ, ὅπερ ἐστὶν, Ἐν ἀρχῇ ἐποίησεν.
β΄ Οὐελεσμὼθ, ὅ ἐστι, Ταῦτα τὰ ὀνόματα.
γ΄ Οὐεκρὰ, ὅ ἐστι, Καὶ ἐκάλεσεν.
δ΄ Ἀμμεσφεκοδὶμ,[1] ὅ ἐστι, Ἀριθμοί.
ε΄ Ἐλεαδεβαρὶμ, Δευτερονόμιον, Οὗτοι οἱ λόγοι.
ϛ΄ Ἰσσοῦε Βενουῆ,[2] Ἰησοῦς ὁ τοῦ Ναυῆ.
ζ΄ Ἰωσοφατὴμ, Κριταί.
η΄ Ῥούθ.
θ΄ Σαμουὴλ, ὅπερ (112a2) ἑρμηνεύθη,[3] Ὁ κλιτός.[4]
ι΄ Οὐαμμὲλ[5] Δαβὶδ, ὅ ἐστι, Βασιλεὼς[6] Δαβίδ.
ια΄ Δαβρὴ Ἰωακεὶμ,[7] ὅ ἐστι, Λόγοι ἡμερῶν.
ιβ΄ Ἔσδρας, ὅπερ ἐστὶ, Βοηθὸς, Βίβλος.
ιγ΄ Σεφαρθελλὶμ, ὅ ἐστι, Βίβλος ψαλμῶν.
ιδ΄ Μελδὼθ, Παροιμίαι.
ιε΄ Ὁ Κωὲλ,[8] Ἐκκλησίας τύπος.
ιϛ΄ Σισὰμ σιρὶμ,[9] Ἆσμα ἀσμάτων.
ιζ΄ Προφῆται ιβ΄.
ιη΄ Ἡσαΐας.
ιθ΄ Ἰερεμίας.
κ΄ Ἰεζεκιήλ.
κα΄ Δανιήλ.
κβ΄ Ἰώβ.
Ἔξω δὲ τούτων· Ἐσθὴρ, καὶ τὰ Μακκαβαϊκὰ, ἅπερ ἐπιγέγραπται, Σαρβὴθ Σαβαναϊέλ.

---

[1] In their notes FGM suggest emending to Ἀμμεσθεκωδειμ.
[2] GM Βενουη.
[3] GM ἡρμηνευθη.
[4] *Lc* FGM κλητος.
[5] *Lc* FGM Οὐαμμελεχ.
[6] *Lc* FGM Βασιλευς.
[7] *Lc* FGM Ἰαμμημ.
[8] *Lc* FGM Κωελεθ.
[9] *Lc* FGM Σιρ ἀσσιριμ.

<CANON, LITERATURE, AND MEASUREMENTS (25-28)>

**25.** – The twenty-two books covenanted (*endiatheto*) in the Old:[1]
1. Briséth, which is, In the beginning he made.[2] (Gn)
2. Ouelesmôth, which is, These are the names. (Ex)
3. Ouekra, which is, And he called. (Lv)
4. Ammesphekodim, Numbers.
5. Eleadebarim, Deuteronomy, These are the words.
6. Issoue Benoué, Iésous son of Naué. (Js)
7. Iôsophatém, Judges.
8. Ruth.
9. Samouél, which is translated "called." (1-4 Bas)
10. Ouammelech Dabid, which is, King David. (1 Par)
11. Dabré Iammém, Words of days. (2 Par)
12. Esdras, Helper, book.
13. Sepharthellim, which is, book of Psalms.
14. Meldôth, Proverbs.
15. The Kôeleth, type of the church.[3]
16. Sir assirim, Song of Songs.
17. Prophets XII.
18. Ésaias.
19. Ieremias.
20. Iezekiél.
21. Daniél.
22. Iôb.

Outside these, Esther and the Maccabaean books, entitled Sarbéth Sabanaiel.[4]

---

[1] Cf. the discussion of early lists in Robert M. Grant, *The Formation of the New Testament* (London: Hutchinson, 1965) 36–41. The number twenty-two was considered important because this is the number of letters in the Hebrew alphabet.

[2] Origen rightly omits "he made" from Briséth.

[3] *Ekklésias-typos* for *ekklésias-tés*.

[4] Origen omits the Maccabees; the Hebrew name may mean "History of the house of warriors" (McNeile in Hugh J. Lawlor-John E. L. Oulton, *Eusebius* [2 vols.; London: SPCK, 1928] 2.217), or according to Brownlee's suggestion, it may attempt to render ספר בת סרכי אל , the Aramaic equivalent of ספר בת חשמנאים, or "The Book of the House of the Princes of God" (See William H. Brownlee, "Maccabees, Books of," IDB 3 [1962] 203).

ΚϜ'. + Ὀνομασίαι καὶ ἑρμηνεία τῶν παρ' Ἑβραίοις στοιχείων. (112b1)
"Αλφ, μάθησις. Βὲθ, οἴκου. Γήμελ,[1] πλήρωσις. Δάλεθ, δέλτων. Ἤ, αὕτη.
Οὐαὺ, ἐπ' αὐτῇ. Ζαὶ, ζῇ. "Ηθ, ζωή.[2] Τὴθ, καλή. Ἰὼθ, ἀρχή. Κὰφ, ὅμως.
Λάμδ,[3] μάθετε. Μὴν, ἐξ αὐτῶν. Νοὺν, αἰώνια. Σάμχ,[4] βοήθεια. Ἀΐν, πηγὴ
ἢ ὀφθαλμοῦ.[5] Φῆ, στόμα. Σαδὶ, δικαιοσύνη. Κὼφ, κλῆσις. Ῥῆς, κεφαλῆς.
Σένω,[6] ὀδόντες. Ταῦ, σημεῖα.
    Ὁμοῦ ἀπαρτίζει τοιαύτην διάνοιαν· Μάθησις οἴκου, πλήρωσις δέλτων
αὕτη,[7] ἐν[8] αὐτῇ ζῇ ὁ ζῶν· καλὴ ἀρχὴ, ὅμως μάθετε ἐξ αὐτῶν αἰώνια.
Βοήθεια ὀφθαλμοὺς,[9] στόμα καὶ δικαιοσύνην,[10] κλῆσις (112b2) κεφαλῆς καὶ
ὀδόντων σημεῖα.

ΚΖ'. + Μῆνες Ἑβραίων, Αἰγυπτίων, Μακεδόνων, Ῥωμαίων.
    δ' Νησὰν, Φαρμουθὶ, Ξανθικὸς, Ἀπρίλλιος.
    ε' Εἴαρ, Πάχων, Ἀρτεμίσιος, Μάϊος.
    ϛ' Σιουὰν, Ναϋνὴ,[11] Δέσιος, Ἰούνιος.

---

[1] Lc FGM Γιμελ.
[2] Lc FGM ζων.
[3] Lc FGM Λαμεδ.
[4] Lc FGM Σαμεχ.
[5] GM ὀφθαλμοι.
[6] Lc FGM Σιν.
[7] FGM omit αὐτη.
[8] FGM omit ἐν.
[9] Lc FGM ὀφθαλμου.
[10] Lc FGM δικαιοσυνη.
[11] Lc FGM Παϋνι.

Origen's list cited by Eusebius omits the XII Prophets by mistake and so totals only twenty-one.[1] Cyril of Jerusalem in 350 lists twenty-two names in Greek,[2] while later Epiphanius provides different Hebrew names.[3] Joseph's list includes the XII and separates Ruth from Judges. His total would reach twenty-three if he did not treat Esther as deutero-canonical. (Cod.A has a completely different list.)

**26.** – Names and meanings of the letters among the Hebrews (112b):
Alph, learning. Beth, of a house. Gimel, fullness. Daleth, of writing tablets. Hé, this. Ouau, on it (her). Zai, he lives. Héth, the living. Téth, good. Iôth, beginning. Kaph, yet. Lamed, learn. Mén, from them. Noun, eternal. Samech, aid. Ain, fount or of the eye. Phé, mouth, Sadi, justice. Kôph, calling. Rés, head. Sin, teeth. Thau, signs.
Joined together, these make the meaning thus: Learning of the house, this is fulness of writing tablets; the one who lives lives by it. A good beginning, yet learn eternal things from them. An aid to the eye is the mouth and justice. The calling of the head and signs of the teeth.[4]

**27.** – The months of Hebrews, Egyptians, Macedonians, Romans:
4. Nésan (first as in c. 68), Pharmouthi, Xanthikos, April
5. Eiar, Pachôn, Artemisios, May
6. Siouan, Pauni, Desios, June

---

[1] Origen's list: Brésith (In the beginning), Ouellesmôth (These are the names), Ouïkra (And he called), Ammesphekôdeim, Elleaddebareim, Iôsue ben Noun, Sôphteim, Samouél, Ouammelchdauid, Dabréïamein, Ezra, Sphartheleim, Melôth, Kôelth, Sirassireim, Iessia, Ieremia, Daniél, Iezekiél, Iôb, Esthér, Sarbéthsabanaiél (Maccabees) (Eusebius *HE* 6.25.2). A quite different list in Epiphanius *Weights and Measures* 23 (PG 43, 277C–280A); Greek names only, ibid. 4 (243B); cf. James E. Dean, *Epiphanius' Treatise on Weights and Measures: The Syriac Version* (Chicago: University of Chicago Press, 1935) 44–45.

[2] Cyril *Cat.* 4.35 (PG 33, 500A–B): (1–5) Pentateuch, (6) Josh, (7) Jd with Ruth, (8) 1–2 Rg, (9) 3–4 Rg, (10) 1–2 Par, (11) 1–2 Esd = Ez-Neh, (12) Esther, (13–17) five poetic books (Job, Ps, Prv, Ec, Ca); (18–22) five prophetic (XII, Is, Jer, Ez, Dn).

[3] Hebrew in Epiphanius *Weights and Measures* 23 (PG 43, 277C–280B); Greek names only, *Weights and Measures* 4 (243B); cf. Dean, *Weights and Measures*, 44–45.

[4] From Eusebius *Gospel Preparation* 10.5.4–9 (Mras I 574,11–575,6); cf. 11.6.34–35 (II 18,19–19,2). Jerome makes use of the same material in his *Epistula* 30.5–13. See "Tetragrammon." Eusebius cites the mnemonic poem for apologetic reasons, while here the purpose is more in keeping with its original mnemonic intent.

ζ' Θαμυοὺζ,[1] Ἐπὶφ,[2] Πάνεμος,[3] Ἰούλιος.
η' Ἄβ, Μεσσορῆ, Λῶος, Αὔγουστος.
θ' Ἐλοὺς,[4] Θὼθ, Γορπιαῖος, Σεπτέμβριος.
ι' Ὀσρὶ,[5] Φαοφὶ, Ὑπερβερεταῖος, Ὀκτώβριος.
ια' Μαρσαβᾶν, Ἀθὺρ, Δῖος, Νοέμβριος.
ιβ' Χασελεῦ, Χυὰκ,[6] Ἀπηλλαῖος, Δεκέμβριος.
α' Τηβὴθ, Τύβυ, Αὐδυναῖος, Ἰανουάριος.
β' Σαβὰθ, Μεχὴρ, Περίτιος, Φευρουάριος.
γ' Ἀδάρ, Φαμενουθὶ, Δύστρος, Μάρτιος.

**ΚΗ'.** + ⟨Α.⟩ Ὅπως τὸ ἱερὸν κατεσκευάζετο χρίσμα;
Ἄνθους σμίρνης[7] ἐκλεκτῆς σίτλοι[8] φ'. Ποιεῖ γόμορ . ⟨. . . . .⟩[9] κε.[10]
**(113a1)** ⟨. . . . .⟩[11] γίνονται,[12] ϩϩτ'.[13]
Ἐν τῷ ἁγίῳ σταθμῷ[14] ὁ σίτλος[15] ὁ εἷς νόαρ, ἤγουν ϩϩ.[16] ⟨. . . . .⟩[17] ἑξ.

---

[1] *Lc* FGM Θαμουζ.
[2] *Lc* FGM Ἐπιφι.
[3] FGM Παμενος.
[4] *Lc* FGM Ἐλουλ.
[5] In their Latin translations FG note that the form is wrong. M suggests emending to Θισρι.
[6] *Lc* FGM Χοϊακ.
[7] FGM σμυρνης.
[8] *Lc* FGM σικλοι.
[9] *Lc* FGM, who assume a *lacuna*.
[10] Emend to ρκε' based on Ex 30:23.
[11] *Lc* FGM, who assume a *lacuna*.
[12] FGM γινονι.
[13] The ϩ sign is here used to represent a similar sign in the ms. which apparently indicates some type of measure since it is set in apposition to the biblical measures. FGM render this numeration θθ'.
[14] FGM των ἐν τω ἁγιω σταθμω.
[15] *Lc* FGM σικλος.
[16] FGM render this θθ'.
[17] Although CFGM do not so indicate, there is a probable *lacuna* here.

7. Thamouz, Epiphi, Panemos, July
8. Ab, Mesoré, Lôos, August
9. Eloul, Thôth, Gorpiaios, September
10. Osri (Tisri), Phaophi, Hyperberetaios, October
11. Marsaban, Athyr, Dios, November
12. Chaseleu, Choiak, Apéllaios, December
1. Tébéth, Tyby, Audynaios, January
2. Sabath, Mechér, Peritios, February
3. Adar, Phamenouthi, Dystros, March[1]

**28.** – <A.> How was the sacred chrism prepared? (Cf. C. 69[9])

Of **flower of choice myrrh, 500 shekels**; it makes <1>25 gomers (113a). They equal ℌℌ 300.

Of those by the sacred standard, the shekel is one coin, 1 1/2, they count it as ℌℌ 6.

[1] See Elias Bickerman, *Chronology of the Ancient World* (rev. ed., London: Thames & Hudson, 1980); Werner Eisenhut, "Kalender," *KP* 3 (1969) 58–63; Walther Sontheimer, "Monat," *KP* 3 (1969) 1405–8; cf. *Hastings Dictionary of the Bible* (ed. Grant-Rowley; New York: Scribner's, 1963) 1001–2.

Κινναμώμου[1] εὐώδους τὸ C'·[2] σίτλοι[3] σν'. Γόγο[4] ξβC'. γίνονται ϞϞϵ'.[5]
Καλάμου εὐώδους σίτλοι[6] σν'. ϞϞϵ'.[7]
Ἱερεως σίκλοι φ' ϞϞτ'.[8]
Ἐλαίου ἐξ ἐλαιῶν, ἕν,[9] ᾧ[10] ποιεῖ χ‹όεις› θ',[11] ὁμοῦ λλλ'.[12]

+ ‹Β.› Ὅπως τὸ ἱερὸν κατεσκευάζετο θυμίαμα;
Στακτὴν, ὄνυχα, χαλβάνην, λίβανον, δάφνην, ἴσον ἴσῳ, φησὶν, ἔσται.

---

[1] Μ Κιναμωμου.
[2] This sign apparently indicates 1/2.
[3] Lc FGM σικλοι.
[4] Emend to Γόμορ.
[5] FGM render this θθϵ'.
[6] Lc FGM σικλοι.
[7] FGM render this θθϵ'.
[8] FGM render this θθτ'.
[9] FGM εἰν; lege ἕν.
[10] FGM omit ᾧ.
[11] FGM λλλ'; C reads χθ', but emendation seems necessary.
[12] FGM render this λλλ'.

**Of fragrant cinnamon, half as much, 250 shekels;**
62 1/2 gomers. They make ꟿꟿ 5.
**Of fragrant reed, 250 shekels:** ꟿꟿ 5.
**Of iris, 500 shekels,** ꟿꟿ 300:
**Of olive oil a <hin>** [Ex 30:23-24], makes ch<oeis> 9,
together 1830.[1]

<B.> How was the sacred incense prepared?
**Stakte, onycha, galbanum, frankincense, shall be in equal parts,** it says
[Ex 30:34].

Josephus combines incense with ointment and then says he is not
describing the ingredients of the incense "for fear of wearying my
readers" (3.198), while Irenaeus cites both texts from Exodus as
providing numbers which Gnostic heretics could not allegorize
(*Heresies* 2.24.3). *b. Kerithoth* (6a) gives a different list of
ingredients in the compound of incense used in the Temple: balm,
onycha, galbanum, frankincense (3500 sacred shekels each), myrrh,
cassia, spikenard, saffron (800 shekels each), costus, 600 shekels,
aromatic reed, 150 shekels, and cinnamon, 450 shekels.[2]

---

[1] In 3 Rg 7:24 the Hebrew *bath* (plural, 7:38) is rendered *choeis*, but this does not
clear up our text. The editors express thanks to R.W. Allison of Bates College for his
guidance. For the amounts cf. Josephus *Ant*. 3.197. The *gomor* (*'omer*) is defined as a
solid measure by Epiphanius *Weights and Measures* 21 (PG 43, 273A), and the *shekel*
and the *hin* in C. 24 (285A, 284C); cf. Dean, *Weights and Measures*, 138–41, also
Friedrich Hultsch, *Metrologicorum scriptorum reliquiae* 1 (Leipzig: Teubner, 1864; repr.
1971) 169–71 ("De notis mensuarum et pondium"). Add Theodoret *Questions on Exodus*
64 (PG 80, 289C, relying on Josephus *Ant*. 3.197 for *hin* = 2 Attic choeis; other measures,
*Questions on Ezekiel* 45:9–15 (PG 81, 1237A–B). See also Procopius of Gaza on Exodus
(PG 87, 660A,C). The trouble, as Allison notes, arises because the totals "don't yet seem
to make sense." Very little help comes from Marcellin Berthelot–C.-E. Ruelle, *Collection
des anciens alchimistes grecs* (Paris: Steinheil, 1888) 92–126 ("Signes et notations
alchimiques"); Paul Tannery, "Sur les abréviations dans les manuscrits grecs," *Revue
archéologique*, Ser. 3,12 (1888) 210–13; Edward M. Thompson, *An Introduction to
Greek and Latin Palaeography* (Oxford: Clarendon, 1912) 81–84; Wilhelm Weinberger,
"Kurzschrift," *PWRE* 11 (1922) 2219–22; Herbert Boge, *Griechische Tachygraphie und
tironischen Noten* (Berlin: Akademie, 1973) Tafeln 4–5.

[2] *Hebrew-English Edition of the Babylonian Talmud* (London: Soncino, 1989); cf.
John A. Thompson, "Perfume," *IDB* 3 (1962) 730–32. Almost all these plants are
discussed by Harold N. Moldenke and Alma L. Moldenke, *Plants of the Bible* (Waltham

**ΚΘ'.** + Τίνες γεγόνασι[1] γίγαντες;

Πρῶτοι ἐκεῖνοι, οἱ ταῖς θυγατράσι[2] τῶν ἀνδρῶν συμπλακέντες[3] τῶν δαιμόνων, γεννηθέντες, δι' οὓς καὶ ὁ κατακλυσμὸς **(113a2)** ἐγένετο, εἴκοσι καὶ ἑκατὸν ἐτῶν γεγονότων αὐτῶν, περὶ ὧν καὶ Μωϋσῆς φησιν· Ἐκεῖνοι ἦσαν[4] οἱ γίγαντες οἱ ἀπ' αἰῶνος ἄνθρωποι[5] οἱ ὀνομαστοί.

Δεύτερος ὁ Νεβρὼθ[6] ὁ κυνηγός, ὁ τῆς Βαβυλῶνος ἀρξάμενος βασιλεύς, περὶ οὗ καὶ Μωϋσῆς μέμνηται ὡς ἐν παραδείγματι μυθευομένου, λέγων· Διὰ τοῦτο ἐροῦσιν, ὡς Νεβρὼθ[7] γίγας κυνηγὸς ἔναντι τοῦ Θεοῦ.

‹γ'› Ἐγένοντο δὲ καὶ ἐν Ἀσταρὼθ Χαρνὲμ γίγαντες, οὓς κατέκρυψε[8] Χοδολογόμορ[9] βασιλεὺς Ἐλλάμ.

‹δ'› Μετὰ ταῦτα ἐν τῇ Χεβρὼν τρεῖς οἱ τοῦ Σεννὰκ[10] υἱοί· οὕστινας **(113b1)** Χάλεβ ὁ τοῦ Ἰεφωνῆ, λαβὼν ἐν κλήρῳ τὴν πόλιν, ἐξωλόθρευσε.

‹ε'› Καὶ ἐπὶ τοῦ βασιλέως Δαβὶδ γεγόνασι γίγαντες δ', οὓς καὶ ἀναιροῦσιν οἱ τοῦ Δαβὶδ στρατηγοὶ· Ἰεσβὴ, ὃν ἀνεῖλεν Ἀβισὰ, Σὲθ, ὃν ἀνεῖλε Σοβοχῆς ὁ Ἀστοθοῦ, Ἐλαῖαν, ὃν ἀνεῖλεν Ἀριὼ ὁ Βηθλεεμίτης. Τέταρτος δὲ μᾶλλον ὁ ἑξαδάκτυλος, ὃν ἐπάταξεν Ἰωνάθαν υἱὸς Σαμαίου, ἀδελφοῦ Δαβίδ.

‹ς'› Καὶ Γολιὰθ δὲ ὁ Χετταῖος ἐν τοῖς γίγασιν ἀριθμεῖται, ὃν νέος ὢν Δαβὶδ σφενδονίσας ἀνεῖλεν· οὗ καὶ τὸ δόρυ ἀνελόμενος, ἀνέθηκεν εἰς τὸ ἱερόν.[11]

---

MA: Chronica Botanica, 1952); cf. Michael Zohary, *Plants of the Bible* (Cambridge: Cambridge University Press, 1982) esp. 196–207.

[1] GM γεγονασιν.

[2] GM θυγατρασιν.

[3] Lc FGM συμπλακεντων.

[4] FGM εἰσιν.

[5] FGM οἱ ἄνθρωποι.

[6] Lc FGM Νεβρωδ.

[7] Lc GM Νεβρωδ.

[8] In their notes FGM suggest emending to κατεκοψε based on Gn 14:5.

[9] Lc FGM Χοδολλογομορ.

[10] FGM seem to assume that C reads Σενναδ; they propose emending to Ἐνακ on the basis of Js 15:13-14 and Jd 1:20.

[11] Beyond the written ennumerations for the first two items, neither C nor the editions number the items in this chapter.

## <GIANTS AND PROLIFIC MEN (29-30)>

**29.** – Who were giants?[1]

First, those born to the daughters of men who had intercourse with the demons, because of whom the deluge took place 120 years after their birth; of whom Moses said, "They were the giants of old, famous men" [Gn 6:4].

Second, Nebrôd the hunter who was the first king of Babylon, whom Moses mentions as an example of a story, "Therefore they will say, 'Like Nebrôd the giant, a hunter before God'" [Gn 10:9].

<3> Also there were giants in Astaroth-Charnem, whom Chodollogomor king of Ellam hid [cut off, Gn 14:1,5].

<4> Later in Chebrôn there were the three sons of Sennak (Sennach, Cod.G), whom (113b) Chaleb son of Iephôné killed when he chanced to take the city [Js 15:13-14].

<5> And under King David there were four giants whom David's generals killed [2 Rg 21:18-22]: Iesbé, whom Abisa killed [21:16-17]; Seth, whom Sobochés son of Astothos [Astatôthei, Cod.B] killed [21:18]; Elaian, whom Ariôg [Ariôrgeim, Codd. A,B] the Béthleemite killed [error based on 21:19]; and more notably the fourth, who had six fingers, was killed by Jonathan son of Samaios, [Semeei, Codd.A,B] the brother of David [21:20; 1 Par 20:6].

<6> Also Goliath the Chettaean is counted among the giants, the one whom the young David killed with a stone from a sling [1 Rg 17:49]. Then taking his spear he dedicated it in the Temple [21:9].

---

[1] Compare Hyginus 28: "Otos and Ephialtes."

**Λ'.** + Τίνες πολύπαιδες γεγόνασιν;
‹α'› Ἰακὼβ τρεῖς καὶ δέκα παῖδας **(113b2)** ἐσχήκει.
‹β'› Γεδεὼν ὁ κριτὴς ο', οὓς καὶ ἀνεῖλεν ὁ νῶθος[1] αὐτοῦ παῖς Ἀβιμέλεχ, τὴν ἀρχὴν ἑαυτῷ τοῦ λαοῦ περιποιούμενος.
‹γ'› Ἰαεὶρ ὁ κριτὴς ὁ Γαλααδίτης λβ' παῖδας καὶ οὗτος ἐσυστήσατο.
‹δ'› Λάβδων καὶ αὐτὸς ἐν τοῖς κριταῖς γεγονώς, λ' πατὴρ παίδων γεγόνει.[2]
‹ε'› Δαβὶδ κβ' τοὺς πάντας ὁ βασιλεύς[3].
‹ς'› Ῥοβοὰμ ὁ τοῦ Σολομῶνος υἱός, υἱοὺς κη' καὶ θυγατέρας ξ'.
‹ζ'› Ἀβίας υἱός, υἱοὺς κβ' καὶ θυγατέρας ιγ'.[4]
‹η'› Ἀχαὰβ ὁ τοῦ Ἰσραὴλ βασιλεὺς ο' υἱούς, οὓς ἀπέκτεινεν Ἰηοῦ.[5]

**ΛΑ'.** + Ὅπως κατενεμήθη ὁ λαὸς τὴν γῆν τῆς ἐπαγγελίας, ὡς ὁ Ναυῆ Ἰησοῦς αὐτοῖς ἐκληροδότησεν. **(114a1)**
‹α'› Φυλὴ Ῥουβὶμ καὶ Γάδ, καὶ ἥμισυ φυλῆς Μανασσῆ. Πρῶτοι οὗτοι παρὰ Μωϋσέως τὴν πέραν τοῦ Ἰορδάνου χώραν παρειλήφασιν, τὴν πρότερον οὖσαν Ἀμορραίων καὶ Ῥαφίμ, τὴν Βασσαανῖτιν ἅπασαν.
‹β'› Φυλὴ Μανασσῆ, τὸ ἕτερον ἥμισυ σκῆπτρον, πέραν καὶ τοῦτο τοῦ Ἰορδάνου περὶ Γαδάραν Γεργεσαίων χώραν, καὶ τὴν νῦν λεγομένην Σκυθόπολιν, μέχρι τῆς παρὰ Λίδωρον.[6]

---

[1] *Lc* FGM νοθος.
[2] FGM γεγονεν.
[3] In FGM ὁ βασιλευς follows immediately after Δαβιδ.
[4] Emend to ις', based on 2 Par 13:21.
[5] The items in this chapter are not numbered in CFGM.
[6] *Lc* FGM παραλιας Δωρ.

**30.** – Who were prolific?

<1> Jakôb, who had thirteen sons [Gn 35:23-26].[1]

<2> Gedeôn, the judge who had seventy sons whom his bastard son Abimelech killed and obtained rule over the people for himself [Jd 9:5].

<3> Iaeir the judge, a Galaadite, who had thirty-two sons [10:4].

<4> Labdôn, himself among the judges, was the father of thirty sons [forty, 12:13].

<5> David the king had twenty-two sons in all [2 Rg 3:2-5, 5:14-16, 12:23-24, 13:1].

<6> Roboam the son of Solomôn, twenty-eight sons and sixty daughters [2 Par 11:21].

<7> Abias <his> son, twenty-two sons and sixteen (thirteen) daughters [2 Par 13:21].

<8> Achaab king of Israél, seventy sons whom Iéou killed [4 Rg 10:7].

Presumably this chapter (see C. 38) is inspired by the lost treatise of Eusebius *On the Polygamy with Many Offspring* (*polypaidia*) *of the Ancients Beloved by God*, mentioned in his *Gospel Demonstration* 1.9.20 and *Gospel Preparation* 7.8.29. Eusebius also wrote on the allotment of the land to the twelve tribes (*Onomasticon* praef., p. 2, 7-9 Klostermann); see C. 31.

<THE PROMISED LAND (31-36)>

**31.** – How the people divided the land of promise, as Iésous (114a) distributed it to them.

<1> The tribe of Roubim and Gad and half the tribe of Manassé. These first received from Moses the region across the Jordan formerly belonging to the Amorites, and Raphim [Raphaeim, Js 15:8 Cod.A], all Basanitis [13:8-11].

<2> The tribe of Manassé, the other half tribe, the region **across Jordan** about Gadara, belonging to the Gergesenes and **now called Scythopolis**, **as far as** the coast at **Dôr** [17:11].[2]

---

[1] Genesis lists 12; Fabricius (55, note a) suggests that our author counts Joseph's two sons (Gn 48:5) in his place.

[2] Josephus *Ant.* 5.83–84 (also 6.374) with mention of Scythopolis, which Stephen C. Goranson notes as the "retirement home" of the Count Joseph known to Epiphanius (*The Joseph of Tiberias Episode in Epiphanius* [Ann Arbor: U.M.I. Dissertation Services, 1992] 147).

‹γ'› Φυλὴ Ἰούδα, τὴν ἐπάνω τῆς Ἰδουμαίας χώρας¹ ἅπασαν, διήκουσαν μέχρι τῆς Σοδομίτιδος, πόλεις δὲ (114a2) κατὰ θάλασσαν ἔχουσα,² Γάζαν καὶ Ἀσκάλωνα.

‹δ'› Φυλὴ Συμεὼν, τὴν Ἰδουμαίαν, τὴν Αἰγύπτῳ καὶ Ἀραβίᾳ πρός ὅρον³ ἔχουσα παρ' ἄλλον,⁴ τὴν ἐπέκεινα Γάζης.

‹ε'› Φυλὴ Βενιαμὶν, Ἱεριχοῦντα καὶ Βεθὴλ, καὶ Ἱεροσόλυμα ἕως θαλάσσης, ἐν στενῷ ἀπὸ τοῦ Ἰορδάνου ποταμοῦ μέχρι Γαβαὼ, Εὐαίων, Ἀμορραίων περὶ Βεθὴλ, Ἰεβουσαίων περὶ Ἰερουσαλήμ.

‹ς'› Φυλὴ Ἐφραὶμ, ἀπὸ Βεθὴλ ἐπὶ τὸ μέγα πεδίον, μέχρι Γαζάρων, ἀπὸ τοῦ Ἰορδάνου, Φερεζαίων, Ἀμορραίων, Σαμορραίων.⁵

‹ζ'› Φυλὴ Ἰσσάχαρ, Κάρμηλον τὸ ὄρος καὶ Ἰταβύριον⁶ ὄρος, (114b1) τέρμονα τὸν ποταμὸν ἔχοντες. Φερεζαίων καὶ αὕτη ἡ χώρα.

‹η'› Φυλὴ Ζαβουλὼν, ἀπὸ τοῦ ποταμοῦ μέχρι τῆς Γεννησαρίτιδος λίμνης, καὶ τὴν κοιλάδα καλουμένην. Φερεζαίων καὶ⁷ ὁ χῶρος.

‹θ'› Φυλὴ Ἀσὴρ, τὰ περὶ Σιδῶνα τετραμμένα, ἐν οἷς καὶ πόλις Κεῖ.⁸ Χαναναίων ἡ χώρα.

‹ι'› Φυλὴ Νεφθαλεὶμ, τὰς⁹ περὶ Δαμασκὸν, Γαλιλαίας καθύπερθεν καὶ τῶν Ἰορδάνου πηγῶν, αἱ τὸ ῥεῖν ἐκ τοῦ ὄρους ἔχουσι. Τούτου¹⁰ Κιναίων ἡ χώρα.

‹ια'› Φυλὴ Δὰν, τὰ περὶ Ἄζωτον, Ἰαμνίαν καὶ Γίτταν, ἀπὸ Ἀκκάρωνος ἕως ὄρους, (114b2) ἐξ οὗ ἡ Ἰούδα ἤρκται¹¹ φυλή.

Αἱ δὲ κληρουχίαι πᾶσαι, ἀπὸ ἀνατολῆς ἐπὶ δύσιν ἐγένοντο τῶν πασῶν φυλῶν, καὶ τὴν παρ' ἄλλων¹² νειμαμένων Παλαιστίνης καὶ Φοινίκης.¹³

---

¹Lc FGM χωραν.
²Lc FGM ἔχουσαν.
³FGM print προσορον.
⁴Lc FGM ἔχουσαν παραλιον.
⁵In their notes FGM propose emending Σαμορραιων to Χαναναιων.
⁶In their notes FGM wrongly report that the manuscript reads Ἰλαμυριον at this point.
⁷FGM και ὁδε.
⁸Lc FGM Ἀρκης.
⁹Lc FGM τα.
¹⁰Lc FGM Τουτο.
¹¹FGM ηρκται; emend to ἄρχεται or οἴχεται?
¹²Lc FGM παραλιον.
¹³The items in this chapter are not numbered in CFGM.

<3> The tribe of Iouda had **the whole region of upper Idoumaia extending as far as <Lake> Sodomitis**, with the coastal **cities Gaza and Askalôn**.[1]

<4> The tribe of Symeôn, **Idoumaia bordering on Egypt and Arabia**[2] with a coastal region beyond Gaza.

<5> The tribe of **Beniamin, Jerichô and Bethél and Hierosolyma to the sea** [Js 18:21-28]. **In the narrow strip from the Jordan river** to Gabaô of the Euaites, the Amorrites around Bethél, the Iebousites around **Jerusalem**.[3]

<6> **The tribe of Ephraim, from Bethél to the great plain up to Gazara. From the Jordan**,[4] of the Pherezaioi, Amorites, Samorrites [cf. Js 9:1].

<7> The tribe of **Isachar, Mount Karmél and Mount Itabyrion**, (114b) with **the river as a limit**.[5] The land of the Pherezaioi itself.

<8> The tribe of Zaboulôn, from the river **to the lake of Gennesarit**, with the region called Hollow; this too was the region of the Pherezaioi.[6]

<9> The tribe of Asér, bordering **on Sidôn**, where **the city of Arkés** is. The land of the Chanaanites.[7]

<10> The tribe of Nephthaleim, up to **Damascus, upper Galilee and the sources of the Jordan, which flows from the mountain**.[8] This is the land of the Kinaioi.

<11> The tribe of Dan, **about Azôtos, Iamnia, and Gittan, from Akkaronos to the mountain where the tribe of Iouda starts**.[9]

<These are> all the portions of all the tribes from east to west, and bordering on the seacoast of Palestine and Phoenicia.

---

[1] Josephus *Ant.* 5.81, simplified from Joshua 15.

[2] Josephus *Ant.* 5.82, simplified from Joshua 19:1–8.

[3] Josephus *Ant.* 5.82. Iebous is Ierousalém, Joshua 18:28.

[4] Josephus *Ant.* 5.83.

[5] Josephus *Ant.* 5.84.

[6] Josephus *Ant.* 5.84 (assigning "Hollow" to Asér).

[7] Josephus *Ant.* 5.85.

[8] Josephus *Ant.* 5.86.

[9] Josephus *Ant.* 5.87.

**ΛΒ'.** + Τίνες εἰσὶν αἱ φυγαδευτήριοι πόλεις, εἰς ἃς κατέφευγον οἱ ἀκούσιον φόνον δεδρακότες;
‹α'› Ἐν μὲν τῷ πέραν τοῦ Ἰορδάνου ἐν πεδίῳ φυλῆς Ῥουβίμ· Βοσορὴ[1] πρὸς τῇ ἐρήμῳ.
‹β'› Ἐν δὲ τῇ φυλῇ Γάδ· τὴν Ῥαμὼθ, πρὸς τῇ Γαλαὰδ χώρᾳ.
‹γ'› Ἐν δὲ[2] τῇ φυλῇ Μανασσῆ· τὴν Γαῦλον, πρὸς τὴν Βασὰν χώραν.
‹δ'› Ἐν δὲ ταῖς (115a1) ἐννέα φυλαῖς καὶ ἡμισὶ· τὴν καὶ Ἐδὲς[3] ἐν τῇ Γαλιλαίᾳ ἐν ὄρει Νεφθαλλείμ.[4]
‹ε'› Καὶ τὴν Συχεὶμ ἐν ὄρει Ἐφραίμ.
‹ς'› Καὶ τὴν Χεβρὼν ἐν ὄρει Ἰούδα.
Αὗται αἱ[5] πόλεις ἑξ, ἀμφὶ τὸν Ἰορδάνην κείμεναι.[6]

**ΛΓ'.** + Τίνες εἰσὶν αἱ μη' πόλεις,[7] αἱ τοῖς Λευΐταις ἀφορισθεῖσαι;
‹α'-β'› Ἀπὸ φυλῆς Ἰούδα, καὶ φυλῆς Συμεών· πόλις Καριαθαρβὸκ ἥ ἐστι Χεβρὼν, πόλις Ἐλὼμ, καὶ τὴν Τεέλλαν, καὶ τὴν Δαβὴρ, καὶ τὴν Ἄσαν, καὶ τὴν Ἀχὰν, καὶ τὴν Βεθσαμὶς, καὶ τὴν Ἐλβὰ, καὶ τὴν Βεθούρ.[8]
‹γ'› Ἀπὸ φυλῆς Βενιαμίν· τὴν (115a2) Γαβαὼν, καὶ τὴν Γαβεὲ, καὶ τὴν Ἀνὰχ, καὶ τὴν Γαλαμάθ. Αὗται πόλεις ιγ'.[9]
‹δ'› Ἀπὸ φυλῆς Ἐφραίμ· τὴν Συχὲμ, καὶ τὴν Γαζὲρ, καὶ τὴν Γαβαῖν, καὶ τὴν Βεθθορών.[10] Αὗται πόλεις δ'.
‹ε'› Ἀπὸ φυλῆς Δάν· τὴν Ἐλθακὼλ, καὶ τὴν Γεβαὼν, καὶ Ἐδὼμ, καὶ τὴν Γεερέμ. Καὶ αὗται πόλεις δ'.
‹ς'› Ἀπὸ ἡμίσους φυλῆς Μανασσῆ·[11] τὴν Καναχὴ, καὶ τὴν Βετσάν. Αὗται πόλεις β'. Ἀπὸ ἑτέρου ἡμίσους φυλῆς Μανασσῆ·[12] τὴν Γαῦλον, καὶ τὴν Βοσσόρον. Καὶ αὗται πόλεις β'.

---

[1] *Lc* F, who in his Latin translation assumes a reading of Βοσορ. GM emend to Βοσορ ἡ.
[2] GM omit δε.
[3] *Lc* FGM ἡμισεια· Κεδες.
[4] *Lc* FGM Νεφθαλειμ.
[5] FGM omit αἱ.
[6] The items in this chapter are not numbered in CFGM.
[7] FGM Τινες αἱ μητροπολεις.
[8] Emend by adding Αυται πολεις θ'.
[9] Emend to Αυται πολεις δ'. Πασαι πολεις των Λευϊ υἱων ιγ'.
[10] *Lc* FGM Βεθορων.
[11] *Lc* GM Μανασσης.
[12] *Lc* GM Μανασσης.

**32**. – What are the cities of refuge to which those fled who had committed manslaughter?

<1> Across the Jordan in the plain of the tribe of Roubim, Bosor[é] by the desert [Js 20:8].

<2> In the tribe of Gad, Ramôth, near the land of Galaad [20:8, Cod.A].

<3> In the tribe of Manassé, Gaulon near the land of Basan [20:8, variant in mss].

<4> In the (115a) nine and a half tribes, Kedes [Cod.A] in Galilaia on the mountain of Nephthaleim [Arm.], and

<5> Sicheim on the mountain of Ephraim, and

<6> Chebrôn on the mountain of Judah [20:7].

These six cities lie on both sides of the Jordan.

**33**. – What forty-eight cities were set apart for the Levites?

<1-2> From the tribe of Iouda and the tribe of Symeôn: the city Kariatharbok [Cod.A,Arm], which is Chebrôn [Js 21:11]; the city Elôm [21:14] and Teella (Tema, Gella) and Daber [21:14-15] and Asan and Achan (Tanu) and Bethsamis and Elba and Bethour; <these are nine cities> [21:16].

<3> From the tribe of Beniamin: Gabaôn [21:17] and Gabee and Anach and Galamath [21:18]; these are <four cities> [21:22]. <All thes cities of Leuï are> are thirteen cities [Js 21:19].

<4> From the tribe of Ephraim: Sichem and Gazer and Gabain and Bethorôn; these are four cities [21:20-22].

5> From the tribe of Dan: Elthakôl (Elthakol] and Gebaôn and Edôm (Ailôn) and Geerem (Gethremmôn, Cod.A); these too are four cities [21:23-24].

<6> From half the tribe of Manassé: Kanaché [Tanachei] and Betsan [Bethsan, Arm.]; these are two cities [21:25]. From the other half of the tribe of Manassé: Gaulon and Bossoron [Bosorran]; these too are two cities [21:27].

‹ζ'› Ἀπὸ φυλῆς Ἰσσάχαρ· τὴν Κισσώ, καὶ τὴν Ῥαμὰθ, καὶ τὴν Δεββαθὰ, καὶ τὴν (115b1) Ἠλίη.¹ Αὗται πόλεις δ'.

‹η'› Ἀπὸ φυλῆς Ἀσῆρ· τὴν Μασαλὰ, καὶ τὴν Ἀβδὼθ, καὶ τὴν Χελκὰθ, καὶ τὴν Ῥαάβ. Αὗται πόλεις δ'.

‹θ'› Ἀπὸ φυλῆς Νεφθαλείμ· τὴν Κεδὲς τὴν² ἐν τῇ Γαλιλαίᾳ, καὶ τὴν Ἐμὰθ, καὶ τὴν Καρεῖν. Αὗται πόλεις γ'.

‹ι'› Ἀπὸ φυλῆς Ζαβουλών·τὴν Ἰεκκὼμ, καὶ τὴν Κασεὶρ,³ καὶ τὴν Ῥεμμὼν, καὶ τὴν Ἑλλάν. Αὗται πόλεις δ'.

‹ια'› Ἀπὸ φυλῆς Ῥουβίμ· πέραν τοῦ Ἰορδάνου, τὴν Βόσορ, καὶ τὴν Ἰαζεὶρ, καὶ τὴν Κεδμὼθ, καὶ Ἀφαάθ. Αὗται πόλεις δ'.

‹ιβ'› Ἀπὸ φυλῆς Γάδ· τὴν Ῥαμὼθ, καὶ Ματθανὴν, καὶ τὴν Ἐσεβῶν, καὶ τὴν Ἀζείρ. Καὶ (115b2) αὗται πόλεις δ'.⁴

**ΛΔ'.** + Τίνας εἰλήφασι πόλεις καὶ βασιλεῖς, Ἰησοῦς καὶ Καλέφ οἱ πιστοί;

‹α'› Τὸν βασιλέα Ἰεριχώ.

‹β'› καὶ τὸν βασιλέα τῆς Γαί, ἥ ἐστι πλησίον Βεθήλ.

‹γ'› βασιλέα Ἰερουσαλήμ.

‹δ'› βασιλέα Χεβρῶν.

‹ε'› βασιλέα Λάχις.

‹ς'› βασιλέα Ἰεριμούθ.

‹ζ'› βασιλέα Γαζέρ.

‹η'› Βασιλέα Αἰγλώμ.

‹θ'› βασιλέα Ἀδέρ.

‹ι'› Βασιλέα Δαβήρ.

‹ια'› βασιλέα Ὀδολλάμ.

‹ιβ'› βασιλέα Ἑρμᾶ.

‹ιγ'› βασιλέα Θαπφοῦ.

‹ιδ'› βασιλέα Δεβνᾶ.⁵

‹ιε'› βασιλέα Βέκ.

‹ις'› βασιλέα Μακιδά.⁶

‹ιζ'› βασιλέα Σαμρῶν.

‹ιη'› βασιλέα Ὀφέρ.

‹ιθ'› βασιλέα Ἀχσάφ.

---

¹ *Lc* M Ἤλιν.
² GM omit την.
³ *Lc* FGM Κασσειρ.
⁴ The items in this chapter are not numbered in CFGM.
⁵ *Lc* FGM Λεβνα.
⁶ *Lc* FGM Μακηδα.

<7> From the tribe of Isachar: Kissô [Keisôn, Cod.B] and Ramath [Remmath, Cod.B] and Debbatha [some mss] and (115b) Hélis [Régéb éliou, one ms]; these are four cities [21:28-29].

<8> From the tribe of Aser: Masala (Masaal, Cod.A) and Abdath [Abdôth, some mss] and Chelkath [Arm.] and Raab; these are four cities [21:30-31].

<9> From the tribe of Nephthaleim: Kedes [Cod.A] in Galilee and Emath and Karein [Karain]; these are three cities [21:32].

<10> From the tribe of Zaboulôn: Iekkôm and Kasseir and Remmôn and Ellan; these are four cities [21:34-35, Heb.].

<11> From the tribe of Roubim: across the Jordan, Bosor and Iazeir and Kedmôth and Aphaath (Maphaath,some mss); these are four cities [21:36-37].

<12> From the tribe of Gad: Ramôth [Cod.B] and Matthanén [Mathanin, some mss] and Esebôn [Cod.A,Arm.] and Azeir [Azér, Cod.A,Arm.]; these too are four cities [21:38-39].

**34**. – What [cities and] kings did the faithful Iésous and Kaleph (Chaleb) take?

<1> The king of Hierichô [Js 12:9].

<2> And the king of Gai, near Bethél [12:9; Geth, Cod.A].

<3> The king of Hierousalém [12:10].

<4> The king of Chebrôn [12:10].

<5> The king of Lachis [12:11b].

<6> The king of Hierimouth [12:11a].

<7> The king of Gazer [12:12b].

<8> The king of Aiglôm [Eglôm, 12:12a Cod.A].

<9> The king of Ader (12:14 Cod.A).

<10> The king of Dabér [12:13].

<11> The king of Odollam [12:15].

<12> The king of Herma [12:14 Cod.A].

<13> The king of Tapphou [Phaphphout, 12:17 Cod.A].

<14> The king of Lebna [12:15].

<15> The king of Bek [Aphek, 12:18 Cod.A].

<16> The king of Makéda [12:16 Cod.A].

<17> The king of Samrôn [12:20 Cod.A].

<18> The king of Opher [12:17].

<19> The king of Achsaph [12:20 Cod.A].

‹κ'› Βασιλέα Ἀσώρ. **(116a1)**
‹κα'› βασιλέα Μελδών.
‹κβ'› Μαρρών.[1]
‹κγ'› βασιλέα Κέδες.
‹κδ'› βασιλέα Θανάκ.
‹κε'› βασιλέα Ἰεκονὰμ τοῦ Χερμέλ.
‹κϛ'› βασιλέα Δῶρ.
‹κζ'› τοῦ Ναφὲρ Δῶρ.[2]
‹κη'› βασιλέα Γωὴμ[3] τῆς Γογέλ.
‹κθ'› βασιλέα Θερσά.
Πάντες οὗτοι βασιλεῖς κθ' οὓς ἀνεῖλεν Ἰησοῦς σὺν ταῖς πόλεσιν αὐτῶν, καὶ ἐκληροδότησεν αὐτὰς τοῖς υἱοῖς Ἰσραήλ.[4]

**ΛΕ'.** + Τίνες εἰσὶ βασιλεῖς οἱ ἐπελθόντες[5] τῇ ἅλυκι[6] πεδιάδι οὓς ἐπάταξεν Ἀβραάμ;
Μαρφὰλ, βασιλεὺς Σενναάρ. Ἀρειὼχ,[7] βασιλεὺς Ἑλλαά. Χοδολογόμορ,[8] βασιλεὺς Ἑλλάμ.[9] Θαργὰλ,[10] βασιλεὺς ἐθνῶν.

**ΛϜ'.** + Τίνες εἰσὶ βασιλεῖς[11] οὓς διέσωσεν **(116a2)** Ἀβραὰμ μετὰ τοῦ Λώτ; Ἑλλὰμ, βασιλέα Σοδόμων. Μεγαβερσᾶν, βασιλέα Γομόρρας. Σενναὰρ, βασιλέα Ἀδαμῶν. Σομοβὸρ, βασιλέα Σεβώημ. Βαλὰκ, βασιλέα Σεγόρ. Τούτους Ἀβραὰμ ἐπιδιώξας καὶ ἀνελὼν ἐκ τῆς ἀπαγωγῆς, ὑφεξείλατο,[12] ἐπιστρατούσας[13] αὐτοῖς τοὺς ἑαυτοῦ παῖδας, ὄντας τὸν ἀριθμὸν τιη'.

---

[1]*Lc* FGM βασιλεα Μαρρων.
[2]*Lc* FGM βασιλεα του Ναφερ Δωρ.
[3]*Lc* FGM Γωιμ.
[4]The items in this chapter are not numbered in CFGM.
[5]*Lc* FGM Τινες οἱ Βασιλεις ἐπελθοντες.
[6]FGM άλυκη.
[7]*Lc* FGM Ἀριωχ.
[8]*Lc* FGM Χοδολλογομορ.
[9]*Lc* FGM Ἑλαμ.
[10]*Lc* FGM Θαργαρ.
[11]FGM Τινες οἱ βασιλεις.
[12]M ὑπεξειλατο.
[13]*Lc* FGM ἐπιστρατευσας.

<20> The king of Asôr [12:19 Cod.A] (116a).
<21> The king of Meldôn [Madon, 12:19 Heb].
<22> The king of Marrôn [12:20 Cod.A].
<23> The king of Kedes [12:22 Cod.A].
<24> The king of Thanak [12:21 Cod.A].
<25> Iekonam king of Chermel [12:22 Cod.A].
<26> The king of Dôr [king Addôr, 12:23 Cod.A].
<27> The king of Napher Dôr [12:23 Cod.A].
<28> The king of Gôim of Gogel [Gôeim king of Gelgea, 12:23 Cod.A].
<29> The king of Thersa.

All these twenty-nine [31 according to Js 12:24 LXX and Heb] kings Iésous destroyed with their cities and allotted them to the sons of Israel [12:7].

**35.** – Who are the kings who went out in the salt valley and were struck down by Abraam?

Marphal [some mss], king of Sennaar; Ariôch, king of Ellaa (Ellasar); Chodollogomor, king of Elam; Thargar (Thalga), king of the gentiles [Gn 14:1].

**36.** – Who were the kings whom Abraam saved with Lôt?

Ellam (Balla) king of Sodom; Megabersan (*meta* Barsa[1]) king of Gomorrha; Sennaar king of Adamians (Adama); Somobor king of Sebôém; Balak king of Segor (Balak, that is, Ségor) [Gn 14:2].[2] Abraam excluded them after pursuing them and saving them from captivity, when he marched out against them with his own children, who were 318 in number [14:14].[3]

---

[1] Or with several minuscule mss, *epoiésan* **mega** *polemon*.

[2] Here Joseph is certainly not following Josephus, who confusedly lists Balas, Balaias, Synabanés, Symmobor, and the king of the Baléni (*Ant.* 1.171).

[3] Joseph pays no attention to the common early fantasy that the number (in Greek tau, iota, eta) stood for the cross and the first two letters of the name Jesus; but cf. C. 151.

ΛΖ'. + Τίνες Ἑβραῖοι γυναῖκας ἐθνικὰς ἠγάγοντο;

‹α'› Ἰούδας· τὴν Σουά, ἐξ ἧς ἔσχεν υἱούς, τὸν Σεὶρ, καὶ τὸν Αὐνᾶ, καὶ τὸν Σιλώμ. Ἔλαβε δὲ γυναῖκα τὴν Θάμαρ τῷ υἱῷ αὐτοῦ Σεὶρ, καὶ τούτου ἀποθανόντος, ἔδωκεν αὐτὴν (116b1) τῷ Αὐνᾷ γυναῖκα. Καὶ τούτου δὲ ἀποθανόντος, καὶ μὴ ἀπολύοντος αὐτὴν ἑτέρῳ γαμηθῆναι, δόλῳ ἡ Θάμαρ ἔσχεν ἐξ αὐτοῦ υἱούς, τὸν Φαρὲς καὶ τὸν Ζαρά.

‹β'› Μωϋσῆς· τὴν Σεπφόραν, ἐξ ἧς ἔσχε τὸν Γερσὼν καὶ τὸν Ἐλιέζερ.

‹γ'› Σαλμών· τὴν Ῥαὰβ τὴν πόρνην τὴν[1] τοὺς κατασκόπους κατακρύψασαν, ἐξ ἧς τὸν Βοόζ.

‹δ'› Βοόζ· τὴν Μωαβίτιν Ῥούθ,[2] ἐξ ἧς ἔσχε τὸν Ἰωβὴδ, τὸν τοῦ Ἰεσσαὶ πατέρα, ἐξ οὗπερ γεννᾶται ὁ Δαβίδ. Οὗτοι μὲν οὖν, οἱ τεχθέντες ἐκ τῶν ἐθνικῶν γυναικῶν, καὶ εἰς τὴν τοῦ Σωτῆρος συντελοῦσι σάρκωσιν, ἐπὶ δὲ βλάβῃ τῇ[3] ἑαυτῶν (116b2) ἔσχον ἐθνικὰς γυναῖκας.

‹ε'› Σαμψὼν τὴν Δαλιλά, δι' ἧς ἀπατηθεὶς, καὶ τὸν ἁγιασμὸν τοῦ ναζηραίου διεφθάρη, καὶ ἐκτυφλωθεὶς, ἀδοξῶν τελευτᾷ.

‹ς'› Σολομὼν τὴν τοῦ Αἰγυπτίου θυγατέρα ἀγόμενος, καὶ Μωαβίτιδας, καὶ Ἀμμωνίτιδας, Σύρας καὶ Ἰδουμαίας, Χετταίας καὶ Ἀμορραίας.[4]

ΛΗ'. + Τίνες πολλὰς ἤγαγον γυναῖκας;

‹α'› Ἰακὼβ δ', τὴν Λίαν, τὴν[5] Ῥαχὴλ, τὴν Βαλλὰν, τὴν Ζελφάρ·[6] ἐξ ὧν καὶ παῖδες αὐτῷ γεγόνασι ιγ'.

‹β'› Γεδεὼν ‹. . . . . . . . . .›[7] ἐξ ὧν καὶ ο'[8] παῖδες αὐτῷ[9] γεγόνασιν.

‹γ'› Δαβὶδ πλείους ἢ ι', τὴν Ἀχιναὰν, καὶ τὴν (117a1) Μελχὼλ, τὴν Ἀβιγαίλαν,[10] τὴν Ἐγγήθ, τὴν Βιττάλ, τὴν Αἰγλήν, τὴν Βηρσαβεὲ,[11] καὶ ἄλλαι,[12] ἃς ἔλαβεν εἰς τὴν Ἰερουσαλὴμ πλήρης[13] τὴν βασιλείαν ἀπολαβών· ἐξ ὧν καὶ ιγ' υἱοὺς ἐκτήσατο. Ὧν γυναικῶν τὰ ὀνόματα οὐκ ἀναγέγραπται.

---

[1] *Lc* FGM omit την.
[2] FGM omit ἐξ ἧς τον Βοοζ. Βοοζ την Μωαβιτιν Ῥουθ.
[3] FGM omit τῃ.
[4] The items in this chapter are not numbered in CFGM.
[5] FGM omit την.
[6] *Lc* FGM Ζελφαν.
[7] C gives no indication of a break. FGM surmise a *lacuna*.
[8] FGM locate ο' after γεγονασιν.
[9] FGM τούτῳ.
[10] *Lc* FGM Ἀβιγαἰλ.
[11] *Lc* FGM Βεθσαβεε.
[12] *Lc* FGM ἀλλας.
[13] *Lc* GM πληρη.

<PROBLEMS WITH WOMEN (37-42)>

**37.** – What Hebrews married gentile wives?

<1> Ioudas married Soua, from whom he had as sons Seir (Ér) and Auna and Silôm [mss, Gn 38:2-5]. He took Thamar as a wife for his son Seir and when he died he gave her (116b) as a wife to Auna, and after he too died he did not allow her to marry another, but by craft Thamar had her sons Phares and Zara by him [38:6-30].

<2> Moses, Sepphora, from whom he had Gersôn and Eliezer [Ex 18:3-4].

<3> Salmôn, the prostitute Raab, who concealed the spies, and had Booz [Js 2:1; Mt 1:5].

<4> Booz, the Moabite Ruth, by whom [Ru 4:10] he had Iôbed the father of Iessai by whom David was born [Mt 1:5]. These, then, who were born of gentile women also contributed to the incarnation of the Savior but harmed themselves because they had gentile wives.

<5> Sampson, Dalila, by whom he was deceived and corrupted the sanctity of his Nazarite vow, and after being blinded, he died ingloriously [Jd 16:4,17-21]. Cf. C. 39(2).

<6> Solomon who married the daughter of an Egyptian and some Moabites and Ammonites, Syrians and Idoumaians, Hittites and Amorites [3 Rg 11:1]. Cf. C. 39(6).

**38.** – Who had many wives?

<1> Jakôb four: Lia, Rachél, Balla, and Zelpha [Gn 29-30], from whom thirteen children were born to him.

<2> Gedeôn <had many wives> [Jd 8:30] from whom <seventy> sons were born.

<3> David more than ten: Achinaan [1 Par 3:1], (117a) Melchôl [Môcha, 3:2], Abigail [Abeigaia, 3:1], Eggéth [Aggéth, 3:2, one ms], Bittal [Abital, 3:3 Cod.A], Aiglé [Aigla, 3:3 some mss], Bethsabeë [3:5],[1] and others whom he took to Jerusalem when he fully obtained the kingdom, by whom he had thirteen (nine) sons whose mothers' names are not recorded [3:6-7]. He had Abissa

---

[1] Here and in C. 86(2) the Cambridge MS spells her name Bérsabeë as in Cod.B (Bersabé in *Ant*. 7.348–49; 8.3, 6–7). The similar form Birsabeë occurs in C. 40(7) and 73. The form Béthsabeë, frequently found in Cod.A, occurs in C. 114(3) (Beethsabé in Josephus *Ant*. 7.130, 146).

Ἔσχε δὲ καὶ Ἀβισσᾶ τὴν Σουναμῖτιν, τὴν θερμαίνουσαν αὐτὸν διὰ τὴν τοῦ σώματος ἀπόψυξιν.

‹δ'› Ὁ δὲ Σολομὼν τὰς γυναῖκας καὶ παλλακὰς τ' ἐσχηκὼς,[1] ἕνα μόνον υἱὸν, τὸν καὶ τῆς βασιλείας ἐγκρατῆ γεγενεῖσθαι[2] μὴ δυνάμενον, ἔσχηκεν ἀπὸ Ναβᾶν[3] τῆς Ἀμμωνίτιδος, (117a2) ἢ ὡς ἄλλη ἔκδοσις ἔχει, ἀπὸ Θάμαρ θυγατρὸς Ἀβεσσαλώμ.[4]

**ΛΘ'.** + Ὅσαι γυναῖκες τοὺς ἄνδρας διέφθειραν;
‹α'› Εὔα· τὸν Ἀδὰμ, ἀπατηθεῖσα καὶ αὐτὴ πρὸς τοῦ διαβόλου.

‹β'› Δαλιδὰ[5] τὸν Σαμψὼν ἀποξυράσασα καὶ δέσμιον τοῖς πολεμίοις παραδοῦσα, καὶ διὰ ταύτην ἀναιρούμενον, ἐκτυφλωθέντα πρότερον αἰσχρῶς.

‹γ'› Καὶ τοῦ λαοῦ δὲ τοῦ Ἰσραηλιτικοῦ τὴν ἀναίρεσιν αἱ τῶν Ἀμορραίων ἐποιήσαντο γυναῖκες, κατὰ γνώμην τοῦ μάντεως Βαλαὰμ, τὴν τῷ Βαλὰκ εἰσηγηθεῖσαν, εἰς ἀπόστασιν αὐτοὺς[6] ἐπαγαγομένων.[7]

‹δ'› Ἡ Αἰγυπτία, (117b1) ἡ τὸν ἀρχιμάγειρον τοῦ βασιλέως, μετὰ τὸ μὴ δυνηθῆναι τὸν Ἰωσὴφ ἀπατῆσαι, συμπείσασα, ὡς ἐπελθόντος αὐτῇ τοῦ Ἰωσὴφ, καὶ ποιήσασα αὐτὸν ἐγκατάκλειστον τὸν σώφρονα.

‹ε'› Ἡ τοῦ Ἰὼβ γυνὴ, ἐπιχειροῦσα πείθειν τὸν εὐσεβέστατον Ἰὼβ λαλεῖν ῥῆμά τι πρὸς Κύριον, ἀλλ' οὐ δυνηθεῖσα διὰ τὸ ἰσχυρόγνωμον τοῦ εὐσεβοῦς.

‹ς'› Οὕτω δὴ καὶ τὸν σοφώτατον Σολομῶντα γυναῖκες, ἃς παρανόμως ἠγάγετο, εἰς[8] τοὺς ναοὺς οἰκοδομεῖν οἷς αὗται δαίμοσιν ὡς θεοῖς ἐτίμων ἀνέπεισαν.

‹ζ'› Ἰεζάβελ τὸν Ἀχαὰβ τῇ Ἀστάρτῃ θείνη[9] ἠπάτησεν, καὶ τὸν προφήτην (117b2) ἐκδιώκειν Ἠλίαν, διὸ καὶ τετιμώρηνται.

‹η'› Γοθολία ἡ τοῦ Ἀχαὰβ καὶ τῆς Ἰεζάβελ θυγάτηρ, τὸ τοῦ Δαβὶδ γένος ἀφανίσαι διὰ τῶν ἐπηκόων αὐτῆς μηχανομένη.[10]

---

[1]FGM ἐπτακοσιας γυναικας, και παλλακας ἐσχηκως; *lege* ἐπτακοσιας γυναικας και παλλακας τ' ἐσχηκως.

[2]*Lc* FGM γεγενησθαι.

[3]*Lc* FGM Νααμα.

[4]The items in this chapter are not numbered in CFGM.

[5]*Lc* FGM Δαλιλα.

[6]GM omit αὐτους.

[7]*Lc* GM ἀπαγαγομενων.

[8]Delete εἰς.

[9]*Lc* FGM θυειν.

[10]*Lc* FGM μηχανωμενη.

(Abeisa) the Sounamitis (Sômaneitis), who warmed him because of the frigidity of his body [3 Rg 1:1-4].

<4> Solomon, who had 700 wives and 300 concubines [11:3], had only one son <Roboam>, who could not keep firm hold of the kingdom. He was from Naama the Ammonite [14:21 Cod.A] or, as another version has it, from Thamar the daughter of Abessalôm [2 Rg 14:27, wife of Roboam].

> Presumably this chapter, like C. 30, is inspired by the lost treatise of Eusebius *On the Polygamy with Many Offspring of the Ancients Beloved by God.* See the note on C. 30.

**39.** – What women corrupted their husbands? [1]

<1> Eua, Adam, being seduced herself by the devil [Gn 3:17].

<2> Dalila who shaved Sampson and delivered him bound to the enemies; he was destroyed on her account after being blinded shamefully [Jd 16:19-21].

<3> The women of the Amorites brought about the destruction of the Israelite people when they led them into apostasy, in accordance with the declaration the seer Balaam delivered to Balak [cf. Nm 31:16].

<4> The Egyptian woman (117b) who persuaded the king's chief cook, after she failed to seduce Iôséph, that Iôséph attacked her, and got this chaste one imprisoned [Gn 39].

<5> The wife of Iôb, who tried to persuade the most pious Iôb to say something against the Lord, but failed because of the strong will of the pious one [Job 2:9-10].

<6> Likewise, his wives (whom he had married illegally) persuaded the most-wise Solomon to build the temples in which they honored demons as gods [3 Rg 11:1-8].

<7> Iezabel led Achaab astray to sacrifice to Astarte [18: 19] and persecute the prophet Elijah; therefore both were punished [4 Rg 9:36].

<8> Gotholia (Codd.A,B),[2] daughter of Achaab and Iezabel, who tried to destroy the family of David through those who obeyed her [11:1].

---

[1] Compare Hyginus 240: "Who killed their husbands?"

[2] C. 41(7) and 42(3) use "Godolia," the form of the name characteristic of the Armenian tradition.

⟨θ⟩ Ἡρωδιὰς τὸν Ἡρώδην φονεύειν τὸν Βαπτιστὴν Ἰωάννην, διὰ τῆς εὐρύθμως ὀρχησαμένης τῆς ἑαυτῆς θυγατρὸς ἐπαγαγομένη.[1]

**Μ΄.** + Ὅσαι γυναῖκες τοὺς ἄνδρας εὐεργέτησαν,[2] καὶ δι᾽ ὧν ἔδρασαν εὐάρεστοι τῷ Θεῷ γεγόνασι;

⟨α⟩ Σάρρα πεισθεῖσα τῷ Ἀβραὰμ, καὶ λέγουσα ἀδελφὴ[3] αὐτοῦ εἶναι κατὰ τὰς ὑποθέσεις αὐτῷ,[4] πρὸς τὸ[5] διὰ **(118a1)** τὸ κάλλος αὐτῆς ἐπηρείας. Καὶ πάλιν παρακαλοῦσα[6] αὐτὸν συγγενέσθαι τῇ παιδίσκῃ τῇ Ἄγαρ, ἵνα καταστήσαιτο παιδίον, πρὸς τὸ μὴ δι᾽ αὐτὴν στεῖραν οὖσαν, ἄπαιδον[7] καὶ αὐτὸν ἀποθανεῖν.

⟨β⟩ Ῥαχὴλ καὶ Λία ὑπακούουσαι τῷ ἀνδρὶ, καὶ ἀκολουθοῦσαι αὐτῷ εἰς τὴν Χαναναίαν, τὸν πατρῷον οἶκον καταλιμπάνουσαι.

⟨γ⟩ Ῥεβέκκα δὲ ὁμοίως, τοῦ μόνον ὀνομασθέντος ἀνδρὸς αὐτῆς Ἰσαὰκ πόθῳ, κατέλιπε τὴν πατρῴαν ἑστίαν, καὶ πρὸς τὸν μνηστῆρα ἐξανάγοιτο.[8]

⟨δ⟩ Ἡ τοῦ Γεδεὼν γυνὴ, δείσαντα τὸν **(118a2)** ἄνδρα τὴν τοῦ ἀγγέλου ἐπιφάνειαν ῥώννυσιν ἀπὸ τοῦ δέους, πίστιν αὐτῷ τὴν ἀπὸ γνώμης ἐντιθεῖσα σωτήριον.[9]

⟨ε⟩ Μελχὼλ, τὸν Δαβὶδ ἀναιρεῖσθαι ὑπὸ τοῦ Σαοὺλ μέλλοντα, καθημώσασα[10] διὰ θυρίδος, καὶ δρασμὸν αὐτῷ τὸν ἀπὸ τοῦ φόνου περιποιησαμένη.

⟨ϛ⟩ Ἡ Ἀβιγαῖα,[11] ἡ τὸν Ναβὰλ πανώλεθρον ἀναιρεῖσθαι μέλλοντα, τὸν Δαβὶδ ἐνυβρίσαντα, ῥυσαμένη τῆς διαφορᾶς διὰ τῆς παρακλήσεως τῆς πρὸς Δαβὶδ, δώροις αὐτὸν ὑπὲρ τοῦ ἀνδρὸς ἐξευμενισαμένη.

---

[1] The items in this chapter are not numbered in CFGM.
[2] *Lc* GM εὐηργέτησαν.
[3] *Lc* FGM ἀδελφην.
[4] *Lc* FGM αὐτου.
[5] *Lc* FGM τας.
[6] *Lc* GM παρακαλουσαν.
[7] M ἀπαιδα.
[8] *Lc* FGM ἐξαναγεται.
[9] Emend to σωτηριου.
[10] *Lc* FGM καθιμωσασα.
[11] *Lc* FGM Ἀβιγαϊλ.

<9> Hérôdias, who led Hérôd to kill the Baptist Iôannés through the rhythmic dancing of her daughter [Mt 14:6].

**40**. – What women helped their husbands and were pleasing to God through what they did?

<1> Sarra obeyed Abraam and claimed to be his sister, as was agreed between them, so that she might not be sought out because of (118a) her beauty [Gn 12:11-13]. She also persuaded him to lie with her maid Agar so that he might get a child from her, so that though she was sterile he might not die childless [16:1-3].

<2> Rachél and Lia regarded their husband and followed him to Chanaan, leaving their father's house [31:14].

<3> Similarly, Rebekka, solely for the love of her husband, who was named Isaak, left her paternal hearth and went to her betrothed [24:58].

<4> The wife of Gedeôn, when her husband was afraid at the appearance of an angel, he was restored from his fear when she implanted faith in him, which came from the knowledge of salvation [Jd 13:21-23].

<5> Melchôl, when David was about to be killed by Saul, let him out through a window and arranged his escape from the murder [1 Rg 19:11-17].

<6> Abigail delivered the destructive Nabal[1] from danger when he was going to be killed because he insulted David, through her encouragement to David, mollifying him on behalf of her husband by her gifts [1 Rg 25].

---

[1] 1 Rg 25:3 calls him a Cynic.

‹ζ΄› Ἡ δὲ τοῦ Σολομῶνος μήτηρ ἡ Βιρσαβεέ,[1] ἡ κατὰ τοῦ προφήτου (118b1) Νάθαν ὑποθήκας,[2] τὴν βασιλείαν τῷ υἱῷ περιποιησαμένη, διδάξασα τὸν Δαβὶδ τὰ τῷ Ἀδονίᾳ[3] τετολμημένα.

‹η΄› Ῥαὰβ δὲ διὰ πίστεως εὐδοκιμεῖ παρὰ τῷ Θεῷ, διασώζουσα τοὺς κατασκόπους, καὶ δι᾽ ἄλλης ὁδοῦ τούτους ἀπολύουσα, καὶ συνθήκας περὶ σωτηρίας πρὸς αὐτοὺς ποιουμένη.

‹θ΄› Ῥοὺθ ἡ Μωαβίτις, ἡ τῆς ἐκύρας[4] διὰ πόθον ἱερὸν ἀχώριστος, καὶ εἰς Ἐκκλησίαν Κυρίου καταταττομένη.

‹ι΄› Καὶ ἡ γυνὴ, ἡ τὸν ἐναγέστατον Ἀβιμέλεχ, τὸν δεινὰ κατὰ τοῦ λαοῦ ἐργασάμενον, μέγιστόν τι κατώρθωσε τῷ λαῷ, μίλου[5] (118b2) ἠλάσματι[6] τοῦτον ἐκ τοῦ τείχους, κατὰ τοῦ κράνους αὐτοῦ ἀπορριφέντι, ἀνελοῦσα.

‹ια΄› Καὶ ἡ τὸν Σαβεὲ δὲ, τὸν τοῦ Βοχορὶ, προκατειληφότα τὰ[7] τὴν Ἄβελ καλουμένην πόλιν, ἀπὸ τοῦ βασιλέως ἀποστάντα Δαβὶδ ἀποκτείνασα, καὶ τήν κεφαλὴν αὐτοῦ διὰ τοῦ τείχους τῷ Ἰωὰβ ῥίψασα, καλὸν καὶ σοφὸν ἔργον ἐπεδείξατο,[8] ὅλην πόλιν πολιορκίας ῥυσαμένη.

‹ιβ΄› Σοφὴ δὲ καὶ ἡ Θεκουῖτις, ἡ τὸν Ἀβεσσαλὼμ τῆς φυγῆς ὑπὸ τοῦ πατρὸς κληθῆναι ποιησαμένη, ταῖς τοῦ Ἰωὰβ ὑποθήκαις.

‹ιγ΄› Σαβὰ τε[9] ἡ τῶν (119a1) Αἰθιόπων Βασιλὶς τῆς σοφίας εἵνεκα[10] Σολομῶνος εἰς τὴν Ἰουδαίαν σταλεῖσα, ἐπὶ σοφίᾳ καὶ αὐτὴ δικαίαν ἀπηνέγκατο[11] τιμήν.

‹ιδ΄› Ἡ χήρα, ἡ ἐν Σαράφθοις[12] τὸν Ἠλίαν δεξιωσαμένη, ἐπὶ τιμῇ τῇ παρὰ Θεοῦ.

---

[1] Lc FGM Βηθσαβεε.
[2] FGM τας του προφητου Ναθαν ὑποθηκας.
[3] Lc FGM Ἀδωνιᾳ.
[4] Lc FGM ἑκυρας.
[5] Oddly, CM here agree against FG's μυλου. Lege μυλου.
[6] Lc FGM κλασματι.
[7] Lc FGM omit τα.
[8] Lc GM ἀπεδειξατο.
[9] Lc FGM δε.
[10] Lc FGM ένεκα.
[11] FG ἀπηνεματο; M ἀπενειματο.
[12] Lc FGM Σαρεφθοις.

<7> Béthsabeë, the mother of Solomon, who acquired the kingdom for her son according to the precepts of the prophet (118b) Nathan, teaching David what Adônias ventured to do [3 Rg 1:18-19].

<8> Raab, who found favor with God through faith [Hb 11:31], saved the spies and released them through another way and made agreements about safety with them [Js 2:1,6:25].

<9> Ruth the Moabitess, who because of a sacred desire did not let herself be separated from her mother-in-law and was inducted into the Church of the Lord [Ru 1:14,4:14].

<10> The woman who killed the detestable Abimelech when he was working the greatest harm upon the people did something great for the people by hitting his head with a piece of millstone from the wall [Jd 9:53].

<11> The woman who killed Sabeë the son of Bochori, who had previously occupied the city called Abel while revolting against King David, and threw his head through the wall to Iôab. She exhibited a good and wise work, delivering the whole city from siege [2 Rg 20:22].

<12> The wise Tekoan woman who had Abessalôm recalled from flight by his father, at Iôab's counsel [14:1-3].

<13> Saba (119a) queen of the Ethiopians, who came to Ioudaia because of Solomon's wisdom and herself received due honor for wisdom [3 Rg 10:1-2,13].[1]

<14> The widow among the Sarephthans who received Élias as a guest for the sake of honor with God [17:10-24].

---

[1] Cf. Josephus *Ant*. 8.175–76.

‹ιε'› Ἡ γυνὴ ἡ Σουμανῖτις,[1] ἡ τὸν Ἐλισσαῖον δεξιουμένη, καὶ οἶκον αὐτῷ σχολαῖον εὐτρεπίσασα, μεγάλα καὶ τὸν ἄνδρα καὶ τὸν ἑαυτῆς οἶκον ὤνησεν. Υἱόν τε γὰρ οὐ πρότερον ὄντα αὐτῇ ἐκτήσατο, καὶ τοῦτον ἀποθανόντα, ζῶντα ἀπειλήφει.

‹ις'› Ἐν δὲ τῇ χάριτι τῇ κατὰ Χριστῷ,[2] τὴν τοῦ κόσμου σωτηρίαν Μαρία διηκονίσατο,[3] (119a2) γεννήσασα ἡμῖν σαρκὶ τὸν μονογενῆ Υἱὸν τοῦ Θεοῦ, τὸν Κύριον ἡμῶν Ἰησοῦν Χριστόν.

‹ιζ'› Ἐλισάβετ, ἡ τοῦ Ζαχαρίου γυνὴ, τὸν πρόδρομον τοῦ Κυρίου Ἰωάννην τὸν Βαπτιστὴν συλλαβοῦσα, καὶ προφητεύειν ἠξίωται.

‹ιη'› Τὴν τε ἀνάστασιν τοῦ Κυρίου αἱ τρεῖς Μαρίαι πρῶται θεασάμεναι, τοῖς μαθηταῖς ἀπήγγελλον.[4]

‹ιθ'› Ἀλλὰ καὶ Ἰωάννα ἡ τοῦ ἐπιτρόπου Ἡρώδου γυνὴ, μετὰ καὶ ἄλλων πιστοτάτων γυναικῶν ἀκολουθοῦσα τῷ Κυρίῳ, τὰ χρήματα ἐπιφερομένη κατανάλου[5] εἰς τὴν διακονίαν τῶν ἑπομένων τῷ Σωτῆρι.[6]

**ΜΑ'.** + Τίνες ἄνδρες ἐπὶ σοφίᾳ θαυμαστοὶ γεγόνασι; (119b1)

‹α'› Σὴμ καὶ Ἰάφεθ, ὀπισθοφανεῖς ἐπιβαίνοντες τὴν τοῦ πατρὸς καλύψαι[7] γυμνότητα.

‹β'› Ἰωσὴφ, τὰς καθ’ ἑαυτὸν ὑποφέρων σοφῶς συμφορὰς, καὶ τὰ ὀνείρατα διαλύων, καὶ τὸν καιρὸν τῶν εὐφοριῶν καὶ τοῦ λιμοῦ πανσόφως οἰκονομῶν.

‹γ'› Βεσελεὴλ[8] ὁ τοῦ Ὀρὶ, καὶ Ἐλιὰβ ὁ τοῦ Ἀρχισαμὰκ[9], οἱ τὴν ἱερὰν σκηνὴν ἐργασάμενοι.

‹δ'› Χουσὶ, ὁ τοῦ Δαβὶδ σύμβουλος, τὴν τοῦ Ἀχιτόφελ σοφίαν μεταχειρισάμενος.

‹ε'› Σολομὼν, ὁ τῆς σοφίας χάρισμα κομισάμενος.

‹ς'› Οἱ υἱοὶ Μαοὺλ, Αἰθὰν καὶ Ἐσρὰν καὶ Ἡμὰν καὶ Χαλχὰλ καὶ Δαρδᾶν.

---

[1] Lc FGM Σουναμιτις.
[2] Lc FGM Χριστον.
[3] Lc FGM διηκονησατο.
[4] F ἀπηγγελαν; lc GM ἀπηγγειλαν.
[5] FGM κἀτηναλου.
[6] The items in this chapter are not numbered in CFGM.
[7] GM κατακαλυψαι.
[8] Lc FGM Βεσσελεηλ.
[9] Lc FGM Ἀχισαμαχ.

<15> The Sounamitis woman who received Elissaios and made her house an attractive place of rest for him, and benefited her husband and her house, for she acquired the son she had had; though he was dead, she received him back alive [4 Rg 4:36-37].

<16> In the time of the grace of Jesus Christ, Maria ministered to the salvation of the world, for she bore in the flesh the only-begotten Son of God, our Lord Jesus Christ.

<17> Elisabet wife of Zacharias conceived the Forerunner of the Lord, Iôannés the Baptist, and was deemed worthy of prophesying [Lk 1:42].

<18> The three Marias first saw the resurrection of the Lord and told the disciples [Mt 28:1; Mk 16:1,9; Lk 24:10; Jn 20:18].

<19> But also Iôanna wife of the procurator of Hérôdés with other faithful women followed the Lord, provided money and spent it to serve those who followed the Savior [Lk 8:3].

**41.** – What men were marvelous for their wisdom?[1] (119b)

<1> Sém and Iapheth who came with averted faces to cover their father's nakedness [Gn 9:23].

<2> Iôséph, wisely enduring the disasters that came upon him, interpreting dreams, and most wisely administering the times of fertility and famine [Gn 41].

<3> Besseleél son of Ori and Eliab son of Achisamach, who made the sacred tabernacle [Ex 31:2,6].

<4> Chousi counselor of David, who overturned the wisdom of Achitophel [2 Rg 17:7].

<5> Solomon who obtained the gift of wisdom [3 Rg 3:12].

<6> The sons of Maoul, Aithan and Esra and Éman and Chalchal and

---

[1] Compare Hyginus 254: "What men were most pious?"

Περὶ ὧν καὶ οἱ ἐν ταῖς Βασιλείαις, ὡς σοφῶν, καὶ (119b2) τὰ¹ τοῦ Σολομῶνος, μνήμη γίνεται.

‹ζ'› Ἰωδαὲ ὁ ἀρχιερεὺς, ὁ τὴν Γοδολίαν² ἀποκτείνας, καὶ τὸν ἐκ τοῦ Δαβιδικοῦ γένους Ἰωὰς σοφῶς εἰς βασιλείαν προαγαγών.

‹η'› Δανιήλ, ὁ τὰ μυστικὰ τῶν βασιλέων θεάματα ἀποκαλύπτων, περὶ οὗ καὶ πρὸς τὸν διάβολον εἴρηται· Μὴ σὺ σοφώτερος εἶ τοῦ Δανιήλ;

‹θ'› Ἔσδρας, ὁ τῶν ἱερῶν Γραφῶν, μετὰ τὴν ἐκ Βαβυλῶνος τοῦ Ἰουδαϊκοῦ λαοῦ ἐπάνοδον, μνήμην ποιησάμενος.³

**ΜΒ'.** + Τίνες ἐπὶ σοφίᾳ γυναῖκες θαυμασταὶ γεγόνασι;

‹α'› Θάμαρ, ἐπὶ παιδογονίᾳ⁴ τὸν Ἰούδαν σοφισαμένη.

‹β'› Ῥεβέκκα, τῷ Ἰακὼβ τὰς (120a1) παρὰ τοῦ πατρὸς εὐλογίας οἰκονομήσασα δοθῆναι, καὶ εἰς τὴν Μεσοποταμίαν αὐτὸν πρὸς τὴν ἑαυτῆς συγγένειαν ἐκπέμπουσα, διὰ τὴν τοῦ Ἡσαῦ μῆνιν.

‹γ'› Ἰωσαβὲτ,⁵ ἡ τοῦ βασιλέως Ἰωρὰμ θυγάτηρ, Ἰωδαὲ δὲ τοῦ ἀρχιερέως γυνὴ, κρύψασα Ἰωὰς τὸν Ὀχοζίου τοῦ ἀδελφοῦ αὐτῆς υἱόν, ἵνα μὴ πρὸς τῆς Γοδολίας ἀναιρεθῇ, καὶ φυλάξασα εἰς τὴν τῆς Δαυϊτικῆς βασιλείας ἔκφανσιν.

‹δ'› Σοφὴ καὶ ἡ Σουναμῖτις, ἡ τὸν προφήτην Ἐλισσαῖον δεξιωσαμένη, τῇ τε τῆς οἰκίας παρασκευῇ, καὶ τῇ παραμονῇ τῇ τοῦ προφήτου.⁶

**ΜΓ'.** + Τίνες ἐπὶ δεινότητι γενόμενοι (120a2) σοφοί, διὰ τῆς ἑαυτῶν σοφίας ἀπώλοντο;

‹α'› Οἱ τὸν πύργον οἰκοδομεῖν ἕως οὐρανοῦ βουλόμενοι, διελύοντο τῇ πολυφωνίᾳ.

‹β'› Φαραὼ κατασοφιζόμενος τὴν τοῦ λαοῦ διαφθορὰν, καὶ κατέχειν εἰς δούλους βουλόμενος, συναπολλύμενος τῇ τοιαύτῃ ἐπιχειρήσει.

‹γ'› Ἀβιμέλεχ ὁ τοῦ Γεδεὼν υἱὸς, σοφιζόμενος ἑαυτῷ τὴν ἀρχὴν περιποιήσασθαι, καὶ τοὺς ο' ἀδελφοὺς φονεύσας, ὑπὸ γυναικὸς ὡς κύων ἀναιρούμενος.

---

¹FGM print κατα τα, although in his notes M suggests μετα (or μετα τα?). Emend to και τουτου.

²FGM Γοθολιαν.

³The items in this chapter are not numbered in CFGM.

⁴Lc GM παιδογονιαν.

⁵Lc FGM Ἰωσαβελ.

⁶The items in this chapter are not numbered in CFGM.

Dardan, who are mentioned in the books of Reigns as being wise, along with <the wisdom> of Solomon [4:27].[1]

<7> Iôdaë the high priest who killed Godolia[2] and wisely made Iôas, who was of David's line, king [4 Rg 11:15].

<8> Daniél who explained the mystical visions of kings; of whom it was said even to the devil, "You are not wiser than Daniél, are you?" [Ez 28:3].

<9> Esdras who remembered the sacred scriptures after the return of the Jewish people from Babylon [cf.1 Es 18:8].[3]

**42.** – What women were marvelous for their wisdom?[4]

<1> Thamar who outwitted Ioudas in order to have children [Gn 38].

<2> Rebekka (120a) arranged for the father's blessing to be given to Iakôb and sent him to her relatives in Mesopotamia to escape the wrath of Ésau [Gn 27].

<3> Iôsabél the daughter of King Iôram and wife of Iôdaë the high priest, who hid Iôas the son of her brother Ochozias so he would not be killed by Godolia [Arm.][5] and preserved him until his emergence to rule the Davidic kingdom [4 Rg 11:1-12:1].

<4> The wise Sounamitis who received the prophet Elissaios with the house prepared for him and her persistence with the prophet [4:10,36-37].

<MORAL EXAMPLES (43-62)>

**43.** – What wise men became too clever and perished because of their wisdom?

<1> Those who wanted to build the tower to heaven and were divided into many languages[6] [Gn 11:9, cf. C. 57].

<2> Pharaô, who plotted the destruction of the people and wanted to keep them as slaves, and perished in his own enterprise [Ex 5-14].

<3> Abimelech son of Gedeôn, when he thought he could acquire the first rank and killed his seventy brothers but was killed like a dog by a woman [Jd 9:53-56].

---

[1] Maoul (Origen); Aithan (Eusebius); Esra (Esdraités, Eusebius); Éman (Cod.A); Chalchal (Cod.A, Eusebius).

[2] In C. 39(8), this name is spelled "Gotholia."

[3] Irenaeus *Her* 3.21.2.

[4] Cf. Hyginus 254 (and 256): "What women were most pious?"

[5] In C. 39(8), this name is spelled "Gotholia."

[6] *Polyphônia*, as in Josephus *Ant.* 1.117.

⟨δ⟩ Σαοὺλ μηχανόμενος¹ τὴν τοῦ Δαβὶδ ἀναίρεσιν, καὶ τὸ δόρυ κατ' αὐτοῦ βάλλων, **(120b1)** ὑπὸ τοῦ ἰδίου ξίφους διολλύμενος.

⟨ε⟩ Ἀχιτόφελ δεινὰ σοφιζόμενος καὶ παρευδοκιμηθεὶς πρὸς τὸν Ἀβεσσαλώμ, ὑπὸ τοῦ Χουσὶ,² ἀγχόνῃ χρησάμενος.

⟨ϛ⟩ Οἱ τὸν Δανιὴλ συσκευασάμενοι τοῖς λέουσιν ἐκδοθῆναι, αὐτοὶ τοῖς θηρίοις ἐκδοθέντες.

⟨ζ⟩ Καὶ ἔτι πρότερον, οἱ τοῦ Ἰωσὴφ ἀδελφοὶ, ἀφανίζειν αὐτοῦ τὴν ἐκ τῶν ὀνειράτων ἐπίδοξον προσδοκίαν σοφισάμενοι, ὑπὸ τὴν κρίσιν αὐτοῦ περὶ τοῦ παντὸς ἔκειντο.³

**ΜΔ'.** + Τίνες ἐπικρύψει τῆς ἀληθείας σοφοὶ, σωτηρίαν εὕραντο; **(120b2)**

⟨α⟩ Ἀβραὰμ ἀδελφὴν ἑαυτοῦ λέγων εἶναι τὴν Σάρραν, ἵνα μὴ ὑπὸ τῶν Αἰγυπτίων δι' αὐτὴν ἀναιρεθῇ.

⟨β⟩ Μωϋσῆς πρὸς τὸν Αἰγύπτιον λέγων, τριῶν ἡμερῶν τὸν λαὸν ἐπὶ τὴν θεοῦ λατρείαν ἀπάξειν.

⟨γ⟩ Σαμουὴλ χρίων τὸν Δαβὶδ εἰς βασιλέα, ἐπὶ θυσίαν φάσκων εἰς τὴν Βηθλεὲμ ἀφικνεῖσθαι.

⟨δ⟩ Ἰωνάθαν λέγων πρὸς τὸν ἑαυτοῦ πατέρα τὸν Σαοὺλ περὶ τοῦ Δαβὶδ, ὡς ὑπ' αὐτοῦ παρακληθεὶς εἴη εἰς τὴν Βηθλεὲμ ἀπιέναι.

⟨ε⟩ Ὁ Δαβὶδ φεύγων τὸν Σαοὺλ, πρὸς τὸν ἱερέα τὸν Ἀβιμέλεχ φάσκων, ὡς ὑπὸ τοῦ βασιλέως ἀπεσταλμένος **(121a1)** εἴη ἐπί τι πρᾶγμα προσῆκον αὐτῷ. Καὶ πρὸς τὸν ἀλλόφυλον ἐλθὼν, δείσας μὴ, ὡς στρατηγὸς ὢν τοῦ λαοῦ, ἀποθάνῃ, μανίαν ἐσκέψατο,⁴ πρᾶγμα προβαλλόμενος οὐκ ἀληθὲς, διὰ σωτηρίαν.

⟨ϛ⟩ Καὶ Μελχὼλ δὲ, τοῦ πατρὸς ἐπαγανακτοῦντος αὐτῇ διὰ τὴν τοῦ Δαβὶδ ἀπόλυσιν, ἀναιρεῖσθαι λέγουσα πρὸς αὐτὸν,⁵ εἰ μὴ τοῦτο πεποιήκει.⁶

---

¹ Lc FGM μηχανωμενος.
² Lc FGM Χουση.
³ The items in this chapter are not numbered in CFGM.
⁴ Lc FGM ἐσκηψατο.
⁵ Lc FGM αὐτου.
⁶ The items in this chapter are not numbered in CFGM.

<4> Saul, plotting the destruction of David, and casting the spear at him [1 Rg 19:10], perished (120b) by his own sword [31:4].

<5> Achitophel, making evil plans and being surpassed by Chousé in the esteem of Abessalôm, hanged himself by a rope [2 Rg 17:23].

<6> Those who plotted to deliver Daniél to the lions, were themselves delivered to the beasts [Dn 6:24].

<7> And still earlier, the brothers of Iôséph who plotted to make his glorious expectation derived from dreams disappear, but were entirely dependent on his decision [Gn 37; 42–47].

**44.** – What wise men found safety by concealing the truth?

<1> Abraam, saying that Sarra was his sister so that he would not be killed by the Egyptians because of her [Gn 12:13]. [1]

<2> Moses, saying to the Egyptian <king> that he should lead the people away for three days for the worship of God [Ex 5:3].

<3> Samouél, anointing David as king and saying that he came to Béthleem for sacrifice [1 Rg 16:13].

<4> Iônathan, telling his father Saul that David asked him for permission to go to Béthleem [20:6].

<5> David, when he fled from Saul, saying to the priest Abimelech (Amimelech, Cod.A) that he was sent (121 a) by the king on business related to him [21:1-2]. And coming to the Philistine (Geth) and fearing lest as general of the people he would be killed, he pretended to be mad, creating a false impression for the sake of safety [21:12-13].

<6> And Melchôl, when her father Saul was indignant with her because David had escaped, said he had threatened her with death unless she did this [19:17].

---

[1] The story appears again in Gn 20:2, 13 and 26:7.

**ΜΕ'.** + Τίνες δὲ δόλῳ δικαιοσύνης ἔργα διεπράξαντο;
‹α'› Ἀὼδ ὁ κριτὴς τὸν Αἰγλὼμ, τὸν τῶν Μωαβιτῶν βασιλέα, ὡς ὑπήκοος
παρ' αὐτοῦ[1] μετὰ δώρων ἐλθὼν, ἀνελὼν δόλῳ. **(121a2)**
‹β'› Ἰαὴλ, ἡ τοῦ Κιναίου Χαβὲρ γυνὴ, τὸν Σισάρα φεύγοντα φιλοφρόνως
δεχομένη, καὶ γάλακτι ποτίζουσα κατακοιμήσασά τε, τὴν κεφαλὴν αὐτοῦ
τελευταῖον πασσάλῳ διελάσασα.

**ΜϚ'.** + Τίνες πρὸς σχήματι[2] χρηστότητος ἢ εὐσεβαίας, θάνατον
κατειργάσαντο;
Πρῶτος ὁ ὄφις τὴν Εὔαν διὰ χρηστότητος ἔπεισεν ἐφάπτεσθαι τοῦ τῆς
γνώσεως φυτοῦ, ὡς θεῶν γινομένων εἰ φάγοιεν, καὶ διὰ ταύτης εἰς θάνατον
ἐνέβαλε.
‹β'› Κάϊν τὸν ἀδελφὸν φιλοφρόνως ὡς **(121b1)** εἰς ἑώρησιν[3]
προτρεπόμενος. Διέλθωμεν εἰς τὸ πεδίον, φάμενος, οὕτως ἀναιρῶν.
‹γ'› Ἡ Ἰεζάβελ πρὸς σχήματι[4] νηστείας Θεῷ προσαγομένης ὑπὲρ τοῦ
βασιλέως, τὸν Ναβουθαὶ συκοφαντοῦσα.
‹δ'› Ὁ Ἰσμαὴλ φιλίας πρὸς σχήματι[5] πρὸς τὸν προστάτην τοῦ
ὑπολειφθέντος εἰς τὴν Ἰερουσαλὴμ λαοῦ, τὸν Γοδολίαν, παραγενόμενος, καὶ
τοῦτον οὕτως ἀνελών.[6]

**ΜΖ'.** + Τίνες δίκαιοι ἀνῃρέθησαν;
‹α'› Ζαχαρίας ὁ τοῦ ἀρχιερέως Ἰωδαὲ υἱὸς, ἐπιπλήττων δυσσεβοῦντι τῷ
Ἰωᾶς, λιθόλευστος ἀναμέσον τοῦ ναοῦ καὶ τοῦ θυσιαστηρίου **(121b2)**
ἀναιρεῖται.
‹β'› Οὐρίας ὁ προφήτης, φεύγων τὰς ἀπειλὰς τοῦ λαοῦ, ἐπείπερ παρήνει
μὴ δυσσεβεῖν, κληθεὶς ἀπὸ τῆς Αἰγύπτου εἰς τὴν Ἰερουσαλὴμ, ἐφονεύετο.

---

[1] Lc FGM προς αὐτον.
[2] Lc FGM προσχηματι.
[3] Μ αἰωρησιν.
[4] Lc FGM προσχηματι.
[5] Lc FGM προσχηματι.
[6] After Πρωτος, the items in this chapter are not numbered in CFGM.

**45.** – Who through craft performed works of righteousness?

<1> Aôd the judge, who killed Aiglôm king of the Moabites with a ruse, by coming to him as a vassal with gifts [Jd 3:21].

<2> Iaél the wife of the Kenite Chaber, who amicably received the fugitive Sisara, gave him milk to drink and put him to sleep, finally driving through his head with a peg [4:17-21].

**46.** – Who on the pretext of kindness or piety produced death?

First the serpent who through kindness persuaded Eua to touch the tree of knowledge because if she ate from it they would become gods, and through this cast them into death [Gn 3].

<2> Kain, who amicably encouraged his brother to go forth as (121b) for exercise, saying to him, "Let us go to the plain" [4:8], and thus killed him.

<3> Iezabel, on the pretext of fasting to God on behalf of the king, denouncing Nabouthai [3 Rg 21:9].

<4> Ismaél, coming on the pretext of friendship to the governor of the people remaining in Jerusalem, Godolias, and thus killing him [4 Rg 25:25; Jer 41:2].

## GOOD AND BAD MEN AND WOMEN

**47.** – What righteous ones were slain? [See C. 61.]

<1> Zacharias son of the [high] priest Jodaë, when he rebuked the impious Iôas, was stoned and died between the Temple and the altar [2 Par 24:21; Lk 11:51 = Mt 23:35 (son of Berachiah)].

<2> Ourias the prophet, fleeing from the threats of the people, since he exhorted them against impiety, was called from Egypt to Jerusalem and put to death [Jer 26:23].

‹γ› Ναβουθὲ[1] ὁ Ἰσραηλίτης[2], τὸν ἑαυτοῦ πατρικὸν ἀμπελῶνα μὴ βουληθεὶς δοῦναι τῷ Ἀχαάβ, ὑπὸ τῆς Ἰεζάβελ συκοφαντούμενος, λίθοις βαλλόμενος ἀνήρητο.

‹δ› Γοδολίας, ὁ τοῦ λαοῦ μετὰ τὴν αἰχμαλωσίαν προϊστάμενος, ὑπὸ Ἰσμαήλου διὰ τὸ εἶναι προστάτης[3] ἀνήρητο.

‹ε› Ὀσαΐας[4] ὁ προφήτης ὑπὸ Μανασσῆ ἐπρίσθη, ὡς ἡ παράδοσις ἔχει, οὔτε γὰρ (122a1) ἡ Γραφὴ τοῦτο ἔφησεν.

‹ς› Ἰούδας ὁ Μακκαβαῖος, καὶ οἱ Ἀσαμοναίου παῖδες, ὑπὸ Ἀντιόχου τοῦ Ἐπιφανοῦς ἐπ᾽ εὐνομίᾳ δεινῶς αἰκισθέντες ἀνηρέθησαν.

‹ζ› Ἰάκωβος ὁ ἀδελφὸς τοῦ Κυρίου, ὁ διὰ τὴν ὑπερβάλλουσαν ἀρετὴν δίκαιος ἐπικληθεὶς, ὑπὸ τοῦ λαοῦ ἀνηρέθη.[5]

**ΜΗʹ.** + Τίνες ἀδελφοὺς ἀπέκτειναν;
‹α› Κάϊν, τὸν Ἄβελ.
‹β› Ἀβιμέλεχ ὁ τοῦ Γεδεὼν υἱὸς, τοὺς οʹ.
‹γ› Ἀβεσσαλὼμ, τὸν Ἀμνών.
‹δ› Σολομὼν, τὸν Ἀδωνίαν.
‹ε› Ἰωρὰμ ὁ τοῦ Ἰωσάφατ υἱὸς, τοὺς εʹ ἀδελφοὺς αὐτοῦ.[6]

**ΜΘʹ.** + Τίνες παρὰ τὸ δοκοῦν τῷ Θεῷ χρηστευσάμενοι ἀναιροῦνται; (122a2)
‹α› Σαοὺλ μὴ ἀποκτείνας Ἄγαγ τὸν τοῦ Ἀμαλὴκ βασιλέα, προσταχθεὶς πανώλεθρον αὐτὸν διαφθεῖραι, ἀλλὰ φεισάμενος αὐτοῦ παρὰ τὸ δοκοῦν τῷ Θεῷ, κατακρίνεται ὑπὸ τοῦ προφήτου Σαμουὴλ τὴν καθαίρεσιν στῆναι[7] τῆς βασιλείας.

‹β› Ἀχαὰβ παραλαβὼν τὸν τοῦ Ἄδερ υἱὸν βασιλέα Συρίας εἰς ἀναίρεσιν, τὴν τοῦ Θεοῦ βουλὴν[8] ἐλεεῖ τὸν ἐκδοθέντα αὐτῷ εἰς θάνατον, καταφρονητὴν γεγονότα τοῦ Θεοῦ, Ἰσραήλ. Διόπερ αὐτὸς ἐξεδόθη τῇ παγγενῆ[9] διαφθορᾷ.

---

[1] Lc FGM Ναβουθαι.
[2] Lc FGM Ἰεζραηλιτης.
[3] Lc FGM προστατην.
[4] Lc FGM Ἡσαϊας.
[5] The items in this chapter are not numbered in CFGM.
[6] The items in this chapter are not numbered in CFGM.
[7] FGM omit στηναι.
[8] Lc FGM παρα την του Θεου βουλην.
[9] Lc FGM παγγενει.

<3> Nabouthai the Iezraélite (Arm.), who did not want to give his ancestral vineyard to Achaab and was slandered by Iezabel and stoned to death [3 Rg 21:1-14].

<4> Godolias, in charge of the people after the captivity, was killed by Ismaél because he was in command [Jer 41:1-2].

<5> Ésaias the prophet was sawn asunder by Manassés, as tradition says; (122a) the scripture did not say this.[1]

<6> Ioudas Makkabaios and the <other> sons of Asamonaios were cruelly killed by Antiochos Epiphanés for keeping the law.[2]

<7> Iakôbos the Lord's brother because of his surpassing virtue was called "the Just," and was slain by the people.[3]

**48.** – Who killed their brothers?[4]

<1> Kain <killed> Abel [Gn 4:8].

<2> Abimelech son of Gedeôn <killed> seventy brothers [Jd 9:5].

<3> Abessalôm <killed> Amnôn [2 Rg 13:29].

<4> Solomon <killed> Adônias [3 Rg 2:25].

<5> Iôram son of Iôsaphat <killed> his five brothers [six in 2 Par 21:1-4].

**49.** – Who were merciful, contrary to God's will, and perished?

<1> Saul, who did not kill King Agag son of Amalek when ordered to extirpate him, but spared him against God's will and was condemned by the prophet Samouél to lose the kingdom [1 Rg 15:23; 28:18].

<2> Achaab when he took the king of Syria, the son of Ader, to destroy him but contrary to the will of God took pity on the one given to him for death and became a despiser of the offspring of God, Israel. Therefore he himself was delivered to the general destruction [3 Rg 21:31-42].

---

[1] Hebrews 11:37 probably refers to this event, reported in the apocryphal *Ascension of Isaiah* and mentioned by Justin (*Dialogue* 120.5), Tertullian (*Patience* 14.1; *Scorpiace* 8.3), Hippolytus (*On Antichrist* 30, p. 20, 13 Achelis), and Origen (*Commentary on Matthew* 10.18 (Klostermann p. 24, 6). See Bar Hebraeus, cited on C. 75(5).

[2] Apparently a garbled version of the Maccabaean mother and her seven sons (4 Maccabees; 2 Maccabees 7).

[3] Cf. C. 153; Eusebius *HE* 2.23.7 (scribes and Pharisees, 2.23.10–16); cf. *2 Apoc. Jas.* 61–62 in James M. Robinson, ed., *The Nag Hammadi Library in English* (3d ed.; San Francisco: Harper & Row, 1988) 275 (apparently priests).

[4] Cf. Hyginus 238: "Who killed their daughters?" (the missing cc. 226–37 could have contained a heading like Joseph's).

‹γ'› Ὁ κελευσθεὶς ὑπὸ τοῦ προφήτου πατάσσειν αὐτόν, εἰς ἔλεγχον τῆς τοῦ (122b1) Ἀχαὰβ ἀνηκόου τοῦ Θεοῦ φιλανθρωπίας, καὶ μὴ πατάξας, λέοντι περιπίπτειν ἀκούει διὰ τὴν παρακοὴν τῷ θηρίῳ. Καὶ τούτῳ περιπεσὼν κατὰ τὴν ὁδόν, ὑπ' αὐτοῦ καὶ ἀναιρεῖται.

‹δ'› Ὁ προφήτης ἐπὶ[1] τοῦ Ἱεροβοὰμ εἰς τὴν Βεθὴλ ἀποσταλεὶς, προλέγειν τὴν τῶν ψευδοπροφητῶν ἐσομένην ἐπὶ τοῦ θυσιαστηρίου κατάκαυσιν, καὶ κελευσθεὶς εἰς τὴν τοῦ Ἰσραὴλ μὴ ἑστιαθῆναι χώραν, παρακρουσθεὶς[2] ὑπὸ τοῦ ψευδοπροφήτου χρηστότητα,[3] ὑπὸ λέοντος θηρίου κατὰ τὴν ὁδὸν ἐφονεύετο.[4]

**Ν'.** + Τίνες μισθὸν δικαιοσύνης (122b2) τὸ ἀποθανεῖν ἐκομίσαντο, καὶ τίνες δι' ἀσεβείας ἐπεβίωσαν;

‹α'› Ὁ τοῦ Ἱεροβοὰμ βασιλέως Ἰσραὴλ[5] υἱός, νέος ὢν ἀποθνήσκει, ἐπειδὴ εὑρέθη ῥῆμα ἀγαθὸν ἐν αὐτῷ περὶ[6] Κυρίου, ὡς Ἀχίας ὁ προφήτης πρὸς Ἀνὼ τὴν μητέρα αὐτοῦ, περὶ τῆς ζωῆς αὐτοῦ ἐρωτῶσαν, ἔφη.

‹β'› Ἰωσίας εὐσεβήσας ὁ βασιλεύς, ἐπὶ δικαιοσύνῃ ἀποθνήσκει, ἀκούσας παρὰ τῆς προφήτιδος Ὀλδῆς· Τάδε λέγει Κύριος· Ἰδοὺ ἐγὼ προστίθημί σε πρὸς τοὺς πατέρας σου, καὶ προστεθήσῃ ἐν εἰρήνῃ, (123a1) ἵνα μὴ ἴδωσιν οἱ ὀφθαλμοί σου πάντα τὰ κακά, ἃ ἐγὼ ἐπάγω ἐπὶ τὸν τόπον τοῦτον καὶ πάντα τὸν λαόν.

‹γ'› Κάϊν, ἵνα εἰς ἑβδόμην γενεὰν ‹.....›[7] τὴν τῆς ἀδελφοκτονίας.

‹δ'› Καὶ τὰ Χαναναίων ἔθνη, ἵνα πληρωθῶσιν αὐτῶν αἱ ἁμαρτίαι.[8]

**ΝΑ'.** + Τίνες, οὐ νοσήσαντες, ἀποθνήσκειν ἐκελεύοντο;

‹α'› Ἀαρὼν, εἰς τὸ ὄρος ἀνελθεῖν κελευόμενος, ἵνα ἀποθάνῃ.

‹β'› Μωϋσῆς, ἔμβα[9] καὶ τελεύτα, ἀκούων.

---

[1] Lc FGM ὑπο.
[2] FGM παρακουσθεις.
[3] FGM omit ὑπο του ψευδοπροφητου χρηστοτητα.
[4] The items in this chapter are not numbered in CFGM.
[5] FGM omit Ἰσραὴλ. Emend to του Ἰσραηλ.
[6] FGM παρα.
[7] C shows no break, but FGM rightly suggest a *lacuna* at this point.
[8] The items in this chapter are not numbered in CFGM.
[9] Instead of C's ἐμβα, FGM unnecessarily emend to ἀναβηθι εἰς το ὄρος Ναβαυ.

<3> The man who was ordered by the prophet[1] to strike him as proof of (122b) the kind-heartedness of Achaab, who was hostile to God. When he did not strike, he heard that he would encounter a wild lion because of his disobedience. And when he fell upon it on the road he was killed by it [20:35-36].

<4> After the prophet was sent by Ieroboam to Bethél to foretell the future burning of the sanctuary of the false prophets and was ordered not to eat in Israel, when he was led away from excellence by the false prophet he was killed by a wild lion on the road [13:1,13].[2]

**50**. – Who received death as the wages of righteousness, and who lived on through impiety?

<1> The son of Ieroboam king of Israel died young after there was found a good word in him concerning the Lord, as Achias the prophet said to his mother Anô [3 Rg 12:24, Cod.B], who was asking about his life.[3]

<2> Iôsias the pious king dies because of righteousness, hearing from the prophetess Olda, "Thus says the Lord, Behold I gather you to your fathers, and you shall be joined to them in peace (123a), so that your eyes may not see all the evils that I am bringing upon this place and the whole people" [4 Rg 22:20].

<3> Kain to the seventh generation [Gn 4:15] <remained alive in punishment for> killing his brother.

<4> The nations of the Chanaanites [Js 17:13; Jd 1:28], that their sins might be filled up.

**51**. – Who were not sick but commanded to die?

<1> Aaron, ordered to go up to the mountain to die [Nm 20:25].

<2> Moses, hearing: "Go forth and die" [Dt 32:49-50].

---

[1] Identified as Micaiah in Josephus *Ant.* 8.389.

[2] Identified as Iadôn in Josephus *Ant.* 8.231 (408).

[3] The story does not appear in Cod.A or Arm.

‹γ'› Δανιὴλ ἀκούων παρὰ τοῦ ἀγγέλου· Καὶ σὺ βάδιζε, καὶ ἀναπαύου. Καὶ ἀναπαύσῃ καὶ ἀναστήσῃ εἰς τὴν δόξαν σου, εἰς προθεσμίαν ἡμερῶν. ‹δ'› Ἰωάννης (123a2) ὁ εὐαγγελιστής.[1]

ΝΒ'. + Τίνες τῶν ἁγίων, τυφλοὶ τὴν ὅρασιν γεγονότες, ἀπέθανον; ‹α'› Ἰσαάκ. ‹β'› Ἰακώβ. ‹γ'› Ἡλεῖ ὁ ἱερεύς. ‹δ'› Ἀχίας ὁ προφήτης ὁ Σκαλωνίτης.[2]

ΝΓ'. + Τίνες διέμειναν, οὐκ ἀπέθανον;[3] ‹α'› Ἐνὼχ ἐν ἑβδόμῃ γενεᾷ τῇ ἀπὸ τοῦ Ἀδὰμ μετετέθη, καὶ οὐχ εὑρίσκετο. ‹β'› Ἡλίας ἐν ἅρματι πυρὸς ἀναληφθεὶς ὡς εἰς τὸν οὐρανόν. ‹γ'› Τοῦ δὲ Μελχισεδὲκ θάνατος οὐ γέγραπται, ἐπεὶ μηδὲ γέννησις. Τέθνηκε γοῦν ἐπειδὴ καὶ γεγέννηται, διὰ δὲ τὸ τύπον αὐτὸν εἶναι τῆς ἀρχιερωσύνης[4] Χριστοῦ, οὐκ ἀναγέγραπται.[5] (123b1)

ΝΔ'. + Τίνες ἀποθανόντες ἀνέζησαν; ‹α'› Ὁ τῆς χήρας τῆς Σαραφθινῆς υἱὸς ὑπὸ Ἡλίου τοῦ προφήτου. ‹β'› Ὁ τῆς Σουναμίτιδος υἱός, ὃν Ἐλισσαῖος ἀνέστησεν. ‹γ'› Ὁ ἐκκομιζόμενος, καὶ διὰ τὴν ἔφοδον τῶν λῃστῶν, δεισάντων τῶν ἐκκομιζόντων, ἐπιρριφεὶς τῷ τοῦ Ἐλισσαίου μνήματι, ἀναστὰς καὶ πεφευγὼς μετὰ τῶν καταρριψάντων αὐτόν.

Ὑπὸ δὲ τοῦ Σωτῆρος τρεῖς ἀνέστησαν νεκροί· ‹δ'› ἡ τοῦ Ἰαήρου θυγάτηρ ἡ δωδεκαετής, ‹ε'› ὁ τῆς χήρας μονογενὴς υἱὸς ἐκκομιζόμενος πρὸς αὐτὸ (123b2) τὸ μνῆμα, ‹ς'› Λάζαρος τετραήμερος ὀδωδὼς ἀπὸ τοῦ μνήματος κληθείς. Τρεῖς ἐν τῇ Παλαιᾷ, τρεῖς ἐν τῇ Νέᾳ.

Καὶ διὰ τῶν ἀποστόλων· ‹ζ'› ἡ Δορκὰς ἐν Ἰόππῃ ὑπὸ Πέτρου, ‹η'› Εὔτυχος ὑπὸ Παύλου ἐν Τρωάδι.[6]

---

[1] The items in this chapter are not numbered in CFGM.
[2] Lc FGM Σιλωνιτης. The items in this chapter are not numbered in CFGM.
[3] Lc FGM και οὐκ ἀπεθανον.
[4] GM ἀρχιεροσυνης.
[5] The items in this chapter are not numbered in CFGM.
[6] The items in this chapter are not numbered in CFGM.

<3> Daniél, hearing from the angel: "And you too go away and rest, and you will rest and rise up in your glory on the appointed day" [Dn 12:13].

<4> Iôannés the Evangelist [Jn 21:23].

**52**. – Which of the saints became blind and died?

<1> Isaak [Gn 27:1].

<2> Iakôb [48:10].

<3> Éli the priest [1 Rg 3:2].

<4> The prophet Achias the Silonite [3 Rg 14:4].

**53**. – Who survived and did not die?

<1> Enoch in the seventh generation from Adam was translated and not found [Gn 5:24].

<2> Élias was taken up to heaven in a chariot of fire [4 Rg 2:11].

<3> The death of Melchisedek, like his birth, was not recorded. He died, since he was born, but since he was a type of the high priesthood of Christ, it was not recorded [Gn 14:18-20].[1] (Cf. C. 115[2].) (123b)

**54**. – Who died and lived again?

<1> The son of the Saraphthiné widow, raised by Élias the prophet [3 Rg 17:22].

<2> The son of the Sounamitis, whom Elissaios raised [4 Rg 4:35].

<3> The man who was carried to be buried and because of the arrival of bandits was thrown into the tomb of Elissaios, arose and escaped [13:21] with those who had thrown him there.

By the Savior three dead persons arose: <4> the daughter of Iaéros, twelve years old [Mk 5:41]; <5> the only son of the widow, brought to the tomb [Lk 7:14]; <6> Lazaros, dead for four days and stinking, called from the tomb [Jn 11:39, 43]. Three in the Old, three in the New.

And through the apostles: <7> Dorkas in Ioppé by Petros [Ac 9:40]; <8> Eutychos by Paul in Troas [20:9-10].

---

[1] Cf. Epiphanius *Pan.* 55.3.2–3: no genealogies for Melchizedek, Daniel, Shadrach, Mishak, Abednego, Elijah.

**ΝΕ'.** + Τίνες στεῖραι τετόκασι;[1]

‹α'› Σάρρα ἡ τοῦ Ἀβραὰμ γυνὴ τὸν Ἰσαὰκ γεννήσασα.

‹β'› Ῥεβέκκα ἡ τοῦ Ἰσαὰκ γυνὴ τοὺς διδύμους, τὸν Ἡσαῦ καὶ τὸν Ἰακὼβ, γεννήσασα.

‹γ'› Ῥαχὴλ ἡ τοῦ Ἰακὼβ, ἡ τὸν Ἰωσὴφ καὶ τὸν Βενιαμὶν γεννήσασα.

‹δ'› Ἄννα ἡ τοῦ Ἑλκανᾶ, ἡ τὸν προφήτην (124a1) Σαμοὴλ[2] γεννήσασα.

‹ε'› Ἡ Σουμανῖτις,[3] ἡ παρὰ τοῦ Ἐλισσαίου λαβοῦσα τὸν υἱόν, καὶ ἀποθανόντα αὖθις λαβοῦσα.

‹ς'› Ἐλισάβετ ἡ Ζαχαρίου γυνή, ἡ τὸν βαπτιστὴν Ἰωάννην γεννήσασα.[4]

**ΝϜ'.** + Τίνες πατέρα[5] ἠτίμασαν;

‹α'› Χὰμ τὸν[6] Νῶε, τὴν γύμνωσιν αὐτοῦ τοῖς ἀδελφοῖς ἐξαγγείλας.

‹β'› Ἡσαῦ, παρὰ τὴν τοῦ πατρὸς γνώμην γυναῖκας Χαναναίας ἀγαγόμενος.

‹γ'› Ἀβεσσαλώμ, ἐπαρθεὶς κατὰ τοῦ Δαβὶδ καὶ πολεμῶν αὐτῷ, καὶ τὰς γυναῖκας αὐτοῦ μιάνας.

‹δ'› Ἀδωνίας, αὐτοχειροτόνητον ἑαυτὸν (124a2) βασιλέα, παρὰ τὴν τοῦ πατρὸς γνώμην, ἀναδεῖξαι πειραθείς.[7]

**ΝΖ'.** + Τίνες ἀλαζονευσάμενοι κατηνέχθησαν;

‹α'› Οἱ τὸν εἰς οὐρανὸν διήκοντα βουληθέντες οἰκοδομεῖν πύργον, τῇ πολυγλώσσῳ διασχισθέντες φωνῇ.

‹β'› Φαραὼ ἐπὶ τῇ ἑαυτοῦ δυνάμει θρασυνόμενος, καὶ λέγων· Τὸν Θεὸν οὐκ ἐπίσταμαι, καὶ τὸν λαὸν οὐκ ἀποστέλλω· μετὰ τὰς δέκα πληγὰς, ὑπὸ βυθὸν πανστρατιᾷ καλυπτόμενος.

‹γ'› Ῥοβοὰμ καταφρονήσας τοῦ λαοῦ καὶ μείζω τοῦ Σολομῶνος τοῦ ἑαυτοῦ (124b1) πατρὸς θελήσας φρονεῖν, τῆς πνευματικῆς[8] ἐξέπεσεν ἀρχῆς.

‹δ'› Γολιάθ μέγα φρονήσας κατὰ παρατάξεως ὅλης τοῦ ἱεροῦ λαοῦ, ὡς κύων, λίθῳ νεανίου βάλοντος[9] αὐτὸν, κατέπεσεν.

---

[1] GM τετοκασιν.

[2] Lc FGM Σαμουηλ.

[3] Lc FGM Σουναμιτις.

[4] The items in this chapter are not numbered in CFGM.

[5] GM πατερας.

[6] GM mistakenly print των.

[7] The items in this chapter are not numbered in CFGM.

[8] Lc FGM πατρικης.

[9] FGM βαλλοντος.

**55.** – What women were sterile but gave birth?

<1> Sarra wife of Abraam, who bore Isaak [Gn 21:1-3].

<2> Rebekka wife of Isaak, who bore the twins Ésau and Iakôb [25:24].

<3> Rachél the wife of Iakôb, who bore Iôséph and Beniamin [30:22-24; 35:18].

<4> Anna the wife of Elkana, who bore (124a) Samouél the prophet [1 Rg 1:19-20].

<5> The Sounamitis woman who from Elissaios the prophet received a son and when he died received him back [4 Rg 4:17,36].

<6> Elisabet the wife of Zacharias, who bore the Baptist Iôannés [Lk 1:36,60].

**56.** – Who dishonored a father?

<1> Cham, Nôé, announcing his nakedness to his brothers [Gn 9:22].

<2> Ésau, against his father's will marrying Canaanite wives [28:8-9].

<3> Abessalôm, rising against David and warring with him, and defiling his wives [2 Rg 16:22].

<4> Adônias, who publicly dared to make himself king by his own decision against the will of his father [3 Rg 1:5].

**57.** – Who were thrown down because of arrogance? [Contrast C. 58.]

<1> Those who wanted to build a tower reaching to heaven were dispersed into a polyglot voice [Gn 11:9, cf. C. 43].

<2> Pharaô, emboldened by his own might and saying "I do not know God" [Ex 5:2] and "I am not sending the people away," after ten plagues was covered up in the deep with his whole army [14:28].

<3> Roboam despising the people and wishing to know more than his (124b) father Solomon, fell from his father's power [3 Rg 12:14].

<4> The great Goliath after despising the whole military of the sacred people fell like a dog, struck by the stone of a young man who threw it [1 Rg 17:50].

‹ε'-ϛ'› Ἀβεσσαλὼμ ἐπὶ κόμῃ, καὶ Ἀδωνίας ἐπὶ κάλλει ἐπαρθέντες, ἀτίμωτον ἑαυτοῖς βίον κατέστρεψαν.

‹ζ'› Ὁ τῶν Βαβυλωνίων βασιλεὺς Σενναχιρεὶμ[1] μέγα θρασυνθεὶς ἐπὶ τῇ τῶν ἐθνῶν παραλήψει, καὶ κατὰ τοῦ Ἐζεκίου, ὡς μὴ δυναμένου βοηθεῖσθαι, διὰ Ῥαψάκου κατεπαρθεὶς, τὸν ἑαυτοῦ στρατὸν θεηλάτῳ (124b2) πλήγῃ ὑπὸ μίαν καιροῦ ῥοπὴν ἀπολλὺς, καὶ δραπέτης, μόνος ἀποδιδράσκων εἰς τὴν ἑαυτοῦ γῆν, κἀκεῖσε πρὸς τῶν οἰκείων παίδων ἀναιρούμενος.

‹η'› Ὁ Συρίας βασιλεὺς Ἀδάδου ὁ υἱὸς, πάντα τὸν τοῦ Ἰσραὴλ λαὸν ἀφανίζειν ἀπειλῶν διὰ παιδαρίων σλβ'· μυρίους πολεμιστὰς ἑαυτοῦ ἀπόλλυσι, καὶ τὴν ὅλην ἑαυτοῦ βασιλείαν διεφθείρετο.

‹θ'› Ὀζίας ὁ βασιλεὺς ἐπὶ δικαιοσύνῃ μέγα φρονήσας, καὶ ἱερᾶσθαι βουλόμενος, λεπρωθεὶς, οὐ μόνον τῆς βασιλείας, ἀλλὰ καὶ τῆς οἰκίας ἐξεβάλλετο.

‹ι'› Ναβουχοδονόσορ ἐπὶ τῇ πάντων (125a1) κρατήσει τῶν ἐθνῶν καὶ τῇ[2] τῆς Βαβυλῶνος αὐξήσει, ὑπὲρ ἄπαντας ἐπαρθεὶς, τὴν τοῦ ἀνθρώπου διάνοιαν ἀφαιρεθεὶς, θηρίου ψυχὴν καὶ τρόπον ἔσχηκε.

‹ια'› Καὶ Φαρισαῖος ἐπὶ τῇ ἑαυτοῦ δικαισύνῃ μέγα φρονήσας, καὶ ἐπὶ ταύτῃ κατὰ τοῦ τελώνου θρασυνθεὶς, τὴν δικαιοσύνην ἀπώλωλε.[3]

**ΝΗ'.** + Τίνες διὰ ταπεινοφροσύνην εἰς δόξαν καὶ ὕψος ἤχθησαν;

‹α'› Ἰωσὴφ, ταπεινοφρονήσας ἐφ' οἷς ὑπέμεινε χαλεποῖς παρὰ τῶν ἀδελφῶν καὶ τῆς νομισθείσης δεσποίνης, εἰς τὸ κρατεῖν τῆς Αἰγύπτου (125a2) προήγετο.

‹β'› Ἰακὼβ, φεύγων τὰς τοῦ ἀδελφοῦ ἀπειλὰς, καὶ ξένην ἀντὶ τῆς πατρῴας, οὐ ἑστίας[4] ἀλλαξάμενος, πλούσιος ἐπανήρχετο καὶ τίμιος.

‹γ'› Ἰούδας, ἐπιπεσὼν τῷ Ἰωσὴφ ἐφ' οἷς εἰς αὐτὸν ἐπλημμέλησαν, βασιλικοῦ γένους ἀξιοῦται γενέσθαι φύλαρχος.

‹δ'› Γαβαωνῖται, τὸν Ἰησοῦν ὑπελθόντες ἐν τῇ τῶν ἐθνῶν παραλήψει, διὰ ταπεινοφροσύνης ἐν τοῖς οἰκείοις μεμενήκασι, τῆς σωτηρίας τετυχηκότες.

‹ε'› Δαβὶδ, δι' ὅλου ταπεινοφρονῶν ἐφ' οἷς ὑπὸ τοῦ Σαοὺλ ὑπέμεινε, καὶ τὴν βασιλείαν (125b1) ἀπελάμβανεν.

‹ϛ'› Ἰερεμίας, ὑπτόμενος[5] καὶ φυλακιζόμενος ἐπὶ ταῖς ἀληθέσι

---

[1] FGM Σενναχηρειμ.
[2] FGM omit τη.
[3] *Lc* GM απολωλε. The items in this chapter are not numbered in CFGM.
[4] *Lc* FGM ξενην αντι της πατρωας εστιαν.
[5] *Lc* FGM τυπτομενος.

<5-6> Abessalôm, proud of his hair, and Adônias, of his beauty, had a dishonorable end to their lives [2 Rg 18:9, 3 Rg 1:6].

<7> The king of Babylon Sennachireim, haughty over the defeat of the nations and against Ezekias as one who could not be helped, elated by the report of Rapsakos [4 Rg 18:17]. He lost his army by a divine blow in the briefest moment of time, and running back to his own land he alone escaped, and there he was killed by his sons [19:37].

<8> The king of Syria son of Adados,[1] when he had threatened to destroy the whole people of Israel through 232 servants. Countless warriors were lost and his whole kingdom destroyed [3 Rg 20:15-21].

<9> Ozias the king, haughty because of his justice, and desiring to sacrifice, was made a leper and was cast out of not only his kingdom but also his house [2 Par 26:15-16].

<10> Nabouchodonosor, because of his (125a) victory over all nations and the growth of Babylon, exalted himself above all; deprived of his human reasoning, he had the life and manners of a beast [Dn 5:19-21].

<11> And the Pharisee, haughty because of his righteousness and therefore insulting the tax-collector, lost righteousness [Lk 18:10-14].

**58.** – Who were brought to glory and exaltation because of humility?

<1> Iôséph, after humbly enduring the troubles inflicted by his brothers and supposed mistress, was advanced to rule Egypt [Gn 39-43].

<2> Iakôb, fleeing from the threats of his brother and exchanging an alien hearth for a paternal one, returned with wealth and honors [27:43, 32:14].

<3> Ioudas, falling before Iôseph because of what they had done to him, was deemed worthy to become an officer of the royal family [44:18].

<4> The Gabaônites, after tricking Iésous during the war on the gentiles, through humility remained in their own homes and obtained safety [Js 9].

<5> David, who was constantly humble in what he suffered from Saul, and (125b) received the kingdom [e.g. 1 Rg 24:9-10].[2]

<6> Ieremias, beaten and imprisoned for his true predictions and bearing it

---

[1] Ben-Hadad, Hebrew; son of Adados, Josephus *Ant.* 8.363; son of Ader, LXX. The next number, 232, is shared with Cod.A and Josephus *Ant.* 8.374.

[2] Compare 1 Clement 18 on the humility of David.

προρρήσεσι, καὶ φέρων ταπεινοφρόνως, προστάτης τοῦ λαοῦ κατὰ τὸν καιρὸν ἐγίνετο τῆς πολιορκίας.

‹ζ›› Νηνευῖται,[1] ταπεινοφρονήσαντες ἐπὶ τὸ τοῦ Ἰωνᾶ κήρυγμα, ἐλέους τετυχήκασιν ἀπήμαντοι διαμείναντες.

‹η›› Καὶ ὁ Κύριος δὲ τὸν Τελώνην πολλῇ ταπεινοφροσύνῃ εἰς τὸ ἱερὸν ἀνεληλυθότα, καὶ ἑαυτὸν ἐπὶ ταῖς πλημμελείαις κατακρίναντα, δεδικαιῶσθαι ἔφη ὑπὲρ τὸν μεγαλορήμονα[2] Φαρισαῖον.[3]

**ΝΘ'.** + Τίνες ἐπὶ φόνοις ἔδρασαν[4] (125b2) ἀπεδέχθησαν, καὶ εὐάρεστοι παρὰ Θεῷ γεγόνασι;

‹α›› Μωϋσῆς τὸν Αἰγύπτιον ἀνελὼν, καὶ ἐκδικίαν τοῦ ἀδικουμένου Ἑβραίου ποιησάμενος.

‹β›› Φινεὲς ὁ τοῦ < Ἐλεαζαρ ὁ τοῦ>[5] Ἀαρὼν υἱὸς, τὸν Ζαμβρὴν καὶ τὴν Χασβὴν διελάσας, καὶ οὕτω τὴν κατὰ τοῦ λαοῦ δικαίαν τοῦ Θεοῦ μῆνιν ἐξιλασάμενος.

‹γ›› Σαμουὴλ ὁ ἱερεὺς καὶ προφήτης, τὸν τῶν Ἀμαληκιτῶν βασιλέα τὸν Ἀγὰγ ἀνελὼν, καὶ πληρώσας βουλὴν Θεοῦ, ἣν ὁ Σαοὺλ οὐκ ἐπλήρωσεν.

‹δ›› Οἱ εἰς τὴν ἔρημον προσδεδραμηκότες καλοῦντι τῷ Μωϋσῇ, καὶ τοὺς προσήκοντας αὐτοῖς, ἐπιμεμενηκότας (126a1) τῇ δυσσεβεῖ γνώμῃ τῆς εἰδωλολατρείας ἀποσφάξαντες.

‹ε›› Δαβὶδ τὸν νεανίαν τὸν[6] Ἀμαληκίτην, τὸν καυχώμενον ἐπ’ αὐτοῦ, ὡς τὸν Σαοὺλ αὐτὸς ὁ[7] ἐπισφάξας εἴη· καὶ τὸν Ῥιχὰβ, καὶ τὸν Βαανὰν, τοὺς τοῦ Ῥεμμὼθ υἱοὺς τοῦ Βηρροθέου, τοὺς τὸν Μεμφιβοσθὲ τὸν τοῦ Σαοὺλ υἱὸν, ὡς πρὸς αὐτοῦ χάριν ἀπεκτανκότας,[8] καὶ τὴν κεφαλὴν αὐτοῦ κομίσαντας αὐτῷ.

‹ϛ›› Ἡ γυνὴ, ἡ τοῦ[9] Ἀβιμέλεχ ἀπὸ τοῦ τείχους, κλάσματι μύλου ἐπιρριφότι αὐτῷ ἀνελοῦσα.

‹ζ›› Ἡ γυνὴ τὸν Ἀβεσσᾶ μέλλοντα πολιορκίαν κινεῖν τῇ πόλει ἀναιρεθῆναι ποιήσασα, (126a2) καὶ τὴν κεφαλὴν αὐτοῦ τῷ Ἰωὰβ ἀπὸ τοῦ τείχους ἀποντίσασα.[10]

---

[1]*Lc* FGM Νινευιται.
[2]*Lc* FGM μεγαλορρημονα.
[3]The items in this chapter are not numbered in CFGM.
[4]FGM Τινες ἐφ’ οἷς ἐδρασαν φονοις.
[5]Emend to Φινεὲς ὁ τοῦ Ἐλεαζαρ ὁ τοῦ on the basis of Nm 25:7.
[6]*Lc* FGM omit τον.
[7]FGM omit ὁ.
[8]FGM ἀπεκτακοτας.
[9]*Lc* FGM τον.
[10]The items in this chapter are not numbered in CFGM.

humbly, was made leader of the people when the city was besieged [Jer 39:11-12].

<7> The Ninivites, who were humble at the preaching of Iônas and, obtaining mercy, remained free from harm [Mt 12:41].

<8> And the Lord said that the tax-collector, going up to the Temple with much humility and condemning himself for his sins, was justified beyond the magniloquent Pharisee [Lk 18:14].

**59.** – Who in spite of the murders they committed were accepted as pleasing with God?

<1> Moses killed an Egyptian, avenging a mistreated Hebrew [Ex 2:11-12].

<2> Phinees son of <Eleazar, son of> Aaron transfixed Zambrés and Kosbé and thus expiated the just wrath of God against the people [Nm 25:7-8, 25-26].

<3> Samouél priest and prophet, who killed Agag king of the Amalekites and fulfilled the will of God which Saul had not fulfilled [1 Rg 15:33].

<4> Those who ran forward in the desert at Moses' call and slaughtered their relations who remained (126a) in the impious opinion of idolatry [Ex 32:27-32].

<5> David killing the Amalekite young man who boasted that he himself had slain Saul [2 Rg 1:15]; and also Richab and Baanas sons of Remmôth the Bérrothite, who said they killed the son of Saul Memphibosthe for his [David's] favor and brought his head to him [4:12].

<6> The woman who killed Abimelech from the wall by throwing a piece of millstone on him [11:21].

<7> The woman who had Abessa killed because he was going to raise a revolt in the city and sent his head to Iôab from the wall [20:21].

Ξ'. + Τίνες ἐπὶ παρανομίαις[1] λιθόλευστοι ἀνῃρέθησαν, καὶ τίνες ἐπ' εὐσέβεια;[2]

‹α'› Ὁ Σαλωμὶθ υἱὸς τῆς θυγατρὸς Δαρείου,[3] ἐπὶ βλασφημίᾳ, μετὰ ἑτέρου αὐτοῦ μαχόμενος,[4] Θεὸν ἐβλασφήμησεν.

‹β'› Ὁ ἐν Σαββάτῳ ξύλα ἐκλέξας εἰς τὴν ἔρημον.

‹γ'› Ἀχάρ ὁ ἱερόσυλος, ὁ ἐκ τῶν ἀναθημάτων τῆς Ἱεριχοῦς ἀποκρυψάμενος.[5]

ΞΑ'. + Καὶ τίνες δίκαιοι ἐπ' εὐσεβείᾳ;

‹α'› Ναβουθὲ[6] ὁ Ἰσμαηλίτης,[7] συκοφαντηθεὶς ὑπὸ τῆς Ἰεζάβελ ὡς καταρασάμενος (126b1) Θεὸν καὶ βασιλέα.

‹β'› Ζαχαρίας ὁ ἀρχιερεὺς ὁ τοῦ Ἰωδαὲ, ὑπὸ Ἰωᾶς βασιλέως, ἀναμέσον τοῦ ναοῦ καὶ τοῦ θυσιαστηρίου λιθασθεὶς, ὅτι παρῄνει[8] αὐτῷ μὴ δυσσεβεῖν.[9]

ΞΒ'. + Τίνες παρανόμους μίξεις πεποίηντο;

‹α'› Λὼτ ταῖς θυγατράσι συμμιχθείς.

‹β'› Ῥουβὶμ τῇ τοῦ πατρὸς παλλακῇ.

‹γ'› Οἱ ἐν Γαβαᾷ τῆς φυλῆς Βενιαμὶν, τῇ τοῦ Λευΐτου γυναικὶ· ἐπιξενωθέντας[10] αὐτοῖς συγχρησάμενοι, ὡς καὶ ὀχληθεῖσαν ἀποθανεῖν. Ἐφ' ᾗ πράξει καὶ πολὺς τοῦ λαοῦ φόνος ἐγένετο.

‹δ'› Ἀμνὼν[11] τὴν ἀδελφὴν Θάμαρ (126b2) παρθένον φθείρας, καὶ μετὰ τὴν ὕβριν τῆς ἑαυτοῦ οἰκίας[12] ἀποπέμψας.

‹ε'› Ἀβεσσαλὼμ τὰς τοῦ πατρὸς γυναῖκας ἐπ' ἀτιμίᾳ τοῦ πατρὸς, γνώμῃ τοῦ Ἀχιτόφελ, διαφθείρας.[13]

---

[1] FGM παρανομιας

[2] *Lc* FGM omit και τινες ἐπ' εὐσεβεια (nearly replicated in Chapter 61).

[3] *Lc* FGM Δαβρει.

[4] *Lc* FGM ὁς μετα ἑτερου μαχομενος.

[5] The items in this chapter are not numbered in CFGM.

[6] *Lc* FGM Ναβουθαι.

[7] *Lc* FGM Ἰεζραηλιτης.

[8] GM παρηνου.

[9] The items in this chapter are not numbered in CFGM.

[10] *Lc* FGM ἐπιξενωθεντος.

[11] FGM Ἀμων. *Lege* Ἀμμων.

[12] GM οἰκειας.

[13] The items in this chapter are not numbered in CFGM.

**60**. – Who perished by stoning because of lawlessness?

<1> The son of Salômith the daughter of Dabrei, for blasphemy; when fighting with another he blasphemed God [Lv 24:11].

<2> He who collected wood on a Sabbath in the desert [Nm 15:32].

<3> Achar the sacrilegious, who hid some of the consecrated loot from the city of Jericho [Js 7:25].

**61**. – Who were righteous because of piety? [See C. 47.]

<1> Nabouthai the Iezraélite, slandered by Iezabel as having cursed (126b) God and king [3 Rg 21:13].

<2> Zacharias [the high priest], son of (the priest) Iôdaë, stoned between the Temple and the altar by King Iôas, because he urged him not to be impious [2 Par 24:20, 22; Mt 23:35].[1]

**62**. – Who had illicit intercourse?[2]

<1> Lôt had intercourse with his daughters [Gn 19:31].

<2> Roubim, with his father's concubine [35:22; 49:4].

<3> Those in Gabaas of the tribe of Beniamin, with the wife of a Levite, making common use of their host. She died after abuse by them, and because of the crime there was a great slaughter of the people [Jd 19:25-28; 20:21, 25, 35, 46].

<4> Ammôn (Cod.A) violated his virgin sister Thamar and after the insult sent her away from his house [2 Rg 13:14-18].

<5> Abessalôm corrupted the wives of his father to his father's dishonor, on the advice of Achitophel [16:21-22].

---

[1] Joseph follows Matthew in calling Azarias by the name Zacharias, although Joseph avoids the problematic "son of Barachias" of Zch 1:1. It is unclear whether Joseph identifies the Iddo (Addo) of Zch 1:1, 7, etc. with Iôdaë. Azarias the son of Iôdaë is not described as high priest in the Bible (although note the Azarias of 1 Par 6:10) and he is not found in the list of high priests in C. 2 above. However, his father Iôdaë is called "the priest" in 4 Rg 11:9–15 and 2 Par 24:20, and he does appear in the list in C. 2. Presumably Joseph here inferred that the son followed the father in office.

[2] Same heading in Hyginus 253.

ΞΓ'. + Τίνες διώνυμοι γεγόνασι;[1]
‹α'› Ἰωθὼρ[2] ὁ τοῦ Μωϋσέως γαμβρὸς, καὶ Ῥαγουὴλ καὶ Ἰωβάβ κικλήσκεται.

‹β'› Ὁ βασιλεὺς Γὲθ, παρ' ὃν Δαβὶδ φευγὼν[3] κατήγετο.

‹γ'› Ἰώσηππος δέ φησι, Μελχίαν ὀνομάσθαι[4] ὑπὸ τῶν γονέων Μωϋσῆν ἐν τῇ περιτομῇ, ὑπὸ δὲ τῆς ἀναλαβούσης αὐτὸν τῆς τοῦ Φαραὼ θυγατρὸς, Μωϋσέα προσονομάσθαι.[5]

‹δ'› Γεδεὼν ὁ κριτὴς, (127a1) ᾧ αὐτός ἐστιν Ἱεροβαάλ.

‹ε'› Ἀδονίας, ὁ καὶ Ὀρνίας.

‹ς'› Ὀχοζίας, ὁ καὶ Λαζίας.

‹ζ'› Ἡλιακεὶμ, ὁ καὶ Ἰωακείμ.

‹η'› Ἰδιθοὺμ ὁ ψαλτῳδὸς,[6] ὁ καὶ Ἐθάμ.

‹θ'› Χειρὰμ ὁ ἐπὶ τοῦ Σαλομῶνος τὸν ναὸν δειμάμενος, ὁ καὶ Ἐχίας.

‹ι'› Ἔσδρας, ὁ καὶ Σαλαθιήλ.

‹ια'› Ναθανίας, ὃν μετονόμασεν[7] Ναβουχοδονόσορ Σεδεκίαν.

Καὶ ἐν τῇ Νέᾳ·

‹ιβ'› Πέτρος, ὁ καὶ Σίμων καὶ Συμεὼν καὶ Κηφᾶς.

‹ιγ'› Θωμᾶς, ὁ καὶ Δίδυμος.

‹ιδ'› Θαδδαῖος, ὁ καὶ Λεββαῖος καὶ Ἰούδας Ἰακώβου.

‹ιε'› Μάρκος, ὁ καὶ Ἰωάννης.[8]


ΞΔ'. + Τίνες δευτέρῳ ὀνόματι ἐπωνομάσθησαν; (127a2)
‹α'› Ἀβρὰμ ἐπωνομάσθη Ἀβραάμ.

‹β'› Ἰακὼβ, Ἰσραήλ.

‹γ'› Ἰωσὴφ, Κόμφθομ βανήχ.

‹δ'› Ἀνανίας, Σεδράχ.

---

[1] GM γεγονασιν.
[2] Lc M Ἰοθορ.
[3] Lc FGM φυγων.
[4] FGM ὠνομασθαι.
[5] GM προσωνομασθαι.
[6] Lc GM ψαλμῳδος.
[7] Lc FGM μετωνομασεν.
[8] The items in this chapter are not numbered in CFGM.

## <TWO NAMES (63-64)>

**63.** – Who had two names?

<1> Iothor father-in-law of Moses [Ex 3:1] was also called Ragouél [Ex 2:18, Nm 10:29] and Iôbab [Jd 4:11].

<2> The king of Geth, by whom David was harbored when in flight [1 Rg 27:3].

<3> Iôséppos (Josephus) says Moses at his circumcision was named Melchias by his parents,[1] but was called Moses by the daughter of Pharaô who retrieved him.

<4> Gedeôn the judge, (127a) who is the same as Ierobaal [Jd 6:32].

<5> Adonias [1 Par 3:2], also called Ornias [2 Rg 3:4].[2]

<6> Ochozias, also called Lazias [Azia, 4 Rg 11:2, Cod.A].

<7> Éliakeim [Cod.A], also called Iôakeim [1 Par 24:12].

<8> Idithoum the psalm-singer [Ps 38, 61, 76], also called Etham [Aitham, Ps 87:1 Cod.A].

<9> Cheiram, who built the Temple for Solomon, was also named Echias [a second Cheiram, 3 Rg 7:1?].

<10> Esdras, also named Salathiél [2 Es (4 Ezra) 3:1].

<11> Nathanias (Nathanian, LXX mss), whom Nabuchodonosor renamed Sedekia[s] [4 Rg 24:17].

And in the New Testament:

<12> Petros, also called Simôn [Jn 1:42] and Symeôn [Ac 15:14; 2 Pt 1:1] and Képhas [Jn 1:42; contrast C. 137].

<13> Thômas, also called Didymos [Jn 21:2].

<14> Thaddaios [Mt 10:3, Mk 3:18], also called Lebbaios [Cod.D, Old Lat.] and Ioudas the son of Jakôbos [Lk 6:16, Ac 1:13].

<15> Markos, also called Iôannés [Ac 15:37].

**64.** – Who were called by a second name?

<1> Abram was renamed Abraam [Gn 17:5].

<2> Iakôb, Israel [32:28].

<3> Iôséph, Komphthom Banéch [Psonthomphanéch, 41:45 Cod.A].

<4> Ananias, Sedrach.

---

[1] Named Moses, Josephus *Ant.* 2.228 (Ex 2:10); Clement (*Str.* 1.153.1) says that he was first named Joakim and "had a third name (Melchi) in heaven after his assumption, according to the initiates."

[2] GM compare Procopius of Gaza on 3 Rg 1:5 (PG 87, 1148C–D): "Ornia son of Aggeth <and> David: Adônias, for he was two-named."

‹ε'› Ἀζαρίας, Μισάκ.
‹ϲ'› Μισαὴλ, Ἀβδεναγώ.[1]
‹ζ'› Δανιὴλ, Βαλτάσαρ.
‹η'› Πασχὼρ, μέτοικος.
Καὶ ἐν τῇ Νέᾳ·
‹θ'› Σίμων ἐπωνομάσθη Πέτρος.
‹ι'-ια'› Ἰωάννης καὶ Ἰάκωβος οἱ ἀπόστολοι, Βοανεργὲς, ὅ ἐστιν, υἱοὶ Βροντῆς.[2]

## ΒΙΒΛΟΣ Β'.

**ΞΕ'.** + Τίνα ἐστὶ[3] τὰ ἐπὶ τῆς μιᾶς θεότητος παραλαμβανόμενα;
‹α'› Ἄκουε Ἰσραὴλ, Κύριος ὁ Θεός σου, Κύριος εἷς ἐστιν.
‹β'› Ἐγώ εἰμι Κύριος ὁ Θεός σου.
‹γ'› Καὶ γνώτωσαν ὅτι σὺ Κύριος, σὺ[4] μόνος ὕψιστος ἐπὶ πᾶσαν τὴν γῆν.
‹δ'› Καὶ ὁ Κύριός φησιν· Ἵνα γινώσκωσί (127b1) σε τὸν μόνον ἀληθινὸν Θεόν.
‹ε'› Καὶ ἡ κιβωτὸς ἐν ᾗ ὁ Νῶε διεσώθη, εἰς ἕνα πῆχυν συνετελεῖτο.
‹ϲ'-η'› Εἷς ὁ ναὸς, ἐν ᾧ ὁ Θεὸς ἐλατρεύετο, εἷς ὁ νόμος, ἡ κιβωτὸς μία.[5]

**ΞϹ'.** + Τίνα δὲ τὰ ἐπὶ δυαδικῆς ὑποστάσεως;
‹α'› Ποιήσωμεν ἄνθρωπον κατ' εἰκόνα ἡμετέραν, καὶ καθ' ὁμοίωσιν.
‹β'› Ἰδοὺ γέγονεν Ἀδὰμ, ὡς εἷς ἐξ ἡμῶν.
‹γ'› Τί τὸ ὄνομα αὐτοῦ, ἢ τί ὄνομα[6] τῷ υἱῷ αὐτοῦ;
‹δ'› Καὶ ὁ Κύριός φησιν· Ἐγὼ καὶ ὁ Πατὴρ ἕν ἐσμεν, καὶ Ἵνα γινώσκωσί σε τὸν μόνον ἀληθινὸν Θεὸν, καὶ ὃν ἀπέστειλας Ἰησοῦν Χριστὸν εἰς τὸν κόσμον. Καὶ πάλιν· Ἐλευσόμεθα ἐγὼ καὶ ὁ πατὴρ, (127b2) καὶ μονὴν παρ' αὐτῷ ποιησώμεθα.[7]

---

[1] FGM Ἀβδενεγω.
[2] The items in this chapter are not numbered in CFGM.
[3] FGM omit ἐστι.
[4] FGM omit συ.
[5] The items in this chapter are not numbered in CFGM.
[6] Lc FGM ἡ τι το ὄνομα.
[7] Lc FGM ποιησομεθα.

<5> Azarias, Misach [Dan 1:7: Misaél, Misach].

<6> Misaél, Abednego [Azarias, Abednego]

<7> Daniél, Baltasar [Dn 1:7].

<8> Paschôr, *metoikos* (sojourner) [Jer 20:3].

And in the New:

<9> Simôn was renamed Petros [Mt 16:18].

<10-11> The apostles Iôannés and Iakôbos, Boanerges, that is, sons of thunder [Mk 3:17].

## BOOK II

### <THEOLOGICAL MYSTERIES (65-67)>

**65**. – What testimonies are there to the one Deity?

<1> "Hear, Israel, the Lord your God, the Lord is one" [Dt 6:4].

<2> "I am the Lord your God" [Ex 20:5].

<3> "And let them know that thou art the Lord, thou alone art the Most High above all the earth" [Ps 82:18].

<4> And the Lord said, "That they may know (127b) thee the only true God" [Jn 17:3].

<5> And the ark in which Nôé was saved was completed to one cubit [Gn 6:16; see C. 67(6)].

<6-8> One is the Temple in which God was worshipped, one the law, one the ark [i.e., the ark of the covenant].

**66**. – What <testimonies are there to> the dyadic [1] nature (*hypostasis*)?

<1> "Let us make man after our image and after the likeness" [Gn 1:26].

<2> "Behold, Adam has become like one of us" [3:22].

<3> "What is his name? or what is the name of his son?" [Prv 30:4].

<4> And the Lord said, "I and the Father are one" [Jn 10.30] and "that they may know thee the only true God and Jesus Christ whom thou hast sent into the world" [17:3], and again, "We shall come (I and the Father) and make our abode with him" [14:23].

---

[1] Plutarch *Generation of the Soul* 26 (1025C), part of soul.

‹ε'› Ἐν δύο πλαξὶν ὁ νόμος ἐνεγέγραπτο.[1]

‹ς'› Δύο καὶ ἐν τῷ μυστικῷ ᾄσματι τοῦ νυμφίου οἱ μασθοὶ, οἷς ἡ νύμφη τρέφεται, ἐν νόμῳ καὶ ἐν[2] χάριτι.

‹ζ'› Δύο καὶ τῆς νύμφης, τὸ ἱερατικὸν καὶ λαϊκὸν τάγμα.[3]

**ΞΖ'.** + Τίνα τὰ ἐντριαδικῆς[4] παραλαμβανόμενα;

‹α'› Δεῦτε, καταβάντες συγχέωμεν ἐκεῖ τὰς γλώσσας αὐτῶν.

‹β'› Τὸ βάπτισμα τὸ ἐν Τριάδι, εἰς τὸ ὄνομα τοῦ Πατρὸς, καὶ τοῦ Υἱοῦ, καὶ τοῦ Ἁγίου Πνεύματος.

‹γ'› Τρία νοερὰ τάγματα· οὐρανίων, ἀερίων, ἐπιγείων.

‹δ'› Τρεῖς τοῦ παντὸς γένους ἀνθρώπων γενάρχαι· Σὴμ, Χὰμ, Ἰάφεθ.

‹ε'› Τρεῖς οἱ τοῦ λαοῦ **(128a1)** πατριάρχαι· Ἀβρὰμ,[5] Ἰσαὰκ, Ἰακώβ.

‹ς'› Ἡ κιβωτὸς ἐν ᾗΝῶε διεσώζετο, τρεῖς ἀριθμοὺς ἔφερε, τὸν Λ', τὸν Ν', τὸν Τ' καὶ εἰς ἕνα πῆχυν συνεπληροῦτο, ἡ μονὰς ἐν Τριάδι γνωρίζεται.

‹ζ'› Τρεῖς ἄγγελοι τῷ Ἀβραὰμ ὤφθησαν, τὴν ἐπαγγελίαν τοῦ ἐκ στείρας υἱοῦ ποιούμενοι.

‹η'› Τρεῖς ἑορταὶ νόμιμοι, ἐτήσιοι· ἑορτὴ τὸ[6] Φασὲκ, ἑορτὴ τῆς Πεντηκοστῆς, ἑορτὴ τῶν Σκηνοπηγιῶν.

‹θ'› Τριῶν ἀνδρῶν ἡ μαρτυρία ἀληθής ἐστι.

‹ι'› Τρεῖς τὸ Πνεῦμα μαρτυρίας φέρει· περὶ ἀληθείας, καὶ[7] περὶ δικαιοσύνης, καὶ περὶ κρίσεως.

‹ια'› Τρεῖς ὁ Κύριος ἐν Ἅδου πεποίηκεν ἡμέρας,[8] οὗ τύπος ἦν ὁ Ἰωνᾶς.[9] **(128a2)**

---

[1] FGM ἐγγεγραπτο.

[2] FGM omit ἐν.

[3] The items in this chapter are not numbered in CFGM.

[4] Lc FGM τα ἐπι τριαδικης.

[5] Lc FGM Ἀβρααμ.

[6] Lc FGM του.

[7] FGM omit και.

[8] FGM Τρεις ἐν Ἁδου ὁ Κυριος πεποιηται ἡμερας.

[9] The items in this chapter are not numbered in CFGM.

<5> The law was written on two tablets [Ex 31:18].

<6> There are two breasts of the bridegroom in the mystical Song [7:3, 4:5], by which the bride is nourished, the law and grace.

<7> And the two of the bride [8:8] are the priestly and the lay orders.[1]

**67.** – What <testimonies are there to> to the triadic <*hypostasis*>?[2]

<1> "Come let us go down and confuse their speech there" [Gn 11:7].

<2> Baptism in the Trinity (*trias*), in the name of the Father and the Son and the Holy Spirit [Mt 28:19].

<3> Three intelligible ranks (*noera tagmata*): heavenly, aerial, and earthly.

<4> Three common parents of all humanity: Sém, Cham, Japheth [Gn 10:1].

<5> Three are the (128a) patriarchs of the people: Abraam, Isaak, Iakôb [Ex 3:6].

<6> The ark in which Nôé was saved bore three numbers: 30, 50, 300 (300, 50, 30), and was completed to one cubit [Gn 6:15-16; C. 65(5)], the monad in the triad being made evident.

<7> Three angels appeared to Abraam and made him a promise about a son from his sterile wife [Gn 18:2, 19:1].

<8> Three prescribed annual festivals: the feast of Phasek, the feast of Pentecost, the feast of Tabernacles [see C. 126].

<9> The testimony of three men is true [Dt 17:6; Mt 18:16].

<10> The Spirit bears three testimonies: concerning truth, concerning righteousness, and concerning judgment [Jn 16:8].

<11> The Lord spent three days in Hades, of which Iônas was a type [Mt 12:40]. (Continued at C. 128)

---

[1] With these moderate examples of "two" we may compare Irenaeus' investigation of "five" (*Against Heresies* 24,4).

[2] Cf. John of Damascus (PG 94, 1444C) in PGL 1404: *to triadikon tôn hypostaseôn*.

## ‹ΒΙΒΛΟΣ Γ'› [1]

ΞΗ'. + Τίνες εἰσίν οἱ σταθμοὶ τῆς πορείας τοῦ λαοῦ, οἱ ἀπ' Αἰγύπτου;

Τῷ πρώτῳ μηνί, τῇ πέντε καὶ δεκάτῃ τοῦ μηνὸς (οὗτος δέ ἐστιν ὁ παρὰ Μακεδόσι ξανθικὸς), ἀπῆραν ἀπὸ Ῥαμεσσῆ, τῇ ἐπαύριον τοῦ πάσχα, φαγόντες τὸ πρόβατον τὸ Φασὲκ εἰς τὴν Αἴγυπτον.

Πρῶτον τοίνυν σταθμὸν ἦλθον εἰς Σοχώθ.[2]

β' Εἰς Βουθάν.

γ' Εἰς Πηρώθ.

δ' Ἀπέναντι Μαγδόλου.[3]

ε' Ἀπέναντι Ἡρώθ.

ϛ' Διέβησαν τὴν θάλασσαν εἰς τὴν ἔρημον, ὁδὸν τριῶν ἡμερῶν περάσαντες, ἦλθον εἰς Πικρίαν τρίτῃ ἡμέρᾳ τὴν διαίρεσιν τῆς θαλάσσης (128b1) ὁδεύσαντες.

Ἕβδομον σταθμὸν, ἦλθον ἀπὸ τῆς Πικρίας, ἥ ἐστι Μερρὰ πηγὴ, εἰς Ἐλίμ,[4] ἔνθα ηὗρον[5] πηγὰς ιβ', καὶ φοίνικας ο'.

η' Σταθμὸν, ἀπὸ τῆς Ἐλὶμ[6] ἦλθον εἰς θάλασσαν Ἐρυθράν.

θ' Ἀπὸ θαλάσσης Ἐρυθρᾶς εἰς Ῥαφικά.

ι' Εἰς ἄλλην Ἐλίμ.[7]

ια' Εἰς Ῥαφιδίμ.[8] Ἐν τῇ Ῥαφιδὶμ ἐπῆλθεν ὁ Ἀμαλὴκ τῷ λαῷ, καὶ ταῖς ἐπάρσεσι τῶν Μωϋσέως χειρῶν κατεβλήθη.

ιβ' Ἐν τῇ ἐρήμῳ Σινᾷ.

ιγ' Ἐν μνήματι τῆς ἐπιθυμίας, ἔνθα πολλὰ γογγύσαντες, ἐπείπερ εἰς ἀνάμνησιν ἦλθον ὧν ἤσθιον ἄρτων ἐν Αἰγύπτῳ καὶ κρεῶν, κατεβόων (128b2)

---

[1] This book division is not noted in CFGM. In C, the words ΒΙΒΛΟΣ Β' appear before the beginning of C. 65, and then no further book division is noted until after the heading to C. 69, where the words ΒΙΒΛΟΣ Δ' appear. The lack of a reference to a Book III points clearly to a significant gap in the text. While the lacuna might be construed to lie between Chapters 68 and 69, the subject matter of the surrounding chapters makes a gap between Chapters 67 and 68 more likely. It is the editors' conjecture that a number of chapters originally contained between Chapters 67 and 68 have fallen out, including all but the last chapter of the third book.

[2] *Lc* FGM Σοκχωθ.

[3] *Lc* FGM Μαγδωλου.

[4] *Lc* FGM Ἐλειμ.

[5] FGM εὑρον.

[6] *Lc* FGM Ἐλειμ.

[7] *Lc* FGM Ἐλειμ.

[8] F Ῥαφιδιμ, ὅπου ἐπῆλθεν; GM Ῥαφιδειμ, ὅπου ἐπῆλθεν.

## <BOOK III>

### <EXODUS STATIONS (68) (from C. 36)>

**68.** – What are the stations of the people on the way from Egypt?

In the first month and the fifteenth day of the month [Nm 33:3] (For the Macedonians this is Xanthikos [C. 27,1].), they departed from Ramessé, on the day after the Pascha, after they ate the sheep, the Phasek, in Egypt.

For the first station, then, they came to Sokchôth.

2. To Bouthan

3. To Pérôth

4. Opposite Magdôlou

5. Opposite Hérôth

6. They crossed the sea into the desert, making a three-days' journey. They came to the bitter <waters> on the third day (128b) after crossing the divided sea.

The 7th station. They came from the bitter <waters>, which is the spring of Merra, to Eleim, where they found twelve springs and seventy palm trees [Nm 33:9].

The 8th station. From Eleim they came to the Red Sea.

9. From the Red Sea to Raphika

10. To another Eleim.

11. To Raphideim. In Raphideim Amalek attacked the people and was cast down by the raising of Moses' hands.

12. In the Sinai desert [33:15].

13. At the Monument<s> of Lust, where many grumbled, since they remembered the bread and meat they were accustomed to eat in Egypt. They

τοῦ Μωϋσέως, τοῦ μάννα τοῦ ἐξ οὐρανοῦ νειφομένου[1] βρώματος τὴν ὑπόσχεσιν ἐκομήσαντο.[2] Ἀπὸ τοῦ τῆς ἐπιθυμίας μνήματος, Τεσσαρισκαιδέκατον σταθμὸν ἦλθον εἰς Ἀσηρώθ.

ιε' Εἰς Ῥαθαμά.[3]
ις' Εἰς Ῥεμμωφερές.
ιζ' Εἰς Ἐλβῶνα.
ιη' Εἰς Δεσελέθ.
ιθ' Εἰς Μακελάθ.[4]
κ' Εἰς Σαφάρ.
Ἐικοστὸν πρῶτον σταθμὸν εἰς Χαραδάθ.[5]
κβ' Εἰς Μακελώθ.
κγ' Εἰς Χαττοάθ.
κδ' Εἰς Ταράθ.
κε' Εἰς Ματγεκά.
κς' Εἰς Σελμῶνα.
κζ' Εἰς Μασουρούθ.
κη' Εἰς Βάμεθ.[6]
κθ' Εἰς τὸ ὄρος Γαλαάδ.
λ' Εἰς Σεγεβαθά.[7]
λα' Εἰς Σεβρωνά.
λβ' Εἰς Γεσιῶν γαβέρ.
λγ' Ἐν (129a1) μηνὶ τρίτῳ ἀπὸ τῆς ἐξόδου, ἐν τῇ ἐρήμῳ Σινᾷ. Ἐνταῦθα Ἰωθὼρ[8] ὁ Μωϋσέως γαμβρὸς παραγίνεται πρὸς αὐτὸν, ἄγων αὐτῷ τὴν γυναῖκα αὐτοῦ[9] καὶ τοὺς υἱούς. Ἐνταῦθα Θεοῦ ἐπιφάνεια πρὸς Μωϋσῆν, καὶ διδασκαλία πρὸς τὸν λαὸν καὶ νουθεσία, καὶ τοῦ λαοῦ δυσσέβεια ἐπὶ τῇ μοσχοθεσίᾳ.[10] Ἐπεὶ δὲ δυσσεβείαις τιμωρούμενος ὁ λαὸς πρὸς τὸ μὴ ἐπιβῆναι τῇ γῇ τῆς ἐπαγγελίας, περιείλετο κατὰ τὴν ἔρημον πλανώμενος.

---

[1] GM νιφομένου.
[2] Lc FGM ἐκομισαντο.
[3] Lc FGM Ῥαμαθα.
[4] FGM have Εἰς Εἰσμακελαθ by dittography.
[5] FGM κα' Εἰς Χαραδαθ.
[6] Lc FGM Βαβεθ.
[7] Lc FGM Σεναβαθα.
[8] Lc M Ἰοθορ.
[9] FGM omit αὐτου.
[10] Lc FGM μοσχοθυσια.

shouted against Moses and obtained the promise of the manna falling like snow from heaven.

From the Monument<s> of Lust they came to the 14th station at Asérôth [33:17].

15. To Ramatha.
16. To Remmôpheres.
17. To Elbôna.
18. To Deseleth.
19. To Makelath.
20. To Saphar.

The twenty-first station to Charadath.

22. To Makelôth.
23. To Chattoath.
24. To Tarath.
25. To Matgeka.
26. To Selmôna.
27. To Masourouth.
28. To Babeth.
29. To the mountain of Galaad.
30. To Senabatha.
31. To Sebrôna.
32. To Gesiôn Gaber.

33. In the (129a) third month after the Exodus, in the desert of Sinai. There Iothor the father-in-law of Moses came to him, bringing his wife and children. There, the epiphany of God to Moses and teaching and warning to the people, and the impiety of the people with the worship of the calf. Because of the impiety the populace was punished so that it did not enter the land of promise, but wandered about in the desert.

Καὶ τριακοστὸν τέταρτον σταθμὸν εἰς τὴν ἔρημον Φαγὰν κατήγετο, ἥ ἐστι Κάδης.[1]

λε΄ Ἀπὸ Κάδης, εἰς τὸ ὄρος πλησίον[2] τῆς (129a2) Ἐδώμ. Ὧδε ἀποθνήσκει Ἀαρὼν, ἐν ἔτει τεσσαρακοστῷ τῆς ἐξόδου ἀπὸ Αἰγύπτου τοῦ λαοῦ, τῷ πέμπτῳ μηνὶ (ὅ[3] ἐστι παρὰ Μακεδόσι Λῶος) μιᾷ τοῦ μηνὸς, ἦν δὲ ἐτῶν ρκγ΄.

‹λϛ›[4] Ἀπὸ Ὢρ τοῦ ὄρους, τριακοστὸν ἕκτον σταθμὸν, ἦλθον εἰς Ἐλμῶνα.

λζ΄ Εἰς Φινώ.

λη΄ Εἰς Ὠβώθ.

λθ΄ Εἰς Γαὶ, ἐπὶ τῶν ὁρίων Μωάβ. Ἐν τούτοις τοῖς ὁρίοις τῶν Μωαβιτῶν βασιλεὺς[5] καλεῖ τὸν μάγον τὸν Βαλαὰμ, καταράσασθαι τὸν λαόν. ‹Τεσ›σαρακοστὸν σταθμὸν,[6] ἀπὸ τοῦ Μωάβ, τιμωρηθεὶς ἐπὶ τῷ τελεσθῆναι τὸ[7] Βεελφεγὼρ, ἦλθον εἰς Ζαρέθ.

μα΄ Εἰς σο (129b1)περὰν[8] Ἀρνών.

μβ΄ Εἰς Φρέαρ.

μγ΄ Εἰς Δεβωγγάδ.[9]

μδ΄ Εἰς Γαιμῶν Δεβλαθέμ.

με΄ Εἰς τὰ ὄρη τὰ Ἀμωρῆ, ἀπέναντι Ναβαῦ.

μϛ΄ Ἐπὶ δυσμῶν Μωάβ, κατὰ Ἱεριχώ.

μζ΄ Ἐπὶ τὸν Ἰορδάνην, ἀναμέσον Σιμὼθ ἕως Μελσὰτ, τὸ κατὰ δυσμάς. Ἐνταῦθα Μωϋσῆς κατέληξε, καὶ τὸ Δευτερονόμιον γράψας πέραν τοῦ Ἰορδάνου ἐν τῇ ἐρήμῳ πρὸς δυσμὰς, κατέλεξε τῷ λαῷ, ἐν ἔτει τεσσαρακοστῷ τῆς ἐξόδου, ἐν τῷ[10] ἑνδεκάτῳ μηνὶ (οὗτος δέ ἐστι Δύστρος[11] κατὰ Μακεδόνας[12]), νεομηνία τοῦ μηνός. Καὶ κελευσθεὶς

---

[1] GM Καδες.
[2] FGM omit πλησιον.
[3] FGM ὅς.
[4] This item is not numbered in CF.
[5] FGM ὁ βασιλευς των Μωαβιτων.
[6] The omission of the initial part of the word is due to scribal carelessness, but the restoration is obvious. FGM have μ΄ Σταθμον.
[7] Lc FGM τῳ.
[8] In their notes GM rightly suggest emending to το περαν.
[9] Lc FGM Δεββωγαδ.
[10] FGM omit ἐν τῳ.
[11] GM Διστρος.
[12] FGM παρα Μακεδοσι.

And the 34th station. <The populace> was led down to the desert of Phagan, which is Kadés.

35. From Kadés to the mountain near Edom, where Aaron dies, in the fortieth year from the exodus of the people from Egypt, in the fifth month (It is Lôos according to the Macedonians [C. 27,5].), on the first day of the month, being 123 years old [Nm 33:38-39].

36. From Mount Ôr, the thirty-sixth station, they came to Elmôna [Nm 33:41].

37. To Phinô.

38. To Ôbôth.

39. To Gai in the regions of Môab. In these regions the king of the Môabites summons the magician Balaam to curse the people.

The fortieth station, from Môab, when the people had been punished for being initiated to Beelphegôr [Nm 25], they came to Zareth.

41. To the region (129b) beyond Arnôn.

42. To Phrear.

43. To Debbôgad.

44. To Gaimôn Deblathem.

45. To the Amorite mountains opposite Nabau.

46. To the west, Moab by Jericho.

47. By the Jordan between Simôth as far as Melsat to the west [Nm 33:1-49]. There Moses stopped and after writing Deuteronomy [Dt 31:24] across the Jordan in the western desert, he read it before the people, in the fortieth year from the Exodus from Egypt, the eleventh [twelfth] month (This is Dystros according to the Macedonians), on the new moon of the month. After being

ἀνελθεῖν ἐπὶ τῇ κορυφῇ (129b2) τοῦ ὄρους Φασγᾶ, καὶ θεάσασθαι πᾶσαν τὴν τῆς ἐπαγγελίας γῆν πόρρωθεν, ἐκεῖ γενόμενος ἐτῶν ἑκατὸν εἴκοσι τελευτᾷ.

‹ΒΙΒΛΟΣ Δ'.›

**ΞΘ'.** + Τίνα ἐστὶν ἃ τεθέαται Μωϋσῆς[1] θαυμάσια καὶ δι' αὐτοῦ κατέργασται;[2] [ΒΙΒΛΟΣ Δ'.][3]

‹α'› Ἐν τῷ Σινᾷ ὄρει τὴν βάτον ὁρᾷ καιομένην, ἀλλὰ χλοάζουσαν καὶ μὴ κατακαιομένην.

‹β'› Σημεῖον αἰτήσας παρασχεῖν τὴν[4] εἰς τὴν Αἴγυπτον αὐτοῦ ἀποστολῆς, τὴν ῥάβδον τὴν ποιμενικὴν ῥίπτειν ἐκελεύετο, ‹ἢ μετέβαλεν εἰς ὄφιν›[5] καὶ πάλιν τὸν ὄφιν ἀπὸ τῆς κέρκου δραξάμενος, εἰς ῥάβδον ἐπανῆγε.

‹γ'› Τὴν χεῖρα ἀποκρύπτειν εἰς τὸν κόλπον (130a1) κελευόμενος, λευκὴν ὡσεὶ χιὼν καὶ παρηλλαγμένην ἐξήγαγε, καὶ πάλιν ἀποκρύψας αὐτὴν, εἰς τὸ κατὰ φύσιν ἀποκαταστᾶσαν ἐπανήγαγε.[6]

‹δ'› Κατιὼν ἐπὶ τὴν προτεθεῖσαν αὐτῷ λειτουργίαν εἰς τὴν Αἴγυπτον, ἀγγέλῳ περιτυχὼν ἀπεπνίγετο, ἀλλ' ἡ γυνὴ γνοῦσα, τὸν ἄγγελον ἐξευμενισαμένη· Νυμφίος σύ μοι δι' αἱμάτων, αὐτῷ φήσασα, τῆς ἐπιθέσεως ἀπεῖρξε.

‹ε'› Κατελθὼν εἰς τὴν Αἴγυπτον, τὸ δαμαζόμενον τοῦ λαοῦ πλῆθος ὑπὸ τῇ τῶν Αἰγυπτίων δουλαγωγίᾳ παρεμυθήσατο, ὡς ὑπὸ Θεοῦ ἦ[7] ἀπεσταλμένος τὴν ἐλευθερίαν αὐτοῖς πωρίσασθαι.[8] (130a2) Καὶ τῷ βασιλεῖ ἀπειθοῦντι συγχωρεῖν τὸν λαὸν ἐπὶ Θεοῦ λατρείαν ἐξιέναι, τὰς δὲ κατὰ πληγὰς[9] ἐπήγαγε, τοῦ λαοῦ συνιόντος[10] τοῖς Αἰγυπτίοις, καὶ μηδὲν ἐκ τῶν πληγῶν διὰ τὴν συνουσίαν ὑφισταμένου.

Πρώτη μὲν γάρ πληγῇ τὰ Αἰγύπτου ὕδατα εἰς αἵματα μετέβαλε, καὶ πάλιν παρακληθεὶς ἀντεκαθίστη.

‹β'› Πληγῇ βατράχων πλήθει τὴν ἄπασαν Αἴγυπτον ἐπλήρου.

---

[1]FGM ὁ Μωϋσῆς.
[2]GM κατειργασται.
[3]Emend to locate ΒΙΒΛΟΣ Δ' immediately before C. 69.
[4]Lc FGM της.
[5]Conjectural emendation; the context makes clear that something has fallen out.
[6]GM ἐπανηγαγεν.
[7]FGM εἴη.
[8]Lc FGM πορισασθαι.
[9]Lc FGM τας δεκα πληγας.
[10]Lc FGM συνοντος.

ordered to go up to the top of Mount Phasga and view the whole land of promise from afar, he died there in the 120th year of his age [Dt 34:7].

## <BOOK IV>

### <WONDERS AND PREDICTIONS IN ISRAEL><69-96>

**69**. – What wonders did Moses see and what wonders were effected through him? [BOOK IV]

<1> On Mount Sinai (Horeb) he saw the bush burning but budding and not burned up [Ex 3:2].

<2> When he asked for a sign of his divine mission in Egypt, he was ordered to cast down the pastoral rod, <which became a serpent,> and again catching the serpent by the tail he turned it back into a rod [4:1-5].

<3> Ordered to conceal his hand in his bosom, (130a) he brought it forth white as snow and altered; and when he hid it again he brought it forth restored to its natural state [4:6-7].

<4> Proceeding to Egypt to the task imposed on him, he was choked by an angel whom he encountered, but his wife knew about it and propitiated the angel; saying to Moses, "Surely you are a bridegroom through blood," she saved him from the attack [4:24-26].

<5> When he went down to Egypt, he informed the multitude of the people oppressed in slavery to the Egyptians that he had been sent by God to provide liberation for them. And he brought the ten plagues upon the king, who would not let the people go for the worship of God. The people mingled with the Egyptians but suffered no harm from the plagues in spite of their association.

In the first plague he turned the waters of Egypt into blood [7:20], and again when asked restored them. [1]

<b> In the second plague he filled all Egypt with a swarm of frogs [8:6].

---

[1] Not in Exodus or Josephus *Ant.* 2.295.

‹γ'› Ἐπεὶ δὴ[1] καὶ τούτους εἰπών, συνήγαγε[2] σκνιπῶν[3] ἄπλετον γένος, τὸν ἀέρα τῆς Αἰγύπτου συνεμέστωσε.

‹δ'› Κυνόμυιάν τε ἐπὶ τούτοις τὴν ἀναισχυντοτάτην (130b1) ἐπέφερε τοῖς Αἰγυπτίοις, οὐκ[4] ἐνδιδόντων τὸν λαὸν εἰς τὴν τοῦ Θεοῦ λατρείαν προελθεῖν.

‹ε'› Εἰργάσατο ‹.......›[5]

‹ζ'› Ἐπὶ δὲ τούτοις, χάλαζαν ἐπήγαγεν ἀναιροῦσαν ἅπερ ὕπεθρα[6] κατελαμβάνετο.

‹η'› Ἔπειτα ἀκρίδων νέφη,[7] τοὺς καρποὺς ἅπαντας καταλώσασα.[8]

‹θ'› Σκότος τε μόνους σκοτίζων[9] τοὺς Αἰγυπτίους, τοῖς Ἑβραίοις οὐ μελαινόμενον.

Δεκάτην δὲ καὶ τελευταίαν ἐπέρριψεν αὐτοῖς πληγήν, τὸν τῶν πρωτοτόκων, ἀθρόον ὑπὸ μίαν καιροῦ ῥοπὴν θάνατον.

‹ς'› Μετὰ δὲ τὴν ἔξοδον τοῦ λαοῦ τὴν ἐπ' Αἰγύπτου,[10] ἐπιδιώκοντος αὐτὸν τοῦ Αἰγυπτίου (130b2) στρατοῦ, τὴν Ἐρυθρὰν διεῖλε[11] θάλασσαν εἰς δίοδον τοῦ λαοῦ, καὶ πάλιν ἐπήγαγε[12] ταύτην κατὰ τοῦ διώκοντος βασιλέως, ὃν ἐπεκάλυψε τῷ τῆς θαλάσσης βυθῷ, πλήξας ῥάβδῳ τὴν θάλασσαν,[13] ὥσπερ αὐτὴν εἰς τὴν τοῦ λαοῦ δίοδον καὶ πρότερον ἔπληξε.

‹ζ'› Τὸ πικρὸν ὕδωρ Μερρᾶς τῆς πηγῆς μετέβαλεν εἰς νᾶμα[14] πότιμον, ξύλον βάψας ἐν αὐτῇ, ὥσπερ δὴ καὶ ἐκελεύετο. Μάννα προεῖπεν[15] ὕειν τὸν

---

[1]FGM δε.

[2]FGM τουτοις απειπον συναγαγων; lege τουτους απειπων συνηγαγε.

[3]FGM print σκιπων; in their notes FG suggest κνιπων. Lege σκνιφων, following Ex 8:16.

[4]FGM Αἰγυπτιοις, ἤν, οὐκ.

[5]The accounts of the fifth and sixth plagues have fallen out, but one word may remain. In C Εἰργάσατο is presented as part of the preceding sentence, but there it appears to be superfluous.

[6]Lc FGM ὑπαιθρα.

[7]Emend to νεφελη?

[8]FGM καταναλωσασαι. Emend to καταλυσασα or καταναλωσασα.

[9]Lc FGM σκοτιζον.

[10]Lc FGM ἀπ' Αἰγυπτου.

[11]GM διειλεν.

[12]GM ἐπηγαγεν.

[13]FGM την θαλασσαν ραβδω.

[14]FGM εἰς ναμα μετεβαλε.

[15]GM προειπε.

<c> Since they disobeyed these signs, he brought a huge swarm of gnats and filled the air of Egypt [8:17].

<d> After this (130b) he brought the most shameless dog fly [LXX 8:21] upon the Egyptians, when they did not let the people go forth to the worship of God [8:24,31].

<e> He did <. . . . . .>[1]

<g> Next he brought hail, which destroyed whatever happened to be outside [9:23].

<h> Then clouds of locusts, which consumed all the fruits [10:12].

<i> Darkness, which darkened only the Egyptians and was not black for the Hebrews [10:22-23].

Tenth and last, he cast a plague on them, the simultaneous and widespread death of the first-born [12:29].

<6> After the exodus of the people from Egypt, when the Egyptian army was in pursuit he divided the Red Sea for the passage of the people and again brought it back against the pursuing king, whom he covered in the depth of the sea, smiting the sea with the rod, as he smote it before for the passage of the people [14].

<7> He changed the bitter water of the spring Merra into a flowing river by dipping a piece of wood in it, as he was ordered [15:25]. He predicted that God

---

[1] Here the 5th plague on livestock (9:6) and the 6th plague of boils (9:10) have dropped out. Josephus *Ant.* 2.303 replaces flies with "beasts" and also omits the plague on livestock.

Θεὸν εἰς τὴν ἐρήμῳ τοῦ λαοῦ διατροφὴν,[1] καὶ οὕτως ἐγίνετο. Ὀρτυγομήτραν καθήπτασθαι[2] προειπὼν, **(131a1)** ἐπιθυμήσαντος κρέα φαγεῖν τοῦ λαοῦ, εἰς θεογνωσίαν τὸν λαὸν ἐπαιδαγώγει. Ἐκ ξηρᾶς πέτρας ῥάβδῳ πληγείσης, ποταμίων ὑδάτων ἀθρόον ῥύσιν προίκατο.[3] ‹η'› Χειρῶν ἐκτάσει πολέμου νίκην κατὰ τοῦ ἐπελθόντος στρατοῦ τῷ λαῷ τοῦ Ἀμαλὴκ[4] εἰργάσατο.

‹θ'› Νόμον ἐδόξατο[5] παρὰ Θεοῦ ἐν διπτύχῳ γραφέντα πλακὶ τεσσαράκοντα νηστεύσας ἡμέρας. Καὶ πάλιν διὰ τὴν τοῦ λαοῦ δυσσέβειαν, τὰς θεογράπτους συντρίψας πλάκας, δεύτερον ἐπιβὰς τῷ Σινᾷ ὄρει, καὶ νηστεύσας ὁμοίως ἄλλας ἡμέρας τεσσαράκοντα, τὸν νόμον **(131a2)** ἐν αἷς ἀνεκόμισε λαξεύσας πλαξὶν, ἀνενεώσατο. Τὸ πρόσωπον κατέβη δεδοξασμένος, ὡς μήτε τὸν λαὸν ἐνορᾶν αὐτῷ δύνασθαι. Καὶ αὐτὸς δὲ ἐνομοθέτησε πᾶσι δικαιώμασι[6] τοῦ λαοῦ γεγένηται. Θείας ὀπτασίας παρὰ πάντας τοὺς προφήτας ἠξίωται.

Τῆς νοερᾶς οὐσίας θαυμαστοὺς χαρακτῆρας ἐθεασάτο, πρὸς οὓς τὴν ἱερὰν σκηνὴν κατασκευάζειν ἐκελεύετο. Τὴν ἱερὰν σκηνὴν ἀντίτυπον τῆς νοερᾶς κατεσκεύασεν οὐσίας.

Τὸ ἱερὸν χρίσμα, ἐν ᾧ τὴν ἱερωσύνην καθεσθεὶς, συνέθηκεν. **(131b1)** Ἀρχιερέας ἀπέδειξε τὸν ἀδελφὸν Ἀαρὼν καὶ τοὺς τούτου παῖδας, δι' οὗ κατεσκεύασται[7] χρίσματος. Τὴν ἱερὰν σκηνὴν καὶ πάντα τὰ ἐν αὐτῇ τῷ ἁγίῳ χρίσματι χρίσας ἡγίασε.

‹ι'› Σάββατον αὐτὸς πρῶτος ὡρίσατο, δείξας αὐτὸ, διὰ τῆς διπλῆς ἐκλογῆς τοῦ μάννα, καὶ τῆς ἀσήπτου διαμονῆς αὐτοῦ, οὐ πρότερον ἐγνωσμένον. Τρεῖς νομίμους ἑορτὰς τῷ λαῷ παρέδωκε τοῦ ἐνιαυτοῦ τῷ Θεῷ[8] ἑορτάζειν. Τοὺς μοσχοποιήσαντας ἐτιμωρήσατο διὰ τῶν προσδεδραμηκότων αὐτῷ, τρισχιλίους τοὺς ἀνεπιστρέπτους ἀποκτείνας.

Τὸν λαὸν ἐνομοθέτησεν. **(131b2)** Ἀπηρίθμησε καὶ τοὺς Λευίτας ἀπ' αὐτῶν διελών. Περὶ θυσιῶν αὐτοῖς διετάξατο, καὶ ἀπάρεως τῆς ἱερᾶς σκιμῆς, καὶ πορείας εὐτάκτου. Πῦρ ἐπὶ τὸ θυσιαστήριον κατὰ τὴν πρώτην πρόοδον ἐξ οὐρανοῦ καταβιβαζόμενον ἔδειξεν, ὃ καὶ διέμεινεν ἄσβεστον.

---

[1] Lc FGM ἐν τη ἐρημω εἰς την του λαου διατροφην.
[2] Lc FGM καθιπτασθαι.
[3] Lc GM προηκατο.
[4] Lc FGM στρατου του Ἀμαληκ, τω λαω.
[5] Lc FGM ἐδεξατο.
[6] Lc FGM νομοθετης ἐπι πασι τοις δικαιωμασι.
[7] Lc FGM κατεσκευασε.
[8] FGM omit τω Θεω.

would rain[1] manna in the desert for feeding the people, and thus it happened [16:15]. (131a) By predicting that quail would fly down since the people wanted meat to eat, he instructed the people in the knowledge of God [16:13]. Striking a dry rock with his rod, he produced a great flow of river water [17:6].

<8> By stretching out his hands he won victory in war for the people against the oncoming army of Amalek [17:11].

<9> He received the law from God written on two tablets [31:18], after fasting forty days. And again after breaking the tablets written by God because of the people's impiety, he went up Mount Sinai a second time and after fasting in the same manner another forty days, he renewed the law on the tablets of stone he had taken with him [34:4]. He came down with such a radiant face that the people could not look at him [34:29-30; 2 Cor 3:7]. He was the legislator for all the laws of the people. He was worthy of more divine visions than all the prophets.

He beheld the marvelous characters of the spiritual substance, after which he was ordered to construct the sacred tabernacle. He constructed the sacred tabernacle as a copy of the spiritual substance.[2]

He made the sacred chrism (C. 28) by which he instituted the priesthood. (131b) He appointed as high priests his brother Aaron and his sons, through whom he made the chrism [Ex 28:41]. He consecrated the sacred tabernacle and everything in it, anointing it with the holy chrism [30:22-33].

<10> He was the first to institute the Sabbath, previously unknown, pointing to it through the double collection of the manna and its preservation without spoiling [Ex 16:23-24]. He provided the people with three lawful festivals to celebrate for God each year (C. 67, 126). He punished those who made the calf through those who ran to him, killing three thousand of the obstinate [Ex 32:28].

He legislated for the people. He counted the Levites separately from them. He made arrangements for them about sacrifices and the departure of the sacred tabernacle and an orderly march. He showed them fire descending from heaven on the altar at the first advance [Lv 9:24] and remaining inextinguished. He

---

[1] *Huein ton theon*; see Index B.

[2] See Philo *Life of Moses* 2.74–76 for Moses' vision of "the incorporeal ideas of future objects." *Noera ousia*: see Index B.

Τοὺς προσαγαγόντας οὐκ ἐκ τούτου πυρὸς, Ναβὰδ[1] καὶ Ἀβιοὺδ τοὺς ἀρχιερεῖς, θεηλάτῳ πληγῇ καταπεσόντας ἀπέδειξε. ‹ια'› Καθαρῶν καὶ μὴ καθαρῶν ζώων διάκρισιν ἐποιήσατο. Ὑπὲρ ἁμαρτιῶν λύσεως τὰς ἀφορισμένας[2] θυσίας ἐπήταξε[3] δεῖν προσάγεσθαι. (132a1) Λεπρῶν καὶ ἀναπήρων διακρίσεις ἀπὸ τῆς ἱερᾶς συναγωγῆς ὑπέδειξε, καὶ περὶ καθάρσεως αὐτῶν τίνα προσάγεσθαι καὶ ὅπως χρὴ διετάξατο. ‹ιβ'› Τοὺς Ἀμορραίους ἀναιμωτὶ κατελθὼν, τὴν γῆν αὐτῶν ταῖς δύο φυλαῖς τῇ τοῦ Ῥουβὶμ καὶ τῇ τοῦ Γὰδ[4] ἀπένειμεν εἰς κλήρους. Τὸν τῶν Μαδιανιτῶν ἀνεῖλε βασιλέα, καὶ τὸν μάντην[5] βαλαὰμ κακοσύμβουλον αὐτῷ κατὰ τοῦ λαοῦ γενόμενον. Τοὺς τελεσθέντας τῷ Βεελφεγὼρ ἐκ τοῦ λαοῦ δισμυρίους τετρακισχιλίους ἀναιρεθησομένους προεῖπε. Σημεῖον καὶ (131a2) τύπον τοῦ σωτηρίον σταυροῦ τοῦ Κύριου[6] ἐν ᾧπερ ἀνέστησεν ὄφει χαλκῷ προκατεβάλετο, ᾧ προσέχοντες οἱ δακνόμενοι ὑπὸ τῶν ὄφεων οὐκ ἀπόλλυντο.[7]

‹ιγ'› Πέντε βίβλους τῷ λαῷ συνέταξεν, εἴς τε μελέτην διηνεκῆ καὶ διδασκαλίαν λόγων ἱερῶν, καὶ μνήμην τῶν ὑπὲρ αὐτῶν καὶ εἰς αὐτοὺς γεγενημένων, καὶ προφητείαν τῶν ἐπιόντων αὐτοῖς δεινῶν, ῥαθυμίαν[8] τε ἀπὸ τῆς εὐσεβείας, καὶ ἀποκλίσει τῇ ἐπὶ δυσσέβειαν, κατέλιπεν. Ἀλλὰ καὶ ᾠδὴν αὐτοῖς, μετὰ τὴν ἐπὶ τὴν διὰ θαλάσσης σωτηρίαν καταλεχθεῖσαν, ἑτέραν ᾖσεν, (132b1) ὡς τὰ ἔθνη προτιμηθήσεται αὐτῶν δυσσεβησάντων, τὰ πρότερα ἀσύνετα, καὶ ὑπὸ Θεοῦ προσληφθήσεται πρὸς παροργισμὸν αὐτῶν, τῶν ἐπὶ ταῖς πολλαῖς εἰδωλολατρείαις παροργισάντων τὸν Θεόν. Ἔστι δὲ τὰ πέντε αὐτοῦ βιβλία Γένεσις, Ἔξοδος, Λευϊτικὸν, Ἀριθμοὶ, Δευτερονόμιον.[9]

---

[1] *Lc* GM Ναδαβ.

[2] GM ἀφωρισμενας.

[3] *Lc* FGM ἐπεταξε.

[4] GM ταις δυο φυλαις του Ῥουβιν και του Γαδ.

[5] *Lc* FGM μαντιν.

[6] FGM omit του Κυριου.

[7] *Lc* GM ἀπωλλυντο.

[8] FGM ῥᾳθυμιᾳ.

[9] With the exceptions of the first, second (which is not numbered in C), and tenth plagues, the items in this chapter are not numbered in CFGM.

showed that those who did not offer with this fire, the priests Nadab and Abioud, were killed by a divine blow [10:1-2].

<11> He made a distinction between clean and unclean animals [11]. He gave orders for offering the appointed sacrifices for the remission of sins. (132a) He prescribed the separation of lepers and cripples from the sacred assembly, and prescribed certain offerings for their cleansing.

<12> Overcoming the Amorites without bloodshed,[1] he allotted their land to the two tribes of Roubin and Gad. He killed the king of the Madianites as well as the seer Balaam who gave him bad counsel against the people. He foretold that the 24,000 of the people who were initiated to Beelphegôr would be killed [Nm 25:9]. He set forth a sign and example of the salvific cross of the Lord in the bronze serpent he raised, at which those bitten by snakes looked and did not perish [Nm 21:9; Jn 3:14].

<13> He composed five books for the people and left them for constant meditation and the teaching of sacred words and the memorial of what things were done for them and to them, and for prediction of the penalties coming upon them and their neglect of piety and inclination to impiety. But beyond the ode recited upon their escape through the sea [Ex 15] he sang another [Dt 32], that if they were impious (132b) the gentiles would be preferred, formerly ignorant but taken up by God to anger those who frequented idols and angered God. His five books are Genesis, Exodus, Leviticus, Numbers, Deuteronomy.

---

[1] This contradicts Nm 21:23 (Dt 29:7).

Ο΄. + Τίνα ἐστὶ¹ τά διὰ Ἰησοῦ τοῦ Ναυῆ ἐπιτελεσθέντα σημεῖα, καὶ δι᾽ αὐτοῦ τῷ λαῷ κατεργασθέντα θαύματα;

‹α᾽› Τὸν Ἰορδάνην ποταμὸν, εἰς τὸ παρελθεῖν τὸν λαὸν ἐπὶ τὴν τῆς ἐπαγγελίας γῆν, (132b2) διέλε.

‹β᾽› Δώδεκα λίθους, κατὰ ἀριθμὸν τῶν δώδεκα φυλῶν, ἐκ τοῦ ποταμοῦ ἀνακομισθῆναι μεγάλους ἐκέλευσεν,² εἰς μνημόσυνον ἀποτεθειμένους τῷ λαῷ τῆς πορείας αὐτοῦ, τῆς διὰ τοῦ ξηροῦ γενομένου ποταμοῦ.³

‹γ᾽› Τὰς ἑξήκοντα μυριάδας τοῦ λαοῦ πετρίναις περιέτεμε μαχαίραις.

‹δ᾽› Τὰ ἐν Ἱεριχὼ τείχη σαλπίγγων ἠχῇ κατεστρέψατο.

‹ε᾽› Τὸν ἱεροσυλήσαντα Ἀχαραῖον, ὁ λαὸς⁴ ἡττᾶτο, κληρωτὸν ἀνεύρηκε, καὶ λιθόλευστον ἀνεῖλε.

‹ϛ᾽› Τὰς πόλεις τῶν ἐθνῶν, καὶ τοὺς βασιλεῖς αὐτῶν ἀναιμωτὶ παρείληφεν. (133a1) Ὑπὲρ Γαβαωνιτῶν, τῶν αὐτομόλων τῷ λαῷ γεγονότων, πολεμῶν, εἰς τελείαν νίκην τὴν ὑπὲρ αὐτῶν τὸν ἡλίου δρόμον ἔστησε.

Ταῖς φυλαῖς κατὰ κλήρους αὐτῶν τὴν γῆν, ἣν παρειλήφει παρὰ τῶν ἐθνῶν, κατένειμε. Τῷ πιστοτάτῳ Χαλὲβ τῷ τοῦ Ἰεφωνῆ, τὸν ἄξιον αὐτοῦ κλῆρον ἀπένειμε. Τὴν Ῥαὰβ, τὴν τοὺς κατασκόπους δεξαμένην, ἐτίμησε, τῷ λαῷ συγκατατάξας αὐτήν. Τοῖς ἱερεῦσι καὶ τοῖς Λευΐταις τὰς πόλεις καὶ τὰ προήστεια⁵ ἀποδέδωκε. Τὰς φυγαδευτηρίους ἓξ πόλεις ἀπέδειξε, (133a2) πάντα κατορθώσας κατὰ τοῦ⁶ Μωυσέως⁷ ὑποθήκας. Ἀπολύων τὸν λαὸν ἐπὶ τοὺς κλήρους, οὓς κατένειμεν αὐτὸς, λίθον ἔστησεν εἰς μαρτύριον τῶν ἐπ᾽ αὐτοῦ⁸ λεγομένων αὐτοῖς, ὡς ἀληθῆ εἴη. Ἃ δὲ ἦν, ὡς μετ᾽ αὐτὸν καταλείψουσι τὸν σωτῆρα καὶ προστάτην αὐτῶν γενόμενον Θεόν, καὶ τοῖς τῶν ἐθνῶν εἰδώλοις προστεθήσονται, ὅθεν καὶ αὐτοὶ παραλειφθέντες ὑπὸ Θεοῦ, δαίμοσιν οἷσπερ εἵλαντο ἐκδοθήσονται, καὶ μετὰ πολλὰς τιμωρίας, ἃς καὶ ἐν τοῖς πατρῴοις κλήροις ὑποστήσονται, τὴν ἐκβολὴν τὴν (133b1) ἀπὸ τῆς γῆς, καὶ εἰς τὰ ἔθνη διασπορὰν γενησομένην αὐτῶν ἄτιμον ἐπιγνώσονται.⁹

---

¹ FGM omit ἐστι.
² FGM omit ἐκελευσεν.
³ FGM insert προσεταξεν after ποταμου.
⁴ *Lc* FGM Ἀχαραιον, δι᾽ ὃν ὁ λαος.
⁵ *Lc* FGM προαστεια.
⁶ *Lc* FGM τας.
⁷ FGM Μωσέως.
⁸ *Lc* FGM ὑπ᾽ αὐτου.
⁹ The items in this chapter are not numbered in CFGM.

**70.** – What are the signs performed through Iésous son of Naué and the wonders worked through him for the people?

<1> He divided the Jordan river for the people to cross to the land of promise [Js 3].

<2> He ordered twelve huge stones taken from the river according to the number of the twelve tribes and set up by the people as a memorial of their passage through the dry river [4].

<3> He circumcised 600,000 of the people with stone knives [5:2].

<4> He overturned the walls of Jericho by the sound of trumpets [10:12].

<5> By lot he discovered sacrilegious Acharaion, because of whom the people were inferior in battle, and killed him by stoning [7:18].

<6> He captured the cities of the gentiles and their kings without bloodshed (C. 34 above). (133a) When fighting for the Gabaônites who had spontaneously given themselves to the people, he checked the course of the sun for a total victory on their behalf [10:12].

He distributed the land he had taken from the gentiles to the tribes according to their lots (C. 31 above). He assigned a worthy lot to the most faithful Chaleb son of Iephôné [15:13]. He honored Raab, who had received the spies, enrolling her among the people [6:25]. He gave cities and suburbs to the priests and the Levites [21:1-42]. He indicated six cities of refuge [20:7-8]. He set everything in order according to the statutes of Moses and sent away the people with the lot that he assigned them. He set up a stone in testimony that what he had said to them was true, that is, that afterwards they would abandon God their Savior and Ruler [Dt 32:15], and would join the idols of the gentiles: wherefore they would be abandoned by God and delivered to the demons whom they chose; and after they would undergo many punishments in their ancestral lots, they would experience expulsion (133b) from the land and a disgraceful dispersion among the gentiles [Js 24:25-27].

**OA'.** + Τίνα ἐστὶ[1] τὰ διὰ τῶν κριτῶν θαυμάσια γενόμενα;

‹α'› Τὸν Ἀδωνιβεζὲκ βασιλέα τῶν Ἀλλοφύλων, ἑβδομήκοντα βασιλεῖς ἀκρωτηριάσαντα,[2] πολεμήσαντες ποδῶν καὶ χειρῶν ἐξέτεμον, καὶ μυρίους αὐτοῦ στρατιώτας διὰ τῆς τοῦ Ἰούδα φυλῆς ἀνεῖλε.[3]

‹β'› Τὸν βασιλέα Μωαβιτῶν δουλαγωγοῦντα τὸν λαόν, Ἐδὼμ[4] δὲ οὗτος ἐκαλεῖτο, Ἀὼδ ὁ κριτὴς ἐπελθών, ὡς εὔνους αὐτῷ περὶ τὴν ὑπακοὴν ἐσόμενος, καὶ (133b2) δωροδοκήσας, ἀνεῖλε δόλῳ. Ἀμφοτεροδέξιος γὰρ ὢν ὁ Ἀὼδ, καὶ δὴ[5] βουλόμενος αὐτῷ τῶν συμφερόντων ἰδίᾳ ἢ διάτι λέγειν,[6] τῇ εὐωνύμῳ χειρί, παρόντος οὐθενός, εἰς τὸν κοιτῶνα αὐτὸν διεχειρίσατο.

‹γ'› Τὸν Σισάρα πάλιν[7] κρατοῦντα τοῦ λαοῦ διὰ τὸ δυσσεβεῖν, Δεβόρρα τις γυνὴ στείλασα ὑπὸ τῆς Νεφθαλεὶμ φυλῆς Βαρὰκ Βασιλέα τῶν Χαναναίων τυγχάνοντα κατεπολέμησε,[8] καὶ τετρακισχιλίους μὲν αὐτοῦ στρατιώτας ἀναιρεῖ, αὐτὸν δὲ τὸν Σισάρα μόνον ἀποδράντα τοῦ πολέμου, Ἰαζήλ τις μαινομένη (134a1) φεύγοντα γυνὴ[9] πρὸς τὴν ἑαυτῆς οἰκίαν, ὡς εἰς καταφυγὴν προσικαμένη,[10] ποτίζει γάλακτι διψῶντα, καὶ κατακοιμίζει πρὸς τῷ ἐδάφει. Ἀποκαθευδήσαντα δὲ αὐτόν, πασσάλῳ[11] διὰ τοῦ κράνους πειράσαι,[12] διαχρᾶται. Ζητοῦντι δὲ αὐτὸν καταλαβεῖν τῷ Βαρὰκ, δείκνυσιν Ἰαζὴλ ἐν τῇ γῇ καταπεπαρμένον.

‹δ'› Πάλιν Μαδιναίων ἐπικειμένων τῷ λαῷ, διὰ τὸ ἐπὶ ταῖς δυσσεβείαις ὑπὸ Θεοῦ ἐκκαταλελεῖφθαι,[13] Γεδεὼν δι' ἀγγέλου προβάλλεται κριτής. Καὶ σημεῖον οὗτος αἰτεῖ, εἰ προστῆναι οἷός τε εἴη τοῦ λαοῦ, τοιοῦτον αὐτῷ (134a2) δοθῆναι. Πόκον ἀποθέμενος ἐν τῇ γῇ, τοῦτον ᾔτει δρόσου[14]

---

[1] FGM omit ἐστι.
[2] FGM ἀκρωτηριασαντα.
[3] Lc FGM ἀνειλον.
[4] GM Ἐδων; emend to Ἐγλωμ.
[5] Lc FGM, who replace και δη with ὡς.
[6] Lc FGM αὐτῳ ἰδιᾳ τι λεγειν των συμφεροντων.
[7] FGM place βασιλεα των Χαναναιων following παλιν.
[8] FGM στειλασα τον Βαρακ, τον ἐκ φυλης Νεφθαλειμ, τουτον κατεπολεμησε.
Emend to στειλασα ἀπο της Νεφθαλειμ φυλης Βαρακ (Ιαβιν βασιλεα των Χαναναιων τυγχανοντα) κατεπολεμησε.
[9] FGM place γυνη before φευγοντα.
[10] Lc FGM προσηκαμενη.
[11] Lc FGM πασσαλον.
[12] Lc FGM περασασα.
[13] M ἐγκαταλελειφθαι.
[14] FGM δροσῳ.

**71.** – What wonders took place through the judges?

<1> They warred on Adônibezek king of the Philistines (C. 23), who had mutilated seventy kings, and cut off his feet and hands, and killed ten thousand soldiers through the tribe of Iouda [Jd 1:4-7].

<2> The judge Aôd coming upon the king of the Moabites who enslaved the people (he was called Eglôm), as if, being friendly, he was there for obedience, killed him by craft. Since Aôd was ambidextrous, as if he wanted to tell him something useful in private, he killed him with his left hand in his bedroom with no one present [3:19-22].

<3> A certain Deborra, sending Barak of the tribe Nephthaleim (when Iabin was king of the Chanaanites) warred against Sisara, who was ruling the people because of its impiety, and killed four thousand of his soldiers. Only Sisara escaped, and a certain (134a) mad woman named Iazél took him into her house as if for refuge, gave milk to him in his thirst, and let him sleep on the ground. While he slept she killed him by piercing a peg through his skull. Iazél showed him, transfixed on the ground, to Barak who was seeking to capture him [4:17-22]. [1]

<4> Again, when the Madianites were attacking the people because they were abandoned by God for their impiety, Gedeôn was appointed judge through an angel [6:11]. And he asked for a sign to be given him if he were were such as to rule the people. Placing a fleece on the ground, he asked for it to be filled

---

[1] A different version in C. 45.

πληροῦσθαι, τῇ[1] περὶ τὸν πόκον γῆς μηδ᾽ ὅλως[2] ὑγραινομένης. Ὡς δὲ οὕτως ἐγίνετο, πάλιν ᾔτει, τὸ μὲν περὶ τὸν πόκον ἔδαφος ὑγραίνεσθαι, τὸν δὲ πόκον ἄψετον μένειν. Ὡς δὲ εἶδεν[3] οὕτω γενόμενον ὡς ἑστήκει,[4] ἐνεχείρει τοῖς προτεταγμένοις.[5] Καλεῖ γοῦν συνάρασθαι αὐτῷ τοὺς βουλομένους τοῦ λαοῦ ἐπὶ τὸν ἐχθρῶν πόλεμον. Καὶ συνέρχονται δισχίλιοι καὶ τρισμύριοι.[6] Πολλοὺς δὲ αὐτῷ τοὺς συνεληλυθότας ὁ Θεὸς εἰπὼν εἶναι, ἀποπέμπειν ἐκελεύετο τοὺς δειλούς. (134b1) Μένουσι δὴ, τούτων ἀποπεμφθέντων, μύριοι.

Βουλόμενος δὲ ὁ Θεὸς αὐτῷ δεικνύειν, ὡς οὐ πολεμούντων πλήθει περιέσται τῶν πολεμίων ἀπείρων ὄντων, ἀλλὰ θείᾳ χειρί, πάλιν αὐτῷ κελεύει κατιέναι πρὸς τῷ παρακειμένῳ ποταμῷ, κἀκεῖσε δεικνύει τοὺς συνελευσομένους ἐν τῇ μάχῃ. Ὡς δὲ εἰς ὕδωρ πιεῖν οἱ μύριοι κατέβησαν, ἐπιτηρεῖσθαι κελεύεται τὰ τοῖς στόματα[7] τοῖς ὕδασι καταβάλλοντας, κατακαμπτομένους ἐν τῷ πίνειν, καὶ ταῖς[8] χερσὶν ἀνιμωμένους τὸ ποτὸν, καὶ λάπτοντας ὡσεὶ κύνες. Οὗτοι δὲ ὤφθησαν ὄντες μόνοι (134b2) τριακόσιοι. Καὶ πάλιν ὁ[9] πέμψας τοῦς[10] ἑπτακοσίους καὶ ἐννεακισχιλίους, ἀκούει ὡς διὰ τῶν τριακοσίων τοὺς πολεμίους ἀμαχητὶ τροπώσηται.[11] Ὑδρείας[12] οὖν αὐτοῖς ἐπιφέρεσθαι καὶ λαμπάδας ἐν τῇ εὐωνύμῳ χειρὶ κελεύεται,[13] καὶ σάλπιγγας ἐν τῇ δεξιᾷ· εἶτα ἀπορρίψαντας τὰς ὑδρείας,[14] σαλπίζειν καὶ ἐπιβοᾶν· Ῥομφαία τῷ Κυρίῳ[15] καὶ τῷ Γεδεών. Τούτων δὲ οὕτω τελουμένων, οἱ πολέμιοι δι᾽ ἑαυτῶν ἐκόπτοντο, πλῆθος ὄντες ἄπειρον,

---

[1]Lc FGM της.
[2]FGM μηδόλως.
[3]FGM εἶδε.
[4]Lc FGM ἤτηκει. While ὡς ἑστηκει ("as he stood there") makes sense, it does not follow the biblical account.
[5]FGM προστεταγμενοις.
[6]FGM wrongly emend to δισμυριοι.
[7]F κελευεται τους τα στοματα. Lc GM κελευεται τα στοματα.
[8]Lc FGM τους.
[9]Lc FGM omit ὁ.
[10]FGM omit τους.
[11]FGM τροπωσεται.
[12]FGM Ὑδριας.
[13]Lc FGM κελευει.
[14]FGM ὑδριας.
[15]FGM replace Κυριω with Θεω.

with dew, with the earth around the fleece not at all dampened. As it happened thus, he asked again for the ground around the fleece to be dampened but the fleece to remain dry. As he saw what he had asked take place, he undertook the appointed tasks [6:36-40]. He called together those of the people who wanted war against the enemies, and 32,000 assembled. God said that those who assembled were <too> many and ordered him to send away the fearful; (134b) when they were dismissed ten thousand remained [7:2-3].

When God wanted to show him that he would be victor not by the number of warriors even if they were without limit, but by the divine hand, again he ordered him to go down to the nearby river and there he would show those who would assemble for the fight. As the ten thousand went down to drink he was ordered to watch those who put their mouths in the water, bending down to drink, and those who drew the drink up with their hands and lapped it like dogs; these were only three hundred [7:4-8]. And again when he sent away 9,700 he heard that he would put the enemies to flight with the three hundred without a fight. He ordered them to bring him jars and lamps in their left hand and trumpets in the right, then breaking the jars to blow the trumpets and shout, "A sword for the Lord and Gedeôn!" [7:15-18] When these things were done, the enemies were struck down by one another [7:22], being an innumerable multitude, and he caught and beheaded four hostile kings,

καὶ τέσσαρας βασιλεῖς τοὺς πολεμίους χειρωσάμενος πελεκίζει, τὸν Ὠρὴβ, (135a1) <καὶ τὸν Ζὴφ,>¹ καὶ Ζεδεέ,² καὶ Σαλμανᾶ, Μαδιανιτῶν καὶ Ἀμαληκιτῶν τοὺς βασιλέας. ‹ε'› Μετὰ δὲ ταῦτα πάλιν ἁμαρτῶντι³ τῷ λαῷ καὶ δυσσεβοῦντι, ἐπικρατεῖς οἱ πολέμιοι γίνονται. Κριτὴς Ἰεφθάε ὁ Γαλααδίτης προβάλλεται, ὃς πολεμῶν τὸ τῶν Ἀμμανιτῶν ἔθνος, ἐπηύξατο πρὸς τῇ νίκῃ, τὸν ἀπαντῶντα αὐτῷ ἀνίοντι ἐκ τῆς ἑαυτοῦ πρῶτον οἰκίας προσαγαγεῖν ὑπὲρ τῆς νίκης εἰς θυσίαν. Ἀπαντᾷ γοῦν αὐτῷ μονογενὴς παρθένος, ἣν εἶχε θυγάτηρ, καὶ προσήγαγε ταύτην, ἐπιδούσης ἑαυτὴν καὶ τῆς κόρης. (135a2) ‹ς'› Πάλιν⁴ ἀπὸ τῆς εὐσεβείας ἀπορᾳθυμήσαντι⁵ τῷ λαῷ καὶ καταπονουμένῳ⁶ πρὸς τὴν Φυλιστιαίων,⁷ καὶ ἀπὸ⁸ θρηνοῦντι τὴν ἐπάνθειαν, Σαμψὼν Ναζηραῖος τῇ ἀναστροφῇ γίνεται κριτὴς, ὃς ἐν ταῖς θριξὶν εἶχε τὴν δύναμιν. Καὶ πρῶτον μὲν λέοντα κατὰ τὴν ὁδὸν αὐτῷ περιτετυχηκότα ἔκτεινε, ταῖς χερσὶ περιδραξάμενος. Ἔπειτα εἰσελθὼν εἰς θέαν τοῦ νεκροῦ λέοντος, καὶ εὑρὼν ἑσμὸν⁹ μελισσῶν ἐπικαθεζόμενον¹⁰ αὐτοῦ τῷ κρανίῳ, μέλι λαβὼν ἐξ αὐτοῦ βέβρωκεν. Ἀθετούμενος δὲ,¹¹ γυναῖκα ἣν ἐθνικήν οὖσαν ἠγάγετο, παρὰ τοῦ (135b1) ταυτῆς πατρός,¹² τιμωρεῖται τοὺς συμφύλους αὐτοῦ ταύτῃ. Τριακοσίους ἀλώπεκας συλλαβόμενος, καὶ κατὰ δύο προσδήσας αὐτῶν τὰς κέρκους λαμπάσιν ἐξημμέναις, κατὰ τὰς χώρας ἀπέλυσεν. Οὕτω γοῦν αὐτῶν ἅπαντας τοὺς καρποὺς (καὶ γὰρ ἦν ἀμητοῦ καιρὸς) ἐνέπρησεν. Ἔπειτα πολεμοῦσι τοῖς Ἀλλοφύλοις τὸν λαὸν διὰ τὴν τοιαύτην τοῦ Σαμψὼν ἀδικίαν, λύσις ὁμολογεῖται¹³ τοῦ πολέμου γενέσθαι, εἰ τὸν Σαμψὼν δέσμιον αὐτοῖς παραδῷεν. Καὶ δήσαντες ἑκόντα οἱ προσήκοντες καλωδίοις, παρέδοσαν τοῖς Ἀλλοφύλοις. (135b2) Ὁ δὲ

---

¹ The phrase καὶ τον Ζηφ has fallen out of C; FGM restore it.
² FGM καὶ τον Ζεδεε.
³ M ἁμαρτοντι.
⁴ FGM Παλιν δε.
⁵ Lc GM ἀπορρᾳθυμησαντι.
⁶ GM καταπατουμενῳ.
⁷ F προς Φυλισταιων; GM προς Φιλισθαιων.
⁸ Lc FGM omit ἀπο.
⁹ Emend to ἑσμον.
¹⁰ Lc FGM ἐπικαθεζομενον.
¹¹ FGM replace δε with δια.
¹² FGM παρα του πατρος αυτης.
¹³ Lc FGM ὁμολογειται.

Ôréb (135a) <and Zéb> [7:25] and Zebeë and Salmana [8:5 Cod.A,Arm], kings of the Madianites and Amalekites.

<5> After this when the people sinned again in impiety the enemies ruled. Iephthaë the Galaadite was appointed judge and warred against the Ammanite people, and he made a vow for victory that he would offer as a sacrifice for victory the one who first met him on his return to his own house. There met him the only virgin daughter he had, and he led her forth when the girl offered herself [11:29-40].

<6> Again, when the people neglected piety and was downtrodden by the Philistines when complaining of burdens, Sampson by life-style a Nazérite became a judge; he had his power in his hair. First he killed with his hands a lion that met him by the road [14:5-6]. Then going to see the dead lion he found a swarm of bees sitting on its skull, and taking honey he ate of it [14:8-9]. Rejected by the (135b) father of the woman he had married, who was a gentile, he took vengeance on his fellow tribesmen in this way. Collecting three hundred foxes and binding their tails two by two with lighted torches, he freed them throughout the land [15:4]. By this, he burned all of their crops, for it was harvest time. Then when the Philistines warred upon the people because of the injustice of Sampson, it was agreed that the war would cease if they delivered Sampson in bonds to the Philistines. And those present bound <their> willing <victim> with ropes and delivered him to the Philistines. He immediately broke

παραυτίκα τὰ δεσμὰ διαρρήξας, καὶ σιαγώνος[1] ὀστέου περιτυχὼν ὄνου, χιλίους αὐτῶν ἐν αὐτῷ παίων ἀπέκτεινεν. Ἐκ δὲ τοῦ κόπου τῆς ἀναιρέσεως αὐτῶν δίψῃ[2] φλεγόμενος, ἀπώλλυτο. Καὶ πάλιν ἀπολαβὼν τὴν σιαγώνα,[3] ὕδωρ αὐτῷ ῥύσασαν, ὅσον ἰάσασθαι τὴν δίψαν ἠδύνατο, εὕρατο. Ἄλλοτε προσλαβὼν[4] τῇ Γαζαίων πόλει, καὶ καθεσθήσας παρά τινι γυναικὶ, ἐφυλάττετο πρὸς[5] τῶν πολιτῶν πρὸς ἀναίρεσιν. Ὁ δὲ νύκτωρ ἐγερθεὶς, καὶ τοὺς φύλακας θεασάμενος ἐν ταῖς πύλαις καθεύδοντας,[6] ἐφ' ὤμων[7] μετὰ τῶν παραστάδων, μοχλοῖς (136a1) αὐτοῖς καὶ ἀψίσι, τὰς πύλας ἀράμενος, εἰς τὸν κατάντικρυ τῆς πόλεως βουνὸν ἀπέθετο, δέκα σταδίους ἔχοντα.[8]

Ἡττηθεὶς δοὺς τοῦ ὕστερον[9] ἀλλοεθνοῦς πόθῳ γυναικὸς, καὶ τὴν ἀλκὴν ἐν τίνι κέκτηται βιασαμένης αὐτὸν ἐξειπεῖν, προὐδόθη τοῖς πολεμίοις. Ἐπεὶ γὰρ ἔγνω τὴν ἀλκὴν τὸ γύναιον[10] ἐν ταῖς θριξὶν αὐτῷ παρεῖναι, ἀναλκῆ διέδειξεν αὐτὸν[11] ἀποξυράσασα. Λαβόντες δὲ αὐτὸν, εἶχον αἰχμάλωτον[12] οἱ πολέμιοι, καὶ κατέπαιζον αὐτοῦ παρὰ τοὺς ἑαυτῶν θεοὺς εὐωχούμενοι, (136a2) καὶ τοῖς ὄμμασιν αὐτὸν πηρώσαντες ἐκόλαζον. Ὡς δὲ ἐπέγνω τὰς τρίχας αὐτοῦ προϊέναι, καὶ τὴν ἀλκὴν ἐγγίνεσθαι, ἐπεύχεται τῷ Θεῷ τὴν ἐκδίκησιν αὐτοῦ ποιεῖσθαι. Καὶ βληθεὶς, εὐωχουμένων τῶν ἐχθρῶν παρὰ τοὺς ἐκείνων θεοὺς, εἰς τὸ καταπαίζεσθαι, ἠξίου τὸν ὁδηγὸν, παρὰ τοὺς κίονας ἄγειν αὐτὸν,[13] τοὺς τὸν ναὸν ὑποφέροντας. Ὡς δὲ ἦγεν οὐχ ὁρῶντα, δραξάμενος τῶν δύο κιόνων, καὶ μέγα βοήσας πρὸς τὸν Θεὸν, καθ' ἑαυτοῦ καὶ τοῦ συναλισθέντος[14] εἰς τὴν ἐφ' ὕβριν θέαν αὐτοῦ πλήθους,[15] τὸν ναὸν ἐπεσπάσατο. Οὕτω γοῦν τὸν τε ναὸν κατέσπασε,[16] καὶ

---

[1] Lc FGM σιαγονος.

[2] FGM διψει.

[3] Lc FGM σιαγονα.

[4] FGM Ἄλλοτε δε προσβαλων. Emend to Ἄλλοτε προσβαινὼν?

[5] Lc FGM, who replace προς with παρα.

[6] FGM τους φυλακας ἐν ταις πυλαις καθευδοντας θεασαμενος.

[7] Lc GM ἐπ' ὤμων.

[8] Lc FGM ἀπεχοντα.

[9] FG Ἡττηθεις δ' εἰς θ' ὑστερον . Lc M Ἡττηθεις δ' εἰς ὑστερον.

[10] FGM το γυναιον την ἀλκην.

[11] Lc FGM, who replace αὐτον with τουτον.

[12] FGM αἰχμαλωτον εἰχον.

[13] FGM omit αὐτον. Emend to τουτον.

[14] FGM unnecessarily emend to συναυλισθεντος.

[15] FGM unnecessarily replace πληθους with λαου.

[16] GM κατεσπασεν.

the bonds and finding the jawbone of an ass killed thousands of them by striking with it. Burning with thirst from the labor of killing, he weakened. And again taking the jawbone he found running water to cure his thirst [15:9-20]. Another time, going to the city of the Gazaeans he stayed with a certain woman and was watched by the citizens so as to destroy him. But he arose in the night and saw the watchers asleep in the gates, and he lifted on his shoulders the gates with the doorposts (136a) and their bars and loops, to put them down on a hill opposite the city, ten stadia away [16:1-3].[1]

Afterwards, overcome by lust for an alien woman and forced by her to explain the source of his strength, he was betrayed to the enemies. The woman knew that his strength resided in his hair and she shaved him and made him weak. The enemies took him captive and made fun of him, sporting with him at feasts with their gods, and blinded him [16:21]. When he knew that his hair was growing and his strength was back he prayed God to do vengeance for him. He was brought in, when the enemies were feasting with their gods, to make sport of him, and asked his guide to lead him to the pillars which held up the temple [16:26]. So he went, although sightless, grasped two columns and shouted to God for the destruction of himself and the (136b) multitude who had assembled to look at him with disdain, and he pulled the temple down. Thus he

---

[1] "Before Hebron," 1 Rg 16:3; "above Hebron," Josephus *Ant.* 5.305; "nearly 40 miles away," Thackeray-Marcus, *Josephus* 5 (LCL, 1934) 137 note c.

ἑαυτὸν μετὰ τοῦ τῆς πόλεως πλήθους ἀνεῖλε, πλείους ἀποκτείνας ἐν τῷ θνήσκειν, εἴπερ[1] ζῶν ἀπέκτεινεν.[2]

ΟΒ'. + Τίνα ἐστὶ τὰ διὰ Σαμουὴλ διαπεπραγμένα θαύματα;

‹α'› Μειράκιον ὢν ἔτι, θείας ἤκουε φωνῆς ἐν τῇ ἱερᾷ σκηνῇ τρεφόμενος, ὡς Ἠλεὶ ὁ ἀρχιερεὺς πανέστιος ἀπὸ τῆς ἀρχιερωσύνης[3] καθαιρεῖται. Ἱερεὺς ὁμοῦ καὶ προφήτης καὶ κριτὴς γενόμενος τοῦ λαοῦ, ἐν ἀριστοκρατίᾳ (136b2) πρυτανεύσας διέπρεψεν ἐν ἅπασι. Τὸν λαὸν εὐνομεῖν ἐδίδασκε, καὶ τῶν Ἀλλοφύλων πολεμεῖν, κατὰ τὸν τῆς διδασκαλίας[4] καιρὸν ἐπελθόντων παρεθάρρυνε, παραινῶν μὴ διδειέναι[5] τοῦ πλήθους τῶν πολεμίων τὴν ἔφοδον. Παραυτίκα δὲ τῆς ἐντεύξεως ἱερουργῶν, τοὺς πολεμίους ἐτρέψατο, καὶ τὴν κατ' αὐτῶν ἀπεδίδου τῷ λαῷ νίκην, πλουσίους ἐξ ὧν κατειλήφασι σκύλων μετὰ τὴν αἵρεσιν αὐτῶν ποιησάμενος.

‹β'› Αἰτήσαντι τῷ λαῷ τοῖς ἔθνεσιν ἴσα βασιλεύεσθαι, κέχρικε (137a1) βασιλέα[6] τὸν Σαοὺλ, καὶ προεῖπεν αὐτῷ χρισθέντι τὰ κατὰ τὴν ὁδὸν ἀπιόντι πιστοτικὰ[7] τὰ[8] τῆς βασιλείας ἀπαντήσοντα τὰ[9] σύμβολα. Δημηγορήσας τῷ λαῷ περὶ τῆς ἑαυτοῦ πρότερον ἀριστοκρατίας, καὶ διδάξας εὐνομεῖν, καὶ τὴν βασιλέως ἐξουσίαν·[10] οὐδὲ γὰρ ᾔδεισαν ἡλίκη. Ἀναδείκνυσιν αὐτοῖς τὸν κεχρισμένον βασιλέα. Πρὸς δὲ πίστωσιν αὐτοῦ τῶν ἀληθινῶν καὶ τῷ Θεῷ[11] εὐδοκήτων λόγων, ἐν ὥρᾳ θέρους[12] ὄμβρους αἰτῆσαι[13] τὸν Θεὸν παρασχεῖν. Καὶ παραυτίκα βροντῶν καὶ θεοσημειῶν γινομένων,[14] ὗσεν ὁ Θεὸς τοσοῦτον, (137a2) ὡς δείσαντα τὸν λαὸν τὴν ἐπομβρίαν, ὁμολογῆσαι γνῶσιν ἔχειν δι' αὐτοῦ τοῦ Θεοῦ, καὶ δεηθῆναι τοῦ Θεοῦ τοῦ προφήτου, περὶ τῆς τῶν ὄμβρων ἀνοχῆς.

---

[1] Lc FGM ἤπερ.
[2] The items in this chapter are not numbered in CΓGM.
[3] GM ἀρχιεροσυνης.
[4] Emend by substituting προσευχης for διδασκαλιας.
[5] Lc FGM διδιεναι.
[6] FGM omit βασιλεα.
[7] M πιστωτικα.
[8] FGM omit τα.
[9] FGM omit τα.
[10] FGM την βασιλειας ἐξουσιαν.
[11] FGM και των Θεῳ.
[12] FGM omit ἐν ὥρᾳ θερους.
[13] Lc GM αἰτησας.
[14] Lc FGM γενομενων.

destroyed the temple and killed himself and a multitude of the city, killing more in his dying than he killed when alive [16:30].

**72.** – What wonders were worked through Samouél?

<1> When still a child and brought up in the sacred tabernacle he heard a divine voice say that the high priest Élei and his house would be deprived of the high priesthood [1 Rg 3:12-14]. Becoming a priest and a prophet and a judge of the people, he held the presidency in the aristocracy and was suitable in every respect.[1] He taught the people to observe the laws, and aroused them to fight the Philistines, who were attacking at the time of prayer,[2] exhorting them not to fear assault by a numerous enemy [7:9]. Immediately making an offering after his supplication he turned the enemies to flight and gave the people victory against them, making them rich from the spoils they took after they killed them.[3]

<2> When the people asked that like the gentiles they should be governed by a king, he anointed (137a) Saul as king and predicted to him that most reliable signs of the kingship would meet him on the way. Calling an assembly of the people he taught them about his earlier aristocracy and on obedience to the laws and the nature of royal authority, for they did not know what it was. He showed them the anointed king [8-10]. So that they would believe in his true words, well pleasing to God, when it was hot he asked God to provide a storm [7:10]. Immediately, as it thundered and divine portents appeared, God rained[4] so much that the people feared the heavy rain and asked the prophet of God about stopping the showers.

---

[1] Samuel and aristocracy, Josephus *Ant.* 6.36; also in Moses' farewell address, *Ant.* 2.223.

[2] The corruption "teaching" may have been based on reading *edidaxen* or *edidasken* for *edikazen* (1 Rg 7:6).

[3] Prosperity, Josephus *Ant.* 6.21.

[4] *Hysen ho theos*; see Index B.

⟨γ⟩ Ἁμαρτῶντι[1] τῷ Σαοὺλ καὶ ἀνηκουστοῦντι περὶ τὰ προστασσόμενα, περὶ καθαιρέσεως προεῖπε[2] τῆς βασιλείας, καὶ ὡς ἑτέρῳ δέδοται, ζῶντος ἔτι αὐτοῦ, παρὰ τοῦ Θεοῦ. Τὸν Δαβὶδ υἱὸν Ἰεσσαὶ τοῦ Βηθλεεμίτου χρεῖ[3] βασιλέα, κρατοῦντος ἔτι τοῦ Σαοὺλ, καὶ προεῖπεν αὐτῷ ὡς εὐάρεστος ἔσται τῷ Θεῷ. Γηραιὸς γενόμενος εἰς τὴν ἑαυτοῦ πόλιν τελευτᾷ, (137b1) υἱοὺς καταλείψας οὐκ ἐπαξίους[4] τῆς ἑαυτοῦ διαδοχῆς.[5]

ΟΓ'. + Τίνα ἐστὶ τὰ τῷ Δαβὶδ πεπραγμένα, καὶ εἰς αὐτὸν θαύματος ἄξια πραχθέντα;

⟨α⟩ Χρισθεὶς εἰς βασιλέα ἔμενε τὰ τοῦ πατρὸς νέμων ποίμνια, τέως τοῖς ἀνθρώποις ὢν ἄγνωστος. Τὸν Γετθαῖον Γολιὰθ ἄνδρα γίγαντα κατὰ παντὸς τοῦ Ἑβραίων στρατοπέδου κατακενοτομοῦντα κατέβαλεν ἑνὸς λίθου βολῇ. Λέοντας ἀναιρεῖ καὶ ἄρκους,[6] ἀποπνίγων[7] χειρὶ τοὺς ἐπιόντας αὐτοῦ ποιμνίῳ.[8]

⟨β⟩ Τὸν ἐνοχλοῦντα δαίμονα τῷ Σαοὺλ ψάλλων ἔπαυεν[9] (137b2) τῆς ἐνοχλήσεως, καὶ κατεπράϋνε τῷ[10] Σαοὺλ ἄχθος.

Τοὺς δεκαπλασίους ἐπαίνους[11] παρὰ τὸν βασιλέα Σαοὺλ[12] μαρτυρούμενος ἔχειν παρὰ προφητευουσῶν ἐν χορείαις παρθένων, οὐκ ἐπαίρετο[13] τοῖς ἐπαίνοις, ἀλλ' ἐφθονεῖτο πρὸς τοῦ βασιλέως. Τὰς τοῦ φθονοῦντος, ἀναιρεῖν αὐτὸν ὁρμήσαντος πολλάκις,[14] προνοίᾳ Θεοῦ[15] διέφυγε χεῖρας. Τὰς ὁρισθείσας αὐτῷ ὑπὲρ μνηστείας τῆς Μελχὸλ κατὰ δεινότητα τοῦ πατρός, ἑκατὸν ἐκόμησεν[16] ἀκροβυστίας. Τοὺς πεμφθέντας ὑπὸ τοῦ Σαοὺλ ἄγειν αὐτὸν ἐπ' ἀναιρέσει, προφητεύοντας (138a1) ἔβλεπεν

---

[1]M Ἁμαρτοντι.
[2]FGM wrongly emend to προσειπε.
[3]Lc FGM χριει.
[4]FGM ἀξιους.
[5]The items in this chapter are not numbered in CFGM.
[6]Lc FGM ἀρκτους.
[7]FGM ἐπιπνιγων.
[8]FGM τω αὐτου ποιμνιω.
[9]Lc FGM ἐπαυε.
[10]Lc GM, who in their notes suggest το.
[11]GM omit ἐπαινους.
[12]FGM τον βασιλεα τον Σαουλ.
[13]Lc GM, who in their notes suggest ἐπηρετο.
[14]FGM πολλακις ὁρμησαντος.
[15]FGM προνοια του Θεου.
[16]Lc FGM ἐκομισεν.

<3> He predicted to Saul, who sinned and rejected the commandments, that he would be deprived of the kingdom and it would be given to another by God while he was still living [13:14]. He anointed David son of Iessai the Béthleemite as king, while Saul still was ruling, and predicted to him that he would please God [16:13]. When he was an old man he died in his own city [25:1], (137b) leaving sons unworthy to succeed him.

**73.** – What wonders were done by David and for him?

<1> After being anointed as king, he continued to feed his father's flock, remaining unknown to men [1 Rg 16:13]. He felled the Getthite giant Goliath, whom the whole army of Hebrews opposed in vain, by casting one stone [17:4,50]. He killed lions and bears by choking them with his hand when they invaded his flock [17:34-35].

<2> He checked the trouble of the troubling demon by playing the lyre for Saul and freed Saul from his burden [16:23].

He received tenfold the praises of King Saul, attested by the virgins[1] who prophesied in choruses [18:6-7]. He was not affected by the praise but rather envied by the king [18:8]. By the providence of God he escaped from the hands of the envious one, who often tried to kill him [18:10-11]. He acquired a hundred foreskins, the price to marry Melchol, which was set in accordance with her father's sternness [18:25]. Those who were sent by Saul to lead him to death,

---

[1] Not biblical but from Josephus *Ant*. 6.193, 354.

αὐτοῦ τὴν βασιλείαν. Καὶ πάλιν τοὺς ἄλλους πεμφθέντας, τὰ αὐτὰ τοῖς προτέροις προφητεύοντας. Ἐπειδὴ[1] παρεγίνετο, μὴ πιστεύων τοῖς ἀπαγγέλλουσι περὶ τῶν προφητευόντων, ὁ Σαοὺλ τὴν[2] ἀναίρεσιν αὐτοῦ δι' ἑαυτοῦ ποιεῖσθαι βουλόμενος, καὶ αὐτὸς ἐβλέπετο προφητεύων ἀσχημόνως τὴν τοῦ Θεοῦ βασιλείαν· ἐξ ἑαυτοῦ γὰρ γενόμενος, καὶ γυμνούμενος ἐν ὑπέθρῳ,[3] ταῦτα ἀγνοῶν ἀνεφθέγγετο. Φεύγων τὸν Σαοὺλ, εἰς τὴν ἱερατικὴν ἀπελθὼν[4] πόλιν, τὴν τοῦ Γολιὰθ ἐκομίζετο μάχαιραν, τὴν ὑπ' αὐτοῦ πρότερον (138a2) ἀνατεθεῖσαν, καὶ τοὺς ἱεροὺς ἤσθιεν ἅμα τοῖς αὐτῷ συνοῦσιν ἄρτοις.[5] Ὑφ' ἧς εἰλήφει κακοσχόλῳ τοῦ πατρὸς γνώμῃ γυναικὸς πρὸς ἀναίρεσιν, ὑπὸ ταύτης διεσώζετο, διὰ θυρίδος αὐτὸν ἐκ τῶν φθονικῶν[6] τοῦ πατρὸς χειρῶν εἰς φυγὴν ἐκπεμψάσης.

Εἰς βασιλέα τῆς Γιττίνης[7] ἐλθὼν τὸν[8] Ἀγχοῦς, καὶ ἐπιγνωσθεὶς αὐτὸς ὢν ὁ τὸν Γολιὰθ καταβαλὼν, ἐπιλειψίαν[9] σοφισάμενος, καὶ διὰ ταύτην οἰκτισθεὶς, ἀπελύετο τῆς ἀναιρέσεως.

Τοῦ Σαοὺλ διὰ τὴν αὐτοῦ δεξίωσιν ἀνελόντος τοὺς τν' ἱερεῖς, πεφευγότα τὸν (138b1) Ἀβιάθαρ ὑποδέχεται, καὶ αὐτὸς ἐν φυγαῖς διάγων, καὶ ἐν τοῖς δέουσιν ἱερωμένον.[10] Τοὺς ἐπιόντας πολεμίους τῷ λαῷ ἐκδιωκόμενος τῆς Ἰουδαίας, ἐπὶ ὧν ἐπολέμει, καὶ τοῖς ἐκδιώκουσιν αὐτὸν ἔπεμπεν ἀφαιρούμενος ἀπὸ τῶν πολεμίων ἐθνῶν τὰ σκῦλα.

⟨γ'⟩ Ἐπελθόντα τὸν Σαοὺλ δεύτερον, οὐκ ἀνεῖλεν, ἀλλὰ καὶ σημεῖα τῆς ἐκδόσεως αὐτοῦ, πῆ μὲν τὰ τῆς χλαμύδος κράσπεδα, πῆ δὲ τὸ δόρυ καὶ τὸ νυκτιπότιον ἀφελόμενος ἀπεδίδου, δεικνὺς ὡς Θεὸς[11] ἀναμένει τὸν ἀμυνόμενον, καίπερ λαβὼν παρ' αὐτοῦ τοῦ δύνασθαι τὴν ἐξουσίαν. (138b2)

⟨δ'⟩ Ἐν τοῖς ὄρεσι καὶ ἐν[12] ταῖς ἐρημίαις κατὰ τὸν τῆς φυγῆς καιρὸν διάγων, φύλαξ ἐγίνετο τῶν ποιμνίων, καὶ τοῖς τὰ ποίμνια κεκτημένοις, ἦν καὶ ἐν[13] τούτοις ἐπίκουρος. Ἐνυβρίσαντα τὸν Νάβαλ αὐτὸν ἐν καιρῷ τῆς

---

[1] FGM Ἐπει δε.
[2] FGM omit την.
[3] *Lc* FGM ὑπαιθρῳ.
[4] *Lc* FGM ἐπελθων.
[5] *Lc* FGM ἀρτους.
[6] *Lc* FGM φονικων.
[7] *Lc* FGM Γετθινης.
[8] *Lc* FGM, who omit τον.
[9] *Lc* FGM ἐπιληψιαν.
[10] *Lc* FGM ἱερωμενων.
[11] FGM Θεον.
[12] FGM omit ἐν.
[13] *Lc* FGM, who omit ἐν.

he saw (138a) predicting his kingdom. And again the others who were sent sent predicted the same as the first [19:20-21]. When he arrived not believing those who announced what was predicted, Saul wanted to kill him himself, and he was seen shamelessly predicting the kingdom of God; for he was ecstatic and naked in the open air, speaking in ignorance of these things [19:23-24].[1] In flight from Saul, he came into the priestly city and took the sword of Goliath earlier dedicated by him, and he ate the sacred loaves with his companions [21:6-9]. He was saved by the wife he had taken from the malevolent plan of her father to kill him, when she let him through a window to escape the murderous hands of her father [19:12].

Coming to Anchous (Achish) king of Getthiné (Gath) and recognized as the one who defeated Goliath, he simulated epilepsy, and was therefore pitied and escaped death [21:10-13].

He harbored Abiathar, who fled when Saul killed the 350 priests on account of [their] approval of him. (138b) He himself was in flight [22:20-22] and in need of those who performed sacred rites. He drove from Ioudaia the enemies who attacked the people, and to his pursuers he sent spoils taken from hostile gentiles.

<3> When Saul came out a second time he did not kill him but gave back signs of his generosity such as the skirt of his robe or the spear and the jar of water [24:11, 26:16], showing that God remained his protector even if he had received power from him to do the deed.

<4> Living in mountains and deserts at the time of his flight, he became a guardian of the flocks and defender of those who possessed flocks. When Nabal

---

[1] 1 Rg gives no indication that Saul predicted the kingdom of God, though it connects the Spirit of God with ecstasy (1 Rg 19:20-24).

κουρᾶς τῶν προβάτων, εὐλογίας ὑπὲρ τῆς φυλακῆς τῶν ποιμνίων αἰτήσαντα, τὴν ὕβριν οὐχ ὑποίσας, ἔμελλεν ἀναιρεῖν ὁρμήσας, εἰ μὴ σοφή τις ἡ τοῦ Νάβαλ γυνὴ (Ἀβιγαία δὲ ἦν ὄνομα αὐτῇ) ἀπαντιάσασα[1] τοῖς δώροις αὐτὸν, καὶ προφητικοῖς ἐξευμενίσατο[2] λόγοις. Ἐκδικεῖται πρὸς τοῦ Θεοῦ, τοῦ (139a1) Νάβαλ τὴν ταχίστην ἀποθανόντος. Ἀνανήψας γὰρ οὗτος ἐκ τῆς μέθης, καὶ γνοὺς ἅπερ ἐνύβρισε, καὶ ἃ πάσχειν ἤμελλε,[3] φόβῳ καταπλαγεὶς ἀποθνήσκει.[4]

‹ε'› Τὸν Ἀγχοῦς βουλόμενον ἔχειν αὐτὸν σύμμαχον ἐν τῷ κατὰ Σαοὺλ πολέμῳ, οὐκ εἴων οἱ τούτῳ προσήκοντες, καίπερ καὶ τοῦ Δαβὶδ βουλομένου. Ἄλλην καὶ νῦν ἐπ' αὐτοῦ τοῦ Θεοῦ πρόνοιαν.[5] Καὶ βουλομένου[6] συμμαχεῖν αὐτὸν[7] τοῖς Ἀλλοφύλοις ἐπὶ τῇ τοῦ Σαοὺλ καὶ τοῦ Ἰωνάθαν ἀναιρέσει, ἀποπεμφθεὶς (139a2) ὑπὸ τοῦ Ἀγχοῦς, ἀπὸ τῆς πρὸς τὸν ἑαυτοῦ λαὸν μάχης, ἔγνω τὰς τοῦ Ἰούδα πόλεις ὑπὸ Ἀμαληκιτῶν ἐσκυλεῦσθαι, καὶ καταδιώξας ἀναιρεῖ μὲν τοὺς πολεμίους, ἀποστέλλει[8] τοῖς ἐσκυλευμένοις τὰς ἑαυτῶν γυναῖκας καὶ τὰ τέκνα, καὶ προστάτης οὕτω καὶ κηδεμὼν ἀντὶ πολεμίου τοῖς οἰκείοις ἐγίνετο. Ἐνταῦθα νόμον ἔθετο, τὰ ἐκ πολεμίων σκύλα σκευοφύλαξι καὶ πολεμισταῖς ἐξ ἴσου δασμολογεῖσθαι, ἐπείπερ οἱ φαῦλοι τῶν μετ' αὐτοῦ καταδιωξάντων τοὺς Ἀμαληκίτας οὐκ ἐβούλοντο (139b1) τῆς λίας[9] ἀπονέμειν τοῖς δι' ἀρρωστίαν παραμεμενηκόσι τὴν[10] τοῖς κοινοῖς ἐφοδίοις.

‹ς'› Ἀποθανόντα τὸν Σαοὺλ ἐν τῇ πρὸς τὸν[11] Ἀλλόφυλον Ἀγχοῦς μάχῃ, οὐχ ὡς πολέμιον[12] ἤκουσε πεσόντα, ὡς δὲ γνήσιον ἐθρήνησε, καὶ κηδεμόνα, καὶ τὸν ἐπιτάφιον αὐτοῦ[13] τε καὶ τῷ υἱῷ συνέγραψεν ὕμνον. Τὸν δὲ κομίσαντα τὰ βασιλέως τοῦ Σαοὺλ σημεῖα, καὶ τὴν ἀναίρεσιν αὐτοῦ μηνύσαντα, καὶ δὴ πρὸς χάριν αὐτοῦ δεδρακέναι τι εἰς αὐτὸν φήσαντα, καὶ

---

[1] FGM ἀντιασασα.
[2] Lc GM ἐξευμενισε.
[3] FGM ἐμελλε.
[4] FGM ἀπεθανετο.
[5] In their notes, GM suggest that ἐλαβεν or something similar has fallen out.
[6] FGM Και γαρ βουλομενου.
[7] Lc GM, who in their notes suggest αὐτου.
[8] Lc GM, who in their notes insert δε at this point.
[9] Lc FGM λειας.
[10] GM note that this την appears redundant.
[11] FGM omit τον.
[12] FGM πολεμιος.
[13] Lc FGM αὐτῳ.

insulted him during the time of his keeping sheep, when he was asking blessings for the guardian of the flocks, he could not bear the insult and was going to kill him had not a certain wise woman, the wife of Nabal (Abigail was her name) mollified him with gifts and prophetic words [25:1-35]. He was vindicated by God (139a) when Nabal suddenly died; for since he sobered up from his stupor and knew the insults he had given and what he was going to suffer, he died overcome by fear [25:36-38].

<5> When Anchous wanted to have him as an ally in the war against Saul [28:2], his companions did not allow it although David also wanted it [29]. <This provides> another exhibition of the providence of God. When he himself wanted to fight with the Philistines in the battle where Saul and Iônathan were slain, he was sent by Anchous out of the battle against his own people, for he knew that the cities of Iouda were being despoiled by the Amalekites; on the one hand he pursued and destroyed the enemy forces, and on the other hand he returned their wives and children to those who had been despoiled, and became a leader and protector instead of an enemy to his own poeple. Therefore he laid down the law that booty taken from enemies was to be divided equally among the supply corps and warriors, since certain evil men among those who pursued the Amalekites with him did not want (139b) to share the booty with those who remained in camp because of sickness [30:21-25].

<6> When Saul died in the fight against Anchous the Philistine, he heard of his fall not as an enemy but mourned him as a relative and protector and wrote a funeral hymn for him and his son. The one who brought him Saul's insignia and informed him of his destruction, and supposed he had won favor by what he told

ὡς εὐαγγέλιον[1] αὐτῷ παραγεγονέναι δόξαντα, ὡς κακὸν ἄγγελον ἀνεῖλε. (139b2)

‹ζ'› Τρίτον εἰς βασιλείαν χρίεται. Πρότερον μὲν ὑπὸ[2] τοῦ ἱερέως Σαμουὴλ εἰς τὴν ἑαυτοῦ οἰκίαν τὴν Βηθλεέμ· δεύτερον ὑπὸ[3] τοῦ Ἰουδαϊκοῦ δήμου· καὶ τρίτον ὑπὸ[4] παντὸς ὁμοῦ τοῦ λεὼς,[5] εἰς ἣν διέτριβε πόλιν, τὴν Χεβρῶν.

‹η'› Τοὺς τὰ λείψανα τοῦ Σαοὺλ καὶ τοῦ υἱέως περιστείλαντας (ἀπὸ δὲ πόλεως ἦσαν Ἰαβῆς οὕτω καλουμένης) καλέσας, μεγαλοπρεπῶς ἠγάσθη, καὶ ἠξίωσεν εὐλογίας. Ἐπ' ἐχθροῖς οὐχ ἥσθη πώποτε ἀναιρουμένοις. Καὶ γὰρ τοὺς ἀνελώντας[6] τὸν τοῦ Σαοὺλ υἱὸν Μεμφιβοσθὶ,[7] (140a1) παρά τισι τιμώμενον, καὶ τὴν τοῦ πατρὸς ἀρχὴν, ὡς ὀφειλομένην αὐτῷ, δεῖν ὑπ' αὐτοῦ κατέχεσθαι[8] βουλομένους,[9] τοσοῦτον[10] οὐκ ἐπεδέξατο,[11] ἀλλὰ καὶ τισάμενος, ἀνεσκολοπισμένα παντὶ τῷ λαῷ τὰ σώματα αὐτῶν περὶ τὰς λεωφόρους ἀπεδείξατο. Ἐμίσει καὶ τοὺς ὑπὲρ αὐτοῦ δοκοῦντάς τι δρᾶν ἐπ' ἀναιρέσει[12] τῶν οὐκ ὀφειλόντων διδόναι δίκας. Ἰωὰβ ὃν γοῦν[13] στρατηγὸν αὐτοῦ γεγονότα, ἀποκτείναντα τὸν τοῦ Μεμθιβοστοῦ[14] στρατηγὸν, Ἀβηννὴρ δὲ ἦν ὄνομα τούτῳ, τοσοῦτον ἀπεστράφη, ὡς καὶ ἐν τοῖς ἐχθροῖς ἀριθμεῖν, καὶ φυλάττειν (140a2) αὐτῷ τὴν ὑπὲρ τοῦ κακῶς ἀναιρουμένου οὐκ ἀνεκδίκητον τίσιν.[15]

‹θ'› Ἕνεκα τῶν ἀκροβυστιῶν, ἠγάγετο γυναῖκα τὴν Μελχὸλ, παρὰ[16] τοῦ πατρὸς ἐκδοθεῖσαν ἑτέρῳ τινὶ τῷ Φαλτίᾳ. Ταύτην ἀνειλήφει ἀπολαβὼν τὴν βασιλείαν, οὔτε τὸν Φαλτίαν ἀδικεῖν, οὔτε μοιχαλίδα τὴν Μελχὸλ γεγονέναι λογισάμενος. Τῆς ψυχῆς οἰκεῖα δείγματα ἔχοντας σώματα τοὺς

---

[1] Lc GM, who in their notes suggest εὐαγγελον.
[2] FGM ἀπο.
[3] FGM ἀπο.
[4] FGM ἀπο.
[5] GM print λεων. Lc GM, who propose λεω in their notes.
[6] Lc FGM ἀνελοντας.
[7] Lc FGM Μεμφιβοσθε.
[8] Emend to δεῖν αὐτον κατεχεσθαι.
[9] FGM print βουλομενος; GM suggest βουλομενοις in their notes.
[10] Lc FGM, who print οὐ μονον in place of τοσουτον.
[11] Lc FGM ἀπεδεζατο.
[12] FGM omit ἐπ' ἀναιρεσει.
[13] FGM Τον Ἰωαβ γουν.
[14] Lc FGM Μεμθιβοσθου.
[15] Lc GM δικην.
[16] Lc FGM ἠν παρα.

him, considering himself a messenger of good, he slew as a wicked messenger [3 Rg 1:1-16].

<7> He was anointed as king three times, first by the priest Samouél in his native Béthleem [1 Rg 16:13]; second by the Judaic citizenry (*démos*) [2 Rg 2:4], and third by the whole people (*leôs*)[1] together in the city of Chebrôn, where he was staying [5:3].

<8> Summoning those who buried the remains of Saul and his son (they were from the city called Iabés) he greatly admired and blessed them [2:4-5]. He never rejoiced over slain enemies. He not only did not receive those who, wanting him to be controlled, had killed Saul's son Memphibosthe, (140a) honored by some who wanted his father's kingdom restored to him as his due, but instead he punished them, impaling their corpses on public roads before the whole people [4:11-12]. He hated those who on his behalf seemed to do destructive things to those who did not deserve punishment. When his general Iôab had killed Memphibosthe's general named Abénnér, he turned from him and considered him among his enemies and kept for him the penalty, not without punishment, for the one whom he had murdered.

<9> Because of the foreskins he married Melchol [1 Rg 18:27], who was given by her father to a certain Phaltias [25:44]. He took her as his wife again when he received the kingdom but did not think that Phaltias had acted wrongly or that Melchôl was an adulteress. When the Iebousites who had bodies

---

[1] Galicciolli (p. 36 n. 6; Migne p. 80 n. 78) notes that Joseph does not (ordinarily) use *leôs* for *laos*, and suggests that the chapter is an interpolation. Josephus *Ant.* 6.63 mentions two anointings of Saul by Samuel but only one anointing of David, again by Samuel, 6.165. See Index B s.v. *démos*, *leôs*.

Ἰεβουσαίους· χωλοὶ γὰρ ἐτύγχανον καὶ τυφλοὶ πάντες· εἴργειν αὐτῷ πειρωμένους τὴν εἰς τὴν πόλιν εἴσοδον, κατασχὼν τὴν πόλιν, τὴν ἀναίρεσιν δὲ μὴ ὢν[1] εἰργάσατο. (140b1) Τὰ ἐπικείμενα τῷ λαῷ πολεμικὰ ἔθνη, καὶ τοὺς περιοίκους ἐχθροὺς τοῦ λαοῦ, τοὺς Ἀλλοφύλους, Μωαβίτας τε καὶ Σύρους, καὶ μὴν Ἀμμανίτας καὶ Ἀμαληκίτας καθελὼν τῆς οἰκείας κατὰ τοῦ λαοῦ δυναστείας, ὑποφόρους αὐτῷ πεποίηται, καὶ τὸν ἑαυτοῦ λαὸν τὸν Ἰσραὴλ, ἀνειμένον ἐκ τῶν πάλαι πολεμίων, καὶ φοβερὸν ἅπασι τοῖς ἔθνεσι κατεστήσατο.

‹ι› Τὴν ἱερὰν κιβωτὸν, τὴν ὕπεθρον[2] καὶ ἀσκήνωτον[3] ἔτι οὖσαν, εἰς τὴν ἑαυτοῦ πόλιν μετὰ δημοτελοῦς ἀνήγαγεν εὐωχίας, καὶ αὐτὸς τοῖς χορεύουσιν ἐπὶ τῇ (140b2) ταύτης ἐπανόδῳ συσκιρτῶν, ἐπὶ Θεοῦ δόξῃ τὴν βασιλέως ἀξίαν ἀποτιθέμενος, τὴν δὲ ἰδιώτου περιχάρειαν προαιρούμενος. Βουληθεὶς ναὸν οἰκοδομῆσαι τῷ Θεῷ, διὰ τοῦ προφήτου Νάθαν ἐκωλύετο, διδασκόμενος τὸν ἐν πολέμοις κεκμηκότα μὴ δεῖν τέμενος ἱερωσύνης παριστᾷν, τῷ δ' ἐξ αὐτοῦ φύντι παρέχειν τὸν Θεὸν εἰρηναίαν τὴν βασιλείαν, καὶ τὴν τοῦ ναοῦ κατασκευὴν ὁ προφήτις[4] ὑπισχέειτο.[5]

‹ια› Καταφονούμενον ἐπιγνοὺς τὸ τοῦ Σαοὺλ γένος, διὰ τὴν περὶ αὐτὸν εὐλάβειάν τε (141a1) καὶ τιμὴν ἐπιζητεῖσθαι κελεύει τοὺς ἐκεῖ[6] προσήκοντας, ὅπως αὐτοὺς ἀξιώσῃ τιμῆς τε καὶ εὐνοίας. Καὶ δὴ μηνυθέντος αὐτῷ παιδὸς Ἰωνάθα[7] (Μεμφιβάαλ δὲ ἦν ὄνομα αὐτῷ), ὃς καὶ τοὺς πόδας πληγεὶς πεπήρωτο, περιλελημμένου[8] τινὸς, φιλοφρονεῖται αὐτὸν, καὶ ὁμέστιον εἶχε, καὶ τὴν οὐσίαν ἅπασαν αὐτῷ δίδωσι τὴν Σαοὺλ ἐπίτροπον αὐτῷ δοὺς πάντων ὁμοῦ πραγμάτων, Σιβᾶν ὄνομα,[9] δοῦλον αὐτῷ πατρῷον γεγενημένον. Οὕτως ἦν καὶ περὶ τοὺς οἰχομένους ὁσιότατος.[10] (141a2) Ὁ τῶν Ἀμμανιτῶν βασιλεὺς, φεύγοντα δεξιωσάμενος αὐτὸν, ἐν τοῖς φίλοις ἠριθμεῖτο· ἐπειδὴ τεθνήκει, τὴν ἐκείνου μνήμην τιμῶν, ἀπέστειλεν ἐπὶ τὸν τούτου παῖδα Ἀνανὸν τοὺς παρακαλέσοντας, διάδοχον αὐτὸν τῆς πατρικῆς φιλίας εἶναι βουλόμενος. Ὁ δὲ, ὡς κατασκόπους αὐτοῦ

---

[1] Delete ὤν.
[2] Lc FGM ὕπαιθρον.
[3] Lc FGM ἀσκήνητον.
[4] Lc FGM προφήτης.
[5] Lc FGM ὑπισχνεῖτο.
[6] Lc FGM ἐκείνῳ.
[7] Lc FGM Ἰωνάθαν.
[8] Lc FGM περιλελειμμένου.
[9] Lc FGM ὀνόματι.
[10] Lc FGM ὁσιώτατος.

indicative of their soul, for they were all lame and blind, tried to keep him out of their city, he took the city but did not destroy it [2 Rg 5:6-10]. (140b) The neighboring nations hostile to the people and the surrounding enemies of the people — the Philistines, Moabites, Syrians, Ammanites and Amalekites [8:12] — he destroyed their power over the people and made them pay tribute to himself, and he made his people Israel at rest from its former enemies and fearful to all the gentiles.

<10> He brought the sacred ark, which was still in the open and without a tabernacle, into his city with public festivities, and he himself danced with choruses at his arrival, for the glory of God putting off his royal dignity and preferring the joy of a private citizen [6:14-23]. Desiring to build a temple to God, he was forbidden through the prophet Nathan and taught that one wearied with wars should not erect a holy precinct, but the prophet promised that God would provide a peaceable kingdom and the building of the Temple to his son [7:1-17].

<11> Learning that the family of Saul had been put to death, because of reverence (141a) and honor toward him he ordered a search for those related to him so that he might pay them honor and esteem. And when he learned that a certain son of Iônathan named Memphibaal survived, though crippled in both feet, he received him humanely and treated him as a guest and gave him the whole property of Saul. He assigned as steward of all his property a certain Siban who had been his father's slave [9:1-13]. Thus he was most pious in regard to the departed. The king of the Ammanites, who had received him as a fugitive, was counted among his friends, and when he died, honoring his memory he sent messengers to console his son Ananos, desiring him to succeed to the father's friendship. But thinking the consolers had been sent as spies of his

τῆς βασιλείας τοὺς ἐπὶ τὴν παράκλησιν ἐσταλμένους[1] νομίσας, ξυρεῖ τοὺς πώγωνας αὐτῶν, καὶ τὰς χλαμύδας ἀποτέμνει. Γνοὺς δὲ ὁ Δαβὶδ τὴν ἄφρονα τούτου πρᾶξιν, τοὺς μὲν οἰκείους κατὰ χώραν μένειν ἐκέλευεν,[2] (141b1) ἄχρι τῆς τῶν τριχῶν ἀναφύσεως, τὸν δὲ 'Ανανὸν πρὸς τῇ πονηρᾷ πράξει ἐκπολεμεῖν αὐτῷ παρεσκευασμένων[3] κατεπόρθησε διὰ στρατηγοῦ τοῦ 'Ιωὰβ,[4] σὺν ἑτέροις πέντε βασιλεῦσιν, οὓς συμμάχους ὁ 'Ανανὸς[5] συνεπηγάγετο.

‹ιβ'› Περιπεσὼν ἁμαρτάδι πικρῶς ἐδάκρυσε, καὶ περὶ συγγνώμης ἱκέτευσε[6] τὸν Θεὸν εὐθύμως. Γυναῖκα γὰρ θεασάμενος εὐπρεπῆ τὴν Βιρσαβεὲ,[7] ταύτην οἴκαδε καλέσας ἐκτήσατο. Ὡς δὲ ἑαυτὴν ἔγνω γενομένην ἐγκύμονα, δηλοῖ τῷ Δαβὶδ ὅπερ ἐπεγνώκει, καὶ δὴ μηχανώμενος (141b2) τὸν ἄνδρα τὸν αὐτῆς διαλαθεῖν τὴν αὐτοῦ τε καὶ τῆς αὐτοῦ γυναικὸς συνουσίαν, καταπέμπεται τοῦτον ἀπὸ τοῦ στρατοπέδου· καὶ γὰρ ἦν ἀνδρεῖός τε καὶ εὔνους στρατιώτης. Ὡς δὴ γωρίσαντα τῷ βασιλεῖ τὰ κατὰ τὴν παράταξιν τοῦ πολέμου δεδρασμένα. Ὡς δὲ ἀφικώμενος εἶπεν ἕκαστα[8] εἰς τὴν ἑαυτοῦ οἰκίαν ἀπιέναι προσετάττετο. Ὁ δὲ οὐκ ἀπῄει, στρατιώτης γὰρ ἦν ἀνδρεῖος, ἀλλ' ἔμεινεν ἐπὶ τῆς παρατάξεως, λογισάμενος ἔτι μένειν ὡπλισμένος ὑπέθριος.[9] Ἐπεὶ δὴ ὁ βασιλεύς (142a1) ἔγνω πρὸς ἂν τὴν αὐτοῦ ταῖς μηχαναῖς τὴν Οὐρίου[10] (καὶ γὰρ οὕτως ἐκεκλήσκετο[11]) προβεβλημένην ἀνδρίαν τὸ . . . . . . . . τὸν ἄνδρα.[12] Οὕτω γοῦν λογισάμενος, γράφει τῷ τοῦ πολέμου στρατηγῷ μετιέναι τὸν Οὐρίαν κἀκεῖ[13] τέχνῃ χρησάμενον. Καὶ γενομένου τούτου, ἔλεγχος αὐτῷ τῆς ἐναγοῦς πλημμελείας Νάθαν ὁ προφήτης ἀποστέλλεται. Ὡς δὲ ἔγνω μὴ

---

[1] GM ἐπεσταλμενους.
[2] Lc FGM ἐκελευσεν.
[3] Lc FGM παρεσκευασμενον.
[4] Lc FGM δια του στρατηγου 'Ιωαβ.
[5] FGM ὁ 'Ανανος συμμαχους.
[6] FGM ἱκετευε.
[7] Lc FGM Βηθσαβεε.
[8] Lc FGM, who replace Ὡς δὴ γωρισαντα κτλ. with Ὡς δε ἀφικομενος ἐγνωρισε τω βασιλει, και εἰπεν ἑκαστα τα κατα την παραταξιν του πολεμου δεδρασμενα.
[9] Lc FGM ὑπαιθριος.
[10] Lc FGM Ἐπει δε τουτο τω βασιλει ἀνηγγελθη, ἐγνω μηχαναις καταβαλειν την του Οὐριου.
[11] Lc FGM ἐκικλησκετο.
[12] FGM omit το . . . τον ἄνδρα. Approximately nine letters are illegible.
[13] GM suggest κακῃ.

kingdom, he shaved their beards and cut up their mantles. When David learned of this senseless crime, he or(141b)dered his people to stay in place until their hair grew again, and Ananos, who was preparing to war against him for the wicked deed, he devastated through his general Iôab, along with five other kings whom Ananos brought as allies [10:1-19].

<12> When he fell into sin he wept bitterly and supplicated God zealously. For when he saw the beautiful Béthsabeë, he called her to his house and possessed her. When she knew that she was pregnant she explained what she knew to David [11:2-5]. Plotting to conceal his intercourse with her from her husband, he recalled him from the army–for the husband was a brave and loyal soldier. Upon arriving, he reported the army's deeds in battle to the king, who ordered him to go to his house. He did not go, for he was a brave soldier, but he returned to the army and remained in the formation, reasoning that, as one bearing arms, he should remain outside [11:6-13]. When that was (142a) reported to the king, he plotted against the famous courage of Ourias (as he was called) . . . . . . . . the man. With this in mind he wrote to his general to kill Ourias by a wicked stratagem [11:14-17]. When this happened, Nathan the prophet was sent to convict him of his impious crime. And when he knew that he

δεδυνῆσθαι κρύπτειν τὸν Θεὸν τὸ μεμηχανημένον, καταθρηνεῖ καὶ κατολοφύρεται τὴν δεινὴν ἑαυτοῦ¹ πρᾶξιν, καὶ πικρὸν σχετλιάσας (142a2) τὸν οἶκτον ἐξηγεῖτο,² ὅπερ³ ὁ προφήτης αὐτῷ πάλιν ἐλθὼν ἔφη δεδόσθαι, δι᾽ ἧσπερ ἐπιούσης ἐκδέξεται⁴ δίκης. Ἐπεὶ δὴ⁵ ταύτῃ τῇ πλημμελείᾳ ἄσχετα δεινὰ κατὰ πάσης αὐτοῦ τῆς οἰκίας, καθὼς ἥμάρτησεν·⁶ ἔδραμε⁷ γὰρ Ἀμνὼν ὁ υἱὸς αὐτοῦ ἀδελφῆς ἑαυτοῦ πρὸς πατρὸς τῇ Θάμαρ,⁸ καὶ τυχὼν ἧς εἴρα,⁹ πλεῖον οὗπερ αὐτῆς εἴρα¹⁰ παραυτίκα.¹¹ Ἀναιρεῖ δὲ τοῦτον τὸν Ἀμνὼν Ἀβεσσαλὼμ, ὁ ἀδελφὸς τῆς Θάμαρ καὶ πατρὸς γεγενημένος,¹² τὴν αἰσχρῶς διϋβρισμένην διεκδικεῖν βουλευσάμενος. Ἐπανίσταται δὲ ὁ τοῦ ἀδελφοῦ (142b1) φονεὺς Ἀβεσσαλὼμ καὶ αὐτῷ τῷ πατρὶ καὶ πληροῖ λύθρων τὴν τοῦ πατρὸς ὅλην οἰκίαν. Ὁ δὲ μὴ φέρων υἱὸς¹³ πρὸς μάχην ἀκροβολίζειν, καὶ νικᾷν ἥττης οὐκ ἐλάσσω ἀνείκειν,¹⁴ ἀπανίσταται τῆς βασιλικῆς αὐτοῦ οἰκίας, ἀποδιδράσκων ἐπὶ τὴν ἔρημον· καὶ ὑπέφερεν οὐ μόνον ἅπερ ἔφερεν ἑαυτῷ γυμνόπους βαδίζων καὶ ἀλύων ἄχθει,¹⁵ ἀλλὰ καὶ ὑβριζόμενος ὑπὸ¹⁶ Σεμεῆ τινὸς οἰκέτου τοῦ Σαοὺλ γεγονότος, κόνην¹⁷ καταπάσσοντος αὐτὸν, καὶ χέρμασι κατακοντίζοντος καὶ λοιδορουμένου. (142b2) Ἀλλ᾽ οὐκ ἡμύνατο¹⁸ διὰ¹⁹ τὸν κακόστομον, καίπερ δυνάμενος διὰ τῶν ἑπομένων, ἐλογίζετο δὲ ταῦτα ταῖς οἰκείαις προσήκειν ἁμαρτάσιν. Ἐπιτείνων δὲ ὁ Ἀβεσσαλὼμ τὴν αὐτοῦ πατρολῷον²⁰ πρᾶξιν, τολμᾷ καὶ τὰς

---

¹FGM αὐτου.
²*Lc* FGM ἐξητεῖτο
³*Lc* FGM ὅν περ.
⁴*Lc* FGM ἐπιουσης αὐτῳ ἐκδεξεται.
⁵*Lc* FGM Ἐπι δε.
⁶*Lc* FGM ἥμαρτησε πεπονθεν.
⁷*Lc* FGM ἡρασθη.
⁸*Lc* FGM, who replace ἀδελφης ἑαυτου κτλ. with της προς πατρος ἀδελφης αὐτου Θαμαρ.
⁹*Lc* FGM ἡρα.
¹⁰*Lc* FGM ἡρα.
¹¹*Lc* FGM, who emend to παραυτικα ἐμισησεν.
¹²*Lc* FGM Ἀβεσσαλωμ, ὁ και προς μητρος ἀδελφος της Θαμαρ γεγενημενος.
¹³*Lc* FGM υἱον.
¹⁴*Lc* FGM οὐκ ἐλασσονα νικην.
¹⁵*Lc* GM ἀχθη.
¹⁶FGM ἀπο.
¹⁷*Lc* FGM κονιν.
¹⁸*Lc* FGM ἡμυνετο.
¹⁹FGM omit δια.
²⁰In their notes GM wrongly suggest πατραλῳαν.

could not hide his deed from God, he lamented and bewailed his evil action and grieving and groaning asked for mercy. When the prophet came again he said it was given him because of the future penalty to be exacted. Therefore, because of this great crime he suffered immutable evils against his whole house, for his son Amnôn loved his sister (on his father's side) Thamar and, aware of whom he loved, immediately <hated> her more than he had loved her [13:14-15]. Abessalôm, Thamar's full brother, killed Amnôn since he wanted to avenge her who was shamefully insulted [13:29]. The brother's (142b) murderer Abessalôm even rose up against his father and filled the whole paternal house with blood. Unwilling to endure skirmishing with his son and to win victory not less than defeat, he left the royal house and fled into the desert, where he not only suffered harm by walking barefoot and weary but was insulted by Semeé a servant of Saul, who threw dust on him, hit him with stones, and cursed him. But he did not take revenge for the abuse, though he could have done so through those who followed him, but considered that these things were suited to his own sins [2 Reg 16:5-12]. Abessalôm, worsening his patricidal act, also ventured in

τοῦ πατρὸς διαφθείρειν ἐν ὑπέθρῳ[1] γυναῖκας, αἳ κατάλλασσον,[2] δεικνὺς τοῖς ὑπαχθεῖσιν αὐτοῦ τῇ κακοπραγίᾳ τὴν κατὰ τοῦ πατρὸς ἐπανάστασιν. Καὶ ταῦτα καταπραξάμενος, ἔπεισι[3] κατὰ τὴν ἔρημον, καθελεῖν ἀπὸ τῆς ἀρχῆς τὸν πατέρα κατεπειγόμενος.

‹ιγ'› Καὶ συμβουλῆς ἐπ'[4] κατ' αὐτοῦ γινομένης, (143a1) κατηντιβόλει τοὺς ἑαυτοῦ στρατιώτας ὁ Δαβὶδ φείδεσθαι τοῦ Ἀβεσσαλὼμ, καὶ προσέχειν ὅπως μηδὲν πάθοι δεινόν. Ἐν γοῦν τῇ μάχῃ τρέπεται, καὶ νῶτα δίδωσιν[5] ὁ ὑπαχθεὶς ἄθλιος τοῦ Ἀβεσσαλὼμ δῆμος. Αὐτὸς δὲ ὁ πατρωλυίας[6] ὑπὸ τῆς δίκης ἐλαυνόμενος, ὑπὸ κλάδων ἀναρτᾶται δρυός, καὶ γὰρ ἔτρεφε κόμας ἐφ' αἷς ἤπερτο,[7] καὶ τὴν ἧτταν ἐπιγνούς, ἱππότης ἀποδιδράσκειν ἠπείγετο. Οὕτω γοῦν αὐτὸν[8] ἀνηρτιμένον[9] κατειληφότες οἱ τῷ βασιλεῖ προσήκοντες κατατοξεύσαντες ἀνακρούουσι, (143a2) καὶ καθελόντες, κολοσσιαῖον[10] κατὰ τῆς ἀπεριστάλτου ταφῆς αὐτοῦ σωρὸν ἐπήγειραν λίθων. Ὁ δὲ Δαβὶδ μαθὼν τὴν ἔνδικον τίσιν, οὐχ ὡς ἐπὶ πατρωλυίᾳ[11] πεσόντι γεγήθει, ὡς δὲ ἐπὶ παιδὶ γνησίῳ τεθνηκότι[12] διεθρήνει, καὶ τὸν θάνατον αὐτοῦ περιπαθῶς ὠλοφύρετο. Ἔνθεν οὕτω, τῶν[13] διὰ τὸ πλημμεληθὲν αὐτῷ συνολαρτηθέντων[14] δεινῶν ἀπηλλαγμένην,[15] αὖθις ἀπειλήφει τὴν βασιλείαν.

‹ιδ'› Ἐπανελθὼν εἰς τὰ βασίλεια, τοὺς μὲν ἁλόντας αὐτοῦ[16] πολεμίους γεγονέναι οὐκ[17] ἐτιμωρήσατο, (143b1) τοὺς δὲ συνελθόντας αὐτῷ καὶ δεξιωσαμένους αὐτὸν ἐν τῇ φυγῇ, καὶ ἐτίμησε καὶ συνεστίους ἐποιήσατο. Ἐν παρατάξει πολέμου διάγων, καὶ τῶν πολεμίων τὴν περὶ τὸν ἑαυτοῦ

---

[1] Lc FGM ὑπαιθρῳ.

[2] FGM print κατηλασσον; in their notes GM suggest κατηλλασσον. Based on 2 Rg 16:21, emend to κατηφυλασσον τον οικον.

[3] GM ἐπεισιν.

[4] Lc FGM, who omit ἐπ'.

[5] Lc ΓGM διδους.

[6] Lc FGM πατραλοιας.

[7] Lc FGM ἐπηρετο.

[8] FGM omit αὐτον.

[9] Lc FGM ἀνηρτημενον.

[10] FGM κολοσιαιον.

[11] Lc FGM πατραλοια.

[12] FGM omit τεθνηκοτι.

[13] FGM place των after αὐτῳ.

[14] Lc FGM συνομαρτηθεντων.

[15] Lc FGM ἀπαλλαγεις.

[16] FGM αὐτῳ. Emend to ὑπ' αὐτου?

[17] FGM wrongly omit οὐκ, as can be seen from 2 Rg 19:22–23.

the outdoors to defile his father's wives, who were guarding the house, and by his wicked action showed his followers his revolt against his father [16:21-22]. And after he did this he went away into the desert, hastening to drive his father from power.

<13> And when a plot was laid (143a) against him, David asked his soldiers to spare Abessalôm and to take care that he should not suffer harm. In the battle he was put to flight and the unhappy people of Abessalôm in retreat turned their backs on him. The parricide himself, driven by justice, was hung up on the branches of an oak, for he let grow the hair on which he was caught up when, realizing defeat, he was hastening to escape on horseback. Thus, then, the king's soldiers caught him suspended and thrust into him with arrows, and taking him down they erected a colossal heap by his unguarded tomb [18:14-17]. But when David learned of the just penalty he did not rejoice as over a fallen parricide but lamented as over a genuine deceased son and passionately grieved for his death. In this way he was freed from the evils attendant upon his crime, and immediately recovered his kingdom.

<14> Returning to the palace, he (143b) did not punish prisoners for having been his enemies, but he honored and provided with food those who came with him and received him in his flight. And when he did something in the line of battle and the enemy had occupied the whole countryside around his army, he

στρατὸν ἄπασαν χώραν προκατειληφότων, ὕδατος ἐπεθύμησεν ἐξ ἰδίου λάκκου τοῦ ἐν Βηθλεέμ. Οἱ δὲ στρατηγοὶ τὴν τῶν πολεμίων διακόψαντες φάλαγγα, ὥρμησαν εἰς τὴν Βηθλεέμ, καὶ τὸ ὕδωρ αὐτῷ διεκόμισαν. Ὁ δὲ ἀποθαυμάσας αὐτοὺς τῆς τε[1] ἀνδρείας καὶ τῆς περὶ αὐτὸν ἐννοίας,[2] οὐκ ἤνεγκε τοῦ ὕδατος πιεῖν. (143b2) Αἷμα αὐτὸ τῶν στρατηγῶν εἶναι λογισάμενος, τῷ δὲ Θεῷ τοῦτο δῶρον ἔσπεισε θάψας.

‹ιε›' Ἐπενόησε, παρὰ τῷ[3] Θεῷ δοκοῦν, ἐπαριθμῆσαι τὸν λαὸν οὗπερ ἦρχεν. Ὑπομένει δὲ ἀγανάκτησιν ἐπὶ τούτῳ, καὶ δι' αὐτὸν ὑπομένει θεήλατον ὁ λαὸς πληγήν. Καὶ θεασάμενος ἄπειρον πεσὸν τοῦ λαοῦ ἐν ἡμέρᾳ μιᾷ πλῆθος, ἑαυτὸν ἠξίου καταληφθῆναι, προσπεσὼν τῷ Θεῷ, τῇ τιμωρίᾳ· Ἐγώ, λέγων, ὁ ποιμὴν ἥμαρτον καὶ ἐγὼ ἐκακοποίησα· καὶ τὸ ποίμνιον τί ἐποίησε; Βουληθεὶς ὂν ἐπέγνω χῶρον ἐπιτήδειον εἰς τὴν τοῦ ναοῦ κατασκευὴν εἶναι, πρίασθαι (144a1) παρὰ Ὄρνου τινὸς, τοῦ τοῦτον τότε κεκτημένου, προῖκα τοῦτον αὐτῷ προσάγοντος, οὐκ ἐδέξατο τὸν τόπον, οὐκ εὐαγῆ οὐδὲ εὐπρόσδεκτα λογισάμενος εἶναι τὰ ἐκ δωροδοκίας τῷ Θεῷ καθωσιωμένα· ἀλλὰ χρήματα δοὺς ὅσαπερ ἐκεῖνος ἐβούλετο, τὴν ἐκ δικαιοσύνης οὕτως ἀνέθετο τῷ Θεῷ κτῆσιν.

‹ις›' Πᾶσαν αὐτοῦ συγγραφὴν ἐφ' ἑκάστῳ τῶν συμπιπτόντων δι' ὕμνον[4] συνεγράψατο, καὶ τὸν ἅπαντα βίον τὸν ἑαυτοῦ Θεὸν ὑμνῶν διετέλει. Καὶ ψαλτήριον δὲ μουσικὸν ὄργανον ἠχοῦν εἶχεν ἐν τούτῳ. Χοροὺς δὲ ἔστησε ψαλτῳδοὺς,[5] τὸ Λευϊτικὸν (144a2) γένος ἅπαν, ὑπὲρ τοὺς τρισμυρίους τότε, ὑπὸ τρεῖς ποιησάμενος χοροδιδασκάλους, εἰς τὸ ψάλλειν διηνεκῶς καὶ ὑμνεῖν τὸν Θεόν, τοὺς ἑαυτοῦ ὕμνους ἐντάξας. Καὶ πεποίηται μὲν ψαλμοὺς ἀπείρους, οὓς καὶ κατέλεξε τοῖς τῶν Λευϊτῶν χοροδιδασκάλοις. Ἀλλ' ὁ βασιλεὺς Ἐζεκίας τὸ ψαλμῶν πλῆθος[6] εἰς ὀλιγωρίαν[7] ἄγον τοὺς Λευίτας ἐπιγνοὺς, τοὺς ἑκατὸν τούτους καὶ πεντήκοντα ψαλμοὺς, διὰ τῶν ἐν τῷ λαῷ σοφῶν, ἀπὸ τοῦ τοσούτου πλήθους ἐποίησεν ἐπιλαχθῆναι.[8]

‹ιζ›' Διάδοχον τῆς αὐτοῦ βασιλείας (144b1) τὸν υἱὸν ἐποιήσατο, τὸν Σολομῶν, ὃν ἐκ τῆς Βιρσαβεὲ[9] ἐκτήσατο, καὶ χρισθέντα διὰ τοῦ προφήτου

---

[1]FGM omit τε.
[2]*Lc* FGM εὐνοίας.
[3]FGM το.
[4]*Lc* FGM ὕμνων.
[5]GM ψαλμῳδοὺς.
[6]FGM το των ψαλμων πληθος.
[7]*Lc* FGM ἐν ὀλιγωρια.
[8]*Lc* FGM ἐπιλεχθηναι.
[9]*Lc* FGM Βηθσαβεε.

wanted water from his own cistern in Béthleem. His generals broke through a phalanx of the enemy and got to Béthleem and brought the water to him. He marveled at their courage and their love of him, but could not drink the water. Regarding it as his generals' blood, he poured it on the ground as a gift to God [23:13-17].

<15> He planned, against God's will, to count the people whom he ruled, but he suffered indignation because of this and on account of him the people suffered a plague sent by God. And seeing a countless multitude of the people falling on one day he prayed that be himself would be taken as punishment, and falling before God he said, "I the shepherd sinned and did wrong; but what did the flock do?" [2 Reg 24:17] Desiring to buy a place that he knew was suitable for the building of the Temple (144a) from a certain Ornos (Orna), who then owned it and offered it to him free, he did not accept the place, believing that places consecrated to God out of free gifts were neither undefiled nor acceptable, but by paying as much money as he wanted, he offered the property to God out of justice [24:18-25].

<16> He wrote down in hymns his account of whatever happened to him and spent his whole life hymning his God. And he had a psaltery, a resounding musical instrument, for this, and instituted a chorus of psaltery-players, the whole Levitical race, over thirty thousand, whom he subjected to three choirmasters, to sing psalms and hymns to God continually, setting his own hymns in order. He composed innumerable psalms, which he assigned to the choirmasters of the Levites; but King Ezekias, recognizing that the number of the psalms made the Levites negligent, retained 150 Psalms out of so many, through the wise among the people.

<17> He made Solomon, his son by Béthsabeë, the successor to his kingdom, anointed through the prophet Nathan; he reverenced him by

Νάθαν, αὐτὸς ἐπικυρῶν αὐτῷ τὴν βασιλείαν προσεκύρωσε,[1] παρήνει δὲ αὐτῷ τὴν πρὸς τὸν[2] Θεὸν εὐσέβειαν εἰλικρινῆ διατηρεῖν, τῆς ἀρίστης [ἀρίστης][3] ἀρχῆς ταύτην ὑπόθεσιν εἶναι λέγων. Καὶ τὸν ναὸν δὲ ἐκέλευσεν οἰκοδομεῖν αὐτῷ,[4] τὴν ὕλην[5] αὐτοῦ διάθεσιν, μέτρα τε καὶ χρήματα[6] τῆς ὅλης αὐτοῦ δομήσεως παραδούς, καταλείψας αὐτῷ τῆς μεγαλοπρεποῦς καὶ πολυτελοῦς κατασκευῆς ἐπάξια δαπανήματα· (144b2) χρυσοῦ τε καὶ γὰρ ἦν τάλαντα δεκάκις μύρια καὶ ἑκατονάκις, ἀργύρου μύρια τάλαντα.[7] Χαλκιοῦ γὰρ καὶ[8] σιδήρου σταθμὸς ὅσος ἦν[9] [ὑπὲρ] εἰς ἀριθμὸν[10] ἐλθεῖν οὐκ ἠδύνατο. Καὶ τοὺς ἐνυβρίσαντας αὐτῷ κατὰ τὸν τῆς δυσπραγίας καιρόν, οὐκ εἴασεν ἀγνῶτας. Κατέλεξε γὰρ καὶ τούτους τῷ Σολομῶν, ὅπως αὐτοὺς ὑποβλέπηται. Τεσσαράκοντα δὲ βασιλεύσας ἐνιαυτοὺς, εὐκλεῶς τελευτᾷ, τῷ Σαλομῶν παραδοὺς τὴν βασιλείαν.[11]

ΟΔ'. + Τίνα ἐστὶ τὰ τῷ Σολομῶνι δεδρασμένα;
   ‹α› Δωδεκαετὴς[12] τῆς βασιλείας (145a1) ἐφαψάμενος, τὸν ἀδελφὸν τὸν[13] αὐτοῦ, ὃς ἑαυτῷ[14] τὴν βασιλείαν ἔτι ζῶντος τοῦ πατρὸς ἁρπάζειν ἐπηράθη,[15] αἰτήσαντα δὲ καὶ γυναῖκα λαβεῖν τὴν συνευναθεῖσαν τῷ Δαβὶδ παρθένον διαμείνασαν τὴν Ἀβισσὰν, ἀνεῖλε. Τὸν Ἀβιάθαρ ὃς ἦν

---

[1] Lc FGM προσεκυνησε.
[2] FGM omit τον.
[3] Lc FGM, who omit the second αριστης, as a dittography.
[4] FGM αυτω οικοδομειν.
[5] Lc FGM ολην, although C may possibly be correct.
[6] Lc FGM σχηματα, although again C may possibly be correct.
[7] FGM omit μυρια ταλαντα.
[8] FGM replaces Χαλκιου γαρ και with δε και.
[9] In a note GM calls this ἦν redundant, suggesting τοσουτος ἦν, ὅσος εἰς.
[10] F ὑπ' ἀριθμον. GM omit ὑπερ εἰς before ἀριθμον. Emend to omit ὑπερ
[11] Several manuscripts quote from this chapter, although they identify it as C. 100 of the *Hypomnestikon* of Josephus. The quotations begin with item 16 and continue to the end of the chapter. For more on this, see Menzies, "Interpretive Traditions," 15-22.
    The items in this chapter are not numbered in CFGM.
[12] FGM print Δωδεκακετης, but GM correct it in their notes.
[13] FGM omit τον.
[14] FGM αυτω.
[15] Lc FGM ἐπειραθη.

confirming his kingship and warned him to keep his piety pure toward God, saying that this was the foundation of the best rule. He also ordered him to build the Temple, delivering his whole plan <with> the measurements and appearances of the whole building, and he left adequate sums for constructing the magnificent and expensive structure, 1,100,000 talents of gold, tens of thousands of talents of silver, and an incalculable weight of bronze and iron.[1] Nor did he leave those who had insulted him in difficult times unavenged, for he enumerated them for Solomon so that he might deal with them [3 Rg 2:5-9]. When he had reigned gloriously for forty years he died and passed on the kingdom to Solomon.

**74.** – What was done by Solomon?
<1> When he assumed the throne (145a) at the age of twelve,[2] he killed his brother, who had tried to seize the kingdom while his father was still alive and had sought to take as wife David's companion Abissa (Abeisa, 3 Rg 2:17), still a virgin. He drove from the priesthood the high priest Abiathar, who had joined

---

[1] Gold: 100,000 talents; silver: 1,000,000 (1 Par 22:14).
[2] Twelve, 3 Rg 2:12 (Cod.A); fourteen (94 minus 80), Josephus *Ant.* 8.211.

ἀρχιερεὺς, τῆς ἱερωσύνης ἐξήγαγε, συνελθόντα[1] τῷ ᾿Αδονίᾳ[2] εἰς τὴν τῆς βασιλείας ἐπιχείρησιν. Τὸν ᾿Ιωὰβ ὃς ἦν τοῦ πατρὸς στρατηγὸς, εἰς τὸ θυστιαστήριον καταφυγόντα διὰ τὸ συμπράττειν τῷ ᾿Αδωνίᾳ, καὶ αὐτὸν ἀνεῖλεν, ὑπομνήσας αὐτὸν,[3] ὡς ἐπώφειλε τὸν τοιοῦτον θάνατον, ἀποκτείνας (145a2) παρὰ τὴν τοῦ πατρὸς γνώμην δύο στρατηγοὺς εὐαρέστους αὐτῷ, τὸν ᾿Αβεννὴρ υἱὸν Νὴρ, καὶ τὸν ᾿Αβεσσὰ υἱὸν ᾿Ιεθὼρ,[4] γεγενημένους. Τὸν Σεμεῆ, τὸν τοῦ ᾿Αβεσσαλὼμ δοῦλον, ὡς[5] δυσπραγοῦντα τὸν πατέρα θεασάμενος κατηρᾶτο καὶ ἐλίθαζεν, εἰς τὴν ᾿Ιερουσαλὴμ περιώρισε, καὶ μηνυθέντα αὐτῷ[6] τὴν πόλιν ποῦ προεληλυθέναι, ὡς ὑπέρφρονα[7] τῆς[8] βασιλέως γνώμης ἀπέκτεινε. Χιλιόμβην πρώτην ποιούμενος ἀπὸ τῆς ἑαυτοῦ βασιλείας θυσίαν, ἔθυσεν εἰς τὴν Γαβαῶν τῷ Θεῷ, ὧδε γὰρ εἵλετο προσαγαγεῖν, (145b1) τῆς ᾿Ιερουσαλὴμ οὐδέπω[9] δομησθείσης.[10] ᾿Επὶ τῇ εὐσεβεῖ θυσίᾳ κελευσθεὶς δι᾿ ὀνειράτων θέας αἰτῆσαί τι παρὰ τοῦ Θεοῦ, σοφίαν ἤτησε,[11] δι᾿ ἧς τὰς ἐνδίκους οἷός τε εἴη τοῦ λαοῦ κρίσιν[12] ἐκφέρειν. ᾿Αποδεχθεὶς δὲ ἐπὶ τῇ τοιαύτῃ αἰτήσει, καὶ τὴν σοφίαν εἰλήφει, καὶ ἅπερ οὐκ ᾐτήκει, πλοῦτον, καὶ δύναμιν, καὶ τὴν εἰρηναίαν διαγωγήν.

‹β᾿› Δύσλυτον ἔλυσε δύο γυναικῶν προλεχθουσῶν[13] αὐτῷ κρίσιν, περὶ ζῶντος καὶ τεθνεῶτος κρινομένων παιδίων. ᾿Επιγνοὺς εἴπερ[14] εἰλήφει σοφίᾳ, καὶ τὸ ζῶν (145b2) ποίας εἴη γυναικὸς, στοργῇ τῇ τοῦ παιδίου, καὶ τὸ τεθνηκὸς ὡς τῆς ἑτέρας, διὰ τῆς περὶ αὐτὸ τὸ ζῶν ἀφιδίας.[15]

---

[1] FGM τον συνελθοντα.

[2] Lc FGM ᾿Αδωνια.

[3] FGM αὐιῳ.

[4] FG ᾿Ιωθωρ; lc M ᾿Ιοθορ.

[5] Lc FGM ὁς.

[6] Lc FGM, who omit αὐτῳ.

[7] F mistakenly prints ὑπερφονα.

[8] FGM του.

[9] FGM print οὐπω in place of οὐδε πω.

[10] FGM δομισθεισης.

[11] FGM ἠτησε σοφιαν.

[12] Lc FGM κρισεις.

[13] Lc FGM προσελθουσων.

[14] Lc FGM, who omit εἰπερ.

[15] Lc FGM ἀφειδιας.

Adônias in his attempt upon the kingdom.[1] He killed Iôab, general for his father, who fled to the altar because of what he did with Adônias, after warning him that he was liable to such a death because contrary to his father's will he had killed two generals approved by him, Abennér son of Nér and Abessa {2 Rg 20:10 Arm.] son of Iothôr. He commanded Semeé slave of Abessalôm, who saw his father doing badly and cursed him and stoned him, to remain in Jerusalem, and when he learned he had left the city as despising the will of the king, he killed him [3 Rg 3:36-46]. He made the first sacrifice of a thousand oxen from his kingdom, and offered it to God at Gabaôn, for there he chose to make offering (145b) when the Temple at Jerusalem had not yet been built. After the pious sacrifice he was ordered through dreams to ask something from God and he asked for wisdom to be just and make judgments for the people. He was heard for this request and he received wisdom and, what he had not asked for, wealth and power and a peaceful life [3:4-14].

<2> He solved the difficult question raised by two women who came to him about a live and a dead child, for in his wisdom he knew the woman to whom the living one (146a) belonged, from her love toward the child, and the one to whom the dead one belonged, because she did not want the living one spared [3:16-28].

---

[1] Josephus *Ant.* 8.3, 5, 9–10.

‹γ'› Ἀπόλεμον καὶ εἰρηναῖον ἀπὸ τῶν περιοίκων καὶ τῶν ἄλλων ἐθνῶν, τὸν τῆς ἑαυτοῦ[1] βασιλείας διετέλεσε χρόνον, ὑπὸ τὰς ἑαυτὸν ἐκείνας[2] τοῦ λαοῦ διάγοντος. Ἐν εὐφορίαις ἀνειμένος, τὸν ναὸν ᾠκοδόμησεν ἐν τῇ Ἱερουσαλήμ, κατὰ τοῦ πατρὸς ὑποθήκας,[3] ἐν ἓξ καὶ εἴκοσι[4] ἐνιαυτοῖς αὐτὸν ἐκτελέσας, καὶ τὴν ἱερὰν κιβωτόν, ἣν Μωϋσῆς κατεσκεύασεν, ἀναθεὶς εἴσω. Βοῶν τε[5] εἴκοσι καὶ δύο χιλιάδας διὰ τῶν ἱερέων καταθύσας, καὶ (146a1) τὸν λαὸν τῶν δώδεκα φυλῶν εἰς τὸν ἐγκαινισμὸν συγκαλέσας, ἐφ' ἡμέρας δὶς[6] ἑπτὰ θύσας,[7] ἀπέλυσεν ἀγαλλομένους.[8]

‹δ'› ‹Ἀγαλλόμενος› τὴν Αἰθιόπων βασιλίδα (Σαβὰ δὲ ἦν ὄνομα αὐτῇ),[9] τῆς αὐτοῦ σοφίας εἵνεκα πρὸς αὐτὸν ἀφιγμένης, ἐξέπληξεν ἐπὶ τῇ φρονήσει, καὶ περὶ πάντων ὧνπερ μαθεῖν ἐβουλήθη,[10] γνῶσιν αὐτῆς[11] παρέδωκεν ἀτρεκεστάτην. Πάσας τὰς ἔξωθεν κειμένας, ὑποτελεῖ[12] τῇ ἑαυτοῦ σοφίᾳ ἐποιήσατο βασιλείας, καὶ ἐκόμιζον ἐτησίους εἰσφορὰς πάντες ἑκοντὶ, χρυσοῦ τε καὶ ὧν εἶχον ἐξαιρέτων ἐν δώροις ἐπιχωρίων ἐπιτηδείων. (146a2)

‹ε'› Τρεῖς βίβλους ἐξέδωκε πρὸς παίδευσιν καὶ ἱερὰν ὠφέλειαν τῷ λαῷ τιμιωτάτας, καὶ τὴν μὲν Παροιμίαν,[13] τὴν δὲ Ἐκκλησιαστήν, τὴν δὲ ἐπέγραψεν ᾆσμα ᾀσμάτων.[14] Εἰσὶ δὲ αὐτοῦ[15] καὶ ἕτεροι πλεῖστοι λόγοι, οὓς ἀπέκρυψεν ὁ εὐσεβὴς βασιλεὺς Ἐζεκίας, οὐδὲν ἐπιγνοὺς[16] ὄφελος[17]

---

[1] FGM omit ἑαυτου.

[2] FGM print ἑκαινας; lc the emendation proposed in the notes of GM: ὑπο τας ἑαυτου συκας.

[3] FGM τας του πατρος ὑποθηκας.

[4] Lc FGM εἰκοσιν.

[5] Lc FGM δε.

[6] Lc FGM δε.

[7] Lc FGM θυσας.

[8] M reads ἀγαλλομενος for ἀγαλλομενους and construes the sentence to end with την Αιθιοπων βασιλιδα, (Σαβα δε ἦν αὐτη ὄνομα). Emend to Ἀγαλλομενος and begin a new sentence with it.

[9] FGM αὐτη ὄνομα.

[10] FGM ἠβουληθη.

[11] Lc FGM αὐτη.

[12] Lc FGM ὑποτελεις.

[13] Emend to τας μεν Παροιμιας.

[14] FGM ᾀσμα ᾀσματων ἐπεγραψεν.

[15] FGM omit αὐτου.

[16] FGM omit ἐπιγνους.

[17] F ἰφελος by mistake.

<3> He completed the time of his reign without war and in peace with the surrounding peoples and the other gentiles, while the people lived <under its own vine and its fig-tree> [4:25].[1] Being devoted to constructive pursuits, he built the Temple in Jerusalem according to the counsel of his father, completing it in twenty-six years,[2] and placing inside the sacred ark which Moses constructed. He sacrificed 22,000 oxen through the priests and (146a) he called together the people of the twelve tribes for the dedication; after sacrificing for seven days he worshiped and sent them away [8:63-65].

<4> Although he honored the queen of the Ethiopians (Saba was her name) when she came to him because of his wisdom, he astonished her with his prudence, and concerning all that she wanted to learn about, he delivered the most exact knowledge to her [10:1-3]. He made all the kingdoms lying outside subject to his wisdom, and they all gladly paid annual tribute in gold and other native products suitable for gifts [10:14-15].

<5> He published three books highly honored among the people for instruction and sacred usage and wrote Proverb<s>, Ekklésiastés, and the Song of Songs. There are also many other works of his which the pious king Ezekias hid, not recognizing any benefit to be found in many spells having to do with

---

[1] Emending with G (p. 40; Migne col. 89 n. 88) in accordance with 3 Rg 4: 24: "each under his vine and under his fig-tree" (Cod.A,Arm).

[2] Seven years according to 3 Rg 6:38 (Josephus *Ant.* 8.99); add 20 years from 2 Par 8:1? But *Ant.* 8.130 has 7 + 13 (20.141).

ἐπὶ πολλοῖς εὑρίσκεσθαι λόγοις τοὺς δὲ δαιμόνων ἐφεκτικούς,[1] καὶ παθῶν
ἰατρικοὺς, καὶ κλεπτῶν φωρατικούς. Οἱ τῶν Ἰουδαίων ἀγύρται παρ' ἑαυτοῖς
φυλάσσουσιν ἐπιμελέστατα, τῶν πιστῶν τῆς ἁγίας Ἐκκλησίας (146b1)
τούτοις οὐ κεχρημένων, διὰ τῇ τοῦ Χριστοῦ πίστει[2] καθοσιοῦν ἑαυτοὺς
δεδιδάχθαι.

‹ς'› Ἑνδεκαετὴς καὶ πρὸ τῆς βασιλείας υἱὸν φαίνεται γεννήσας.
Δωδεκαετὴς γὰρ γενόμενος ἐφήψατο τῆς βασιλείας, βασιλεύει δὲ τὰ πάντα
τεσσαράκοντα ἔτη, καταλιπὼν Ῥοβοάμῳ τῷ υἱῷ τὴν βασιλείαν. Ἐνιαυτῶν
ἑνὸς καὶ τεσσαράκοντα[3] γεγονὼς .... τελευτᾷ, γυναῖκας ἑπτακοσίας[4] καὶ
παλλακὰς τριακοσίας κλητησάμενος.[5] Οὐκ εὐκλεῶς ἀποθνήσκει, ἐπείπερ
ταῖς ἐθνικαῖς αὐτοῦ χαριζόμενος γυναιξὶ, ναοὺς τοῖς (146b2) ἑαυτῶν[6] θεοῖς
ᾠκοδόμησε.[7]

**ΟΕ'.** + Τίνα ἐστὶ[8] τὰ ὑπὸ Ἡσαΐου τοῦ προφήτου πεπραγμένα θαύματα;
‹α'› Περὶ τῆς τοῦ Σωτῆρος παρουσίας πολλοῖς καὶ ποικίλοις τρόποις
προεφήτευσεν. Ὀφθαλμοφανῆ τὴν δόξαν τοῦ Σωτῆρος τὴν θεϊκὴν τοῖς
προφητικοῖς ὀφθαλμοῖς ἐθεάσατο. Τῆς παρθενικῆς[9] γεννήσεως τοῦ Κυρίου
τὸν τύπον ἐπιδεῖξαι, ἐν τῷ Ἐμμανουὴλ τεχθέντι αὐτῷ κατὰ προφητείαν υἱῷ
ἠξίωται. Τὴν ἀγνωσίαν τοῦ λαοῦ, τὴν περὶ τὸν Σωτῆρα, καὶ τὴν διὰ τοῦτο
ἐπιβουλὴν αὐτῷ, καὶ τὴν τῶν ἐθνῶν ἀντεισαγωγὴν διὰ πλειόνων (147a1)
ἐξέφαινεν. Ὡς καὶ ἐκ τῆς ῥίζης Ἰεσσαὶ ὁ[10] Κύριος ἀναφάνησε,[11] τὸ[12]
αὐτὸς ὢν ὁ δίκαιος κριτὴς, καὶ ἐξημερῶν τὰ θηρία πρὸς ἀνθρώπους, εἰς τὸ
καὶ ἡμέρως συνεῖναι τοῖς αὐτῶν κτήνεσιν. Προεῖπεν ὡς τὰ εἴδωλα πάντα
σὺν αὐτοῖς ναοῖς καθαιρεθήσεται.[13] Φανερῶς ἐξεῖπεν, ὡς καὶ τὸν[14] εἰς

---

[1] FGM ἐκφευκτικους.
[2] *Lc* FGM δια το τῃ Χριστου πιστει.
[3] FGM omit ἑνος και τεσσαρακοντα.
[4] GM ἑπτακοσιους.
[5] *Lc* FGM κτησαμενος.
[6] *Lc* FGM αὐτων.
[7] The items in this chapter are not numbered in CFGM.
[8] FGM omit ἐστι.
[9] *Lc* FGM παρθενικης.
[10] FGM omit ὁ.
[11] F emends ἀναφανησε, το to ἀναφανησαιτο; G emends to ἀναφανησαιται; *lc* M,
who emends to ἀναφανησεται.
[12] FGM do not print το. See note above.
[13] GM καθαιρεθησονται.
[14] *Lc* FGM των.

stopping demons, healing diseases and finding theives.[1] The begging priests (*agyrteis*) of the Jews keep them most diligently, but the believers of the holy Church (146b) do not use them because they have been taught to sanctify themselves in the faith of Christ.

<6> He seems to have generated a son in his eleventh year, even before his reign, for at the age of twelve he assumed the throne.[2] He reigned forty years in all and left the kingdom to his son Roboam [3 Rg 11:42-43]. Being forty-one ... he died,[3] and had seven hundred wives and three hundred concubines. He did not die gloriously, since to please his gentile wives he built temples for their gods [11:3-8].

<PREDICTIONS AND MIRACLES (75-101)>

**75.** – What are the miracles wrought by Ésaias the prophet?

<1> He prophesied concerning the advent of the Savior in many and diverse ways. He plainly saw the divine glory of the Savior with prophetic eyes [Is 6:1-3]. He was judged worthy of showing the type of the virginal generation of the Lord in the prophecy of his son Emmanouél [7:14].[4] Through additional coments he (147a) indicated the ignorance of the people about the Savior and the consequent plot against him, and he disclosed the substitution of the gentiles; and how the Lord would come from the stem of Jesse and would be a righteous judge, taming the beasts for men so that they would be tame for their flocks [11:1-10]. He foretold that all the idols would be destroyed with the temples. He plainly stated that the cities of those who remained in impiety would

---

[1] Jopsephus *Ant.* 8.45–49 (Solomon's magic); Theodor Hopfner, *Griechisch–Ägyptischer Offenbarungszauber* 2.2 (Amsterdam: Hakkert, 1990) 496–98.

[2] Solomon reigned for 40 years (3 Rg 11:42; 2 Par 9:30) but Rehoboam was 41 when he became king (3 Rg 12:13; 1 Par 14:21). The figure twelve appears in 3 Rg 2:12 (Cod.A).

[3] The number 52 is missing; Josephus *Ant.* 8.211 assigns 80 years to the reign and 94 to the life.

[4] Goranson ("The Joseph of Tiberias Episode," 149–50) rightly points out that it is most unusual for a Christian author to suggest that Emmanuel was born to Isaiah's wife. Likely this interpretation has resulted from use of Aquila, Symmachus, or Theodotion, which all describe Immanuel's mother as ἡ νεᾶνις rather than the Septuagint's ἡ παρθένος. See also C. 151.

δυσσέβειαν ἐναπομεινάντων πόλεις ἀνατρα[τρα]πήσονται,[1] καὶ μετὰ
ῥητοὺς χρόνους ἀνακτισθήσονται. Τῆς Χριστοῦ θεότητος πρὸς ἐπίγνωσιν
πολλαχῶς προεῖπεν.

⟨β'⟩ Ἑκατὸν ὀγδοήκοντα καὶ πέντε χιλιάδων ἀναίρεσιν (147a2)
Βαβυλωνίου στρατοῦ τῇ Ἱερουσαλὴμ ἐπικειμένου, ἐπὶ τοῦ βασιλέως
Ἐζεκίου, προεῖπεν ἔσεσθαι. Κατ' ἐκείνην ἣν προεφήτευσεν ἡμέραν, ὁ
τοσοῦτος θεηλάτῳ πληγῇ νεκρὸς ἔκειτο στρατός, ὑπὸ μίαν καιροῦ ῥοπὴν ἐν
νυκτί. Ἀλλὰ καὶ Σενναχιρείμου[2] τοῦ βασιλέως τούτου τοῦ τοσούτου
στρατοῦ προεῖπε τὴν ἀπὸ τοῦ ἐπικεῖσθαι τῇ Ἱερουσαλὴμ μόνου φυγὴν, καὶ
τὴν παραυτίκα ἐν τῇ οἰκίᾳ αὐτοῦ γενησομένην αὐτὴν[3] ἀναίρεσιν, καὶ οὕτω
τὴν ταχίστην ἐγίνετο.[4]

Ἀπαγορευθέντι[5] τῷ βασιλεῖ[6] Ἐζεκίᾳ νοσοῦντι, (147b1) καὶ ἀκούσαντι
ἐντείλεσθαι περὶ τῆς βασιλείας ὡς τεθνηξόμενον, κλαύσαντι τῷ βασιλεῖ ἐπὶ
τῇ τοῦ ζῆν ἀπογνώσει, προεῖπεν ὡς οὐ τεθνήξοιτο, ἀλλ' ὅτι καὶ
πεντεκαίδεκα ἐνιαυτοὺς εἰς τὸ βιῶναι ἔτι προσειλήφει. Τὸν ἥλιον προεῖπεν
ἀπὸ δυσμῶν ἐπ' ἀνατολῇ ἀνατρέχειν, σημεῖον τῆς ὑγιείας διδοὺς τῷ
Ἐζεκίᾳ βασιλεῖ. Καὶ τοῦτο μὲν ἐγίνετο,[7] ἀπὸ τῆς ἑνδεκάτης ὥρας ἐπὶ
πρώτην ἐπαναδεδραμηκότος[8] τοῦ ἡλίου. Ὡς ὁ πρῶτος[9] Ἰσραὴλ αἰχμάλωτος
εἰς τὴν Βαβυλωνίαν, (147b2) διὰ τὰς δυσσεβείας ἀπαχθήσοιτο, προεῖπεν,
ὅπερ ἐγεγόνει, τῆς προρρήσεως μετὰ ἔτη ὀκτὼ πληρωθείσης. Ὡς καὶ
Ἰούδας εἰς τὴν Βαβυλωνίαν αἰχμάλωτος διὰ τὰς αὐτὰς τῷ Ἰσραὴλ
δυσσεβείας ἀπαχθήσοιτο προεῖπεν. Ἀλλὰ καὶ Ἐζεκίᾳ τῷ βασιλεῖ, τοῖς ἀπὸ
τοῦ Βαβυλωνίου ἐπὶ σκέψιν αὐτοῦ ἀποσταλεῖσιν ἐπιδείξαντι τὸν ἑαυτοῦ
πλοῦτον, καὶ τὰ κειμήλια, προεῖπεν ὡς τὴν Βαβυλωνίαν[10] ταῦτα
ἀπαχθήσοιτο σκῦλα γενησόμενα, καὶ οἱ αὐτοῦ ἔγγονοι παράληπτοι τοῖς
Βαβυλωνίοις ἔσονται. (148a1)

⟨γ'⟩ Καὶ Κῦρον τὸν Περσῶν βασιλέα, μετὰ πεντήκοντα καὶ ἑκατὸν
ἐνιαυτοὺς τῆς αὐτοῦ προφητείας τίκτεσθαι μέλλοντα, καθαιρήσοντα τὴν

---

[1] Lc FGM, who emend to ἀνατραπησονται, recognizing the dittography.
[2] Lc FGM Σενναχηρειμου.
[3] In their notes GM suggest αὐτου.
[4] Lc GM ἐγενετο.
[5] Lc FGM Ὑπαγορευθεντι.
[6] GM omit τῳ βασιλει.
[7] Lc GM ἐγενετο.
[8] FGM print ἐπαναδραμηκοτος, but GM correct it in their notes.
[9] FGM move πρωτος from here to just before προειπεν.
[10] Lc FGM εἰς την Βαβυλωνιαν.

be destroyed, and rebuilt after a fixed time. He set forth the knowledge of the deity of Christ in many ways.

<2> He foretold the destruction of 185,000 men of the Babylonian army against Jerusalem under King Ézekias. On the same day that he prophesied, such a great army lay dead of a divinely sent plague, in one moment of time by night [37:36]. But also he foretold the escape of Sennachéreimos, this king of so great an army, alone from the siege of Jerusalem, and his imminent destruction in his house, and thus it immediately took place [4 Rg 19:36-37].

When King Ézekias was diagnosed as being sick and (147b) heard that he should give commandment about the kingdom because he was about to die, to the king who was lamenting over his despair of life[1] he indicated that he would not die but had received fifteen more years of life [38:5]. He predicted that the sun would move from west to east, giving a sign of health to King Ézekias. And that took place, with the sun having moved back from the eleventh to the first hour [38:7-8]. He foretold the first exile of Israel to Babylonia because of impious acts, which took place with the prophecy fulfilled after eight years, and foretold that Iouda would be led captive to Babylonia because of the same impieties as Israel. And to King Ézekias, who showed his wealth and treasures to those sent from Babylon to inspect it, he foretold that these would be taken as spoils to Babylonia, and his sons would be captured by the Babylonians [c. 39].

<3> (148a) And he predicted that Kyros (Cyrus) king of the Persians, to be born a hundred and fifty years after his prophecy, would destroy the empire of

---

[1] This expression (*tou zēn apognôsis*) appears in Dionysius of Halicarnassus 1.81.6.

Βαβυλωνίων[1] ἀρχὴν προηγόρευσε, καὶ ὡς τοὺς Ἰουδαίους ἀπὸ τῆς αἰχμαλωσίας ἀνήσειν.

‹δ'› Ὡς καὶ ἐπαναχθεὶς ὁ Ἰουδαίων λαὸς αὖθις ἐκδοθήσοιτο τῇ ἐν ἅπασι τοῖς ἔθνεσιν αἰχμαλωσίᾳ, διὰ τὸ ἀπειθῆσαι ἐν εὐτελεῖ σχήματι παραγινομένῳ Χριστῷ, ἐμφανῶς προεφήτευσεν. Ὡς τὰ ἔθνη προσλήψεται Χριστὸς, διὰ τῆς εἰς αὐτὸν πίστεως, καὶ τιμήσει, τοῦ ἀχαρίστου λαοῦ ἀποβληθέντος, (148a2) ἐκήρυξεν. Ὡς μετὰ τὴν ἀποβολὴν πάλιν, ὁ λαὸς ἀπὸ τῆς τῶν ἐθνῶν διασπορᾶς, Χριστῷ πιστεύσας ἐπαναχθήσεται, τὰς πρὸς τοὺς πατέρας ἀγαθὰς ὑποσχέσεις πληρούμενος, μετὰ τὴν ἔκτησιν[2] τῶν διὰ τὴν εἰς Χριστὸν τόλμαν τιμωριῶν, πολλὰς προρρήσεις ἐξεῖπεν.

‹ε'› Ἐπ' ἔτη δὲ ἑκατὸν πεντεκαίδεκα προφητεύσας, ὑπὸ Μανασσῆ τοῦ βασιλέως, ὡς ἡ παράδοσις ἔχει, πρισθεὶς ἀναιρεῖται. Ὡς δὲ τὸ γράμμα τῆς προφητείας αὐτοῦ δηλοῖ, ἐπὶ ὀκτὼ καὶ ὀγδοήκοντα ἔτη προεφήτευσεν.[3]

**ΟΓ'.** + Τίνα ἐστὶν ἃ Ἱερεμίας (148b1) προεφήτευσε, καὶ προφητεύων ὑπέμεινε;

Πρῶτον ἰσχὺς αὐτῷ δίδοται παρὰ Θεοῦ, πρὸς τὸ δύνασθαι φέρειν τὰς κατ' αὐτοῦ κινουμένας τοῦ λαοῦ καὶ τῶν ἀρχόντων ἐπαναστάσεις, προλέγων τῷ λαῷ τὰ ἐπερχόμενα διὰ τὴν ἀπείθειαν δεινά, καὶ μὴ πιστευόμενος, ὑπέμενε τέως μόνος τὰ χαλεπά. Εὐχὰς προσάγειν τῷ Θεῷ ἀπὸ[4] τοῦ λαοῦ διεκωλύετο, ὡς οὐκ ἀκουσθησόμενος διὰ τὸ ὑπερβάλλειν τὰς τοῦ ἔθνους ἁμαρτίας, τὰς ὑπὲρ αὐτῶν τῶν ἁγίων πρεσβείας. Τῶν ψευδοπροφητῶν τἀναντία αὐτῶν,[5] καὶ τὰ (148b2) πρὸς ἀρέσκιαν[6] τοῦ λαοῦ προφητευόντων καὶ πιστευομένων, ὕβριν ὑπέμεινε, καὶ χαλεπῶς ἠνιᾶτο. Προὔλεγε καὶ ὡς ὁ Ἰσραὴλ τῆς σωτηρίας, τῆς τῷ λαῷ ὑπεσχημένης, ἐκβληθήσεται, καὶ τὰ ἔθνη ταύτης τεύξηται.[7]

‹β'› Τύπους ὑποδειγματικοὺς ἐθεάσατο τῶν μὲν τὴν παντελῆ διαφθορὰν καὶ ἀνεπίστρεπτον ὑπομενόντων τοῦ λαοῦ, ἐν τῷ κεραμείῳ, τοῦ πεσόντος κεράμου καὶ συντριβέντος δεικνυμένην· τῶν δὲ ἀνακληθησομένων, ἐν τῷ ἀποπεσόντι ἐκ τῶν χειρῶν τοῦ κεραμέως ἀπὸ τοῦ ὀργάνου σκεύη,[8] καὶ

---

[1] FGM των Βαβυλωνιων.
[2] Lc FGM ἔκτισιν.
[3] The items in this chapter are not numbered in CFGM.
[4] Emend to ὑπερ.
[5] Lc FGM αὐτῳ.
[6] Lc FGM ἀρέσκειαν.
[7] GM τευξεται.
[8] Lc FGM σκευει.

the Babylonians and liberate the Jews from their captivity [45:1].

<4> He also prophesied plainly that when the people of the Jews was restored it would again be handed over to captivity among all nations because it was disobedient to the Christ who came in lowly fashion [53:2-3]. He proclaimed that Christ would accept and honor the gentiles because of their faith in him, rejecting the ungrateful people. Again he set forth many predictions of how after the rejection the people from the dispersion among the gentiles would be recalled after believing in Christ, fulfilling the good promises made to the fathers, after the payment of the punishments because of the crime against Christ.

<5> When he had prophesied for 115 years he was sawn asunder [cf. Hb 11:37] by King Manassés, as the tradition has it, but as the letter of his prophecy explains, he prophesied for 88 years.[1]

**76.** – What are the things that Ieremias (148b) predicted, and suffered for his prophecy?

First, strength was given him by God so that he could bear the movements of the people and the rulers against him, when he predicted to the people what bad things would happen because of disobedience, and when he was not believed he alone suffered difficulties. He was forbidden to offer prayers to God for the people so that he would not be heard, because the sins of the nation surpassed the embassies of the saints on their behalf. When the false prophets prophesied contrary to him to please the people and were believed, he endured insult and was greatly distressed. He predicted that Israel would be excluded from the salvation promised to the people and that the gentiles would obtain it.

<2> He beheld exemplary prefigurations: of those enduring the complete and irrevocable destruction, shown when the pot, namely the people, fell and shattered in the potter's house; of those who will be recalled, when the vessel fell from the wheel out of the hands of the potter and was (149a) taken up again

---

[1] Partly repeated from C. 47(5). Prophecy for 115 (113) years = sum of the reigns of Ozias (52 years), Iôatham (16), Achaz (16), and Ezekias (29) (Is 1:1 [Fabricius, 183 n.u]). Eighty-eight: Fabricius (183 n.y) cites Bar Hebraeus: (a) prophecy under Ozias, 24 years; (b) silence under Ozias "because he did not reprove him," 28 years; (c) later prophecy, 61 years (total prophecy, 85). Bar Hebraeus adds that Menasseh "killed him by putting him between two boards and sawing him asunder" (English translation from John H. Hicks, *The Scholia of Barhebraeus on the Book of Isaiah*, Diss. Chicago [Divinity School], 1933, p. 49).

πάλιν ἀναληφθέντι (149a1) ὑπ’ αὐτοῦ ἀπὸ¹ τοῦ ἐδάφους, καὶ ἀναπλασθέντι. Βασιλεῖ τοῦ Ἰούδα τῷ Ἰωάχαζ, πρὸ ἑνῶς² αἰχμάλωτος ἀχθεὶς τὸ πρὸς τοῦ Βαβυλωνίου,³ καὶ τῆς βασιλείας παντελῶς ἐκπεσεῖται. Ἀλλὰ καὶ τῷ Σεδεκίᾳ προέλεγεν, ὡς πανέστιος αἰσχρῶς τὴν ἑαυτοῦ καταστρέψαι⁴ βασιλείαν.

‹γ›︎ Καὶ τὴν Βαβυλωνίων ἀρχὴν μετὰ οʹ ἔτη τῆς τοῦ Ἰεχονίου ἀποικίας, καθαιρεθήσεσθαι προεφήτευσε, καὶ τὸν λαὸν μετὰ τὴν τῆς βασιλείας ἐπαναχθήσεσθαι καθαίρεσιν. Τοῖς μετὰ Ἰεχονίου⁵ εἰς τὴν Βαβυλωνίαν ἀποικισθεῖσιν, ὑπὸ ψευδοπροφητῶν (149a2) ἀπατωμένοις, ὡς ἐπαναχθήσονται τὴν ταχίστην, ἐπέστελλε μὴ πείθεσθαι τούτοις, ἀλλ’ ἐκδέχεσθαι καὶ τοὺς ἐν τῇ Ἰουδαίᾳ μετὰ τοῦ Σεδεκίου μεμενηκότας, ἅμα αὐτοῖς ἀποικίσεσθαι.⁶

ΟΖʹ. + Τίνα ἐστὶν ἃ προεφήτευσε⁷ Σοφονίας;
‹αʹ›︎ Ὡς ἐκκάθαρσις τῆς κακίας γενήσεται.
‹βʹ›︎ Ὡς ἡ Ἱερουσαλὴμ τὰ Χαναναίων πράξασα, τὰ Χαναναίων πείσεται.
‹γʹ›︎ Κατὰ τῶν ἐθνῶν προλέγει τῶν ἐπαναστάντων τῷ λαῷ, ὡς τιμωρηθήσονται.
‹δʹ›︎ Καὶ κατὰ τῆς Νινευῆ,⁸ ὡς ἐπαρθεῖσα κατενεχθήσονται.⁹ (149b1)

ΟΗʹ. + Τίνα προεφήτευσεν Ἀγγαῖος;
‹αʹ›︎ Μετὰ τὴν ἐπάνοδον τοῦ λαοῦ τὴν ἀπὸ τῆς αἰχμαλωσίας, προφητεύων αἰτιᾶται τοῖς ἐπανελθοῦσιν, ὅτι ῥᾳθυμώτερον¹⁰ προσφέρονται τῇ τοῦ ναοῦ οἰκοδομῇ, καὶ προτρέπεται ταύτης ἔχεσθαι.

---

¹GM omit ἀπο.
²FGM ὡς προ ἑνως; emend to προ ἑνος ἑτους.
³FGM print προ του Βαβυλωνιου in place of το προς του Βαβυλωνιου. Emend to εἰς Βαβυλωνα.
⁴Lc FGM καταστρεψει.
⁵FGM μετα του Ἰεχονιου.
⁶Lc FGM ἀποικισθησεσθαι. The second and third items in this chapter are not numbered in CFGM.
⁷GM προεφητευσεν.
⁸FGM Νινευι.
⁹Lc FGM κατενεχθησεται. The items in this chapter are not numbered in CFGM.
¹⁰Lc GM ῥᾳθυμοτερον.

by him from the ground and reshaped; to the king of Iouda Iôachaz (Iôakeim), that within a year he would be led as a captive to Babylon and that he would completely fall away from the kingdom [43:30]. But he also predicted to Sedekias that he would ingloriously lose the kingdom for his house [22:30, cf. C. 118(2)].

<3> And the rule of the Babylonians would be overthrown seventy years after the exile of Iechonias [25:12] and the people would be brought back after the destruction of the kingdom. He sent letters to those who were deported to Babylon with Iechonias and were deceived by false prophets as about to return very soon [28]. He urged them not to believe them but to wait for those who had remained in Ioudaia with Sedekias soon to be sent from their homes to them (i.e., those in Babylon) [29:4-9].[1]

**77.** – What are the things that Sophonias predicted?

<1> That there would be a cleansing of wickedness [1:2].

<2> That Jerusalem, doing the deeds of the Chanaanites, would share the punishment of the Chanaanites [3:1-7].

<3> And he predicted that the gentiles who arose against the people would be punished [3:14-20].

<4> And against Ninevé, that though exalted it would be (149b) humbled [2:13].

**78.** – What did Aggaios predict?

<1> After the return of the people from captivity, in prophecy he blamed those who came back because they advanced the building of the Temple too slowly and exhorted them to take it up [1:2].

---

[1] Other points about Jeremiah: C. 18(3–7), 58(6).

⟨β'⟩ Τότε[1] Ζοροβάβελ, καὶ τῷ τοῦ Ἰωσεδὲκ Ἰησοῦ τοῖς τοῦ λαοῦ ἡγεμόσι προφητεύει, ὡς ἔχουσι τὸν Θεὸν προστάτην, ἐπί τε τῇ τοῦ ναοῦ οἰκοδομῇ καὶ τῇ τοῦ λαοῦ ἐπιστασίᾳ.

⟨γ'⟩ Καὶ πρὸς τοὺς ἱερεῖς ἀποτείνεται, ὡς ἡ δικαιοπραγία τὸν ἁγιασμὸν, οὐχ ἡ τῶν ἱερῶν βρωμάτων (149b2) ἡ[2] βρῶσις παρέχεται.[3]

**ΟΘ'.** + Τίνα προεφήτευσε[4] Ζαχαρίας;

⟨α'⟩ Ὑπόμνησιν ποιεῖται τῶν προγονικῶν δυσσεβειῶν τοῦ λαοῦ, δι' ἃς ἀπήχθησαν εἰς αἰχμαλωσίαν. Δι' ὀπτασίας τῆς τῶν ἵππων εἰδέας, καὶ ἐπιβάτου ἵππου, τὴν γεγενημένην δι' ἀγγέλων, ὁρᾷ τοῦ[5] λαοῦ, μετὰ τὴν ἐπάνοδον κηδεμονίαν, καὶ τῶν τεσσάρων βασιλειῶν τῶν ἐκπολεμησάντων[6] τῶν λαῶν[7] τὴν καθαίρεσιν ὁρᾷ, ἐν τέσσαρσι κέρασι, διὰ τεσσάρων τεκτόνων γενησομένην. Ὁρᾷ καὶ τῆς Ἰερουσαλὴμ τὴν ἐντελῆ θείαν οἰκοδομίαν, καὶ τὴν ἐκ τῆς διασπορᾶς τοῦ λαοῦ (150a1) ἐπάνοδον γενησομένην, καὶ τὴν ἐπανάστασιν τοῦ διαβόλου, τὴν κατὰ Ἰησοῦ τοῦ Ἰωσεδὲκ τοῦ[8] ἀρχιερέως, ὃς καὶ ἦν τοῦ Κυρίου ἡμῶν Ἰησοῦ τοῦ οὐρανίου ἀρχιερέως τύπος. Ὁρᾷ καὶ τὴν ἐξ ἐπιτιμήσεως Θεοῦ πτῶσιν γεγενημένην τοῦ διαβόλου. Τὴν τοῖς ἐπιορκοῦσι πανώλεθρον ἐθεάσατο διαφθορὰν, καὶ τὴν τῶν δυσσεβούντων εἰς βυθὸν ᾅδου κατάπτωσιν.

⟨β'⟩ Τὴν περικόσμον[9] ἀγγελικὴν ἐπιστασίαν τεθέαται ἐν τύπῳ τεσσάρων ἁρμάτων, ποικίλοις ἵπποις ὑπεζευγμένων ἐπιδειχθεῖσαν. (150a2) Εἶδε καὶ τὸν ἐν τύπῳ τοῦ Σωτῆρος ἀρχιερέα, τὸν ἐν τῇ ἐπανόδῳ τοῦ λαοῦ ἀρχιερατεύσαντα, Ἰησοῦ[10] τὸν τοῦ Ἰωσεδὲκ, ἐξ ἀδοξίας εἰς δόξαν προεληλυθότα.

Προεφήτευσε καὶ περὶ τῆς[11] τῶν ἐθνῶν ἐν πίστει προλήψεως,[12] καὶ τῆς τοῦ Ἰσραὴλ μετὰ ταῦτα γενησομένης· καὶ ὡς ὁ Ἀντίχριστος ἐπιθήσεται τῇ τοιαύτῃ προσλήψει, εἰς δύο ῥάβδους περικοφθησομένας τὰς δύο κλήσεις

---

[1] *Lc* FGM Τῳ τε.
[2] *Lc* FGM, who omit ἡ.
[3] The items in this chapter are not numbered in CFGM.
[4] GM προεφητευσεν.
[5] FGM print ὁρᾷ την του, with the την modifying κηδεμονιαν.
[6] GM suggest ἐκπολεμησασων in their notes.
[7] *Lc* FGM τον λαον.
[8] FGM omit του.
[9] *Lc* FGM περικοσμιον.
[10] *Lc* FGM Ἰησουν.
[11] GM omit της.
[12] *Lc* GM, who mention the possibility of emending to προσληψεως.

<2> He prophesied to Zorobabel and to Iésous son of Iôsedek, the leaders of the people, that they would have God as helper in building the Temple and ruling the people [2:2-5].

<3> He declared to the priests that good works, not the eating of sacred foods, bring sanctity [2:11-14].


**79.** – What did Zacharias predict?

<1> He recalled the ancestral crimes of the people because of which they were led into captivity [Zch 1:2-6]. Through a vision of the form of horses and a rider he saw the care of the people by angels after their return [1:8-17], and he saw the destruction of four kingdoms warring upon the people, in four horns through four craftsmen [1:18-21]. He also saw the divinely completed building of Jerusalem [2:1-5] and the (150a) future return of the people from the dispersion [2:6-13] and the revolt of the devil against Iésous son of Iôsedek the high priest, who was a prefiguration of our Lord Jesus the heavenly high priest. He also saw the fall of the devil because of God's rebuke [3:1-2]. He beheld the complete destruction of perjurors and the fall of the impious to the depths of Hades [c. 5].

<2> He also saw angelic care for the whole world typified by four chariots yoked to various kinds of horses [6:1-8]. He also saw the high priest as a type of the Savior, high priest at the return of the people, Iésous son of Iôsedek, who came from disgrace to glory [6:11-13].

He also prophesies about the gentiles in their advance in faith and that of Israel afterwards; and how the Antichrist would oppose such an advance. (The act of) being broken into two rods signifies the two callings [11:10,14].

ἐπιτυπῶν. Προεῖπε καὶ περὶ τῆς τοῦ Κυρίου προδοσίας, ὡς ἀντὶ τῆς ὀφειλομένης αὐτῷ παρὰ τοῦ λαοῦ τιμῆς εὐεργεσίας,[1] τριάκοντα χρυσῶν αὐτὸν (150b1) ἐτιμήσαντο, ὡς ὑπὲρ τῆς προδοσίας ὁ Ἰούδας εἰλήφει, καὶ ὡς ἐν τῷ γαζοφυλακίῳ τὸ χρυσίον ἐβάλετο, καὶ πάλιν εἰς τιμὴν τοῦ ἀγροῦ τοῦ κεραμέως ἐξοδιάζετο.

‹γ'› Καὶ περὶ τοῦ Ἀντιχρίστου πάλιν, ὡς ἐπιθήσεται τοῖς ἁγίοις, καὶ καθαιρεθήσεται. Προεφήτευσε[2] καὶ περὶ τοῦ σωτηρίου πάθους Χριστοῦ, καὶ τῆς ἐνδόξου παρουσίας αὐτοῦ, καὶ ὡς ἐπὶ τοῦ ὄρους τοῦ ἐλαιῶνος φανήσοιτο. Προεῖπε καὶ τὴν τοῦ Γὼγ καὶ Μαγὼγ ἔφοδον κατὰ[3] τῶν ἁγίων τόπων, γενησομένην ἐν τέλει, καὶ τὴν θεήλατον αὐτοῦ τιμωρίαν, (150b2) ἀλλὰ καὶ ὡς εἰς ὕστερον τὰ ἔθνη τοῦτον πορισμὸν ἕξουσι σωτηρίας, τὴν εἰς τὴν Ἱερουσαλὴμ Θεῷ τελουμένην προσκύνησιν, ὑπ' αὐτῶν ἐπιτελεσθησομένην.[4]

**Π'.** + Τίνα προεφήτευσε[5] Μαλαχίας;

‹α'› Ὀνειδίζει τὸν λαὸν, ὡς, γεγονότες υἱοὶ τοῦ Ἰακὼβ, τοῦ προτιμηθέντος ὑπὸ Θεοῦ παρὰ τὸν Ἡσαῦ, ἀγνώμονες περὶ τὸν τετιμηκότα πεφήνασιν.

‹β'› Ἐγκαλεῖ καὶ τῷ ἱερατικῷ[6] τάγματι, ὡς ἐκλεχθέντες ἐν τῷ Λευῒ εἰς τὸ[7] ἱερατεύειν, ἀμελεῖς περὶ τὴν (151a1) ἱερωσύνην ἁλίσκονται.

‹γ'› Μέμφεται καὶ τοῖς τὰς γαμετὰς ἀδίκως ἀπολύουσι,[8] καὶ τοῖς τὴν παρὰ Θεοῦ δικαίαν κρίσιν περὶ πάντων ἐκφέρεσθαι μὴ προσδοκῶσι.[9]

‹δ'› Κατακρίνει καὶ τοὺς τὰς νομίμους ἀπαρχὰς καὶ δεκατίας μὴ προσάγοντας τοῖς ἱερεῦσι, καὶ τοὺς ἐξουθενοῦντας τὴν θείαν λατρείαν.

‹ε'› Προφητεύει καὶ ὡς ἡ δικαία κρίσις τοῦ Θεοῦ περὶ πάντας ἐκφανήσεται.[10]

---

[1] *Lc* FGM τιμης και ευεργεσιας.
[2] GM Προεφητευσεν.
[3] FGM replace κατα with και.
[4] The items in this chapter are not numbered in CFGM.
[5] GM προεφητευσεν.
[6] FGM ιερω.
[7] FGM omit το.
[8] GM απολυουσιν.
[9] GM προσδοκωσιν.
[10] The items in this chapter are not numbered in CFGM.

He foretold the betrayal of the Lord, how instead of the honor and benefit due him by the people they would value him at thirty pieces of gold[1] (150b) that Judas would receive for the betrayal and would cast into the treasury and would be spent for the price of the potter's field [11:12-13]

<3> And again of the Antichrist, that he would oppose the saints and be destroyed. He also predicted the salvific passion of Christ and his glorious coming and how he would appear on the Mount of Olives [14:4]. He predicted the invasion of Gôg and Magôg[2] against the holy places that would occur at the end, and his divine penalty, but how finally the gentiles would have this means of salvation, the perfected worship of God at Jerusalem, to be performed by them [14:16; Jn 4:20].

**80.** – What did Malachias predict?

<1> He cursed the people who, though sons of Iakôb whom God preferred to Ésau, seemed ungrateful to the one who preferred them [1:2-5].

<2> He also rebuked the priestly order who, though called in Leui to be priests, were indifferent to the (151a) priesthood [1:6-14].

<3> He also condemned those who unjustly divorced their wives [2:14-16] and those who did not expect a just judgment of everything from God [2:17].

<4> He condemned those who did not bring the lawful first-fruits and tithes to the priests and who despised the divine worship [3:8-10].

<5> He predicted that God's just judgment of everything would be manifest [4:1-6].

---

[1] Zch 11:12 (Mt 27:3–10) mentions silver not gold. The same mistake occurs in C. 146.

[2] Gôg and Magôg appear in Ez 38–39 and Rv 20:8, not Zch.

**ΠΑ'.** + Τίνα ἐστὶ τὰ διὰ Ἠλία[1] γεγονότα θαυμάσια σημεῖα;[2]
«α'»[3] Ἐξ ὀλιγήστου[4] ἀλεύρου καὶ ἐλαίου, ἐν καιρῷ λιμοῦ πεμφθεὶς εἰς Σαραφθᾶ τῆς Σιδωνίας, γυναῖκα χήραν (151a2) καὶ τὸν ταύτης υἱόν, καὶ ἑαυτὸν ἐπὶ τριετῆ διέθρεψε χρόνον.
Δεύτερον, υἱὸν τῆς σταθμοχοῦ[5] τῆς χήρας ἀποθανόντα ἀνέστησε.
Τρίτον, πῦρ ἐξ οὐρανοῦ ἐπὶ τὰ ἱερεῖα κατήγαγε.
Τέταρτον, ὑετὸν ἐξ ἀνομβρίας προειπὼν ἔσεσθαι, εὐθέως ἐπήγαγε.
Πέμπτον, πεντηκόνταρχον ἐπ' αὐτὸν ἐλθόντα, παραστάσεως εἵνεκα τῆς πρὸς βασιλέα,[6] καὶ τοὺς πεντήκοντα αὐτοῦ, φορᾷ πυρὸς οὐρανίου ἐνέπρησε. Καὶ «ἕκτον»,[7] πάλιν τὸν ἐλθόντα δεύτερον ὁμοίως ἀνεῖλεν.
Ἕβδομον, τῇ μηλωτῇ τὸν Ἰορδάνην περάσας,[8] διεῖλε πλημμυροῦντα ποταμόν, εἰς (151b1) πάροδον αὐτοῦ[9] τε καὶ Ἐλισσαίου.

**ΠΒ'.** + Τίνα ἐστὶ τὰ διὰ Ἐλισσαίου γεγονότα διπλᾶ[10] ἐν πνεύματι Ἠλιοῦ θαυμαστὰ σημεῖα;
«α'»[11] Ἰορδάνην ποταμὸν τῇ τοῦ Ἠλιοῦ μηλωτῇ διελών, παρελήλυθε.
β' Τὰ ἐν Ἰεριχῷ ὕδατα ἄγονα ἰάσατο.
γ' Τεσσαράκοντα παῖδας διαπαίζοντας αὐτόν, ἄρκοις[12] δυσὶν ἐξελθεῖν κελεύσας ἀπὸ τοῦ δρυμοῦ, διεχειρίσατο.[13]
δ' Ἀτέκνῳ γυναικὶ στείρᾳ οὔσῃ τῇ Σουναμίτιδι υἱὸν ἐδωρήσατο.
ε' Καὶ τοῦτον πενταετῆ γενόμενον, καὶ ἀποθανόντα, ἀναζῆσαι ἐποίησε.
ϛ' Θανάσιμον βρῶμα δι' ἀλεύρου (151b2) ἐπιβληθέντος ἀβλαβὲς ἀπετέλεσεν.
ζ' Ἐξ ἄρτων κριθίνων ι' ἑκατὸν ἄνδρας ἐν καιρῷ λιμοῦ χορτάσας, καὶ περισσεῦσαι ἐποίησεν.
η' Νεεμᾶν λεπρωθέντα Σύρον τῆς λέπρας ἰάσατο.

---

[1] *Lc* FGM Ἠλιου.
[2] *Lc* FGM, who emend to θαυμαστα σημεια or emend to θαυμασια και σημεια.
[3] This first item is not numbered in CFGM.
[4] *Lc* FGM ὀλιγιστου.
[5] Lc GM, who in their notes suggest σταφμουχου.
[6] FGM τον βασιλεα.
[7] Emendation seems necessary. Ἑκτον is not found in CFGM.
[8] In their notes GM suggest περασων.
[9] *Lc* GM ἑαυτου.
[10] In their notes GM suggest διπλῳ.
[11] This first item is not numbered in CF.
[12] *Lc* FGM ἀρκτοις.
[13] FGM διεχρησατο.

**81**. – What miraculous signs were wrought through Élias?

<1> At a time of famine when sent to Saraphtha of Sidônia, he fed a widow, her son, and himself for three years with a little meal and oil [3 Rg 17:12].

Second, he recalled the dead son of the widow-householder to life [17:19].

Third, he brought down fire from heaven upon the sacrifices [18:38].

Fourth, predicting rain after a drought he brought it down at once [18:41].

Fifth, when a commander of fifty troops came to take him to the king he burned him up along with the fifty by a fall of heavenly fire [4 Rg 1:9-10].

And <sixth>, again he likewise destroyed a second one who came [1:11-12].

Seventh, in order to cross the Jordan, he divided the flood waters with a sheepskin so that (151b) he and Elissaios could cross [2:8].

**82**. – What miraculous signs doubled by the spirit were wrought through Elissaios?

1. Dividing the Jordan river with the cloak of Élias, he crossed it [4 Rg 2:14].

2. He cured the polluted waters in Jericho [2:21].

3. He slew forty (42) boys who had derided him by ordering two bears to come out of the woods and slay them [2:24].

4. To the childless sterile woman, the Sounamitis, he gave a son [4:16], and

5. when this boy died at the age of five, he brought him back to life [4:34].

6. He made deadly food harmless by putting meal in it [4:41].

7. With ten barley loaves he filled a hundred men at a time of famine and had some left over [4:42, Old Latin].

8. He cured the leprosy of a leper, the Syrian Neeman [5:14].

θ' Τὸν Γιεζῆ χρήματα παρ᾽ αὐτοῦ κομισάμενον ἐλέπρωσεν.
ι' Σίδηρον ἀναπλεῦσαι ἀπὸ βυθοῦ τῇ τοῦ στηλαίου ἐποίησεν¹ ἐπῳδῇ.
ια' Τοὺς ἐπ᾽ αὐτὸν ἐλθόντας στρατιώτας Σύρους ἀορασίᾳ περιβαλὼν, εἰς τὴν πόλιν εἰσήγαγε.
ιβ' Πολιορκουμένῳ βασιλεῖ, καὶ συνερχομένῳ εἰς τὴν Σαμάρειαν, τῶν πολεμίων ἐπικειμένων, καὶ (152a1) διὰ τοῦτο λιμῷ πάντων τῶν ἐν τῇ πόλει φθειρομένων, ἀφθονίαν σίτου καὶ κριθῶν ἀθρόον προεῖπεν ἔσεσθαι, καὶ ἀγγελικῇ δυνάμει οἱ πολέμιοι ἐξηλαύνοντο, καὶ αἱ τροφαὶ εὕρηντο.
ιγ' Τρεῖς βασιλεῖς καὶ στρατὸν ἄπειρον διὰ δίψαν ἀπολλύμενον ὑδάτων ἀθρόον² ἐπιφορᾷ ῥαγδαίῳ ποτῷ διέσωσε.
ιδ' Ἐλαίου ῥύσιν χήρᾳ γυναικὶ, μελλόντων δουλοῦσθαι διὰ πατρῷον χρέος τῶν υἱῶν αὐτῆς, πρὸς τὴν τῶν χρεῶν ἔκτισιν καὶ διατροφὴν αὐτῶν καὶ τῆς μητρὸς ἐποιήσατο.
‹ιε᾽›³ Ἐν δὲ τῷ μνήματι αὐτοῦ νεκρὸς ὑπὸ (152a2) τῶν ἐκκομιζόντων αὐτὸν, ἐπιρριφεὶς⁴ ἀνήπτατο,⁵ καὶ μετὰ τῶν ἐπιρριψάντων αὐτὸν ἔθεεν ἐπὶ τὴν πόλιν· καὶ γὰρ ἦσαν ὁρμῶντες εἴσω τῆς πόλεως, λῃστὰς ἐπιδιώκοντας αὐτοὺς ἀποδιδράσκοντες.

ΠΓ'. + Τίνα ἐστὶν ἃ προεφήτευσεν Ἡλίας;
‹α᾽› Βασιλεῖ τοῦ Ἰσραὴλ τῷ Ἀχαὰβ εἶπεν, ὡς οὐ μὴ βρέξῃ⁶ ἕως οὗπερ πάλιν⁷ αὐτὸς τὸν ὄμβρον ἐπικαλέσοιτο, καὶ οὕτως ἐγίνετο.
‹β᾽› Ὀχοζίᾳ τῷ τοῦ Ἀχαὰβ υἱῷ νοσοῦντι, καὶ ἀποστείλαντι παρὰ τῷ ἐν τῇ Ἀκκαρῶν θεῷ ἐπερωτᾶν εἰ ζήσεται, τοῖς ἀγγέλοις αὐτοῦ (152b1) περιτυχὼν, προεῖπε λέγειν αὐτῷ καὶ ὅτι⁸ δυσσεβῶν παρὰ δαιμόνων περὶ τοῦ ζήσεσθαι τὰς μαντείας αἰτεῖ, καὶ διὰ τοῦτο οὐ ζήσεται.⁹

ΠΔ'. + Τίνα ἐστὶν ἃ Ἐλισσαῖος προεφήτευσεν;
‹α᾽› Ἐλθὼν εἰς τὴν Δαμασκὸν Ἀζαήλῳ προεῖπεν, ὡς ὁ μὲν τῆς Δαμασκοῦ βασιλεὺς ὁ Ἄδερ τεθνήξεται. Ἐτύγχανε δὲ ἀπεσταλμένος¹⁰ ὑπ᾽

---

¹In their notes GM suggest that ἐπιβολη would be a more fitting verb.
²Lc FGM ἀθρουν.
³This item is not numbered in CF.
⁴Emend to ἐπιρραφεις.
⁵Lc M ἀνιστατο.
⁶Lc GM βρεξει.
⁷FGM omit παλιν. Emend by moving παλιν so as to follow οὐ μη or βρεξει.
⁸FGM transpose to ὅτι και.
⁹The items in this chapter are not numbered in CFGM.
¹⁰FGM δ᾽ ἀπεσταλμενος.

9. He sent leprosy upon Giezi (Gehazi) who received money from Neeman [5:27].

10. He made iron float from the deep by the spell which he made on a post [6:6].

11. He struck with blindness the Syrian soldiers coming against him and led them into the city [6:18].

12. He predicted, when the king besieged and came against Samaria with soldiers lying in wait, and (152a) because of this there was a famine for all who were perishing in the city [6:24-25], that there would be a great supply of wheat and barley [7:1], and by angelic power the enemies were driven away and food was found [7:6].

13. He rescued three kings and a huge army perishing because of thirst by providing a violent flow of flood water for drink [3:16-17].

14. He made a supply of oil flow for a widow who was going to enslave her sons in their father's debt, for the payment of the debts and the feeding of themselves and their mother [4:1-7].

15. When a dead man was thrown into his tomb by those who were carrying him, he arose wrapped in a winding sheet and ran to the city with those who had thrown him in. They were hastening within the city in order to escape the robbers pursuing them [13:21].

**83.** – What are the things that Élias predicted?

<1> To Achaab king of Israel he said it would not rain again until he called down rain with prayers, and so it was [3 Rg 17:1; 18:45].

<2> When Ochozias son of Achaab was sick and he had sent to ask the god in Accaron (Ekron) if he would live, meeting his messengers (152b) he (Elijah) told them to tell him that he had acted impiously with demons when he asked oracles about living and therefore he would not live [4 Rg 1:16-17].

**84.** – What did Elissaios predict?

<1> On coming to Damaskos he predicted to Azaél that Ader (Ben-hadad) king of Damaskos (Syria) would die–it happened that he had been sent by him

αὐτοῦ κακουμένου, πευσόμενος αὐτὸν εἰ ζήσεται. Αὐτὸς δὲ διάδοχος αὐτοῦ τῆς βασιλείας ἔσται, καὶ πάμπολλα τοῦ¹ Ἰσραὴλ ἐνδείξεται δεινά.

‹β'› Καὶ τὸν Ἰοῦ² (152b2) προεῖπε τοῦ Ἰσραὴλ ἐπὶ τετάρτην αὐτοῦ γενεὰν βασιλεύσειν, ἐπὶ καθαιρέσει τοῦ οἴκου τῆς τοῦ Ἀχαὰβ βασιλείας, προβεβλημένον εἰς τὴν βασιλείαν.

‹γ'› Παραγενομένῳ πρὸς αὐτὸν τῷ Ἰηοῦ προεῖπεν, ὡς τρίτον προσβαλεῖ τῇ βασιλείᾳ Δαμασκοῦ, καὶ νικήσει τὸν κατ᾽ αὐτῆς πόλεμον. Καὶ ἐπειδὴ ἐκέλευσεν αὐτῷ τοξεύειν³ συντονώτατα, τρίτον ἀκοντήσας⁴ τὸ βέλος, ἐπέσχε τὴν βολήν. Λυπηθεὶς δὲ ὁ προφήτης ἔφη τὸ τρίτον ἔκνικᾶν. Εἰ γὰρ πέμπτον ἠκόντισεν ἂν, πλήρης τὴν Δαμασκινῶν⁵ ἤμελλε καθαίρειν (153a1) βασιλείαν.⁶

**ΠΕ'.** + Τίνα ἐστὶν ἃ Γὰδ προεφήτευσεν;

Ἀπαριθμήσαντι τῷ Δαβὶδ παρὰ τὸ δοκοῦν τῷ Θεῷ τὸν λαὸν, ἀγανακτεῖν ἔφη τὸν Θεὸν κατ᾽ αὐτοῦ, καὶ ἐκ τριῶν ἐπικειμένων τιμωριῶν, διὰ δὴ⁷ τοῦ λιμοῦ τριετοῦς,⁸ πολέμου τριμηνιαίου, λοιμοῦ⁹ τριημέρου, ἑλέσθαι ἣν ἂν βούλοιτο.

**ΠϜ'.** + Τίνα ἐστὶν ἃ προεφήτευσε Νάθαν;

‹α'› Βουληθέντι τῷ Δαβὶδ τὸν ναὸν οἰκοδομεῖν, μὴ βούλεσθαι τὸν Θεὸν δι᾽ αὐτοῦ τὴν οἰκοδομὴν ἀπήγγειλε γίνεσθαι. Τὸν δὲ ἐξ αὐτοῦ γενησόμενον υἱὸν, τὸν Σαλομῶν, οὐδέπω τεχθέντα, (153a2) τοῦτον προεῖπε μέλλειν αὐτὸν προβαλέσθαι καὶ συμπληροῦν.

‹β'› Τὸ εἰς τὴν Βηρσαβεὲ καὶ τὸν Οὐρίαν πλημμελῆσαι, ἤλεγξε τὸν Δαβὶδ, καὶ τὴν ἐπὶ τῇ πλημμελείᾳ παίδευσιν ἐπιοῦσαν αὐτῷ προεῖπε, καὶ τὴν ἐπὶ τῇ ταπεινοφροσύνῃ αὐτοῦ τοῦ ἁμαρτήματος λύσιν.

‹γ'› Τὸν παρ᾽ αὐτοῦ προφητευθέντα τὴν Ἰερουσαλὴμ οἰκοδομεῖν, τὸν υἱὸν αὐτοῦ τὸν Σαλομῶντα, αὐτὸς εἰς τὴν βασιλείαν προηγάγετο, ὑπομνήσας τὸν Δαβὶδ τῆς ὑποσχέσεως, καὶ τὸν ἐπαναστῆναι τῇ βασιλείᾳ πειραθέντα (153b1) τὸν Ἀδωνίαν, σοφῶς καθαιρεθῆναι παρασκευασάμενος.

---

¹GM suggest τω in their notes.
²Lc FGM Ἰηου.
³FGM print ἐκελευσε τοξευειν, omitting αὐτῷ.
⁴Lc FGM ἀκοντισας.
⁵Lc FGM Δαμασκηνων.
⁶The items in this chapter are not numbered in CFGM.
⁷FGM print δηλαδη in place of δια δη.
⁸FGM τριετους λιμου.
⁹Lc FGM και λοιμου.

when he was ill to ask the prophet if he would live—and he himself would succeed to his kingdom and would greatly harm Israel [4 Rg 8:7].

<2> And he predicted that Iéou would reign over Israel to the fourth generation, after he had been thrust into the kingship on the destruction of the house and the kingdom of Achaab [10:30].

<3> And when Iéou (Iôas) came to him he predicted that for the third time he would fight with the kingdom of Damascus and win the war against it. And since he ordered him to shoot arrows vigorously, after firing three he stopped shooting. The prophet grieved and said he would win three times, but if he had shot a fifth arrow he would have completely destroyed the (153a) kingdom of the Damascenes [13:19].

**85.** – What are the things that Gad predicted?

When against the will of God David counted the people he said that God was angry with him and he could choose one of the three punishments that were in store for him: famine for three years, war for three months, or pestilence for three days [2 Rg 24:13].

**86.** – What are the things that Nathan predicted?

<1> When David wanted to build the Temple, he announced that God did not want the building begun and finished by him, but that it would be the son who would be born from him Solomon, who was not yet born, who would lay the foundation and bring the work to completion [2 Rg 7:7-17].

<2> He blamed David for sinning against Bérsabeë and Ourias [12:1] and foretold the punishment that would come for the sin as well as the remission of sin because of his humility [12:13-14].

<3> Predicting that his (i.e., David's) son Solomon would build Jerusalem, he promoted him for the kingship, recalling David's promise and (153b) wisely undertaking to destroy Adônias, who tried to rebel against the kingdom [3 Rg 1:11-14].

**ΠΖ'.** + Τίνα προεφήτευσεν Ἀχίας ὁ Σιλωνίτης;

‹α›· Ἰεροβοὰμ¹ προεῖπεν, ὡς τῶν δέκα τοῦ Ἰσραὴλ φυλῶν βασιλεύει.² Διαρρήξας³ γὰρ τὸ ἱμάτιον αὐτοῦ εἰς δώδεκα μέρη πεποίηκε, καὶ ἐκέλευσεν αὐτῷ δέκα μέρη λαμβάνειν ἐκ τούτων, προειπὼν αὐτῷ, ὡς δέκα φυλῶν τοῦ Ἰσραὴλ βασιλεύει.⁴

‹β›· Ἀνονί[τη]⁵ τῇ τοῦ⁶ Ἰεροβοὰμ γυναικὶ πρὸς αὐτὸν μετ' ἐπικρύψεως ἡκούσῃ, περὶ παιδὸς ἀρρωστοῦντος ἐπερωτῶν⁷ εἰ ζήσεται· **(153b2)** ταύτην μὲν ἐξ ὀνόματος ἐκάλει, μὴ σημάνασαν ἑαυτὴν, καίπερ τυφλὸς διὰ τὸ γῆρας τυγχάνων. Προεῖπε⁸ δὲ αὐτῇ, ὡς καὶ τὸν υἱὸν οὐ καταλήψεται ζῶντα, ὁ δὲ Ἰεροβοὰμ ἀπὸ τῆς βασιλείας οἰκτρῶς καταστραφήσεται.⁹

**ΠΗ'.** + Τίνα Σαμαίας προεφήτευσε;

‹α›· Ῥοβοὰμ τῷ τῆς Ἰερουσαλὴμ βασιλεῖ ἐν δεκαδύο μυριάσι στρατιωτῶν ἐπιόντι πολεμεῖν κατὰ τῶν δέκα τοῦ Ἰυραὴλ τῶν ἀποστασῶν αὐτοῦ φυλῶν, κατὰ τὴν πορείαν περιτυχὼν, ἀναστρέφειν ἐπὶ τὰ οἰκεῖα, καὶ μὴ συμφύλων πόλεμον παρατάττειν ἔλεγε, καθαίρεσιν **(154a1)** αὐτοῦ παντελῆ, καὶ τοῦ στρατοῦ ἧτταν προφητεύων, εἰ πολεμήσουσι.

‹β›· Προεῖπε καὶ τῷ Ῥοβοὰμ καὶ τῷ λαῷ, ὡς ἐγκαταλείψαντα¹⁰ τὸν Κύριον, ἐγκαταλειφθήσονται ὑπ' αὐτοῦ.

‹γ›· Καὶ τῷ Ἰεροβοὰμ δὲ προεῖπεν, ὡς τῶν δέκα τοῦ Ἰσραὴλ κρατήσει σκήπτρων, τοῖς αὐτοῖς τοῦ Ἀχία σημείοις τῶν τοῦ ἱματίου ῥηγμάτων χρησάμενος.

**ΠΘ'.** + Τί προεφήτευσεν Ἰάδων;

Οὗτός ἐστιν, ὁ εἰς τὴν Βεθὴλ παραγενόμενος, τοῦ Ἰεροβοὰμ τὸ θυσιαστήριον ἐγκαινίζοντος, καὶ προειπὼν τὸν Ἰωσίαν βασιλεύσειν, ὡς¹¹ κατακαίειν **(154a2)** ἤμελλε τοὺς ἱερωμένους ἐν τῷ θυσιαστηρίῳ, σημεῖον

---

¹*Lc* FGM Τῳ Ιεροβοαμ.
²*Lc* FGM βασιλευσει.
³GM Διαρρησας.
⁴*Lc* FGM βασιλευσει.
⁵Emend to Ἀνονι to correct the dittography; Ἀνω τη is suggested by G (p. 45, note 3) and M (col. 101, note 4). Ἀνω is also mentioned in Chapter 50.
⁶M printed που by mistake.
⁷*Lc* FGM επερωτησουσα.
⁸GM προειπεν.
⁹The items in this chapter are not numbered in CFGM.
¹⁰In their notes GM suggest εγκαταλειψαντες.
¹¹*Lc* FGM ὁς.

**87.** – What did Achias the Silonite predict?

<1> He predicted to Ieroboam that he would reign over the ten tribes of Israel, for he rent his garment into twelve parts and ordered him to take ten parts from these and predicted that he would be king over ten tribes of Israel [3 Rg 11:30-31].

<2> He called by name Anô the wife of Ieroboam, who had come to him in concealment to ask if her sick son would live [C. 50], even though she did not identify herself and had become blind because of old age [14:4-6]. He predicted to her that her son would not live and that Íeroboam would wretchedly lose the kingdom [14:16].

**88.** – What did Samaias predict?

<1> He went to meet Roboam king of Jerusalem with 120,000 [LXX] soldiers advancing in war against the ten tribes of Israel which had defected from him, and told him to return home and not war upon their fellow tribesmen, predicting that (154a) he and his army would be completely destroyed if they waged war [3 Rg 12:22; 2 Par 11:1].

<2> He also predicted to Roboam and to the people that because they had abandoned the Lord they would be abandoned by him [2 Par 12:5].

<3> And he predicted to Ieroboam that he would rule the ten tribes[1] of Israel, using the same signs as Achias, the parts of the garment [3 Rg 12:24 ms].

**89.** – What did Iadôn predict?[2]

This is the one who came to Bethél when Ieroboam was dedicating an altar, and predicted that Iôsias would be king and he was about to burn up those who

---

[1] Literally "scepters." This is a Hebraism, since *Shevet* can mean either "tribe" or "scepter." This usage is found in the LXX (e.g. 3 Rg 11:13).

[2] Named not in 3 Rg but in Josephus *Ant.* 8.231.

παραυτίκα δοὺς τοῦ θυσιαστηρίου τὴν διάρρηξιν, τοῦ τὸ προρρηθὲν γενήσεσθαι.

Ϟ'. + Τί προεφήτευσε Βαασά;
Τῷ βασιλεῖ τοῦ Ἰσραὴλ, Βαασᾶ καὶ αὐτῷ λεγομένῳ, προεῖπεν, ὡς τεθνήξεται τὴν ταχίστην, διὰ τὰς δυσσεβείας.

ϞΑ'. + Τί προεφήτευσε Μιχαίας;
Τῶν ψευδοπροφητῶν ἀπατώντων τὸν Ἀχαὰβ, ὃς ἦν τοῦ Ἰσραὴλ βασιλεὺς, ὡς πολεμήσας τὸν Σύρον βασιλέα τὸν Ἄδερ, ἀφαιρήσεται παρ' αὐτοῦ τὴν Γαλααδῖτιν (154b1) χώραν, ἣν οἱ Σύροι πάλαι παρὰ τῶν Ἰσραηλιτῶν ἀφείλοντο, κληθεὶς καὶ αὐτὸς εἶπε,[1] τί δέοι περὶ τοὺς πρὸς τοὺς[2] Σύρους πολέμους πράττειν, προεῖπεν, ὡς συμβαλὼν ἀναιρεθήσεται, τοῦ Θεοῦ τῇ διαβόλου ἀπάτῃ ἐκδεδωκότος αὐτὸν, διὰ τῶν ψευδοπροφητῶν, ὅπως διὰ τὰς δυσσεβείας ἀναιρεθήσεται.

ϞΒ'. + Τίνα προεφήτευσεν Ἀζαρίας υἱὸς Σαδώκ;
Ὡς ὁ λαὸς ἐγκαταλείψει τὸν Κύριον, καὶ ἐγκαταλειφθήσεται ἐπὶ πολλαῖς ἡμέραις[3] ὑπὸ Θεοῦ· καὶ πολλὰ διὰ τῆς καταλείψεως τιμωριθείς,[4] εἰς ὑετὸν[5] προσλειφθήσεται,[6] (154b2) γνοὺς τὸν παιδευτὴν καὶ σωτῆρα, καὶ τῶν ἐπαγγελιῶν πληρωτήν.

ϞΓ'. + Τίνα προεφήτευσεν Ἰησοῦ[7] ὁ τοῦ Ἀνανῆ;[8]
Ἰωσαφὰτ τῷ τοῦ Ἰούδα[9] βασιλεῖ συμμαχοῦντι τῷ Ἀχαὰβ, ἐν τῇ πρὸς τοὺς Σύρους περὶ τῆς Ῥεμμὼθ Γαλαὰδ μάχῃ, ἐκφυγόντι ἐκ τῆς ἅμα τῷ Ἀχαὰβ ἀναιρέσεως, ὑπαντήσας ἔφη κακῶς πεπραχέναι, συμμαχήσαντι τῷ δυσσεβεῖ καὶ ὑπὸ Θεοῦ μισουμένῳ φίλον γεγονότα. Καὶ εἰ μὴ αὐτὸς εὐσεβὴς φανεὶς, τὰ εἴδωλα τοῦ Ἰούδα καθεῖλεν, ὀργῆς ἂν ἐπειρᾶτο Θεοῦ, διὰ τὴν τοῦ Ἀχαὰβ σύμπραξιν. (155a1)

---

[1] Lc FGM εἴπειν.
[2] FGM omit τους.
[3] Lc FGM πολλας ἡμερας.
[4] Lc FGM τιμωρηθεις.
[5] Lc FGM υἱον.
[6] Lc FGM προσληφθησεται.
[7] Lc FGM Ἰησους.
[8] Lc FGM Ἀνανι.
[9] FGM του λαου Ἰουδα.

sacrificed in the sanctuary, when giving a sign that it would be as he predicted, the altar was broken [3 Rg 13:1-10].

**90.** – What did Baasa (Eiou) predict?

To the king of Israel, himself named Baasa, he foretold that he would soon die because of his impious acts [3 Rg 16:1-4].

**91.** – What did Michaias predict?

When the false prophets deceived Achaab king of Israel as if by waging war on the Syrian king Ader he would take the region of (154b) Galaad (Ramoth-Gilead) from him, which the Syrians had previously taken from the Israelites, Michaias was summoned to speak about what would be necessary to make war against the Syrians, and he predicted that he would be killed in battle since through the false prophets God had given him over to the deceit of the devil so that he would be destroyed for impiety [3 Rg 22:1-28].

**92.** – What did Azarias son of Sadôk predict?

That the people would abandon the Lord and would be abandoned for many days by God and would suffer many punishments through the abandonment, but would be received as a son, recognizing the Chastiser and Savior and Fulfiller of promises [2 Par 15:1-7].

**93.** – What did Iésous (Iéou) son of Anani predict?

Having come to Iôsaphat king of Judah, an ally of Achaab in the battle against the Syrians at Rémmôth Galaad who fled to avoid being killed with Achaab, the prophet said that he (ie., Iôsaphat) had acted badly., having become a friend to his impious ally, a man hated by God. Furthermore, had he not destroyed the idols of Judah, thus appearing to be righteous, he would have experienced the wrath of God on account of this alliance with Achaab [2 Par 19:2] (155a).

ϘΔ'. + Τίνα προεφήτευσεν Ἰζιὴλ¹ ὁ προφήτης;

Τῷ Ἰωσαφὰτ πολεμοῦντι πρὸς Ἀμμανίτας καὶ Μωαβίτας, καὶ τοὺς ἀπὸ τοῦ² Ἡσαῦ ἐπελθόντος³ τῷ Ἰούδᾳ, προεῖπεν, ὡς δι᾽ εὐχῆς καὶ σαλπίγγων αὐτοὺς καθαιρίσῃ.⁴ Καὶ οὕτως ἐγίνετο.⁵

ϘΕ'. + Τίνα προεφήτευσεν Ἐλιὰδ ὁ τοῦ Ὀβδία;

Τῷ Ἰωσαφὰτ φιλίαν ἀσπασαμένῳ πρὸς Ὀχοζίαν τοῦ Ἀχαὰβ,⁶ καὶ τῶν πλοίων κοινωνὸν αὐτὸν ποιησαμένων,⁷ τῶν εἰς Αἰθιοπίαν ἀποπλεόντων ἐπ᾽ ἐμπορίᾳ, προεῖπεν, ὡς καὶ αἰνίαις⁸ (155a2) ναυαγήσως,⁹ καὶ αὐτὸς οὐκ εὐάρεστος Θεῷ γενόμενος, διὰ τοῦτο τεθνήξεται.

ϘϜ'. + Τίνα προεφήτευσεν Ὀλδᾶ, ἡ τοῦ Σελὶμ γυνή;

Ἰωσίᾳ τῷ βασιλεῖ εὐσεβεῖ γενομένῳ, καὶ τὸν ναὸν ἐρειπωθέντα ἀνανεουμένῳ,¹⁰ καὶ διαρρήξαντι τὰ ἱμάτια αὐτοῦ ἐπὶ τῇ ἀναγνώσει τοῦ εὑρεθέντος βιβλίου Μωϋσέως, ἐν ἐπιλησμονῇ τῶν θείων νόμων τοῦ λαοῦ γενομένου, ἐπέστειλεν, ὡς ὁ λαὸς μὲν εἰς αἰχμαλωσίαν ἐκδοθήσεται διὰ τὴν ἀποραθύμησιν¹¹ τὴν ἀπὸ Θεοῦ, αὐτὸς δὲ πρὸ τῆς τῶν κακῶν ἐπαγωγῆς τεθνήξεται, (155b1) διὰ τὴν φιλόθεον αὐτοῦ γνώμην, ἵνα μὴ ἴδῃ τὰ ἐπιόντα κακά.

ϘΖ'. + Τίνα ἐστὶν ἃ Ζαχαρίας ὁ ἀρχιερεὺς προεφήτευσεν;

Ἐπὶ τῇ γεννήσει Ἰωάννου τοῦ Βαπτιστοῦ πεπληρῶσθαι τὰς τοῦ Θεοῦ πρὸς τὸν Ἀβραὰμ ἔλεγεν ἐπαγγελίας, τὸν Θεὸν ἀνυμνῶν, καὶ ἐπὶ τούτῳ τετάχθαι τὸν Ἰωάννην, πρόδρομον τοῦ ὑψίστου Θεοῦ γενόμενον, ἐφ᾽ ὅτε¹² τὴν ὁδὸν αὐτοῦ εἰς κόσμον ἐρχομένου ἑτοιμάσαι,¹³ σωτήριον οὖσαν τοῦ

---

¹Lc FGM Ὀζιιλ.
²GM omit του.
³Lc FGM ἐπελθοντας.
⁴Lc FGM καθαιρηση.
⁵Lc GM ἐγενετο.
⁶FGM τον του Ἀχααβ.
⁷Lc FGM ποιησαμενῳ.
⁸Lc FGM ἀνιαις.
⁹Lc FGM ναυαγησεως.
¹⁰FGM print ἀνανεομενῳ, but GM correct it in their notes.
¹¹Lc GM ἀπορραθυμησιν.
¹²Lc FGM ἐφ᾽ ᾧ τε.
¹³Emend to ἑτοιμασθαι.

**94**. – What did Oziél (Iahaziel) the prophet predict?

To Iôsaphat warring against the Ammanites and Moabites and those who had come from Esau to Judah, that through prayer and trumpets he would destroy them. And so it took place [2 Par 20:14-23].

**95**. – What did Eliad son of Obdias predict [Eliezer son of Ôdia, 2 Par 20:37, Cod.A]?

To Iôsaphat who entered upon a treaty of friendship with Ochazias son of Achaab and joined him in building ships to sail to Ethiopia for trade, he predicted that he would die in the distress of shipwreck, since he was not pleasing to God [20:35-37].

**96**. – What did Olda wife of Selim predict?

To Iôsias the pious king who renewed the ruined Temple and rent his garments upon the reading of the discovered book of Moses, when the people had forgotten the divine laws, she wrote a letter to say that the people would be given into captivity for their neglect of God, but because he himself had a (155b) God-loving mind he would die before such evils came so that it would not be necessary for him to see the future evils [2 Par 34:22-28 = 4 Rg 22:14-20].

<MIRACLES AND PREDICTIONS AMONG CHRISTIANS (97-101)>

**97**. – What did Zacharias the high priest[1] predict?

At the birth of Iôannés the Baptist he said, praising God, that the prophecies made to Abraam were fulfilled, and for this purpose Iôannés was appointed as the precursor of God Most High, through whom (i.e., Iôannés) the way of his (i.e., Christ's) coming into the world was prepared, to be salvific for the people

---

[1] Lk 1:9 says that "it fell to [Zacharias] by lot to enter the Temple of the Lord and burn incense." Joseph misunderstands this verse to imply that he was high priest. On casting lots to determine who will offer incense, see *m Tamid* 5.2–6.3 (esp. 6.3, which makes it clear that the one offering incense need not be a high priest). Cf. Index A, s.v. "high priest."

λαοῦ, καὶ ἐπίλαμψιν τοῖς ἐν σκότει καθημένοις καὶ σκιᾷ θανάτου· καθὼς διὰ τῶν ἁγίων αὐτοῦ προφητῶν, (155b2) τῶν ἀπ' αἰῶνος προκηρυττόντων τὴν παρουσίαν αὐτοῦ, λελάληκεν.

ϞΗ'. + Τίνα ἐστὶν ἃ Συμεὼν προεφήτευσεν;
Οὗτος θεασάμενος ὃν ὁ[1] Ζαχαρίας Θεὸν ὕψιστον προεκήρυξεν, ἐπίλαμψιν[2] τοῖς ἐν σκότει καθημένοις, ὑπὸ τῆς μητρὸς Μαρίας εἰς τὸ ἱερὸν, τεσσαρακονθήμερον βρέφος ἔτι ὄντος,[3] ἀναφερόμενον, ὑπὸ τοῦ Ἁγίου Πνεύματος ἀχθεὶς, δεξάμενος τὸ παιδίον ἐβόα· Νῦν ἀπολύεις τὸν δοῦλόν σου, Δέσποτα, κατὰ τὸ ῥῆμά σου, ἐν εἰρήνῃ. Ὅτι εἶδον οἱ ὀφθαλμοί μου τὸ σωτήριόν σου, ὃ ἡτοίμασας κατὰ πρόσωπον (156a1) πάντων τῶν λαῶν, φῶς εἰς ἀποκάλυψιν ἐθνῶν, καὶ δόξαν λαοῦ σου Ἰσραήλ. Προεφήτευσε καὶ τὸν Μαρίας ἐπὶ τῷ σταυρῷ σκανδαλισμόν.

ϞΘ'. + Τί προεφήτευσεν Ἐλισάβετ;[4]
Θεασαμένη τὴν Παρθένον Μαρίαν πρὸς αὐτὴν ἐληλυθυῖαν, εὐλογημένην εἶπεν εἶναι ἐν γυναιξὶν, καὶ εὐλογημένον τὸν καρπὸν τῆς κοιλίας αὐτῆς. Καὶ πόθεν μοι τοῦτο, ἵνα ἔλθῃ ἡ μήτηρ τοῦ Κυρίου μου πρός με; Ἰδοὺ γὰρ, ὡς ἐγένετο ἡ φωνὴ τοῦ ἀσπασμοῦ σου εἰς τὰ ὦτά μου, ἐσκίρτησεν ἐν ἀγαλλιάσει τὸ βρέφος ἐν τῇ κοιλίᾳ μου. Ἐφ' οἷς καὶ τοὺς πιστεύοντας τοῖς (156a2) οὕτω λελαλημένοις ἐκφανησομένοις μακαρίους ἀπέφηνεν.

Ρ'. + Τίνα ἐστὶ τὰ διὰ τῆς Παρθένου Μαρίας προφητευθέντα;
Μεγαλύνει καὶ αὐτὴ τὸν Θεὸν, ἐπὶ τὸ εἰς αὐτὴν ἐκφαινομένῳ μυστηρίῳ τοῦ Θεοῦ τόκου. Ἀγάλλεται τῷ ἐν[5] Πνεύματι, λέγουσα μακαρίζεσθαι αὐτὴν ἐν πάσαις ταῖς γενεαῖς, ἀπὸ τοῦ νῦν μεγίστου πράγματος ὑπὸ τοῦ[6] Θεοῦ ἐπ' αὐτῇ ἐκφαινομένου.

Καὶ τίνα ἐστὶν ἃ Ἰωάννης ὁ Βαπτιστής;
Ὅτι ὁ ὀπίσω αὐτοῦ, τοῦτ' ἔστιν, ὁ μετ' αὐτὸν γεννηθεὶς, πρὸ αὐτοῦ ὑπῆρχεν. Ὅτι ἄνωθέν ἐστιν ἐξ οὐρανοῦ Χριστός. Ὅτι τοὺς (156b1) δικαίους ἀπὸ τῶν ἀδίκων Χριστὸς διακρινεῖ.

---

[1] GM omit ὁ.
[2] FGM εἰς ἐπιλαμψιν.
[3] Lc FGM ὄν.
[4] GM Ἐλιζαβετ.
[5] FGM omit ἐν.
[6] FGM omit του.

and a light to those sitting in darkness and in the shadow of death [Lk 1:79], as he spoke through his holy prophets who have always predicted his coming [1:70].

**98.** – What did Symeôn predict?

He saw the one whom Zacharias foretold, God Most High, a light to those sitting in darkness, carried by his mother Maria into the Temple while still being an infant of forty days. Inspired by the Holy Spirit, taking the child he shouted, "Lord, now let your slave depart in peace according to your word; for my eyes have seen your salvation, which you have prepared before the face (156a) of all peoples, a light for revelation to the gentiles, and the glory of your people Israel." He also predicted to Maria the scandal upon the cross [Lk 1:27-35].

**99.** – What did Elisabet predict?

Seeing the Virgin Maria coming to her, she said she was "blessed among women and blessed was the fruit of her womb; and whence is it to me that the mother of my Lord comes to me? For behold, as the word of your greeting struck my ears, the babe leapt for joy in my womb." Hence also she declared "blessed those who believe that what was thus spoken will be fulfilled" [Lk 1:41-45].

**100.** – What are the things predicted through the Virgin Maria?

She too magnified God for the mystery that would befall her, that of the birth of God,[1] rejoicing in the Spirit and saying that she was blessed in all generations because of the greatest deed now manifested by God in her [Lk 1:46-49].

And what through Iôannés the Baptist?

That he who came after him — that is, born after him — existed before him [Jn 1:30], for Christ is from above [3:31], from heaven, and (156b) Christ will separate the just from the unjust.

---

[1] This could also be translated "the offspring of God." This expression may reflect what is commonly called "Alexandrian christology." Cf. C. 1(70).

**ΡΑʹ.** + Τίς ἄκων προεφήτευσεν ἐν τῷ Εὐαγγελίῳ;

Καϊάφας ὁ ἀρχιερεὺς τὸ σωτήριον τοῦ Χριστοῦ πάθος προαγορεύων, πρὸς τοὺς Ἰουδαίους φησίν· Ὑμεῖς οὐκ οἴδατε οὐδέν, οὐδὲ διαλογίζεσθε, ὅτι συμφέρει ὑμῖν, ἵνα εἷς ἄνθρωπος ἀποθάνῃ ὑπὲρ τοῦ λαοῦ, καὶ μὴ ὅλον τὸ ἔθνος ἀπόληται· ἐφ᾽ οἷς ἐπήγαγεν ὁ Εὐαγγελιστής· Τοῦτο δὲ ἀφ᾽ ἑαυτοῦ οὐκ εἶπεν, ἀλλ᾽ ἀρχιερεὺς ὤν, προεφήτευσεν, ὅτι ἤμελλεν Ἰησοῦς[1] ἀποθανὼν, ὑπὲρ τοῦ ἔθνους ἀποθνήσκειν, καὶ οὐχ ὑπὲρ τοῦ **(156b2)** ἔθνους μόνον, ἀλλ᾽ ἵνα καὶ[2] τὰ ἐσκορπισμένα τοῦ[3] Θεοῦ πρόβατα συναγάγῃ εἰς ἕν.

Ἐν δὲ τῇ Παλαιᾷ ἄκοντες προφητεύουσι·

‹αʹ› Βαλαὰμ ὁ μάντης.[4]

‹βʹ› Καὶ οἱ ἀποσταλέντες ὑπὸ τοῦ Σαοὺλ ἐπὶ τὸν Δαβίδ.

‹γʹ› Καὶ αὐτὸς ὁ Σαοὺλ ἐπελθὼν αὐτῷ.[5]

## ΒΙΒΛΟΣ Εʹ.

**ΡΒʹ.** + Τίνες εἰσὶν οἱ τοῦ Δαβὶδ δυνατοί;

‹αʹ› Ἰεσβοὸς διεκόσμει τὴν διασκευὴν αὐτοῦ. Εἶχεν ὑπ᾽ αὐτὸν ἐννακοσίους.

‹βʹ› Ἀδινών, ὃς τῶν τραυμάτων ἐπεμελεῖτο.

‹γʹ› Ἐλεάζαρ υἱὸς ἀδελφοῦ τοῦ Δαβίδ.

‹δʹ› Σωσιὼς μόνος τοῖς πολεμίοις ἀνθίστατο, κελεύων **(157a1)** τοῖς ὑπ᾽ αὐτὸν κυλεύειν[6] τοὺς πίπτοντας.

‹εʹ› Σαμᾶ, ὃς τῶν πολεμίων διωκόντων τὸν τοῦ λαοῦ στρατόν, μόνος[7] ἀπέστρεφε τοὺς διώκοντας.

‹ϛʹ› Ἀβεσσά, ὃς ἑξακοσίοις ἐν πολέμῳ μόνος ἀνθίστατο.

‹ζʹ› Βαναίας, Ἐλιὰβ υἱὸς τοῦ ἀδελφοῦ Δαβίδ, ὃς καὶ τοὺς δύο στρατηγοὺς ἀνεῖλε, καὶ λέοντας ἀπέκτεινε, καὶ τὸν Αἰγύπτιον ἄνδρα δυνατὸν ὄντα ὤλεσεν.

‹ηʹ› Ἀσαῆλος τριάκοντα ἐφεστήκει ἄρχουσιν.

‹θʹ› Ἐλεηνᾶν, ὃς ἦν καὶ αὐτὸς υἱὸς ἀδελφοῦ του Δαβίδ.

---

[1] FGM ὁ Ἰησοῦς.
[2] FGM omit καί.
[3] FGM omit του.
[4] Lc FGM μαντις.
[5] The items in this chapter are not numbered in CFGM.
[6] Lc FGM σκυλευειν.
[7] F μονους; GM print μονους, but indicate in their notes that they prefer μονος.

**101**. – Who in the gospel predicted unwillingly?

Kaiaphas the high priest predicted the salvific passion of Christ and said to the Jews, "You do not know anything, nor do you consider that it is expedient for you that one man die for the people and the whole nation not perish" The evangelist added that "He did not speak on his own but since he was high priest he predicted that Jesus would die for the nation, and not only for the nation but that he might also gather the scattered sheep of God into one" [Jn 11:49-51].

In the Old Testament these prophesied unwillingly:

<1> The seer Balaam [Nm 24:1].

<2> And those sent by Saul against David [1 Rg 19:19-21].

<3> And Saul himself coming to him [1 Rg 19:23-24;24:21].

## BOOK V

### <DAVID AND SOLOMON (102-4)>

**102**. – Who were the mighty men of David? [2 Rg 23:8; 1 Par 11:10][1]

<1> Iesboos who decorated his armor and had nine hundred under him [cf. 2 Rg 23:8, 1 Par 11:11][2]

<2> Adinôn who cared for wounds [23:8, *traumatias*, Cod.B].

<3> Eleazar son of the brother of David [Heb.: son of Dôdî or *Dôdô*, his uncle; LXX 23:9: his uncle, son of Sousei/Sôsei].

<4> [Sôsiôs], who alone resisted the enemies and ordered (157a) those who fought under him to despoil the fallen.[3]

<5> Sama (Samaa, Arm.), who when the enemy pursued the army of the people alone forced the pursuers to retreat [23:11-12].[4]

<6> Abessa (Abishai), who alone resisted six hundred in battle[5] [23:18].

<7> Banaias son of Eliab brother of David,[6] who killed two generals and slew lions (a lion) and destroyed a mighty Egyptian [23:20-21, cf. C. 147].

<8> Asaél[os] was among thirty rulers [23:24].

<9> Eleénan, himself the nephew of David (LXX, son of his uncle, Doudei = *Dôdô*) [23:24].

---

[1] Cf. Josephus *Ant.* 7.307–17. A military list occurs in Hyginus 97: "Who went to fight at Troy and how many ships?"

[2] Decorated armor, killed nine hundred soldiers, LXX MSS.

[3] Josephus *Ant.* 7.308–9 (also corrupt).

[4] Josephus *Ant.*. 7.309–10 (Sabaias).

[5] Josephus *Ant.* 7.315, with some manuscripts of 1 Par 11:20.

[6] In 2 Rg 23:20: Banaias son of Iôdaë.

‹ι›> Σεμὰν ὁ Μυδαῖος.
‹ια›> Ἀλλῆς ὁ τοῦ Κελθῆ.
‹ιβ›> Ἑλλᾶς ὁ τοῦ Φελλαθί.
‹ιγ›> Ἱερᾶς υἱὸς Ἐσκὰθ ὁ Θεκοΐτης. **(157a2)**
‹ιδ›> Ἀνεζὰρ ὁ Ἀνωθίτης.
‹ιε›> Ἑλαὼν ὁ Λωΐτης.
‹ις›> Νοερίων ὁ Φατίτης.
‹ιζ›> Ἀλλοὺς υἱὸς Φαφά.
‹ιη›> Ἑναῦ ὁ Νεφθαλίτης.
‹ιθ›> Ἐτθὶ[1] υἱὸς Ῥεβαέχ.
‹κ›> Σαβεὲθ Ἀδδαὴ ὁ ἀπὸ Γαασσῆ.
‹κα›> Ἀβιελβὼν ἀπὸ τῆς πεδιάδος.
‹κβ›> Ἀδδὰδ ἐκ Ναχάλ.
‹κγ›> Ἰασβιὴλ ἀπὸ Σαράθ.
‹κδ›> Ματθί.
‹κε›> Ἰωὰβ Ἀρσαμίτης.
‹κς›> Ἐλίας ὁ Σαλαβωνίτης.[2]
‹κζ›> Ἰωνάθαν υἱὸς Ἀσάν.
‹κη›> Σωμνᾶν ὁ Ἀρρωδίτης.
‹κθ›> Ἐλίαν ὁ Ἀραθίτης.
‹λ›> Ἀλιφαλέτ.
‹λα›> Ἀλιὰφ υἱὸς Ἀχιτόφελ.
‹λβ›> Ἀσαραὴ ὁ Καρμήλιος.
‹λγ›> Φαρὰς ὁ Ἀρχίτης.
‹λδ›> Γαὰλ υἱὸς Νάθαν.
‹λε›> Σαβαβωναὴ ὁ Γαδδίτης.
‹λς›> Ἐλιὲφ ὁ Ἀμμαρίτης.
‹λζ›> Γελωραὶ **(157b1)** ὁ Βεροθέος.
‹λη›> Ἰαδδάδ.[3]
‹λθ›> Θερρή.
‹μ›> Γεράς.
‹μα›> Ἐθέρ.

---

[1] *Lc* FGM Ἔζθι.
[2] GM Σαλαβονιτης; *lc* the Armenian Σαλαβωνειτης.
[3] *Lc* GM Ἰαδαδ.

<10> Seman the Mydaian (Sammai the Aroudaios) [23:25, Cod.A].

<11> Allés son of Kelthé [23:26 Ellés, Cod.A; the Kelôthei, Arm].

<12> Ellas son of Phellathi (Allas Fellataeus) [23:26, Arm.].

<13> Hieras (Eiras) son of Eskath the Thekoïtés [23:26].

<14> Anezar (Abiezir) the Anôthités [23:27].

<15> Elaôn the Lôités (Ellôn) [23:28].

<16> Noeriôn the Phatités (Noere the Entôphateités) [23:28].

<17> Allous son of Phapha (Alaph ... Baanaai) [23:29 Cod.A].

<18> Enau the Nephthalïtés (Ela ... Baana the Netôphathités, LXX var.) [23:28].

<19> Ezthi son of Rebaech (Esthaei ... Reiba) [23:29].

<20> Sabeeth Addaé from Gaassé (Addai of the brook of Goas) [23:30 Arm].[1]

<21> Abielbôn from the plain [23:31 Arm].

<22> Addad (Addai) from Nachal [23:31 Arm].

<23> Iasbiél from Sarath (Gasbiel the Arabadita)[23:31 Arm].

<24> Matthi [perhaps = Machatai, 23:34 Cod.A].

<25> Iôab the Arsamités (son of Sarouia) [23:18].

<26> Elias the Salabôneités [23:32 Arm].

<27> Iônathan, son of Asan [23:32 Arm].

<28> Sômnan the Arrodités (Samnan the Arôdeités) [23:33].

<29> Elian the Arathite (Abialbon the Arbathite) [23:31].

<30> Aliphalet [23:34].

<31> Aliaph (Eliab) son of Achitophel [23:34].

<32> Assaraé (Asarai) the Karmelian [23:35].

<33> Pharas the Archite (Pharaei the Aracheieis, Cod.A) [23:35].

<34> Gaal son of Nathan [23:36].

<35> (Sababonaé) the Gaddités (son of Gaddi, Cod.A) [23:36].

<36> Elieph the Ammarités (Eleïë the Ammanités) [23:37].

<37> Gelôrai the Berothean (157b) (Gelôre the Béthôraian, the armor-bearer of) [23:37].

<38> Iadad (Iôab) [23:37].

<39> Therré (Eiras the Aitheiraios) [23:38].

<40> Geras (Gérab) [23:38].

<41> Ether (the Ethennaios) [23:38].

---

[1] Armenian readings come from Brooke-McLean-Thackeray, *The Old Testament in Greek* II.1 (Cambridge: At the University Press, 1927) 195.

**ΡΓ'.** + Τίνες οἱ τοῦ Σαλομῶντος ἄρχοντες;
‹α'› Βαναίας στρατηγὸς ἀντὶ τοῦ Ἰωάβ.
‹β'› Σαδὼκ, καὶ ὁ υἱὸς αὐτοῦ Ἀζαρίας, ἱερεῖς.
‹γ'› Ζαμβοὺχ, ἱερεὺς ἕτερος τοῦ Σαλομῶν.
‹δ'› Ἐλιαρέφ.
‹ε'› καὶ Ἀχιὰβ υἱοὶ Σισᾶ.
‹ϛ'› Ἰωσαφὰτ υἱὸς Ἀχιλλίδ.
‹ζ'› Ἀδωνειρὰν υἱὸς Ἀβδωθὼ, ἐπὶ τὸν φόρον.


Καὶ οἱ κατὰ μῆνα τὰ δέοντα χορηγοῦντες·
‹η'› Βεοὺρ ἐν ὄρει Ἐφραὶμ, υἱὸς Κακών.
‹θ'› Ἐμμακμὲς υἱὸς Ἐσδῆ.
‹ι'› Ἐρραβὼθ υἱὸς Ἀμινᾶς δεύτερος ἐν χώρᾳ Ταασσή.
‹ια'› Βεναὰν υἱὸς Ἀλιοὺθ ἐν Θαανάς.  (157b2)
‹ιβ'› Μεγεδὼ υἱὸς Γάβερ.

**103.** – Who were the princes of Solomon?[1]

<1> Banaias (Banaiou), general in place of Iôab [3 Rg 2:35].
<2> Sadôk and his son Azarias, priests [2:35,4:1 Cod.A].
<3> Zambouch another priest of Solomon [Zambouth, 4:5 Cod.A].
<4> Eliareph (Arm) and
<5> Achiab sons of Sisa [Seisa, 4:3 Cod.A].
<6> Iôsaphat (Cod.A) son of Achillid [Achilleid, 4:3 ms].
<7> Adôneiran son of Abdôthô [Abdô, Arm], in charge of tribute [4:6].

And those who supplied the provisions every month [4:7]:

| (Names) | (Places) |
|---|---|
| <8> Beour,[2] | in Mount Ephraim [4:8] |
| son of Kakôn [3] [4:9] | |
| <9> Emmakmes[4] [4:9]], son of Esdé[5] [4:10]. | |
| <10> Errabôth[6] second son of Aminas,[7] | in the land of Taassé.[8] |
| <11> Benaan,[9] son of Aliouth,[10] | in Thaanas[11] [4:12]. |
| <12> Megedô[12] [4:12], son of Gaber [4:13]. | |

---

[1] Josephus *Ant.* 8.35–36; much closer to 3 Rg 2:35, 4:1–19; cf. Alfred Rahlfs, *Septuaginta-Studien* 3 (Göttingen: Vandenhoeck & Ruprecht, 1911) 224–39, (but Joseph is certainly not following the "Lucianic" text).

[2] LXX: Baiôr; MT: ben-Chur.

[3] Cod.A and Arm: son of Dakar; MT: son of Deqer.

[4] This is a corruption of the geographic reference "in Machmas" found in Cod.A and Arm. Cod.B has "in Machemas"; MT "in Maqats."

[5] Cod.A and Arm: son of Esd.

[6] This is a corruption of the geographic reference "in Arabôth" from 4:10 found in Cod.A and Arm.

[7] From 4:11. Cod.A, Arm, MT read "son of Aminadab."

[8] From 4:11. Cod.A and Arm read "in the land of Nephthadôr"; MT "all of Naphath Do'r." Cod.B has a complete muddle.

[9] Cod.A [4:12]: Baana.

[10] MT: 'Achilud; Cod.A [4:12]: Eloud.

[11] Cod.A: Thaanach; Arm: Thanach.

[12] Cod.B and Arm: Mekedô. This is a corruption of the geographic reference preserved in the MT: in Ta'anakh and Megiddo. Cod.A: Memagedaô.

‹ιγ'› Ἑρραμὼθ υἱὸς Ἀδδή.

‹ιδ'› Ἐμμαενώ.

‹ιε'› Ἀχειμαὰς ἐν Νεφθαλείμ.

‹ις'› Βασιλείας υἱὸς Χουσῆ ἐν Ἀσὴρ καὶ ἐν Βααλώθ.[1]

‹ιζ'› Ἰωσαφὰτ υἱὸς Φαρροῦ ἐν Ἰσάχαρ.

‹ιη'› Σεμεῆ υἱὸς Ἠλᾶ ἐν Βενιαμίν.

‹ιθ'› Γάβερ υἱὸς Ἀδαὴ ἐν Γαλαάδ, καὶ ἐν γῇ Γηῶν βασιλέως Ἀμμορραίων, καὶ Ὢγ βασιλέως Βασάν.

‹κ'› Καὶ Νασὴφ ἐν γῇ Ἰούδα παρέστηκεν, ὑποδεχόμενος τὰ παρ' ἑκάστῳ τεταγμένα.

---

[1] Lc FGM Βααλαωθ.

\<13\> Erramôth[1] [4:13] son of Addé[2] [4:14].

\<14\> Emmaenô[3] [4:14].

| | |
|---|---|
| \<15\> Acheimaas | in Nephthaleim [4:15].[4] |
| \<16\> Chousé, son of the queen[5] | in Aser and in Baalaôth[6] [4:16]. |
| \<17\> Iôsaphat son of Pharrou[7] | in Isachar [4:17 in MT].[8] |
| \<18\> Semeé[9] son of Éla | in Benamin [4:17; 4:18 in MT]. |
| \<19\> Gaber[10] son of Adaé | in Galaad[11] and in the land of Géôn[12] king of the Amorites and of Og king of Basan [4:18; 4:19 MT]. |

\<20\> And Naséph stood by in the land of Iouda, receiving what was ordered of each one [4:18 + *hekastos kata tén syntaxin autou*, 4:21].

The Biblical material which Joseph uses has suffered greatly in tranbsmission. In this chapter, as elsewhere, the text of the *Hypomnestikon* exhibits similarities to Cod.A and Arm. In general, the MT seems superior to the LXX at 3 Rg 4:8ff., and the chief virtue of Cod.A and Arm is their relative similarity to the MT. Cod.B., on the other hand, is a complete mess.

Joseph (or a source) was disturbed that in his Bible some individuals ("son of Kakôn," "son of Esdé," etc.) were named only by patronymics. In an attempt to "correct" the text, several place names have been converted into personal names.

---

[1] Cod.A, Arm: en Ramôth. This is a corruption of the geographic reference preserved in the MT: in Ramoth Gil'ad.

[2] Arm: Ainadab, son of Addo; Cod.A: Ainadab son of Sadôk; MT: 'Achiynadab son of 'Iddo'.

[3] Cod.A: Maanaim; MT: Machanaymah. Although this is probably a geographic reference, here this is is obscured even in the MT.

[4] At this point the LXX adds that "he took Basemmath daughter of Salômôn" (+ "as wife," Cod.A, Arm). Josephus *Ant.* 8.36–37 omits Acheimaas, giving "Basima" as wife to Achinadab; then notes Banakités (Baana) and \<Iô\>saphatés, Soumouis, and Gabarés, ending with "one more as ruler" (so Heb "nesib" of 4:19, Joseph's Naseph).

[5] Cod.A, Cod.B, Arm, and MT: Baana son of Chousei.

[6] Joseph follows Cod.A., Arm, and MT at this point against Cod.B.

[7] Joseph here follows Cod.A and Arm. Cod.B reads Phouasoud.

[8] Cod.B places "Iôsaphat son of Phouasoud in Issachar" in 4:20, at the end of the list.

[9] Cod.B omits Semeé.

[10] Cod. B omits Gaber.

[11] Joseph's Galaad accords with Cod.A and Arm. Cod.B reads: "in the land of Gad."

[12] LSS: Séôn.

ΡΔ'. + Τίνα ἦν τὰ καθ᾽ ἑκάστην ἡμέραν ἐξοδιαζόμενα τῷ Σαλομῶν;

Σεμιδάλεως κόροι λ', ἀλεύρου κόροι ξ', μόσχοι ἐκλεκτοὶ ι', βόες νομάδες κ', (158a1) πρόβατα ρ', ἐκτὸς ἐλάφων, καὶ ζορκάδων,[1] καὶ ὀρνίθων. Ἦσαν δὲ αὐτῷ τετράκις μύριοι τοκάδες ἵππων εἰς ἅρματα, καὶ δώδεκα χιλιάδες ἱππέων.

ΡΕ'. + Περὶ τοῦ ναοῦ τῆς Ἱερουσαλὴμ, οὗ[2] ᾠκοδόμησε Σαλομῶν.

Ἤρξατο τῆς οἰκοδομῆς ἐν ἔτει ἀπὸ τῆς ἐξ Αἰγύπτου ἐξόδου τοῦ λαοῦ πεντηκοστῷ καὶ ἑξακοσιοστῷ, ἐν τῷ τετάρτῳ μηνὶ, οὗτός ἐστι κατὰ Μακεδόνας Πάνεμος, δευτέρᾳ τοῦ μηνὸς, λίθους μὲν ἑτοιμαζόμενος καὶ ξύλα ἀπὸ πρώτου ἔτους τῆς βασιλείας αὐτοῦ ἐπὶ ἔτη τρία. Ἀρξάμενος δὲ τῆς οἰκοδομῆς (158a2) ἀπὸ τετάρτου ἔτους τῆς βασιλείας αὐτοῦ. Εἰς δὲ τὴν ἐργασίαν παρέστησεν ἐργάτας ἑπτακισμυρίους, ἐπιστάτας τρισχιλίους ἑξακοσίους. Ἀρχιτέκτονας[3] δὲ τῆς ὅλης ἐργασίας ἀπὸ Τύρου λαμβάνει τὸν Χηρὰμ υἱὸν γυναικὸς χήρας ἀπὸ φυλῆς Νεφθαλὴ πατρὸς Τυρίου. Συνηρᾶτο δὲ αὐτῷ καὶ ὁ Τύρου βασιλεὺς, εἰς τὴν ναοῦ οἰκοδομὴν, ὁ Χιρὰμ, ξύλα κέδρινα καὶ πεύκινα διδοὺς ἀπὸ τοῦ Λιβάνου. Ἐχορήγει δὲ ὁ Σαλομῶν αὐτῷ κατ᾽ ἐνιαυτὸν εἰς ἀναλώματα τῶν κοπτόντων τὰ ξύλα, καὶ καταγόντων αὐτὰ ἕως θαλάσσης, (158b1) σίτου κόρους β',[4] ἐλαίου βάτους β'·[5] καὶ ἀπέστελλεν ἐκ τοῦ λαοῦ τοῦ[6] Ἰσραηλιτικοῦ εἰς τὸν Λίβανον μυρίους ἐργάτας κατὰ μῆνα ἀλλασσομένους, καὶ εἶχον ἔξαρχον οὗτοι τὸν Ἀδωνειράμ.

ΡϚ'. + Ὁποῖος ἦν ὁ ναὸς, ὃν Σαλομῶν ᾠκοδόμησεν;[7]

‹α›Μέσος οἶκος ἦν στοαῖς[8] σταδιαῖος,[9] κατὰ τὰς τέσσαρας πλευρὰς περιβεβλημένος, Ἁγίασμα καλούμενος, ἔχων μῆκος πήχεις ξ', πλάτος πήχεις κ', ὕψος πήχεις λ', πρὸς δὲ ἀνατολὰς ἀπέβλεπεν. Εἶχε δὲ καὶ προναΐον[10] ἰσόπλατον τῷ ναῷ, πήχεις ἔχων κ', καὶ ὕψος ἴσον τῷ ναῷ· τριάκοντα (158b2) γὰρ πηχῶν ἦν καὶ τοῦτο, εἰσάγων ἐπὶ πήχεις κ',

---

[1] FGM δορκαδων.
[2] Lc FGM ὀν.
[3] Lc FGM ἀρχιτεκτονα.
[4] Emend to ͵β'.
[5] Emend to ͵β'.
[6] FGM omit του.
[7] FGM ᾠκοδομησε.
[8] FGM omit στοαις.
[9] Emend to σταδιαις.
[10] M προναον.

**104**. – What were Solomon's daily provisions?

30 kors of wheat flour, 60 kors of meal, 10 fatted oxen, 20 pastured oxen, (158a) 100 sheep, apart from stags, gazelles, and birds. He also had 40,000 brood-mares for chariots, and 12,000 horses [3 Rg 4:22-23,24 Cod.A, Arm].[1]

## <THE TEMPLE AND THE TABERNACLE (105-111)>

**105**. – About the Temple of Jerusalem that Solomon built.[2]

He began the building in the 650th year after the exodus of the people from Egypt,[3] in the fourth month which is Panemos for the Macedonians, on the second day of the month,[4] when he had prepared the stones and the wood for three years from the first year of his reign [3 Rg 5:17]. He began the building from the fourth year of his reign. He provided 70,000 workmen for the work and 3,600 supervisors [5:15-16, not Cod.A; 2 Par 2:18]. He took as architect of the whole work Héram from Tyre, son of a widow from the tribe of Nepththalé and a Tyrian father [7:2, not Cod.A]. The king of Tyre, Hiram, assisted him in building the Temple, providing cedar and cypress wood from Lebanon [5:8-9]. For his expenses in cutting the wood and transporting it to the sea Solomon supplied him with (158b) 2<0,000> cors of wheat and 2<0,000> baths of oil [5:11]. And he sent 10,000 workmen from the Israelite people to Lebanon, changed every month, and they had Adôneiram in charge [5:14].[5]

**106**. – Of what sort was the Temple that Solomon built?

<1> The middle house, called Sanctuary, was surrounded on four sides with pillared colonades, with a length of sixty cubits, a width of twenty cubits, and a height of thirty cubits [3 Rg 6:6]. **It faced toward the east.[6] It also had a porch of the same width as the Temple, twenty cubits, and a height equal to the Temple, for this too was of thirty cubits, leading into twenty cubits, and**

---

[1] Josephus *Ant.* 8.40–41.

[2] Cf. Hyginus 225, "Who first built the temples of the gods?"

[3] This contradicts 3 Rg 6:1 (440th, LXX [Heb 480th] year, 2nd month = Ziv; cf. 2 Par 2:2) as well as Josephus *Ant.* 8.61 (592 years after, 2nd month called Artemisios or in Hebrew Iar) and 20.230 and *Against Apion* 2.19 (612 years).

[4] Fourth year of Solomon, 2nd month (3 Rg 6:1).

[5] *Dismyrioi* (20,000), Adôramos in Josephus *Ant.* 8.57, 859.

[6] Josephus *Ant.* 8.64 (height sixty; east).

περιοίκοιτο[1] δὲ οἴκοις βραχέσι λ', πενταπήχεσιν ἰσοπλεύροις, ἐπὶ τρία στέγη, εἰς κ' πήχεις τῶν τριῶν στεγῶν τούτων ἠρμένων. Τοῖς δὲ οἰκίσκοις τούτοις τοῖς λ' ἄνοδοι κεκρυμμέναι γεγένηντο, διὰ μικρῶν θυρῶν ἐπὶ τὰ στέγη ἀνάγουσαι. Οἱ δὲ τῶν οἰκίσκων τούτων δέκα πήχεις ὑπέρτεροι, ἀνειμένην παρεῖχον τοῦ Ἁγιάσματος οἴκῳ[2] τὴν τῶν φώτων βολήν. Ἀπὸ δὲ τῶν ἑξήκοντα πηχῶν τοῦ ναοῦ, οἱ ἐσώτατοι[3] τῷ Ἁγίῳ τῶν ἁγίων διήρηντο, οἱ δὲ ἄλλοι μ', τῷ ἐξοτάτῳ[4] (159a1) ἁγίῳ κεκλήρωντο. Αἱ δὲ θύραι τοῦ ναοῦ πρὸς τὸ εὖρος κ' πηχῶν γεγένηντο, ἔσωθεν καὶ ἔξωθεν διόλου κεχρυσωμέναι. Καταπέτασμα δὲ ἦν τὸ ἐπ' αὐταῖς καθηπλωμένον,[5] ἐκ βύσσου καὶ ὑακίνθου καὶ πορφύρας καὶ κοκκίνου ὑφασμένον. Καὶ ἦν ἅπας ὁ ναὸς καὶ τὰ ἐν αὐτῷ πάντα ἔσωθεν καὶ ἔξωθέν διόλου χρυσῷ καταπεπλασμένα. Καὶ τὸ ἔδαφος δὲ χρυσῷ παχεῖ κατέστρωτο, οἵ τε τοῖχοι φοίνικος[6] καὶ Χερουβὶμ ἐγγεγλυμμένους[7] καὶ τετορνευμένους[8] διόλου διέκειντο. Οὕτω τοίνυν ὁ ναὸς κατεσκεύαστο.

⟨β'⟩ Περιέκειτο (159a2) δὲ κύκλῳ τοῦ ναοῦ γῆ Σιὼν[9] εἰς τρεῖς πήχεις ἀνατείνων[10] τὸ ὕψος, ἔργον[11] δὲ τοὺς πολλοὺς τῆς[12] εἰς τὸ ἱερὸν εἰσόδου, μόνοις δὲ ἀνειμένον τοῖς ἱερεῦσι.[13]

**ΡΖ'.** + Τίνα ἦν τὰ ἐν τῷ Ἁγιάσματι ἀνακείμενα ἀφιερώματα;

⟨α'⟩ Εἰς μὲν τὸν ἅγιον οἶκον, τὸν εἰκοσάπηχυν καὶ ἰσόπλευρον, ἡ κιβωτὸς, ἣν Μωϋσῆς ἐποιήσατο, ἔνδον ἀνατεθεῖσα, ὑπὸ τῶν Χερουβὶμ σκεπομένη, οἵτινες[14] ἦσαν δύο ἀνὰ δύο πτέρυγας[15] ἔχοντα πενταπήχεις,

---

[1]FGM print περιοικειτο. *Lc* GM, who in their notes suggest emending to περιῳκειτο.

[2]FGM τῳ του Ἁγιασματος οἰκῳ .

[3]*Lc* GM, who in their notes suggest emending to οἱ ἐσωτατοι κ'.

[4]*Lc* GM ἐξωτατῳ.

[5]GM καθηλωμενον.

[6]*Lc* GM, who in thier notes suggest emending to φοινιξι .

[7]*Lc* FGM ἐγγεγλυμμενοις .

[8]*Lc* FGM τετορνευμενοις .

[9]*Lc* FGM, who print γεισιον in place of γη Σιων.

[10]*Lc* FGM ἀνατεινον.

[11]*Lc* FGM εἰργον .

[12]FGM omit της.

[13]The items in this chapter are not numbered in CFGM.

[14]FGM ἀτινα.

[15]FGM print ἦσαν δυο πτερυγας. Emend to ἦσαν δυο ἀνα πτερυγας.

surrounded by thirty small chambers, five cubits broad and equilateral, raised on three stories to twenty cubits.[1] There were thirty concealed steps leading to the roofs through little doors. The upper ten cubits of these chambers provided a free opening of light to the house of the Sanctuary.[2] Of the sixty cubits of the Temple, the innermost twenty belonged to the Holy of Holies and the other forty to the (159a) outer Holy [3 Rg 6:16-17]. The doors of the Temple were twenty cubits in width, completely gilded on the inside and outside. A veil was hung upon them, woven of undyed linen and blue and purple and scarlet.[3] And the whole Temple and everything in it inside and outside was made entirely of gold. And the floor was covered with thick gold[4] and the walls were entirely covered with palms and the Cherubim, carved and sculpted [3 Rg 6:28-29]. Thus the Temple was built.

<2> A parapet lay around the Temple with a height reaching three cubits and keeping the multitude from the entrance to the sacred place, open only to the priests.[5]

107. – What were the consecrated vessels in the sanctuary?[6]

<1> In the equilateral sanctuary with a breadth and length of twenty cubits was the tabernacle which Moses made, placed within, covered by the Cherubim each with two wings five cubits long, standing on each side of the

---

[1] An interpretation of Josephus *Ant.* 8.65–66.

[2] Josephus *Ant.* 8.70–71.

[3] Josephus *Ant.* 8.75,71–72; 2 Par 3:14.

[4] Josephus *Ant.* 8.74–75; 3 Rg 6:28–29.

[5] Josephus *Ant.* 8.95.

[6] 3 Rg 7:15–50 (2 Par 3:3–4:22); Josephus *Ant.* 3.115–33; 8.71–88.

ἐξ ἑκατέρου τῆς κιβωτοῦ παρεστῶσαι.¹ Καὶ μία μὲν πτέρυξ πρὸς τὸν τοῖχον ἐξέτατο, (159b1) μία δὲ πρὸς τὴν κιβωτόν, καὶ συναπτόμεναι δὲ ἑαυταῖς, αἱ δύο πτέρυγες ἔσκεπον τὴν κιβωτόν, πρὸς ἀνατολὰς βλέπουσαν. Καὶ ἡ στεφάνη δὲ ἔκειτο τῇ κιβωτῷ, εἰς ἣν Μωϋσῆς ἔμφασιν τῆς τοῦ Θεοῦ σημασίας ἐνέγραψε, τὸ τετράγραμμον δὲ ἦν τούτῳ² ὄνομα, ἄρρητον, οὐκ ἀλλοιουμένη, ἀλλά γε εἰς ἀεὶ διαμένουσα. Ἐπέκειντο δὲ αἱ δίπτυχοι πλάκες ἐν τῇ κιβωτῷ, ἐν αἷς ὁ θεόγραφος ἐνεγέγραπτο δεκάλογος, ἃς Μωϋσῆς ἐδέξατο παρὰ τοῦ Θεοῦ ἐν τῷ Σινᾷ ὄρει, τὸν λαὸν νομοθετῶν. Ἐν δὲ τῷ Ἁγίῳ τῶν (159b2) ἁγίων τούτῳ οἴκῳ μόνος ὁ ἀρχιερεὺς ἅπαξ τοῦ ἐνιαυτοῦ εἰσήει.

⟨β'⟩ Ἐν δὲ τῷ ἁγίῳ τῷ τεσσαρακονταπήχει, τῷ πρὸ τούτου, στύλοι χάλκεοι παρειστήκεισαν, ὕψος πηχέων ιη', περιμέτρου πηχέων ιβ', πάχους κεχωνευμένων³ δακτύλων δ'. Ἐφ' ἑκάστῃ δὲ κεφαλῇ τῶν κιόνων, κρίνον ἐπέκειτο ἐπὶ πέντε πήχεις ἐγγεγραμμένον,⁴ καὶ τούτῳ περιέκειτο δίκτυον χάλκεον, ἀφ' οὗ καὶ ῥοαὶ διακόσιαι⁵ ἀπήρχοντο.⁶ Ἐκαλεῖτο δὲ ὁ μὲν ἐκ δεξιῶν κίων, Ἴδρυσις, ὁ δὲ ἐξ εὐωνύμων, Δύναμις. Κατὰ δὲ τὸ δεξιὸν μέρος εἰσιόντων, λουτὴρ ἦν ἰδρυμένος, (160a1) χονευτός,⁷ χάλκεος, Θάλασσα διὰ τὸ μέγεθος καλούμενος, διάμετροι⁸ πηχῶν δέκα, ἐν δὲ κύκλῳ τριάκοντα πήχεσι καὶ ἑνὶ μετρούμενος, πάχει παλαιστιαίῳ πεπαχυμμένος, βάτους δεχόμενος ὕδατος τρισχιλίους. Εἰς τοῦτον οἱ ἱερεῖς εἰσιόντες λειτουργεῖν, τὰς χεῖρας ἀπενίπτοντο, καὶ τοὺς πόδας ἀπερραίνοντο. Ἐπέκειτο δὲ ὁ λουτὴρ ἐπὶ σπείρας πηχυαίας, ἐνέα⁹ πήχεις διάμετρον ἐχούσης, καὶ μόσχοι δώδεκα τὰ ὀπίσω πρὸς τὴν πείραν¹⁰ ἔχοντες, τὰ δὲ πρόσωπα πρὸς τὰ τέσσαρα κλίματα βλέποντες, (160a2) τριῶν μόσχων κατὰ πλευρὰν ἱδρυμένων, οἳ τὸ¹¹ τοῦ λουτῆρος ὑπέκειντο κύκλῳ.

⟨γ'⟩ Καὶ ἄλλοι δέκα λουτῆρες, πέντε μὲν ἐκ δεξιῶν, πέντε δὲ ἐξ εὐωνύμων καθίδρυντο, βάσεις χαλκᾶς τετραγώνους ὑπέχοντες, μήκους

---

¹FGM παρεστωτα. Emend to παρεστωτες.
²In their notes, GM suggest emending to τουτο.
³Lc GM, who in their notes suggest emending to κεχωνευμενοι.
⁴Lc FGM ἐγηγερμενον.
⁵FGM διακοσιοι.
⁶Lc FGM ἀπηρτητο.
⁷Lc FGM χωνευτος.
⁸Lc FGM διαμετρος.
⁹Lc FGM ἐννεα.
¹⁰Lc FGM σπειραν.
¹¹Lc FGM τῳ.

tabernacle. **And one wing extended to the wall,** (159b) **one to the tabernacle, and where they were joined they covered the tabernacle,** which faced to the east [cf. 3 Rg 6:23-27; 8:6-7]. And a crown lay on the tabernacle, on which Moses engraved an imprint of the signification (*sémasia*) of God (the *Tetragrammon* was his ineffable *name*), not changeable but enduring forever.[1] Also in the tabernacle lay the two tablets on which the Decalogue, written by God, was inscribed, tablets which Moses received from God on Mount Sinai, legislating for the people [Ex 25:16]. Into the Holy of Holies building only the high priest entered, once a year [Ex 30:10].

<2> In the forty-cubit Holy, lying before this, stood **bronze pillars eighteen cubits high, with a circumference of twelve cubits, moulded to a width of four fingers. On the capital of each column lay a lily rising to a height of five cubits, and around this was a bronze net from which two hundred pomegranates were suspended. The column on the right was** called Building (*Hidrysis*), **that on the left,** Power (*dynamis*).[2] On the right side on entering was **a worked bronze basin,** (160a) **called Sea because of its size, with a diameter of ten cubits** and a circumference of thirty-one cubits,[3] **in thickness a palm broad** and **holding three thousand *baths*[4] of water. The priests who were going in to serve washed their hands and feet in it.**[5] The basin lay on a rounded moulding of a span, with a diameter of nine cubits, and twelve calves with their backs toward the moulding and their faces looking in four directions, with three calves on each side under the hemisphere of the basin [3 Rg 7:13].

<3> And ten other basins, five to the right and five to the left, having underneath **rectangular bronze bases with a length of five cubits, a width of**

---

[1] High priest wears crown with name of God: Josephus *Ant.* 3.172, 187. *Tetragrammon onoma*, Clement *Str.* 5.34.4 (*tetragrammaton onoma*, Philo *Life of Moses* 2.115).

[2] Josephus *Ant.* 8.77–78. "Setting up" (*katorthôsis*) and "strength" (*ischys*), 2 Par 3:17.

[3] 3 Rg 7:23 (2 Par 4:2) has diameter 10, circumference 30; Joseph or a source has corrected to 31, with *pi* at 3.14.

[4] Josephus *Ant.* 8.79–80.

[5] Josephus *Ant.* 8.87; 2 Par 4:5–6.

πήχεις¹ ε', πλᾶτος πήχεις δ', ὕψος πήχεις ϛ'. Ἑκάστῃ δὲ βάσει δ' κιονίσκοι κατὰ γωνίαν ἑστῶτες προσέκειντο, ἐφ' ὧν οἱ λουτῆρες ἐπέκειντο ὕψους πήχεις δ', χωροῦντες ἀνὰ χοᾶς² μ'· διεστήκασι δὲ ἀπ' ἀλλήλων τέτρασι³ πήχεσι. Καὶ χεῖρες δὲ ἦσαν χαλκαῖ, πρὸς τὸν ὑποκείμενον κύκλον ἐρει[ρει]σμέναι,⁴ (160b1) ὕψους πηχῶν ι', ὧν οἱ ὦμοι τοὺς λουτῆρας ὑπέφερον. Λέοντες δὲ καὶ μόσχοι καὶ ἀετοὶ καὶ φοίνικες περὶ τοὺς κιονίσκους, κατὰ τὴν τῶν τεσσάρων πηχῶν διάστασιν εἱστήκεισαν. Ταῦτα δὲ πάντα ἐπὶ τεσσάρων τροχῶν ἐωρούμενα⁵ ἐπέκειντο. Οἱ δὲ λουτῆρες οὗτοι, εἰς τὸ καθαίρειν τὰ ἐντὸς τῶν ὁλοκαυτουμένων ζώων, καὶ τοὺς πόδας «αὐτῶν»⁶ ἀπονίπτειν προύκειντο.

‹δ'› Ἐν τούτῳ δὲ⁷ τῷ οἴκῳ καὶ θυσιαστήριον ἵδρυτο χάλκεον, μῆκος πηχῶν κ', «εὖρος τοσούτων»,⁸ ὕψος πηχῶν ι', πρὸς τὰς ὁλοκαυτώσεις. Καὶ τὰ σκεύη δὲ αὐτοῦ ἦν (160b2) χάλκεα· ποδηστῆρες⁹ καὶ ἀναληπτῆρες.¹⁰ Καὶ τράπεζα δὲ χρυσῆ, ἐφ' ἧς οἱ τῆς προθέσεως ἄρτοι δώδεκα ἐπέκειντο, καὶ λυχνία, ἡ τοὺς ἑπτὰ λύχνους κατὰ τὴν Μωϋσέως διάταξιν ἀπαστράπτουσα, χρυσῆ καὶ αὐτή. Καὶ βωμὸς χρύσεος μέσος τούτων πάντων ἵδρυτο. Καὶ ἄλλαι δὲ τράπεζαι χρυσαῖ, καὶ λυχνίαι ποικίλαι ποικίλως εἰργασμέναι, μικραὶ καὶ διάφοροι. Ἐν αἷς ἐπετίθετο τὰ ἱερὰ σκεύη, φιάλαι καὶ σπονδία. Ταῦτα πάντα εἶχεν ὁ τῶν μ' πηχῶν οἶκος "Αγιος, πρὸ τοῦ καταπετάσματος τοῦ (161a1) ἀδύτου τοῦ Ἁγίου τῶν ἁγίων, ἐν ᾧ ἡ Κιβωτὸς ἀνέκειτο.¹¹

**ΡΗ'.** + Τίνα ἦν τὰ κατασκευασθέντα καὶ ἀνατεθέντα ὑπὸ τοῦ Σαλομῶνος εἰς ἱερουργίαν τὰ¹² κειμήλια;

Οἰνοχοαὶ ὀκτακισμύριοι χρυσαῖ, ἀργυραῖ δὲ διπλασίονες. Φιαλῶν, μυριάδων δέκα χρυσαῖ, ἀργυραῖ δὲ διπλασίονες. Πίνακες εἰς τὸ προσφέρειν

---

¹GM omit πηχεις.
²Lc FGM χοας.
³M τεσσαρσι.
⁴Lc FGM, who eliminate the dittography, printing ἐρεισμεναι.
⁵FGM αἰωρουμενα.
⁶The word αὐτων is not found in CFGM, but is found in Josephus *Ant.* 8.87.
⁷Lc FGM Ἐν δε τουτῳ.
⁸The words εὖρος τοσουτον are not found in CFGM, but probably should be read based on Josephus *Ant.* 8.88.
⁹Lc FGM ποδιστηρες.
¹⁰In their notes GM suggest ἀναλημπτηρες.
¹¹The items in this chapter are not numbered in CFGM.
¹²Lc FGM, who omit τα.

**four cubits, and a height of six cubits** [7:14]. On each base there were **four little columns standing at the corners**, on which the basins lay to a **height of four cubits, each holding forty measures.** They stood **four cubits** apart. And there were bronze hands (160b) fixed to the hemisphere, with a height of ten cubits, whose shoulders held up the basins. Lions and calves and eagles and palm trees stood around the columns with an interval of four cubits. **All these were raised upon four wheels. These basins were appointed for cleansing the entrails of the** slaughtered **animals and** for washing <their> feet. [1]

<4> In this house there also stood **an altar of bronze, with a length of twenty cubits, <a width the same> and a height of ten cubits, for the whole burnt-offerings. And its vessels were of bronze, the tripods and buckets.** And the table was **of gold** on which the twelve **loaves** of show-bread lay, and the seven-branched candelabrum **according to the ordinance of Moses** was of gold. **An altar of gold was set in the middle of all this,** and **other tables** were **of gold,** and artful candelabra intricately worked, small and varied, among which were set **the** sacred **vessels, bowls and cups. All these things were within the Holy House of forty cubits, before the veil of the** (161a) **shrine of the Holy of Holies, where the ark lay.** [2]

**108.** – What were the vessels prepared and dedicated by Solomon for divine worship?

**Eighty thousand gold pitchers. Double the number in silver. A hundred thousand gold bowls. Double the number in silver. Eighty thousand gold**

---

[1] Josephus *Ant.* 8.81, 85, 87.

[2] Josephus *Ant.* 8.88–90.

ἐν αὐταῖς σεμίδαλιν πεφυρμένην, χρυσοῖ ὀκτακισμύριοι, ἀργυραῖ δὲ διπλασίονες. Μέτρα δὲ ἦν[1] καὶ ἀσσαρὶ, ὡς Μωϋσῆς ἐξέδωκε, χρυσᾶ μὲν μύρια, ἀργυρᾶ δὲ διπλασίονα. Θυμιατήρια χρυσᾶ δισμύρια, καὶ ἄλλα (161a2) μύρια, ἐν οἷς τὸ πῦρ ἀπὸ τοῦ μεγάλου βωμοῦ «ἐτίθετο»,[2] πεντακισμύρια.

**ΡΘ'.** + Τίνα ἦν τὰ ἱερεῦσι[3] καὶ Λευΐταις εἰς τὰς λειτουργίας κατασκευασθέντα ὑπὸ Σαλομῶντος αἰσθήματα;[4]

Στολαῖς ἱεραῖς[5] σὺν ποδήρεσι, καὶ ἐπωμίσι, καὶ λογίῳ, καὶ λίθοις τοῖς ἀρχιερεῦσι, χίλιαι. Ζῶναι ἐκ βύσσου καὶ πορφύρας μυριάδες ρ'.[6] Σαλπίγγων μυριάδες κ'· καὶ Λευΐταις, ἐκ βύσσου στολαῖς,[7] μυριάδες κ'· καὶ τὰ ὄργανα τὰ μουσικὰ, νάβλαι καὶ κιννύραι πρὸς τὴν ὑμνῳδίαν ἐξευρημέναι, ἐξ εἰλέκτρου[8] (161b1) κατασκευασμέναι[9] τετρακισμύριαι.

**ΡΙ'.** + Ὁποία ἦν[10] ἡ σκηνὴ, ἡ ὑπὸ Μωϋσέως ἀνασταθεῖσα, κατὰ τὴν ὑπόδειξιν, ἣν ἐθεάσατο ἐν τῷ ὄρει;

‹α'› Περίβολος ἦν αἰθέριος μήκους πηχῶν ρ', πλάτους πηχῶν ν'. Ἡ δὲ στάσις ἦν τοῦ περιβόλου ὀρθίοις κάμαξι περιβεβλημένη χαλκέοις πενταπήχεσι τὸ ὕψος, εἴκοσι μὲν κατὰ τὸ μῆκος, δέκα δὲ κατὰ τὸ πλάτος. Κιονόκρανα δὲ ἀργύρεα καὶ βάσεις χαλκαῖ ἑκάστῳ κάμακι πεποίηνται, πέντε δὲ πήχεσιν ἀπ' ἀλλήλων (161b2) διεστήκασιν οἱ κάμακες καταπεπηγμένοι. Κρίκοι δὲ τοῖς κάμαξι προσηλοῦντο, πρὸς τὸ μῆκος καὶ τὸ πλάτος ἀποβλέποντες. Καὶ τῶν κρίκων ἐξήπτετο καλοδία,[11] ἥλων χαλκῶν πηχέων[12] εἰς τὸ ἔδαφος καθηλωμένων ἐκδεδεμένα,[13] πρὸς τὸ τὴν σκηνὴν ἀκίνητον ὑπὸ τῆς τῶν ἀνέμων βίας διαφυλάττειν. Σινδόναι δὲ κατετείχιζον τὴν σκηνὴν ἐκ βύσσου καὶ ὑακίνθου καὶ πορφύρας καὶ κοκκίνου διυφασμέναι, πεντάπηχεις, τετράγωνοι, ἀπὸ τοῦ κράνους μέχρι τῆς

---

[1] *Lc* FGM ἰν.
[2] *Lc* FGM
[3] *Lc* FGM τα τοις ἱερευσι.
[4] *Lc* FGM ἐσθηματα.
[5] *Lc* FGM Στολαι ἱεραι.
[6] Emend ρ' (ἑκατον) to ἑκαστον, as in Josephus *Ant.* 8.93 (εἰς ἑκαστον μυριας).
[7] *Lc* FGM στολαι.
[8] *Lc* FGM ἠλεκτρου.
[9] GM wrongly emend to κατεσκευασμεναι.
[10] FGM omit ἦν.
[11] *Lc* FGM καλῳδια.
[12] *Lc* FGM πηχυαιων.
[13] GM ἐνδεδεμενα.

platters to carry the mixed fine flour, and double the number in silver. Measures such as Moses delivered, the *hin* and the *assarôn*, of gold ten (twenty) thousand, and double the number in silver. Twenty thousand gold censers and fifty thousand other censers in which the fire from the great altar <was placed.>[1]

**109.** – What were the vestments prepared by Solomon for the priests and Levites for the liturgies?

**A thousand** sacred **vestments for the high priests, with long robes and upper garments and oracle and stones. Girdles of linen and of purple, ten thousand each. Two hundred thousand trumpets and, for the Levites, two hundred thousand robes of linen. As for the musical instruments, he made forty thousand** *nablai* and *kinnyrai* **for leading the singing of hymns, formed of** (161b) **electrum.**[2]

**110.** – Of what sort was the tabernacle set up by Moses according to the model which he saw on the mountain [Ex 26 and 36]?

<1> **It was a courtyard with a length of a hundred cubits and a breadth of fifty cubits.** The position of the enclosure was surrounded by **bronze shafts fifty cubits high,** twenty on the long sides and ten on the broad.[3] **The capitals** of each pole **were made of silver and the sockets of bronze**, and the poles were **fixed in the ground** five cubits apart. Rings were attached to the poles, looking at the length and the breadth. **Cords were fastened from the rings and fastened to bronze pegs a cubit long, which were nailed to the ground to keep the tabernacle unmoved by the force of the winds.**[4] **Linens** covered the tabernacle, **woven of linen and colored blue and purple and scarlet,** five cubits long and square, from the peak to the base, and were spread out from the

---

[1] Josephus *Ant.* 8.91–92. Thackeray-Marcus, *Josephus* 5 (London: Heinemann, 1950) 621 note a, point out that Josephus invented all these numbers (therefore Joseph used Josephus, the only source of Cc. 108–9).

[2] Josephus *Ant.* 8.93–94 (musical instruments described in 7.306).

[3] Josephus *Ant.* 3.109 (twenty shafts on each of the two longer sides, ten broadwise on the rearward side).

[4] Josephus *Ant.* 3.108–10.

βάσεως, κατὰ μέσου (162a1) τῶν καμακίων ἕως ἐδάφους κεχυμέναι. Καὶ αἱ μὲν τρεῖς πλευραὶ τοῦτον ἐστήκασι τὸν τρόπον.

‹β›› Ἡ δὲ τετάρτη πλευρά, ἣν καὶ πρώτην μᾶλλόν τις εἴποι καλῶς εἶναι (εἴσοδος γὰρ ἦν εἰς τὴν σκηνὴν αὕτη, πεντήκοντα πήχεις ἔχουσα) πύλης μὲν εἰκασμένην μέσην εἴκοσι πηχέων εἶχεν εἴσοδον, δύο δὲ κάμακας ἑκάστῃ πλευρᾷ τῆς εἰσόδου καταπέπηκτο, παραστάδας ὥσπερ ἀποτελούσας. Ἑκατέροθε [1] δὲ τῆς εἰσόδου ἀνὰ ‹τὰ ἱστία›[2] δεκαπέντε πήχεις ἀπέμενον,[3] ἑκάστου μέρους τρεῖς κάμακας καταπεπηγμένου (162a2) καὶ ἐρεισμένου κατὰ τὴν τῶν τριῶν τῶν ἄλλων πλευρῶν ἐργασίαν καὶ περίφραξιν. Τὸ δὲ μέσον τῆς εἰσόδου κατεπετέταστο[4] τῷ τῶν κ' πηχῶν καταπετάσματι, τῷ τῶν τεσσάρων βαθμῶν καθυφασμένῳ. Εἴσω δὲ τῆς εἰσόδου, λουτὴρ χάλκεος ἦν, τὴν βάσιν χαλκέαν[5] ἔχων, ἐξ ὃ τοῦ[6] οἱ ἱερεῖς τὰς χεῖρας ἀποπλύνειν, καὶ τῶν ποδῶν κατασχεῖν τοῦ ὕδατος τοῦ[7] ἐν αὐτῷ παρῆν. Καὶ ὁ μὲν περίβολος οὕτως ἦν, ὁ τοῦ αἰθρίου.[8]

**ΡΙΑ'.** + Ὁποῖον ἦν τὸ Ἁγίασμα τὸ μέσον[9] τοῦ περιβόλου, (162b1) ὃ Μωϋσῆς κατεσκεύασε;

‹α›› Τὸ δὲ Ἁγίασμα μέσον τοῦ περιβόλου, μῆκος ἔχον ἐπὶ πήχεις λ', πλάτους πήχεις γ',[10] πρὸς ἀνατολὰς βλέπον. Τὸ δὲ μῆκος τῶν τριάκοντα πηχῶν ἐν κίοσιν ἵδρυτο κ', τετραγώνοις, ξυλίνοις, καταχρύσοις, ἑκάστης πλευρᾶς ἑνὸς ἡμίσεος[11] πήχεος ἀλλήλων ἀφεστηκόσιν. Ὁ δὲ κατὰ δύσιν τοῖχος πηχῶν τριῶν[12] ἐν ἓξ κίοσι συνέστηκε. Συνῆσαν δὲ ἀλλήλοις ἡρμοσμένοι, ὥστε δοκεῖν ἕνα τοῖχον τὴν συντέλεσιν ὁλόχρυσον εἶναι, μεμυκότων τῶν ἁρμῶν ἔσωθε[13] καὶ ἔξωθεν. Εἶχε γὰρ ἕκαστος κίων (162b2)

---

[1] *Lc* FGM Ἑκατερωθε.

[2] The words των ιστιων are not found in CFGM. This emendation is suggested by the LXX text of Ex 27:14–15.

[3] FGM ανεμεινον. Emend to απομετρουμενον?

[4] *Lc* GM κατεπεπεταστο.

[5] GM χαλκην.

[6] *Lc* FGM ἐξ οὑ.

[7] *Lc* FGM ὁτου.

[8] The items in this chapter are not numbered in CFGM.

[9] FGM omit το μεσον.

[10] Emend to ι', based on Josephus *Ant.* 3.115.

[11] *Lc* FGM ἡμισεως.

[12] Emend to ἐννέα on the basis of Josephus *Ant.* 3.119 or to δέκα based on what follows.

[13] FGM ἐσωθεν.

middle (162a) of the poles to the ground. **Such were three sides of the enclosure.**

**<2> On the fourth side,** which one might more correctly call the first (for **this was the entrance into the tabernacle, with fifty cubits**), **it had a middle entrance like a door, of twenty cubits, and two poles were fixed to each side of the entrance,** functioning as vestibules. **On each side of the entrance stood three poles** with each part attached and made firm, <with hangings of> fifteen cubits [Ex 27:14-15]. The middle of the entrance was covered with a veil of **twenty cubits,** woven with four colors. **Within the entrance was a bronze mixing-bowl with a bronze base, from which the priests washed their hands and could wash their feet with the water that was in it. And such was the enclosure in the courtyard.** [1]

**111.** – Of what sort was the Holy in the middle of the enclosure (162b) which Moses constructed [cf. Ex 26 and 36]?

**<1> The Holy was in the middle of the court, with a length of thirty cubits and a breadth of ten cubits, facing eastward. That length of thirty cubits was sustained by twenty pillars, rectangular, wooden, gilded, with each side separated from the others by half a cubit.** [2] **The wall to the west was of three cubits with six columns, fitted together so that it seemed there was one wall all of gold with tightly fitted clamps inside and outside.** [3] Each pillar was of three spans so that the length of thirty cubits was completed

---

[1] Josephus *Ant.* 3.111–14.
[2] Josephus *Ant.* 3.115–19.
[3] Josephus *Ant.* 3.117.

τρεῖς σπιθαμὰς,[1] ὥστε συμπληροῦσθαι τὸ μῆκος τῶν τριάκοντα πηχῶν ὑπὸ τῶν εἴκοσι κιόνων, καὶ τῶν δέκα ὑπὸ τῶν ἕξ. Ἐγγώνιοι δὲ δύο κίονες ἦσαν ὀπίσω, ἀπὸ πήχους ἑνὸς συνάπτοντες τῷ πλάτει τὸ μῆκος. Διὰ δὲ πάντων τῶν κιόνων ἐπέκειτο διατρέχουσα μία συμπλεκομένη σανίς, γιγγλισκοῖς[2] θήλεσι καὶ ἄρρεσι κατεχομένη, πρὸς τὸ μήθ᾽ ὑπ᾽ ἀνέμων κραδαίνεσθαι τὴν σκηνὴν, ἀλλ᾽ ἐν ἠρεμίᾳ πολλῇ διαφυλάττεσθαι. Τὸ δὲ ἔνδον τῆς σκηνῆς εἰς τρία διῄρετο[3] κατὰ πηχῶν ι', καὶ (163a1) ἦν τὸ μὲν ἐσώτατον ἄδυτον πηχῶν ι', τοῖς ἱερεῦσιν ἄβατον. Τέσσαρες δὲ κίονες ἴσοι τοῖς ἄλλοις διεῖργον τὸ ἄδυτον τοῦ ἐξοτάτου.[4] Οἱ δὲ λοιποὶ πήχεις εἴκοσι, οἱ πρὸ τοῦ ἀδύτου, τοῖς ἱερεῦσι μόνοις ἐξέκειντο. Τὸ δὲ μέτωπον, ἐξ οὗπερ ἡ εἴσοδος ἦν, πέντε κίοσι διαχρύσοις, ἴσοις τοῖς ἄλλοις, συνίστατο, χαλκιαῖς[5] βάσεσιν ἐφεστῶτες.[6]

‹β'› Εἶχε δὲ καταπέτασμα ἐκ βύσσου καὶ πορφύρας καὶ ὑακίνθου καὶ κοκκίνου βαφῆς ἔμπηχον ι', καὶ διαιροῦντο[7] οἱ δέκα πήχεις τοῦ ἀδύτου τούτῳ τῷ καταπετάσματι. (163a2)

Καὶ ὁ μὲν ναὸς Ἅγιος ἐκαλεῖτο, ὁ ἐξότατος.[8] Ἅγιον δὲ ἁγίων, τὸ ἄδυτον. Τὸ δὲ πρῶτον[9] τῶν κ' πηχῶν μέρος ἱερεῦσιν ἀνεῖτο ὑπολυομένοις.[10] Τὸ τῶν ι' δὲ πηχῶν προεισόδιον καὶ πρὸ τοῦ μετώπου, φάρσος ἐφελκόμενος ἀπὸ κάλων, ἐπὶ θάτερα κρίκοις ἐπισυναγόμενος πρός τε τοῦ[11] ἐκπετάννυσθαι καὶ συνεφέλκεσθαι κατὰ γωνίαν. Καὶ γὰρ ἐν ταῖς ἐπισήμοις ἡμέραις ἐπισυνήγετο πρὸς τὸ κατοπτεύεσθαι. Ἦσαν δὲ καὶ σινδόναι περιτιθέμεναι τῷ ἁγιάσματι. Καὶ ἐπὶ ταῖς (163b1) σινδόσιν,[12] βεβαμμένων ποικίλαις βαφαῖς ἕτερα καλύμματα, πρὸς τὸ τοὺς χειμῶνας ἐπέχειν. Καὶ ἐπάνω τούτων ἄλλαι διφθέραι πεποιημέναι, καλύπτουσαι τὸ σκεπάσματα ἐν τοῖς ὑετοῖς.

---

[1] Lc FGM σπιθαμας.
[2] Lc FGM γιγγλυμοις.
[3] Lc FGM διηρητο.
[4] Lc FGM ἐξωτατου.
[5] M χαλκαις. Emend to χαλκειαις.
[6] Lc FGM ἐφεστωσιν. Ἐφεστωτες may be the author's own error, caused by relying on Josephus *Ant.* 3.124.
[7] Lc FGM διηρηντο.
[8] Lc FGM ἐξωτατος.
[9] Emend to δευτερον, based on Josephus *Ant.* 3.127.
[10] Lc FGM (and Josephus *Ant.* 3.127) ὑποδυομενοις.
[11] Lc FGM το.
[12] Lc FGM σινδοσι.

by the twenty pillars, and of the ten by the six. Two pillars in the back were square, of one cubit when combining the length with the breadth. **Through all the pillars was one bar, held together with "female" and "male" screws so that the tabernacle would not be shaken by winds but would be kept in complete calm. The inside of the tabernacle was divided in three parts measuring ten cubits.** Even (163a) the inmost shrine was of ten cubits, and **was closed to the priests. Four pillars** equal to the others separated the shrine from the outside. The remaining parts, those in front of the shrine, were of twenty cubits and were **open** only **to the priests. The front, through which they entered, consisted of five gilded pillars equal to the others, standing on bronze bases.**[1]

<2> It had **a veil of linen, dyed purple and blue and scarlet, of ten cubits, and the ten cubits of the shrine were separated by this veil.**

And **the Temple was called Holy** for the outmost part, and **Holy of Holies** for the shrine.[2] **The second part** of the twenty cubits **was allowed as a passage for priests entering.** The vestibule, before the front, of ten cubits, was **the part pulled over by cords held together on both sides by rings, so that it could be spread out or drawn back in a corner. On important days it was opened up to be seen. There were linen cloths hung up in the sanctuary, and in addition to the** (163b) **linens other veils dyed with various dyes, to resist bad weather. And above these were other elaborate skins covering the cloths during rains.**[3]

---

[1] Josephus *Ant.* 3.121–24. Screws, 121, 130.

[2] Josephus *Ant.* 3.124–25.

[3] Josephus *Ant.* 3.127–33.

‹γ'› Ἡ δὲ κιβωτὸς ἦν εἰς τὸ Ἅγιον τῶν ἁγίων, ἐκ ξύλων ἀσήπτων, μήκους σπηθαμῶν[1] ε', πλάτους καὶ βάθους σπηθαμῶν[2] τριῶν, χρυσῷ ἔξωθε καὶ ἔσωθε κατακεκρισμένη.[3] Αὕτη δέ, ὁπότε δέοι, ὑπὸ τῶν ἱερέων ἐφέρετο,[4] κρίκοις χρυσοῖς ἐνηλωμένη, καὶ ἐπ' ὤμων ἀρτῆρσιν[5] ἀγομένη. Ἐπῆσαν δὲ αὐτῇ δύο (163b2) Χερουβὶμ, μορφῇ δὲ οὐδενὶ ταύτῃ[6] τῶν ὑπὸ ἀνθρώπων ἑωραμένων παραπλήσια. Ἐν ταύτῃ καὶ αἱ δύο πλάκες ἀπέκειντο τῆς δεκαλόγου. Ἐν δὲ τῷ ναῷ τῷ πρὸ τῶν Ἁγίων, τράπεζα ἵδρυτο μήκους πηχῶν β', πλάτους πηχῶν α', ὕψους σπηθαμῶν[7] τριῶν, κρίκοις χρυσοῖς ἐνηλωμένη, καὶ ἀρτῆρσι[8] φερομένη χρυσοῖς, ἐν ᾗ οἱ τῆς προθέσεως ἄρτοι δώδεκα, ἐν δυσὶν ἑξάσιν κατὰ πᾶν σάββατον ἐναλλασσόμενοι, ἄζυμοι ἐτίθεντο. Καὶ ἐπάνω δύο φιάλαι χρυσαῖ τῶν [ν'] ἄρτων[9] θυμιαμάτων πλήρης,[10] πρὸς δὲ ἀρκτῷον ἔκειντο πλευρόν. (164a1) Λυχνία δὲ ἦν πρὸς τὸ μεσημβρινὸν πλευρόν, ἐκ χρυσοῦ κεχονευμένη,[11] διάκενος, σταθμοῦ μνῶν ρ'· πεποίητο δὲ ἐκ κρίνων, καὶ ῥοΐσκων, καὶ κρατηριδίων, εἰς ἑπτὰ μέρη διαιρουμένη, ἑκάστου μέρους δέκα συνθέσεις ἐκ κρίνων καὶ ῥοῶν[12] καὶ κρατηριδίων ἔχοντος, οἵ εἰσιν οἱ πάντες ο'· καὶ ἐπὶ ταύτης λύχνοι ἑπτά.

‹δ'› Μέσον δὲ τῆς λυχνίας καὶ τῆς τραπέζης, θυσιαστήριον ἦν πηχυέον[13] κατὰ πλευρὰν ἑκάστην, ὁμοίως ἐκ ξύλων ἀσήπτων, χρυσῷ περιεληλασμένων, ὕψους πηχῶν β'. Ἐπῆν δὲ αὐτῷ αἰσχάρα[14] χρυσέα, καὶ κατὰ (164a2) γωνίαν χρύσεοι στέφανοι ἐπέκειντο, ὡς[15] καὶ σκυταλίδες καὶ

---

[1] *Lc* FGM σπιθαμων.

[2] *Lc* FGM σπιθαμων.

[3] F χρυσω εσωθεν και εξωθεν κατακεχρισμενη; GM print χρυσω εσωθεν κατακεχρισμενη, omitting και εξωθε; in their notes, however, GM suggest χρυσω εσωθεν κατακεχρυσωμενη; Josephus (*Ant.* 3.134) uses the verb περιεληλαστο (or the variant περιεληλατο).

[4] FGM print εφηρετο, but GM suggest εφερετο in their notes.

[5] Emend to αρτησιν.

[6] In their notes, GM suggest emending to τουτων.

[7] *Lc* FGM σπιθαμων.

[8] Emend to αρτησι.

[9] FGM print Και επανω των ν' αρτων δυο φιαλαι χρυσαι, but in their notes GM suggest emending the ν' to ιβ'. However, the number ν' is best explained as a dittograph. *Lege* Και επανω των αρτων δυο φιαλαι χρυσαι.

[10] *Lc* FGM πληρεις.

[11] *Lc* FGM κεχωνευμενη.

[12] Emend to ῥοϊσκων.

[13] *Lc* FGM πηχυαιον.

[14] *Lc* FGM εσχαρα.

[15] *Lc* FGM, who omit ὡς.

<3> The ark was in the Holy of Holies, made of rot-free wood, with a length of five spans and a width and depth of three spans, with gold rubbed on the outside and the inside. When it had to be carried by the priests it had gold rings infixed and was carried about with carrying rods on their shoulders. On it were two cherubim, in form similar to nothing seen by men, and on it were the two tables of the decalogue. In that part of the Temple before the Holy was a table two cubits long, one cubit wide, and three spans high. It had gold rings attached and was carried about with gold carrying rods. On it were the twelve unleavened loaves of the show-bread in two sixes, changed every Sabbath. And above these loaves were two gold cups full of incense, placed to the north. (164a) There was a candelabrum to the south of cast gold, weighing when empty a hundred minas; it was made of lilies and small pomegranates and small mixing-bowls and was divided into seven parts, each part having ten combinations of lilies and small pomegranates and small mixing bowls; in sum they were seventy, and there were seven lamps on it.

<4> Between the candelabrum and the table was the altar, a cubit on each side, also of rot-free wood covered with gold, two cubits high, and on it was a golden brazier, and golden crowns lay at each corner, and rods and

κρίκοι, πρὸς τὸ αὐτὸ διὰ τῶν ἱερέων φέρεσθαι συνέκειντο.

Πρὸ δὲ τῆς σκηνῆς ἵδρυτο βωμὸς χάλκεος ὑπόξυλος, κατὰ πλευρὰν ἑκάστην ε' πήχεις ἐκμετρημένος,¹ τὸ δὲ ὕψος τρίπηχυς, ὁμοίως χρυσῷ κεκοσμημένος,² ἐσχάραν ἐπικειμένην ἔχων δικτυοτὴν,³ τὸ καταφερόμενον πῦρ ἐξ αὐτῆς, γῆς ἐκδεχομένης,⁴ καὶ ἐτίθετο ἀντικρὺ τοῦ χρυσέου. Σκεύη δὲ πρὸς τὴν τούτων λειτουργίαν ἦν πολλὰ καὶ διάφορα· οἰνοχοαὶ καὶ **(164b1)** φιάλαι, καὶ θυΐσκαι, καὶ κρατῆρες, χρύσεα πάντα, πρὸς τὰς ἱερουργίας πεποιημένα. Αὕτη ἡ σκηνή.

**ΡΙΒ'.** + Πόσος ἦν ὁ λαός, ὁ ὑπὸ Δαβὶδ ἀριθμηθεὶς παρὰ τὸ δοκοῦν τῷ Θεῷ;

Ἀπὸ μὲν τοῦ Ἰσραὴλ ρι' μυριάδες, ἀπὸ εἰκοσαετοῦς ἕως πεντηκονταετοῦς, ἀνδρῶν μαχητῶν. Ἀπὸ δὲ τοῦ Ἰούδα, τῆς αὐτῆς ἡλικίας, μ' μυριάδες. Αἵτινες πᾶσαι διὰ τοῦ Ἰωὰβ ἠριθμήθησαν.

**ΡΙΓ'.** + Πόσοι ἀπώλοντο τοῦ λαοῦ ἐπὶ τῇ ἁμαρτίᾳ τοῦ Δαβὶδ, τῆς ἐξαριθμήσεως τοῦ λαοῦ; **(164b2)**

Εἰς ἓξ ὥρας, τὰς ἀπὸ πρωῒ ἕως ἀρίστου, μυριάδες ζ'.

**ΡΙΔ'.** + Τίνες πορνεύσασαι γυναῖκες, εἰς γάμους εὐδοκήμησαν;⁵

‹α'› Θάμαρ ἡ Χαναναία, εἰς τὸν Ἰούδαν σοφῶς πορνεύσασα, τὸν Φαρὲς καὶ τὸν Ζαρὰ ἐξ αὐτοῦ γεννήσασα.

‹β'› Ῥαὰβ, ἡ τοὺς κατασκόπους κατακρύψασα, ἐκ τοῦ Σαλμὼν τὸν Βοὸζ γεννήσασα.

‹γ'› Βηθσαβεέ, ἐκ τοῦ Δαβὶδ τὸν Σαλομῶνα γεννήσασα.

‹δ'› Γόμερ, ἡ τοῦ Δεβηλαεὶμ, ἐκ τοῦ Ὡσηὲ τὸν Ἰερραὲλ γεννήσασα.⁶

**ΡΙΕ'.** + Τίνες ἐν τοῖς προφήταις ἄγαμοι μεμενήκασιν;

‹α'› Ἄβελ ὁ τοῦ Ἀδάμ.

‹β'› Μελχισεδὲκ ὁ ἀρχιερεὺς τοῦ Θεοῦ **(165a1)** τοῦ ὑψίστου.

‹γ'› Ἠλίας ὁ ἀναληφθείς.

‹δ'› Ἐλισσαῖος ὁ τούτου μαθητής.

‹ε'› Ἰερεμίας ὁ κελευσθεὶς ὑπὸ Θεοῦ μὴ λαμβάνειν γυναῖκα.⁷

---

¹ In their notes GM suggest emending to ἐκμεμετρημενος. *Lege* ἐκμετρουμενος.
² FGM κεκονιημενος.
³ *Lc* FGM δικτυωτην.
⁴ *Lc* FGM της γης ἐκδεχομενης.
⁵ *Lc* FGM εὐδοκιμησαν.
⁶ The items in this chapter are not numbered in CFGM.
⁷ The items in this chapter are not numbered in CFGM.

rings so that it could be carried by the priests.

Before the tabernacle was located a wooden altar covered with bronze with sides of five cubits and a height of three cubits, similarly adorned with gold, with a latticed brazier on top, the earth catching the fire that fell from it (i.e., the brazier). And it (i.e., the altar) was set opposite the golden altar. The vessels for the service of these were many and various: ladles and (164b) bowls and censers and mixing-bowls, all of gold, made for the sacred ritual. Such was the tabernacle.[1]

<DAVID'S CENSUS (112-13)>

**112.** – How many were the people counted by David contrary to God's will?

From Israel there were 1,100,000, from the age of twenty to fifty, fighting men. From Iouda, of the same age, 400,000; all these were counted through Joab.[2]

**113.** – How many of the people perished because of the sin of David when he counted the people?

In six hours from early morning to the noon meal, seventy thousand [2 Rg 24:15].

<MORALS OF WOMEN AND MEN (114-16) (from C. 62)>

**114.** – What sexually immoral women turned were distinguished in marriage?

<1> Thamar the Chananaian wisely was a prostitute for Ioudas and bore Phares and Zara from him [Gn 38:11-30].

<2> Raab who hid the spies and bore Booz from Salmôn [Js 2:1; Mt 1:5].

<3> Bethsabeë who from David bore Solomon [2 Rg 12:24].

<4> Gomer daughter of Debélaeim, who from Ôséë bore Ierraël [Hos 1:3].

**115.** – Who among the prophets remained unmarried?

<1> Abel son of Adam [Gn 4:17].

<2> Melchisedek high priest of the (165a) highest God [14:18].[3]

<3> Élias who was taken up [4 Rg 2:1].

<4> Elissaios his disciple [3 Rg 19:20].

<5> Ieremias, ordered by God not to take a wife [Jer 16:1].

---

[1] Josephus *Ant.* 3.134–50.

[2] Josephus *Ant.* 7.320 gives 900,000 and *400,000*, while 2 Rg 24:9 has 800,000 and 500,000; but 1 Par 21:5 gives *1,100,000* and 470,000.

[3] Priest in Gn 14:18; but cf. Hb 5:10; 6:20; see Index A s.v. "priest."

**ΡΙϚ'.** + Τίνες ἐν τοῖς ἀποστόλοις γυναῖκας ἔσχον;
‹α'›..θαι¹ Πέτρος· καὶ γὰρ θυγατέρα ἐκέκτητο.
‹β'› Φίλιππος· καὶ γὰρ τρεῖς ἔσχε θυγατέρας προφήτιδας, αἳ κεκοίμηνται ἐν τῇ Ἀσίᾳ, ἅγιαι παρθένοι.
‹γ'› Παῦλος, ὁ² καὶ ἐπιστέλλων φησίν· Καὶ σὺ, σύζυγε, προλάβου³ αὐτάς.⁴

**ΡΙΖ'.** + Τίνες οὐκ ἐτάφησαν ἐν τοῖς βασιλικοῖς τοῦ Δαβὶδ τάφοις βασιλεῖς, διὰ τὸ δυσσεβῆσαι;
‹α'› Ἰωράμ.
‹β'› Ἰωᾶς.
‹γ'› Ὀζίας.⁵
‹δ'› Ἀχάζ. **(165a2)**
‹ε'› Μανασσῆς.
‹ϛ'› Ἀμών.
Ὀζίας δὲ διὰ τὸ λεπρωθῆναι.⁶

**ΡΙΗ'.** + Τίνες οἱ ἐκ τοῦ Δαβὶδ βασιλεῖς ἔκβλητοι ἐκ τῆς τοῦ Σωτῆρος γενεαλογίας γεγόνασι, καὶ διατί;
‹α'› Ὀχοζίας ὁ τοῦ Ἰωρὰμ υἱὸς, καὶ Ἰωᾶς ὁ τοῦ Ὀχοζίου, καὶ Ἀμασίας ὁ τοῦ Ἰωᾶς. Οὗτοι οὐ γενεαλογοῦνται ἐν τῷ Εὐαγγελίῳ. Ἐπείπερ ὁ Ἰωρὰμ θυγατέρα τοῦ Ἀχαὰβ καὶ τῆς Ἰεζάβελ ἠγάγετο γυναῖκα, τὴν Γοδολίαν, ἥτις ταῖς τῆς Ἰεζάβελ δυσσεβείαις τεθραμμένη, καὶ τὸν Ἰωρὰμ ἐπηγάγετο καὶ τὸν Ἰωρὰμ ἐπηγάγετο δυσσεβεῖν, καὶ τὸν υἱὸν αὐτοῦ τὸν Ὀχοζίαν. Καὶ τοῦ Ὀχοζίου ἀποθανόντος **(165b1)** τὸ βασιλικὸν γένος τὸ ἐκ τοῦ Δαβὶδ ἐπεχείρησεν ἀφανίσαι, εἰ μὴ Ἰωσαβεὲ ἡ τοῦ Ὀχοζίου ἀδελφὴ, γυνὴ δὲ Ἰωδαὲ τοῦ ἀρχιερέως, βρέφος ὄν⁷ ἔτι τοῦ⁸ Ἰωᾶς, υἱὸν τοῦ ἀδελφοῦ αὐτῆς Ὀχοζίου κλέψασα, καὶ κατακρύψασα ὀκταετῆ⁹ γεγονότα, ἔδειξε τῷ

---

¹*Lc* FGM, who emend by omission. In C, approximately two illegible letters precede the letters θαι.

²*Lc* FGM ὁς.

³In their notes, GM suggest reading προσλαβου. In the best witnesses to Phil 4:3, the word is συλλαμβανου.

⁴The items in this chapter are not numbered in CFGM.

⁵FGM omit Ὀζίας.

⁶The items in this chapter are not numbered in CFGM.

⁷In their notes GM suggest ὄντα.

⁸*Lc* GM, who in their notes suggest τον.

⁹Emend to ἐξετη on the basis of 4 Rg 11:3.

**116.** – Who among the apostles had wives?

<1> Petros, for he had a daughter.[1]

<2> Philippos, for he had three daughters, prophetesses, who are buried in Asia, holy virgins.[2]

<3> Paulos, for he says in a letter, "And you, help-meet, aid them [Phil 4:3]."[3]

<KINGS (117-19) (from C. 17)>

**117.** What kings because of their impiety are not buried in the royal tombs? of David?

<1> Iôram [2 Par 21:20].

<2> Iôas [24:25].

<3> Ozias [2 Par 26:23].

<4> Achaz [28:27].

<5> Manassés [33:20; 4 Rg 21:18].

<6> Amôn [4 Rg 21:26].

But Ozias because he had leprosy.

**118.** – What kings descended from David were omitted from the genealogy of the Savior, and why?

<1> Ochozias son of Iôram [Jehoram, 4 Rg 8:25], Iôas son of Ochozias [4 Rg 12:1], and Amasias son of Iôas [14:1]. These are not mentioned in the Gospel in the genealogy [of Christ], since Iôram married Godolia, daughter of Achaab and Iezabel, and she, brought up in the impieties of Iezabel, led both Iôram and his son Ochozias to sin. When Ochozias died (165b) she tried to extirpate the royal line of David, except that Iôsabeë the sister of Ochozias and wife of the high priest Iôdaë secretly hid the infant Iôas, son of her brother Ochozias, for six[4] years [4 Rg 11:1-3] and then showed him to the high priest Iôdaë, who

---

[1] Children, Clement *Str.* 3.52.5; Eusebius *HE* 3.30.1; daughter, *Acts of Peter* in Edgar Hennecke-Wilhelm Schneemelcher, *New Testament Apocrypha* (2 vols.; Philadelphia: Westminster, 1965) 2.276.

[2] Eusebius *HE* 3.31.3–5.

[3] Clement *Str.* 3.53.1; Eusebius *HE* 3.30.1.

[4] Brooke-McLean-Thackeray, *The Old Testament in Greek* 2.2 (Cambridge: At the University Press, 1930) 336, cite Anon.1 for *octo* in 11:3.

ἀρχιερεῖ Ἰωδαὲ, ὃς ἀποκτείνας τὴν Γοδολίαν, εἰς τὸν Ἰωᾶς κατεστήσατο τὴν βασιλείαν.

‹β'› Ἀλλ᾽ οὐδὲ Σεδεκίας γενεαλογεῖται ἀνηκουσθήσας[1] Θεοῦ, καὶ κατάραν ὑπομεῖναι,[2] τὴν διὰ τοῦ προφήτου Ἱερεμίου φήσαντος· Γράψον τὸν ἄνδρα τοῦτον ἐκκήρυκτον.[3] **(165b2)**

**ΡΙΘ'.** + Τίς ἰατροῖς κακωθεὶς χρησάμενος, καὶ μὴ παρὰ τῷ Θεῷ τὴν ἴασαν αἰτήσας, ἀποθνήσκει;
Ἀσὰ, ὁ τοῦ Ἰούδα βασιλεὺς, τοὺς [τὸν φ'][4] πόδας μαλακισθεὶς, καὶ μὴ ἐκζητήσας τὸν Κύριον, ἀλλὰ τοὺς ἰατροὺς ἀποθνήσκει.

**ΡΚ'.** + Τίνα ἐστὶ τὰ μνημονευόμενα ἐν ταῖς Γραφαῖς βιβλία ὡς ὄντα, οὐχ εὑρισκόμενα δέ;[5]
‹α'› Ναθὰν, καὶ Ἀδδὼ, καὶ Ἀχιὰ τοῦ Σιλωνίτου, καὶ Σεμεΐ, καὶ Ἰηοῦ ἐν τῇ βίβλῳ τῶν Βασιλειῶν γέγραπται εἶναι βιβλία. Προφῆται δέ εἰσιν οὗτοι, ὁ[6] γεγράφασι περὶ **(166a1)** ὅ[7] προεφήτευσεν,[8] ἃ οὐχ εὑρίσκεται.

‹β'› Ψαλμοὶ τρισχίλιοι λέγονται ἐν Παραλειπομέναις εἶναι τοῦ Δαβὶδ, μόνους δὲ αὐτῶν τοὺς ἑκατὸν πεντήκοντα ὑπὸ τῶν φίλων Ἐζεκίου τοῦ βασιλέως[9] ἐξελέσθαι,[10] τοὺς δὲ ἄλλους ἀποκεκρύφθαι.

‹γ'› Πεντακισχιλίας παροιμίας ὑπὸ τοῦ Σαλομῶνος[11] ἐκδεδώσθαι[12], φησὶν ἡ τῶν Παραλειπομένων Γραφή. Ἀλλ᾽ οὔκ εἰσι[13] νῦν ἢ μόναι τρεῖς αἱ ἐκκλησιαζόμεναι· τὸ Ἀσμα ἐξ ᾀσμάτων πλειόνων τὸ μυστικὸν ἐξειλέχθαι ἐπιγέγραπται.

---

[1] Lc M ἀνηκουστησας.
[2] Lc FGM ὑπομεινας.
[3] The items in this chapter are not numbered in CΓGM.
[4] The bizarre τὸν φ' may be a corruption of σφοδρα (see 2 Par 16:12). Lc FGM, who simply omit it.
[5] FGM omit δε.
[6] Lc FGM οἱ.
[7] Lc FGM ὧν.
[8] Lc FGM προεφητευσαν.
[9] FGM print των φιλων του βασιλεως Ἐζεκιου του βασιλεως, but GM note the redundancy.
[10] FGM ἐξειλεχθαι.
[11] FGM Σαλομωντος.
[12] Lc FGM ἐκδεδοσθαι.
[13] GM εἰσιν.

killed Godolia and restored the kingdom to Iôas [11:16–20]. [1]

<2> Furthermore, Sedekias is not mentioned in the genealogy, since he disobeyed God [24:18-20] and underwent a curse pronounced by the prophet Ieremias: "Write that this man was rejected" [Jer 22:30]. [2]

**119**. – Who died because in sickness he used physicians and did not ask healing from God?

Asa king of Iouda had a foot ailment and did not ask of the Lord but of physicians, and died [2 Par 16:12–13]. [3]

<BIBLICAL LITERATURE (120–22) (from C. 26)>

**120**. – What books mentioned in the Scriptures are not extant? [4]

<1> The books of Nathan and Addô (Iôél) and Achias (Achia, Cod.A) the Silonités [2 Par 9:29] and Semei [Samaia, Cod.A] and Iéou [Addô, Cod.A] are recorded in the book of Reigns [2 Par 12:15]. [5] These were prophets who wrote down (166a) what they predicted, but they are not now extant.<2> In Paralipomena there are said to be 3,000 psalms of David, but only 150 of them were selected by the friends of King Ezekias; the others were hidden.

<3> The book of Paralipomena says that 5,000 proverbs were published by Solomon, [6] but only three (books) are now read [in church]. [7] The title, "the Song of" – many – "Songs," indicates its mystical meaning.

---

[1] In fact, however, the son of Iôram (Jehoram) is called Ozias (Ahaziah) in the genealogy (Mt 1:8).

[2] In fact, he was substituted for Jehoiachin by the alien king Nebuchadnezzar (4 Rg 24:17).

[3] Josephus *Ant.* 8.314, obviously not Joseph's source, says Asa died happy.

[4] Diekamp (*Hippolytos von Theben*, 149 n. 1) notes that in other Byzantine manuscripts this chapter is anonymous, as are Cc. 122, 124, 135, 145, and 152.

[5] Joseph obviously reverses the names Addô and Iéou.

[6] Neither statement appears in Par, but 3 Rg 4:28 says that Solomon uttered 3,000 parables and his odes were 5,000, while Josephus mentions 1,005 books of odes and songs (5,000 LXX) and 3,000 books of parables and similitudes (Josephus *Ant.* 8.44).

[7] "Proverb<s>, Ekklésiastés, Song of Songs," C. 74(5). Here as in C. 26(15) the name Ekklésiastés may have led to confusion with *ekklésia*.

‹δ'› Ἰώσηππος δὲ ἱστορεῖ, δύο βιβλία προφητείας τὸν προφήτην Ἰεζεκιὴλ (166a2) γεγραφέναι, ἓν δὲ μόνων[1] ἐπιγινώσκομεν εὑρίσκεσθαι.[2]

**ΡΚΑ'.** + Τίνες εἰσὶν αἱ ὑπὸ τῶν ἀποστόλων μαρτυρίαι παραγενόμεναι,[3] ὧν τὰς γραφὰς οὐκ ἔχομεν;

‹α'› Ματθαῖός φησιν ἐπὶ τῇ οἰκήσει τοῦ Ἰωσήφ, ἀπὸ τῆς ἐξ Αἰγύπτου ἀνόδου εἰς τὴν Ναζαρὲθ[4] μετὰ τοῦ Κυρίου· Ἐλθὼν δὲ ᾤκησε τὴν Ναζαρὲθ,[5] ἵνα πληρωθῇ τὸ γεγραμμένον, ὅτι Ναζωραῖος κληθήσεται.

‹β'› Παῦλος ἐν τῇ πρὸς Ἐφεσίους φησί· Διὸ λέγει· Ἔγειρε,[6] ὁ καθεύδων, καὶ ἐπιφαύσει σοι ὁ Χριστός.

‹γ'› Καὶ πάλιν· Γέγραπται, Ἐγένετο (166b1) ὁ πρῶτος ἄνθρωπος εἰς ψυχὴν ζῶσαν, ὁ[7] δεύτερος εἰς πνεῦμα ζωοποιοῦν.

‹δ'› Καὶ τοῖς ἐν Μιλήτῳ πρεσβυτέροις διαλεγόμενός φησι· Μνημονεύετε μᾶλλον ἢ λαμβάνειν.[8]

**ΡΚΒ'.** + Τίνες εἰσὶν οἱ τὰς ἱερὰς Γραφὰς ἑρμηνεύσαντες;

Πρῶτον ἐπὶ Πτολεμαίου τοῦ Φιλαδέλφου ἐν Ἀλεξανδρείᾳ οἱ οβ' τῶν Ἰουδαίων Σοφοί, ὑπὸ Ἐλεαζάρου τοῦ ἀρχιερέως εἰς τὸ ἑρμηνεῦσαι αὐτῷ τὰς Γραφὰς ἀποσταλέντες.

Δεύτερος δὲ[9] Ἀκύλας ἑρμηνεύει, ἐπὶ τοῦ βασιλέως Ἀδριανοῦ γεγονώς, ὃς ἐξ Ἑλλήνων ὤν, καὶ προστεθεὶς τῷ Ἰουδαϊσμῷ, πονήσας περὶ (166b2) τὴν Ἑβραΐδα, ἐπιγνούς τε ὡς οὐκ ἀκριβῶς ἡρμήνευσαν οἱ οβ' σοφοί, τὸ[10] μὴ τὴν Ἑλλήνων φωνὴν ἀκριβοῦν, ἡρμήνευσεν ἀκριβέστερον.

---

[1]*Lc* GM, who in their notes suggest emending to μονον or μονως.

[2]Several manuscripts quote the material in this chapter, but identify it as being from C. 158 of the *Hypomnestikon* of Josephus. For more on this, see Menzies, "Interpretive Traditions," 15-22.

The items in this chapter are not numbered in CFGM.

[3]In their notes, GM suggest emending to παραγομεναι.

[4]FM Ναζαρετ; G Ναζαρεν by mistake.

[5]FGM Ναζαρετ.

[6]FGM Ἔγειραι.

[7]GM ὁ δε.

[8]FGM print μαλλον διδοναι ἢ λαμβανειν. *Lc* GM, who in their notes suggest the reading: Μνημονευετε ὅτι μακαριον ἐστι μαλλον διδοναι ἢ λαμβανειν.

The items in this chapter are not numbered in CFGM.

[9]FGM omit δε.

[10]*Lc* FGM, who emend to δια το.

<4> Josephus relates that the prophet Iezekiél wrote two books of prophecy, [1] but we know of the existence of only one.


**121**. – What are the testimonies adduced by the apostles from writings we do not possess?

<1> Matthew, speaking of Joseph's domicile after he returned from Egypt to Nazareth with the Lord, says, "He came and dwelt in Nazareth so that what is written might be fulfilled, He shall be called a Nazôraios" [Mt 2:23].

<2> Paul says in the <letter> To the Ephesians, "Wherefore it says, Awake, sleeper, and Christ will shine upon you" [Eph 5:14].

<3> And again, "It is written, The first (166b) man became a living soul, the second, a life-giving spirit" [1 Cor 15:46].

<4> And when he spoke with the presbyters at Miletus he said, "Remember that it is more blessed to give than to receive" [Ac 20:35].


**122**. – Who are those who translated the sacred Scriptures?

First under **Ptolemy Philadelphos at Alexandria were the seventy-two wise men of the Jews** sent by Eleazaros the high priest to translate the scriptures for him.[2]

The second translator was **Aquila, who lived in the time of the emperor Hadrian; of Greek origin, he embraced Judaism and labored in Hebrew.** He understood that the seventy-two wise men had not translated accurately because they did not know Greek well, and he translated more accurately.

---

[1] Josephus *Ant.* 10.79.

[2] Seventy translators in C. 2(36) and Eusebius *HE* 5.8.12 (from Irenaeus); 6.16.4; seventy-two in Epiphanius *Weights and Measures* 9 (PG 43, 249B–C).

Τρίτος ἡρμήνευει[1] Σύμμαχος ἐπὶ Σεβήρου καὶ Ἀντωνίνου, τοῦ Γέτα ἐπικεκλημένου, γενόμενος. Τοῦτόν φασι Σαμαρείτην ὄντα, καταγνώντα[2] αὐτῶν, ἀπ᾽ αὐτῶν ἀπεστᾶναι, φιλοπονήσαντά τε περὶ τὰς Ἑβραϊκὰς γραφὰς, ἐξενέγκαι αὐτῶν τὰς ἑρμηνείας.

Τέταρτος ἑρμηνεύει Θεοδοτίων, Ποντικὸς τὸ γένος, καὶ[3] αἵρεσιν Μαρκιωνιστής, ἔπειτα προστεθεὶς Ἰουδαίοις, (167a1) καὶ ζηλώσας τὴν Ἑβραΐδα, ἡρμήνευσε καὶ αὐτὸς τὰς Γραφὰς, οὐ πάνυ τῆς τῶν οβ᾽ ἑρμηνείας παραλλάξας.

Πέμπτη δὲ ἔκδοσις εὑρέθη ἐν Ἱεριχῷ, ἐν πίθοις χαλκοῖς κεκρυμμένη, οὐκ ἐπιγεγραμμένη τὸν ἑρμηνέα. Φασὶ δὲ αὐτὴν ὑπὸ γυναικὸς ἑρμηνεῦσθαι, τὸ[4] καὶ ἐν οἰκίᾳ γυναικὸς ἐπιμελοῦς ἐν τοῖς ἱεροῖς λόγοις εὑρᾶσθαι τοὺς πίθους.

Ἕκτη δὲ ἄλλη εὑρέθη ἐν Νικοπόλει τῇ πρὸς Ἀκτίοις, μετὰ τὸν Οὐήρου[5] διωγμόν.

Ἐξ οὗ[6] αἱ ἑρμηνεῖαι τῶν Γραφῶν εἰσὶ, καὶ σώζονται.[7]

**ΡΚΓ´.** + Ποσάκις πορθεῖται ἡ Ἱερουσαλήμ;

(167a2) Πρῶτον, ὑπὸ Ναβουχοδονόσορ τοῦ Βαβυλωνίου, ἐπὶ Σεδεκίου βασιλέως καὶ Ἱερεμίου τοῦ προφήτου, ἐπὶ ο´ ἔτη.

Δεύτερον, μετὰ ἔτη υνε´, ὑπὸ Ἀντιόχου τοῦ Ἐπιφανοῦς, ἐπὶ ἡμέρας ,βσ´, κατὰ τοὺς Μακκαβαίων χρόνους.

Τρίτον, ὑπὸ Πομπίνου,[8] τοῦ Ῥωμαίων ἡγουμένου, Ἀριστοβούλου καὶ Ὑρκανοῦ περὶ[9] ἱερωσύνης μαχομένων, οἳ ἦσαν ἀδελφοὶ, καὶ ἐπαγαγομένων

---

[1] Lc FGM ἡρμήνευσε.

[2] M καταγνοντα.

[3] Lc GM, who in their notes emend to κατα.

[4] Lc GM, who in their notes suggest emending to τῳ.

[5] In their notes F suggests emending to Σεβηρου and GM to Σευηρου, following Epiphanius. Lc GM.

[6] Lc FGM οὖν.

[7] A number of Byzantine Octateuchs have three short lists attached, two of which (this chapter on the translators of the OT, and C. 124 on the captivities of Israel) seem to be taken indirectly from the *Hypomnestikon*. The third is a list of divine names unrelated to C. 151. R. Devreesse suggests that this traditional collocation may be the work of Nicephorus since these lists appear in the *Catena Nicephori* I, 29-31. See Robert Devreesse, *Codices Vaticani Graeci*, vol. 2: *Codices 330-603* (Vatican City: Typus Polyglottus Vaticanus, 1937) 3; also see Menzies, "Interpretive Traditions," 26-28.

[8] Lc FGM Πομπηϊου.

[9] FGM unnecessarily replace περι with ἐπι.

The third translator was **Symmachus, in the time of Severus** and Antoninus surnamed Geta. They say **he was a Samaritan** but condemned his compatriots and was rejected by them, and applied himself to the Hebrew scriptures and published translations of them.

The fourth translator was **Theodotion**, of **Pontus** by nation, a **Marcionite** by sect. [1] He then **joined the Jews**, (167a) studied Hebrew, and translated the scriptures in a manner he thought not far from the version of the 72 translators.

The fifth edition was found at Jericho, hidden in bronze jars with no translator's name inscribed. They say it was translated by a woman, since the jars were found in the house of a woman who was a student of the sacred literature. [2]

The sixth was found **at Nicopolis near Actium**, after the persecution of <Se>verus. [3]

There are six translations of the scriptures and they are still preserved. (Continued in C. 130)

<HEBREW HISTORY (123-27)>

**123.** – How many times was Jerusalem besieged?

First, by Nabouchodonosor the Babylonian, in the time of Sedekias the king and Ieremias the prophet, for seventy years [4 Rg 25; Jer 52].

Second, after 455 years, by Antiochos Epiphanés for 2200 days, in the times of the Maccabees [2300 days, Dn 8:14 LXX].

Third, by Pompéios the Roman general, when the brothers Aristoboulos and Hyrkanos were fighting over the priesthood; when they introduced him to the

---

[1] For Aquila, Symmachus, Theodotion *cf*. Epiphanius *Weights and Measures* 14–17 (PG 43, 261B–264D).

[2] Joseph combines a translation found at Jericho (Epiphanius *Weights and Measures* 18, PG 43, 268A; Eusebius *HE* 6.16.4 mentions a jar) with a book by Symmachus which Origen received from Juliana of Caesarea in Cappadocia. See Palladius *Lausiac History* 64; Edward C. Butler, *The Lausiac History of Palladius* 2 (Texts and Studies 6.2; Cambridge: Cambridge University Press, 1904) 160,6–14. For Juliana, Eusebius *HE* 6.17.

[3] Nicopolis: Eusebius *HE* 6.16.2 (Epiphanius *Weights and Measures* 18, PG 43, 268A). For the last two (columns of Origen's *Hexapla*) see Eusebius *HE* 6.16.2–3; cf. Nautin, *Origène: Sa vie et son oeuvre* (Paris: Beauchesne, 1977) 303–61.

αὐτῶν¹ εἰς τὸν ναὸν, καὶ ἐπὶ μῆνας τρεῖς μιάναντα αὐτὸν, καὶ πάντα τὰ ἔνδον ἀφελόμενον.

Τέταρτον, ὑπὸ Σωσίου τοῦ Ῥωμαίων στρατηγοῦ, ὃν Ἡρώδης ἀπηγάγετο² κατὰ (167b1) Ἀντιγόνου, τοῦ Ἀριστοβούλου περὶ ἀρχιερωσύνης ἀνισταμένου, δέξασθαι βασιλέα τῆς Ἰουδαίας τὸν Ἡρώδην. Ἐπολιορκήθη δὲ ἐπὶ τούτου μῆνας ἕξ.

Πέμπτον, μετὰ ἔτη ρ' τῆς ὑπὸ Σωσίου πολιορκίας. Μετὰ δὲ τὴν τοῦ Κυρίου ἄρνησιν,³ καὶ ἄνοδον αὐτοῦ τὴν εἰς οὐρανὸν⁴ εἰς ἔτη λη', ὑπὸ Οὐεσπασιανοῦ καὶ Τίτου Ἰουδαία πᾶσα πεπόρθηται, καὶ ὁ ναὸς παντελῶς ἥλω.⁵

**ΡΚΔ'.** + Ποσάκις, καὶ πότε ἐπορθήθησαν οἱ ἐξ Ἰσραήλ;

α'⁶ Ἐπὶ Ἱεροβοὰμ,⁷ Σωσάκις ὁ Αἰγυπτίων βασιλεύς.

β' Ἐπὶ Ἀζαὴλ βασιλέως Ἀσσυρίων ἐπῳκίσθησαν (167b2) εἰς Ἀσσυρίους.

γ' Ἐπὶ Ἐζεκίου δὲ αἱ δέκα φυλαὶ μετῳκίσθησαν εἰς Μήδων⁸ καὶ Χαλδαίων.

δ' Ἐπὶ Ναβουχοδονόσορ ὅτε καὶ τὸν Ἰεχωνίαν⁹ ἐξετύφλωσε, καὶ τὸν Σεδεκίαν.¹⁰

ε' Ἐπὶ Νέρωνος βασιλέως Ῥωμαίων.¹¹

ϛ' Ἐπὶ Οὐεσπασιανοῦ στρατηγοῦ Ῥωμαίων.

ζ' Πτολεμαῖος ὁ Λαγῶς¹² δόλῳ παραλαβὼν τὰ Ἱεροσόλυμα, μετῆρεν εἰς Αἴγυπτον.

---

¹Lc FGM αὐτον.

²Lc FGM ἐπηγαγετο.

³FGM emend to ἀναστασιν.

⁴FGM τον οὐρανον.

⁵FGM ἐαλω.

⁶FGM spell out Πρωτον.

⁷Emend to Ῥοβοαμ based on 3 Rg 14:25–26 in the LXX.

⁸C leaves a blank space large enough for three or four letters between εἰς and Μηδων. FGM print εἰς ὁρια Μηδων. *Lege* εἰς ὁρη Μηδων, following 4 Rg 18:11 in the LXX.

⁹Lc FGM Ἰεχονιαν.

¹⁰Emend to τον και Σεδεκιαν or τον και Σεδεκιαν κεκλημενον.

¹¹Clearly items five and six of this list are not correctly located and should be placed between items nine and ten (as the English translation reflects). Perhaps a marginal note supplementing the list or a copyist's marginal correction of an inadvertent omission was improperly inserted by a later copyist.

¹²M Λαγου.

Temple he polluted it for three months and stole everything inside.[1]

Fourth, by Sôsios (Sossius), the Roman general whom Hérôdés brought in against (167b) Antigonos, when Aristoboulos rebelled because of the high priesthood, so that they might receive Hérôdés as king of Ioudaia. It was besieged under him for six months.[2]

Fifth, a hundred years after the siege under Sôsios (Sossius). But in the thirty-eighth year after the denial of the Lord and his ascension into heaven, **all Ioudaia** was devastated by Vespasian and Titus and **the Temple** was **completely** destroyed.[3]

**124.** – How often and when were the Israelites led into captivity?[4]

1. Under [Ie]roboam by Sôsakis king of the Egyptians [3 Rg 14:25-26; Sousakeim, LXX].

2. Under Azaél king of the Assyrians, resettled in Assyria [4 Rg 17:3-6; Salmanasar, Cod.A].

3. Under Ezekias the ten tribes were resettled to the lands of the Medes and the Chaldaeans [18:11].

4. Under Nebouchadonosor when he blinded Iechonias also known as Sedekias [4 Rg 25:7].[5]

7. Ptolemaios (I) Lagôs by craft took Jerusalem and resettled the inhabitants in Egypt.[6]

---

[1] See above, C. 2(50); contradicts Josephus *Ant.* 14.72.

[2] Josephus *Ant.* 14.468–91, cf. *War* 1.351.

[3] Eusebius *HE* 3.5.4–5. Julian is aware that the temple was overthrown three times (*Epistle* 89, p. 135,18 Bidez-Cumont).

[4] Captivities, Hippolytus *Chr* 29 = *LG* 1.22, quales captivitates populi.

[5] Hippolytus *Chr* 718 = *LG* 1.332 (50): Sediciam qui et Ieconias dictus... Ieconiam et Sediciam. Hippolytus *Dn Comm* 1.3: Iechonias = Sedekias.

[6] Josephus *Ant.* 12.6–7.

η' Ἐπὶ Ἀντιόχου τοῦ Ἐπιφανοῦς, ὃς καὶ ἐπὶ βδελύγμασιν ἠνάγκασε,[1] βασιλεὺς Συρίας.

θ' Πόμπιος[2] στρατηλάτης Ῥωμαίων, ὑποφόρους ἐποίησε πολεμήσας Ἰεροσόλυμα, Ὑρκανοῦ βασιλεύοντος καὶ (168a1) ἱερατεύοντος.[3]

Ἕως αὐτοῦ τοίνυν Ὑρκανοῦ, ἡ βασιλεία τοῦ Ἰσραήλ. Καὶ λαμβάνει τὴν βασιλείαν Ἡρώδης ἀλλόφυλος, ἀπὸ τῶν Ῥωμαίων, ὃς καὶ πλησιάζει τῇ τοῦ Χριστοῦ παρουσίᾳ.

ι' Τίτος ὁ υἱὸς Οὐεσπασιανοῦ, κατὰ τὸν καιρὸν τῆς τοῦ πάσχα,[4] κατασκάψας τὰ Ἰεροσόλυμα, ἐν ᾧ πάντες ἑόρταζον[5] οἱ τοῦ ἔθνους συναχθέντες, ἀνεῖλε μυριάδας ρι', καὶ ἄλλας ρ' μυριάδας ‹αἰχμαλώτους›,[6] οὓς διαπέπρακεν ἐσχάτῃ ἁλώσει.[7]

## ΡΚΕ'. + Κεφάλαιον Ἰωσήππου ἕτερ‹ου›.[8]

Γυνή τις, τοῦ λιμοῦ διὰ τῶν σπλάγχνων καὶ μυελῶν παρεισδύνοντος,[9] ἐπὶ τὴν φύσιν ἐχώρει, καὶ τὸ τέκνον (168a2) (ἦν δὲ αὐτῇ[10] ὑπομάσθιος παῖς) ἁρπασαμένη εἶπε· Βρέφος ἄθλιον ἐν πολέμῳ καὶ λιμῷ καὶ στάσει, τίνι σε τηρῶ; Γενοῦ μοι τροφὴ, καὶ τῷ βίῳ μῦθος. Καὶ ταῦτα λέγουσα, σφάζει τὸν υἱὸν, καὶ ὀπτήσασα, τὸ μὲν ἥμισυ κατεσθίει, τὸ δὲ λοιπὸν καλύψασα ἐφύλαττεν. Εὐθέως οἱ στασιασταὶ παρῆσαν, καὶ τῆς ἀθεμίτου κνίσης[11]

---

[1] Emend to ἐπι βδελυγμασιν τον λαον ἠναγκασε.

[2] Lc FGM Πομπηϊος.

[3] Emend to ἀρχιερατευοντος.

[4] Lc FGM της του πασχα ἑορτης.

[5] Lc G, who suggests in a note, and M, who prints, ἑωρταζον.

[6] C does not have the word αἰχμαλωτους. The restoration is based on the list of Israelite captivities found in the manuscript of the *Chronographeion Syntomon* which Angelo Mai found in the Vatican Library, but which has subsequently disappeared. See Angelo Mai, ed., *Scriptorum veterum novae collectionis e vaticanis codicibus* (10 vols.; Rome: Burliaeum, 1825–1836) 1,2.3–4.

[7] A number of Byzantine Octateuchs preserve the material found in this chapter (usually in modified form). See note at the end of C. 122 above.

In C, each entry of this chapter uncharacteristically begins at the left margin of the column, and the item numbers appear in the gutter to the left of the column.

[8] C abbreviates this word ἑτερ. FGM print ἑτερον. However, this chapter is an interpolation and most likely the interpolator is attempting to distinguish Flavius Josephus from the author of the *Hypomnestikon*, whom he also believes (probably incorrectly) to be named Josephus.

[9] GM παρεισδυοντος.

[10] FGM αὐτο.

[11] FGM κνισσης.

8. Under Antiochos Epiphanés, who as king of Syria forced <the people> to abominations.[1]

9. Pompéios commander of the Romans made them subject to tribute when he warred on Jerusalem, when Hyrkanos was king and <high> (168a) priest.

Up to this Hyrkanos Israél was a kingdom, and the foreigner Hérôdés received it from the Romans; he was close to the advent of Christ.[2]

5. Under Nero king of the Romans.

6. Under Vespasian general of the Romans.

10. Titus son of Vespasian, capturing Jerusalem at the time of the feast of Passover when all those of the people came together for the feast killed 1,100,000 and made another 1,000,000 obtained in this last devastation captives.[3]

**125. – A chapter of the other Iôséppos.[4]**

**A certain woman, with famine penetrating her bowels and marrow, outraged nature when she seized her child (a babe at the breast) and said, "Unhappy infant, amid war and famine and revolt for what am I preserving you?[5] Become food for me, and to the world a tale of horror...." This said, she slays[6] her son and after roasting him, eats half and kept the remainder concealed. The rebels suddenly arrived and when they smelled the lawless**

---

[1] Josephus *Ant.* 12.246–56.

[2] Josephus *Ant.* 14.58–74; 15.195.

[3] Josephus *War* 6.420. Joseph's figures approximate the three million Eusebius (*HE* 3.5.5) ascribes to Josephus (*War* 6.425–28).

[4] Joseph reverses the sequence found in both Josephus and Eusebius and may rely on Eusebius. Note that in C. 82(12) he does not relate the similar story in 4 Rg 6:28–29 and also omits the similar prediction by Jeremiah (19:9) from C. 76.

[5] Present tense, Joseph and Eusebius; future, Josephus.

[6] *Sphazei*, Joseph; *kteinei*, Josephus and Eusebius.

σπασάμενοι, ἠπείλουν, εἰ μὴ δὴ[1] τὸ παρασκευασθὲν, ἀποσφάττειν αὐτὴν ταχέως. Ἡ δὲ τὰ λείψανα τοῦ υἱοῦ διεκάλυψε. Τοὺς δὲ εὐθέως φρίκη καὶ φρενῶν ἔκστασις ἔλαβε, καὶ παρὰ τὴν ὄψιν ἐπεπήγησαν. (168b1) Ἡ δὲ εἶπεν· Ἐμὸν τοῦτο τὸ τέκνον γνήσιον, καὶ τὸ ἔργον ἐμόν. Φάγετε, καὶ γὰρ ἐγὼ βέβρωκα. Μὴ γίνεσθε μήτε μαλακώτεροι γυναικὸς, μήτε συμπαθέστεροι μητρός. Εἰ δὲ ὑμεῖς εὐσεβεῖς, καὶ τὴν ἐμὴν ἀποστρέφεσθε θυσίαν, καὶ τὸ λοιπὸν[2] ἐμυνάτω.[3]

Τὸ δὲ ἀπὸ τοῦ λιμοῦ φθειρόμενον κατὰ τὴν πόλιν πλῆθος ἔπιπτε, καὶ καθ᾿ ἑκάστην οἰκίαν ὅπου τροφὴ παρεφάνη, πόλεμος ἦν ἐν αὐτῇ, καὶ διὰ χειρῶν ἐχώρουν οἱ φίλοι πρὸς ἀλλήλους. Πίστις δὲ ἀπορίας οὐδὲ τοῖς ἀποθνήσκουσιν, ἀλλὰ τοὺς ἐμπνέοντας οἱ λησταὶ διερεύνων,[4] καὶ ὑπὸ (168b2) ἀμηχανίας τοὺς αὐτοὺς οἴκους εἰσεπήδων δὶς ἢ τρὶς ὥρᾳ μιᾷ.

PKϚ'. + Πόσαι ἑορταὶ παρὰ Ἰουδαίοις ἄγονται;

Νόμιμοι μὲν αἱ τρεῖς, ἐν αἷς καὶ τρὶς τοῦ ἐνιαυτοῦ εἰς τὴν Ἰερουσαλὴμ ἀνίεσαν.

Πρώτην τὴν τοῦ Φασὲκ, ἥ ἐστιν ὑπέρβασις, ἐν ᾗ τὸ ἄζυμον ἤσθιον, διαβατήριον καλουμένην, ἐν τεσσαρισκαιδεκάτῃ[5] τοῦ πρώτου μηνὸς ἐπιτελουμένην.

Δευτέραν, τὴν Πεντηκοστὴν, μετὰ ν' ἡμέρας τοῦ Φασὲκ ἐπιτελουμένην, ἐν ᾗ τὰ πρωτογεννήματα προσῆγον, ἐπείπερ καὶ αἱ δίπτυχοι πλάκες τῆς νομοθεσίας ἐν ταύτῃ τῇ ἡμέρᾳ (169a1) τῷ Μωϋσῇ ἐν τῷ Σινᾷ ὄρει ἐπεδόθησαν.

Τρίτην, ἐν τῷ ἑβδόμῳ μηνὶ, τὴν τῶν Σκηνοπηγίων· ἐν ᾧ μηνὶ, νεομηνίᾳ μὲν τοῦ μηνὸς σαλπίζειν ἐν κερατίναις[6] ἐπετάττοντο σάλπιξι,[7] τῇ δὲ δεκάτῃ νηστείαν μετὰ κακουχίας ἄγειν. Ἀπὸ δὲ πεντεκαιδεκάτης ἕως ἡμερῶν ἑπτὰ σκηνοποιεῖσθαι. Αὗται μὲν οὖν αἱ νόμιμοι τρεῖς ἑορταί.

‹δ'› Ἐφευρέθησαν δὲ καὶ ἄλλαι τέσσαρες ἑορταὶ, πραγμάτων εὐεργεσίας ἐνεγκάντων τινάς. Ἐν αἷς λυχνοβατοῦσι, μηνὶ Ἀδὲρ, ὅς ἐστι Δύστρος, ὑπὲρ τῆς ἀναιρέσεως Ἀμάνου, ὃς συνεσκευάσατο ἐπὶ τῶν Περσῶν ὅλον τὸ ἔθνος ἐν μιᾷ ἡμέρᾳ ἀπὸ (169a2) συνθήματος ἐξαφανισθῆναι.[8]

---

[1] Lc FGM, who replace δη with δειξειν.
[2] GM λειπον.
[3] Lc FGM μεινατω.
[4] FGM διηρευνων.
[5] Lc FGM τεσσαρεσκαιδεκατη.
[6] FGM κερατινοις.
[7] Lc FGM σαλπιγξι.
[8] G ἐξαφαισθαι; lc M ἐξαφανισαι.

odor they threatened to slay her at once unless she showed them what she had prepared. The woman revealed the remains of her son. At once horror and amazement overcame them and they were paralyzed at the sight. (168b) But she said, "This is my own son, and my deed. Eat, for I too have eaten. Do not be softer than a woman or more compassionate than a mother. If you are pious and turn from my sacrifice, let the rest remain for me" [Josephus *War* 6.204-11; Eusebius *HE* 3.6.23-26].

Those who fell as victims of famine throughout the city were a boundless multitude and in each house when food appeared it meant war and friends fell to fighting one another. Credit for being in want was not given the dying, but the robbers searched those who were expiring, out of incompetence rushing into[1] the same houses two or three times in an hour [Josephus *War* 6.193-96; Eusebius *HE* 3.6.17-18].

**126.** – How many festivals are celebrated among the Jews?

The prescribed festivals were three [C. 67, 69] when, three times a year, they went up to Jerusalem.

First was Phasek, which is "passing over,"[2] the feast called "crossing"[3] on which they ate the unleavened bread, celebrated on the fourteenth day of the first month.[4]

The second is Pentecost, celebrated fifty days after Phasek, on which they brought forward the first fruits as the two tables of the legislation handed down (169a) to Moses on Mount Sinai on this day.[5]

The third, the festival of Tabernacles, occurs in the seventh month, in which at the new moon of the month they were ordered to sound the trumpet with trumpets of horn, and on the tenth to fast in sadness, but from the fifteenth for seven days, to make a tabernacle.[6] These are the three prescribed festivals.

<4> But four other festivals were added because of successes and benefits for which they proceeded with lamps, in the month of Ader, which is Dystros, because of the killing of Amman, who under the Persians had tried to destroy the

---

[1] *Eis...eispédôntes*, Josephus; Eusebius (TBDM) omits *eis* with Joseph.

[2] *Hyperbasis*, Josephus *Ant.* 2.313.

[3] *Diabatérion*, Philo *Special Laws* 2.145.

[4] Josephus *Ant.* 3.248.

[5] Josephus *Ant.* 3.252.

[6] Josephus *Ant.* 3.240–47; 2 Macc 1:9.

Μαρδοχαῖος δὲ πείσας Ἐσθὴρ᾿ σύγκοιτον γενομένην Δαρείου τοῦ Ἀσουήρου, τὴν συσκευὴν αὐτοῦ ἀνέτρεψε, καὶ αὐτὸν ἀνεσταύρωσεν. Ἑορτάζουσι γοῦν ταύτην ἡμέραν,[1] καὶ καλεῖται αὕτη ἡ ἑορτὴ παρ᾿ αὐτοῖς Φρουραί.

‹ε›᾿ Μηνὶ τῷ αὐτῷ ὑπὲρ τῆς ἀναιρέσεως Νικάνορος τοῦ ἀποσταλέντος ἐπὶ Δημητρίου ἐπὶ τῶν[2] Μακεδόνων λαὸν καὶ[3] τὸν λαὸν ἀφανίσαι. Ἀλλὰ τούτῳ συμβαλὼν Ἰούδας ὁ Μακκαβαῖος, ἐνίκησε, καὶ τὴν κεφαλὴν αὐτοῦ καὶ τὰς[4] χεῖρας ἀποκόψας, ἤγαγεν εἰς τὴν Ἰερουσαλὴμ τῇ τρισκαιδεκάτῃ τοῦ **(169b1)** Δύστρου μηνός. Ἐν ᾗ ἡμέρᾳ καὶ τὴν ἑορτὴν ἕως τοῦ παρόντος ἐπιτελοῦσι.

‹ς› Μηνὶ δὲ Χασλεὺς,[5] ὅς ἐστιν Ἀπρίλλιος,[6] πέμπτῃ καὶ εἰκοστῇ, ἄλλην ἑορτὴν, τὰ Φῶτα καλουμένην, ἐπιτελοῦσι, τῆς καθαιρέσεως τοῦ ναθὰβ[7] μνήμην ποιούμενοι, ὃν ἐμίανεν Ἀντίοχος ὁ Ἐπιφανής.

‹ζ› Μηνὶ δὲ Νησᾶν, Ξανθικὸς δέ ἐστιν οὗτος, ἄλλην ἄγουσιν ἑορτὴν, ὑπερεύσημον, ὁ[8] Ματταθίου τὴν ἄκραν ἐκαθαίρισε.[9]

**ΡΚΖ'. + Ποίας νηστείας Ἰουδαῖοι νηστεύουσι;**

Νόμιμον μὲν οὖν νηστείαν, τὴν ἐν τῷ ἑβδόμῳ μηνὶ, δεκάτῃ τοῦ μηνὸς, νηστεύειν παρειλήφασιν. Εἰσὶ **(169b2)** δὲ καὶ ἄλλαι δ᾿ αὐτοῖς παρειλημμέναι νηστεῖαι, καὶ παρὰ τῷ προφήτῃ Ζαχαρίᾳ μνημονευόμεναι, περὶ ὧν φησι· Νηστεία ἡ τετάρτη,[10] καὶ νηστεία ἡ πέμπτη,[11] καὶ νηστεία ἡ ἑβδόμη,[12] καὶ νηστεία ἡ δεκάτη[13] ἔσται τῷ οἴκῳ Ἰούδα εἰς χαρὰν καὶ εἰς εὐφροσύνην, καὶ εἰς ἑορτὰς ἀγαθάς.

Καὶ ἡ μὲν τοῦ τετάρτου μηνὸς νηστεία, ἔστιν ἐν ᾧ μηνὶ ἡ πόλις ὑπὸ τοῦ Ναβουχοδονόσορ ἐρράγη. Ἡ δὲ τοῦ πέμπτου, ἐν ᾧ ἐνεπρήσθη ὁ ναός.

---

[1] FGM ταυτην την ημεραν.

[2] Lc FGM τον.

[3] FGM replace και with ἐπι τῳ.

[4] FGM omit τας.

[5] Lc FGM Χασλευ.

[6] Emend to Ἀπηλλαιος. The notes of FGM show that they were aware of a problem at this point.

[7] Lc FGM ναου.

[8] Lc FGM ὅτε ὁ.

[9] G ἐκαθαιρισεν; lc M ἐκαθαρισεν.

Only the first three items of this chapter are numbered in CFGM.

[10] FGM τεταρτου.

[11] FGM πεμπτου.

[12] FGM ἑβδομου.

[13] FGM δεκατου.

whole nation on a signal in one day. But Mardochaios persuaded Esthér, the wife of Dareios Asouéros, and she overturned the plot and crucified him. They keep this day as a festival and it is called Phrourai by them [11.295].

<5> In the same month, for the destruction of Nicanor, sent by Demetrius for the Macedonian people to suppress the people, but Ioudas Makkabaios fought and defeated him and, cutting off his head and hands, brought him to Jerusalem on the thirteenth of the month (169b) Dystros, on which day they celebrate the festival until now [12.412; 1 Macc 7:49; 2 Macc 15:36].

<6> On the twenty-fifth of the month Chislev, which is Apéllaios,[1] they celebrate another festival which they call Lights, recalling the consecration of the Temple which Antiochos Epiphanés defiled [1 Macc 6:52].[2]

<7> And in the month of Nisan, which is Xanthikos, they celebrate another solemn festival, when the son of Mattathias purified the citadel [1 Macc 13:51-52, 23 Artemision[3]].

**127.** – What fasts do the Jews keep?

They received by tradition the prescribed fast on the tenth day of the seventh month. There are four other fasts received by them and mentioned by the prophet Zacharias [Zch 8:19]: "The fast of the 4th and the fast of the 5th and the fast of the 7th and the fast of the 10th will be to the house of Iouda for joy and gladness and for good feasts."

The fast of the 4th month is when the city was broken by Nebouchadonosor; that of the 5th, when the Temple was burned; the 7th, when Godolias was slain

---

[1] Cf. C. 27(9).

[2] Josephus *Ant.* 12.318–19, 325.

[3] Josephus has stopped following 1 Macc at 13.214 = 1 Macc 13:42. Perhaps our Joseph is simply confused; cf. Josephus *Ant.* 3.201.

The fact that two festivals commemorating the purification of the temple are mentioned, each on the twenty-fifth of some month, suggests that a corrupt text may have led to this bifurcation. Ralph Marcus in his edition of Josephus notes that Laurentianus plut. 69, codex 20 sates that the festival of purification was celebrated on the twenty-fifth of Xanthikos (=Nisan) rather than the twenty-fifth of Chislev.

Ἑβδόμου δὲ, ἐν ᾧ Γοδολίας ἀνηρέθη ὑπὸ Ἰσμαήλου.¹ Καὶ δεκάτου, καθ᾽ ὃν μῆνα τοῖς οὖσιν ἐν Βαβυλῶνι ἀνηγγέλει² τὰ γενόμενα ἐν Ἰερουσαλὴμ ἅπαντα κακά. **(170a1)**

**ΡΚΗ´.** + Τίνα ἐστὶν, ἃ μὴ χρὴ ζητεῖν, ὅτι καὶ ἀκατάληπτα;

‹α›› Τὴν πρὸ³ τῆς γενέσεως τῆς ἀβύσσου, περὶ τῆς⁴ νοερᾶς οὐσίας, πρότερον⁵ ὑπεράνω τῶν οὐρανῶν ἐστιν, ἔνθα τὰ ὕδατα ἐναπελείφθη, τῆς ἀβύσσου τὰ μεταδιακριθέντα· ἐπὶ τῆς γῆς, ἢ ὑπὸ τὴν γῆν, ἢ ἐν αἰθερίῳ τῷ ὑπὸ τὸν οὐρανόν. Ὧν γὰρ ἡ οὐσία καὶ πρὸ τῆς διακοσμήσεως καὶ πρὸ τῆς ἀβύσσον τὴν ὑπόστασιν ἔσχε, τόπου τινὸς οὐκ ἐπινοουμένου τὸ τηνικαῦτα, ἐν ᾧ τὴν μονὴν εἶχε, τούτων τὴν μονὴν οὐδὲ μετὰ τὴν γεῦσιν⁶ τοῦδε τοῦ παντὸς ζητητέον, ἢ μόνον ὅτιπερ **(170a2)** τῷ ποιητῇ Θεῷ παρειστήκει.

Περὶ τοῦ ὑπὸ γῆν ὕδατος, οὗ πέρας οὐ προσήκει ζητεῖν. Ἀλλ᾽ εἴτε μετέωρον⁷ ἀνήρτηται δυνάμει Θεοῦ, κατὰ τοῦ κρημνοῦ· Τὴν δὲ γῆν⁸ ἐπ᾽ οὐδενί·⁹ εἴτε ἐπὶ στερεοῦ φέρεται, κατὰ τό· Ἐγὼ ἐστερέωσα τοὺς στύλους αὐτῆς· εἴτε ἐπ᾽ ἀπείρων ὑδάτων ἐστὶν, κατὰ τό· Ἀβύσσῳ ὡς ἱματίῳ ἑλίξεις αὐτήν. Παραιτέον¹⁰ τὴν περὶ τῶν βαθυτέρων ἔρευναν, τῷ σοφῷ πειθομένους λόγῳ.

‹β›› Τὸ αὐτὸ καὶ περὶ τοῦ συμπεράσματος τῶν ὑδάτων, τῶν ὑπεράνω τῶν οὐρανῶν, βαθὺ τὸ ζητεῖν. Ὡς γὰρ τοῦ ὑπὸ τὴν γῆν τέλους **(170b1)** ἀνεύρητος ἡ ἔρευνα, οὕτω καὶ ἡ ζήτησις ‹τῶν ὑπερουρανίων›.¹¹

‹γ›› Ἄρρητα ἀκηκοέναι ῥήματα ὁ Ἀπόστολος ἁρπαγεὶς ἕως τρίτον¹² οὐρανοῦ ἔφη. Οὐδὲ ταῦτα τίνα ἐστὶ χρὴ ζητεῖν. Ἃ γὰρ οὐκ ἐξὸν ἀνθρώπῳ λαλῆσαι, καὶ αὐτὸς ὁ Ἀπόστολος ἔφη. Ἰωάννης εἶπεν· Ἃ ὀφθαλμὸς οὐκ

---

¹GM wrongly emend to Ἰσραηλου.

²FGM ἀνηγγελη; emend to ἀνηγγελθη.

³In their notes, FGM suggest that here the word μονην has either fallen out or is implied, resulting in the reading. Την μονην προ.

⁴FGM emend περι της to ποιητης. Emend to ἡ περι της.

⁵*Lc* FGM ποτερον.

⁶*Lc* FGM γενεσιν.

⁷*Lc* FGM μετεωρος.

⁸*Lc* FGM, who replace κατα του Κρεμμου· Την δε γην with κατα το Κρεμαζων γην (following the LXX of Job 26:7). Oddly, when F reports how his MS reads, it difers from C in order. He reports κατα του κρημνου επ᾽ ουδειν την δε γην.

⁹*Lc* FGM ἐπ᾽ ουδενος.

¹⁰*Lc* FGM Παραιτητεον.

¹¹The words των ὑπερουρανιων are not found in CFGM, but in their notes GM suggest adding των ὑπερουρανιων ανεισοδος.

¹²*Lc* FGM τριτου.

by Ismaél [Jer 41:2]; and the 10th, the month in which all the evil events in Jerusalem were reported to those in Babylon (170a).[1]


<THEOLOGICAL MYSTERIES (128) (from C. 67)>


**128**. – What are the things one must not investigate, because they are incomprehensible?

<1> The time before the generation of the abyss, or concerning the intelligible being (*noera ousia*), whether it is above the heavens, where the waters of the abyss were taken up after they were separated, or on the earth or under the earth, or in the ethereal region under the heaven. For the being (*ousia*) had a real existence (*hypostasis*), before the constitution of the world and before the abyss, even though at that time no place could be conceived in which it could subsist. For the subsistence of such things is not to be sought after creation or from the universe, only that it is present with God the Creator.

Of the water under the earth, whose limit it is not right to seek. But whether the land is suspended on high by the power of God, according to "Suspending the earth on nothing" [Job 26:7] or on a firm foundation, according to "I made solid its columns" [Ps 74:3], or on immeasurable waters, according to "You encircled it with the abyss as a garment" [Ps 103:6, 101:27], we must avoid searching the deeper matters, in obedience to the wise word.

<2> Similarly it is a deep matter to search for the limit of the waters above the heavens [Gn 1:7-8]. For as inquiry into the end under the earth leads (170b) to no discovery, so also does the search <for things above the heavens>.

<3> And it is not right to inquire about what the hidden words were which the Apostle says he heard in the third heaven. For "it is not lawful for a man to speak" them, as the Apostle himself said [2 Cor 12:4]. John (Paul) says, "What

---

[1] According to Josephus *Ant.* 10.146, Nabouchodonosor set fire to the temple "on the new moon of the 5th month" (cf. 4 Rg 25:8; Jer 52:13); Godolias slain in 7th, 4 Rg 25:25.

ἴδε,[1] καὶ οὓς οὐκ ἤκουσε, καὶ ἐπὶ καρδίαν ἀνθρώπου οὐκ ἀνέβη, ἃ ἡτοίμασεν ὁ Θεὸς τοῖς ἀγαπῶσιν αὐτόν. Πῶς καὶ ταῦτα νοῆσαί τις οἷός τε εἴη, ἃ μήτε αἰσθήσει, μήτε νοήσει ὑποπίπτειν δυνατόν;

‹δ'› Τὸ διάστημα, τὸ πρὸ τῆς τοῦ φωτὸς γενέσεως, τῶν χρόνου μυρίων[2] οὐκ ὄντων, οὐ καταληπτόν, μόνῳ Θεῷ ἐγνωσμένον. (170b2) Τοιοῦτο καὶ τὸ κατὰ[3] τὴν ἐσομένην τοῦ κόσμου συναίρεσιν, ἕως ἀναδείξεως τῆς καινῆς κτίσεως, ἐννοοῦμεν.

‹ε'› Αἱ νοεραὶ οὐσίαι τὰ ἐασθητὰ[4] καὶ σωματικὰ πῶς ὁρῶσι, κρείττους αἰσθήσεως οὖσαι; Τοῦ Θεοῦ τὴν ὀφθαλμοφανῆ θέαν, ἀοράτου τὴν φύσιν ὄντος. Θεὸν γάρ, φησὶν, οὐδεὶς ἑώρακε πώποτε. Τὸ γὰρ μόνῃ καθαρᾷ καρδίᾳ θεώμενον, αἰσθητοῖς ὀφθαλμοῖς ὁρᾶσθαι[5] πῶς οἴονται;[6]

‹ς'› Δυσκαταλήπτοις[7] καὶ ἡ τοῦ Ἰσραὴλ σωματικὴ εὐλογία, ἐν οε' ψυχαῖς τοῦ Ἰακὼβ κατελθόντες εἰς Αἴγυπτον, καὶ κατὰ τετάρτην γενεὰν[8] (171a1) ἐν ξ' μυριάσιν ἀνδρῶν ἐξεληλυθότος.

‹ζ'› Περὶ γὰρ τῆς ἡμέρας τῆς παρουσίας τοῦ Κυρίου καὶ αὐτὸς ὁ Κύριος ἀπέδειξεν· Οὐχ ὑμῶν γάρ ἐστι, χρόνους ἢ καιροὺς εἰδέναι, πρὸς τοὺς ἀποστόλους ἔφη, οὓς ὁ Πατὴρ ἔθετο ἐν τῇ ἰδίᾳ ἐξουσίᾳ.[9]

ΡΚΘ'. + Ὅσα δι' ἐνυπνίων τισὶν ἐμπεφάνισται;

‹α'› Ὁ Ἰακὼβ κλίμακα ὁρᾷ εἰς οὐρανὸν[10] ἀπὸ γῆς διήκουσαν.

‹β'› Ἰωσὴφ τὰς ἀδελφῶν δραγμὰς, τὴν αὐτοῦ προσκυνούσας δραγμὴν, καὶ τοὺς ἀστέρας πάλιν, καὶ τὸν ἥλιον καὶ τὴν σελήνην ποιοῦντας τὸ αὐτό.

‹γ'› Οἱ ἐν Αἰγύπτῳ μετὰ τοῦ Ἰωσὴφ καθειργμένοι·[11] (171a2) ὁ μὲν ἀπολυόμενος τοὺς τρεῖς βότρυας ἐκθλίβων, καὶ τὸν οἶνον ἐπιδιδοὺς τῷ βασιλεῖ, ὁ δὲ κολαζόμενος τοὺς ἐπὶ τοῦ κανοῦ τρεῖς φέρων ὑπὸ τῶν ὀρνέων ἐσθιομένους ἄρτους.

---

[1] Lc FGM εἶδε.
[2] Lc FGM μοριων.
[3] Lc GM, who in thier notes suggest emending κατα to μετα.
[4] Lc FGM αἰσθητα.
[5] GM θεασθαι; emend to ὁρᾶν?
[6] FGM οἰον τε.
[7] Lc FGM Δυσκαταληπτος.
[8] Lc FGM κατα την τεταρτην γενεαν.
[9] The items in this chapter are not numbered in CFGM.
[10] GM οὐρανους.
[11] GM print καθειγμενος, but suggest καθειργμενοι, the reading of CF, in their notes.

eye has not seen or ear heard nor has it risen into the heart of man, what God has prepared for those who love him" [1 Cor 2:9]. How then can anyone understand these things which cannot fall under sense or thought?

<4> The interval before the creation of light, when no divisions of time existed [Gn 1:1-3], is incomprehensible to man and known to God alone. Such also we understand to be <the situation after> the future destruction of the world until the manifestation of the new creation [Rv 10:6].

<5> How will the intelligible beings (*noerai ousiai*) see objects of sense and body, being superior to sense? How will we see with our eyes the God who is by nature invisible? For it says [Jn 1:18], "No one has ever seen God." How do they expect to see with the eyes of sense the one seen only by a pure heart [Mt 5:8]?

<6> The corporeal blessing of Israel is hard to understand, when it was given to seventy-five souls [Ac 7:14; Gn 46:27 LXX; see C. 6] as Jacob went down to Egypt, and in the fourth generation came out (171a) with 600,000 men [Ex 12:37; Nm 11:21].[1]

<7> Concerning the day of the Lord's coming, the Lord himself signified: "It is not yours to know the times or seasons," he said to the apostles, "which the Father has set in his own authority" [Ac 1:8].

<BIBLICAL LITERATURE (129-33) (from C. 28)>

**129.** – What is revealed to some through dreams?

<1> Iakôb saw a ladder reaching heaven from earth [Gn 28:2].

<2> Iôséph saw the sheaves of his brothers worship his sheaf, and stars, sun, and moon doing the same [37:7, 9].

<3> Those imprisoned with Iôséph in Egypt: one was released when he crushed three branches of grapes and gave the wine to the king, while another was punished when he brought three loaves in a basket and they were eaten by birds [40:9-19].

---

[1] Philo *Life of Moses* 1.147 emphasizes the number "over 600,000" and adds an extra crowd of mixed descent; in *Special Laws* 2.146 he treats the total as more than two million. Josephus *Ant.* 2.176–83 names the "seventy" who went to Egypt and mentions the growth from 70 to 600,000 (ibid. 214) and the 600,000 just "of military age" who came out (ibid. 317). Two hundred fifteen years had elapsed (ibid. 318; 216 years according to Fabricius, 269 note s; 430 years in Ex 12:40 and Ac 7:6). See C. 6 for Joseph's list.

‹δ'› Ὁ Φαραὼ τοὺς ἑπτὰ λιπαροὺς βόας, καὶ στάχυας εὐστραφεῖς[1] ἑπτὰ, καὶ πάλιν κατησχυνομένους[2] βόας ἑπτὰ, καὶ τοσούτους στάχυας.

‹ε'› Ὁ τὴν κοιλιομένην[3] κριθίνην μαγίδα[γιδα][4] θεώμενος Μαδιανίτης ἐπὶ τοῦ Γεδεὼν, καὶ τὴν σκηνὴν καταστρέψασαν, τὴν τοῦ Μαδιάμ.

‹ϛ'› Ναβουχοδονόσορ τὸν ἀνδριάντα θεώμενος τὸν πολύυλον, ὑπὸ τοῦ λίθου συντριβόμενον, τοῦ ἄνευ (171b1) χειρῶν[5] ἐπ' αὐτὸν ἐξ ὄρους καταβάντος.

‹ζ'› Καὶ πάλιν τὸ ὑψηλότατον δένδρον, τὸ ἐκτέμνεσθαι κελευόμενον, καὶ μεθ' ἑπτὰ βλαστάνον ἐνιαυτούς.

‹η'› Ὁ Δανιὴλ περὶ τῶν ἀνισταμένων καὶ καθαιρουμένων δ'[6] εὐ[7] μορφαῖς θηρίων, βασιλειῶν, καὶ περὶ τῆς τελευταίας βασιλείας, τῆς καθαιρουμένης τοῦ Ἀντιχρίστου, κέρατος βραχυτάτου φανέντος αὐτῷ. Καὶ περὶ τῆς ἐξ οὐρανῶν ἤκουσεν αἰωνίου Χριστοῦ[8] βασιλείας. [καθαιρουμένης τοῦ Ἀντιχρίστου, κέρατος βραχυτάτου φανέντος αὐτῷ. Καὶ περὶ τῆς ἐξ οὐρανῶν ἤκουσεν αἰωνίου Χριστοῦ βασιλείας.][9]

‹θ'› ὁ Ἀπόστολος (171b2) ἀκουῶν[10] τοῦ Κυρίου λέγοντος αὐτῷ· Θάρσει, Παῦλε, ἀκούων, ὡς γὰρ διεμαρτύρω περὶ ἐμοῦ εἰς τὴν Ἰερουσαλήμ, οὕτω σε δεῖ καὶ εἰς Ῥώμην μαρτυρῆσαι.

‹ι'› Καὶ χειμαζόμενος ἐν τῷ πλεῖν, ἄγγελον ὁρᾷ καθ' ὕπνους αὐτῷ λέγοντα· Ἰδοὺ κεχάρισταί σοι ὁ Θεὸς πάντας τοὺς πλέοντας μετὰ σοῦ.[11]

ΡΛ. + Τὴν τῶν Βασιλειῶν βίβλον[12] τίς κατέγραψε;

‹α'› Τοῦ μὲν Σαοὺλ τὰς πράξεις Σαμουὴλ ὁ προφήτης ἀναγραψάμενος, ἔθηκεν ἐπὶ τῆς Σκηνῆς. Τοῦ δὲ Δαβὶδ, τὰς προτέρας μὲν ὁ αὐτὸς Σαμουὴλ, Γὰδ δὲ καὶ Νάθαν οἱ προφῆται τὰς μετὰ ταύτας.

---

[1]FGM εὐτραφεις.

[2]Lc FGM καταισχυνομενους.

[3]Lc FGM κυλιομενην.

[4]Lc FGM, who correct the obvious dittograph to μαγιδα.

[5]FGM χειρος.

[6]FGM move δ' so that it follows ἀνισταμενων. Instead, perhaps δ' should be moved closer to the noun it modifies, i.e., either immediately preceding or following βασιλειων.

[7]Lc FGM ἐν.

[8]GM omit Χριστου.

[9]Lc FGM, who omit the bracketed material as a dittography.

[10]FGM omit ἀκουων.

[11]The items in this chapter are not numbered in CFGM.

[12]Emend to Τας των Βασιλειων βιβλους.

<4> Pharaô saw seven fat cows and seven well-twisted sheaves of wheat, and again seven gaunt cows and as many sheaves [41:1-6].

<5> The Madianite who saw a barley-cake rolling for Gedeôn and overturning the tent of Madiam [Jd 7:13].

<6> Nebouchadonosor who saw a statue made of various materials crushed by the stone which without (171b) a hand upon it came down from a mountain [Dn 2:31-35].

<7> Again, a very tall tree was ordered cut down and grew again after seven years [4:10-17].

<8> Daniél, concerning four kingdoms that rose and fell in the guise of beasts [7:3], and concerning the final kingdom of Antichrist to be destroyed, with a very small horn that appeared to him [7:8]; and he heard concerning the eternal kingdom of Christ from the heavens [7:14, 27].

<9> The apostle heard the Lord say to him, "Be of good cheer, Paul, for as you have borne witness to me in Jerusalem, so you must bear witness at Rome" [Ac 23:11].[1]

<10> And when he was storm-tossed when sailing, he saw an angel in a dream who said to him, "Behold, God has given you all who sail with you" [27:25].

**130.** – Who composed the book<s> of Reigns?[2]

<1> Samouél the prophet recorded the deeds of Saul and put them in the tabernacle [1 Rg 10:25]. The same Samouél, <recorded> the earlier deeds of David, and the prophets Gad and Nathan the later ones [1 Par 29:29].

---

[1] The quotations from Ac 23:11 and 27:24 are reversed between C. 129 and C. 153.

[2] An analogous but much simpler analysis in Theodorus Schermann, *Prophetarum vitae fabulosae* (Leipzig: Teubner, 1907) 39, 9–23.

⟨β'-δ'⟩ (172a1) Τοῦ δὲ Σολομῶνος, τὰς μὲν προτέρας πράξεις Ναθὰν ἀνεγράψατο, τὰς δὲ μετέπειτα Ἀχίας ὁ Σιλωνίτης καὶ Ἰωήλ.

⟨ε'-ς'⟩ Τοῦ δὲ Ῥοβοὰμ Σαμαίας καὶ Ἰαδών.

⟨ζ'⟩ Τοῦ δὲ Ἀβιᾶ Ἀδών, καὶ τοῦ Ἀσᾶ.

⟨η'⟩ Τοῦ δὲ Ἰωσαφὰτ Ἰησοῦς ὁ τοῦ Ἀνανῆ. Οὗτος δὲ ὁ Ἰησοῦς ἑκάστας τῶν βασιλέων τοῦ Ἰσραὴλ ἀναζητήσας πράξεις, ἀνεγράψατο.

⟨θ'⟩ Τῶν δὲ ἑξῆς βασιλέων τοῦ Ἰούδα, τοῦ Ἰωρὰμ καὶ τοῦ Ὀχοζίου, καὶ Ἰὰς[1] καὶ Ἀμασίου, γέγονε τῶν πράξεων ἀναγραφὴ, καὶ ἀπέκειτο ἐν τοῖς βασιλείοις. Ὀζίου[2] δὲ καὶ Ἰωάθαμ, καὶ Ἀχὰς καὶ Ἐζεκίου, οὐ μόνον δημόσιος (172a2) τὰς πράξεις συνέλεξε βίβλους,[3] ἀλλὰ καὶ Ἡσαΐας ὁ προφήτης αὐτὰς ἀνεγράψατο.

⟨ι'⟩ Τοῦ δὲ Μανασσῆ οἱ ὁρῶντες, οἵτινές εἰσιν οἱ τότε προφῆται, τὰς δυσσεβεῖς ἀνεγράψαντο πράξεις, καὶ ἐν τοῖς βασιλείοις ἀπέθεντο. Ἀμασίου δὲ καὶ Ἰωσίου καὶ Ἰωακεὶμ ἀναγραφαὶ δημόσιοι γεγένηνται τῶν πράξεων, καὶ ἐν τοῖς βασιλείοις ὁμοίως ἀνετέθεισαν.[4]

⟨ια'⟩ Ἰεχωνίου δὲ καὶ Σεδεκίου, ἐφ' ὧν καὶ ὁ λαὸς εἰς αἰχμαλωσίαν ἀπήχθη, καὶ ὁ ναὸς ἥλω, καὶ ἡ βασιλεία κατηνέχθη, Ἰερεμίας ὁ προφήτης τοὺς οἰκτοὺς[5] ἀνεγράψατο βίους.

⟨ιβ'⟩ Ὁμοῦ δὲ τῶν βασιλέων τὰς (172b1) πράξεις, καὶ τὰ τέλη, Ἔσδρας ὁ σοφὸς ἐν τῇ ἐπανόδῳ γενόμενος τοῦ λαοῦ, τῇ ἀπὸ τῆς αἰχμαλωσίας, ἀπομνημονεύσας ἅπασαν τὴν βίβλον τῶν Βασιλειῶν, τῶν τε εὐσεβῶς βιωσάντων τὰς πράξεις. Μετὰ δὲ ταῦτα ἐπιγνοὺς τίνα ἐστὶ τὰ παραλειφθέντα αὐτῷ ἐν τῇ Βασιλειῶν βίβλῳ, ἰδίᾳ ταῦτα πάλιν ἀνενέγκας ἐξέθετο, ἐπείπερ ἡ προτέρα βίβλος ἡ ἐκδοθεῖσα, παρὰ πολλῶν ἐξείλειπτο.[6] Ἥντινα βίβλον ἐν δυσὶ τόμοις ἐγγραφεῖσαν, Ἰουδαῖοι μὲν, Λόγοι ἡμερῶν, ἡ δὲ Ἐκκλησία Παραλειπομένων βίβλον ἐπέγραψεν.[7] (172b2)

---

[1] Lc FGM Ἰωας.
[2] M Ὀσιου.
[3] Lc FGM βιβλος.
[4] M ανετεθησαν.
[5] Lc FGM οἰκτρους.
[6] M ἐξελελειπτο.
[7] The items in this chapter are not numbered in CFGM.

<2-4> (172a) Of Solomon, Nathan recorded the earlier deeds, Achias the Silônite and Iôél the later ones [2 Par 9:29].

<5-6> Of Roboam, Samaias and Iadôn [Adô, 12:15].

<7> Of Abias and Asa, Adôn (Adô) [13:22, cf. 16:11].

<8> Of Iôsaphat, Iésous [Cod.B] son of Anani; this Iésous also, after investigating the deeds of the kings of Israel, recorded them [20:34].

<9> A record was made of the deeds of the rest of the kings of Judah, Iôram Ochozias Iôas Amazias [25:26], included in the books of Reigns [24:27]. Not only did the public record describe the deeds of Ozias [26:22], Iôatham [27:7], Achas [28:26], and Ezekias [32:32], but Ésaias the prophet [26:22, 32:32] also recorded them.

<10> Eyewitnesses, that is, the prophets of his time [4 Rg 21:10], recorded the impious deeds of Manassé and set them in the books of Reigns [4 Rg 21:1-18]. The public records of the acts of Amasias [2 Par 25:26] and Iôsias [35:27] and Iôacheim [36:8] were also composed and similarly set in the books of Reigns.

<11> Ieremias the prophet recorded the miserable lives of Iechonias and Sedekias, under whom the people was taken away to captivity, the Temple destroyed, and the kingdom overthrown [Jer 52:4-30 = 4 Rg 24:8-25:12].

<12> Similarly Esdras the wise, who lived at the return of the people from captivity, recorded the (172b) acts of the kings and their deaths in the whole book of Reigns and the acts of those who lived piously. Afterwards he was aware of what he had left out of the book of Reigns and set it forth again, since the book he had set forth earlier had many gaps.[1] The Jews called this book, written in two volumes, "Words of days," while the church entitled it "Book of things left out (*paraleipomenôn*)."

---

[1] 1 Par 36:22–23 = 1 Es 1:1–3.

**ΡΛΑ'.** + Τίνα παραβολικῶς καὶ αἰνιγματωδῶς ἐν ταῖς Γραφαῖς εἴρηται; ‹α'› Ὁ Γεδεὼν τοῖς ἀπὸ τῆς[1] Ἐφραὶμ φυλῆς ἀγανακτοῦσιν αὐτῷ, ὅτι μὴ κέκληκεν αὐτοὺς εἰς τὸν κατὰ Μαδιανιτῶν πόλεμον, φησίν· Οὐχὶ κρεῖττον[2] ἐπιφυλλὶς ἐν Ἐφραὶμ, ἢ τρυγητὸς ἐν Ἐβιάζερ; ‹β'› Ἰωβὰβ ὁ τοῦ Γεδεὼν υἱὸς πρὸς τοὺς Σικιμήτας[3] ἑλομένους τὸν φονέα γενόμενον τῶν ο' αὐτοῦ ἀδελφῶν βασιλεύειν αὐτὸν,[4] τὸν Ἀβιμέλεχ, φησί· Πορευόμενα ἐπορεύθη τὰ ξύλα τοῦ χρῖσαι ἀφ' ἑαυτὰ[5] βασιλέα. Καὶ εἶπε τῇ ἐλαίᾳ· Βασίλευσον ἐφ' ἡμᾶς. Καὶ εἶπεν αὐτοῖς (173a1) ἡ ἐλαία· Ἀφεῖσα τὴν πιότητά μου, ἣν ἐδόξασεν ὁ Θεὸς καὶ ἄνθρωποι,[6] πορευθῶ ἄρχειν τῶν ξύλων; Καὶ εἶπον πάντα τὰ ξύλα τῇ συκῇ· Δεῦρο, βασίλευσον ἐφ' ἡμᾶς. Καὶ εἶπεν ἡ συκῇ· Ἀφεῖσα τὴν γλυκύτητά μου, καὶ τὸ γένημά[7] μου τὸ ἀγαθὸν, πορευθῶ ἄρχειν ξύλων.[8] Καὶ εἶπον τὰ ξύλα τῇ ἀμπέλῳ· Δεῦρο, καὶ βασίλευσον ἐφ' ἡμᾶς. Καὶ εἶπεν αὐτοῖς ἡ ἄμπελος· Ἀφεῖσα τὸν οἶνόν μου, καὶ τὴν εὐφροσύνην τῶν ἀνθρώπων, πορευθῶ ἄρχειν ξύλων;[9] Καὶ εἶπον τὰ ξύλα τῇ ῥάμνῳ· Δεῦρο, βασίλευσον ἐφ' ἡμᾶς. Καὶ εἶπεν ἡ ῥάμνος τοῖς ξύλοις· Εἰ ἐν ἀληθείᾳ (173a2) ὑμεῖς χρίετέ με βασιλέα ἐφ' ὑμᾶς, εἰσέλθετε καὶ ὑποδύσατε ὑπὸ τὴν σκέπην μου. Καὶ εἰ μὴ, ἐξέλθῃ πῦρ ἐκ τῆς ῥάμνου, καὶ καταφάγοι τὰς κέδρους τοῦ Λιβάνου. (173b1)

‹γ'› Σαμψὼν εἰς τὸ μελικήριον ὃ εὖρεν ἐν τῷ στόματι οὗ ἀπέκτεινε λέοντος, καὶ ἔφαγε, πρόβλημα ποιήσας φησίν· Ἐκ στόματος ἐσθίοντος ἐξῆλθε βρῶσις, καὶ ἐξ ἰσχυροῦ γλυκύ.

‹δ'› Καὶ ὁ Δαβὶδ πρὸς τὸν Σαοὺλ φησι· Δικάσαι Κύριος ἀναμέσον ἐμοῦ καὶ σοῦ, καὶ ἐκδικήσαι Κύριος ἐκ σοῦ, καὶ ἡ χείρ μου οὐκ ἔσται ἐπὶ σὲ, καθὼς λέγει ἡ παραβολή· Ἐξ ἀνόμων ἐξελεύσεται πλημμέλεια. (173b1)

‹ε'› Ὁ Ἀχαὰβ πρὸς τὸν Σύρων βασιλέα ἀπειλοῦντα αὐτῷ, πᾶσαν τὴν τοῦ Ἰσραὴλ βασιλείαν ἀνειρεῖν, φησί· Μὴ καυχάσθω ὁ περιζωννύμενος, ὡς ὁ ἀποζωννύμενος.[10]

‹ς'› Ἰωᾶς ὁ τοῦ Ἰσραὴλ βασιλεὺς, Ἀμασίᾳ τῷ τοῦ Ἰούδα βασιλεῖ φιλίαν ἀσπαζομένῳ πρὸς αὐτὸν, ἀλαζονευόμενος αὐτὸν, καὶ ὑπερορῶν αὐτοῦ τοῦ[11]

---

[1]FGM omit της.
[2]*Lc* FGM κρειττων.
[3]*Lc* FGM Σικημιτας.
[4]*Lc* FGM αὐτων.
[5]*Lc* FGM ἐφ' ἑαυτα.
[6]FGM και οἱ ἀνθρωποι.
[7]FGM γεννημα.
[8]FGM ἀρχειν των ξυλων.
[9]FGM ἀρχειν των ξυλων.
[10]FGM ὑποζωννυμενος.
[11]*Lc* FGM, who omit του.

**131.** – What in the scriptures were spoken parabolically and enigmatically?

<1> Gedeôn said to the men of the tribe of Ephraim who were annoyed with him because he had not called them to the war against the Madianites, "Is not the gleaning of the grapes of Ephraim better than the vintage of Abiezer?" [Jd 8:2]

<2> Iôbab son of Gedeôn [Ioatha son of Ierobaal, 9:5 Lat.] said to the Sikémites who chose as king Abimelech, who had killed his seventy brothers, "The trees went forth to anoint a king over them; and they said to the olive, 'Reign over us.' And (173a) the olive said to them, 'Leaving my fatness, which God and men commended, shall I go to rule over trees?' And all the trees said to the fig, 'Come, reign over us.' And the fig said, 'Leaving my sweetness and my good fruit, shall I go to rule over trees?' And the trees said to the vine, 'Come and reign over us.' And the vine said to them, 'Leaving my wine and the cheer of men, shall I go to reign over trees?' And the trees said to the bramble, 'Come, reign over us.' And the bramble said to the trees, 'If in truth you anoint me king over you, come and find refuge in my shade. And if not, let fire come out of the bramble and consume the cedars of Lebanon'" [9:7-15].

<3> Sampson posed a riddle about the honeycomb which he found in the mouth of the lion he killed, and ate, "Out of the eater came food, and sweet out of the strong" [14:14].

<4> And David said to Saul, "May the Lord judge between me and you, and may the Lord avenge me upon you; but my hand will not be against you, as the proverb says, 'Out of the wicked comes forth wickedness'" [1 Rg 24:12-13].

<5> (173b) Achaab said to the king of the Syrians who was threatening him with the loss of the whole kingdom of Israel, "Let not him who girds on his armor boast himself as he who puts it off" [3 Rg 21:11].

<6> Iôas king of Israel made plain to Amasia king of Iouda, who proposed friendship with him but received him arrogantly and disliked meeting him, "A

τὴν σύντευξιν, δηλοῖ πρὸς αὐτόν· Ἡ ἄκανος ἐλάλησε πρὸς τὴν κέδρον τοῦ Λιβάνου λέγουσα· Δὸς τὴν θυγατέρα σου τῷ υἱῷ μου εἰς γυναῖκα. Καὶ διῆλθε τὰ θηρία τοῦ ἀγροῦ ἐν τῷ Λιβάνῳ, (173b2) καὶ κατεπάτησαν τὴν ἄκανον. Τύπτων ἐπάταξας τὴν Ἰδουμαίαν καὶ ἐπῆρέ σε ἡ καρδία σου. ‹ζ´› Ὁ δὲ Σαλομῶν πᾶσαν αὐτοῦ τὴν βίβλον τὴν πρώτην διὰ παραβολῶν ἐξήνεγκε.¹

**ΡΛΒ´.** + Τίνες εἰσὶν αἱ ὑπὸ² τοῦ Κυρίου παραβολαὶ ῥηθεῖσαι;³
‹α´› Περὶ τῆς νέας χάριτος, ὡς μὴ δεῖν ἐπὶ παλαιῷ ἱματίῳ καινὸν ῥάκκος⁴ ἐπιρράπτειν. Ἀσκοῖς παλαιοῖς μὴ δεῖν νέον οἶνον ἐμβάλλειν.
‹β´› Τοὺς ἀποστέλλων⁵ ὡς πρόβατα ἐν μέσῳ λύκων ἀποστέλλειν ἔφησε.
‹γ´› Τὸ κήρυγμα σπέρματι παραβέβληκεν, εἰς μὲν καλὴν γῆν καταβαλλομένῳ, (174a1) καὶ ἐν ρ´ καὶ ξ´ καὶ λ´ καρποφοροῦντι. Ἐν δὲ πέτρᾳ καὶ φραγμῷ καὶ ἀβαθῆ⁶ γῇ, τὸ⁷ ἄκαρπον εἶναι ἀπελέγχεσθαι.
‹δ´› Ζιζανίοις ἐπισπειρομένοις τοὺς τῶν αἱρέσεων λόγους, τῷ ἀγαθῷ σπέρματι, τῷ παρ᾽ αὐτοῦ σπαρέντι ἐπὶ τῆς γῆς.
‹ε´› Σίνηπι, τὸν τοῦ κηρύγματος λόγον, ὑπερτέρῳ τῶν ἀνθρωπίνων τυγχάνοντι κατὰ τὴν αὔξησιν, δογμάτων.
‹ϛ´› Καὶ ζύμῃ παραβέβληται, εἰς ἀλεύρου σάτα τρία ἐμβληθείσῃ.
‹ζ´› Θησαυρῷ κεκρυμμένῳ ἐν τῇ γῇ, καὶ πάντων ἀπεμπωλουμένων εἰς τὴν τούτου κτῆσιν.
‹η´› Μαργαρίτῃ τιμίῳ, (174a2) προτιμωμένῳ τῶν ἤδη κτησθέντων.
‹θ´› Πλουσίῳ κεκτημένῳ ἐν τῷ ταμιείῳ⁸ αὐτοῦ καινὰ καὶ παλαιά, τῆς νέας καὶ παρ᾽ Ἑβραίοις διαθήκης τὴν ἐπίγνωσιν.
‹ι´› Ἀλώπηκι⁹ τὴν Ἡρώδου πονηρίαν ὑποβαλλούσῃ.
‹ια´› Ὡς οὐ τὸ εἰσερχόμενον <ἀλλὰ τὸ ἐξερχόμενον μολύνει τὸν ἄνθρωπον>¹⁰ ὅ ἐστιν, αἱ τῆς κακίας ἔννοιαι καὶ λόγοι.
‹ιβ´› Ἡ τῶν Φαρισαίων ζύμη, τουτέστιν ἡ πονηρία, ἡ καὶ τοὺς ἄλλους κακίζουσα.

---

¹The items in this chapter are not numbered in CFGM.
²FGM ὑπερ.
³FGM ῥηθεισαι παραβολαι.
⁴Lc FGM ῥακος.
⁵Lc FGM ἀποστολους.
⁶Lc FGM ἀβαθει.
⁷FGM omit το.
⁸FGM ταμειω.
⁹Lc GM Ἀλωπεκι.
¹⁰Lc FGM, who insert ἀλλα το ἐξερχομενον μολυνει τον ανθρωπον.

thistle sent to a cedar of Lebanon, saying, 'Give your daughter to my son for a wife.' And the beasts of the field passed through Lebanon and trampled down the thistle. You have smitten Idoumaia, and your heart has lifted you up" [4 Rg 14:9–10].

<7> Solomon wrote his whole first book (Proverbs) in parables.


**132**. – What are the parables of the new grace expressed by the Lord?

<1> How one must not sew a new patch on an old garment, and one must not pour new wine into old skins [Mt 9:16–17].

<2> He said he was sending out the apostles like sheep in the midst of wolves [10:16].

<3> He compared the preaching to a seed cast (174a) upon good ground and bearing fruit 100-, 60-, and 30-fold, but said that the seed cast on rock or hedged or shallow ground would be denounced as fruitless [13:3–9].

<4> He compared the good seed sown by him and oversown with tares to the words of the heresies [13:25],

<5> and the mustard seed to the word of the preaching, in its increase surpassing human doctrines [13:23].

<6> He also compared it to yeast put into three measures of meal [13:33];

<7> to a treasure hidden in the ground and selling everything to acquire it [13:44];

<8> to a valuable pearl, valued more than other possessions [13:46].

<9> He compared to a rich man possessing new and old in his treasury, the knowledge of the New and the Hebrew covenants [13:52].

<10> He compared the malice of Hérôdés to a fox [Lk 13:32].

<11> He taught that not what goes into a man but what comes out defiles him, that is, thoughts and words of wickedness [Mt 15:10–11].

<12> The leaven of the Pharisees, that is, malice, harms others [16:5].

‹ιγ´› Ἡ τῶν παιδίων παράδειξις, πρὸς τὸν[1] ἁπλοῦν τῶν σωζομένων τρόπον.

‹ιδ´› Ἡ τοῦ ἀπολωλότος ἑνὸς προβάτου ζήτησις, τὴν τοῦ γένους τῶν ἀνθρώπων ὑποδεικνύσα σωτηρίαν.

‹ιε´› Ἡ τοῦ τυχόντος (174b1) πολλῶν πλημμελειῶν παρὰ τοῦ δεσπότου τὴν ἄφεσιν, αὐτοῦ δὲ μὴ ἀφιέντος τοῖς συνδούλοις τὰς εἰς αὐτὸν μικρὰς ἁμαρτίας.

‹ιϛ´› Δούλων ἀποσταλέντων ἐπὶ τῇ τῶν καρπῶν λήψει τοῦ ἀμπελῶνος, καὶ ὑβρισθέντων καὶ φονευθέντων, καὶ τοῦ υἱοῦ εἰς τοῦτο ἐλθόντος, καὶ τὰ ἴσα τῶν ἀγνωμόνων[2] τοῖς δούλοις πεπονθότος.

‹ιζ´› Ἡ τῶν ἀπὸ πρώτης ὥρας, καὶ τρίτης, καὶ ἕκτης καὶ ἐνάτης,[3] καὶ πρὸς ἑσπέραν εἰς τὴν ἐργασίαν τοῦ ἀμπελῶνος ἐπίμισθον κομισαμένων.

‹ιη´› Ἡ τῶν εἰς τοὺς γάμους κληθέντων, καὶ μὴ ἀπατησάντων[4] ἀποβολὴ, καὶ τῶν ἀντεισαχθέντων (174b2) ἐκ διεξόδων καὶ τριόδων κλῆσις.

‹ιθ´› Ἡ τοῦ μὴ πρεπόντως ἀπαντήσαντος εἰς τοὺς γάμους ἐκβολή.

‹κ´› Ἡ τῶν δέκα παρθένων ἑτοίμος καὶ ἀνέτοιμος ἀπάντησις.

‹κα´› Ἡ τῶν ἐνεργῶν οἰκονόμων, καὶ πορισάντων εἰς τὰ τοῦ δεσπότου χρήματα, ἀπάντησις, καὶ διὰ τοῦτο τιμωμένων, καὶ ἡ τοῦ ἀργοῦ καὶ ἀπορίστου ἀτιμία.

‹κβ´› Ἡ τῶν ἐκ δεξιῶν προβάτων καὶ τῶν ἐξ εὐωνύμων, τῶν μὲν ἔνδοξος, τῶν δὲ ἐπ᾽ ἀδοξίᾳ παράστασις.

‹κγ´› Ἡ τοῦ ἐμπεσόντος εἰς τοὺς λῃστὰς, καὶ ὑπὸ Σαμαρείτου ἐλεηθέντος, μὴ ἐλεηθέντος δὲ ὑπὸ Φαρισαίου καὶ Λευΐτου, ὑπόδειξις. (175a1)

‹κδ´› Ἡ τοῦ ἐν νυκτὶ τὸν ἄρτον αἰτοῦντος διὰ τῆς παρανόμου ἐκλιπαρήσεως, λῆψις.

‹κε´› Ἡ συκῆ, ἡ διὰ τὴν[5] ἀκαρπίαν μὴ ἐκτμηθεῖσα, ἀλλ᾽ ἵνα καρπὸν ἀγάγῃ ἐπὶ ὑποσχέσει μείνασα.

‹κϛ´› Ὁ κριτὴς ὁ ἀνευλαβὴς καὶ ἀναιδὴς, διὰ γοῦν τὸ ὀχαλεῖσθαι,[6] τῆς προσοχλούσης χήρας ἀκούσας.

‹κζ´› Ἡ τοῦ εὐγενοῦς ἐπὶ βασιλείας λήψει εἰς μακρὰν ἀποδημίαν,[7] καὶ τῶν παραιτουμένων αὐτὸν ἐν τῇ τῆς βασιλείας λήψει, ἀναίρεσις.

---

[1] GM το.
[2] FGM τα ἴσα παρα των ἀγνωμονων.
[3] FGM ἐννατης.
[4] Lc FGM ἀπαντησαντων.
[5] FGM omit την.
[6] Lc FGM ὀχλεισθαι.
[7] Lc GM, who suggest ἀποδημια in their notes.

<13> The setting forth of children for the simple behavior of the saved [18:2–4].

<14> The search for the one lost sheep, indicating the salvation of the human race [Lk 15:4].

<15> The parable of the forgiveness by the master of the man with (174b) many debts who did not forgive his fellow slaves for their minor sins against him [Mt 18:23–35].

<16> The parable of the slaves sent to receive the fruits of the vineyard, insulted and murdered, and when the son came for this, he suffered the same as the slaves from the hard-hearted [21:33–41].

<17> The parable of those hired to labor in the vineyard at the first, third, sixth, and ninth hours and toward evening [20:1–16].

<18> The rejection of those invited to a wedding who did not come, and the calling instead of those from highways and byways [22:1–10].

<19> The ejection of the one who was not suitably dressed to go to the wedding [22:11–13].

<20> The commendation of the ten virgins, ready and unready [25:1–13].

<21> The commendation of the business stewards who were profiting with the master's money and therefore commended, and the disgrace of the idle and unprofitable [25:14–30].

<22> The placing of the sheep <and goats> at right and left, glorious and contemptible [25:33].

<23> The story of him who fell among thieves and was pitied by a Samaritan but not by a Pharisee [1] and a Levite [Lk 10:30–35].

<24> (175a) The acceptance of the one who sought bread at night through unlawful importunity [11:5–8].

<25> The fig tree, not cut down because barren, but left with the expectation of fruit [13:6–9].

<26> The impious and shameless judge because he was troubled, hearing the widow who troubled him [18:2–6].

<27> The long journey of a nobleman to receive a kingdom and the destruction of those who hindered him in receiving it [19:12–27].

---

[1] "Priest" in Lk 10:31.

‹κη'› Ὁ ποιμὴν, ὁ διὰ τῆς θύρας εἰσιὼν εἰς τὴν μάνδραν, καὶ τὰ πρόβατα κατ᾽ ὄνομα καλῶν, καὶ ὁ μὴ διὰ τῆς θύρας, ἀλλὰ ἀλλαχόθεν, κλέπτης ὤν, ἐπιβαίνων.[1] (175a2)

**ΡΛΓ'.** + Τίνων τῶν ἔξωθεν μαρτυριῶν ὁ ἀπόστολος Παῦλος μνήμην ποιεῖται;
‹α'› Ἀπολογούμενος ἐν Ἀθήναις περὶ τοῦ κηρύγματος τοῦ λόγου, φησίν· Ὡς[2] καί τινες τῶν καθ᾽ ὑμᾶς ποιητῶν εἰρήκασι· Τοῦ γὰρ καὶ γένος ἐσμέν.
‹β'› Καὶ Τίτῳ γράφων ἐν τῇ Κρήτῃ διάγοντι, φησίν· Εἶπέ τις ἐξ αὐτῶν, ἴδιος αὐτῶν προφήτης· Κρῆτες ἀεὶ ψεῦσται, κακὰ θηρία, γαστέρες ἀργαί.
‹γ'› Καὶ ὁ Κύριος διεχρήσατο[3] παραβολῇ τῇ ἔξωθεν, εἰπὼν πρὸς ἐν Ναζαρέθ· Πάντως ἐρεῖτέ μοι τὴν παραβολὴν ταύτην· Ἰατρὲ, θεράπευσον σεαυτόν.
‹δ'› Καὶ τῇ ἐπιγραφῇ τῇ ἐν τῷ βωμῷ τῷ ἐν Ἀθήναις, ὁ Παῦλος, (175b1) ἐχούσῃ· Ἀγνώστῳ Θεῷ, ἐχρήσατο μαρτυρίᾳ, Ὃν οὖν ἀγνοοῦντες εὐσεβεῖτε, λέγων, τοῦτον ἐγὼ καταγγέλλω ὑμῖν.[4]

**ΡΛΔ'.** + Πόσοι Ἰάκωβοι ἐν τοῖς ἀποστόλοις γεγόνασιν;
‹α'› Ἰάκωβος ὁ τοῦ Ἰωάννου ἀδελφὸς, υἱὸς Ζεβεδαίου, ὃν καὶ ἀνεῖλεν Ἡρώδης χαριζόμενος Ἰουδαίοις.
‹β'› Ἰάκωβος ὁ τοῦ Ἀλφαίου.
‹γ'› Ἰάκωβος ὁ ἀδελφὸς τοῦ Κυρίου ὁ καλούμενος Δίκαιος, ὃς καὶ τῆς ἐν Ἰερουσαλὴμ Ἐκκλησίας πρῶτος προέστη.[5]

**ΡΛΕ'.** + Πόσοι Ἰωάννοι εἰς τὸ κήρυγμα γεγόνασι καὶ πόσοι Ζαχαρίοι;[6]
‹α'› Ἰωάννης ὁ Βαπτιστὴς, ὃν Ἡρώδης ἀπεκεφάλισεν, (175b2) ὅς καὶ τὸ μαρτύριον ἐν τῇ Παλαιστίνῃ εἶχε σεβαστῇ.
‹β'› Ἰωάννης ὁ τοῦ Ζεβεδαίου υἱὸς, ὁ εὐαγγελιστὴς, ὁ καὶ τὴν ἀποκάλυψιν θεασάμενος, καὶ τὴν καθολικὴν ἀποστείλας, ὃς καὶ ἐν Ἐφέσῳ τὸ μαρτύριον ἔχει.
‹γ'› Ἰωάννης ὁ ἐπικαλούμενος Μάρκος, ὁ Πέτρου ἀκόλουθος, καὶ τὸ Εὐαγγέλιον γράψας, καὶ πρῶτος τῆς Ἀλεξανδρέων Ἐκκλησίας ἐπίσκοπος ἀναδειχθείς.

---

[1] The items in this chapter are not numbered in CFGM.
[2] M Ὠ.
[3] FGM ὁ Κυριος δε ἐχρησατο.
[4] The items in this chapter are not numbered in CFGM.
[5] The items in this chapter are not numbered in CFGM.
[6] *Lc* FGM Ζαχαριαι.

<28> The shepherd who enters through the door and calls the sheep by name, and the one who does not enter through the door but otherwise and is a thief [Jn 10:1–5].

**133**. – What outside witnesses does the apostle Paul mention?

<1> When he made a defence at Athens for the preaching of the word, he said, "As some of your poets have said, 'We are his offspring'" [Ac 17:28].

<2> And writing to Titus in Crete, "One of them, their own prophet, said, 'Cretans are always liars, wicked beasts, idle bellies'" [Tit 1:12].

<3> The Lord also used a parable from outside when he said to those at Nazareth, "Doubtless you will tell me this parable, 'Physician, cure yourself'" [Lk 4:23].

<4> And Paul used the inscription on the altar at Athens, (175b) dedicated "To the unknown God," saying, "The one whom you ignorantly worship, I proclaim to you" [Ac 17:23].[1]

<APOSTLES AND DISCIPLES (134–37)>

**134**. – How many Iakôboi were there among the apostles?[2]

<1> Iakôbos the brother of Iôannés and son of Zebedee, whom Hérôdés killed to please the Jews [Ac 12:2–3].

<2> Iakôbos son of Alphaeus [Ac 1:13].

<3> Iakôbos the Lord's brother, who was called Just, who was first head of the church at Jerusalem.[3]

**135**. – How many Johns were there for the preaching, and how many Zachariases?

<1> John the Baptist whom Hérôdés beheaded, who bore witness in Palestinian Sebasté.[4]

<2> John son of Zebedee, the Evangelist, who also beheld the Apocalypse and sent the General <Epistle>, and was martyred at Ephesus.

<3> John surnamed Mark, who wrote the Gospel and was appointed first bishop of the church of the Alexandrians.[5]

---

[1] Cf. Clement *Str.* 1.59.2 (Titus), 1.91.5, 5.82.4 (Acts); no mention of Lk 4:23.

[2] Compare Demetrius of Magnesia, *On Men of the Same Name*, cited by Diogenes Laertius 1.38.

[3] Cf. C. 47(1,7); Eusebius *HE* 2.1.2–3.

[4] Sebasté (=Samaria) lay in the later Roman Palestine I.

[5] Eusebius *HE* 2.16.1; cf. 24.

Ζαχαρίαι δὲ δ' γεγόνασι.

Πρῶτος ὁ τοῦ Ἰωδαὲ τοῦ ἀρχιερέως υἱός, ὃν ἀπέκτεινεν Ἰωᾶς ὁ βασιλεὺς, ἀναμέσον τοῦ ναοῦ καὶ τοῦ θυσιαστηρίου.

‹β'› Ὁ τοῦ Βαραχίου, οὗ μνήμην ὁ προφήτης **(176a1)** Ἡσαΐας ποιεῖται, εἰς μαρτυρίαν αὐτὸν παραλαβὼν τοῦ τικτομένου παιδίου.

‹γ'› Καὶ ὁ προφήτης.

‹δ'› Καὶ ὁ πατὴρ Ἰωάννου[1] τοῦ Βαπτιστοῦ.[2]

**ΡΛϚ'.** + Ἱππολύτου Θηβαίου, ἐκ τοῦ χρονικοῦ αὐτοῦ συντάγματος.

Ἰάκωβος ὁ ἐπικληθεὶς Δίκαιος,[3] καὶ γενόμενος πρῶτος ἐπίσκοπος Ἱεροσολύμων, ἀδελφὸς μὲν τοῦ Κυρίου κατὰ σάρκα ἐλέγετο εἶναι, υἱὸς δὲ τοῦ τέκτονος Ἰωσὴφ, ἐκ τῆς βιωτικῆς αὐτοῦ γυναικός. Ἀδελφοὶ Συμεών, [Σιδόνιος,][4] Ἰούδα[5] καὶ Ἰωσῆ. Τέσσαρας γὰρ υἱοὺς ἔσχεν ὁ Ἰωσήφ, καὶ δύο θυγατέρας, τήν τε Μάρθαν **(176a2)** καὶ τὴν Μαρίαν, ἐκ τῆς γυναικὸς αὐτοῦ τῆς Σαλώμης, θυγατρὸς Ἀγγαίου, τοῦ ἀδελφοῦ Ζαχαρίου τοῦ ἱερέως, τοῦ πατρὸς Ἰωάννου τοῦ Βαπτιστοῦ, υἱοῦ Βαραχίου, τοῦ υἱοῦ Ἀβιᾶ τοῦ ἱερέως. Καὶ τότε ἐχήρευσεν ὁ Ἰωσήφ. Ὡς τὴν Σαλώμην καὶ τὸν Βαπτιστὴν Ἰωάννην ἀδελφῶν τέκνα ἀρρενικῶν εἶναι. Ὁ γὰρ Ἀγγαῖος υἱὸς Βαραχίου, θεῖος δὲ Ἰωάννου· ὁμοίως δὲ καὶ ὁ Ζαχαρίας ἀδελφὸς Ἀγγαίου, θεῖος δὲ Σαλώμης τῆς γυναικὸς Ἰωσήφ. ‹*Σαλώμην δέ φημι, οὐ τὴν μαίαν, ἀλλὰ τὴν γυναῖκα Ἰωσήφ.*›[6]

Ἡ γὰρ Μαρία[7] ἀπὸ Βηθλεὲμ ἐτύγχανεν, ἀνεψιὰ δὲ αὕτη ἐτύγχανε τῆς Ἐλισάβετ, καὶ τῆς ἁγίας **(176b1)** Παρθένου Μαρίας. ‹καὶ δηλοῖ τὸ κατὰ Λουκᾶν εὐαγγέλιον.›[8] Τρεῖς γὰρ ἦσαν ἀδελφαὶ ἀπὸ Βηθλεέμ, θυγατέρες

---

[1] FGM omit Ἰωαννου.

[2] In CFGM, the only item numbered in this chapter is the one about the first Zacharias.

[3] The words ὁ ἐπικληθεις Δικαιος are not found in the other witnesses to Hippolytus.

[4] Σιδονιος is not mentioned in other texts of Hippolytus of Thebes.

[5] FGM Ἰουδας. C agrees with other texts of Hippolytus.

[6] This sentence is not found in C and likely was never part of the interpolation into the *Hypomnestikon*. It was, however, probably part of Hippolytus' original text. Since Diekamp's edition is not widely available, we have included his reconstructed text within the special markings ‹* and *›. FGM restore the reading on the basis of other texts of Hippolytus of Thebes. See Diekamp, *Hippolytos von Theben*, 8.

[7] Lc FGM, who in their notes suggest replacing Μαρια with μαια, the reading of all other witnesses to Hippolytus.

[8] This sentence is not found in CFGM. The bracketed material is Hippolytus of Thebes, but not interpolated material. See Diekamp, *Hippolytos von Theben*, 8.

There were four Zachariases.

First is the son of Iodaë the high priest, whom King Iôas killed between the Temple and the altat [2 Par 24:21; Mt 23:35].

<2> The son of Barachiah, whom the prophet (176a) Isaiah mentions, taking him as a witness of the child to be born [Is 8:2].[1]

<3> And the prophet.

<4> And the father of Iôannés the Baptist [Lk 1:5].


**136.** – Of Hippolytus the Theban from his *Chronikon Syntagma*.

Iakôbos, surnamed the Just, who became first bishop of Hierosolyma, was said to be the brother of the Lord after the flesh, son of the carpenter Iôséph by his wife in the world (=Salômé). His brothers were Symeôn, [Sidonios,] Iouda, and Iôsé. Iôséph had four sons and two daughters, Martha and Maria [Lk 10:38–42], by his wife Salômé, daughter of Aggaios the brother of the priest Zacharias, the father of John the Baptist, son of Barachias the son of the priest Abias, (then Iôséph was a widower,) so that Salômé and John the Baptist were children of brothers; for Aggaios son of Barachias was the uncle of John, and similarly Zacharias, brother of Aggaios, was uncle of Salômé, wife of Iôséph the carpenter. <*I mean Salômé not the midwife but the wife of the carpenter Iôséph.*>[2]

For [Maria] the midwife (*maia*) came from Bethlehem and was the cousin of Elisabet and the holy (176b) virgin Maria. <*And the Gospel according to Luke makes it clear.*> For there were three sisters from Bethlehem, daughters

---

[1] Mt 23:35 combines #1 with #2.

[2] Throughout this chapter the markings <* and *> delimit material which was in the original text of Hippolytus of thebes, but which had fallen out prior to its interpolation into the *Hpymnestikon*.

Ματθὰν τοῦ ἱερέως καὶ Μαρίας τῆς αὐτοῦ γυναικὸς, ἐπὶ[1] τῆς βασιλείας
Κλεοπάτρου <καὶ Σώπαρος τοῦ Πέρσου>,[2] πρὸ τῆς βασιλείας Ἡρώδου τοῦ
υἱοῦ Ἀντιπάτρου. Ὄνομα τῇ αʹ Μαρία, ὄνομα[3] τῇ βʹ Σουβὴ, καὶ ὄνομα τῇ γʹ
Ἄννα. Ἔγημέν τε ἡ πρώτη ἐν Βηθλεὲμ, καὶ ἔτεκε[4] Σαλώμην τὴν μαίαν.
Ἔγημέν τε καὶ ἡ δευτέρα ἐν Βηθλεὲμ, καὶ ἔτεκε τὴν Ἐλισάβετ. Ἔγημέν τε
καὶ ἡ τρίτη εἰς τὴν γῆν τῆς ἐπαγγελίας,[5] καὶ ἐγέννησε Μαρίαν τὴν
Θεοτόκον ἐν Βηθλεέμ.[6] Ὡς εἶναι Σαλώμην (176b2) τὴν μαίαν,[7] <καὶ τὴν
Ἐλισάβετ>[8] καὶ τὴν ἁγίαν Ἄνναν, τὴν γεννήσασαν[9] Μαρίαν τὴν
παναγίαν[10] Θεοτόκον, [καὶ τὴν ἁγίαν Ἐλισάβετ, τὴν γεννήσασαν τὸν
Πρόδρομον,][11] θυγατέρας ἀδελφῶν τριῶν θηλειῶν. Ἐντεῦθεν οὖν ὁ
Βαπτιστὴς Ἰωάννης, καὶ ὁ Κύριος ἡμῶν Ἰησοῦς Χριστὸς, ἀνεψιοὶ λέγονται
εἶναι. Υἱὸς δὲ τοῦ Ἰωσὴφ ἐνομίζετο,[12] ἐπειδὴ καὶ τῶν υἱῶν αὐτοῦ, τῶν ἐκ

---

[1] FGM περι. Other texts of Hippolytus agree with C. See Diekamp, *Hippolytos von Theben*, 9.

[2] The words και Σωπαρος του Περσου are not found in CFGM. The bracketed material is Hippolytus of Thebes, but not interpolated material. See Diekamp, *Hippolytos von Theben*, 9.

[3] FGM και ὀνομα.

[4] GM ἔτεκεν.

[5] Diekamp (*Hippolytos von Theben*, 9) notes that some mss. of Hippolytus read Γαλιλαιας and some (in addition to the Cambridge ms. of the *Hypomnestikon*) here read ἐπαγγελιας. He prints Γαλιλαιας.

[6] A number of manuscripts of Hippolytus of Thebes omit ἐν Βηθλεεμ, and Diekamp (*Hippolytos von Theben*, 9) does not print these words.

[7] Diekamp (*Hippolytos von Theben*, 9) notes that many manuscripts of Hippolytus do not have the words την μαιαν, and he does not print them.

[8] The words και την Ἐλισαβετ are not found in CFGM. They are found in all other witnesses to Hippolytus. See Diekamp, *Hippolytos von Theben*, 9.

[9] The words Ἀνναν, την γεννησασαν do not appear in the other witnesses to the text of Hippolytus. See Diekamp, *Hippolytos von Theben*, 9-10.

[10] The word παναγιαν does not appear in the other witnesses to the text of Hippolytus and perhaps should be deleted (although ὑπεραγιαν appears in one manuscript). See Diekamp, *Hippolytos von Theben*, 10.

[11] The bracketed material is found in CFGM, but is not found in the other manuscripts of Hippolytus and should be deleted. See Diekamp, *Hippolytos von Theben*, 10.

[12] Some manuscripts of Hippolytus of Thebes have λεγεται here rather than ἐνομιζετο. Diekamp prints λεγεται.

of the priest Matthan and his wife Maria in the reign of Kleopatra <*and Soparos [Sapor?] the Persian*> before the reign of Hérôdés son of Antipater. The name of the first: Mariam. The name of the second: Soubé. And the name of the third: Anna. The first married in Bethlehem and bore Salômé the midwife. The second also married in Bethlehem and bore Elisabet. The third married in the land of promise[1] and generated Maria the God-bearer in Béthleëm, so that Salômé [the midwife], <and Elisabet> and [the holy Anna who generated] the [most] holy Maria the God-bearer [, and the holy Elisabet who generated the Precursor], were daughters of three sisters. Hence John the Baptist and our Lord Jesus Christ are said to be cousins. He was said to be the son of Iôséph, since he was

---

[1]While Hippolytus's text probably read "land of Galilee" rather than "land of promise," the manuscript tradition suggests that the divergence occurred prior to the incorporation of this material into the *Hypomnestikon*.

τῆς πρώτης γυναικὸς, ἀδελφὸς ἐνομίζετο.[1]

Ζαχαρίας ὁ πατὴρ Ἰωάννου ἀδελφὸν ἔσχε συνιερέα καλούμενον Ἀγγαῖον, πρὸ αὐτοῦ τετελευτηκότα. Τούτου τοῦ Ἀγγαῖου θυγατέρα ἠγάγετο πρὸς γάμον Ἰωσὴφ ὁ τέκτων, ἐξ ἧς ἐγέννησε (177a1) δ' υἱοὺς καὶ γ' θυγατέρας, ὧν εἷς ἦν Ἰάκωβος, ὁ ἐπικληθεὶς ἀδελφὸς τοῦ Κυρίου, καὶ πρῶτος ἐπίσκοπος Ἱεροσολύμων. Καὶ τὸ ὄνομα τῆς γυναικὸς Ἰωσὴφ Σαλώμη, οὐχ ἡ μαία, ἀλλ᾽ ἑτέρα. Μετὰ δὲ θάνατον αὐτῆς μνηστεύεται Ἰωσὴφ τὴν Θεοτόκον Μαρίαν, κατὰ τὸ μητρικὸν γένος καταγομένην ἀπὸ τοῦ Ματθὰν τοῦ ἱερέως, καὶ αὐτοῦ ἀπὸ Σολομῶντος τοῦ υἱοῦ Δαβὶδ καταγομένην, ὥς φησι τὸ κατὰ Λουκᾶν Εὐαγγέλιον γενεαλογοῦν. Οὗτος γὰρ ὁ Ματθὰν ἔσχε θυγατέρας[2] ἐκ Μαρίας τῆς γυναικὸς αὐτοῦ, ὧν τὰ ὀνόματα (177a2) Μαρία, Σουβή, Ἄννα. Ἡ οὖν Μαρία γεννᾷ <Σαλώμην τὴν μαίαν· ἡ δὲ Σουβὴ γεννᾷ>[3] τὴν Ἐλισάβετ, τὴν μητέρα Ἰωάννου τοῦ Βαπτιστοῦ. Ἡ δὲ Ἄννα γεννᾷ τὴν ἁγίαν Θεοτόκον ἐν Βηθλεέμ, τὴν κατὰ τὸ ὄνομα τῆς μάμμης καὶ θείας, ἐπικληθεῖσαν Μαρίαν. Ὡς εἶναι τὴν Ἐλισάβετ, ἀνεψιὰν μὲν τῆς Ἄννης, ἐξάδελφον δὲ τῆς Θεοτόκου.

Κυροῦνται τὰ ἑκάτερα του Εὐαγγελίου, διὰ τοῦ διηγεῖσθαι τὸ πατρῷον γένος καὶ σαρκικὸν τοῦ Χριστοῦ. Ἦν γὰρ, φησὶν, ὁ Ἰησοῦς[4] ἀρχόμενος, ὡς ἐτῶν λ', ὃς ἐνομίζετο τοῦ Ἰωσὴφ, τοῦ Ἠλεὶ, τοῦ Ματθὰν.[5] (177b1)

ΡΛΖ΄. + Τίνες εἰσὶν οἱ ἀπὸ μαθητῶν τῶν ο' γνώριμοι;

‹α› Βαρνάβας, ὁ σὺν τῷ Παύλῳ κηρύξας τὸ Εὐαγγέλιον, καὶ τοῖς ἀποστόλοις ἑαυτὸν μαθητὴν γεγονότα τοῦ Εὐαγγελίου, εἰς τὴν Ἱερουσαλὴμ ἐμφανίσας.

---

[1] Rather than ἀδελφος ἐνομιζετο, Deikamp's text of Hippolytus of Thebes reads from this point: ἀδελφος ἐστιν ἐκ της συναναστροφης και της συγγενειας του Ἀγγαιου ἀδελφου Ζαχαριου του ἱερεως.

[2] Lᶜ Dickamp (*Hippolytos von Theben*, 41), who emends to: ὁ Ματθαν τρεις ἐσχε θυγατερας.

[3] The words Σαλωμην την μαιαν· ἡ δε Σουβη γεννᾳ are not found in CFGM; they are suggested by Diekamp (p. 42), based in part on Cosmas Vestitior. Note that Diekamp's spelling of Σοββη has been changed to Σουβη to conform to the pattern found in our text.

[4] Diekamp (*Hippolytos von Theben*, 42) prints Χριστος at this point, in place of Ἰησους. Perhaps the text was corrected to Ἰησους on the basis of Lk 3:23.

[5] According to Diekamp (*Hippolytos von Theben*, LVI-LVIII, 41-42 [Spurious Text #10]) the material beginning with Ζαχαριας ὁ πατηρ Ἰωαννου ἀδελφον ἐσχε and continuing to the end of the chapter was originally penned by Cosmas Vestitior, a writer of the ninth century. This material was joined to the *Chronicle* of Hippolytus of Thebes prior to its incorporation into the *Hypomnestikon*. This is known because these texts are found joined in other manuscripts.

[supposed to be] the brother of his (Joseph's) sons by his first wife.[1]

Zacharias the father of John had a brother who also was a priest, named Aggaios, who died before him. Iôséph the carpenter married the daughter of this Aggaios, and had (177a) four sons and three daughters by her. One of them was Jakôb, called the Lord's brother and first bishop of Jerusalem; the name of Iôséph's wife was Salômé, not the midwife but another. After her death Iôséph married Maria the God-bearer, who traced her mother's line from the priest Matthan and to him from Solomon the son of David, as the Gospel according to Luke traces the genealogy. This Matthan had <three> daughters by his wife Maria; their names are Maria, Soubé, Anna. That Maria generated <Salômé the midwife; Soubé generated> Elisabet the mother of John the Baptist. Anna generated the holy God-bearer in Béthleëm, named Maria after her grandmother and aunt, so that Elisabet was the cousin of Anna and cousin-german of the God-bearer.

Both relations are confirmed by the Gospel, where the paternal descent of Christ after the flesh is set forth. "And at the beginning <Christ> (Jesus) was about thirty years old; he was thought to be the son of Iôséph, son of Éli, son of Matthan" [Lk 3:23] (177b).[2]


**137.** – Who are the better known among the seventy disciples?

<1> Barnabas, who preached the gospel with Paul [Ac 13:2] and showed himself to the apostles at Jerusalem as a disciple of the gospel [15:2].

---

[1] The material from the beginning of the chapter to this point is from Hippolytus of Thebes *Chronicle* Frag. 6 (Diekamp, *Hippolytos von Theben*, 7–10. Diekamp argues that this is not an authentic part of Joseph's work, pp. 150–51).

[2] Hippolytus of Thebes, non-genuine Text 10 (Diekamp, *Hippolytos von Theben*, 41–42), which Diekamp attributes to Cosmas Vestitior, a writer from the ninth century or the first half of the tenth century at the latest; cf. pp. LVI–LVIII, 145–51.

‹β'› Σωσθένης, ὃς ἀντὶ τοῦ Ἰούδα συγκατεψηφίσθη μετὰ τῶν ἀποστόλων, δι᾽ εὐχῆς κληθείς.

‹γ'› Ἰοῦστος, ὃς αὐτὸς τῷ κλήρῳ τῶν ἀποστόλων ὑπεβλήθη.

‹δ'› Θαδδαῖος, ὃς ἐν τῇ Μεσοποταμίᾳ ἐν τῇ Ἐδέσσῃ κήρυξ τοῦ λόγου πρὸς Αὔγαρον βασιλέα ἀπέσταλται.

‹ε'› Καὶ Ἰωάννην δὲ τὸν ἐπικληθέντα Μάρκον ἐξ αὐτῶν γεγονότα ἐπιγνώσκομεν. (177b2)

‹ϛ'-ζ'› Ἰούδας καὶ Σίλας, οἱ ὑπὸ τῶν ἀποστόλων μετὰ Παύλου καὶ Βαρνάβα, διὰ τὸ ζήτημα τὸ περὶ τῆς νομικῶν φυλακῆς, εἰς τὴν Ἀντιόχειαν ἀπὸ τῆς Ἰερουσαλὴμ ἀποσταλέντες.

‹η'› Κλήμης δέ φησι, καὶ τὸν Κηφᾶν, περὶ οὗ φησὶν ὁ Παῦλος· Ὅτε δὲ ἦλθε Κηφᾶς εἰς Ἀντιόχειαν, κατὰ πρόσωπον αὐτῷ ἀντέστην, ὅτι κατεγνωσμένος ἦν, ἔνα τῶν ο' εἶναι· μὴ γὰρ περὶ τοῦ ἀποστόλου Πέτρου ταῦτα λέγειν αὐτόν.

‹ΡΛΗ'›[1] + Πόσοι διωγμοὶ κατὰ τῆς Ἐκκλησίας γεγόνασιν ὑπὸ Ἰουδαίων,[2] ἕως τῆς ἁλώσεως αὐτῶν, καὶ τοῦ ἐμπρησμοῦ τοῦ ναοῦ; (178a1)

Τρεῖς μὲν κατὰ τῶν ἀποστόλων ἐν τῇ Ἰερουσαλὴμ γεγόνασι. Τρεῖς δὲ καὶ κατὰ τοῦ Παύλου, οὐ μόνον ἐν τῇ Ἰερουσαλὴμ γεγόνασιν, ἀλλὰ καὶ ἐν τῇ διασπορᾷ, ὑπὸ τῶν Ἰουδαίων δὲ καὶ οὗτοι.

Καὶ πρῶτος μὲν ἦν ὁ κατὰ τὸν συγκλεισμὸν τῶν ἀποστόλων, ὑπὸ τῶν ἀρχιερέων γενόμενος.

Δεύτερος ὁ ἐπὶ Στεφάνῳ τῷ πρωτομάρτυρι, ᾧ καὶ ὁ Παῦλος συνευδόκει.

---

[1] C does not number this chapter. FGM correct this oversight.

[2] Lc FGM ὑπο των Ἰουδαιων.

<2> Sôsthenes [1 Cor 1:1, Ac 18:17], who was counted among the apostles in the place of Judas.[1]

<3> Ioustos, who was subjected to the lot of the apostles [Ac 1:23].

<4> Thaddaios, who was sent as a herald of the Word to Edessa in Mesopotamia to Abgar.[2]

<5> We read that Iôannés called Mark was one of them [Ac 12:25].

<6–7> Ioudas and Silas were sent along with Paul and Barnabas by the apostles to Antioch from Jerusalem because the dispute over keeping the law [Ac 15:22].

<8> Clement says Képhas also was one of the Seventy, of whom Paul says, 'When Képhas came to Antioch I resisted him to his face, for he stood condemned' [Gal 2:11; cf. 1 Cor 15:5–7]; he would not have spoken thus about the apostle Peter.[3]

All this, apart from the usual errors, comes from Eusebius (*HE* 1.12.1–4); he said no list of the Seventy existed, though this gap was soon filled. Diekamp suggests that the brief summary cannot be later than about 500, when apocryphal materials about the Seventy were flourishing,[4] but in any case Joseph avoids apocryphal works, contrasting them with scripture (C. 47).

## <CHRISTIANS PERSECUTED (138–39)>

**138.**[5] – How many persecutions by the Jews took place against the church before their overthrow and the burning of the Temple? (178a)

Three took place against the apostles at Jerusalem and three were incited by the Jews against Paul, not only at Jerusalem but also in the Dispersion, although these also were by the Jews.

First was the imprisonment of the apostles by the high priests [Ac 5:17].

Second was against Stephen the protomartyr, against whom Paul consented [Ac 6:12;8:1].

---

[1] The name should be Matthias (Ac 1:23; Eusebius *HE* 2.1.1) but Eusebius (after Clement?) did mention Sosthenes as among the Seventy (*HE* 1.12.1).

[2] Eusebius *HE* 1.13.

[3] "Clement in the 5th book of the *Hypotyposes*" (Eusebius *H.E.* 1.12.2); cf. Schermann, *Prophetarum vitae*, 124,3; 131,1; 174,1; 182,14. Contrast C. 63.

[4] Diekamp, *Hippolytos von Theben*,150.

[5] Fabricius (followed in G and M) supplied the correct number, omitted by the scribe of the codex, for this chapter and rightly corrected the subsequent numbers.

Τρίτος ὁ ἐπὶ τῇ ἀναιρέσει Ἰακώβου, καὶ Πέτρου καθείρξει, τῇ ὑπὸ Ἡρώδου γεγενημένῃ, ὅτε καὶ ὁ ἄγγελος τὸν μὲν Πέτρον ἀπὸ τῶν δεσμῶν ἔλυσε, καὶ τοῦ δεσμωτηρίου ἐξήγαγε, τὸν δὲ Ἡρώδην (178a2) μὴ¹ δημηγοροῦντα ἐν Καισαρείᾳ ἀθρόῳ ἐν ὀργῇ πληγεῖν.² Κατὰ δὲ τοῦ Παύλου καὶ τῶν ἀδελφῶν, τέταρτος ἐν Λυκαονίᾳ ὑπὸ τῶν Ἰουδαίων ἐκινήθη διωγμός. Καὶ πέμπτος ἐν Βερυίᾳ³ καὶ Κορίνθῳ. Ἕκτος δὲ ἐν τῇ Ἰερουσαλὴμ, ἐφ᾽ ᾧ καὶ ἐν τοῖς δικαστηρίοις ἐξέτασις πολλάκις ἐγένετο τοῦ κηρύγματος. Καὶ τέλος, ἡ εἰς τὴν⁴ Ῥώμην ἐπὶ Καίσαρος, δεσμίου ἐκπομπήδον.⁵

[ΡΛΗ΄.] ‹ΡΛΘ΄.› + Πόσοι καὶ οἱ δι᾽ Ἑλλήνων διωγμοὶ γεγονότες, καὶ διὰ τίνων;

Πρῶτος Νέρων διωγμὸν ἤγαγε κατὰ Χριστιανῶν, ὃς Πέτρον μὲν σταυροῦσθαι, Παῦλον δὲ πελεκίζεσθαι (178b1) προστάττει, τοῦ Πέτρου κάτω κάραν σταυρωθέντος δεηθῆναι.⁶

Δεύτερος, Δομετιανὸς μέγαν κινεῖ καθ᾽ ἡμῶν διωγμὸν, πονηρὸς καὶ οὗτος γενόμενος, ὃς καὶ τὸν Εὐαγγελιστὴν Ἰωάννην εἰς Πάτμον τὴν νῆσον ἐφυγάδευσε.

Τρίτος διωγμὸς ἐξ ἐπαναστάσεως δήμων κατὰ τὰ ἔθνη κινηθέντων κατὰ Χριστιανῶν συνέστη, τῶν ἀρχόντων μᾶλλον κινησάντων αὐτούς. Τοῦτον δὲ ἐπέσχε Τραϊανὸς ὕστερον τὸ δόγμα διδαχθείς. Ἐπὶ δὲ τοῦ διωγμοῦ τούτου, Πιόνιος καὶ οἱ κατ᾽ αὐτὸν μάρτυρες διέπρεψαν.

Τέταρτος διωγμὸς ὑπὸ Οὐήρου, (178b2) καὶ τοῦ υἱοῦ⁷ αὐτοῦ Ἀντωνίου,⁸ κατὰ τῆς Ἐκκλησίας ἐκχεῖται. Ἐπὶ τούτων Πολύκαρπος ἐν τῇ Ἀσίᾳ μαρτυρεῖ, Μητρόδωρος, Κάρπος, Πάπυλος, Ἀγαθωνίκη, καὶ ἕτερον πλῆθος ἁγίων διὰ τοῦ θείου τελειοῦται μαρτυρίου.

Πέμπτος, ὑπὸ Σευήρου, κατὰ τῆς Ἐκκλησίας μέγας συγκινεῖται διωγμὸς, ἐφ᾽ οὗ Ἰουστῖνος ἐμαρτύρησε, καὶ Λεονίδης⁹ ὁ Ὠρειγένους

---

¹ *Lc* FGM μην.
² *Lc* GM, who in their notes suggest emending to πληγων or ἐπληγεν.
³ *Lc* FGM Βεροια.
⁴ *Lc* FGM, who omit την.
⁵ *Lc* FGM ἐκπομπη.
⁶ *Lc* FGM σταυρωθηναι δεηθεντος.
⁷ *Lc* FGM, who in their notes suggest emending to ἀδελφου (*fratre*). This Antoninus would then be Antoninus Pius, who ruled jointly with Lucius Verus, rather than Commodus Antoninus, Verus' son.
⁸ *Lc* FGM Ἀντωνινου.
⁹ FGM Λεωνιδης.

Third was over the killing of Iakôb and the imprisonment of Peter, when the angel on the one hand freed Petros from his bonds and led him from the prison, and on the other hand as Hérôdés spoke to the crowd at Caesarea struck him with overwhelming wrath [12:2–3; 12:23 garbled].

The fourth persecution was incited by the Jews in Lycaonia against Paul and the brethren [14:19];

and the fifth in Beroea and Corinth.

The sixth, at Jerusalem, where the preaching was frequently investigated in the courts; and finally there was his being sent in bonds to Caesar at Rome [25:12].

**139.** – How many persecutions took place through Greeks, and through whom?[1]

Nero was the first to persecute Christians, ordering Petros crucified and Paul beheaded [Eusebius *HE* 2.25.5] (178b), Petros having requested to be crucified head downward [*HE* 3.1.2].

Second, Domitian aroused a great persecution against us; he was an evil man who banished the evangelist Iôannés to the island of Patmos [*HE* 3.18.1].

The third persecution arose when the populace of various nations was moved against Christians especially by local authorities. Trajan checked this after being taught the doctrine [*HE* 3.33.2]. In this persecution Pionius and other martyrs were eminent [*HE* 4.15.47].

The fourth persecution was brought against the church by Verus and his son Antoni<n>us [*HE* 4.14.9]; under them Polycarp bore witness in Asia [*HE* 4.15.1], also Metrodorus [*HE* 4.15.46],[2] Carpus, Papylus, Agathoniké [*HE* 4.15.48], and many other saints, were perfected through divine martyrdom.

Fifth, by Severus a great persecution was set in motion against the church [*HE* 6.1], when Justin was martyred [*HE* 4.16.1) and Leonides the father of

---

[1] For the text see Moreau, "Observations," 260–62.

[2] According to Eusebius he was a Marcionite.

πατὴρ, καὶ Ποταμίαινα ἡ ἁγία παρθένος, καὶ Βασιλείδης, καὶ πλῆθος θείων τελειοῦται μαρτύρων.

Ἕκτος, Μαξιμῖνος πρώτους πάντες τοὺς ὅποι δ᾽ ἂν, ὡς κληρικοὺς, (179a1) ἀναιρεῖσθαι προστάξας, καὶ τότε τοὺς λέγοντας ἑαυτοὺς εἶναι Χριστιανούς.

Ἕβδομος, Δέκιος σφοδρῶς ἐχρήσατο τῷ διωγμῷ, καὶ μαρτυρεῖ Φλαβιανὸς[1] ἐπίσκοπος Ῥώμης, Ἀλέξανδρος ἐπίσκοπος Ἱεροσολύμων, Βαβύλας ἐπίσκοπος Ἀντιοχείας, Σαραπίων ἐπίσκοπος Ἀλεξανρείας, Ἀπολλωνία παρθένος καὶ Ἀμμωναρίων σὺν ἄλλαις τέσσαρες[2] παρθένοις δεινῶς βασανισθείσας,[3] Ἰουλιανὸς ὁ ποδαλγὸς ἐπὶ καμίνου[4] περιφερόμενος, καὶ τῇ ἀσβέστῳ περιραινόμενος. Ὁ ἐπίσκοπος (179a2) Καργέννης[5] Κυπριανός. Μερκουρία τε καὶ Διονυσία ἡ πολύπαις, παρεστηκότων αὐτῇ τῶν παίδων αὐτῆς. Καὶ βασανιζομένη οὐκ ἔστιξε[6] τῆς Χριστοῦ φιλίας τὴν πολυπαιδίαν. Ἐπὶ δὲ τούτου πλεῖστοι μάρτυρες κατὰ πόλεις ἢ[7] κατὰ κώμας τοῖς οὐρανίοις χοροῖς συγκατελέχθησαν. Ὠρειγένης δὲ οὐκ ἠξιώθη τῆς μαρτυρίας ἐν τούτῳ συσχεθεὶς τῷ χρόνῳ, ἀλλ᾽ ἡττηθεὶς, εἰς μετάνοιαν ἐβίω τὸν λοιπὸν αὐτοῦ χρόνον.

---

[1] Emend to Φαβιανος.
[2] Lc FGM τεσσαρσι.
[3] Lc FGM βασανισθεισαις.
[4] Emend to καμήλου, following Eusebius HE 6.41.18.
[5] Lc FGM Καρθαγενης.
[6] Lc FGM, who in their notes suggest emending to ἐστερξε.
[7] FGM substitute και for ἤ, apparently following Eusebius HE 6.42.1.

Origen [*HE* 6.1], the holy virgin Potimiaina, and Basileides [*HE* 6.5] and a throng of divine martyrs was made perfect.

Sixth, Maximin (Thrax) ordered all the leaders, whoever they were, to be slain as clerics [*HE* 6.28] (179a) and then those who confessed to being Christians.

Seventh, Decius made vigorous use of persecution, and the martyrs were F[l]abian bishop of Rome [*HE* 6.39.1], Alexander bishop of Jerusalem [*HE* 6.39.2–3], Babylas bishop of Antioch [*HE* 6.39.4], Serapion bishop of Alexandria,[1] Apollonia, a virgin [*HE* 6.41.7], Ammonarion with four other virgins who were tortured terribly,[2] Julianus who suffered from gout and was borne on a camel[3] and covered with lime [*HE* 6.41.15], the Carthaginian bishop Cyprian,[4] Mercuria, and Dionysia mother of many children, who was tortured in their presence but did not prefer being prolific to the friendship of Christ [*HE* 6.41.18]. In this persecution there were more martyrs counted with the heavenly choirs in the cities than the villages [Cf. *HE* 6.42.1, where cities and villages are coordinated, not contrasted]. Origen was not worthy of martyrdom, being imprisoned at this time; but shown to be inferior, he lived out his life in penance.[5]

---

[1] Not, in fact, bishop [Eusebius *HE* 6.41.8].

[2] Eusebius says "4 women" and names Ammonarion, the aged Mercuria, and Dionysia, mother of many children [*HE* 6.41.18].

[3] Read *kamélou* after Eusebius; for *kaminou*, "furnace."

[4] Eusebius does not mention Cyprian's martyrdom (not under Decius but Valerian).

[5] Not from Eusebius but a simplified variant of the charge in Epiphanius *Pan.* 64.2 (*not* in *Epitome*). Cf. C. 140 (43).

Ὄγδοος, Οὐαλεριανὸς Χριστιανοὺς ἐπολέμησε, καὶ πολλοὶ καὶ ἐπ' αὐτοῦ μεμαρτυρήκασιν, (179b1) ἐξ ὧν εἰσὶ καὶ οἱ ἐν Καισαρείᾳ τῆς Παλαιστίνης μάρτυρες τρεῖς· Πρίσκος, Μάρκος, Ἀλέξανδρος.[1] Ἔννατος, Αὐρηλιανὸς κινεῖ διωγμὸν, οὐχ οὕτως ἄγριον καὶ ἐμφανῆ. Μόνον γὰρ τῶν ἀρχόντων τῆς συνηθείας τῶν παλαιῶν νόμων κατὰ Χριστιανῶν τί γίνεσθαι μὴ[2] διατάξας.

Δέκατος, ὁ μέγας κατὰ τῆς Ἐκκλησίας ὑπὸ Διοκλητιανοῦ διωγμὸς ἐγείρεται, ἐφ' οὗ καὶ πολλοὶ μάρτυρες, ἄνδρες ἐπιφανεῖς, διέπρεψαν ἐν τῷ μαρτυρίῳ. Ἄνθιμος ἐπίσκοπος Νικομηδείας. Φελαίας[3] ἐπίσκοπος Θμούιος. Ἄδαυκτος, (179b2) καθολικὸς, καὶ ἐν αὐτῷ διαπρέπων τῷ ἀξιώματι. Πελαγία ἡ ἐν Ἀντιοχείᾳ παρθένος, νέα κόρη, ῥίψασα ἑαυτὴν ὑπὸ[4] τριστέγου τῆς ἰδίας οἰκίας. Τυραννίων ἐπίσκοπος Τύρου. Ζηνόβιος πρεσβύτερος Σιδῶνος. Σιλβανὸς ἐπίσκοπος Ἡμιστῶν.[5] Ῥωμανὸς ἐπίσκοπος Ἀντιοχείας. Ζηνόβιος ἀρχιητρὸς[6] Ἀντιοχείας. Σιλβανὸς ἐπίσκοπος Γαζαίων, μετὰ καὶ ἄλλων μ'. Πηλεὺς καὶ Νεῖλος ἐπίσκοποι Αἰγύπτιοι. Πάμφιλος πρεσβύτερος Καισαρείας. Πέτρος ἐπίσκοπος Ἀλεξανδρείας, καὶ σὺν αὐτῷ πρεσβύτεροι (180a1) Φαῦσος,[7] Δῖος, Ἀμμώνιος· ἐπίσκοποι δὲ, Φυλαίας, Ἡσύχιος, Παχούμιος, Θεόδωρος. Γάϊός τε ἐν Λαοδικίᾳ[8] ὑπὸ τῶν δήμων συρεὶς μαρτυρεῖ. Καὶ Σαβινιανὸς, στρατιώτης ὄντων[9] ὁπλιτῶν, ὁμολογήσας Χριστιανὸς εἶναι, πελεκίζεται. Καὶ ἀριθμοὶ δὲ ὁλόκληροι στρατιωτῶν, μετὰ τῶν χιλιάρχων καὶ ἑκατοντάρχων, ἀφαιρεθέντες τῶν ὅπλων ἐμαρτύρησαν.

Μετὰ τοῦτον[10] Μαξιμῖνος ἐνδέκατον διωγμὸν διαδέχεται, ὃν αὐτὸς πάλιν ἔπαυσε διατάγματι. Ἔνθεν ἡ Ἐκκλησία τῶν διωγμῶν ἀνεθεῖσα τῶν ἐξ (180a2) Ἑλλήνων, ἐπὶ Κωνσταντίνου καὶ Κωνσταντίου, καὶ Κώνσταντος βασιλευόντων πολλὴν ὑπέμεινε ταραχὴν ὑπὸ Ἀρειανῶν.

Μετὰ τούτους, Ἰουλιανοῦ βασιλεύσαντος τὰ Ἑλλήνων ἑλομένου, οὐ διώξοντος[11] δὲ τοὺς Χριστιανοὺς, ἀλλὰ βδελυξαμένου καὶ συγγραφομένου κατ' αὐτῶν, τῶν δὲ δήμων κατά τε πόλεις καὶ κώμας, τῆς τοῦ βασιλέως

---

[1] FGM Μαρκος και Ἀλεξανδρος.
[2] Lc FGM, who in their notes suggest emending to χρη.
[3] F Φυλαιας; lc GM Φιλαιας.
[4] Lc FGM ἀπο.
[5] Lc FGM Ἡμισων.
[6] GM ἀρχιατρος.
[7] Lc FGM Φαυστος.
[8] Lc FGM Λαοδικεια.
[9] Lc FGM ὦν των.
[10] GM τουτων.
[11] FGM διωξαντος.

Eighth, Valerian warred on Christians and many underwent martyrdom under him (179b), among whom are three martyrs at Caesarea in Palestine: Priscus, Marcus (Malchus) and Alexander [*HE* 7.12].[1]

Ninth, Aurelian also set in motion a persecution not so cruel and conspicuous, but merely commanded the governors that <it was necessary> to enforce the old laws against Christians [cf. *HE* 7.30.20–21].

Tenth, the great persecution against the church was raised by Diocletian. In it many martyrs, famous men, were distinguished for their martyrdom. Anthimus bishop of Nicomedia [*HE* 8.6.6; 8.13.1], Phileas bishop of Thmuis [*HE* 8.9.7–8], Adauctus the Catholicos who was a martyr in that office [*HE* 8.11.2], Pelagia the virgin at Antioch, a young maiden who threw herself from the third story of her own home,[2] Tyrannion bishop of Tyre [*HE* 8.13.3], Zenobius presbyter of Sidon [*HE* 8.13.3], Silvanus bishop of Emesa [*HE* 8.13.3–4], Romanus bishop of Antioch [*Martyrs of Palestine* 2], Zenobius chief physician of Antioch [8.13.4], Silvanus bishop of Gaza with 40 (39) others [*HE* 8.13.5]. Peleus and Nilus, Egyptian bishops [*HE* 8.13.5]. Pamphilus, presbyter of Caesarea [*HE* 8.13.6], Petros bishop of Alexandria and with him the presbyters (180a) Faustus, Dius, Ammonius, and the bishops Phyleas, Hesychius, Pachomius, Theodorus [*HE* 8.13.7], and Gaius was martyred in Laodicea, being dragged to death by the people; the soldier Sabinianus, a hoplite, was executed after confessing to be a Christian. Whole ranks of soldiers with tribunes and centurions were stripped of arms and underwent martyrdom.[3]

After this, Maximin (Daia) succeeded to an eleventh persecution but stopped it again by edict [*HE* 9.10.7–11]. Hence the Church, accustomed to the persecutions from Greeks, endured much trouble from Arians under Constantine, Constantius, and Constans.

After these, in the reign of Julian, who chose the ways of the Greeks, there was no persecution of the Christians, but he abominated and wrote against them,[4] with the populace assenting to the emperor's view in cities and villages

---

[1] Eusebius also mentions a Marcionite woman.

[2] John Chrysostom devoted a brief homily to her jumping from a roof (PG 50, 579–84; cf. anonymous women in Eusebius *HE* 8.12.2); cf. Victor Saxer, "Pelagia," *Encyclopedia of the Early Church* (2 vols.; New York: Oxford University Press, 1992) 2.665.

[3] Sabinianius and the soldiers are unknown, according to Moreau, "Observations," 275.

[4] *Against Galilaeans*; see Introduction.

γνώμῃ[1] συγχρησαμένῳ,[2] δυνατοῖς Χριστιανοῖς διαθέντων.[3] Ἔνθεν καὶ αἱ[4] αἱρέσεις κατὰ τῆς Ἐκκλησίας ἐπανέστησαν, τῶν τε Ἀρειανῶν καὶ τῶν Ἀνθρωπολατρῶν.

[ΡΛΘ'.] ⟨ΡΜ'⟩ + Πόσαι αἱρέσεις κατὰ τῆς (180b1) ἐκκλησιαστικῆς πίστεως ἐπανέστησαν;

Πρῶτον ἐπὶ τῇ ἐνσάρκῳ τοῦ Κυρίου παρουσίᾳ, γεγόνασί τινες Ἡρωδιανοὶ, Χριστὸν τὸν Ἡρώδην εἶναι λέγοντες.

β' Θευδιανοὶ, Θευδᾶς[5] ἀπατηθέντες. Τούτου μέμνηται καὶ Μαλιῆλος[6] ὁ νομοδιδάσκαλος, γνώμην τοῖς ἀρχιερεῦσιν εἰσηγούμενος, βουλευομένοις τι δρᾶν κατὰ τῶν ἀποστόλων, πρὸς τὸ μηδέν τι κατ' αὐτῶν ἐνεργεῖν λέγων· Πρὸ γὰρ τούτων τῶν ἡμερῶν ἀνέστη Θευδᾶς, λέγων εἶναί τινα ἑαυτόν.

γ' Ἐπὶ τῶν ἀποστόλων ἄλλη (180b2) αἵρεσις ἐν γῇ[7] Ἰερουσαλὴμ Αἰγυπτίου μάγου τινὸς συνέστη, καὶ τούτου μνήμη τις ἐν ταῖς ἀποστολικαῖς Πράξεσι γίνεται, ὅτε φησὶν ὁ χιλίαρχος τῷ Παύλῳ· Ἑλληνιστεὶ[8] γινώσκεις; Οὐκ ἄρα σὺ εἶ ὁ Αἰγύπτιος, ὁ πρὸ τούτων τῶν ἡμερῶν ἀναστατώσας, καὶ ἐξαγαγὼν εἰς τὴν ἔρημον τοὺς τετρακισχιλίους ἄνδρας τῶν σικαρίων;

δ' Σιμωνιανοί. Σίμων καὶ αὐτὸς ἐπὶ τῶν ἀποστόλων μάγος γενόμενος, αἵρεσιν διὰ τῆς τῶν σημείων ἐν τέρασι ψευδοῦς ἐνδείξεως εἰσήγαγε, λέγων (181a1) ἑαυτὸν εἶναι τοῦ Θεοῦ δύναμιν τὴν μεγάλην.[9] Καὶ τούτου μνήμη τις ἐν ταῖς Πράξεσι τῶν ἀποστόλων φέρεται.

---

[1] *Lc* FGM γνωμης.
[2] *Lc* FGM συγχρησαμενων.
[3] *Lc* FGM δεινα τοις Χριστιανοις δειχθεντων.
[4] FGM omit αἱ.
[5] F omits Θευδας; GM in their notes suggest emending to ἀπο Θευδα. Emend to ὑπο Θευδας.
[6] *Lc* FGM Γαμαλιηλος.
[7] *Lc* FGM τη.
[8] *Lc* FGM Ἑλληνιστι.
[9] FGM την μεγαλην δυναμιν; emend to την δυναμιν την μεγαλην.

and bringing to light dangers for the Christians.[1] On account of this, heresies arose against the church, both those of the Arians and the Anthrôpolatroi.[2]

## <HERESIES (140–43)>

**140.** – How many heresies arose against the (180b) church's faith?

First, during the incarnation and advent of the Lord, there were some Herodians, who said that **Hérôdés** was the **Christ** [Epiphanius, *Anakephaleosis* of the *Panarion* (cited as *Epit.*) 1 (I 168, 11–12 Holl); the *Syntagma* attributed to Hippolytus, as preserved in Pseudo-Tertullian, *Adversus Omnes Haereses* (ed. Kroymann; cited as *Adv. Haer.*) 1.1].[3]

2. Theudians were deceived <by> Theudas. Gamaliel, the teacher of the law, mentioned him when he gave advice to the high priests who wanted to take action against the apostles, not to do anything against them, saying, "Before these days there arose Theudas, calling himself someone" [Ac 5:36; cf. Josephus *Ant.* 20.97 (*goés*); Eusebius *HE* 2.11; not Epiphanius, not *Adv. Haer.*].

3. In the time of the apostles another heresy arose in Jerusalem, that of an Egyptian magician, mentioned in the apostolic Acts [21:38] when the tribune said to Paul, "Do you know Greek? Are you not that Egyptian who before these days rebelled and led 4,000 men of the Sicarii into the desert?" [Cf. Josephus *War* 2.261; Eusebius *HE* 2.21; not Epiphanius, not *Adv. Haer.*]

4. **Simonians**. Simon himself was a **magos in the time** of **the apostles** and introduced a heresy by falsely demonstrating signs with wonders, calling (181a) himself the great power of God. He too is mentioned in the Acts of the Apostles [Ac 8:9, etc.; not Josephus, Epiphanius, or *Adv. Haer.*].

---

[1] Julian's policy opposed making martyrs: *Epistle* 83 Bidez-Cumont = 7 Wright; 115 = 40.

[2] The term *anthrôpolatroi* was used by Athanasius against Arians, later against Nestorians: PGL 140. The expression "Arians *and* Anthrôpolatroi" does not prove that the Anthrôpolatroi are different from the Arians. Moreau ("Observations," 248) thinks they could be the orthodox as view ' by Apollinarists. See the Introduction for examples and the full argument. Note that the whole chapter is based primarily on the *Church History* of Eusebius, and that Joseph does not mention Julian's plan to rebuild the temple at Jerusalem.

[3] Throughout the chapter, **bold** text indicates that the corresponding words will be found in one or more of the source documents noted (most commonly *Epit.*). If the notes to an entry suggest that the source of Joseph's description is unknown, **bold** text indicates that corresponding words appear in the *Epit.* even though Joseph has not relied directly on that text.

ε' Ἐβιωναῖοι, καὶ οὗτοι κατὰ τῶν ἀποστόλων χρόνους[1] γεγόνασι, πτωχοὶ ἑρμηνευόμενοι, διὰ τὸ περὶ τὴν πίστιν πτωχεύειν. Τὰ γὰρ σωματικὰ νόμιμα Μωϋσέως ἐπιτελεῖν ἔτι βούλονται τοὺς πιστούς.

ς' Εἰσὶ καὶ ἄλλοι Ἐβιωναῖοι, οἱ καὶ Ναζωραῖοι καλούμενοι, τὰ αὐτὰ μὲν περὶ Μωϋσέως νόμιμα τοῖς ἄλλοις διακείμενοι, οὐ μὴν τὸν Κύριον ἡμῶν Ἰησοῦν Χριστὸν, Θεοῦ Λόγον, προϋπάρχοντα εἶναι Θεὸν καὶ Θεοῦ Υἱὸν δοξάζοντες, (181a2) ἀλλ᾽ ἄνθρωπον τιμῆς υἱοῦ Θεοῦ ἠξιωμένον.

ζ' Μενανδριανοί. Μένανδρός τις ἀπὸ Σίμωνος ἀποσχίσας, ἄνωθεν ἑαυτὸν ἔλεγε[2] καταπέμφθαι[3] εἰς διδασκαλίαν τοῦδε τοῦ κόσμου·[4] ἀγγέλους γεγονέναι πολλούς τινας καὶ ἀναριθμήτους.

η' Σατορνηλιανοί. Ὁ Σάτωρ, νῆλος[5] οὗτος ἀπὸ τοῦ Μενάνδρου διέστη, δι᾽ ἑπτὰ μόνων[6] ἀγγέλων γεγονέναι παραδιδοὺς τὸν κόσμον, ἀλλ᾽ οὐ διὰ πλειόνων, ὡς Μένανδρος ὑπετόπασε.

θ' Βασιλειδιανοί. Ὁ Βασιλείδης ἐν Αἰγύπτῳ γεγόνει.[7] τξε' εἶναι λέγει οὐρανοὺς (181b1) καὶ ὀνόματα τούτοις ἐπιφημίζει, καὶ τὸ ἀβραξᾶς ὄνομα τιμᾷ, ἰσάριθμον ὂν τῶν οὐρανῶν καὶ ἡμερῶν τοῦ ἐνιαυτοῦ. Τριακοσίους γὰρ καὶ ἑξήκοντα πέντε ψήφους φέρει.

ι' Νικολαΐται. Νικόλαος ἀπὸ τῶν ἑπτὰ διακόνων, τῶν ἐν τοῖς ἀποστόλοις, εἷς ἐγένετο, Ἐν τῷ κοινὰ εἶναι τὰ πάντα τοῖς πᾶσι, καὶ τὰς γυναῖκας εἰσηγησάμενος, καὶ ξένα τινὰ ὀνόματα τιμᾶσθαι παραδούς.

ια' Γνωστικοὶ ἐν Αἰγύπτῳ ἤρξαντο αἱρεσιάζειν, ἀλλαχοῦ δὲ Βορβοριανοὶ κικλήσκονται, Αἰσχροποιοί. Οὗτοι τὴν Βαρβιλώτην καὶ (181b2) Βαρβερὼ[8] προφέρουσιν ἐν ταῖς ἑαυτῶν[9] εὐχαῖς.

ιβ' Ὀφῖται. Οὗτοι τὸν ὄφιν τιμῶσι καὶ προτίθενται, ὡς καὶ αἴτιον γνώσεως ἀνθρώποις γενόμενον.

ιγ' Καϊανοὶ τὸν Καῒν ὡς μεγάλην τινὰ δύναμιν γεγονότα δοξάζουσι.

ιδ' Σηθῖται τὸν Σὴθ, ὡς ἀπὸ τῆς ἄνω μητρὸς ἐλθόντα εἰς νέου κόσμου δημιουργίαν, τιμῶσιν, ἀρχὰς καὶ ἐξουσίας θεοποιοῦντες.

---

[1] Lc FGM κατα τους των ἀποστολων χρονους.

[2] GM ἔλεγεν.

[3] Lc GM, who in their notes suggest emending to either καταπεπεμφθαι or καταπεμφθηναι.

[4] The text is clearly corrupt at this point. Lc FGM, who in their notes suggest something like εἰς διδασκαλιαν· κτιστας και δημιουργους τουδε του κοσμου.

[5] Lc FGM Ὁ Σατορνηλος.

[6] GM μονον.

[7] Lc FGM ἐγεγονει.

[8] Emend to Βαρβελω και την Βαρβερω.

[9] Lc GM αὐτων.

5. Ebionites. These also were in the times of the apostles, meaning "poor" because they were impoverished in faith, for they still wanted to keep the commandments of Moses which pertain to the body [Eusebius *HE* 3.27.1–2].

6. There are other Ebionites called Nazôraioi, who keep the same commandments of Moses as the others but consider our Lord Jesus Christ, the Logos of God, but do not glorify him as pre-existent God and Son of God, butregard him as a man worthy of being called Son of God [Eusebius *HE* 3.27.3, except for Nazôraioi].

7. Menandrians. A certain Menander separated **from Simon** and said he himself was sent from above to teach <that the makers> of this **world** were many, indeed innumerable, **angels** [*Epit.* 22, I 234,11–13 Holl, exaggerated].

8. **Satornilians**. This **Satornilos** differed from Menander, handing down that **the world was made through only seven angels**, not by many as Menander supposed [*Epit.* 23, I 235,2–4].

9. **Basileidians.** Basileidés lived in Egypt and said there were **365 heavens**, (181b) calling them by **name**, and held the name Abraxas (**Abrasax**) in honor, corresponding to the number of **days of the year**, for it too contains **the number 365** [*Epit.* 24, I 235,8–11; *Adv. Haer.* 1.5].

10. **Nikolaitans**: Nikolaos was one of the seven deacons who were **with the apostles** [Ac 6:5] and, holding that everything was in common for all [2:44–45], introduced the sharing of wives, and handed down certain foreign names to be honored [not *Epit.* 25, I 235,12–17; some agreement with *Adv. Haer.* 1.6].

11. **Gnôstikoi** began their heresy **in Egypt**. They are otherwise called Borborians (*Epit.* **Borboritai**), doers of **shameful** deeds. In their prayers they bring forward **Barbelô** and **Barberô** [*Epit.* 26, I 235, 18, 21–22].

12. **Ophites**. These honor the serpent (*ophis*) and set it forth as the cause of knowledge (*gnôsis*) for men [*Adv. Haer.* 2.1; not *Epit.* 37].

13. **Kaians glorify Kain** as some great **power** [*Adv. Haer.* 2.5–6; not *Epit.* 38].

14. Séthites (**Séthians**) **honor Séth** as **coming from the Mother above** to create a new world; they deify **principalities and powers** [*Epit.* 39, II 2,8–14; some similarities with *Adv. Haer.* 2.7–9].

15. **Karpokratianoi** were **in Asia** and **honor images** of famous men, depicting them even among the Greeks. And they say the **soul of Jesus** ascended into heaven because it was pleasing to (182a) God [not *Epit.* 27, but cf. I 236, 4–5; not *Adv. Haer.* 3.1–2].

16. **Kérinthianoi**. **Kérinthos** said the law was given the Jews **by an angel** and did not result in good for them [*Adv. Haer.* 3.2–3; not *Epit.* 26].

ιε' Καρποκρατιανοί, ἐν τῇ 'Ασίᾳ γεγόνασιν, εἰκόνας τῶν θαυμασθέντων ἀνθρώπων καὶ παρὰ τοῦ[1] Ἕλλησι, γράψαντες τιμῶσι. Καὶ τὴν Ἰησοῦ ψυχὴν εἰς οὐρανὸν ἀνεληλυθέναι, ὡς εὐάρεστον τῷ (182a1) Θεῷ γεγονυῖαν, φασίν. ις' Κηρινθιανοί. Κήρινθος ἐπαγγέλου[2] τὸν νόμον δεδόσθαι Ἰουδαίοις, οὐκ εἰς ἀγαθὸν αὐτοῖς προβησόμενον ἔφη.

ιζ' Οὐαλεντιανοὶ[3] ἀνάστασιν οὐ φασὶν εἶναι, Παλαιὰν ἀθετοῦσι Διαθήκην, τὸν Χριστὸν ἀπ' οὐρανοῦ σῶμα ἐνηνοχέναι βούλονται.

ιη' Πτολεμαῖοι. Ἀπὸ Οὐαλεντίνου Πτολεμαῖός τις διαστάς, συζυγίας αἰώνων τινῶν λ', τῇ Οὐαλεντίνου αἱρέσει προσήγαγε.

ιθ' Σεκουνδιανοί. Σεκοῦνδός τις ἐγένετο μετὰ Ἰσιδώρου τινὸς καὶ Ἐπιφανοῦς. Οὗτοι τῇ Οὐαλεντίνου τυφλῇ γνώμῃ καὶ αἰσχρουργίας (182a2) προστέθεικαν.

κ' Ἡρακλέονες ἀπὸ Ἡρακλᾶ τινὸς, ὀγδοάδας τινὰς τιμᾶν εἰσήχθησαν, καὶ τοὺς ἀποθανόντας αὐτῶν ἐν Ἑβραϊκαῖς ἐπικλήσεσι, καὶ τῷ τοῦ ἀπὸ βαλσάμου μύρῳ λυτροῦσθαι νομίζουσι.

κα' Μαρκόσιοι. Μάρκος τις γεγένηται Κολωβαρσοῦ συμφοιτητής, δύο ἀρχὰς εἰσάγων, νεκρῶν ἀνάστασιν ἀθετῶν.

κβ' Κολωβαρσίοι. Ὁ Κολωβαρσὸς Μάρκῳ μὲν τὰ αὐτὰ φρονῶν, προσθεὶς δὲ καὶ ὀγδοάδας τινάς.

κγ' Κερδωνιανοί. Κέρδων τις Ἡρακλᾶ διαδέχεται τὴν πλάνην, δύο δὲ ἀρχὰς ἐναντίας ἀλλήλαις ὑπεστήσατο, (182b1) τὸν δὲ Χριστὸν μήτε ἐκ τοῦ Θεοῦ γεννητὸν, μήτε ἐκ Μαρίας εἶναι. Ἀνάστασιν ἀθετεῖ, καὶ τὴν Παλαιὰν Διαθήκην οὐ παραδέχεται.

κδ' Μαρκιωνισταί. Μαρκίων Ποντικὸς γέγονε. Τρεῖς ἀρχὰς εἶναι ἐδόξασεν, ἀγαθὸν δίκαιον, φαῦλον. Τὸν δὲ τὴν Παλαιὰν τῷ Ἰσραὴλ νομοθετήσαντα, ἐναντίαν οὖσαν τῇ Καινῇ, ἕτερον ἔφη Θεὸν εἶναι. Ἀνάστασιν ἀθετεῖ, βάπτισμα πολλάκις τοῖς αὐτοῖς δίδωσιν ἐπὶ ἁμαρτιῶν λύσει. Ὑπὲρ κοιμωμένων βαπτίζουσιν.[4]

κε' Λουκιανισταί. Λούκιός τις, οὐχὶ ὁ Ἀρειανὸς, γέγονε (182b2) μετὰ Μαρκίωνα, τὰ Μαρκίωνος διαδεξάμενος, καὶ ἕτερα αὐτοῖς ἐπιπυρωθεὶς ἀτοπώτερα.

κς' Ἀπαλλιανοὶ[5] ἀπὸ Ἀπελλάου τινὸς ἤρξαντο. Κακίζει δὲ τὴν ποίησιν πᾶσαν, ὡς καὶ ὁ Μαρκίων. Οὐ τρεῖς δὲ ἀρχὰς εἶπεν, ὡς ἐκεῖνος, ἀλλ' ἕνα Θεὸν πεποιηκότα Θεὸν ἕτερον, τὸν τῆς κτίσεως δημιουργόν.

---

[1] Lc FGM τοις.
[2] Lc F ὑπ' ἀγγελου; GM ὑπο ἀγγελου.
[3] Lc GM Οὐαλεντινιανοι.
[4] GM βαπτιζουσι.
[5] FGM Ἀπελλιανοι; emend to Ἀπελληανοι.

17. **Oualent<in>ianoi** say there is **no resurrection, reject the Old Testament**, and say **Christ brought his body from heaven** [name in *Epit.* 31, I 236,23; description, 23–24; 237, 1–2; some similarities with *Adv. Haer.* 4.1–6].

18. **Ptolemaioi**. Ptolemaios **disagreed with Oualentinos on some matters** and added the **conjunctions** of 30 aeons to the heresy of Oualentinos [*Epit.* 33, I 237,10; aeons from *Epit.* 31, I 236, 26; a garbled version of *Adv. Haer.* 4.7?].[1]

19. **Sekoundians**. A certain Sekoundos was with a certain **Isidore** and **Epiphanés**. These added **shameful acts** to the blind opinion of **Oualentinos** [*Epit.* 32, I 237, 4–7].

20. **Héracleônes**, from a certain Héraclas, introduced the honoring of certain **Ogdoads** and think their dead are **redeemed** by **Hebrew invocations** and by **balsamic** myrrh [*Epit.* 36, II 1, 13–17; certainly not from *Adv. Haer.* 4.8 or Epiphanius, who name Hérakleônitai as following Hérakleôn].

21. **Markosians. A certain Markos, who introduced two principles and rejected the resurrection of the dead, was a fellow-disciple with Kolorbasos** [*Epit.* 34, II 1, 3–4].

22. **Kolôrbasians. Kolôrbasos had the same ideas** as Markos, but added certain **Ogdoads** [*Epit.* 35, II 1, 9–12].

23. **Kerdônians**. A certain Kerdôn **succeeded to the error of** Heraclas (*Epit.* **Heracleius**) and proposed **two principles opposed to each other**; (182b) **Christ was not born** either of God or of Maria; **he rejects resurrection and** does not accept **the Old Testament** [*Epit.* 41, II 2, 21–22, 24–3, 2].

24. **Markiônists. Markiôn was a Pontic**. He thought there were **three principles: good, just, evil.** He held there was another god who gave the old legislation to Israel, **contrary to the new. He rejects resurrection and gives baptism many times** for freeing from sins. They **baptize for the dead** [*Epit.* 42, II 3, 7–11].

25. **Loukianists. A certain Loukianos[2] (not the Arian)** was after Markiôn and **accepted Markiôn's doctrines, adding** other more absurd teachings [resembles *Epit.* 43, II 3, 13–15; some similarities to *Adv. Haer.* 6.3].

26. **Apell[i]<é>ans** began from a certain Apellaos. He, **like Marcion,** describes **the whole creation as evil** but **did not speak of three principles** as he did, but of **one god who made a second** god, the demiurge of the creation [*Epit.* 44, II 3, 17–21].

---

[1] According to the *Adv. Haer.*, Valentinos introduced the doctrine of the conjunctions of thirty aeons, and Ptolemaios and Sekoundos added first four, and then four more, to Oualentinos' thirty.

[2] For the text, Moreau, "Observations," 252 n. 3.

κζ' Τατιανοί. Τατιανὸς ἐν τῇ Μεσοποταμίᾳ γεγόνει, τῶν[1] Ἐγκρατητῶν αἵρεσιν συστησάμενος, ἣν ἴσασιν οἱ πολλοί.

κη' Φρύγες. Μωντανός τις καὶ Πρισκίλλα τὴν αἵρεσιν ἐν [ἐν][2] τῇ Φρυγίᾳ συνανεστήσαντο,[3] Πεπουζᾶν Ἱερουσαλὴμ (183a1) αὐτοῖς πόλιν τῆς Φρυγίας ποιησάμενοι.

κθ' Πεπουζιανοὶ ἀπὸ Ἐπούζης[4] τῆς Φρυγίας οὕτω προσαγορευόμενοι, κοινωνίαν ἄθεσμον ποιούμενοι κατὰ τὰ[5] τῶν δυσσεβούντων.

λ' Τεσσαρεσκαιδεκατῖται, τὸ Πάσχα ἐν τῇ[6] τεσσαρεσκαιδεκάτῃ τῆς σελήνας μετὰ Ἰουδαίων τελοῦντες.

λα' Ἄλογοί τινες κληθέντες, διὰ τὸ μὴ δέχεσθαι τὸν Λόγον ἐν ἀρχῇ Θεὸν ὄντα πρὸς τὸν Πατέρα, καὶ διὰ τοῦτο μήτε τὸ[7] Ἰωάννου Εὐαγγέλιον δέχεσθαι, μήτε τὴν Ἀποκάλυψιν αὐτοῦ.

λβ' Θεοδοτιανοί. Θεόδοτός τις ἐν τῷ Βυζαντίῳ γενόμενος, ἄνθρωπον εἶπεν εἶναι Χριστὸν ψιλόν, (183a2) μετοχῆς Θεοῦ ἠξιωμένον.

λγ' Ἀρτεμιανοί.[8] Ἀρτεμία[9] γέγονέ τις ἐν τῇ Ἀσίᾳ, τὴν Θεοδότου αἵρεσιν τιμήσας. Ἄνθρωπον γὰρ εἶπε γεγονότα[10] ψιλὸν τὸν Χριστόν, ἐν αὐτῷ τὸν Θεὸν Λόγον κατοικεῖν εὐδοκήσαντα.

λδ' Μελχισεδεκιανοὶ, δύναμιν Θεοῦ τὸν Μελχισεδὲκ εἶναι νομίζουσι, καὶ εἰς αὐτὸν πάσας τὰς Γραφὰς ἀναφέρουσιν, αὐτὸν εἶναι λέγοντες τὸν Χριστόν.

λε' Ναυᾶτοι. Ναυᾶτος μετανοίας τρόπον[11] τοῖς ἁμαρτάνουσιν οὐ δίδωσιν. Οὗτοι δέ εἰσιν οἱ Καθαροὺς ἑαυτοὺς προσαγορεύσαντες.

λς' Σευηριανοί. Γυναῖκας ὁ (183b1) Σεῦηρος παραιτεῖται, δύναμιν ἀριστερὰν αὐτὴν καλῶν. Τὸν οἶνον ἀποβάλλεται, ἀπὸ μίξεως δράκοντος καὶ τῆς γῆς φῦναι τὴν ἄμπελον φάσκων.

λζ' Βαρδισανῖται. Ἀπὸ Βαρδισάνου τινὸς ἐν τῇ Μεσοποταμίᾳ γεγονότος, οὗτοι δὲ ἀνεφύησαν. Ἀνάστασιν ἀθετοῦσι σώματος, καὶ τὴν σάρκωσιν τοῦ Σωτῆρος κατὰ φαντασίαν γεγενεῖσθαι[12] τίθενται.

---

[1] FGM την; emend to την των.
[2] Lc FGM, who remove the dittograph.
[3] Lc FGM συνεστησαντο.
[4] Lc FGM Πεπουζης.
[5] FGM omit τα, apparently regarding it as a dittograph.
[6] FGM omit τη.
[7] FGM omit το.
[8] Emend to Ἀρτεμανοι.
[9] FGM Ἀρτεμιας; emend to Ἀρτεμα.
[10] Lc F εἰπεν εἰναι; GM εἰπεν.
[11] Lc FGM, who in their notes suggest emending to τοπον. Cf. Hb 12:17.
[12] Lc GM γεγενησθαι.

27. **Tatiani**. Tatian lived in **Mesopotamia** and founded the heresy of the Encratites, which many knew [not *Epit.* 46 but cf. *Epit.* 47, II 211, 4 on Encratites; not *Adv. Haer.* 7.1].

28. Phrygians [**Kata Phrygas**]. **Môntanus and Priscilla** founded the heresy in Phrygia, making **Pepouza, a city** of Phrygia, (183a) their Jerusalem [*Epit.* 48 + 49, II 211, 9–10, 13–15; not *Adv. Haer.* 7.2].

29. **Pepouzians**, so called from **Pepuza, a city of Phrygia**; they held unlawful communion in accordance with the deeds of the impious [not *Epit.* 49].

30. Quartodecimans, who **keep the Pascha** with Jews **on the 14th day of the moon** [*Epit.* 50, II 211, 21–22].

31. Some are **called Alogoi** because they do not accept the **Logos** at the beginning as **God** with the Father, and therefore **do not accept the Gospel of John or his Apocalypse** [*Epit.* 51, II 212, 3–6].

32. **Theodotians**. A certain **Theodotus of Byzantium** said Christ was a **mere man**, worthy of God's indwelling [partly *Epit.* 54, II 212, 19, 22; resembles *Adv. Haer.* 8.2].

33. Artem[i]ans. A certain Artem[i]as in Asia honored the heresy of Theodotus, for he said that Christ was a mere man in whom God the Logos was pleased to dwell [Eusebius *HE* 5.28.1; 7.30.17; not Epiphanius or *Adv. Haer.*].

34. **Melchisedekians** think that **Melchisedek is a power** of God and **refer all** the scriptures **to him**, saying he is the Christ [*Epit.* 55, II 212, 25–27].

35. Nauatianoi. **Nauatos** allows **no room for** the **repentance** of those who have sinned.[1] These are the ones who call themselves **"pure"** (*katharoi*) [*Epit.* 59, II 213, 14–15].

36. **Seuérians**. Seuérus (183b) **blamed women, calling her the Left Power, and rejected wine, saying the vine grew out of the intercourse of the serpent with the earth** [*Epit.* 45, III 3, 23–4, 4].

37. Bardisanitai (**Bardésianistai** in Epiphanius and *Epit.*). Their source was a certain Bardisanos (*Epit.* **Bardésianos**; Epiphanius Bardésianés) who was in **Mesopotamia**. They reject the resurrection of the body and the incarnation of the Savior, who merely appeared to exist [Not *Epit.* 56; not Eusebius].

---

[1] Eusebius called Novatian "Noouatos" (*HE* 6.43,45) and said his followers called themselves *katharoi* (6.43.1). Epiphanius then transformed "Noouatos" into "Nauatos" (*Pan.* 59.1.1 and *Epit.* 59, II 213,14); cf. Aline Pourkier, *L'hérésiologie chez Épiphane de Salamine* (Paris: Beauchesne, 1992) 385.

λη' Ἐλκεσιανοὶ ἐν τῇ Ἀραβίᾳ γεγόνασιν. Οὗτοι ἀπό τινος Ἑλκασᾶ[1] ψευδοπροφητείας φέροντες. Ἐλέγοντο δὲ καὶ Σαμψαῖοι.

λθ' Βυριλλιανοί. Βύριλλός τις (183b2) ἐν τῇ Ἀραβίᾳ καὶ οὗτος γεγονώς, ἄνθρωπον τὸν Χριστὸν ἐνόμισεν, οὐ πρότερον αὐτὸν ὄντα τὸν Χριστὸν Λόγον παραδεξάμενος.

μ' Οὐαλέσιοι. Οὐάλης, ὁ ἐν τῇ Ἀραβίᾳ καὶ οὗτος γενόμενος, εὐνούχιζε τοὺς προσιόντας αὐτῷ, καὶ ἀπέτεμνε, τὴν Παλαιὰν Γραφὴν μὴ δεχόμενος.

μα' Σαβέλλιοι. Σαβέλλιός τις ἐν τῇ Πενταπόλει γεγονώς, τὰς τρεῖς ὑποστάσεις τῆς μιᾶς Θεότητος οὐκ ἀποδεξάμενος, Υἱοπάτορα τὴν Θεότητα, καὶ σύνθεον, παρεφρόνει.

μβ' Ὠρειγένιοι αἰσχροποιοῦσι, καὶ τὴν σωφροσύνην οὐ τιμῶσιν, ἀποχρώμενοι τῇ (184a1) σαρκί. Ἀλλ' οὔκ εἰσιν οὗτοι Ἀλεξανδρέως Ὠρειγένους, τοῦ καὶ Ἀδαμαντίου.

μγ' Ὠρειγενιασταί. Οὗτός ἐστιν ὁ καὶ Ἀδαμάντιος, σωμάτων ἀνάστασιν ἀθετεῖ. Εἰς ἀλληγορίας ἀτόπους τὰς Γραφὰς ἔτρεψεν. Ἀπὸ τῆς Ἑλλήνων φιλοσοφίας ἐλθών, τὸν δὲ Ἑλληνισμὸν οὐκ ἀποπτύσας, τρισκαίδεκα αἱρέσεις τῇ Ἐκκλησίᾳ ἐπεισήγαγε.

μδ' Παυλιανοί. Παῦλος ἀπὸ Σαμωσᾶ,[2] τῆς Ἀντιοχέων γενόμενος ἐπίσκοπος, τὴν Θεοδότου καὶ Ἀρτεμᾶ αἵρεσιν ἀνανεωσάμενος, ἄνθρωπον Θεοῦ τιμῇ τετιμημένον τὸν Χριστὸν, διὰ τὸ τὸν Λόγον, (184a2) τὴν Σοφίαν τοῦ Θεοῦ, ἐνοικῆσαι εἰς αὐτὸν, εἶπε.

με' Μανιχαῖοι. Ἀπὸ τῆς Περσίδος οὗτος κατὰ τῆς Ἐκκλησίας ἀνεφάνη, Μάνης λεγόμενος. Δύο φησὶν ἀρχὰς, ἀγαθήν τε καὶ κακὴν εἶναι. Τὸν νομοθέτην ἐν τῷ Ἰσραὴλ γεγονότα καὶ ποιητὴν πάντων ἀθετεῖ. Ἄστρα σέβεται.

μς' Ἱερακῖται. Ἐν Λεοντῷ[3] τῇ κατ' Αἴγυπτον, Ἱέραξ τις λεγόμενος ἔπειθε σαρκὸς ἀνάστασιν μὴ ἐλπίζειν. Γάμον ἠθέτει. Κοσμικοὺς οὐκ

---

[1] Emend to Ἑλκασαι.
[2] GM Σαμοσα; emend to Σαμωσατεως.
[3] Emend to Λεοντοπολῳ.

38. Helkesians were in Arabia, who introduced false prophecies from a certain Helkasa<i>. They were also called Sampsaioi [Eusebius *HE* 6.38; not Epiphanius].

39. Byrillians (Béryllians). A certain Byrillos (Béryllos) who lived in Arabia considered Christ a man and did not admit that he was previously the Christ Logos [Eusebius *HE* 6.39; not Epiphanius].

40. **Oualesians**. Oualens, who was in **Arabia**, **made eunuchs** of those who came to him and **castrated** them, rejecting the Old Testament [*Epit.* 58, II 213, 8–13].

41. **Sabellians**. A certain Sabellius who lived in the Pentapolis did not accept the three persons (*hypostaseis*) of the one Deity, senselessly spoke of the Deity as Son-Father and composite [Eusebius *HE* 7.6].[1]

42. **Oreigenioi commit shameful deeds** and do not honor (184a) chastity, abusing the flesh. But these are not followers of Origen of Alexandria, also called Adamantius [*Epit.* 63, II 213, 24–25].

43. Oreigeniastai (*Epit.* Other **Oreigenioi**). This is **the one also called Adamantius, who rejects the resurrection** of bodies and distorted the scriptures into absurd allegories, coming from the philosophy of the Greeks and not rejecting Hellenism. He introduced thirteen heresies into the church[2] [*Epit.* 64, II 214, 1–7].

44. Paulians. **Paul** from **Samosata** was made bishop of the Antiochenes. He renewed the heresy of Theodotus and Artemas, and said the Christ was a man honored with honor by God because the Logos, the Wisdom of God, dwelt in him. [not Epiphanius or *Epit.* 65, although the latter mentions that he was bishop of Antioch].[3]

45. **Manichaeans**. The one called **Manes from Persia** appeared against the Church, and said there are **two principalities, good and evil**, rejecting the legislator of Israel and maker of all, but venerates **the stars** [*Epit.* 66, III 1, 10–12, 14–15].

46. **Hierakitai**. A certain **Hierax from Leonto<polis> in Egypt** claimed that **the resurrection of the flesh** was not to be hoped for, and **rejected marriage**. He did not receive laymen (*kosmikoi*) and **denied that children**

---

[1] Epiphanius (*Pan.* 62) locates in Rome and Mesopotamia.

[2] For Origen's Greek ideas, Porphyry in Eusebius *HE* 6.19.7–8 (also Epiphanius *Pan.* 64.71.9); as the source of Arius, Anomians, and others, Epiphanius *Pan.* 64.4.2. Cf. C. 139(7).

[3] Paul reviving heresy of Artemas, Eusebius *HE* 7.30.16–17; for Epiphanius, Huebner, "Die Hauptquelle des Epiphanius (*Panarion, haer.* 65) über Paulus von Samosata," *Zeitschrift für Kirchengeschichte* 90 (1979) 201–20: from Pseudo-Athanasius [Apollinaris of Laodicea?] *Against the Sabellians*.

ἐδέχετο. Τὰ παιδία εἰς τὴν Χριστοῦ βασιλείαν μὴ εἰσέρχεσθαι, ἐπεὶ μηδὲ ἤθλησαν. (184b1)

μζ' Μελετιανοί. Ἐν Αἰγύπτῳ σχηματικός[1] τις γέγονε Μελίτων,[2] μὴ συνευξάμενος τοῖς μετανοήσασιν ἀπὸ τοῦ διωγμοῦ, καὶ δεχθεῖσι παρὰ τῆς συνόδου, καὶ Πέτρου τοῦ ἀποστόλου[3] καὶ μάρτυρος.

μη' Ἀδαμιανοὶ γυμνοὶ ἐν ταῖς εὐχαῖς παρίστανται, ἄνδρες ὁμοῦ καὶ γυναῖκες, τοῦ Ἀδὰμ καὶ τῆς Εὔας τῆς ἁπλότητος μνημονεύοντες.

μθ' Μαριανῖται τὴν Μαρίαν εἰς θείαν οὐσίαν ἀνάγουσι,[4] καὶ φησὶν[5] αὐτὴν εἰς οὐρανὸν ἀνειλῆφθαι, μνήμην αὐτῆς ἐν ἄρτου προθέσει ποιούμενοι. (184b2)

ν' Μασαλλιανοὶ ἐργάζεσθαι οὐ βούλονται, ἀλλὰ φησὶν[6] εὐχαῖς εἰς ἀεὶ διατελεῖν, μισεργεῖν ἀγαπήσαντες.

να' Ἀποστολικοί, περὶ τὴν Πισιδίαν οὗτοι γεγόνασιν, ἀποτακτικὰς[7] μόνους[8] δέχονται. Μετ' οὐδενὸς ἑτέρου εὔχονται.

νβ' Ἀρχοντικοὶ ἀρχὰς καὶ ἐξουσίας τινὰς ἀπαριθμοῦσι, καὶ ὑπὸ ταύτας τιθέασι τὴν καθόλου διοίκησιν, Χριστὸν δὲ εἰς τὴν τούτων τῆς διοικήσεως κρίσιν ἰέναι.

νγ' Ἀγγελικοί. Μέγα πεφρονήκασιν οὗτοι, ὡς ἀγγελικὴν ἰδίαν τάξιν ἔχοντες, καὶ τοῖς συντεταγμένοις.[9]

νδ' Αὐδιανοί. Σχίσμα γεγόνασι (185a1) καὶ οὗτοι, κοσμικοῖς οὐ συνευχόμενοι. Ῥάβδῳ διορύξαντες ἀφ' ἑαυτῶν ταῖς εὐχαῖς τοὺς μὴ κοινωνικοὺς ἀπὸ τῶν.[10] Ἀποκρύφοις βιβλίοις κέχρηνται, καὶ παραδόσεσι ξέναις[11] τισὶ τοῦ ἐξάρχου αὐτῶν.

νε' Μαρκελλιανοί. Μαρκέλλιός[12] τις ἐν Ἀγκύρᾳ γεγόνει τὴν Σαβελλίου δόξαν φρονῶν, ἀνυπόστατον τὸν τοῦ Θεοῦ Λόγον, καὶ τὸ Ἅγιον Πνεῦμα νομίσας.

---

[1] Lc FGM σχισματικος.
[2] GM print Μελιτον; lc FGM, who in their notes suggest Μελιτιος.
[3] Lc GM, who in their notes suggest replacing αποστολου with επισκοπου.
[4] FGM αναγουσιν.
[5] Lc FGM φασιν.
[6] Lc FGM φασιν.
[7] FGM υποτακτικους.
[8] FGM μονον.
[9] In their notes, GM suggest that the word υπισξνουμενοι or something similar has fallen out.
[10] Lc F, who in his notes suggests emending απο των to αυτων. GM emend των to ταις, but in their notes suggest that the word has been dislocated.
[11] GM print ξεναι by mistake.
[12] Emend to Μαρκελλος.

**would enter the kingdom of Christ, since they had not contended** <for the faith> [*Epit.* 67, III 1, 16–2, 2] (184b).

47. **Meletianoi.** In Egypt there was a certain **schism**atic Melitios **would not pray with those who** repented after **the persecution** and were accepted by the synod and by Peter the [apostle] <bishop> and martyr [*Epit.* 68, III 2, 3–5].

48. **Adamians,** who are **naked in the prayers,** both **men and women,** recalling the simplicity of Adam and Eua [*Epit.* 52, II 212, 7–12].

49. Marianites raise up Maria to a divine substance and say she was assumed into heaven; they mention her in the offering of the bread [Collyridians of *Epit.* 79; not the Antidikomariamites of *Epit.* 78].

50. Masallians (**Massalians**) do not want to work but say they are always to be active in prayers, delighting in idleness [not *Epit.* 80] [1]

51. Apostolics were **in Pisidia, receiving only anchorites and praying with no one else** [*Epit.* 61, II 213, 18–21].

52. **Archontikoi** list certain principalities and powers and set the administration of the universe under them. They say that Christ came to judge their administration [not *Epit.* or Epiphanius 40].

53. **Angelics** think highly of themselves as **having their own angelic rank,** shared with those ranked with them [*Epit.* 60, II 213, 16–17]. [2]

54. **Audians, schism**atics (185a) who do not pray with laymen, **separating** from themselves **in prayers** with a rod those with whom they think they should not communicate. **They use apocryphal** books and certain alien traditions from their founder [*Epit.* 70, III 230, 4–7, without the Anthropomorphitism discussed in *Pan.* 70.2.4–8, III 234, 8–31].

55. **Markellians.** A certain **Markell[i]os** was in **Ankyra** and **held the view of Sabellius,** supposing that the Logos of God and the Holy Spirit had no nature (*hypostasis*) [fuller than *Epit.* 72, III 230, 16–17].

---

[1] *Epit.* 80 is the last heresy, as in the *Doctrina Patrum* (p. 269,8 Diekamp); plus "These are the heresies to [the reign of] Marcian" [450–457]) as in John of Damascus (PG 94, 729A).

[2] See Introduction.

νϛ' Ἀρειανοί. Ἄρειός τις γέγονεν ἐν Ἀλεξανδρείᾳ, τὸν Υἱὸν τοῦ Θεοῦ κτιστὸν καὶ ἐξ οὐκ ὄντων γεγονέναι δοξάσας.

νζ' Ἡμιάρειοι. Ἐξ Ἀρειανῶν οὗτοι ἀπέσχισαν, ὁμοούσιον[1] τῷ Θεῷ φάσκοντες (185a2) τὸν Υἱόν, τῶν Ἀρειανῶν μόνον τὸ ὅμοιον εἶναι αὐτὸν[2] λεγόντων.

νη' Φωτειανοί.[3] Φωτεινός τις γέγονεν ἐν τῇ Σειρμίῳ. Τὰ Παύλου τοῦ Σαμωσατέως δοξάζουσιν,[4] ἄνθρωπον θεοφόρον εἶναι λέγων[5] τὸν Χριστόν.

νθ' Ἀετιανοί. Ἀέτιός τις Κίλιξ τὸ γένος, τῶν Ἀρειανῶν χωρισθεὶς ὅμοιον λεγῶν[6] τῷ Πατρὶ τὸν Υἱόν, ἀνόμοιον αὐτῷ εἶναι εἶπεν.[7] Εὐνόμιος δὲ προσέστη[8] μετ' αὐτοῦ ταύτης τῆς αἱρέσεως, ὅθεν καὶ Εὐνομιανοὶ οἱ Ἀνομῖται κέκληνται.

ξ' Ἀεριανοί. Ἀέριός τις γέγονε Ποντικὸς, τῆς Ἀρειανῆς αἱρέσεως ὢν, ἀντεδόξασε[9] (185b1) δὲ αὐτοῖς, καὶ ἐχωρίσθη ἀπ' αὐτῶν διὰ τοιαῦτα· ἐπίσκοπον μηδὲν διαφέρειν πρεσβυτέρου λέγων. Τετράδας καὶ παρασκευὰς μὴ προτιμᾷν τῶν ἐν ἄλλαις ἡμέραις νηστεύων,[10] τινὰ σκηνὴν[11] ὑπερεῖδε

ξα' Μακεδονιανοί. Μακεδόνιός τις ἐν Κωνσταντινουπόλει γίνεται, τὸ Πνεῦμα τὸ ἅγιον ἀθετῶν τῆς τοῦ Θεοῦ Πατρὸς καὶ Υἱοῦ οὐσίας. Διὸ καὶ Πνευματομάχοι κέκληνται οἱ κοινωνικοὶ[12] αὐτοῦ.

ξβ' Ἀνθρωπομορφῖται. Οὗτοι εἰς τὴν Ἐλευθεροπόλεως ἀναπεφήνασι χώραν, ἐν ᾧ[13] ἐστὶν .......... (185b2) σωματικὸν χαρακτῆρα καὶ μορφὴν ἀνθρωπίνην τὸν Θεὸν ἔχειν κατὰ τὴν ὕπαρξιν αὐτοῦ τὴν ἀΐδιον λογιζόμενοι, ὡς καὶ Ἰουδαίων οἱ τῶν Γραφῶν ἀμύητοι νενοήκασιν.

---

[1] Lc FGM ὁμοιουσιον.
[2] FGM omit αὐτον.
[3] Lc FGM Φωτεινιανοι.
[4] Lc FGM δοξαζει.
[5] FGM λεγων εἰναι.
[6] Lc FGM λεγοντων.
[7] GM εἰπε.
[8] Lc FGM προεστη.
[9] GM print ἀνεδοξασε by mistake.
[10] Lc FGM, who in their notes suggest emending to νηστειων.
[11] Lc FGM, who in their notes suggest emending τινα σκηνην to τεσσαρακοστην.
[12] FGM κοινωνοι.
[13] Emend to ᾗ?

56. **Areians**. A certain **Areios** lived in **Alexandria**, and supposed that **the Son of God was created** and existed out of the non-existent [resembles *Epit.* 69, III 2, 6–9].

57. **Semiareians**. These separated from the Arians, saying that **the Son** is **of similar substance** (*homo<i>ousios*) with God, while the Areians say he is only similar (*homoios*) [cf. *Epit.* 73, III 230, 22–231, 4].

58. **Phôteinians**. A certain **Photinus** lived at **Sirmium**. He **held the view of Paul of Samosata**, calling Christ a God-bearing [or "inspired"] man [*Epit.* 71, III 230,12–13].

59. **Aetians**. A certain **Aetios, a Cilician** by race, separated himself from Areians who held that the Son is like the Father; he held that he is unlike. **Eunomios** headed the heresy with him; hence the **Anomi**tes were also **called Eunomians** [partly *Epit.* 76, III 231, 20–232, 13; with less detail].

60. **Aerians**. A certain **Aerius was a Pontic, belonging to the Areian heresy** but holding (195b) views contrary to them, and he was separated from them because of such ideas: **bishops are no different from presbyters, one should not prefer the 4th day and Preparation but fast on other days; he omitted the <fortieth> day** (i.e., Lent) [*Epit.* 75, III 231, 9–19].

61. Macedonians. A certain Macedonius lived in Constantinople, separating the Holy Spirit from the substance (*ousia*) of God the Father and the Son; therefore those who share this view are called **Pneumatomachoi** [not based on *Epit.* 74, III 231, 5–8].[1]

62. Anthropomorphites.[2] These appeared in the vicinity of Eleutheropolis, in which is (space for 12 letters). They think God has a bodily form and human shape according to his eternal existence (*hyparxis*), as also those of the Jews who are not initiated in the scriptures have supposed.[3]

---

[1] Epiphanius identified Pneumatomachoi with Macedonians (*Pan.* pr.4.7; I 159,3 Holl; PGL 824).

[2] Lampe (PGL 140) cites the 5th-century historian Socrates for the name Anthrôpomorphianoi used by Origenists (*HE* 6.27; PG 67,688B); Jerome explicitly attacks the Anthropomorphitae (*Tractatus de Psalmis*, Corpus Christianorum 78, 145 [on Ps 93:8–9]); *Contra Ioannem Hierosolymitum* 11 (PL 23, 380C: *Anthropomorphitarum haeresis*). Jerome also quotes Rufinus' charge that Epiphanius was an Anthropomorphite in his *Apologia contra Rufinum* 3.23 (SC 303, 274–276). For additional discussion, see the Introduction.

[3] Elizabeth Clark, *The Origenist Controversy* (Princeton: Princeton University Press, 1992) 104 n. 145, thanks Goranson for noting that here Anthropomorphism is associated with "Eleutheropolis, Epiphanius' home town," just southwest of Jerusalem. Also see Goranson, "The Joseph of Tiberias Episode," 156. The implication of this passage is that in assessing the Anthropomorphite Controversy, which erupted in 393 and in which Epiphanius was a key figure, Joseph sides with Rufinus and John of Jerusalem

Αὗται μὲν οὖν αἱ κατὰ τῆς ἁγίας Ἐκκλησίας ἐπαναστᾶσαι γεγόνασιν αἱρέσεις, τῆς τὸν Κύριον ἡμῶν Ἰησοῦν Χριστόν, τὸν δι' οὗ τὰ πάντα ἐγένετο, καὶ γεννηθέντα ἐκ Μαρίας τῆς Παρθένου κατὰ σάρκα, καὶ ἐπιδημήσαντα τῇ ἑαυτοῦ κτίσει, αὐτὸν εἶναι τὸν πρὸ τῶν αἰώνων συνόντα τῷ Θεῷ καὶ Πατρί, γεννηθέντα ἐκ τῆς οὐσίας τοῦ Πατρός, καὶ ὄνταόμοούσιον τῷ Θεῷ Πατρὶ παρειληφυίας (186a1) καὶ παραδιδούσης, σὺν τῷ Ἁγίῳ Πνεύματι.[1]

As the evidence cited makes clear, Joseph's list of heresies is based in large part, although certainly not entirely, on the *Epitome*. In all probability, for the first half of his list Joseph also made use either directly or indirectly of the now lost *Syntagma* of Hippolytus, the substance of which has survived in the *Adversus Omnes Haereses* of Pseudo-Tertullian. Judgments in these matters are somewhat difficult since Epiphanius made use of the *Syntagma* as he composed the *Panarion*, and the *Epitome* in turn is based on *Pan*.

While Joseph probably relied on the *Syntagma* for the content found in his descriptions of certain heresies, it is in the order in which Joseph's heresies are presented that the influence of the *Syntagma* is most clearly evident. Apart from Joseph's insertions from Eusebius (Theudians, Egyptian magician, Ebionites, Nazôraioi), at the beginning of his catalogue he moves in lockstep with the order found in the *Adv. Haer.* and the *Epitome* through the heresy of the Nicolaitans (no. 10 in Joseph's list). At this point Joseph follows the sequence of the *Epitome* and makes an entry on the Gnostics (for which there is no equivalent in

---

against Epiphanius and Jerome, although it is questionable whether or not it is fair to label Epiphanius an Anthropomorphite. In this regard, one should also note that (a) Origen receives criticism from Joseph (§ 43 above), (b) Epiphanius himself attacked the Audians as Anthropomorphites in *Pan.* 70.2.4–8 (III 234 Holl), and (c) though he did come from Eleutheropolis [*Life* in Holl I 1,1–2] and later built a monastery there, he connected Archontic heretics with the area (*Pan.* 40.1.3). *Contra* Goranson, the notion that the Anthropomorphites of this passage are Audians is untenable. For more on this see the Introduction. Clark notes that the opponents of Anthropomorphism regarded it as a Jewish tendency.
[1] In C, each entry of this chapter uncharacteristically begins at the left margin of the column, and the item numbers appear in the gutter to the left of the column.

These then are the heresies that have arisen against the holy church, which has received and delivered by means of the Holy Spirit that our Lord Jesus Christ, "through whom all things came to be" [Jn 1:3][1] and was born of Maria the virgin after the flesh, and "lived among men"[2] of his own creating, is the same as he who "before all ages"[3] was with God the Father, begotten of the substance (*ousia*) of the Father, of the same substance (*homoousios*)[4] with God the Father. (186a)

*Adv. Haer.*). Then Joseph picks up the sequence of the *Adv. Haer.* for the next seventeen heresies (through the Phrygians; no. 28 in Joseph's list), not at all following the order of the *Epitome*. From this point Joseph follows the sequence of both the *Adv. Haer.* and the *Epitome* with roughly equal, but not complete, regularity as far as the list contained in the *Adv. Haer.* runs (Melchisedekians/ second Theodotus in next-to-last place [no. 34 in Joseph's list], followed by the puzzling final entry of the *Adv. Haer.* concerning Praxeas).

---

[1] The creed of Eusebius of Caesarea; Hans-Georg Opitz, ed., *Athanasius' Werke*, Vol. 3: *Urkunden zur Geschichte des arianischen Streites* (Berlin: DeGruyter, 1934) 43, 12).

[2] Again, the same creed, ibid. 43, 13; compare the comment of August Hahn, *Bibliothek der Symbole und Glaubensregeln der alten Kirche* (3rd ed., rev. L. Hahn, Breslau: Morgenstern, 1897) 132 n. 369: "frei gebildet" by Eusebius; maybe not.

[3] Opitz, *Athanasius' Werke*, 43, 11–12; Hahn, *Bibliothek*, 132, 2.

[4] The Nicene formula: Hahn, *Bibliothek* 161, 2.

## 306 Ὑπομνηστικὸν βιβλίον

[PM'.]‹**PMA'.**› + Ποῖαι αἱρέσεις παρὰ Ἰουδαίοις γεγόνασι;

α'[1] Φαρισαῖοι, ἑρμηνευόμενοι κεχωρισμένοι ἢ ἀφωρισμένοι, περὶ τὰ φυλακτήρια, καὶ καθαρμοὺς σωματικοὺς, καὶ βαπτισμοὺς ξεστῶν καὶ ἐπενάκων[2] ἠσχολημένοι.

β' Σαδδουκαῖοι, ἑρμηνευόμενοι δίκαιοι, νεκρῶν ἀνάστασιν ἀρνοῦνται, ἀγγέλους εἶναι οὐ λέγουσιν οὐδὲ Πνεῦμα Ἅγιον, οὐ πνεῦμα ἁγίων, ἢ ὅλως ἀνθρώπων, μετὰ τὴν ἀπὸ τοῦ σώματος ἔξοδον, οὐ κρίσιν τῶν πεπραγμένων ἀνθρώποις.

γ' Ἐσσηνοὶ, ἀκριβεῖς περὶ τὰ **(186a2)** νόμιμα, γάμου ἀπέχονται καὶ παιδοποιΐας, καὶ συναλλαγμάτων καὶ προόδων τῆς ἀνοήτου συντυχίας.

δ' Ἔστι δὲ καὶ ἄλλο τάγμα Ἐσσηνῶν, τὰ μὲν νόμιμα ὁμοίως τοῖς ἄλλοις ἀκριβοῦντες, γάμον δὲ καὶ παιδωποιΐαν οὐκ ἀρνούμενοι, ἀλλὰ καὶ τῶν[3] ἄλλων καταγινώσκοντες, ὅτι τὴν τοῦ γένους διαδοχὴν ἀποτέμνουσιν.

ε' Εἰσήχθη δὲ καὶ πέμπτη παρ' αὐτοῖς Ἰούδα τοῦ Γαλιλαίου αἵρεσις, ἀνθρώπων μηδένα κύριον ἢ δεσπότην καλεῖν ἀναπείθουσα, ἡ καὶ τὴν ἀπογραφὴν ἐπὶ Κυρίνου γεγενημένην κωλύουσα καταδέξασθαι.[4] **(186b1)**

[PMA'.]‹**PMB'.**› + Τίνες αἱρέσεις παρὰ Σαμαρείταις γεγόνασιν;[5]

Οἱ πρῶτοι Σαμαρεῖται Περσῶν ἄποικοι γεγόνασιν, εἰς τὴν τοῦ Ἰσραὴλ γῆν μετοικισθέντες ὑπὸ Σαλμανασάρου τοῦ Βαβυλωνίων βασιλέως, τὰ Μωσέως[6] νόμιμα καὶ περιτομὴν ἐκ τῆς Πεντατεύχου παρειληφότες, ἐπιμένοντες δὲ καὶ τῷ σεβασμίῳ τῶν πατρῴων καὶ Περσικῶν θεῶν. Γεγόνασι δὲ καὶ ἄλλαι τέσσαρες αἱρέσεις παρ' αὐτοῖς, Γορθηνῶν,[7] Σεβοαίων,[8] Ἐσσηνῶν, Δοσιθιανῶν.[9]

‹α'› Γορθηνοὶ[10] μὲν γὰρ κατὰ τὰς ἑορτὰς τοῖς ἄλλοις οὐ συμφωνοῦσιν, τὰς ἡμέρας αὐτῶν **(186b2)** ἐναλλάξαντες, καὶ ἔξω δὲ τῆς Σαμαρείας περὶ τὰς βρώσεις ἀδιαφοροῦσι.

---

[1]FGM do not number this first item.
[2]*Lc* FGM πινακων.
[3]GM omit των.
[4]In C, each entry of this chapter uncharacteristically begins at the left margin of the column, and the item numbers appear in the gutter to the left of the column.
[5]FGM γεγονασι.
[6]*Lc* FGM Μωϋσεως.
[7]Emend to Γοροθηνων.
[8]Emend to Σεβουαιων.
[9]*Lc* FGM Δοσιθεανων.
[10]Emend to Γοροθηνοι.

**141**. – What "heresies" [sects] existed among the Jews?

Pharisees, translated as "separated" or "set aside," concerned with phylacteries, cleansings of the body, and washings of cups and plates [*Epit.* 15 (I 167, 8, 16, 12–13)].

2. Sadducees, translated as "just," deny the resurrection of the dead, say there are no angels or Holy Spirit or spirits of the saints or of men in general after departure from the body, nor any judgment of what was been done by men [*Epit.* 16 (I 167, 21–23) and Ac 23:8].

3. Essenes are precise about the laws and abstain from marriage and procreation and from dealings and meetings due to blind chance [Josephus *War* 2.120–21].

4. There is another order of Essenes who similarly observe the laws yet do not reject marriage and procreation but despise the others because they cut off the succession of the race [Josephus*War* 2.160–61; *Ant.* 18.18].

5. A fifth [1] sect of Judas the Galilean was introduced among them, allowing them to call no man Lord or Master and prohibiting them to accept the census that took place under Quirinius (186b).[2]


**142**. – What "heresies" [sects] existed among the Samaritans?[3]

The first **Samaritans** were colonists **of the Persians**, sent to live in the land of Israel by **Salmanassaros** king of the Babylonians. They accept **the legislation of Moses and circumcision from the Pentateuch but continue in the cult of their ancestral Persian gods.** There were four other sects among them: Gor<o>thenes, Sebo<u>aeans, Essenes, and Dositheans [Josephus *Ant.* 9.288–90, 10.184]

<1> The **Gor<o>thenes** do not agree **with the others** as to the **festivals**, exchanging the days for others, and are indifferent toward diet when outside Samaria.[4]

---

[1] Fourth according to Josephus *Ant.* 18.23.

[2] Josephus *War* 2.118 with *Ant.* 18.23–25; Ac 5:37; Eusebius *HE* 1.6.3–6.

[3] On Samaritan sects, see Jarl Fossum, "Sects and Movements," in Alan D. Crown, ed., *The Samaritans* (Tübingen: J. C. B. Mohr, 1989) 293–389.

[4] The Gorothenes also appear in Theodoret of Cyrus' *Haereticarum fabularum compendium* 1.1 and in Sophronius.

‹β'› Σεβουαῖοι δὲ διαφέρονται μὲν πρὸς τοὺς Γορθηνοὺς[1] διὰ τὴν τῶν ἑορτῶν ἐναλλαγήν, τῆς δὲ Σαμαρείας οὐκ ἐξίασιν, ἀκαθάρτους ἡγούμενοι τοὺς ἀπὸ τῆς Σαμαρείας ἀποδημοῦντας.

‹γ'› Οἱ δὲ Ἐσσηνοὶ πρὸς οὐδένα διαφέρονται, ἀλλὰ καὶ προσίενται καὶ συσσιτοῦνται τοῖς ἔξωθεν, ὡς πρὸς αὐτοὺς ἐπιδημοῦσι.[2]

‹δ'› Δοσιδιανοὶ[3] δὲ ἀκριβέστεροι τῶν ἄλλων δοκοῦσιν εἶναι. Καὶ γὰρ ἐγκρατεύονται, καὶ παρθενίαν ἐπιτηδεύουσι, καὶ ἀνάστασιν γενήσεσθαι πιστεύουσιν.[4] **(187a1)**

[PMB'.] ‹**ΡΜΓ'.**› + Τίνες αἱρέσεις παρ' Ἕλλησι γεγόνασι;
‹α'› Ἡ περὶ τῶν Φυσικῶν.
‹β'› Ἡ περὶ Θεολογίας.
‹γ'› Ἡ περὶ τῶν ἑπτὰ Σοφῶν.
‹δ'› Ἡ Ἰσοκρατική.[5]
‹ε'› Ἡ Κυριναϊκή.
‹ϛ'› Ἡ Κυνική.
‹ζ'› Ἡ Ἡλιακή.
‹η'› Ἡ Αἱρετική.[6]
‹θ'› Μεγαρική.
‹ι› Πυθαγόρειος.
‹ια'› Ἐμπεδόκλειος.
‹ιβ'› Ἡρακλείτειος.
‹ιγ'› Ἐλεατική.

---

[1] Emend to Γοροθηνους.
[2] FGM ἐπιδημουσιν.
[3] FGM Δοσιθιανοι; emend to Δοσιθεανοι.
[4] The items in this chapter are unnumbered in CFGM.
[5] *Lc* FGM, who in their notes suggest emending to Σοκρατικη.
[6] *Lc* FGM, who in their notes suggest emending to Ἐρετριακη.

<2> The **Sebouaians differ with the Gor<o>thenians** because of the change of **the festivals**; they do not go outside Samaria, considering impure whoever goes outside Samaria.

<3> The **Essenes differ with no one** but allow outsiders to come in and eat common meals with them.

<4> The Dositheans seem to keep the law more carefully than the others, for they **observe continence, value virginity, and believe in future** (187a) **resurrection** [*Epit.* 10–13, I 166–167 Holl; mostly not].[1]

**143.** – What "heresies" [sects] existed among the Greeks?

<1> Physika.
<2> Theologia.[2]
<3> The seven wise men.[3]
<4> [I]Sokratiké [after teacher, Diogenes Laertius 1.17, p. 7, 7 Long].
<5> Kyrenaïké [after city, Diog. p. 7, 2].
<6> Kyniké [after taunts, Diog. p. 7, 5].
<7> Eleiaké [after city, Diog. p. 7, 2].
<8> [Hairetiké] <Eretriaké> [after city, Diog. p. 7, 2].
<9> Megariké [after city, Diog. p. 7, 2].
<10> Pythagoreios [after teacher, Simplicius].
<11> Empedokleios [after teacher].
<12> Herakleiteios [after teacher, cf. Diog. 9.5].
<13> Eleatiké [after city, Simplicius].

---

[1] Hegesippus (*Apud* Eusebius *HE* 6.22) claimed that the Dositheans existed as a sect in the first century C.E. Origen associates Simon Magus and Dositheus, saying that they both appeared "after the time of Jesus" (*Contra Celsum* 1.57) and "in the time of the Apostles" (*Commentarium in evangelium Matthaei* on 24:4). Additionally, the Pseudo-Clementines depict Simon Magus and Dositheus as rivals to the office left vacant by John the Baptist (*Homilies* 2.23 ff. and *Recognitions* 2.8 ff.).

[2] Sextus Empiricus discusses divisions of philosophy into two or three parts: the two, he says, have been called physics/logic (Xenophanes) or physics/ethics (Archelaus of Athens) or logic/ethics, while the three are physics/ethics/logic (*Adversus Mathematicos* 7.2–3, 14, 16) These divisions are not related to Joseph's list. But Sextus does not note that the Stoic Cleanthes had divided logic into dialectic and rhetoric, ethics into ethics and politics, and physics into physics and theology (Diogenes Laertius 7.41) while still earlier Aristotle had praised "theological philosophy," or metaphysics (*Met.* 1026a19). Joseph omits Cleanthes' first four divisions and keeps the last two as he tries to classify philosophies.

[3] These are listed e.g. in Plato *Protagoras* 343A, Plutarch *Banquet of the Seven Sages* 146B–164D, Diogenes Laertius 1.13 and Clement *Str.* 1.59.1; cf. *Laterculi Alexandrini* p. 9 (col. 8) Diels; Hyginus 221, pp. 144–45 Rose.

‹ιδ'› Δημοκρίτιος.[1]
‹ιε'› Πρωταγόρος.[2]
‹ις'› Περρονεία.[3]
‹ιζ'› Ἀκαδιμαϊκή.[4]
‹ιη'› Περιπατητική.
‹ιθ'› Στοϊκή.[5]
‹κ'› Ἐπικούριος.[6]

Ταύτας τὰς εἴκοσι αἱρέσεις Ἡρακλείδης ὁ Πυθαγορικὸς διεῖλεν, ἐν τῷ περὶ τῆς ἐν φιλοσόφοις αἱρέσεως[7] πραγματείας αὐτοῦ βιβλίῳ.[8] **(187a2)**

Diogenes Laertius, as we see, provides a list that includes schools named after cities (Elians, Megarians, Eretrians, Cyrenaics), places (Academics, Stoics), incidental circumstances (Peripatetics), derisive nicknames (Cynics), and teachers (Socratics, Epicureans). The sixth-century commentators on the *Categories* of Aristotle adhere closely to this pattern, listing seven derivations of the names: from (1) "heresiarchs," such as Pythagoras, Epicurus, Democritus, (2) places where they originated (Cyrene) or (3) taught (Stoa, Lyceum, Academy), (4) way of life (Cynics) and (5) type of philosophical judgment (Ephectic), (6) activity during teaching (Peripatetic), and (7) goal (pleasure for Hedonists).[9] The classification scheme dates back to the second century, for Clement of Alexandria used it in analyzing the varieties of Gnostic sects as

---

[1] *Lc* GM Δημοκριτειος.
[2] *Lc* FGM Πρωταγοριος.
[3] *Lc* FGM Πυῤῥονεια.
[4] *Lc* FGM Ἀκαδημαϊκη.
[5] FGM Στωϊκη.
[6] *Lc* FGM Ἐπικουρειος.
[7] *Lege* αἱρεσεων.
[8] The items in this chapter are unnumbered in CFGM.
[9] Ammonius (*Commentaria in Aristotelem Graeca* 4.4, p. 1, 13 Busse); Simplicius (*CAG* 8, p. 3,3 0 Kalbfleisch); Olympiodorus (*CAG* 12.1, p. 3, 8 Busse); Philoponus (*CAG* 13.1, p. 1, 19 Busse); Elias (*CAG* 18.1, p. 108, 15 Busse).

<14> Demokriteios [after teacher].
<15> Protagorios [after teacher].
<16> Pyrrhoneia [after teacher].
<17> Akadémaïké [after place, Diog. p. 7, 3].
<18> Peripatétiké [after activity, Diog. p. 7, 4; Simplicius].
<19> Stoïké [after place, Diog. p. 7, 3; Simplicius].
<20> Epikoureios [after teacher, Diog. p. 7,7][1] Herakleidés the Pythagorean discussed these twenty sects in his book *On the Systems of the Sect<s> among Philosophers*.

> contrasted with the one apostolic teaching and tradition. They were named after their teachers (Valentinus, Marcion, Basilides) or from a place (Peratics) or nation (Phrygians) or from their practice (Encratites) or from peculiar doctrines (Docetae, Haematitae) or from personages (?) they admire (Cainites and Ophites) or from their immoral behavior (Entychitae among the Simonians).[2]
>
> Joseph's list includes only a few names that go beyond these categories, and he seems not to preserve the point, which presumably indicated the origins of school names. The text was printed by both Usener and Diels.[3] Usener cites Diogenes Laertius 5.94 for the *Succession* (of philosophers) by Herakleides Lembos and 5.79 for the epitome by Sotion, possibly used here.[4] Joseph's theme is not succession, however, but subject matter.

---

[1] The passages come from Diogenes Laertius 1.17 and Simplicius; cf. Ritter-Preller, *Historia Philosophiae Graecae* (10th ed., Gotha: Klotz, 1934) 4–5; cf. Pseudo-Galen *History of Philosophy* 4, pp. 601, 20–602, 11 Diels; also the next note.

[2] Clement *Str.* 7.108. Haemititae *may* have been thought to use blood in their eucharists, while Entychitae were supposed to practice random sexual intercourse; cf. F.J.A. Hort–J.B. Mayor, *Clement of Alexandria Miscellanies Book VII* (London: Macmillan, 1902) 354–55.

[3] Hermann Usener, "Vergessenes, IX," *Rheinisches Museum* 28 (1873) 431; Hermann Diels, *Doxographi Graeci* (Berlin: De Gruyter, 1929) 149–53.

[4] Usener, "Vergessenes," 431. Cf. Daebritz, "Herakleides (47) der Pythagoriker," *PWRE* 8 (1912) 487. He identifies this Herakleides, perhaps originally called a Peripatetic, with the Herakleides Lembos who wrote on philosophers (*PWRE* 8, 488–91).

[ΡΜΓ΄.] ⟨ΡΜΔ΄⟩. + ῞Οσαι εἰσὶ μαντεῖαι παρ᾽ ῞Ελλησιν;
⟨α᾽⟩ ᾽Αστρονομική.
⟨β᾽⟩ Γενεθλιακή.
⟨γ᾽⟩ ᾽Ονειροσκοπική.
⟨δ᾽⟩ Οἰονιστική.[1]
⟨ε᾽⟩ Συμβουλική.
⟨ς᾽⟩ ᾽Αρθρική.[2]
⟨ζ᾽⟩ ῾Η διὰ κλήρων.
⟨η᾽⟩ ῾Η δι᾽ ἀστραγάλων.
⟨θ᾽⟩ ῾Η διὰ πεμπύρων.[3]
⟨ι᾽⟩ ῾Η διὰ λαχμῶν.
⟨ια᾽⟩ Θυτικὴ ζώων.
⟨ιβ᾽⟩ ᾽Ωοσκοπική.
⟨ιγ᾽⟩ ῾Η διὰ τεράτων.
⟨ιδ᾽⟩ ῾Η κατ᾽ ἐνθουσίασιν.

---

[1] *Lc* F Οἰωνιστικη; GM mistakenly print Οἰωνικη.

[2] F reports knowledge of another copy of the *Hypomnestikon* which has ᾽Αθρικη at this point (an error in an apograph of C?). He also mentions Gale's proposed emendation to Αἰθρικης. GM abbreviate F's note.

[3] *Lc* GM, who in their notes suggest emending to ἐμπυρων.

### <DIVINATIONS>

**144.** – How many divinations are there among the Greeks?[1]
[Words in **boldface** come from Porphyry as corroborated by Iamblichus; references are to the edition by Sodano]

<1> *Astronomiké*, astrological.[2]
<2> *Genethliaké*, based on nativities.[3]
<3> *Oneiroskopiké*: interpretation of dreams.[4]
<4> *Oiônistiké*, augury.[5]
<5> *Symbo[u]liké*, divination.
<6> *Arthriké*, joints.
<7> Through *kléroi*, lots.
<8> Through *astragaloi*, dice.
<9> Through *pempyroi* (*empyroi*), fire.[6]
<10> Through *lachmoi*, lots.
<11> *Thytiké zôôn*, animal sacrifices.[7]
<12> *Ôoskopiké*, inspection of eggs.
<13> Through *teratoi*, prodigies.[8]
<14> In accordance with *enthousiasis*, frenzy or ecstatic utterance.[9]

---

[1] Cf. Theodor Hopfner, "Mantike," *PWRE* 14 (1928) 1258–88; Konrad Kinzl, "Mantik," *KP* 3 (1969) 968–76; Wolfgang Fauth, "Orakel," *KP* 4 (1972) 324–25 (Orakel-Arten); ancient treatises: Cicero *Divination* 1–2, Iamblichus *Mysteries* (abbreviated *Myst.*) 3.

[2] Cf. movement of stars, Iamblichus *Mysteries* (hereafter *Myst.*) 3.15, p. 135, 4–5 Parthey; 8.6, p. 268, 14; Porphyry *To Anebo* p. 11, 4 in Angelo R. Sodano (*Porfirio Lettera ad Anebo* [Naples: Arte Tipografica, 1958]). Abraham divined by the shooting stars, Julian *Against Galilaeans* 356C (Cyril of Jerusalem called this *astrologiai*, *Cat.* 4.37, PG 33, 501A).

[3] Iamblichus defends *genethlialogia*, *Myst.* 9.1 (p. 273, 6); 9.5 (p. 279, 12).

[4] Cf. C. 129; used by Jews, Julian *Against Galilaeans* 339E–340A.

[5] Plato *Phaedrus* 244A; reliable, Plutarch *Cleverness of Animals* 975A; false, Galen *De praenotione ad Epigenem* 3 (14.615 Kühn); Cyril *Against Julian* (PG 76, 804B). Cf. Theodor Hopfner, *Griechisch-ägyptischer Offenbarungszauber* 2.1 (Amsterdam: Hakkert, 1983) 183. Abraham's use of augury, Julian *Against Galilaeans* 356C, 358D.

[6] Cyril *Against Julian* (PG 76, 804B).

[7] Animals, Augustine *City of God* 10.11 (from Porphyry *To Anebo*); cf. Galen 14.615; *thytiké* = *hieroskopia*, rejected by Porphyry *Abstinence* 2.50 (p. 177, 2 Nauck, 2d ed.). Julian consulted *thytai* in his youth at Athens (Gregory Nazianzen, PG 35, 692A).

[8] False *teratoskopoi*, Plato *Laws* 933 A, C; Cyril *Against Julian* (PG 76, 804B); Gregory Nazianzen *Against Julian* (*terateia*, PG 35, 693C).

[9] Plato *Phaedrus* 249e, *Myst.* 3.6 (p. 114, 1).

‹ιε›› Ἡ κατ᾽ εἴσκρισίν τινος ἐπιπνοίας.
‹ις›› Ἡ διὰ κληδόνων.
‹ιζ›› Ἡ διά τινος ἐπιπνοίας.[1]
‹ιη›› Ἡ διὰ φήμης.
‹ιθ›› Ἡ διὰ πανικοῦ κινήματος.
‹κ›› Ἡ διὰ μορφοσκοπίας.
‹κα›› Ἡ διὰ χειροσκοπίας.
‹κβ›› Ἡ διὰ πιττακίων ὑπὸ σφραγίδα πιπτόντων.
‹κγ›› Ἡ διὰ κοσκίνου.
‹κδ›› Ἡ διὰ (187b1) λεκάνης μαγικῆς.
‹κε›› Ἡ ἐν φιάλῃ.
‹κς›› Ἡ διὰ κλήσεως αὐτοπτικῆς.
‹κζ›› Ἡ διὰ ψυχοπομπίας.
‹κη›› Ἡ διὰ τῶν ζυγοφορουμένων ἀγαλμάτων.
‹κθ›› Ἡ δι᾽ αὐλῶν.
‹λ›› Ἡ διὰ συμβόλων.
‹λα›› Ἡ διὰ κυμβάλων.
‹λβ›› ‹Ἡ διὰ τυμπάνων› καὶ ‹ὀργάνου› παντὸς μουσικοῦ.[2]
‹λγ›› Ἡ διὰ σαβαζίων. Μυρίζοντες.[3]
‹λδ›› Ἄλλοι κατὰ τὸ φανταστικὸν θυάζουσιν.[4]

---

[1] According to GM: "Hæc videtur temere inserta."

[2] C Ἡ δια κυμβαλων και παντος μουσικου. Lc the emendation of FGM based on Porphyry's *Letter to Anebo* 9, 11-12 (ed. Sodano): Ἡ δια κυμβαλων. Ἡ δια τυμπανων και οργανου παντος μουσικου.

[3] In his notes, F suggests Οἱ δια Σαβαζίου, οἱ μητριζοντες. In their notes, GM suggest Οἱ δια Σαβαζιου μητριζοντες. Emend to Οἱ κοπυβαντιζομενοι και οἱ δια Σαβαζιου κατοιχοι και οἱ μητριζοντες. See *Myst.* 3.9 (=*Anebo* 9.13-14).

[4] Lc FGM θειαζουσιν (and *Anebo* 10, 13).

<15> In accordance with *eiskrisis tinos epipnoias* (penetration of some inspiration).[1]

<16> Through *klédones*, omens.[2]

<17> Through some *epipnoias*, inspiration.

<18> Through *phémé*, chance words.[3]

<19> Through *panic* movement.[4]

<20> Through *morphoskopia*, observing forms.

<21> Through *cheiroskopia*, palmistry.

<22> Through *pittakion hypo sphragida piptonton*, list of those falling under the seal.

<23> Through *koskinos*, sifting.

<24> Through (187b) *lekané magiké*, magic basin.[5]

<25> *En phialé*, bowl.

<26> Through *klésis autoptiké*, a personal and active invocation.[6]

<27> Through *psychopompia*, the guiding of souls.[7]

<28> Through *zygophoroumenon agalmaton*, weighed images.[8]

<29> Through **lyres** [*Anebo* 9.11].

<30> Through auspices.[9]

<31> Through **cymbals**.

<32> or **tympani** or every **musical instrument** [*Anebo* 9,10–12].

<33> <Corybants and those possessed> through [**Sabazii**] <Sabazius> [*myrizontes*, anointing] <kai *métrizontes*, and possessed by the Mother of the gods> [*Anebo* 9,13–14; also see item 53].

<34>Others **are inspired according to the vision** [*Anebo* 10,13].

---

[1] Inspiration (Plato *Laws* 811C); *epipnoia thaumasia*, *Myst*. 3.11 (p. 127, 16–17); *epipnoia* of Pan, 3.10 (p. 122, 5.)

[2] Cf. Cyril of Jerusalem *Cat*. 4.37 (PG 33, 501A).

[3] *Sonis certis quibusdam ac vocibus*, Augustine *City of God* 10.11 (from Porphyry *To Anebo*).

[4] Cf. disordered and troubled movements, *Myst*. 3.24 (p. 156, 11).

[5] Cf. Ptolemaeus *Tetrabiblos* 181; Strabo 16.2.39.

[6] Cf. *deixis*, *Myst*. 2.6 (p. 82, 16–17).

[7] Not Iamblichus, but *psychopompoi* in Porphyry *Cave of the Nymphs* 8 (p. 61, 19 Nauck, 2d ed.); Gregory Nazianzen claims Julian dissected children for *psychagôgia* (PG 35, 692A).

[8] Cf. Artemidorus 2.37.

[9] *Myst*. 2.11 (p. 96, 19); 4.2 (p. 184, 11–12.)

⟨λε'⟩ Ἄλλοι σκότος συνεργὸν λαμβάνοντες.
⟨λς'⟩ Ἄλλοι καταπόσεις.
⟨λζ'⟩ Οἱ δὲ ἐπῳδὰς καὶ συστάσεις.
⟨λη'⟩ Ἄλλοι εἰς ὕδωρ φαντάζονται.
⟨λθ'⟩ Οἱ δὲ ἐν τοίχῳ.
⟨μ'⟩ Οἱ δὲ ἐν ὑπέθρῳ¹ ἀέρι.
⟨μα'⟩ Ἄλλοι ἐν ἡλίῳ, καὶ ἐν τοῖς ἄλλοις, (187b2) τοῖς κατ' οὐρανῶν ἄστροις.
⟨μβ'⟩ Οἱ δὲ διὰ σπλάγχνων.
⟨μγ'⟩ Οἱ δὲ δι' ὀρνίθων.²
⟨μδ'⟩ Οἱ δὲ δι' ἀλφίτων.
⟨με'⟩ Ἄλλοι διὰ τῆς φυσικῆς παρατηρήσεως φθανούσης.
⟨μς'⟩ Ἄλλοι ἐπὶ ζώων παραλλαγὰς, ἢ φυτῶν.
⟨μζ'⟩ Οἱ δὲ δι' ἀριθμῶν.
⟨μη'⟩ Οἱ δὲ διὰ τῆς φυσιογνωμονικῆς.
⟨μθ'⟩ Ἔστι δὲ³ καὶ ἐπιβολὴ ἐνθουσιαστικὴ, καὶ ἐπιβολὴ θεοφορίας.

⟨ν'⟩ Χριστήρια⁴ δὲ διαβόητα παρ' αὐτοῖς ἐστί· τὰ ἐν τοῖς ναοῖς βαιτύλια, διὰ λίθων ἐν τοῖς στοιχείοις προσρασσόντων.

⟨να'⟩ Ἐν Αἰγύπτῳ τὸ Βονὶ,⁵ ὄργανόν τι τρίγωνον ἐναρμώνιον,⁶ ᾧ χρῶνται οἱ ἱεροψάλται ἐν (188a1) τοῖς κώμοις πλεκτριζόμενοι.

⟨νβ'⟩ Ἔξ ἄκαρ αἱ τῆς Ἑστίας παρθένοι· ἱερουργοῦσαι λέγουσι καὶ αὐταὶ τὸ μέλλον, ἀσπέτῳ περιτεκμηρόμεναι.⁷

⟨νγ'⟩ Οἵ τε παρὰ τῷ Διονύσῳ διὰ Κορυβαντιῶν κορυβαντιζόμενοι.

---

¹ *Lc* FGM ὑπαιθρῳ.
² FGM δια ὀρνιθων.
³ FGM omit δε.
⁴ *Lc* FGM Χρηστηρια.
⁵ In their notes FGM suggest emending to Βυνι or (following Gale) to Βουνι.
⁶ *Lc* FGM ἐναρμονιον.
⁷ *Lc* FGM, who in their notes suggest emending to ἀσβεστῳ πυρι τεκμηρομεναι.

<35> **Others take darkness as an aid,**

<36> **others potions,**

<37> **others incantations and communications,**

<38> **others appear in water,**

<39> **others on a wall,** [1]

<40> **others in the open air,**

<41> **others in the sun and other stars of the heaven** [*Anebo* 10,13–16]. [2]

<42> Some established the art **through entrails,**

<43> **through birds** [*Anebo* 11,3], [3]

<44> through **barley-groats** [cf. *Anebo* 11,11]; [4]

<45> Others through observation of nature beforehand; [5]

<46> Others from the alterations (*parallagas*) of animals or plants; [6]

<47> Through numbers; [7]

<48> through *physiognomiké*, study of human features.

<49> There is both an **enthusiastic** impetus and an accession of **inspiration** [*Anebo* 9,6]. [8]

<50> Famous oracles among them: *baitylia* in temples, animate stones colliding in the air. [9]

<51> In Egypt is the triangular musical instrument *boni* (harp), used by temple-singers who pluck it at (188a) the revels. [10]

<52> Six Vestal virgins they say celebrate rites and judge the future by the endless <fire>. [11]

<53> Others serve Dionysus through Corybantic rites,

---

[1] Hopfner, *Offenbarungszauber*, 521.

[2] *Myst.* 3.14 (p. 132, 3–8); 3.15 (p. 135, 4).

[3] *Myst.* 3.15 (p. 135, 4); *orneoskopiai*, Cyril of Jerusalem *Cat.* 4.37 (PG 33, 501A).

[4] Cf. *alphitomanteis*, Cyril *Against Julian* (PG 76, 804B); *Myst.* 3.17 (p. 139, 13); *alphita* (p. 141, 14).

[5] Cf. *Myst.* 10.7 (p. 288, 7–8).

[6] Cf. *theia parallaxis*, *Myst.* 3.9 (p. 116, 15).

[7] Through numbers, Hippolytus *Refutation* 4.14.1.

[8] *Myst.* 3.4, p. 109, 6.

[9] For these meteoric stones, Hopfner, *Offenbarungszauber*, 520–21; Karl Tümpel, "Baitylia," *PWRE* 2 (1896) 2779–81; wolfgang Fauth, "Baitylia," *KP* 1 (1964) 806–8.

[10] The hieroglyphic *bnt* means "harp" (Alan Gardiner, *Egyptian Grammar* (ed. 3, London: Oxford University Press, 1973) 614 (M. H. Grant).

[11] Six, Plutarch *Numa* 10.1; perpetual fire, ibid. 9.5, 11.1.

‹νδ'› Ἐν δὲ Κωλοφωνίῳ ἱερεὺς τοῦ Κλαρίου ὕδωρ πίνων, ἔλεγεν ἑκάστῳ περὶ οὗ καὶ ἀφῖκτο.

‹νε'› Ἐν Δελφοῖς δὲ θεσπίζουσιν αἱ γυναῖκες ἐν τοῖς στομίοις τοῦ ὕδατος¹ παρακαθήμεναι.

‹νϛ'› Καὶ ἐν Βραχεῖ² δὲ πάλιν ἐξ ὑδάτων ἀτμιζόμεναι χρισμολογοῦσιν.³

Ἐπὶ χαρακτήρων⁴ δὲ στάντες πληροῦνται τῶν ἀπηγκρίσεων⁵ (188a2) ἔν τισι ναοῖς τοῦ Ἀπόλλωνος.⁶

‹νζ'› Ἡ δὲ Ποιθεία⁷ ἐπὶ τοῦ τρίποδος ἀσχημόνως ἐπικαθημένη, διὰ τῶν γυναικείων πόρων⁸ τὰς μαντικὰς εἰσκρίσεις ὑποδέχεται.

Porphyry certainly referred to Delphic prophetesses as giving mantic responses when seated at the mouth of a grotto (*Anebo* 10, 2–3).⁹ Iamblichus' statement about the tripod probably comes from Porphyry too, though his mention of illumination as by fire is probably his own.¹⁰

Did Porphyry think that she was penetrated by a spirit or demon? Strabo already says she received a *pneuma enthousiastikon* from beneath, but with no mention of sex.¹¹ The sexual emphasis appears in the Christian author Origen,¹² from whom Porphyry,¹³ as reflected in Joseph, presumably derived it — not the other way round, for Porphyry was only fifteen when Origen's *Against Celsus*

---

¹ Emend ὕδατος to ἀδύτου, following Sodano (*Lettera ad Anebo*, 10).

² *Lc* FGM, who in their notes suggest emending to Βραγχιδαις.

³ *Lc* FGM χρησμολογουσιν.

⁴ FGM χαρακτηριων.

⁵ *Lc* FGM πληρουνται των ἀπεγκρισεων, although *Anebo* 10, 11 reads: πληρουμενοι ἀπο εἰσκρισεων.

⁶ In his edition of *Myst.*, Angelo R. Sodano (*Giamblico I misteri egiziani* [Milan: Rusconi, 1984] p. 129, 14-15) suggests deleting the words ἐν τισι ναοις του Ἀπολλωνος because they are not found in *Myst*. 3, 13.

⁷ *Lc* FGM Πυθια.

⁸ In their notes FGM follow Gale in suggesting μοριων as an alternative to πορων.

⁹ *Myst*. 3.11 (p. 123, 13–14).

¹⁰ *Myst*. 3.11 (p. 126, 4–127, 2).

¹¹ Strabo 9.3.6, 419; cf. Cicero *Divination* 1.38, 79; 2.117 (*anhelitus terrae*) with Arthur S. Pease, *M.Tulli Ciceronis De Divinatione* I (Urbana IL: University of Illinois, 1920) 160–61.

¹² *Against Celsus* 3.25 (*pneuma dia tôn gynaikeiôn*); 7.3 (*dechetai pneuma dia tôn gynaikeiôn porôn*), cf. 7.5.

¹³ Porphyry's knowledge of the Christian Origen: Eusebius *HE* 6.19.5–8.

<54> and **the priest of the Clarian** (Apollo) **in Colophon, drinking water** [*Anebo* 10,1–2], spoke to each what he came to ask about.[1]

<55> **At Delphi women prophesy at the mouth** of the grotto [*Anebo* 10,2–3],

<56> and **at Branchidae** again, they **give oracles with vapor from the waters** [*Anebo* 10,3–4].[2]

Others relying on magical symbols (*charaktéres*) are filled with responses (in some temples of Apollo) [*Anebo* 10,10].[3]

<57> The Pythia sitting indecently on the tripod receives the mantic responses through her female passages (*porôn*).

> appeared. Indeed, Iamblichus claims that the "atheists," that is, Christian authors, had taught Porphyry that all divination was performed by "the evil demon."[4]   In turn, John Chrysostom relied on Porphyry, whom he had just used anonymously for Delphic oracles.[5] He apologized for his description, but he insisted that his hearers had to learn of pagan shame, and added, "I know you felt shame and blushed when you heard this." The Pythia "is said to have sat" on the tripod and spread her legs; then a wicked spirit (*pneuma ponéron*) was given forth from below and entered through her genital organs and filled her with madness; she loosed her hair, became a Bacchant, and emitted foolishness from her mouth."[6]

---

[1] Cf. Origen *Against Celsus* 7.3 (Pythia, Dodona, Clarian Apollo, Branchidae [Apollo at Didyma], Zeus Ammon). Chadwick, *Origen Contra Celsum* (Cambridge: Cambridge University Press, 1953) 396 n. 1, notes Strabo 17.1.43, 813–14 (Zeus Ammon, Sibyl, Delphi, Branchidae) and Lucian *Alexander* 8 (Delphi, Delos, Claros, Branchidae).

[2] *Myst*. 3.11 (p. 123, 12–124, 1 ): "Those who drink water, like the priest of the Clarian at Colophon; those who sit at the mouths, like the women who prophesy at Dephi; those with vapor from the waters, like the prophetesses in Branchidae."

[3] *Anebo* 10,10; Sodano deletes the bracketed words, not found in *Myst*. 3.13 (p. 129, 14–15).

[4] *Myst*. 3.31 (p. 179, 12–14: *ponéros daimón*).

[5] *Homily* 1.29 on 1 Corinthians (PG 61, 241D–242A); cf. Gustav Wolff, *Porphyrii De Philosophia ex oraculis* (Hildesheim: Olms, 1962) 162, 164, from Eusebius *Gospel Preparation* 5.9. For Chrysostom and philosophers cf. Derek Krueger, "Diogenes the Cynic," *VC* 47 (1993) 37–39.

[6] For John's viewpoint, cf. Blake Leyerle, "John Chrysostom on the Gaze," *Journal of Early Christian Studies* 1 (1993) 159–74.

Gregory Nazianzen is vaguer. "The Pythia is filled no longer, I know not with what but myth and nonsense."[1] In fact the description is entirely false. There was no grotto

‹νη'› Πολλὰ δὲ ἐν πλείοσι ναοῖς καὶ διὰ καμπιδῶν ψήφων[2] ἀποκρινόντων συνέστη μαντεία, τοῦ νεωκόρου τὴν ψῆφον ἐφορῶντος, καὶ ἀπὸ βιβλίου τὸν χρισμὸν[3] ἀναγινώσκοντος. Καὶ καθὼς Πορφύριος ἐν τῇ πρὸς Ἀνέβοντά φησιν ἐπιστολῇ· Πολλοῖς γὰρ ὁ γύρτης[4] καὶ τῷ κεχηνότι τῆς προσδοκίας ὑμῶν[5] ἐπιθέμενος.[6]

Porphyry addressed his lost *Letter* against divination and theurgy to the Egyptian priest Anebo (Iamblichus), while Iamblichus answered it directly in his treatise *On the Mysteries of the Egyptians*, where some fragments of the lost work can be found or inferred. Christians who used it include Eusebius,[7] Theodoret (from Eusebius), Augustine (*City of God* 10.11), Cyril of Alexandria (PG 76, 691–92: one fragment from Eusebius, the other from Porphyry), and our Joseph.[8]

Deuteronomy (18:10–11) had already denounced anyone who purifies his son or daughter with fire, does divination or augury or casts spells with drugs, a ventriloquist and a interpreter of prodigies, making requests of the dead. The Jewish commentator Philo reiterates much of the condemnation (*Special Laws* 1.60; 4.48), as do the early Christian *Didache* (3.4) and Clement of Alexandria (*Exhortation* 11.2).

---

[1] *Against Julian* 2 (PG 35, 704C). On Gregory's invectives, see Jean Bernardi, "Un réquisitoire: Les invectives contre Julien de Grégoire de Nazianze," *L'empereur Julien: De l'histoire à la légende* (Paris: Belles Lettres, 1978) 89–98.

[2] In their notes FGM suggest the emendation first proposed by Gale: replacing καμπιδων ψηφων with καλπιδων και ψηφων.

[3] *Lc* FGM χρησμον.

[4] *Lc* FGM γαρ ἀγυρτης.

[5] *Lc* FGM ἡμων.

[6] The items in this chapter are not numbered in CFG, although M numbers them.

[7] *Gospel Preparation* 3.4.1–2; 5.7.3; 5.10.1–11; 14.10.1–2.

[8] Cf. Sodano, *Letter to Anebo*, xli–xlix; Gustav Parthey, *Jamblichi De Mysteriis Liber* (Berlin: Nicolai, 1857); Edouard des Places, *Jamblique Les mystères d'Égypte* (Paris, 1966), with pages of Parthey; and Sodano, *Giamblico*.

with holes for the emission of gases, and the tripod was supported by a column 25 feet high, later taken to Constantinople by Constantine and still partly extant near the Blue Mosque. [1]

<58> Many persons in many temples do divination with urns and boxes [2] of pebbles with answers, with the guardian of the temple inspecting the lot and reading the oracle from a book, and as Porphyry says in the *Letter to Anebo*, [3] "For a begging priest (*agyrtés*) applies himself to our expectant look with many examples" [*Anebo* 17,7–8]. [4]

In the second century Artemidorus (*Oneirocriticon* 2.69, p. 195,12–15 and 19–22 Pack) listed false and true diviners thus (we add sections of Joseph): (a) false: *Pythagorists* (followers of Pythagoras), *physiognômikoi* (feature-interpreters, 48), *astragalomanteis* (dice-diviners, 8), *tyromanteis* (cheese-diviners), *koskinomanteis* (sieve-diviners, 23), *morphoskopoi* (shape-interpreters, 20), *cheiroskopoi* (palmists, 21), *lekanomanteis* (dish-diviners, 24), *nekyomanteis* (necromancers, cf. 27); (b) true: *thytoi* (diviners, 11), *oiônistoi* (augurs, 4), *asteroskopoi* (astrologers, 1), *teratoskopoi* (prodigy-interpreters, 13), *oneirokritai* (dream-interpreters, 3), *hépatoskopoi* (liver-interpreters, 42); but (c) *genethlialogoi* (nativity-casters, 2) *mathématikoi* (astrologers, 1) present a problem.

---

[1] Jean-François Bommelaer–Didier Laroche, *Guide de Delphes: Le Site* (École Française d'Athènes, 1991), 165–66; also 30–32 and 179; Courby, *Fouilles de Delphes* 2.1 (École Française d'Athènes, 1915) 63–65; Leicester B. Holland, "The Mantic Mechanism at Delphi," *American Journal of Archaeology* 37 (1933) 201–19; Robert Flacelière, "Le délire de la Pythie est-il une légende?" *Revue des Études Anciennes* 52 (1950) 306–24; Vincenzo Cilento, "L'oracolo degli uomini," *La Parola del Passato* 6 (1951) 161–81; Herbert W. Parke, *Greek Oracles* (London: Hutchinson, 1967) 77–78; Wolfgang Fauth, "Orakel," *KP* 4 (1972) 326–27 (on Delphi). Cf. also Sodano, *Giamblicho*, 299–300.

[2] Reading *kalpidôn* for *kampidôn* with Gale.

[3] Theodor Hopfner, *Griechisch-Ägyptischer Offenbarungszauber* 2.2 (Amsterdam: Hakkert, 1990) 471–85.

[4] Iamblichus apparently has Porphyry in mind as one who reviles the servants of gods as *agyrteis* (*Myst.* 10.3, p. 287, 6–9). This is Platonic language: cf. *agyrteis kai manteis* (seers), Plato *Republic* 364b. For *agyrteis*, see C. 74 on Solomon's magic.

[ΡΜΔ'.] ‹ΡΜΕ'.› + Διατί οἱ Ἰουδαῖοι τὴν (188b1) δευτέραν τῶν σαββάτων καὶ τὴν πέμπτην νηστεύουσι;[1]

‹α'› Δευτέρα σαββάτου ἐτύγχανεν εἶναι, ὅτε ὁ ναὸς ὑπὸ τοῦ Ναβουχοδονόσορ τὸ πρότερον [ὅτε][2] ἐνεπρήσθη.

‹β'› Πέμπτη δέ, ὅτε ὑπὸ Τίτου τὸ δεύτερον ἔπαθε. Πενθοῦσι γὰρ ἐπὶ τῇ ἐμπρήσει τοῦ ναοῦ κατὰ ταύτας τὰς δύο κατὰ πᾶν σάββατον ἡμέρας, καὶ διὰ τοῦτο νηστεύουσι.[3]

[ΡΜΕ'.] ‹ΡΜϜ'.› + Διὰ τί οἱ Χριστιανοὶ τὴν τετράδα καὶ παρασκευὴν νηστεύουσι;[4]

‹α'› Τετράδι τοῦ σαββάτου Ἰούδας ὁ προδότης τὴν τοῦ διαβόλου τῆς προδοσίας ἐνέργειαν ὑπεδέξατο, (188b2) τοὺς λ' χρυσοῦς παρὰ Καϊάφαν[5] καὶ Ἄννα κομισάμενος.

‹β'› Τῇ δὲ παρασκευῇ τὴν τῆς προδοσίας πρᾶξιν ἐπετέλεσεν. Ἐν ᾗ ἡμέρᾳ καὶ τὸ σωτηριόκοσμον[6] πάθος ὁ Κύριος ὑπέμεινε. Κατὰ δὲ τὴν τῶν δύο ἡμερῶν τούτων περίοδον ἀλλοτριοῦνται μὲν οἱ Χριστιανοὶ τῆς τοῦ διαβόλου πράξεως, οἰκειοῦνται δὲ διὰ τῶν νηστειῶν τῷ σωτηριοκόσμῳ[7] πάθει Χριστοῦ.[8]

[ΡΜϜ'.] ‹ΡΜΖ'.› + Τίνα ἔθνη καὶ πόσα ἐκ τοῦ Ἀβραὰμ συνέστη;

Πρῶτον τὸ ἐκ τῆς Ἅγαρ καὶ τοῦ Ἰσμαὴλ, Ἀγαρηνοὶ καὶ Ἰσμαηλῖταί εἰσιν, οἱ ψευδοσαρακηνοὶ κικλησκόμενοι, (189a1) ἑαυτοῖς ἐπιφημίζοντες τὴν ἀπὸ τῆς Σάρρας, οὐκ ὄντες ἐξ αὐτῆς, ἐπωνυμίαν.

---

[1] FGM νηστευουσιν.
[2] Lc FGM, who omit ὅτε.
[3] The items in this chapter are not numbered in CFGM.
[4] FGM νηστευουσιν.
[5] Lc FGM Καϊαφα.
[6] Lc FGM κοσμοσωτηριον.
[7] Lc FGM κοσμοσωτηριῳ.
[8] The items in this chapter are not numbered in CFGM.

## <FASTING (145–46)>

**145**. – Why do the Jews fast the (188b) second of the week (Monday) and the fifth (Thursday)?

<1> The second of the week was when the Temple was first burned by Nabouchadonosor.

<2> The fifth was when it suffered again under Titus. For they mourn over the burning of the Temple on these two days every week, and therefore fast.[1]

**146**. – Why do Christians fast the fourth day (Wednesday) and the Preparation (Friday)?[2]

<1> On the fourth day of the week [Mt 26:2–5] Judas the traitor gave place to the working of the devil [Jn 13:2] for betrayal, having accepted thirty pieces of gold[3] from Kaiaphas and Annas [cf. Lk 3:2, Ac 4:6; C. 2].

<2> On the day of preparation [Jn 19:14] he performed the act of betrayal, on the day when the Lord endured his world-saving passion. On these two days Christians profess themselves alien to the action of the devil and appropriate the world-saving passion of Christ through the fasts.

**147**. – What nations and how many arose from Abraam?

First from Agar and Ismaél were born the Agarénoi and the Ismaélites, falsely called Sarakénoi (189a), who devoted the name of Sarra to themselves, though they were not from her.[4]

---

[1] Cf. C. 127. Josephus (*War* 6.250) says only that both fires took place on the 10th of the month Lous (cf. Jer 52:12–13). Capture by Sossius same day as by Pompeius (Josephus *Ant*. 14.487).

[2] For these fasts cf. Clement *Str*. 7.75.2; contrast with Jewish fasts, *Didache* 8.1, *Apostolic Constitutions* 7.23 (Funk 1.408), *b. Ta'an.* 12a.

[3] Gold rather than silver also in C. 79; by mistake both places.

[4] Sarakénoi probably refers to Nabataeans (Nabatean Arabs) from Ismaél's son Nabaiôth, Josephus *Ant*. 1.221. In C. 24 Joseph distinguishes Arabs from Sarakénoi. Epiphanius too refers to "Agarénoi who are also Ismaélites, now called Sarakénoi" (*Pan*. 4.1.7; not mentioned in the *Epitome*). This passage could suggest that Joseph is later than the seventh century; cf. John of Damascus *Her*. 101 (PG 94, 764A): "The Ismaélites are descended from Ismaél, born of Agar to Abraam....They call them Sarakénoi as "empty (*kenoi*) from Sarra...'Sarra released me empty' [Gn 21:15?]" — a reference to Muslims. But the tradition that accords Ismaél rather than Isaac the place of honor in the story of Abraham and his family was borrowed from Nabatean traders, not invented by Mohammed, and it is not necessary to regard this passage as anti-Muslim polemic. For additional comments, see the Introduction.

Δεύτερον τὸ Ἰσμαηλιτικὸν,[1] ἀπὸ τοῦ Ἰσραὴλ, ὅ[2] ἐστιν Ἰακὼβ, ἐπικληθεὶς δὲ, Ἰσραὴλ ὠνομαζόμενος.[3]

‹γ'› Καὶ ἀπὸ Χεττούρας[4] ἔθνη γεγόνασι τοῦ[5] Ἀβραὰμ γ', τὸ Σαβᾶ, ὅ ἐστι τὸ Αἰθιόπων, καὶ τὸ Μαδιανιτῶν, οἵ εἰσιν οἱ πρὸς τοῖς Αἰθίοψιν. Οἱ Ἐξομῖται, καὶ οἱ τούτοις πρόσοικοι.

‹δ'› Καὶ τὸ Δεδανιτῶν, ἔθνος δέ ἐστι τοῦτο, ἐξ οὗ καὶ Ἰόθορ, ὁ τοῦ Μωϋσέως γαμβρὸς, καὶ οἱ Φαρανῖται τὴν κατοίκησιν ἔχοντες, καὶ ἄγονται πρὸς (189a2) τῇ Ἐρυθρᾷ θαλάσσῃ.

‹ε'› Ἀλλὰ καὶ ἡ Συρία, Δαμασκὸς[6] δέ ἐστιν αὕτη, τὸ ἔθνος αὐτῷ λελόγισται. Ἐκ γὰρ τοῦ οἰκογενοῦς αὐτοῦ, τοῦ Ἐλιέζερ, ἐξ οὗπερ ὁ Δαμασκὸς τίκτεται, καὶ αὐτὴ συνίσταται.

‹ϛ'› Ἀπὸ δὲ τοῦ Ἡσαῦ, ὃς ἔκγονος τῷ[7] Ἀβραὰμ γεγόνει, τὸ Ἰδουμαῖον ἔθνος ἕτερον ἀναφαίνεται, ὃ καὶ Ἐδὼμ προσαγορεύεται.

‹ζ'› Οὐκ ἔξωθε[8] δὲ τῶν ἐξ αὐτῶν[9] φύντων ἐθνῶν, οὐδὲ τὸ Μωαβιτῶν καὶ Ἀμμανιτῶν ἔθνος ἀριθμεῖται. Ἐκ γὰρ τοῦ Λῶτ οὗτοι γενόμενοι, ὃς ἦν ἀδελφοῦ πατρὸς αὐτοῦ υἱὸς, αὐτῷ πάλιν ἐπιγράφονται.[10]

[PMZ'.] ‹PMH'.› + Τίνα ἐστὶν ἃ προεφήτευσε[11] (189b1) ὁ ἀπόστολος Παῦλος;

‹α'› Ὅσοι θέλουσιν εὐσεβῶς ζῆν, διωχθήσονται.

‹β'› Καὶ, ὡς οὐκ ἀνέξονται τῆς ὑγιοῦς διδασκαλίας οἱ πολλοί. Ἐπαναστήσονται δὲ τῇ πίστει πονηροὶ ἄνθρωποι καὶ γόητες, πλανῶντες καὶ πλανόμενοι,[12] ἔχοντες τὴν μόρφωσιν τῆς εὐσεβείας, τὴν δὲ δύναμιν αὐτῆς ἠρνούμενοι.[13]

---

[1] Lc FGM Ἰσραηλιτικον.
[2] Lc FGM ὅς.
[3] Lc FGM ὀνομαζομενος.
[4] F Χετχουρας, by mistake? GM Χειθουρας.
[5] GM τῳ.
[6] FGM ἡ Δαμασκος.
[7] GM του.
[8] FGM ἐξωθεν.
[9] Lc FGM αὐτου.
[10] F prints ἐπιγραφοινται, apparently by mistake, and GM follow, although in their notes they suggest that the form must be either ἐπιγραφοιντο or ἐπιγραφονται (the reading of C).
Only the first two items of this chapter are numbered in CFGM.
[11] Lc FGM προεφητευσεν.
[12] Lc FGM πλανωμενοι.
[13] Lc FGM ἀρνουμενοι.

Second the Israelitic name from Israel, called Iakôb but named Israel [Gn 32:28; see C. 64].

<3> And from Chettoura three nations were born to Abraam: Saba, which is the country of the Ethiopians, and the country of the Madianites, who are near the Ethiopians, and the Exomites and those near them [Gn 25:1–4; 1 Par 1:32–34].

<4> Then the nation of the Dedanites [25:3] from which came Iothor, Moses' father-in-law [Ex 4:18], and the Pharanites who live by the Red Sea.

<5> But also Syria, that is, the nation Damaskos, is reckoned to Abraam, for from Eliezer, born of his house, arose Damaskos from whom it originated.

<6> From Ésau, a descendant of Abraam, the Idoumaian nation arose, also called Edôm.

<7> The Moabites and Ammonites are not counted outside the nations born from him, for these are from Lôt, the son of his father's brother, and are thus ascribed to him.

**148**. – What are the things which the apostle Paul (189b) predicted?

<1> "Those who wish to live piously will be persecuted" [2 Tim 3:12].

<2> And how "many will not bear the healthy doctrine [4:3], for "evil men and charlatans will" rise up against the faith, "deceiving and deceived" [3:13], "having the form of piety but denying its power" [3:5].

‹γ'› Καὶ, ὅτι χρὴ τὴν¹ ἀπὸ τῆς πίστεως ἀποστασίαν πρῶτον ἐλθεῖν, καὶ τότε ἀποκαλυφθῆναι τὸν υἱὸν τῆς ἀνομίας, τὸν ἀντίχριστον. Ὃν ὁ Κύριος ἀνελεῖ τῷ πνεύματι τοῦ στόματος αὐτοῦ, καὶ καταργήσει τῇ ἐπιφανείᾳ τῆς δόξης αὐτοῦ.

‹δ'› Καὶ, ὅτι τῆς κλήσεως (189b2) τῶν ἐθνῶν πληρουμένης, τότε καὶ ὁ Ἰσραὴλ τῆς κλήσεως τῆς σωτηρίου τεύξηται.²

[PMH'.] ‹PMΘ'.› + Τίνα ἐστὶν ἃ προεφήτευσεν Ἰωάννης ὁ Εὐαγγελιστής;
‹α'› Ὡς ἀποστήσονται πολλοὶ τῆς πίστεως, προεγνωσμένοι παρὰ τῷ Θεῷ μὴ εἶναι τῆς πίστεως.

‹β'› Ὡς ὁ³ Ἀντίχριστος ἐλεύσεται, Ἀντιχρίστων καὶ τῶν νῦν αἱρετικῶν παρ' αὐτοῦ κεκλημένων, οἵ καί εἰσιν οὗτοι πολλοί.

‹γ'› Καὶ ἐν τῇ Ἀποκαλύψει αὐτοῦ, περὶ ἑπτὰ πληγῶν ὑπερχομένων⁴ τῷ κόσμῳ πρὸ τῆς τοῦ Χριστοῦ παρουσίας ἀκήκοε.

‹δ'› Καὶ ὡς ἡ Ἐκκλησία ὑπὸ τοῦ δράκοντος, ὅ ἐστιν ὁ διάβολος, (190a1) εἰς τὴν ἐρημίαν ἐκδιωχθήσεται, ποταμὸν ἐπιφέροντος αὐτῇ, ἐκ τοῦ στόματος αὐτοῦ ἐπικλύζοντος αὐτὴν, ὃ καί ἐστιν ἐκ τῆς αἱρέσεως, καὶ τοῦ Ἀντιχρίστου κατ' αὐτῆς ὁρμή.

‹ε'› Καὶ ὡς ὁ⁵ Κύριος ἀθρόως ἥξει μετὰ τῆς οὐρανίου στρατιᾶς αὐτοῦ, τὴν ἀναίρεσιν τῆς δυσσεβείας ποιούμενος, καὶ τὴν βασιλείαν τοῖς ἁγίοις τὴν αἰώνιον ἀποδιδούς.⁶

[PMΘ'.] ‹PN'.› + Πόσοι χρόνοι εἰσὶν ἀπὸ γενέσεως κόσμου, ἕως οὗ παραγέγονεν ὁ Χριστός;
Ἀπὸ τοῦ Ἀδὰμ ἕως Νῶε, ἔτη ,βσεβ'. Ἀπὸ τοῦ Νῶε ἕως Ἀβραὰμ, ἔτη ,αιε'. (190a2) Ἀπὸ Ἀβραὰμ ἕως Ἐξόδου, ἔτη υλ'. Ἀπὸ Ἐξόδου ἕως Κριτῶν, ἔτη Ϟε'. Ἀπὸ Κριτῶν ἕως Ἡλεὶ καὶ Σαμουὴλ, ἔτη υϟ'. Ἀπὸ Σαμουὴλ ἕως ἀρχῆς βασιλείας, ἔτη Ϟ'. Βασιλειῶν ἕως αἰχμαλωσίας λαοῦ ἔτη υϟ'. ‹Αἰχμαλωσίας λαοῦ ἔτη ο'. Βασιλείας Περσῶν ἔτη σλ'.›⁷ Βασιλείας Μακεδόνων ἔτη τ' ἕως ὀκτωκαιδεκαετοῦς⁸ Ὀκταουίου Αὐγούστου. Ὁ δὲ

---

¹GM omit τὴν.
²The items in this chapter are not numbered in CFGM.
³FGM omit ὁ.
⁴FGM ἐπερχομενων.
⁵M omits ὁ.
⁶The items in this chapter are not numbered in CFGM.
⁷CFGM do not contain Αἰχμαλωσιας λαου ἐτη ο'. Βασιλειας Περσων ἐτη σλ'. Emend to accord with the scheme of Julius Africanus. See Gelzer, *Sextus Julius Africanus*, 1.103.
⁸Emend to πεντεκαιδεκαετους.

<3> And "first, apostasy" from the faith "must come, and" then Antichrist, "the son of iniquity, will be revealed" [2 Th 2:3], "whom the Lord will slay with the breath of his mouth" [2:8], and will nullify "by the appearing" of his glory.

<4> And when the calling of the gentiles is complete, then Israel will obtain the call of salvation [Ro 11:25–26].

**149**. – What was predicted by Iôannés the evangelist?

<1> Many will fall away from the faith who were previously known by God as not of the faith [1 Jn 2:19].

<2> Antichrist will come, Antichrists and the present heretics named after him, of whom there are many [2:18].

<3> And in his Apocalypse he had heard about seven plagues to come upon the world before the coming of Christ [Rv 15:1].

<4> And how the church would be persecuted (190a) in the desert by the dragon [12:6], which is the devil [12:9], pouring a river upon it and inundating it from its mouth [12:15], which also is from heresy and the attack of the Antichrist against it.

<5> And how the Lord will suddenly come with his heavenly host [Mal 3:1] to destroy impiety and give the eternal kingdom to the saints [Dn 7:26–27].

**150**. – How much time is there from the creation of the world until Christ came? [1]

From Adam to Nôe, 2262 years. From Nôe to Abraham, 1015 years. From Abraham to the Exodus, 430 years. From the Exodus to the Judges, 95 years. From the Judges to Eli and Samouél, 490 years. From Samouél to the beginning of the kingdom, 90 years. 490 years of the kingdoms to the captivity of the people. <70 years of the captivity of the people. 230 years of the kingdom of the Persians.> 300 years of the Macedonian kingdom up to the [18th] <15th> year [2]

---

[1] Cf. *Liber generationis* 2.172–82 and 138–48, pp. 129–31 Mommsen.

[2] Unemended, the total of the years given is 5197 (not the 5215 years claimed by Fabricius). The dubious Fragment VIII of Hippolytus of Thebes (Diekamp, *Hippolytos von Theben*, 33ff.) gives the first number as 2242, the second as 1170, the third as 444, Moses to David as 599, and David to Christ as 1045, a correct total of 5500.

Κύριος ἡμῶν Ἰησοῦς Χριστὸς γεννᾶται ἐν Βηθλεὲμ τῆς Ἰουδαίας, ἐν ἔτει μγ' τῆς Ὀκταουίου βασιλείας, ὡς εἶναι ἄλλα ἔτη κε'.[1] Ὁμοῦ τὰ πάντα[2] συνάγεται ἐπὶ τὴν τοῦ Σωτῆρος γέννησιν ἀπὸ Ἀδὰμ ἔτη ,εφ'.

Due to textual corruption, this chronographic summary is missing information about the duration of Israel's Babylonian captivity and the duration of the Persian rule. Up to the lacuna, Joseph's numbers agree perfectly with those of Julius Africanus. According to Gelzer, Africanus reckoned Cyrus' first year to be the last year of the Babylonian captivity, and this year was 4942 *Anno Mundi*.[3] If 70 years (for the duration of the captivity) are added to the preceding durations mentioned in Joseph's account (2262 + 1015 + 430 + 95 + 490 + 90 + 490 + 70), a total of 4942 is computed.

From this point, however, exact correlation of Joseph's numbers with those of Africanus becomes more difficult, despite Joseph's use of the general framework of the famous chronographer. Part of the reason for this may be Joseph's greater willingness to adjust the historical record slightly in order to demarcate epochs more clearly.

Africanus calculated the length of the Persian rule at 230 years, ending with the death of Darius III in 5172 *Anno Mundi*.[4] Like Joseph, Africanus calculated the Greek rule to have lasted 300 years (attributing 6 years to Alexander, 40 to Ptolemy Lagos, 37 to Ptolemy Philadelphos, 25 to Ptolemy Euergetes, 17 to Ptolemy Philopator, 24 to Ptolemy Philotetor, 53 to Ptolemy Euergetes, 36 to his son, 29 to Ptolemy Dionysos, and 22 to Cleopatra).[5] Thus Cleopatra killed herself with the asp in 5472 *Anno Mundi*, in what the text of C asserts to be both the eighteenth year of the rule of Octavius Augustus and twenty-five years before the birth of Christ. Adding 5472 and 25 results in a total of 5497, three years short of 5500. Moreover, Cleopatra died in 30 B.C.E., not 25 B.C.E. Probably the text should be emended by changing the Octavian year in which the three hundred years of Macedonian rule ended, with "in the fifteenth year of Ocatavian Augustus" and "in the

---

[1] Emend to κη'.

[2] GM Ὁμου δε παντα.

[3] Gelzer, *Sextus Julius Africanus*, 1.103.

[4] Gelzer, Ibid.

[5] Gelzer, Ibid., 1.274.

of Octavius Augustus. Our Lord Jesus Christ was born in Bethlehem of Ioudaia in the 43rd year of the reign of Octavius Augustus, so that [25] <28> years are to be added. The total from Adam to the Savior's birth is 5500 years.

thirteenth year of Octavian Augustus" being the leading options.[1] An emendation of this sort does not solve all of the problems associated with this text, however.

Clearly the beginning of Octavian's rule is not being calculated from when he was declared Augustus (in 27 B.C.E.) Gelzer claims that Africanus placed the beginning of Augustus' rule in the consulate of Lepidus and Plancus (42 B.C.E.). Joseph apparently prefers to begin Augustus' rule a year earlier, 43 B.C.E., at the beginning of the triumvirate, in the year following the assassination of Caesar. Thus, according to Joseph's presentation, Caesar is neatly succeeded without interval by Octavian, his adopted son.

Problems of internal consistency remain and an additional emendation (or emendations) of C's text appears to be required. At least three possibilities present themselves: 1) Joseph places the death of Cleopatra (and Antony), 5472 *Anno Mundi* by his calculation, in 28 B.C.E., rather than the correct date of 30 B.C.E.; 2) Joseph does not attribute 230 years to the Persian rule as heretofore assumed, but rather 233, thus placing the death of Cleopatra in the year 5475 *Anno Mundi*, twenty-five years before the birth of Christ; or 3) Joseph believes that Christ was born in 5497 *Anno Mundi*, rather than 5500 as C's text reports.

Of these, the first option is to be prefered. Joseph probably believes that Octavian's elevation to Augustus, which occurred in 27 B.C.E., came immediately on the heels of the death of Cleopatra and Antony, 30 B.C.E. in reality but according to this scenario 28 B.C.E. by Joseph's calculation. Once again, Joseph has shifted dates slightly in order to demarcate major epochs more clearly.

---

[1] Gelzer (1.277) points out that George Synkellos places Cleopatra's death in the eleventh year of Octavian's reign, and he argues that Africanus placed in the twelfth year of Octavian's reign.

[PN'.] ⟨**PNA'.**⟩ + Πόσοις καὶ ποίοις ὀνόμασι προηγορεύετο διὰ τῶν (190b1) ἁγίων Γραφῶν ὁ Κύριος ἐν ἀνθρώποις ἐμφανισόμενος [1] κληθήσεσθαι;

⟨α'⟩ Μωϋσῆς προφήτην αὐτὸν καλεῖ, Καὶ προφήτην ὑμῖν ἀναστήσει Κύριος, λέγων, ἐκ τῶν ἀδελφῶν [2] ὑμῶν, ὡς ἐμέ.

⟨β'⟩ Βαλαὰμ ὁ μάντις [3] ἄκων ἄστρον αὐτὸν ἀναφανήσεται [4] προηγόρευσεν, Ἀνατελεῖ, λέγων, ἄστρον ἐξ [5] Ἰακὼβ.

⟨γ'⟩ Ὁ ἄγγελος ἐρωτώμενος ὑπὸ Μανωὲ τοῦ κριτοῦ, τί τὸ ὄνομα καλέσει τοῦ ἐπιφαινομένου Σωτῆρος, φησὶ πρὸς αὐτόν· Ἵνα τί ἐρωτᾷς τὸ ὄνομά μου; Καὶ αὐτό ἐστι θαυμαστόν.

⟨δ'⟩ Δαβὶδ Χριστὸν αὐτὸν προεῖπεν ἐν δευτέρῳ ψαλμῷ· (190b2) ἐν δὲ ιε', Ὅσιον· ἐν κγ', Κύριον τῶν δυνάμεων, καὶ βασιλέα τῆς δόξης· ἐν δὲ λβ', Λόγῳ [6] Θεοῦ τοὺς οὐρανοὺς στερεώσαντα· ἐν μδ', Θεὸν χριόμενον δι' ἀγάπην δικαιοσύνης καὶ ἀνομίας μῖσος· ἐν μη', ἄνθρωπων λυτρωτὴν, ἀλλ' οὐκ ἀδελφὸν ἀνθρώπων· ἐν δὲ ξζ', Ὁδοποιήσατε, φησὶ, τῷ ἐπιβεβηκότι τὸν οὐρανὸν τοῦ οὐρανοῦ κατὰ ἀνατολάς· Κύριος ὄνομα αὐτῷ. Ὅπερ ὁ Ἀκύλας ἐξέδωκε διὰ τοῦ Ια', [7] ἡ ὀνομασία αὐτοῦ. Ἐν δὲ οα', τὴν βασιλείαν αὐτοῦ καὶ τὴν δικαίαν κρίσιν ἐμφαίνεσθαι προφητεύων, Σαλομῶνα αὐτὸν ⟨βασιλεὰ⟩ [8] κεκλῆσθαι ἐπέγραψε. Φῶς δὲ καὶ (191a1) ἀλήθειαν ἀλλαχοῦ τέ φησιν· Ἐξαπόστειλον τὸ φῶς σου, καὶ τὴν ἀλήθειάν σου· καὶ ἐν ἄλλῳ, λίθον ἀποδεδοκιμασμένον, καὶ τοῦτον γενόμενον εἰς κεφαλὴν γωνίας· καὶ σοφίαν Θεοῦ προεῖπεν αὐτὸν, Πάντα, λέγων, ἐν σοφίᾳ ἐποίησας.

⟨ε'⟩ Ἐν δὲ τῷ Ἄσματι τῶν ἀσμάτων ὁ Σαλομῶν νυμφίον αὐτὸν κέκληκε, καὶ ἀδελφὸν, καὶ ἀδελφιδὸν, καὶ βότρυν κυπρίζοντα, ἄνθος πεδίου, μῆλον ἐν ξύλοις, πηδῶντα ἐπὶ τὰ ὄρη, λευκὸν, πυρρὸν, ἐκλελεγμένον ἀπὸ μυριάδων, Σαλομῶνα, ἡγούμενον.

⟨ς'⟩ Ἐν δὲ τοῖς σοφοῖς (191a2) αὐτοῦ λόγοις, Εἰθιὴλ αὐτὸν καλεῖ, ὅ ἐστιν ἴσος Θεῷ· καὶ Υἱὸν Θεοῦ· φησὶ γὰρ ἀνὴρ τῷ Εἰθιήλ· καὶ πάλιν· Τί ὄνομα τῷ υἱῷ αὐτοῦ;

⟨ζ'⟩ Ἡσαΐας δὲ τικτόμενον αὐτὸν ἐκ παρθένου προκηρύττων, Ἐμμανουὴλ αὐτὸν καλεῖσθαι ἔφη. Καὶ πάλιν ἄλλως [9] ὀνόμασι τεχθέντα προσηγόρευσε.

---

[1] FGM ἐμφανησομενος.

[2] FGM accidentally omit ἀδελφων.

[3] F omitting Βαλααμ prints ὁ μαντις. GM omit Βαλααμ and print ὁ μαντης.

[4] *Lc* FGM ἀναφανησεσθαι.

[5] FGM ἐν.

[6] *Lc* FGM Λογον.

[7] C's scribe completely misunderstands this, taking it as a number rather than a name. *Lc* FGM Ἰα.

[8] βασιλεα is not found in CFGM, but the emendation seems necessary.

[9] *Lc* FGM ἀλλοις.

**151.** – With how many and with what sort of names was the appearance of the Lord among men prophesied through the (190b) holy scriptures?

<1> Moses calls him prophet. "And the Lord will raise up for you a prophet like me from your brothers" [Dt 18:15].

<2> Balaam the seer unwillingly called him a star to appear, saying "A star will rise out of Jacob" [Nm 24:17].

<3> The angel asked by the judge Manôe what the name of the Savior to appear would be, said to him, "Why do you ask my name, and it is Marvelous" [Jd 13:18]?

<4> David foretold Christ in the 2nd Psalm [2:2]; in the 15th, Holy One [15:10]; in the 23rd, Lord of powers and King of glory [23:8]; in the 32nd, Word of God who made firm the heavens [32:6]; in the 44th, anointed God for his love of righteousness and hatred of lawlessness [44:8]; in the 48th, Redeemer of men, but not Brother of men [48:7–8]; in the 67th it says, "Make a way for him who has ascended to the heaven of heavens to the east, Lord is his name" [67:5], which Aquila renders as "Ia is his name." In the 71st, predicting that his kingdom and just judgment would appear, Solomon wrote that he would be called <king> [71:1]. Elsewhere he calls him Light and (191a) Truth: "Send out your light and your truth" [Ps 43:3]. And elsewhere, a Stone rejected and made into the head of the corner [Ps 118:22] and Wisdom of God, saying "You made everything by Wisdom" [Ps 104:24].

<5> In the Song of Songs Solomon [1:1] called him Bridegroom [1:7 with Christos] and Brother [5:8] and Brother's Son [5:10] and Grapecluster in bloom [2:13,15] and Flower of the field [2:1], Melon in trees [2:3], skipping upon the mountains [2:8], shining and ruddy and elect from myriads [5:10], Solomon, leader [Symmachus, 6:11 (12)].

<6> In his "wise words" he calls him Eithiél, that is, like God and Son of God, for he says "the man Eithiél" [Prv 30:1] and again, "What name for his son" [30:4].

<7> Ésaias predicted that he would be born of a virgin and said he would be called Emmanouél [Is 7:14][1] and again he called by other names the one born:

---

[1] See also C. 75.

Κάλεσον, φησὶ, τὸ ὄνομα αὐτοῦ, Ταχέως σκύλευσον, ἐξέως προνόμευσον. Καὶ πάλιν, τὸ τεχθὲν ἐπὶ σημείῳ τῆς τοῦ κόσμου σωτηρίας παιδίον, καλεῖσθαι φησὶ[1] μεγάλης βουλῆς ἄγγελον, θαυμαστὸν, σύμβουλον, ἄρχοντα εἰρήνης, ἐξουσιαστὴν, Θεὸν ἰσχυρὸν, Πατέρα τοῦ (191b1) μέλλοντος αἰῶνος. Καὶ πάλιν, ἀγαπητὸν αὐτὸν καλεῖ καὶ πατράδελφον[2] λέγων, Ἄισω δὴ ἆσμα τοῦ ἀγαπητοῦ τῷ πατραδέλφῳ[3] μου.[4] Καὶ πάλιν, ἐξουδενωμένην ψυχὴν, βδελυκτὸν ἔθνους, δοῦλον ἐξουσιαζόντων, πρόβατον, ἀμνὸν τιθυζόμενον,[5] ῥίζαν ἀπὸ γῆς ἀβάτου, ῥάβδον ἐκ ῥίζης Ἰεσσαὶ, ἄνθος ἐκ τῆς ῥίζης ἀνιὸν, λίθον δοκιμαστὸν,[6] λίθον γωνιαῖον, ἔντιμον, θεμέλιον. Καὶ πάλιν φῶς αὐτὸν καλεῖ, Φωτίζου φωτίζου,[7] λέγων, Ἰερουσαλήμ· ἥκει γάρ σου τὸ φῶς, καὶ ἡ δόξα Κυρίου ἐπὶ σὲ ἀνατέταλκε. Καὶ πάλιν Σωτῆρα αὐτὸν ὀνομάζει, Εἴπατε, (191b2) λέγων, Τῇ θυγατρὶ Σιών· Ἰδοὺ ὁ Σωτήρ σοι παραγέγονε. Καὶ Θεὸν αὐτὸν ἀνακηρύττει λέγων ταῖς πόλεσιν Ἰούδα· Ἰδοὺ ὁ Θεὸς ὑμῶν, ἰδοὺ Κύριος ἔρχεται ἐν κράτει ἰσχύος, καὶ τὸ ἔργον ἑκάστου εἰς πρόσωπον[8] αὐτοῦ.

‹η'› Ἰερεμίας δὲ Ἰωσεδὲκ αὐτὸν, ὅ ἐστι, Θεὸς δίκαιος, καλεῖσθαι προηγόρευε· καὶ Δαβὶδ αὐτὸν προεῖπε, πρὸς ὃν[9] ἐπιστρέφειν καὶ σώζεσθαι τὸν λαόν φησίν.[10]

‹θ'› Ἰεζεκιὴλ δὲ, Θεὸν ἐρχόμενον αὐτὸν εἰς τὸ ποιμαίνειν καὶ σώζειν τὰ ἀπολωλότα πρόβατα τοῦ λαοῦ προλέγων, Δαβὶδ ὁμοίως κέκληκε.

‹ι'› Καὶ Δανιὴλ, ὡς Υἱὸν ἀνθρώπου ἐπὶ τὸ (192a1) κρίνειν τὰ πάντα ἐρχόμενον αὐτὸν ὁρᾷ.

‹ια'› Ὡσὴὲ δὲ, τὸν τύπον τοῦ Σωτῆρος ἐκ τῆς πορνευσάσης συναγωγῆς υἱὸν αὐτῷ τικτόμενον, Ἰσραὲλ,[11] ὅ ἐστι, σπορὰ Θεοῦ, προσαγορεύειν[12] κελεύεται.

‹ιβ'› Μιχαίας δὲ γεννώμενον αὐτὸν ἐν τῇ Βηθλεὲμ προλέγων, Ἡγούμενον ὠνόμασεν, ἔχοντα τὴν πρὸ αἰώνων ἔξοδον.

---

[1] FGM ἔφη.
[2] Emend by replacing πατραδελφον with ἀμπελωνα.
[3] Emend by replacing πατραδελφω with ἀμπελωνι.
[4] Due to haplography, FGM omit και παλιν, ἀγαπητον αὐτον καλει και πατραδελφον λεγων ἀσω δη ἀσμα του ἀγαπητου τω πατραδελφω μου.
[5] FGM τυθιζομενον; emend to τεθυμενον.
[6] FGM δοκιμαστικον.
[7] FGM omit the second θωτιζου.
[8] FGM εἰς το προσωπον.
[9] FGM, who omit ὄν.
[10] GM φησι.
[11] GM Ἰεσραηλ.
[12] *Lc* FGM προσαγορευεσθαι.

"You shall call his name," he said, "'The spoil speeds, the prey hastes'" [8:3]. And again, he said that the child to be born as a sign of the salvation of the world would be called "angel of great counsel, wonderful, counselor, prince of peace, powerful, mighty God, Father of the (191b) age to come" [9:6]. And again, he calls him Beloved and Vineyard, saying, "I will sing a song of the beloved to my vineyard [5:1]. And again, a soul of no repute [Aquila, Symmachus, 49:7], abominable of race and slave of the powerful [49:7], a sheep, a sacrificed lamb [53:7], root from a pathless land [53:2], rod from the root of Iessai [11:1], flower rising from the root [11:1], approved stone, corner stone, precious, foundation [28:16]. And again, he calls him Light, saying, "Shine, shine, Jerusalem, for your light has come, and the glory of the Lord has risen upon you" [60:1]. And again, he names him Savior, saying, "Say to the daughter of Siôn, 'Behold, your Savior is at hand'" [62:11]. And again, he proclaims him as God, saying to the cities of Iouda, "Behold, your God, behold, the Lord comes with the power of might and the work of each one is before him" [40:9–10].

<8> Ieremias predicted that he would be called Iôsedek [Jer 23:6], that is, just God; and he forenamed him David [30 (37):9], to whom, he said the people would turn and be saved.

<9> Iezekiél, predicting God himself as coming to shepherd and save the lost sheep of the people [Ez 34; Mt 10:6], similarly called him David [34:23–24].

<10> Daniél sees him as Son of Man coming to (192a) judge everything [Dn 7:13–14,26].

<11> Ôsée orders the son born to him to be called Iesrael [Hos 1:4], that is, "offspring of God," as a model of the Savior <coming> from the fornicating synagogue.

<12> Michaias, predicting that he would be born in Béthleem, named him "Ruler," having his origin before the ages [Mic 5:2].

‹ιγ'› Καὶ Ζαχαρίας πάλιν, τὸν ἐρχόμενον Σωτῆρα τοῦ λαοῦ, Ἀνατολὴν ἔχειν ὄνομα ἔφη· καὶ νομέα δὲ[1] καὶ Θεοῦ σύμφυλον ἄνδρα αὐτὸν καλεῖ, ῥομφαίας κατ' αὐτοῦ ἐγειρομένας.[2]

‹ιδ'› Ἰησοῦν δὲ αὐτὸν Σωτῆρα κόσμου τικτόμενον, Γαβριὴλ ὁ ἄγγελος εὐαγγελιζόμενος τὴν γέννησιν (192a2) αὐτοῦ, πρὸς τὴν Παρθένον καλεῖσθαι μόνος ἔφησεν.

‹ιε'› Ὅπερ ὄνομα ἐσημαίνετο ἐν τῷ μυστικῷ καὶ ἀρρήτῳ ὀνόματι, τῷ ἐν τῇ στεφάνῃ τῆς ἱερᾶς κιβωτοῦ ἐπιγεγραμμένῳ· διὰ τοῦ, τὸ ἰὼδ καὶ ἦδ, σημαινομένου, ὅ ἐστι, δέκατον καὶ ὄγδοον, σαφῶς ὑποδηλουμένου τοῦ ἁγίου Ἰησοῦ, τοῦ Κυρίου τῆς δόξης ὀνόματος.[3]

[PNA'.] ‹PNB'.› + Αἱ δέκα ἐπεφάνειαι[4] τοῦ Κυρίου τοῖς ἰδίοις γενόμεναι, μετὰ τὸ ἐκ νεκρῶν αὐτὸν ἐγερθῆναι.

Πρῶτον, ταῖς περὶ τὴν Μαρίαν ἐν τῷ μνημείῳ.

Δεύτερον, τῷ Κηφᾷ μόνῳ, ὡς καὶ ὁ Παῦλος ἔφη· Ἔπειτα ὤφθη (192b1) Κηφᾷ.

Τρίτον, τῶν θυρῶν κεκλεισμένων, τοῖς μαθηταῖς, τοῦ Θωμᾶ μὴ παρόντος, τῇ μιᾷ τῶν Σαββάτων.

Τέταρτον, τοῖς περὶ Κλεόπα[5] ἀπιοῦσιν εἰς τὴν Ἐμμαὼ ἐν τῇ κλάσει τοῦ ἄρτου.

Πέμπτον, παρόντος τοῦ Θωμᾶ, καὶ τῶν λοιπῶν μαθητῶν, ὅτε καὶ τὸν Θωμᾶν ἐκάλει τὰς χεῖρας καὶ τὴν[6] πλευρὰν ψηλαφήσαντα.[7]

Ἕκτον, ἐν τῇ Γαλιλίᾳ τῆς θαλάσσης Τιβεριάδος, ἐν τῇ ἄγρᾳ τῶν ρνγ' ἰχθύων.

Ἕβδομον, τοῖς πεντακοσίοις ἐφάπαξ, κατὰ τὸν Παῦλον.

Ὄγδοον, τῷ Ἰακώβῳ, κατὰ τὸν Παῦλον.[8]

Ἔννατον, (192b2) εἰς τὸ ὄρος ἐν τῇ Γαλιλαίᾳ, οὗ ἐτάξατο αὐτοῖς ὁ Κύριος, κατὰ τὸν Ματθαῖον.

Δέκατον, εἰς τὸ ὄρος τῶν Ἐλαιῶν, εἰς τὸν οὐρανὸν ἀνερχόμενος.

---

[1] FGM omit δε.

[2] Lc GM ἐγειρομένης.

[3] The items in this chapter are not numbered in CFGM.

[4] Lc FGM ἐπιφανειαι.

[5] GM Κλεοπαν.

[6] FGM omit την.

[7] In their notes GM suggest emending to ψηλαφησοντα.

[8] By mistake, F omits Τῳ Ἰακωβῳ, κατα τον Παυλον in the Greek, but not his Latin translation. Translating back into Greek from F's translation, GM wrongly insert an αὐτον between τον and Παυλον.

<13> Zacharias, again, said that the future Savior of the people would have the name East [Zch 6:12].[1] And he calls him both a shepherd and a man akin to God, against whom a sword is raised [13:7].

<14> Gabriél the angel, proclaiming his birth, when alone with the Virgin said to her that when born he would be called Jesus, the Savior of the world [Lk 1:31; 2:10].

<15> This name was signified by the mystical and ineffable name inscribed on the crown of the sacred ark, signified through Iôd and Éd, that is, the tenth and the eighth [=IH], clearly indicating the name of the holy Jesus, the Lord of glory.[2]

**152.** – The ten epiphanies of the Lord to his own after he was raised from the dead.

First, to Maria and her companions at the tomb [Mt 28:1].

Second, to Képhas alone, as Paul also says: "Next he appeared to (192b) Képhas" [1 Cor 15:5, Jn 20:19].

Third, to the disciples, with Thômas not present, on the first day of the week, with closed doors [Jn 20:19].

Fourth, to Cleophas and companions leaving for Emmaus, by whom "he was known in the breaking of the bread" [Lk 24:35].

Fifth, with Thômas and the other disciples present, when he called upon Thômas to touch his hands and side [Jn 20:27].

Sixth, in Galilee by the Sea of Tiberias at the catch of 153 fish [Jn 21:11].

Seventh, to five hundred at the same time, as Paul testifies [1 Cor 15:6].

Eighth, to Jakôbos, according to Paul [15:7].

Ninth, on the mountain in Galilee where the Lord gave them orders, according to Matthew [Mt 28:16].

Tenth, on the Mount of Olives when he ascended to heaven [Ac 1:12].

---

[1] See Justin *Dialogue with Trypho* 121.2.

[2] For the inscription of the tetragrammaton, C. 107. Iota Eta for Jesus, Barn 9.8 and later. Joseph's Hebrew is not good since the first two letters of the tetragrammaton are *yodh* and *he*, not *yodh* and *chet* as assumed here. In C. 26 Joseph says Iôth means "beginning" and Héth is "living."

[ΡΝΒ'.] ‹ΡΝΓ'.› + Ποσάκις μετὰ τὴν εἰς οὐρανὸν ἐπάνοδον, ὁ Κύριος τοῖς ἰδίοις ὤφθη μαθηταῖς;

Πρῶτον, Στεφάνῳ τῷ πρωτομάρτυρι ἀναιρουμένῳ ὑπὸ τῶν Ἰουδαίων, τῶν οὐρανῶν ἀνοιχθέντων.

Δεύτερον, Παύλῳ εἰσιόντι εἰς Δαμασκὸν, ἐν τῷ τοὺς ἁγίους δεσμίους ἐθέλειν ἄγειν.[1]

Τρίτον, τῷ Παύλῳ εἰς τὴν Ἰερουσαλὴμ, ὅτε ἐπιφανεὶς αὐτῷ ἔφη· Μὴ φοβοῦ, Παῦλε· ὡς γὰρ διεμαρτύρω περὶ ἐμοῦ εἰς Ἰερουσαλὴμ, οὕτως σε δεῖ καὶ εἰς Ῥώμην μαρτυρῆσαι. (193a1)

Τέταρτον, Ἰακὼβ τῷ δικαίῳ, ὡς Ἡγίσηπος[2] καὶ Κλήμης ἱστοροῦσιν, ἀναχθέντι ὑπὸ τῶν Ἰουδαίων, εἰς τὸ πτερύγιον τοῦ ἱεροῦ, ἵνα εἴπῃ τίς ἡ θύρα τοῦ Ἰησοῦ.

[ΡΝΓ'.] ‹ΡΝΔ'.› + Ποῖα[3] εἰδωλεῖα ἐσεβάσθη ὁ λαός, τὸν Θεὸν καταλείψας;

Πρῶτον, τὸ βούκρανον, ὃ ἐν τῇ ἐρήμῳ Ἀαρὼν ἐποίησε.[4]

Δεύτερον, τελεσθεὶς τῷ Βεὲλ Φεγὼρ εἰδώλῳ Μαδιανιτῶν· ἔπειτα τῷ Φεγὼρ βδελύγματι τῶν Ἰουδαίων, τῇ Βαὰλ καὶ ταῖς Ἀστάρταις, θεαῖς Σιδωνίων· τὸ[5] Δαγὼν καὶ τῇ Μυίᾳ,[6] θεοῖς[7] Ἀκκαρώνυ·[8] τῷ Μωλὼχ, τῷ Χαμὼς εἰδώλῳ Μωάβ· καὶ τὸν Θαμούζως,[9] ἐστὶν ὁ Ἄδωνις, (193a2) ἐθρήνουν αἱ γυναῖκες ἐν τῷ ναῷ, καὶ τοῖς οἴκοις αὐτῶν ἐσεβάσθησαν, καὶ ‹οἱ ἄνδρες›[10] τὸν ἥλιον ἐν τοῖς βουνοῖς καὶ τοῖς δάσεσι θύοντες αὐτά.[11]

‹γ'› Ἀχὰζ δὲ[12] ὁ βασιλεὺς τοῦ Ἰούδα, καὶ τοῖς Δαμασκοῦ θεοῖς ἐλάτρευσε.

---

[1] Based on Ac 9:2, emend to read: ἐθέλειν εἰς Ἰερουσαλημ ἄγειν.

[2] F Ἡγισιπως; lc GM Ἡγησιππος.

[3] FGM Ποσα.

[4] GM ἐποιησεν.

[5] Lc FGM τῳ.

[6] Based on 4 Rg 1:2-3, emend to read τη Βααλ Μυια.

[7] Emend to θεῳ.

[8] Lc FGM Ἀκκαρων.

[9] Lc FGM Θαμουζ, ός.

[10] The words οἱ ἄνδρες are not found in CFGM, but seem to be required by the context.

[11] FGM αὐτοις; emend to αὐτον.

[12] FGM omit δε.

**153**. – How many times after the ascension into heaven did the Lord appear to his disciples?

First, to Stephen the protomartyr when he was slain by the Jews and the heavens were opened [Ac 7:55].

Second, to Paul going to Damascus when he wanted to take the saints bound <to Jerusalem> [9:4].

Third, to Paul at Jerusalem when he appeared to him and said, "Fear not, Paul, for as you testified of me at Jerusalem, so you must bear witness at Rome" [27:24 for 23:11] (193a). [1]

Fourth, to Iakôbos the Just, as Hegesippos and Clement relate, when he was taken by the Jews to the wing of the Temple in order to say what was the gate of Jesus. [2]


**154**. – What idols did the people worship when they abandoned God?

First, the head of a calf which Aarôn made in the desert [Ex 32:4].

Second, the people were consecrated to Beel Phegôr [Nm 25:3], idol of the Madianites [25:17–18], then to Phegôr, abomination of the Jews, and Baal and the Astartes, goddesses of the Sidonians [3 Rg 11:5], to Dagôn [Jd 16:23; 1Rg 5:1–5] and <Baal> the Fly, god[s] of the Akkaroi [4 Rg 1:2–3], to Môlôch, to Chamôs the idol of Môab [3 Rg 11:7]. And Thamouz, who is Adônis, the women lamented in the Temple, and worshipped in their houses, and <the men> sacrificed to the Sun itself on hills and in groves [Ez 8:14–16].

<3> Achaz king of Judah also worshipped the gods of Damascus [4 Rg 16:10–11].

---

[1] See C. 129, where Joseph conversely quotes Ac 23:11 for 27:24.

[2] Eusebius *HE* 2.23.12–13; 2.23.1 and 19 for Hegesippus and Clement. Joseph treats Jacob's saying about the Son of Man as his report of a vision.

‹δ'› Μανασσῇ δὲ καὶ κλειδωνιστὰς¹ καὶ ἐγγαστριμύθους, καὶ γλυπτὰ καὶ βωμοὺς τοῖς δαίμοσιν ἐν τῷ ναῷ εἰς τὴν Ἰερουσαλὴμ ἔστησε,² καὶ ἐν πυρὶ διῆγε τὰ τέκνα αὐτοῦ.

‹ε'› Ὁ δὲ Ἰσραὴλ ἀποστὰς τῆς Ἰερουσαλήμ, ταῖς δαμάλεσιν αἷς³ ἔστησεν ὁ Ἰεροβοὰμ ἐν τῇ Βεθὴλ καὶ ἐν τῇ Δὰν, ἐλάτρευεν.⁴

[ΡΝΔ'.] ‹ΡΝΕ'.› + Τίνες βεβαιοτάταις φιλίαις ἐχρήσαντο; **(193b1)**
‹α'› Δαβὶδ ὁ βασιλεὺς, καὶ Ἰωνάθαν, ὁ τοῦ Σαοὺλ υἱός.
‹β'› Ὁ Ἀβεσσαλὼμ καὶ Ἰακώβ.⁵
‹γ'› Ἀχαὰβ, ὁ τοῦ Ἰσραὴλ βασιλεὺς, καὶ Ἰωσαφὰτ, ὁ τοῦ Ἰούδα.⁶

[ΡΝΕ'.] ‹ΡΝϚ'.› + Τίς μετέβαλεν εἰς θηρίον τὴν ψυχήν;
‹α'› Ναβουχοδονόσορ, ὁ Βαβυλώνιος, τιμωρηθεὶς ἐπ' ἀλαζονείᾳ, ἔτη ζ'.
‹β'› Σαοὺλ, ἐκ δικαίου καὶ ἀγαθοῦ τρόπου, διὰ φθόνον τὸν κατὰ τοῦ Δαβὶδ, εἰς ἄδικον καὶ φαῦλον μετέβαλε τρόπον.
‹γ'› Ἰούδας, κληθεὶς εἰς μαθητείαν, καὶ διὰ φιλαργυρίαν προδότης γενόμενος.
‹δ'› Νικόλαος, ἐκ τῶν ἑπτὰ διακόντων γεγονὼς, καὶ εἰς αἵρεσιν ἐκτραπείς.⁷ **(193b2)**

[ΡΝϚ'.] ‹ΡΝΖ'.› + Τίνες ἐκ φαύλον ἀγαθοὶ γεγόνασι;
‹α'› Ματθαῖος ἐκ τελώνου ἀπόστολος καὶ εὐαγγελιστὴς γενόμενος.
‹β'› Ζαχαῖος καταλείψας τὸ τελωνεῖον, καταδικάσας ἑαυτὸν, τετραπλάσια ἃ ἠδίκησε‹ν ἀποδοὺς›,⁸ καὶ οὕτω τὸν Κύριον δεξάμενος.
‹γ'› Παῦλος ἐκ διώκτου κήρυξ τῆς πίστεως γενόμενος.⁹

---

¹Lc GM, who in their notes suggest emending to κληδωνιστας.
²GM ἐν τῳ ναῳ Ἰερουσαλημ ἐνεστησε.
³Lc FGM ἁς.
⁴Lc FGM ἐλατρευσεν.
Only the first two items in this chapter are numbered in CF. Only the first three items are numbered in GM.
⁵Lc FGM, who in their notes suggest emending to Ἰοαβ, based on 2 Rg 14:21.
⁶The items in this chapter are not numbered in CFGM.
⁷The items in this chapter are not numbered in CFGM.
⁸C ἠδικησε; F ἠδικησε αποδους; lc GM ἠδικησεν αποδους.
⁹The items in this chapter are not numbered in CFGM.

<4> Manassé set up diviners and ventriloquists, images and altars to demons in the Temple at Jerusalem, and led his children through fire [4 Rg 21:3–9].

<5> Israel, apostate from Jerusalem, worshipped heifers which Ieroboam set up in Bethél and in Dan [3 Rg 12:28–30].

**155.** – Who were bound by the firmest friendships?[1] (193b)
  <1> David the king and Iônathan son of Saul [1 Rg 18:1].
  <2> Abessalôm and [Jakôb] <Iôab> [2 Rg 14:21].
  <3> Achaab king of Israel and Iôsaphat king of Iouda [3 Rg 22:4].

**156.** – Who changed his soul into a beast?
  <1> Nabouchadonosor the Babylonian, who because of pride was punished for seven years [Dn 4:32].
  <2> Saul was changed from just and good ways into unjust and evil because of envy toward David [1 Rg 18:8–9].
  <3> Judas, called to discipleship, who through love of money became a betrayer [Mt 26:14–16].
  <4> Nicolaos, one of the seven deacons [Ac 6:5], who turned to heresy [see C. 140,10].

**157.** – Who from evil became good?
  <1> Matthew from tax-collector became apostle and evangelist [Mt 10:3].
  <2> Zacchaeus, leaving the custom-house, condemned himself, gave back four times what he had unjustly collected, and thus received the Lord [Lk 19:8].
  <3> Paul from persecutor became herald of the faith [1 Tim 2:7, 2 Tim 1:11].

---

[1] Compare Hyginus 257: "Who were the closest of friends?"

[PNZ'.] ⟨**PNH'.**⟩ + Τίς μακρόβιος μετὰ Μωϋσέα ἐγένετο;
Ἰωδαὲ ἀρχιερεὺς, ὁ τὴν Γοθολίαν¹ ἀποκτείνας, ζήσας ἑκατὸν καὶ τριάκοντα ἔτη.

[PNH'.] ⟨**PNΘ'.**⟩ + Τίνες λέοντας χερσὶν ἀνεῖλον;
⟨α'⟩ Σαμψὼν ὁ Ναζωραῖος.
⟨β'⟩ Δαβὶδ, ὅτε τὰ τοῦ πατρὸς ἔνεμε ποίμνια.
⟨γ'⟩ Βαναίας ὁ τοῦ Ἰωὰβ, (**194a1**) τοῦ Δαβὶδ ὁ² στρατηγός.³

[PNΘ'.] ⟨**PΞ'.**⟩ + Τίνες ὑπὸ λεόντων ἀνηρέθησαν;
⟨α'⟩ Ἰαὼδ ὁ προφήτης, ὁ τὸ σημεῖον εἰς τὴν Βεθὴλ δοὺς, τὴν τοῦ θυσιαστηρίου διάρρηξιν.
⟨β'⟩ Ὁ ἄνθρωπος ὁ κελευθεὶς⁴ πατάξαι τὸν προφήτην, τὸν βουλόμενον δεῖξαι ἑαυτὸν τετραυματισμένον τῷ Ἀχαὰβ, καὶ μὴ ὑπακούσας.
⟨γ'⟩ Οἱ κατοικισθέντες μετὰ τὴν τοῦ Ἰσραὴλ αἰχμαλωσίαν Βαβυλώνιοι εἰς Σαμάρειαν.⁵

[PΞ'.] ⟨**PΞA'.**⟩ + Τίνες ἐπὶ ἱεροσυλίαις ἀνηρέθησαν;
⟨α'⟩ Ἀχὰρ ἐπὶ Ἰησοῦ τοῦ Ναυῆ, ἐπὶ τοῖς ἀναθήμασι τῆς Ἱεριχῶ.
⟨β'⟩ Ὀφνὶ καὶ Φινεὲς οἱ τοῦ Ἡλεὶ, ἐπὶ τὸ ἑαυτοῖς ἀπάρχεσθαι (**194a2**) τὰ ἱεραῖα.
⟨γ'⟩ Ἀνανίας καὶ Σαπφεῖρα ἡ τούτου γυνή, ἐπὶ τῷ μέρει⁶ τινὰ τιμῆς ἀγροῦ προσάγειν, ἐθέλειν δὲ τὴν ἀποστολικὴν πολιτείαν ἀπατᾶν, ὡς ὅλην τοῦ ἀγροῦ τὴν τιμὴν μὴ προσενέγκαντας.⁷

[PΞA'.] ⟨**PΞB'.**⟩ + Τίνες εἰς λάκκους εἰς τὸ ἀναιρεθῆναι ἐβλήθησαν;
⟨α'⟩ Ἰωσὴφ, ὑπὸ τῶν ἀδελφῶν.
⟨β'⟩ Ἱερεμίας, ὑπὸ τῶν ἀρχόντων τοῦ λαοῦ.
⟨γ'⟩ Δανιὴλ, ὑπὸ Περσῶν.⁸

---

¹FGM Γοδολιαν.
²FGM omit ὁ.
³The items in this chapter are not numbered in CFGM.
⁴FGM κελευσθεις.
⁵The items in this chapter are not numbered in CFGM.
⁶FGM μερη.
⁷The items in this chapter are not numbered in CFGM.
⁸The items in this chapter are not numbered in CFGM.

**158**. – Who was long-lived after Moses?

Iôdaë the high priest, who killed Gotholia and lived for 130 years [see C. 2(15); also see 2 Par 24:15].


**159**. – Who killed lions with their hands?

<1> Sampson the Nazoraios [Jd 14:5–6].

<2> David, when he pastured the flocks of his father [1 Rg 17:34–35].

<2> Banaias son of Iôab (194a) David's general [2 Rg 23:20].


**160**. – Who were slain by lions?[1]

<1> Iaôd the prophet, who gave the broken sanctuary as a sign in Bethél [3 Rg 13:1–10].

<2> The man who was ordered to strike the prophet who wanted to show himself wounded to Achaab, and did not obey the order [3 Rg 20:35–36].

<3> The Babylonians who after the captivity of Israel migrated to Samaria.


**161**. – Who were slain because of sacrilege?

<1> Achar, at the order of Iésous Naué because of the devoted things of Jericho [Js 7:1].

<2> Ophni and Phinees, sons of Éli, because they tasted the first parts of the sacrifices [1 Rg 2:12–17; 4:17].

<3> Ananias and his wife Sapphira wanted to deceive the apostolic community (*politeia*) and brought portions of the price of a field but not the whole price of the field [Ac 5:1–10].


**162**. – Who were cast into pits to be slain?

<1> Iôseph, by his brothers [Gn 37:23].

<2> Ieremias, by the princes of the people [Jer 38:6].

<3> Daniél, by the Persians [Dn 6:16].

---

[1] Compare Hyginus 247: "Who were consumed by dogs?"

[ΡϘΒ'.] ‹ΡϘΓ'.› + Τίνες δίκας ἔδοσαν πλημμελήσαντες;

‹α'› Κάϊν ἀποκτείνας τὸν ἀδελφόν, εἰς ἕβδομην[1] γενεὰν παραλυθείς.

‹β'› Σοδόμων αἱ πόλεις καταφλεχθεῖσαι (194b1) διὰ τὴν τῆς φύσεως παραχάραξιν.

‹γ'› Χαναναῖοι καὶ Ἀμορραῖοι τῶν οἰκείων ἐκβληθέντες διὰ τὴν εἰδωλολατρείαν.

‹δ'› Φαραὼ καὶ οἱ Αἰγύπτιοι θείοις ἐναντιούμενοι σημείοις, εἰς τὸν βυθὸν συσχεθέντες.

‹ε'› Σαοὺλ ἐν πολέμῳ πεσὼν ἅμα τοῖς οἰκείοις, καὶ τοῖς Γαβαωνίταις ἐκδιδομένων τῶν υἱῶν αὐτῶν εἰς ἐξιλέωσιν.

‹ϛ'› Ἡ τοῦ Βενιαμὶν φυλή, ἐπὶ τῇ ἀσελγείᾳ τῆς γυναικὸς τοῦ Βηθλεεμίτου.

‹ζ'› Ἡ Βαβυλὼν, ἐπὶ τῇ βασιλείᾳ ἐπαρθεῖσα,[2] εἰς ἐρημίαν ἐκδοθεῖσα.

‹η'› Ἄχαρ, ἱεροσυλήσας.

‹θ'› Ὁ ἐν τῇ ἐρήμῳ τὸ Σάββατον βεβηλώσας ἐπὶ τῇ (194b2) τῶν ξύλων συλλογῇ.

‹ι'› Ὁ Θεὸν ἐν τῇ μάχῃ βλασφημήσας κατὰ τὴν ἔρημον.

‹ια'› Οἱ τοῦ Ἠλεὶ παῖδες, τῆς ἱερωσύνης μετὰ τιμωρίας καταλυθέντες.

‹ιβ'› Σεδεκίας ἐκτυφλωθεὶς ὑπὸ τοῦ Βαβυλωνίου ‹βασιλέως›.[3]

‹ιγ'› Ὁ λαὸς ὁ Ἰουδαίων, ἐπὶ τῇ κατὰ τοῦ Σωτῆρος ἐπαναστάσει, τὴν ἔτι κατέχουσαν αὐτὸν ὑπομένων μετὰ ἀναισθησίας αἰχμαλωσίαν.[4]

[ΡϘΓ'.] ‹ΡϘΔ'.› + Τίνες πλημμελήσαντες ἐλέους τετυχήκασιν;

‹α'› Οἱ τοῦ Ἰωσὴφ ἀδελφοὶ πεπρακότες αὐτόν, καὶ διατραφέντες ὑπ' αὐτοῦ.

‹β'› Δαβὶδ ταπεινώσας ἑαυτὸν ἐπὶ τῇ πλημμελείᾳ, καὶ ἐκτενῶς ἐξομολογούμενος. (195a1)

‹γ'› Σαλομὼν ναοὺς τοῖς τῶν ἐθνῶν εἰδώλοις δειμάμενος, καὶ διὰ τὸν πατέρα μὴ τιμωρηθείς.

‹δ'› Μανασσῆς ἐν αἰχμαλωσίᾳ ἀπαχθεὶς, καὶ ἐπὶ Θεὸν ἐπιστραφείς, καὶ διὰ τοῦτο ἐπαναχθείς.

‹ε'› Ἰωακεὶμ λυθεὶς ἀπὸ τῶν δεσμῶν, καὶ τιμώμενος βασιλικῇ τιμῇ ὑπὸ τοῦ[5] Βαβυλωνίου ‹βασιλέως›.[6]

---

[1] GM ἕβδομον.
[2] GM ἐγερθεισα.
[3] The word βασιλεως is not found in CFGM, but seems required by the context.
[4] The items in this chapter are not numbered in CFGM.
[5] M τον.
[6] The word βασιλεως is not found in CFGM, but seems required by the context.

**163**. – Who paid penalties for their crimes?

<1> After Kain killed his brother, he paid the penalty to the seventh generation [Gn 4:15].

<2> The cities of the Sodomites were overthrown (194b) because of their perversion of nature [Gn 19:4–5].[1]

<3> The Chanaanites and Amorites were cast out of their homes because of idolatry [Dt 7:1–6].

<4> Pharaô and the Egyptians resisted divine signs and were drowned in the deep [Ex 14:28].

<5> Saul fell in battle along with his people and delivered his sons to the Gabaonites for vengeance [1 Rg 31].

<6> The tribe of Beniamin, because of their indecent behavior toward the wife of the Béthleemite [Jd 20].

<7> Babylon, exalted because of royal rule, was given over to the desert.

<8> Achar, because of sacrilege [Js 7:1] (cf. 161[1]).

<9> He who profaned the Sabbath by collecting wood in the desert [Nm 15:32–36].

<10> He who blasphemed God in the battle in the desert [Lv 24:10–23].

<11> The sons of Élei, deprived of the priesthood with a penalty [1 Rg 4:11?].

<12> Sedekias, blinded by the Babylonian <king> [4 Rg 25:7].

<13> Because the people of the Jews rose up against the Savior, they experienced the captivity that still holds them, though they do not sense it.


**164**. – Who obtained mercy after they sinned?

<1> The brothers of Iôseph, who sold him and later were fed by him [Gn 37:28; 45:11].

<2> David, who humbled himself because of his sin and made a lengthy confession [Ps 51] (195a).

<3> Solomon, who built temples for the idols of the gentiles and because of his father did not pay the penalty [3 Rg 11:12].

<4> Manassés was led into captivity and turned to God and on account of this was returned [2 Par 33:11–13].

<5> Iôacheim, freed from bonds and honored with royal honor by the Babylonian <king> [4 Rg 25:27–30].

---

[1] Epiphanius (*Pan.* 42.11.11) speaks of Marcion's *paracharaxis* of Pauline epistles.

‹ϛ'› Ὁ λῃστὴς ἐπὶ τοῦ σταυροῦ Χριστὸν ὁμολογήσας, καὶ τὴν εἰς παράδεισον ὁδὸν εὑράμενος.

‹ζ'› Ὁ ἀπόστολος Παῦλος διώκων τὴν Ἐκκλησίαν, καὶ κήρυξ ἧς ἐπολέμει Χριστοῦ πίστεως ἀποστελλόμενος.

‹η'› Ἡ Ἐκκλησία ἡ ἐξ ἐθνῶν, ἐπὶ ταῖς τοσαύταις πλημμελείαις[1] (195a2) ἐλεουμένη, καὶ διὰ πίστεως Χριστοῦ τῆς τελείας διακαιώσεως ἀξιουμένη.[2]

[ΡΞΔ'.] ‹ΡΞΕ'.› + Τίνες εἰσὶν οἱ κατορθοῦν τι δόξαντες, καὶ ἐπὶ τοῦτο[3] διαμαρτῶντες;[4]

‹α'› Ὁ τὸν Σαοὺλ ἐπισφάξαι καυχησάμενος τῷ Δαβὶδ, καὶ κομίσας αὐτῷ τὸ τῆς βασιλείας σημεῖον, ὡς αὐτῷ προσηκούσης τῆς βασιλείας, ἀναιρεθῆναι προσταχθεὶς ὑπὸ τοῦ Δαβίδ.

‹β'› Ῥαχαὰβ καὶ Βαναίας, οἱ υἱοὶ Ῥεμμὼν, οἱ Μεμφιβωσθὲ[5] τοῦ υἱοῦ Σαοὺλ τὴν κεφαλὴν κομίσαντες τῷ Δαβὶδ, καὶ μεγάλην αὐτῷ δόξαντες κατατίθεσθαι χάριν, δι' ἧς καὶ εὐδοκιμεῖν ἤλπιζον,[6] ἀναιρούμενον[7] (195b1) διὰ τοῦτο.

‹γ'› Ὀζᾶ ὁ τὴν Κιβωτὸν ἐπικληθεῖσαν[8] ἐπισπασάμενος πρὸς ἑαυτὸν, πρὸς τὸ μὴ περιτραπῆναι ἀπὸ τῆς ἁμάξης, ἀποθανὼν παραυτίκα.

‹δ'› Ὁ κελευσθεὶς ὑπὸ τοῦ προφήτου Μιχαίου πατάσσειν αὐτὸν, καὶ δι' εὐλάβειαν οὐ πατάξας, ἀναιρεθεὶς ὑπὸ λέοντος.

‹ε'› Ὁ Φαρισαῖος ὁ[9] ἐπὶ τῇ οἰκείᾳ δικαιοσύνῃ τοῦ τελώνου κατακαυχώμενος.[10]

[ΡΞΕ'.] ‹ΡΞϚ'.› + Τίνα ἐστὶ τὰ ἔθνη καὶ πόσα τὰ τοῖς ἱεροῖς τόποις ὕστερον ἐπανιστάμενα, καὶ θεήλατον ὑπομείναντα τὴν[11] τιμωρίαν;

‹α'› Γὼγ καὶ Μαγὼγ, οἵ εἰσι Σκύθαι.

‹β'› Μοσώχ, Ἰλλυριοί.

‹γ'› Θωβὲλ, (195b2) Θετταλοί.

---

[1] M prints πλημμελειας by mistake.

[2] The items in this chapter are not numbered in CFGM.

[3] GM τουτῳ.

[4] M διαμαρτοντες.

[5] Lc FGM Μεμφιβοσθε.

[6] FGM και ἠλπιζον εὐδοκιμειν.

[7] Lc FGM ἀναιρουμενοι.

[8] Lc FGM ἐπικλιθεισαν.

[9] FGM omit ὁ.

[10] FGM κατακαυχωμενος. The items in this chapter are not numbered in CFGM.

[11] Lc FGM, who omit την.

<6> The thief who on the cross confessed Christ and found the way to paradise [Lk 23:42–43].

<7> The apostle Paul, persecuting the church, and was sent as a herald of the faith of Christ which he had fought [cf. Gal 1:23].

<8> The church of the gentiles, after so many sins, obtained mercy and through the faith of Christ was considered worthy of perfect justification.

**165.** – Who seemed to themselves to have done something rightly and thus sinned?

<1> The man who boasted to David that he had killed Saul, and therefore offered him the royal insignia, as though the kingdom belonged to him, was ordered slain by David [2 Rg 1:15–16].

<2> Rachaab and Banaias the sons of Remmôn, who brought the head of Saul's son Memphibosthe to David, thinking they would find great favor with him and hoped to be in honor, were (195b) therefore slain [4:5–12].

<3> Oza, who pulled the tottering ark to himself lest it fall from the wagon, immediately died [6:6–7].

<4> The man who was ordered by the prophet Michaias to strike him but from reverence did not strike, was slain by a lion [3 Rg 20:35–36].[1]

<5> The Pharisee who boasted of his own righteousness before the Publican [Lk 18:10–14].

**166.** – What nations were there and how many, that later rose against the holy places and suffered divine punishment [Gn 10:2–7]? [See C. 24, 147]

<1> Gôg and Magôg [10:2; see C. 79], who are Scythians [Hippolytus *Chr* (H2) 58; Josephus *Ant.* 1.123].[2]

<2> Mosôch [10:2], Illyrians [*Chr* (H2) 62; Meschos-Cappadocians in Josephus *Ant.* 1.125].

<3> Thôbel [10:2], Thessalians [*Chr* (H2) 61; Iberians in Josephus *Ant.* 1.124].

---

[1] See C. 49, 91, 160.

[2] In Ez 38:2, by means of a gloss, "the land of Magôg" is linked to Gôg, the head of Meshekh and Tuval, whose invasion of Judah is prophesied. No doubt, the origin of this gloss is Gn 10:2, which depicts a certain Magôg as the eponymous ancestor of a nation. Oddly, Rv 20:8–10 presents both Gôg and Magôg as individuals leading an attack on God's people, an approach that Joseph here follows.

⟨δ'⟩ Γομὲρ, Γαλάται.
⟨ε'⟩ Θεργαμὰ, Ἀρμένιοι.
⟨ς'⟩ Σαβαιῶν, Ἄραβες, οἱ πρῶτοι Ἰνδῶν.
⟨ζ'⟩ Θαρσεῖς, Ἄφροι.
⟨η'⟩ Χοῦς, Αἰθίοπες.
⟨θ'⟩ Φοὺδ, Λίβυες.
⟨ι'⟩ Φρὲς, Πέρσαι.[1]

[PΞΓ'.] ⟨PΞZ'⟩ + Αἱ δυνάμεις τῶν λίθων τῶν ἐν τῇ τοῦ ἀρχιερέως ζώνῃ ἐντιθεμένων.
⟨α'⟩ Ἴασπις, μοιχείας ἀποτρεπτική.
⟨β'⟩ Σάπφειρος, ὀφθαλμοῖς στιλπνωτικὴ λαμπρά.[2]
⟨γ'⟩ Χαλκηδόνιος, σωφροσύνης πρόσφορος.
⟨δ'⟩ Σμάραγδος, δαιμόνων ἀπελαστική.
⟨ε'⟩ Σαρδόνυξ, διαπυρσαίνουσα.
⟨ς'⟩ Σάρδιος,
⟨ζ'⟩ Χρυσόλιθος, ὀδύνας ὀφθαλμῶν ἰῶνται.
⟨η'⟩ Βίρυλλος,[3] (196a1) λύπης ἰατική.
⟨θ'⟩ Τοπάζιος.
⟨ι'⟩ Χρυσόπρασος.
⟨ια'⟩ Ὑάκινθος.
⟨ιβ'⟩ Ἀμέθυσος,[4] μέθης ἀλεξιτήριον.[5]

---

[1] The items in this chapter are not numbered in CFGM.
[2] In their notes GM suggest emending to λαμπρας.
[3] Lc FGM Βηρυλλος.
[4] Lc FGM Ἀμεθυστος.
[5] Lc GM ἀλεξητηριον.

<4> Gomer [10:2], Gauls [Galatians, Josephus *Ant.* 1.1.2].

<5> Thergama [10:3, Cod.A], Armenians [*Chr* (H₂) 68; Phrygians in Josephus *Ant.* 1.126].[1]

<6> Sabaioi [10:7], Arabs, the first of the Indians [*Chr* (H₂) 184; Josephus *Ant.* 1.134].

<7> Tharsians [10:4], Africans [not Josephus *Ant.* 1.239].[2]

<8> Chous [10:6], Ethiopians [so Josephus *Ant.* 1.131; *Chr* (H₂) 131].

<9> Phoud [10:6], (Phoutés) Libyans [Josephus *Ant.* 1.132].

<10> Phres, Persians [Elamites-Persians, Josephus *Ant.* 1.143].[3]


**167.** – Powers of the gems worn on the high priest's girdle.

<1> Jasper [Rv 21:19], averter of adultery.

<2> Sapphire [21:19], radiant brightness for the eyes.

<3> Chalcedony [21:19], conducive to chastity.

<4> Emerald [21:19], drives off demons.

<5> Sardonyx [21:20], with fiery color.

<6> Sardian [21:20] and

<7> Chrysolith [21:20] heals eye pains.

<8> Beryl [21:20] (196a) cures pain.

<9> Topaz [21:20].

<10> Chrysoprase [21:20].

---

[1] Thergama "is traditionally associated with Armenia" (John Skinner, *Genesis* [ICC; Edinburgh: Clark, 1910] 197).

[2] The North African city of Carthage may have been one of the cities known as Tarshish in antiquity. Where the MT reads *TRShYSh* in Is 23:1 and Ez 27:12, the LXX reads *Karchédonos* and *Karchédonoi* respectively.

[3] The explanation for the pairing of Φρες and Περσαι, is readily apparent. In Hebrew, the word for Persia is פרס, which could be rendered into Greek as Φρες. The name of the son born to Judah and Tamar is פרצ, which could also be rendered into Greek as Φρος. The fact that this confusion is found in the *Hypomnestikon* is one more indication that the author of this work did not read much Hebrew.

⟨ιγ⟩ Ἄνθραξ.
⟨ιδ⟩ Ἀχάτης.
⟨ιε⟩ Λιγύριος.
⟨ις⟩ Ὀνύχειος.[1]

+[2] Τέρμα πυκτίδων ἐνταῦθα Ἰωσήππου,
Τὰς ὑποθέσεις τῶν πέντε βίβλων ἔχων.[3]
Πέρας δέδωκα τῷ τελευταίῳ στίχῳ.
Τῷ συντελεστῇ τῶν καλῶν Θεῷ χάρις,
Τῷ συμπέρασμα δόντι μοι λόγους γράφειν,
Εἰς αἶνον εὐχάριστον αὐτοῦ τοῦ Λόγου.

---

[1] The items in this chapter are not numbered in CFGM.

[2] In C (but not FGM) the Colophon/Appendix is set off from the body of the text by a ribbon-shaped rosette, and the beginning of the text of the Colophon/Appendix is marked by a cross, as has been the pattern in each of the preceding chapters.

[3] In their notes GM suggest emending to ἔχον.

<11> Hyacinth [21:20].
<12> Amethyst [21:20] preserves from drunkenness.
<13> Carbuncle [Ex 28:17].
<14> Agate [28:19].
<15> Jacinth [28:19].
<16> Onyx [28:20].

The first twelve names come from the list of foundation stones in Rv 21:19–20, not the high priest's girdle,[1] while the last four names come from Ex 28:17–20, not Revelation. With this confused list Joseph finally comes back to the high priests of C. 2 and the Temple vestments of C. 109.

<Colophon/Appendix>

Here is the end of the volumes of Iôseppos.
Having the materials of five books,
I have finished the work with this final verse.
Thanks be to God, the finisher of good things,
Who allowed me to finish writing the words
For grateful praise to his Logos.

---

[1] These simple moral interpretations are not related to Epiphanius' famous (P.F. Foggini [1743], PG 43, 305–20) treatise *De duodecim gemmis* (ibid. 293–301). Moreover, Ex 28:17–21 (39:10–14) and Josephus *Ant.* 3.166–68 (cf. *War* 5.234) state that there were twelve stones, not sixteen.

BIBLIOGRAPHY

A. ANCIENT AUTHORS

Aristotle, commentators: Ammonius (CAG 4.4 [1897], ed. Adolf Busse); Simplicius (CAG 8 [1907], ed. Karl Kalbfleisch); Olympiodorus (CAG 12.1 [1902], ed. Adolf Busse); Philoponus (CAG 13.1 [1898], ed. Adolf Busse); Elias (CAG 18.1 [1900], ed. Adolf Busse).

Artemidorus *Artemidori Daldiani Oneirocriticon Libri V*. Ed. Roger Ambrose Pack, Leipzig: Teubner, 1963.

*Athanasius Werke* 3: *Urkunden zur Geschichte des arianischen Streites*. Ed. Hans-Georg Opitz. Berlin: De Gruyter, 1934.

Augustine *On heresies*. PL 42, 21–50.

Babrius and Phaedrus. *Fables* Ed. Ben Edwin Perry. (LCL) Cambridge, MA: Harvard University Press, 1965 .

Babylonian Talmud (*Kerithoth*). Hebrew-English Edition of the Babylonian Talmud. London: Soncino, 1989.

*Chronicon Paschale*. Ed. Ludwig August Dindorf, *Chronicon Paschale* 1. Corpus Scriptorum Historiae Byzantinae 16, Bonn: Weber, 1832.

Clement of Alexandria. Ed. Otto Stählin, *Clemens Alexandrinus*. 4 vols. (GCS) Leipzig: Hinrichs, 1905–1936.

Cyril of Alexandria *Against Julian*. PG 76, 509–1064.

Cyril of Jerusalem *Catechetical Orations*. PG 33, 332–1060.

Diogenes Laertius. Tr. Robert Drew Hicks. 2 vols. (LCL) London: Heinemann, 1925. Ed. Herbert Strainge Long. 2 vols. Oxford: Clarendon, 1964 .

Epiphanius *Panarion*. Ed. Karl Holl, *Epiphanius*. 3 vols. (GCS) Leipzig: Hinrichs, 1915–1933. English translation by Frank Williams, *The Panarion of Epiphanius of Salamis*: 2 vols. NHS 35–36, Leiden: Brill, 1987, 1994.

*On Weights and Measures*, PG 43, 237–94.

See also *Epitome*.

*Epitome* (*Anacephalaeosis*). Ed. Karl Holl, *Epiphanius*. 3 vols. (GCS) Leipzig: Hinrichs, 1915–1933: 1.162–168, 1.234–237, 2.1–4, 2.211–214, 3.1–2, 3.230–232, 3.415. English translation by Frank Williams, *The Panarion of Epiphanius of Salamis*: 2 vols. (NHS 35–36), Leiden: Brill, 1987, 1994: 1.8–11, 1.55–57, 1.209–210, 2.1–3, 2.208, 2.401–402, 2.567.

Eusebius of Caesarea *Demonstratio Evangelica*. Ed. Ivar August Heikel. (GCS) Leipzig: Hinrichs, 1913.

*Historia Ecclesiastica* . Ed. Eduard Schwartz. 3 vols. (GCS) Leipzig: Hinrichs, 1903–1909; tr. Hugh Jackson Lawlor and John Ernest Leonard Oulton, *Eusebius: The Ecclesiastical History and the Martyrs of Palestine.* 2 vols. London: SPCK, 1928.

*Onomasticon* . Ed. Erich Klostermann. (GCS) Leipzig: Hinrichs, 1904.

*Praeparatio Evangelica.* Ed. Karl Mras. 2 vols. (GCS) Berlin: Akademie, 1954, 1956.

Georgius Cedrenus. Corpus Scriptorum Historiae Byzantinae 34–35, Bonn: Weber, 1838.

Gregory of Nazianzus *Against Julian.* PG 35, 531–720.

Heraclides Pythagoricus. In Joseph, C. 143.

Hippolytus of Rome *Chronicon.* Adolf Bauer, *Hippolytus Werke IV: Die Chronik* . Ed. Rudolf Helm. (GCS) Leipzig: Hinrichs, 1929; ed. 2, Berlin: Akademie, 1955. See *Liber generationis*.

Hippolytus of Thebes *Chronicon*. Ed. Franz Diekamp, *Hippolytos von Theben: Texte und Untersuchungen.* Münster i.W.: Aschendorff, 1898.

Hyginus *De fabulis*. Ed. Herbert Jennings Rose, *Hygini Fabulae.* Leiden: Sijthoff, c. 1933; 2nd ed., 1963.

Iamblichus *De mysteriis*. Ed. Gustav Parthey, *Jamblichi De Mysteriis Liber*. Berlin: Nicolai, 1857; ed. Édouard des Places, *Jamblique Les mystéres d'Égypte*. Paris, 1966 (with pages of Parthey); tr. Angelo Raffaele Sodano, *Giamblico I misteri egiziani.* Milan: Rusconi, 1984 (with pages of Parthey).

Ignatius *Epistle to the Trallians* (Long Apollinarian recnsion). Pp. 93–110 in Franz Xavier Funk and Franz Diekamp, edd. *Patres apostolici*, Vol. 2: *Epistulae spuriae.* 3d ed. Tübingen: Laupp, 1913.

John Chrysostom *Homily* 1.29 on 1 Corinthians. PG 61, 241D–242A.

John of Damascus *De haeresibus.* PG 94, 675–780.

Joseph *Hypomnestikon*, also called *Liber memorialis*, In Fabricius, Johannes Albertus, *Codex Pseudepigraphicus Veteris Testamenti* (Hamburg: Felginer, 1723) part 2 (separate pagination at the end of the volume); edition of Giovanni Batista Gallicciolli in Vol. 14, pp. 2–84 of Andreas Gallandi, ed., *Bibliotheca Veterum Patrum Antiquorumque Scriptorum Ecclesiasticorum Græco-Latina.* 2d ed. 14 vols. Venice: Zatta & Sons, 1788 (text based on Fabricius); also in PG 106 (Paris, 1863) 15–176 (text based on Gallicciolli).

Josephus. I. *The Life*. *Against Apion.* II–III. *The Jewish War.* IV. *Jewish Antiquities, Books I–IV.* Ed. Henry St. John Thackeray. V. *Jewish Antiquities, Books V–VIII.* Ed. Henry St. John Thackeray—Ralph Marcus. VI. *Jewish Antiquities, Books IX–XI.* VII. *Jewish Antiquities, Books XII–XIV.* Ed. Ralph Marcus. VIII. *Jewish Antiquities* Books XV–XVII. Ed.

Ralph Marcus–Allen Paul Wikgren. IX. *Jewish Antiquities*, Books XVIII–XX. Ed. Louis H. Feldman. (LCL) London: Heinemann, 1926–1965.

Julian *Iuliani Imperatoris Epistulae Leges*. Ed. Joseph Bidez-Franz Cumont. Paris: Belles Lettres, 1922; Wilmer Cave Wright (LCL). 3 vols. London: Heinemann, 1913–1923.

Justin Martyr. In Edgar Johnson Goodspeed, *Die ältesten Apologeten*. Göttingen: Vandenhoeck & Ruprecht, 1914; reprinted 1984.

*Liber generationis*. In Theodor Mommsen, *Monumenta Germaniae historica*. *Auctores antiquissimi*, IX. *Chronica minora*. Berlin: Weidmann, 1992; repr. 1961. Cf. Rudolf Helm, *Hippolytus Die Chronik* (Leipzig: Hinrichs, 1929) 140–227; 2d ed., Berlin: Akademie, 1955) 70–140.

*The Old Testament in Greek*. Ed. Alan England Brooke, Norman McLean, Henry St. John Thackeray. Vol. 1. *The Octateuch*, Part 1. *Genesis*. 1906. Part 2. *Exodus and Leviticus*, 1909. Part 4. *Joshua, Judges and Ruth*, 1917. Vol. 2. *The Later Historical Books*, Part 1. *I and II Samuel*, 1927. Part 2. *I and II Kings*, 1930. Part 3. *I and II Chronicles*, 1932. Cambridge: At the University Press.

*The Old Testament in Greek*. Ed. Henry Barclay Swete. 3 vols. Cambridge: At the University Press, 1909–12.

Origen *Contra Celsum*. Ed. Paul Koetschau, *Origenes Werke*. (GCS) Leipzig: Hinrichs, 1899.

Palladius. Ed. Edward Cuthbert Butler, *The Lausiac History of Palladius* .2 Texts and Studies 6.2. Cambridge: At the University Press, 1904.

Philo. Edd. Francis Henry Colson, George Herbert Whitacker, et al. 10 vols. (LCL) London: Heinemann, 1929–62.

Porphyry, *Letter to Anebo*. Ed. Angelo Raffaele Sodano, *Porfirio Lettera ad Anebo*. Naples: Arte Tipografica, 1958.
  *De philosophia ex oraculis haurienda*. Ed. Gustav Wolff, *Porphyrii De Philosophia ex oraculis*. Hildesheim: Olms, 1962.

Procopius of Gaza. *Commentaries on Genesis*. PG 87, 21–512.
  *On Exodus-Proverbs*, PG 87, 512–1544.

*The Pseudo-Augustinian Hypomnesticon against the Pelagians and Celestians*. Ed. John Edward Chisholm. 2 vols., Paradosis 20–21, 1967, 1980.

Pseudo-Galen *Historia philosopha*. Ed. Hermannus Diels, *Doxographi Graeci* 2nd ed., Berlin-Leipzig: De Gruyter, 1929. 597–648.

Pseudo-Tertullian *Adversus omnes haereses*. Ed. Aemilius Kroymann. Pp. 1399–1410 in *Tertulliani Opera*, Part 2: *Opera Montanistica*. Corpus Christianorum, Series Latina 2. Turnholt: Brepols, 1954.

Sextus Empiricus. Tr. Robert Gregg Bury. 4 vols. (LCL) London: Heinemann, 1933–49.

Strabo. Tr. Horace Leonard Jones. 8 vols. (LCL) London: Heinemann, 1917–32.

Theodoret. *Kirchengeschichte*. Ed. Leon Parmentier. (GCS) Leipzig: Hinrichs, 1911.

Theophilus of Antioch. *Ad Autolycum*. Ed. Robert McQueen Grant. (OCT) Oxford: Clarendon, 1971.

## B. MODERN AUTHORS AND EDITORS

Adler, William. "The Origins of the Proto-Heresies: Fragments from a Chronicle in the First Book of Epiphanius' *Panarion*." *JTS* 41 n.s. (1990) 472–501.

Altaner, Berthold. "Augustinus und Epiphanius von Salamis," *Mélanges J. De Ghellinck* 1 (Gembloux: Duculot, 1951) 265–75.

Bannier, Wilhelm. "Ein Papyrusfragment aus der Chronik des Hippolytus," *Philologus* 81, N.F. 35 (1926) 123–27.

Bardy, Gustave. "La littérature patristique des '*Quaestiones et Responsiones*' sur l'Écriture Sainte," *Revue Biblique* 41 (1932) 210–36, 341–69, 515–37; 42 (1933) 14–30, 211–29, 328–52.

_____, "Le 'de haeresibus' et ses sources," *Miscellanea agostiniana* 2 (Rome, 1931) 397–416.

Bauer, Adolf. *Die Chronik des Hippolytos im Matritensis Graecus 121*. Texte und Untersuchungen 29 (N.F. 14.1). Leipzig: Hinrichs, 1905.

Beck, Hans Georg. *Kirche und theologische Literatur im byzantinischen Reich*. Munich: Beck, 1959.

Bernardi, Jean. "Un réquisitoire: Les invectives contre Julien de Grégoire de Nazianze," in René Braun and Jean Richer, edd., *L'empereur Julien: De l'histoire à la légende* (Paris: Belles Lettres, 1978) 89–98.

Berthelot, Marcellin. and Charles-Emile Ruelle, *Collection des anciens alchimistes grecs*. Paris: Steinheil, 1888.

Bickerman, Elias J. *Chronology of the Ancient World*. Rev. ed., London: Thames & Hudson, 1980.

Boge, Herbert. *Griechische Tachygraphie und tironischen Noten*. Berlin: Akademie, 1973.

Bommelaer, Jean-François.-Didier Laroche. *Guide de Delphes: Le Site*. Athens: École Française d'Athènes, 1991.

Brownlee, William Hugh. "Maccabees, Books of." *Interpreter's Dictionary of the Bible* 3 (4 vols.; 1962) 201–15.

Cadbury, Henry J. *The Making of Luke-Acts*. New York: Macmillan, 1927.

*Catalogue of the Manuscripts preserved in the Library of the University of Cambridge* II. Cambridge University Press, 1877.

Cavallera, Ferdinand. *Saint Jérome: Sa vie et son œuvre*. 2 vols. Spicilegium sacrum lovaniense, Études et documents 1 and 2. Louvain: Spicilegium sacrum lovaniense, 1922.

Cave (Cavius) William (Guilielm). *Scriptorum Ecclesiasticorum Historia Literaria*. 1st ed. 2 vols. London: Richard Chiswell, 1698.

Chadwick, Henry. *Origen Contra Celsum*. Cambridge: Cambridge University Press, 1953.

Charles, Robert Henry. *The Greek Versions of the Testaments of the Twelve Patriarchs*. Oxford: Clarendon, 1908.

Cilento, Vincenzo. "L'oracolo degli uomini," *La Parola del Passato* 6 (1951) 161–81.

Clark, Elizabeth A. *The Origenist Controversy*. Princeton: Princeton University Press, 1992.

Courby, Fernand. *Fouilles de Delphes* 2.1. École Française d'Athènes, 1915.

Crum, W.C. *Coptic Ostraca*. London: Egypt Exploration Society, 1902.

Daebritz, Hermann. "Herakleides (47) der Pythagoriker," *PWRE* 8 (1912) 487.

Dean, James Elmer. *Epiphanius' Treatise on Weights and Measures: The Syriac Version*. Chicago: University of Chicago Press, 1935.

Devreesse, Robert. "Anciens commentateurs grecs sur l'Octateuque," Revue Biblique 44 (1935) 166–91; 45 (1936) 201–20; 364–84 .

_____, *Codices Vaticani Graeci*, Vol. 2: *Codices 330–603*. Vatican City: Typus Polyglottus Vaticanus, 1937.

Diels, Hermannus. *Doxographi Graeci*. 2nd ed., Berlin: de Gruyter, 1929.

_____, "Laterculi Alexandrini aus einem Papyrus Ptolemaeischer Zeit," *Abhandlungen der königlich preussischen Akademie der Wissenschaften* 1904, Philosophisch-historische Classe, II, pp. 1–16.

Dietrich, Albert. "Saraka," *KP* 4 (1972) 1548.

Dummer, Jürgen. "Ein naturwissenschaftliches Handbuch als Quelle für Epiphanius von Constantia," *Klio* 55 (1973) 289–99.

Eisenhut, Werner. "Kalender," *KP* 3 (1969) 58–63.

Flacelière, Robert. "Le délire de la Pythie: Est-il une légende?" *Revue des Études Anciennes* 52 (1950) 306–24.

Fauth, Wolfgang. "Baitylia," *KP* 1 (1964) 806–8.

Gager, John G. *Moses in Greco-Roman Paganism*. Society of Biblical Literature, Monograph Series 16, 1972.

de Gaiffier, Baudouin. "'Sub Iuliano apostata' dans le martyrologe romain," *Analecta Bollandiana* 74 (1956) 5–49.

Gardiner, Alan Henderson. *Egyptian Grammar*, 3rd ed., London: Oxford University Press, 1973.

Gehman, Henry Snyder. "The Armenian Version of I and II Kings," *Journal of the American Oriental Society* 54 (1934) 53–59.

_____, (revised after Frederic George Kenyon)."Greek Versions of OT," in Frederick Clifton Grant–Harold Henry Rowley, edd., *Hastings Dictionary of the Bible*, 347–54.

Gelzer, Heinrich. *Sextus Julius Africanus und die byzantinische Chronologie*. 2 vols. Leipzig: Teubner, 1880–85.

Goody, Jack. *The Domestication of the Savage Mind*. Cambridge: Cambridge University Press, 1977.

Goranson, Stephen Craft. "The Joseph of Tiberias Episode in Epiphanius: Studies in Jewish and Christian Relations." Ph.D. dissertation, Duke, 1990; Ann Arbor MI: UMI Dissertation Services, 1992.

Göttsberger, J. *Barhebräus und seine Scholia zur heiligen Schrift*. Biblische Studien 5, Heften 4–5, 1900.

Gouillard, Jean. "L'hérésie dans l'empire byzantin des origines au xiie siècle," *Travaux et mémoires* 1 (1965) 300–1.

Grant, Frederick Clifton–Harold Henry Rowley. *Hastings Dictionary of the Bible*. New York: Scribner's, 1963.

Grant, Robert McQueen. *The Formation of the New Testament*. London: Hutchinson, 1965.

_____, *Greek Apologists of the Second Century*. Philadelphia: Westminster, 1988.

_____, "Greek Literature in the Treatise *De Trinitate* and Cyril *Contra Julianum*," *JTS* 15 (1964) 265–79.

_____, "Patristica," *Vigiliae Christianae* 3 (1949) 225–29 = *Christian Beginnings: Apocalypse to History*. London: Variorum, 1983, Essay XV.

van Haelst, Joseph. *Catalogue des Papyrus littéraires juifs et chrétiens*. Paris: Sorbonne, 1976.

Hahn, August. *Bibliothek der Symbole und Glaubensregeln der alte Kirche*. 3rd ed., rev. G. Ludwig Hahn, Breslau: Morgenstern, 1897.

Harvey, Julien. "Ézéchiel," *Dictionnaire de Spiritualité* 4 (12 vols.; 1961) 2204–20.

Hennecke, Edgar–Wilhelm Schneemelcher, *New Testament Apocrypha* 2. Philadelphia: Westminster, 1965.

Hicks, John Harden. *The Scholia of Barhebraeus on the Book of Isaiah*, Diss. University of Chicago [Divinity School], 1933.

Holl, Karl. *Die handschriftliche Überlieferung des Epiphanius* (*Ancoratus und Panarion*). Texte und Untersuchungen 36.3. Leipzig: Hinrichs, 1910.

Holland, Leicester B. "The Mantic Mechanism at Delphi," *American Journal of Archaeology* 37 (1933) 201–19.

Hopfner, Theodor. *Griechisch-Ägyptischer Offenbarungszauber* 2.1. Amsterdam: Hakkert, 1983; 2.2, 1990.

_____, "Mantike," *PWRE* 14 (1928) 1258–88.

Hort, Fenton John Anthony–Joseph Bickersteth Mayor. *Clement of Alexandria: Miscellanies, Book VII*. London: Macmillan, 1902.

Huebner, Reinhard M. "Die Hauptquelle des Epiphanius (*Panarion*, *haer*. 65) über Paulus von Samosata," *Zeitschrift für Kirchengeschichte* 90 (1979) 201–20.

Hultsch, Friedrich Otto. *Metrologicorum scriptorum reliquiae* 1. Leipzig: Teubner, 1864; repr. 1971.

Jones, Arnold Hugh Martin. *Cities of the Eastern Roman Provinces*. Oxford: Clarendon, 1937.

de Jonge, Hermann Jacob. "Additional notes on the history of MSS. Venice Bibl. Marc. Gr. 494(k) and Cambridge Univ. Libr. Ff. 1.24(b)." Pp. 107–115 in Marinus de Jonge, ed., *Studies on the Testaments of the Twelve Patriarchs*. Leiden: Brill, 1975.

_____, "La bibliothèque de Michel Choniatès et la tradition occidentale des Testaments de XII Patriarches." Pp. 97–106 in Marinus de Jonge, ed., *Studies on the Testaments of the Twelve Patriarchs*. Leiden: Brill, 1975.

de Jonge, Marinus. "Christelijke elementen in de Vitae prophetarum," *Nederlands Theologisch Tijdschrift* 16 (1961–1962) 161–78.

_____, (ed.) *Testamenta XII Patriarchum*. Edited according to Cambridge University Library MS Ff 1.12 fol. 203a–262b. Leiden: Brill, 1964.

_____, "Robert Grosseteste and the Testaments of the Twelve Patriarchs," *JTS* 42 (1991) 115–25.

_____, "The Transmission of the Testaments of the Twelve Patriarchs by Christians," *VC* 47 (1993) 2–6.

Kannengiesser, Charles. "Jérémie," *Dictionnaire de Spiritualité* 8 (1974) 889–96.

Kelly, John Norman Davidson. *Jerome: His Life, Writings, and Controversies*. New York: Harper & Row, 1975.

Kinzl, Konrad. "Mantik," *KP* 3 (1969) 968–76.

Kotter, Bonifatius Balthasar. "John Damascene, St.," *New Catholic Encyclopedia* 7 (14 vols.; 1967) 1047–49.

Krueger, Derek. "Diogenes the Cynic," *VC* 47 (1993) 37–39.

Lagarde, Paul A. de. *Septuagintastudien*, Part 2. Göttingen: Dieterich, 1892.

Lampe, Geoffrey William Hugo. *A Patristic Greek Lexicon*. Oxford: Clarendon, 1961–1968.

Lawlor, Hugh Jackson–John Ernest Leonard Oulton. *Eusebius*. London: SPCK, 1928.

Leyerle, Blake. "John Chrysostom on the Gaze," *Journal of Early Christian Studies* 1 (1993) 159–74 .

Lipsius, Richard Adelbert. *Zur Quellenkritik des Epiphanios*. Vienna: W. Braumüller, 1865.

Malley, William J. "Four Unedited Fragments of the *De Universo* of the Pseudo-Josephus found in the *Chronicon* of Georgius Hamartolus (Coislin 305)" *JTS* 16 (1965) 13–25.

_____, *Hellenism and Christianity* (Analecta Gregoriana, 210). Rome: Università Gregoriana, 1978.

Menzies, Glen Wesley. *Interpretive Traditions in the Hypomnestikon Biblion Ioseppou.* Ph.D. dissertation, Univerity of Minnesota, 1994; Ann Arbor MI: UMI Dissertation Services, 1994.

Milne, Herbert John Mansfield–Skeat, Theodore Cressy. *The Codex Sinaiticus and the Codex Alexandrinus.* Ed.2. London: British Museum, 1955 (1967).

Moldenke, Harold Norman and Alma Lance Moldenke. *Plants of the Bible.* Waltham MA: Chronica Botanica, 1952.

Montgomery, James A. "The Hexaplaric Strata in the Greek Text of Daniel." *JBL* 44 (1925) 289–302

_____, (ed. Henry Snyder Gehman) *The Books of Kings* (ICC). Edinburgh: T.& T. Clark, 1951.

Mordtmann, Johannes Heinrich. "Saracens," *Brill's First Encyclopaedia of Islam 1913–1936*, 7 (8 vols plus suppl.; Leiden: Brill, 1987) 155–56.

Moreau, Jacques. "Observations sur l'*Hypomnestikon Biblion Ioseppou*," *Byzantion* 25–27 (1955–57) 241–76 = *Scripta Minora* (Heidelberg: C. Winter, 1964) 150–73.

Murphy, Francis X. *Rufinus of Aquileia (345–411): His Life and Works.* Studies in Mediaeval History, n.s. 6. Washington, DC: Catholic University of America, 1945.

Nautin, Pierre. "La controverse sur l'auteur de l'«Elenchos.»" *Revue d'histoire ecclésiastique* 47 (1952) 5–43.

_____, *Lettres et écrivains chrétiens des iie et iiie siècles.* Paris: Cerf, 1961.

_____, "Études de chronologie hiéronymienne (393–397): Parts 1–4." *Revue des études augustiniennes* 18 (1972) 209–218; 19 (1973) 69–73; 19 (1973) 213–39; 20 (1974) 251–84.

_____, *Origène: Sa vie et son oeuvre.* Paris: Beauchesne, 1977.

Oikonomides, Al. N., ed., *Abbreviations in Greek Inscriptions*: *Papyri Manuscripts and Early Printed Books.* Chicago: Ares, 1974.

Opelt, Ilona. "Epitome," *RAC* 5 (1965) 944–73 (specifically 963 [no. 129] and 968).

Parke, Herbert William. *Greek Oracles.* London: Hutchinson, 1967.

Pease, Arthur Stanley. *M. Tulli Ciceronis De Divinatione* I. Urbana, IL: University of Illinois, 1920.

Pourkier, Aline. *L'hérésiologie chez Épiphane de Salamine.* Paris: Beauchesne, 1992.

Quasten, Johannes. *Patrology.* 3 vols. Utrecht: Spectrum: 1950–1960; reprinted Westminster, MD: Christian Classics, 1983.

Rahlfs, Alfred. *Septuaginta-Studien*, 3 (Lucians Rezension der Königsbücher). Göttingen: Vandenhoeck & Ruprecht, 1911.

Regenbogen, Otto. "Pinax," *PWRE* 20 (1951) 1409–82 (1470–72 on Hyginus).

Reitzenstein, Richard. *Historia Monachorum und Historia Lausiaca*. Göttingen: Vandenhoeck & Ruprecht, 1916.

Richard, Marcel. "Nouveaux fragments de Théophile d'Alexandrie," *Nachrichten...Göttingen, Philologisch-historisches Klasse*, 1975, 57–65.

Ritter, Heinrich–Ludwig Preller. *Historia Philosophiae Graecae*. 10th ed., Gotha: Klotz, 1934.

Robinson, James M. *The Nag Hammadi Library in English* (3rd ed., San Francisco: Harper & Row, 1988.

Rossi, Francesco. *Trascrizione di tre manoscritti copti del Museo Egizio di Torino* = Memorie della Reale Accademia delle Scienze di Torino, Serie 2, Tom. 37 (Torino: Loescher, 1885).

Saxer, Victor. "Pelagia," *Encyclopedia of the Early Church* 2 (2 vols.; New York: Oxford University Press, 1992) 665.

Schermann, Theodorus. *Prophetarum vitae fabulosae*. Leipzig: Teubner, 1907.

_____, *Propheten- und Apostellegenden nebst Jüngerkatalogen*. TU 31.3. Leipzig: Hinrichs, 1907 (prophets, pp. 1–133).

Schmidt, Peter L."Hyginus 2. H. Mythographus," *KP* 2 (1967) 1263.

Schneemelcher, Wilhelm. "Epiphanius," *RAC* 5 (1965) 919–20.

Schreckenberg, Heinz. *Die Flavius-Josephus-Tradition in Antike und Mittelalter*. ALGHJ 5, Leiden: Brill, 1972.

Serruys, Daniel. "Un fragment sur papyrus de la *Chronique* d'Hippolyte de Rome," *Revue de Philologie* 38 (1914) 27–31

Skeat, Theodore Cressy. "The provenance of the Codex Alexandrinus," *JTS* n.s. 6 (1955) 233–35.

Skinner, John. *Genesis* (ICC). Edinburgh: Clark, 1910.

Smith, Jonathan Z. *Imagining Religion: From Babylon to Jonestown*. Chicago Studies in the History of Judaism. Chicago: University of Chicago Press, 1982.

Sontheimer, Walther. "Monat," *KP* 3 (1969) 1405–8.

Stokes, George Thomas. "Josephus (31) (Joseppus)" *Dictionary of Christian Biography* 3 (1882) 460–61.

Swete, Henry Barclay. *Introduction to the Old Testament in Greek*. Ed 2. Cambridge: At the University Press, 1914.

Tannery, Paul. "Sur les abbréviations dans les manuscrits grecs," *Revue archéologique*, 3d Ser., 12 (1888) 210–13.

Thompson, Edward Maunde. *An Introduction to Greek and Latin Palaeography*. Oxford: Clarendon, 1912.

Thompson, John Alexander. "Perfume," *Interpreters Dictionary of the Bible* 3 (4 vols.; 1962) 730–32.

Thornton, T.C.G. "The Samaritan Calendar: a source of friction in New Testament times," *JTS* 42 (1991) 577–80.

Thyen, Hartwig. *Der Stil der jüdisch-hellenistischen Homilie.* Forschungen zur Religion und Literatur des Alten und Neuen Testaments, N. F. 47, Göttingen: Vandenhoeck & Ruprecht, 1955.

Torrey, Charles Cutler. *The Lives of the Prophets: Greek text and translation.* Journal of Biblical Literature Monograph Series, 1. Philadelphia: Society of Biblical Literature, 1946.

Tümpel, Karl. "Baitylia," *PWRE* 2 (1896) 2779–81.

Usener, Hermann. "Vergessenes, IX," *Rheinisches Museum* 28 (1873) 430–33.

Vallée, Gerard. *A Study in Anti-Gnostic Polemics: Irenaeus, Hippolytus, and Epiphanius.* Waterloo, Ont.: Wilfrid Laurier University Press, 1981.

Voss, Isaac. *De Sibyllinis . . . oraculis.* Oxford: Sheldonian Theatre, 1680.

Weinberger, Wilhelm. "Kurzschrift," *PWRE* 11 (1922) 2219–22.

Westermann, Anton. *Paradoxographi Graeci.* Brunswick: G. Westermann, 1839.

Wilkinson, John. *Egeria's Travels.* London: SPCK, 1971.

Wolff, Gustav. *Porphyrii De Philosophia ex oraculis.* Berlin, 1856; repr. Hildesheim: Olms, 1962.

Zintzen, Clemens. "Mantik," *KP* 3 (1969) 973–74.

Zohary, Michael. *Plants of the Bible.* Cambridge: Cambridge University Press, 1982.

## SELECT INDEXES [1]

### A. NAMES AND TERMS

Aaron, brother of Moses, 2(1), 10(1), 19(1), 21, 33(3), 51(1), 59(2), 68(35), 69, 154(1)

Abbakoum (Habakkuk), prophet, 14(16)

Abessalôm (Absalom), son of David, 38(4), 40(12), 43(5), 48(3), 56(3), 57(5), 62(5), 73(12,13), 155(2)

Abigail, wife of David, 38(3), 40(6), 73(4)

Abissa (Abishag), companion of David, 38(3), 74(1)

Abraam (Abraham), patriarch, 1(20), 15(3), 35, 36, 40(1), 44(1), 55(1), 64(1), 67(5,7), 97, 147(3)

Achias the Silonite, prophet, 15(11), 52(1), **87**, 120(1)

Adam, 1(1,15), 15(1), 39(1), 53(1), 66(2), 115(1), 140(48), 150

Adamianoi, heretics, 140(48)

Aerios, Aerianoi, heretics, 140(60)

Aetius, Aetianoi, heretics, 149(59)

Agar (Hagar), concubine of Abraam, 40(1), 147(1); see Ismaél

Aggaios (Haggai), prophet, 14(18), **78**

Alogoi, heretics, 140(31)

*alph*, etc., letters, 26; *iôd*, *éd*, 151 (see Tetragrammon)

Amnôn, 73(12); see Amôn

Amôn (Amnon), 62(4)

Angelikoi, heretics, 140(53)

Anna, mother of Maria, 136

Annas, high priest, 2(62), 146(1)

Anô, mother of Ieroboam, 50(1), 87(2)

Anthrôpolatroi, heretics, 139(12)

Anthropomorphitai, heretics, 140(62)

Antichrist, 79(3), 129(8), 148(3), 149(2)

Antiochos Epiphanés, 2(39), 47(6), 123(2), 124(8), 126(6)

Aôd, 11(4), 23(13), 45(1), 71(2)

Apellaos, Apellianoi, heretics, 140(26)

Apostolikoi, heretics, 140(51)

Aquila, Bible translator, 122(2), 151(4,7)

Archontikoi, heretics, 140(52)

Areios, Areianoi, heretics, 139(11), 140(56-57,59)

---

[1] Lists of names, as well as chapters 136 and 139–144, are not wholly included. Numbers in **bold** type indicate longer treatments than usual.

ark, 73(10), 74(3), 107(4), 111(3), 151(15), 165(3); Nôe's, 1(10), 4, 65(5), 67(6)

Artem[i]as, Artemianoi, heretics, 140(33)

Asa, king, 119

Audianoi, heretics, 140(54)

Aurelian, emperor, 139(9)

Azarias, prophet, **92;** with Daniel, 64(5); priest, 103(2)

Baasa, king, 13(3), 90; prophet (error for Iéou), 90

Bardisanitai (Bardisanés), heretics, 140(37)

Barnabas, one of LXX, 137(1)

Basileidés, Basileidianoi, heretics, 140(9)

Bérsabeë (Bathsheba), wife of Ourias, 86(2); see Bethsabeë, Béthsabeë

Béthleem, 29(5), 44(3-4), 72(3), 73(7,14), 151(12), 163(6)

Bethsabeë (Bathsheba), 38(3); Béthsabeë, 40(7), 73, 114(3)

Bethél, 15(22), 31(5-6), 34(2,15), 49(4), 89, 154(5), 160(1)

Bible, canon (Hebrew), 25; Deuteronomy, 68(47); books of Moses, 69(13); Psalms, 73; books of Solomon, 74(5), 120(3), 131(7); book of Reigns (Rg), 41(6), 130; prophets,14; Greek translators, LXX, 2(36), 38(4); LXXII, 122; kings omitted, 118; lost books, 120, 121; heretic Valentinus rejects Old Testament, 140(17); Old Testament only for Israel, 140(24); heretic Oualés rejects Old Scripture, 140(40); Acts, 2(78), 121(4), 140(3,4), 142(2-3), 152(10), 153(1-3), 156(4), 161(3); other New Testament books, see Index B.

Bible text: Armenian (Arm.), 2(15), 71(4), 102(20-23,26-27), 103(9,15-19);
>	Cod.A (Codex Alexandrinus), 15(27), 21, 29(5,8,9), 30(2), 33, 34(9,12,13,15-17,19,20,22,28), 38(4), 41(6), 44(5), 63(6,7), 64(3), 71(4), 74(6), 95, 102(10,11,17,24,35), 103(2,3,5,8,10,14,16,17,19), 104, 120(1), 166(5);
>	Cod.B (Codex Vaticanus), 29(5), 33(7,12), 50(1), 102(2), 103(9,12), 124(2), 130(8);
>	Cod.D (Codex Cottonianus), 63(14);
>	Cod.G (Codex Colberto-Sarravianus), 29(4);
>	names in Anon., 3(1,4,6), 118(1);
>	Heb. (Hebrew), 102(2,35), 103(10,12-14)

Borborianoi, heretics, 140(11)

bronze, 69(12), 107(2-4), 110(1-2), 111(4), 122(5)

Byrillos (Beryllos), Byrillianoi, heretics, 140 (39)

Cham (Ham), son of Nôé, 1(10), 4, 24, 56(1), 67(4)

Chanaan, 11(5), 40(2); Chanaanités, 24(19), 32(9), 50(4), 71(3), 77(2), 163(3)

Christ, 1(70), 40(16), 53(3), 66(4), 74(5), 75(14), 79(3), 100, 101(1), 118(1), 121(2), 124(9), 129(8), 136, 139(7), 140(1,6,17,23,32-34,39,44,46,52,58,63), 149(3), 150, 151(4), 164(6-8)

Gotholia (Athaliah), mother of Ochozias, 39(8), 41(7); see Godolia

Gothoniél, 11(2), 23(12)

Hégésippos, Christian, 153(4)

Helkasai, Helkesianoi, heretics, 140(38)

Hémiareioi (Semiarians), heretics, 140(57)

Héraklas, Hérakleones, heretics, 140(20)

heresies, Christian, 132(4), 140; Greek, 143; Jewish, 141; Samaritan, 142

Hérôdés, king, 2(51-53,56,60), 39(9), 40(19), 123(4), 124(9), 132(7), 134(1),
    135(1), 136, 138(3), 140(1)

Hérôdianoi, heretics (?), 140(1)

Hérôdias, wife of Hérôdés, 39(9)

Hierax, Hierakitai, heretics, 140(46)

Hierosolyma (Jerusalem), 31(5), 136 (See also Jerusalem)

High priest(-hood), 2, 17(5), 41(7), 42(3), 53(3), 69(9), 72(1), 74(1,2), 97,
    101(1), 107(1), 109, 118(1), 122(1), 123(4), 135(b1), 138(1), 140(2), 158,
    167; erroneously so styled, 47, 61(1), 115(2); see Priests

Holy, Holy of Holies, 106, 107, 111; chrism, 69(9); church, 74(5), 140(63);
    Jesus, 151(15); one, 151(4); places, 79(3), 166; prophets,97; scriptures, 151;
    Holy Spirit, see Spirit; virgins, 166(3), cf. 136, 139(5)

Hyrkanos, king and high priest, 2(47,50,51), 123(3), 124(9)

Iadôn, prophet, 15(22), **89**, 130(6); Iaôd, 160(1)

Iaél (so LXX), kills Sisara, 23(14), 45(2); see Iazél

Iakôb (Jacob), patriarch, 1(22), 2, 5, 6, 15(5), 42(2), 52(2), 55(2-3), 58(2), 64(2),
    67(5), 80(1), 129(1), 147(2)

Iakôbos (Jacob or James), apostle, 2(78), 47(7), 64(11), 134, 136, 138(3),
    152(8), 153(4)

Iaôd, see Iadôn

Iazél, kills Sisara, 71(3); see Iaél

Iechonias (king), 1(50), 12(21), 76(3)

Iephthaê (Jephthah), judge, 11(13), 23(16), 71(5)

Ieremias (Jeremiah), prophet, 10(19), 14(6), 18(3-7), 22(19), 58, **76**, 115, 118,
    123(1), 130(11), 151(8), 162(2)

Ieroboam (Jeroboam), son of Solomon, 1(35), 13(1,13), 15(22), 49(4), 50(1),
    87(1-2), 88(3), 89, 154(5)

Jerusalem (Hierousalém), 1(34), 2(43), 18(5), 23(2), 31(5), 34(3), 38(3), 46(4),
    47(2), 74(1,3), 75(2), 77(2), 79(1,3), 86(3), 88(1), 105, 123, 124(7,9,10),
    126, 127, 129(9), 134(3), 136, 137(1,7), 138(1,2), 139(7), 140(3,28),
    151(7), 153(2,3), 154(6,7); (Hierosolyma) 31(5), 136

Iésous (Jesus), 1(70), 40(16), 66(4), 79(1), 101(1), 136, 140(6,15,62), 150,
    151(14,15), 153(4); see Christ; Joshua, 14(2), 23(2,9), 25(6), 34, 58(4), **70**,
    161(1); Iéou son of Anani, prophet, **93**, 130(8); son of Gamaliel, 2(79); son

## B. GREEK TERMS

*agyrtés* (begging priest), gentile, 144(58); Jewish, 74(5)

*aïdios* (eternal), 140(62)

*akatalépta* (incomprehensible), 128

*aristokratia* (aristocracy), 72(1,2)

*arréton* (ineffable), 107(1), 151(15)

*baitylia* (meteorites), 144(50)

*basileia tou theou* (kingdom of God), 73(2); *tou Christou* (of Christ), 129, 140(46)

*boni* (Egyptian harp), 144(51)

*charisma* (spiritual gift), *tés sophias* (of wisdom), 41(5)

*démogoreuein* (call an assembly), 72(2)

*démos* (people, frequent in Nm and Js), 73(7)

*diabatérion* (crossing), 126

*dyadikos* (dyadic), *hypostasis*, 66

*dynamis* (power), 107

*eis aei diamenousa* (enduring forever), 107

*enigma*, introduction 3; *enigmatikôs*, 131

*epangelia* (promise), 136 (error for Galilee?)

*eunomein* (observe laws), 72(1,2)

*hidrysis* (building), 107

*hieratikoi* (priestly), 7-10; *hieratikon kai laïkon tagma* (priestly and lay order), 66; see *kosmikoi*

*homoios* (similar), 140(57)

*homo<i>ousios* (of similar substance), 140(57)

*homoousios* (of the same substance), 140(62)

*hyein* (rain, of Zeus, Homer and Hesiod), of God, 69(7), 72(2); cf. Ex 9:18 (16:4): *hyô*; 9:23: *ebrexen kyrios*

*hyparxis* (existence), 140(63)

*hyperbasis* (passing over), 126(1)

*hypostasis* (substance), 66, (67,) 128(1), 140(55)

*hypotheseis* (materials), Appendix/Colophon line 2

*Ioudaïkos démos* (Jewish people), 73(7); *laos*, 41(9)

*Ioudaïsmos* (Judaism), 122(2)

*ischys* (strength), 107

*katorthôsis* (setting up), 107

*klérikoi* (clerics), 139(6)

*kosmikoi* (laymen), 140(46,54); see *hieratikoi*

*laos*, see People; *leôs* (people), 73(7)

## C. SOURCES, PARALLELS, EDITORS